W9-AXV-241

D0435411

The
Junior League
of Monroe, Inc.
presents
our favorite recipes
the
COTTON COUNTRY
collection

The purpose of the Junior League is exclusively educational and charitable and is to promote voluntarism; to develop the potential of its members for voluntary participation in community affairs; and to demonstrate the effectiveness of trained volunteers.

The proceeds from *the COTTON COUNTRY collection* will be used to promote awareness and provide services for Women and Children-At-Risk in the Ouachita Parish Community.

Copies may be obtained from:

COTTON BAYOU PUBLICATIONS
P. O. Box 7138
Monroe, Louisiana 71211-7138

$16.95 per book
(Please add $3.50 per book order for postage and handling)

ISBN 0-9602364-0-6

First Printing, November, 1972	— 10,000
Second Printing, January, 1973	— 10,000
Third Printing, May, 1973	— 20,000
Fourth Printing, January, 1974	— 20,000
Fifth Printing, January, 1975	— 35,000
Sixth Printing, January, 1976	— 35,000
Seventh Printing, January, 1977	— 40,000
Eighth Printing, January, 1978	— 30,000
Ninth Printing, May, 1979	— 50,000
Tenth Printing, June, 1980	— 60,000
Eleventh Printing, March, 1982	— 50,000
Twelfth Printing, September, 1984	— 50,000
Thirteenth Printing, February, 1987	— 30,000
Fourteenth Printing, October, 1989	— 30,000
Fifteenth Printing, June, 1992	— 30,000
Sixteenth Printing, June, 1994	— 30,000
Seventeenth Printing, July, 1996	— 25,000

Printed in the USA by
WIMMER
The Wimmer Companies, Inc.
Memphis

FOREWORD

The word "collection" carries several meanings and connotations: "To bring together into one body"; to gather or exact from a number of persons or other sources"; "an accumulation gathered for study or comparison." The COTTON COUNTRY collection is all these things . . . and more, in that each recipe represents the finest of its kind. And each kind is very fine, indeed.

From the earliest days, cooks of the Ouachita River area were blessed with an endless supply and variety of raw materials. Even today the designation "Louisiana" denotes the very best in shrimp, rice, oysters, sugar cane, pecans, strawberries, to name a few.

In our Cotton Country there were many influences of different peoples, nationalities, systems of law—and of culinary arts. From the earliest days, the Indians taught the settlers about the delicacies native to Louisiana. Creole ladies in New Orleans know about French sauces; their African cooks contributed new ideas in seasonings. Spanish influence brought a hotter accent. A large number of émigrés who fled the French Revolution were followed in less than five years by the Anglo-Americans coming down the Mississippi from Kentucky after the Louisiana Purchase. And each of these made its own contribution to our Cotton Country ideas.

Although influenced by the cosmopolitan atmosphere of New Orleans and the ever-changing activity of river traffic, the Ouachita area was primarily a rural culture. The plantations along the river and the bayous were almost completely self-sustaining, raising their own food, making their own clothes, building their homes from the materials in the forests. Plantation chatelaines and their cooks, using the unusually lavish gifts of nature and the ideas of many root sources, developed a style of cooking distinctive in its heritage and delicious in its culmination.

Here, then, our COTTON COUNTRY collection, a medley of French sauces with Spanish spiciness and African seasonings, served up over the Indian's native corn or oysters or potatoes or wild turkey. To coin a phrase reflecting our varying influences:

May "y'all come" to "Bon Appetit"

Marillyn Taylor

Many pounds heavier and more worries later, our efforts to bring you one of the finest collections of recipes have been completed. Testing contributions from our Southern homes has been challenging and rewarding. We have "seasoned to taste" and "browned the roux." We have overcome the lengthy process of proofing, typing, and proofing again with our vision still intact. We have lived cookbook from dawn to dark and dark to dawn with the hope of *the Cotton Country collection's* being a book to entice everyone from a novice to a master chef into the kitchen.

My deepest gratitude goes to Lucy Sartor (Mrs. D. R.) and Joy Marshall (Mrs. Ben) who have enhanced the beauty of our book with their artistic talents. Mrs. Sartor's cover and illustrations depicting our "Cotton Country" are collector's items in themselves. The originality of Mrs. Marshall's sketches used throughout the book give us a tableful of delights.

To my committee, for their time, talents, cooperation and hard work, a million "thank you's" would not say it all: Mrs. Jim Greenbaum, Mrs. Lestar Martin, Mrs. Dan Sartor, Mrs. Jim Altick, Mrs. Ed Seymour, Jr., Mrs. Jerry Wolff, Mrs. John Ensminger, Mrs. Jim Geisler, Mrs. Tommy Grant III, Mrs. Bachman Lee, Mrs. Saul Mintz, Mrs. George Snellings III, and Mrs. Don Stinson. My sincere appreciation goes also to Mrs. Jesse McDonald's sustaining committee of Mrs. Jay Adams, Mrs. Harry Bell, Mrs. Joe Dixon, Jr., Mrs. Harry Frazer, Jr., Mrs. Doyle Hamilton, Mrs. William Husted, Jr., Mrs. Jack Inabet, Mrs. DeWitt Milam, and Mrs. Levins Thompson who have assisted us in gathering and testing recipes. And to those Junior Charity League members who have helped us test and type— THANK YOU.

From our "Collection" we know you will find new favorites to add to your own "collection" as we have.

November 1972   *Mrs. Don Irby*

ADDENDUM

We wish to acknowledge the ladies who have chaired *the Cotton Country collection* committees through the years:

1972-	Marilyn Swift Irby	1987-	Adrienne Smith Cole
1973-	Jean Strauss Mintz	1988-	Judy Morrow Edmondson
1974-	Flora Kitchingham Wilkins		Lynda Sadler Gavioli
1975-	Armande McHenry Kennedy	1989-	Posey Daniel Moller
1976-	Noel Standley Culpepper		Anna Corrent Oliver
1977-	Jane Virtue Stephens		Vicki Sanders Williams
1978-	Penny Brooks Doughty	1990-	Sara Moore Greene
1979-	Dottie Teleha Hart	1991-	Peggy Young Bermudez
1980-	Carolyn McCormick Myrick		Susan Thrasher Jackson
1981-	Sylvia Whitehead Loftin	1992-	Peggy Young Bermudez
1982-	Wendy King Brown		Kathy McMurrain Czeschin
1983-	Cathy Sherman Crick	1993-	Sara Moore Greene
1984-	Sally Stowers Oliver	1994-	Donna Williams Kokinos
1985-	Judy Downey Breard	1995-	Donna Williams Kokinos
1986-	Marsha Bell Powell	1996-	Susan Thrasher Jackson

Table of Contents

"Cotton Country" Rum Punch

¾ pound lump sugar
2 quarts water
1 quart lemon juice
2 fifths light rum
1 fifth California brandy
½ cup peach brandy

Dissolve lump sugar in water. Add remaining ingredients. Make at least 2 hours before serving. Serves 30 punch cups.

Mrs. George Smelser

Almond Punch

1 large can frozen orange juice
1 small can frozen lemon juice
1 large can pineapple juice
1 large can apricot nectar
½ cup sugar
½ to ¾ small bottle of almond
  extract

Dilute frozen juices according to directions. Mix all together and chill.

Mrs. Eugene Worthen

Cinnamon Punch

1 cup sugar
½ cup "red hots", Cinnamon
  Imperials
2 cups water
2 large cans sweetened pineapple
  juice
1 cup lemon juice
1 large bottle ginger ale

Melt the first three ingredients together in a large boiler. Add the remaining ingredients. Stir thoroughly. Serve hot or cold. Add cake coloring to make a deeper red. Yields approximately 5 quarts.

Mrs. Harry Liner

Fruit Tea Punch

2 cups sugar
1 cup water
2 cups strong tea
1 cup lemon juice
2½ cups orange juice
2 cups pineapple juice
2 cups frozen strawberries
1 quart ginger ale

Make a syrup of two cups sugar and one cup water. Add tea, fruit juices and enough water to make one and one-half gallons. Stir in strawberries and ginger ale just before serving. Yields about fifty servings.

Mrs. William Ledoux

Plantation Syllabub

5 cups sugar
12 cups apple cider
12 Tablespoons grated lemon rind
1 cup lemon juice
4 teaspoons light corn syrup
2 teaspoons aromatic bitters
8 egg whites
8 cups milk
2 pints Half and Half

Combine 4 cups sugar, cider, lemon juice, rind, corn syrup and bitters in a large bowl. Stir to dissolve. Chill several hours or overnight. Make meringues beating the egg whites and gradually adding the remaining 1 cup sugar until stiff peaks form. Place individual puffs on cookie sheets and freeze. *To serve:* Beat milk and cream into cider mix with whisk until frothy. Pour in a punch bowl and float the meringues on top. Serve a "puff" in each cup. 50 punch cup servings.

Mrs. Ivy Jordan

Cool Coffee Eggnog
Great with warm muffins!

4 cups milk
2 egg yolks, beaten
¼ cup sugar
2 Tablespoons instant coffee
1 teaspoon vanilla
¼ teaspoon salt
2 egg whites, beaten
3 Tablespoons sugar

Stir milk into beaten egg yolks. Add sugar, instant coffee, vanilla and salt. Cook over medium heat, stirring constantly, until mixture coats a metal spoon. Chill. Just before serving, beat egg whites till foamy. Gradually add sugar beating to soft peaks. Add to coffee mixture and mix thoroughly. Yields six to eight servings.

Mrs. Harry Bell

Coffee Punch

4 quarts strong coffee
1 quart whipping cream
5 Tablespoons sugar
5 teaspoons vanilla
2 quarts vanilla ice cream

Early in the day or on the day before, make coffee and refrigerate until chilled. Drip chicory coffee such as Luzianne is definitely best. Just before serving, whip cream, adding sugar and vanilla. Spoon or slice ice cream into large punch bowl. Add whipped cream. Pour cold coffee over it and mix well. Serve in cups. Yields fifty to sixty servings.

Mrs. Wesley Shafto, Jr.

"Tomato Juice Wow"

1- 46 ounce can tomato juice
½ of 6 ounce can orange juice, undiluted
Juice of 2 lemons
Juice of 1 lime
1 Tablespoon Worcestershire
2 teaspoons salt

Blend and refrigerate. Serve in frosted glasses.

Mrs. Bob Tucker

Hot Buttered Lemonade

4½ cups boiling water
¾ cup sugar
1½ teaspoons grated lemon peel
¾ cup lemon juice
2 Tablespoons butter
6 cinnamon sticks

In a saucepan combine water, sugar, lemon peel and juice. Cook, stirring occasionally, till heated through. Pour into mugs; top each with 1 teaspoon of butter. Serve with cinnamon stick stirrers. Makes six servings. Add one ounce bourbon or rum for a delicious toddy.

Hot Cranberry Punch

1 cup water
1⅛ cups brown sugar
⅜ teaspoon salt
⅜ teaspoon nutmeg
¾ teaspoon cinnamon
¾ teaspoon allspice
1⅛ teaspoons ground cloves
1- 46 ounce can unsweetened
   pineapple juice
1 bottle cranberry juice cocktail
Rum flavoring to taste
Red food coloring

Combine water and sugar. Place spices in bag and tie securely. Put bag of spices into pot of sugar and water. Bring only to a boil. This syrup can be made ahead of time and keeps well in the refrigerator. Add pineapple and cranberry juice to above mixture. Mix well. Heat. Add rum flavoring to taste and red food coloring to brighten. Add dots of butter and serve in mugs with cinnamon sticks as stirrers, if desired.

Mrs. W. M. Harper

Mulled Cider

2 quarts apple cider
1 teaspoon whole allspice
6 cloves or more
1 stick cinnamon
½ cup brown sugar
½ cup white sugar
½ cup orange juice
⅓ cup lemon juice

Simmer apple cider with spices and sugar for about thirty minutes. Add juices and strain. Can be served immediately or stored in refrigerator and reheated later. Yields about twenty servings.

Mrs. W. Tom Davis

Hot Tomato Punch

1 quart Bloody Mary mix
2½ cups tomato sauce
½ cup tomato paste
¼ cup lemon juice
¼ cup vinegar
Tabasco, salt and celery salt to
   taste
Unsweetened whipped cream

Mix all ingredients except whipped cream. If you want a tangier taste, add more lemon juice and vinegar. Heat. Serve in demi-tasse cups and top with dollops of whipped cream.

Mrs. Jamar Adock

Spiced Tea

3 quarts water
1 teaspoon whole cloves
1 stick cinnamon
½ teaspoon whole allspice
6 tea bags
2 cups sugar
1 can frozen orange juice
1 can frozen lemonade

Boil one quart water, cloves, cinnamon and allspice together for five minutes. Remove from heat and add tea bags. Cover pan and let cool completely. Add two quarts water, sugar, orange juice and lemonade. Stir together. Makes three quarts.

Mrs. James Dennis

Lou's Wassail

2 sticks of cinnamon
½ teaspoon whole cloves
1 Tablespoon nutmeg
½ teaspoon grated allspice
2 quarts of apple cider
⅔ cup of pure lemon juice
2 cups orange juice

Make a spice bag with the spices and place the bag in the juices. Bring mixture to a boil; remove from heat. Store in the refrigerator until ready to serve. Heat and remove spice bag. This is very tart.

Mrs. J. M. Rickerson

French Chocolate
This is a delicious hot chocolate

2½ squares Baker's unsweetened chocolate, cut in pieces
½ cup water
¾ cup sugar
Dash of salt
½ cup cream, whipped
6 cups of hot milk

Combine water and chocolate and cook over low flame until smooth, stirring constantly for about four minutes. Add sugar and salt; continue to cook stirring until thick for about four minutes longer. Cool. Whip cream. Fold chocolate mixture into cream. To serve, place two heaping tablespoons of mixture in a mug. Fill with hot milk. A peppermint stick to stir is pretty for a party. Chocolate mixture may be easily doubled or tripled. Make the chocolate mixture the day before and store covered in the refrigerator.

Mrs. Don Irby

Simple Syrup

1 cup water
1 cup sugar

Boil until sugar is dissolved. Keeps indefinitely in the refrigerator. Use for mixing drinks or in a punch base. Yields two cups.

Mint Syrup
Delicious to make and keep in the refrigerator during those long, hot summer months

2½ cups water
2 cups sugar
6 lemons, juiced
2 oranges, grated peel and juice
4 large handsful of mint

Wash and clean mint well. Dissolve sugar in water and boil together for ten minutes. Pour hot syrup over fruit juices and mint. Cover and let steep several hours. Strain. Pour in jars and refrigerate. This keeps well several weeks. Use in iced tea, mixed drinks, or freeze to a slush and serve in sherbet glasses.

Mrs. Lionel V. Swift
Marietta, Georgia

Hot Chocolate Mix
Delicious and marvelous for gift-giving!

2 pound box Nestles Quik
1 pound box powdered sugar
11 ounce jar Coffeemate
8 quart box powdered milk

Mix together and sift. Store in jars. Fill cup half full of mix and finish filling with hot water.

Mrs. Daniel Dupree

Russian Tea Mix

½ cup instant tea
2½ cups sugar
2 scant cups Tang
2 packages Twist lemonade, small
2 teaspoons cinnamon
1 teaspoon cloves

Mix and store in jar. Add two teaspoons to one cup hot water. Keeps indefinitely.

Mrs. Jerry Wolff

Champagne Peach Cup
Divine, light dessert for luncheon or summer supper

2 packages frozen sliced peaches
  or 3 cups fresh peaches, sliced
  and sweetened
Juice of ½ lemon
2 jiggers simple syrup
2 cups crushed ice
1 pint champagne
Peach slices for garnish

Divide ingredients in half and whirl in a blender. Pour in sherbets and serve with spoons. This may be made a few hours before serving and stored in the freezer Whirl again for a few seconds. Serves 6 to 8.

Deepfreeze Daiquiri

2- 6 ounce cans frozen pink
  lemonade
1-6 ounce can frozen limeade
1 fifth light rum
6 lemonade cans of water

Mix all ingredients. Store in glass jar in deep freeze for 8 to 12 hours before serving. About 30 minutes before serving, remove from freezer. Mixture should be icy. Any portion not used may be frozen again. You may want to omit one can of pink lemonade and add a 10 ounce package of strawberries. For a tart taste, add juice of 2 lemons. This will never freeze solid. This recipe makes about 2 quarts or 20 to 25 cocktails.

Mrs. Elton Upshaw, Jr.

Galliano Daiquiri

¾ ounce Liquore Galliano
¾ ounce light rum
Juice of ½ lime
1 teaspoon powdered sugar

Add one cup crushed ice and blend all ingredients in the blender for 30 to 60 seconds.

Fresh fruit such as peaches, strawberries or very ripe bananas may be added to any daquiri made in a blender.

"Fruit Cocktail"

1½ ounces orange juice
½ ounce lemon juice
1½ ounces Cognac
2 teaspoons sugar
½ fresh banana
1 scoop vanilla ice cream, optional

Place ingredients in blender and serve in champagne glasses or brandy snifter and garnish with cherry and orange slices. To serve as a before dinner drink, frappé with a little crushed ice. To serve as an after dinner drink add the vanilla ice cream if desired. Serves 2.

Mrs. Don Phillips

Piña Colada

6 ounces rum
½ cup Piña Colada mix
2 cups pineapple juice
Crushed ice
Pineapple sticks

Fill blender with first three ingredients and raise to 3/4 full with crushed ice. Blend until frothy. Garnish with stick of fresh pineapple. May pour over crushed ice. Serves 4.

George M. Snellings III

Velvet Hammer

1- 10 ounce package frozen sliced strawberries or frozen peaches
1 cup light rum
Juice of 2 lemons, less than ½ cup
Crushed ice

Put strawberries, rum and lemon juice in blender for a few seconds. Add 1 tray of ice to fill blender. Blend until mixture is icy. Pour into daiquiri glasses. Makes 6 to 8 drinks.

Mrs. Elton Upshaw, Jr.

Harvey Wallbanger
Taking Bloody Mary's place at brunch.

1-6 ounce can frozen orange juice
4 ounces vodka
2 ounces Galliano

Dilute frozen orange juice according to directions. Mix together and serve over ice. The orange juice gives it the freshness of morning. Serves four.

Cassis Punch

3 fifths dry white wine
1½ cups crème de cassis
3 oranges, juiced
Juice of 1½ lemons

Combine wine, cassis and juices. Garnish with orange slices and strawberries. Serve in punch bowl with ice block made of lemonade and filled with blackberries if available. Serves 25 punch cups.

Citrus Punch

Juice of 2 limes
Juice of 1 lemon
3-6 ounce cans frozen orange juice
1- 6 ounce can frozen lime juice
1- 6 ounce can frozen lemon juice
1- 46 ounce can pineapple juice
1 teaspoon almond extract
½ teaspoon salt
1½ quarts water
1- 28 ounce bottle chilled
  ginger ale
1 fifth bottle chilled sauterne

Several hours ahead, combine ingredients except gingerale and wine. Chill. At serving time, stir in gingerale and sauterne. Serve over block of ice or fruit mold in a punch bowl. Serves 40.

Mrs. Don Phillips

Lakeshore Bolo

1 diced fresh pineapple
1 cup simple syrup
1 fifth bourbon
2 fifths champagne

Mix pineapple, simple syrup and bourbon. Let set for 12 hours. When ready to serve, place a decorative block of ice or a whole fresh frozen pineapple in a punch bowl. Pour pineapple mixture over it and add the champagne.

Mrs. Rudolph Weinman
New Orleans, Louisiana

Sangria

2 gallons California Zinfandel
2 quarts orange juice
2 cups lemon juice
1 cup sugar
1 cup brandy
½ cup Cointreau
2 quarts soda water
3 oranges, sliced
3 lemons, sliced

Mix and chill wine, orange juice, lemon juice, sugar, brandy and Cointreau. Pour in punch bowl; add soda, sliced oranges and lemons just before serving. Float frozen fruit arrangement in bowl or decorated ice ring. Makes 13 quarts or about 100 punch cups.

Mrs. Max Williams
Dallas, Texas

New Year's Eve Punch
A great punch for men!

1 fifth bourbon
1 large can unsweetened grapefruit
  juice
¾ cup grenadine
9 cups sparkling water

FOR 40:
6 fifths bourbon
8 quarts grapefruit juice
4½ cups grenadine
14 quarts sparkling water

Mix bourbon, grapefuit juice and grenadine ahead. Add sparkling water to punch bowl just before serving. Serves 32 punch cups.

Mrs. John Cram
Corpus Christi, Texas

Whiskey Cup for 25

2 quarts bourbon
1½ cups sugar
Juice of 3 lemons
½ cup grenadine
2 quarts soda, chilled
2 oranges sliced
1 cup pineapple chunks

Combine bourbon, sugar, lemon juice, grenadine and chill. Just before serving add chilled soda. Garnish with sliced oranges and pineapple chunks.

Mrs. John Cram
Corpus Christi, Texas

Red Devil

1½ ounces Tequila
5 ounces Clamato juice
1 ounce lemon juice
Dash of Worcestershire sauce

Mix ingredients together and serve in a 10 ounce glass over ice.

Mrs. Wilbur Marsh
Dallas, Texas

Bloody Bull

1½ cans consomme
4-6 ounce cans V-8 juice
3 Tablespoons lemon juice
2 Tablespoons Worcestershire
2 Tablespoons celery salt
Tabasco to taste
1½ ounces vodka per drink

Combine first six ingredients. Per drink: Place 1½ ounces vodka in glass with ice and fill with mixture.

Refrigerator Martini

2 cups gin
1 cup vodka
1/2 cup vermouth

Mix in an empty fifth bottle. Store in the refrigerator.
Will keep as long as they last.

Jim Geisler

Milk Punch

8 ounces milk
1 jigger brandy or bourbon
1/2 jigger crème de cacao

Add whiskey and liqueur to milk. Serve over ice.

Ed Seymour, Jr.

Whipped Milk Punch

1 quart vanilla ice cream
1 pint milk
2 teaspoons vanilla
6 ounces whiskey
Nutmeg

Use a blender if possible. Put in all ingredients and
blend until smooth. Otherwise, use electric mixer to
whip until smooth. Garnish each glass with ground
nutmeg. Serves 6.

Jack Ratliff

Egg Nog

8 eggs
1/2 cup sugar
1 cup whiskey
1 pint heavy cream

Separate the eggs. Beat whites until stiff but not dry
and set aside. Beat yolks; add sugar beating well and
continue to beat while adding whiskey. Whip the
heavy cream. Fold in whipped cream and beaten egg
whites. This is a perfect eggnog to eat with a spoon.

George M. Snellings, Jr.

Brandy Ice

6 scoops vanilla ice cream
6 ounces brandy
3 ounces white crème de cacao
1 1/2 ounces white crème de menthe,
    optional
8 ice cubes

Place in blender and blend quickly. Serves 4 to 6.

Allen H. Coon

Pink Squirrel

1 pint vanilla ice cream
2 jiggers brandy
2 jiggers crème de noyaux
8 cubes of ice

Put half of ice cream in blender with brandy and creme de noyaux. Blend, adding ice cubes and remaining ice cream. The mixture should be the consistency of a thick milk shake. If the mixture is not this thick, add more ice cream. Serve in long stem champagne glasses. Serves 6 to 8.

Tommy Godfrey

"Pepper Upper"

8 cups warm coffee
1 gallon vanilla ice cream
1 fifth bourbon whiskey

Put ice cream in a bowl and mash to soften. Pour warm coffee over this and add whiskey. You can make this strong or weak to taste. Ladle in punch cups or Old Fashion glasses. Good as a "Pepper Upper" on New Year's Day or after a celebration. Serves 20 to 25.

Mrs. Rupert Evans
Lake Providence, Louisiana

Irish Coffee

½ ounce Irish whiskey
½ ounce rum
½ teaspoon sugar
Strong dripped coffee
Whipped cream
Freshly shredded coconut

Per Irish whiskey mug: Stir whiskey, rum and sugar in the bottom of the cup until sugar is dissolved. Fill with coffee. Top with whipped cream and freshly shredded coconut. If preparing for a crowd, mix proportional amounts of whiskey, rum and sugar ahead.

Mrs. John Hunt

Café Brûlot

1 cup brandy
40 whole cloves
45 lumps sugar
2 sticks whole cinnamon, broken fine
½ lemon, sliced very thin
½ orange, sliced very thin
1 quart strong drip coffee
Brûlot bowl

In small saucepan, heat brandy over low flame. Combine spices, sugar lumps, orange and lemon slices in Brûlot bowl. Flame brandy; pour into the bowl. Allow to burn 3 to 4 minutes. Pour in the hot coffee slowly. Stir well to dissolve sugar. Serve immediatley, stirring after each cup. NOTE: A chafing dish may be substituted for a Brûlot bowl. Serves 12 demitasse cups.

Mrs. J.B. Dawkins

Hot Buttered Rum Batter

¼ pound butter
1 pound dark brown sugar
¼ teaspoon cinnamon
¼ teaspoon nutmeg
¼ teaspoon ground cloves
Dark rum

Cream butter and sugar. Sprinkle spices and mix thoroughly. Store in refrigerator in a covered container.

THE DRINK:
Place 1 heaping Tablespoon of batter in a mug. Add 1 1/2 ounces dark rum. Fill with boiling water. Stir and serve.

Egg Rolls

FILLING:
1/2 cup finely chopped celery
3/4 cup shredded cabbage
3 Tablespoons oil
1/2 cup diced cooked shrimp
1/2 cup diced cooked pork, ham,
   beef, veal, or chicken
4 scallions, finely chopped
1 clove garlic, minced
1/4 cup Soy sauce

EGG ROLL SKINS:
3/4 cup sifted flour
1 Tablespoon cornstarch
1 teaspoon salt
2 eggs, beaten
Pinch of sugar
1 1/2 cups water
1/4 cup oil

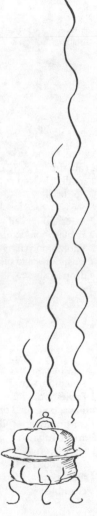

Parboil celery and cabbage in 1/2 cup water. Drain and set aside. Heat oil in skillet, add shrimp and pork. Fry for 3 minutes, stirring constantly. Add remaining ingredients and cook for 5 minutes. To make egg roll skins: sift flour, cornstarch and salt into a bowl. Beat eggs and a pinch of sugar. Add water slowly, beating until batter is smooth. To make each skin, grease a hot 6 inch skillet with about 1 teaspoonful of oil. Pour about 3 Tablespoons of batter over bottom. Fry over medium heat until batter shrinks from sides of skillet. Turn skin and fry for 1 minute on the other side. Remove and cool. Makes 12 skins, for hors d'oeuvres make smaller. *To assemble the egg rolls:* place 2 or 3 Tablespoons of filling on the center of each egg roll skin. Fold 2 sides over edge of filling and roll up. Seal with flour paste. Fry in hot oil until golden brown. Serves 10 to 12.

Mrs. W.S. Shafto, Jr.

Avocado Dip

4 avocados
Garlic salt
Salt
Onion salt
Tabasco
1 Tablespoon Lea & Perrins
Juice of 3 lemons
Mayonnaise

Mash the avocados with a fork and add the seasonings to taste. Squeeze the lemons over the avocados. It is very important to get enough lemon juice or it will taste bland. Mix all of this with mayonnaise to make it creamy. Use Doritos to dip. Makes 2 cups.

Mrs. James Dennis

Guacamole Salad or Dip

1 small onion
1 tomato
1 small dried red pepper,
    optional
6 peeled avocados
2½ teaspoons salt
2 Tablespoons lemon juice
2 Tablespoons mayonnaise
1 teaspoon salad oil
4 drops Tabasco

On a chopping board, chop fine the onion, tomato and dried red pepper. Chop, do not mash the avocados and add the salt, lemon juice, mayonnaise, salad oil, and Tabasco. Mix all ingredients together Serve in a bowl or on greens. Makes 8 servings.

Mrs. William Kelly

Guacamole With Bacon

2 cups mashed avocados, about
    4 medium size
2 Tablespoons lime juice
1 teaspoon grated onion
2 teaspoons olive oil
8 drops Tabasco
½ teaspoon salt
½ teaspoon MSG
4 slices bacon, fried and
    crumbled

Mash avocados and add the rest of the ingredients. Serve with Doritos. Makes 2 cups.

Mrs. Don Irby

There is not a better sauce for fresh vegetables than ½ cup mayonnaise, ¼ cup soy sauce, 2 Tablespoons of lemon juice, salt and pepper to taste.

Quick Guacamole Dip

1 carton sour cream
1 package onion soup mix
2 cans avocado dip
Dill seed to taste or crushed
    dill weed

Mix all ingredients and chill. Serve with Fritos.
Makes about 2 cups.

Mrs. Carrick Inabnett

Curry Dip for Raw Vegetables

1½ cups mayonnaise
2 teaspoons curry powder or
    more to taste
1 Tablespoon grated onion
½ teaspoon dry mustard
½ teaspoon salt
Black pepper to taste
Tabasco to taste

Mix all ingredients together. Good served with crisp
vegetables. This is better if it is made a day before
using. Serves 10 to 12.

Mrs. Paul Lansing
New Orleans, Louisiana

Green Goddess Dip

2- 3 ounce packages cream cheese,
    softened
1 cup mayonnaise
1 cup sour cream
2 Tablespoons lemon juice
4 Tablespoons tarragon vinegar
1 scant Tablespoon garlic salt
½ cup chopped green onions,
    using more tops than bottoms
⅔ cup chopped fresh parsley

Mix all ingredients together. Serve as a dip with
fresh vegetables. Suggested vegetables are: sliced
cucumbers, sliced squash, sliced turnips, cauliflower,
cherry tomatoes, carrot sticks, and celery sticks.

Mrs. Ralph King

Lake Charles Dip

½ pint sour cream
1 package Good Seasons Italian
  Salad Dressing Mix
1 Tablespoon mayonnaise
Juice of ½ lemon
½ avocado, chopped finely
½ tomato, chopped
Dash of Tabasco

Mix all ingredients. Serve immediately or refrigerate. This is delicious with chips or as a dip for raw vegetables.

Mrs. Tommy Godfrey

Mexican Hot Sauce Dip

1-15 ounce can stewed tomatoes
1-11 ounce can Rotel tomatoes
1-8 ounce can jalapeño pepper
  relish

Mix all together in a blender until smooth. Serve with Doritos. Makes 1 quart. Very good on all Mexican food and as a dip.

Mrs. Dick Ethridge

Vegetable Dip

⅓ cup chili sauce
1 cup mayonnaise
2 Tablespoons horseradish
1 small onion chopped finely
1 teaspoon mustard seed
Dash of Tabasco

Mix all ingredients in blender. Use as a dip for cauliflower, celery, carrots, bell pepper or with shrimp.

Mrs. Robert Harrison

Broccoli Cheese Dip

1 package chopped broccoli,
  cooked and drained
3 stalks celery, chopped finely
1 medium onion, chopped finely
2 Tablespoons butter
1 can cream of mushroom soup
1 roll garlic cheese
Worcestershire sauce to taste
Tabasco to taste

Sauté onion and celery in the butter. Add cooked broccoli, mushroom soup, garlic cheese, Worcestershire sauce and Tabasco to taste. You may add 1/2 can of Rotel tomatoes if desired, or just use the juice. One pound of fresh lump crabmeat or 2 cans of crabmeat is a delicious addition also.

Mrs. John Dryden

Lemon Mushrooms
Different and delicious

1 pound butter
2 cups flour
12 large cans mushrooms
6 cans beef bouillon
4 cans mushroom juice
12 lemons, juice and rind
2 cups chopped parsley
Black pepper
Kitchen Bouquet

Make a medium roux of butter and flour. Add drained mushrooms, reserving juice. Add beef bouillon, mushroom juice, and lemon juice to taste. Add parsley, pepper, and Kitchen Bouquet for color. If not thick enough, thicken with corn starch. This recipe freezes well and may also be halved. Serve hot in a chafing dish with Melba rounds.

Mrs. R. L. Davis, Sr.
Mrs. Edmund Brown

Antipasto

2 heads cauliflower, separated
   into flowerets
3 green peppers, cut in strips
2 packages carrots, cut in sticks
1 bunch celery, cut in sticks
1 pound button mushrooms
1½ cups oil, salad and olive
3 cups tarragon vinegar
½ to ¾ cup sugar
3 cloves garlic, minced
1 Tablespoon prepared mustard
1 Tablespoon salt
2 teaspoons tarragon leaves
Pepper to taste

Prepare vegetables. Combine remaining ingredients and pour over vegetables. Taste for seasonings. Cover and chill at least twelve hours, but overnight is better. They should be turned occasionally. Slices of yellow squash and cucumbers are good to add in the summer. Add them a few hours before serving. Drain well to serve. It goes a long way and your weight-watcher friends will love it. Will keep for weeks in the refrigerator. Serves fifty.

Mrs. Jerry H. Wolff

Artichoke Balls

14 ounce can artichoke hearts,
   drained and mashed
1 cup Progresso seasoned bread
   crumbs
2 Tablespoons olive oil
1 Tablespoon lemon juice
2 Tablespoons Romano or
   Parmesan cheese
2 eggs
2 cloves garlic, crushed

Combine all ingredients. Roll in small balls. Roll in extra cheese, using the same kind you put into balls. Heat in 350 degree oven for ten minutes. Do not let them dry out. They may be frozen. Makes four to six dozen depending on size of balls. Very good!

Mrs. Edwin Preis
Newellton, Louisiana

Avocado Cocktail Ring

3 Tablespoons gelatin
2/3 cup cold water
2 1/2 Tablespoons boiling water
Salt
3 Tablespoons vinegar
Tabasco
1 to 1 1/2 cups grated cucumber
1/4 cup grated onion
3 large ripe avocados
Juice of 1 lemon
1/2 cup mayonnaise
1/2 cup sour cream
Dash of celery salt

Soften gelatin in cold water for 10 minutes; add boiling water and dissolve. Add salt, vinegar, and Tabasco; stir well. Set aside to cool. Grate cucumber and onion. Mash avocados and add lemon juice. Stir together cucumber, onion, mayonnaise, sour cream, and celery salt. Blend in gelatin mixture and taste for seasoning. Pour into a 4 cup ring mold that has been rinsed in cold water. Put into the refrigerator to congeal. Unmold and garnish center with one of the following: watercress, parsley, or shrimp. Serve with crackers as an appetizer. Will serve about 50 at a cocktail party.

Mrs. Don Stinson

Pickled Carrots

6 cups water
2 cups vinegar
1/2 cup salt
Carrots
Garlic
Red pepper
Alum
Dill

Make a syrup of water, vinegar and salt, boiled together. Clean and slice raw carrots into stalks. Fill pint jars with carrots and into each jar place one tooth of garlic, red pepper to taste, a pinch of alum and a little dill. Pour your syrup mixture over carrots and seal. Chill before serving. Do not use for two or three weeks. Great for hors d'oeuvres. Nice to keep in refrigerator for drop-in guests!

Mrs. George M. Snellings, Jr.
"Cook with Marie Louise"

Pickled Eggplant

2 medium eggplants
2 medium onions
1/2 cup olive oil
1/2 cup salad oil
1/4 cup wine vinegar
1/2 cup chopped olives
1 teaspoon marjoram
1 teaspoon oregano
1/4 teaspoon basil
Salt and pepper
1/2 teaspoon onion powder

Cook eggplant in salted water until just tender. Drain and dice. Put cut onion rings in bottom of dish. Put eggplant on top of onion rings. Mix the remaining ingredients and pour over the vegetables. Refrigerate overnight. A little messy, but worth it.

Mrs. Jerry H. Wolff

Sicilian Olives

1 quart olives, green with seed
2 teaspoons oregano
2 teaspoons basil
1/2 cup olive oil
3 fresh green onions, chopped
1/2 cup vinegar
1/4 cup wine vinegar
Juice of 2 lemons
1 teaspoon salt

Drain liquid from olives. Using meat cleaver or wooden mallet, bruise each olive by pounding lightly. Return to jar. Combine other ingredients. Pour over olives. Cover. Allow seasonings to blend at room temperature for twenty-four hours. Invert jar occasionally to improve distribution of seasonings. Save liquid after using olives. It makes an excellent salad dressing. You may want to add a little more lemon juice to reduce calories.

Dr. Agnes Miller
Ruston, Louisiana

Pickled Okra

8 cups vinegar
8 cups water
1 cup salt
1 teaspoon dill seed
2 cloves garlic
2 small hot peppers
Fresh okra

Boil vinegar, water, and salt for 10 minutes. Pack washed okra pods, which have had the stems cut off, into pint jars. Place the listed amounts of dill, garlic, and peppers into each jar. Pour the hot mixture over okra to cover. Seal. Allow 3 weeks to pickle. Yields about 10 pints. Chill before serving.

Marinated Raw Mushrooms

1 pound mushrooms
¾ cup olive oil
3 Tablespoons tarragon vinegar
½ teaspoon salt
Fresh ground pepper
2 teaspoons minced parsley
½ teaspoon dried tarragon

Wash mushrooms and slice them lengthwise. Combine all ingredients and mix well with mushrooms. Let stand approximately six hours at room temperature before serving.

Mrs. Gene Worthen

Pickled Mushrooms

3-8 ounce cans button mushrooms
1¼ cup Progresso wine vinegar
2 packages Good Seasons Italian dressing
4 teaspoons shredded green onions
2½ teaspoons dehydrated parsley flakes
1 teaspoon Worcestershire sauce
Dash Tabasco

Drain mushrooms. Combine the remaining ingredients in a bowl. Let sit about 15 minutes, until the parsley and green onions soften. Pour in drained mushrooms. Marinate overnight. Will last for several weeks in the refrigerator if tightly covered.

Mrs. Saul Mintz

Spiced Mushrooms

1 large can button mushrooms
Wine vinegar
2 heaping Tablespoons minced green onions
1 large bayleaf
3 whole cloves
1 clove garlic, minced
1 dash Tabasco
Salt and pepper
Salad oil

Drain liquid from mushrooms. Place in bowl and cover generously with wine vinegar. Put in refrigerator for one hour or longer. Take mushrooms from bowl and put into a jar. Add onions and all seasonings. Pour in oil to barely cover mushrooms. Close jar tightly and refrigerate for two days. Serves about 20.

Mrs. Bob Hand

Stuffed Mushroom Canapé

¼ pound butter
3 ounces chopped green onions
2 cloves of garlic, chopped
¼ teaspoon thyme
⅛ teaspoon Accent
1 cup wet bread
½ cup cracker meal
Salt and pepper to taste
½ pound lump crabmeat
4 fresh mushrooms, 4 or 5 inches
Hollandaise Sauce

Melt butter in saucepan, add green onions, garlic, thyme, and Accent; cook for five minutes. Add wet bread and mix well; blend in cracker meal and cook on a low fire for fifteen minutes. Add salt and pepper to taste. Fold in crabmeat. Let cool. Roll into balls, stuff fresh mushrooms, and bake in the oven at 500 degrees until brown. Top with Hollandaise Sauce. Serves 4. This dressing is also adequate for 12 to 14 two inch mushrooms.

Mushrooms Stuffed with Sausage

1 pint of fresh mushrooms or
  Monarch's for grilling
1 pound of Bryan's hot sausage

Wash mushrooms and remove stems. Chop stems finely or put through blender and mix them with the sausage. Stuff mushrooms and bake in 375 degree oven for 30 minutes. May be prepared ahead but must be served as soon as cooked. Good for brunch.

Mrs. Elton Upshaw, Jr.

Stuffed Mushrooms

2-16 ounce cans deluxe mushroom buttons
2 Tablespoons butter
¾ to 1 pound lean ground meat
Salt and pepper to taste
2 teaspoons Blue Cheese salad mix
Bread rounds
Paprika
Parsley flakes

Remove inside of mushrooms, chop fine and sauté in butter. Cool slightly and mix ground meat and mushrooms. Add salt, pepper, and blue cheese seasoning. Stuff mushroom buttons with a small amount of meat. Toast rounds on one side only. Place button on untoasted side. Sprinkle with paprika and parsley flakes. You may freeze these and use as needed. Heat at 350 degrees for 10 to 15 minutes. Makes about 48 mushrooms.

Mrs. Sidney Opotowsky
Newellton, Louisiana

Sauté crown mushrooms, chicken livers and gizzards in butter seasoned to your taste. Serve hot in a chafing dish. Men love this!

Onion Canapé

6 large onions
½ pound hot sausage
Pepperidge Farm dressing mix
Bouillon
Salt to taste
Cayenne pepper to taste

Boil the onions until soft; drain and cool. Cook the sausage until crumbly and brown. Add enough dressing mix and bouillon to make a thick stuffing. Season to taste with salt and cayenne. Separate the onions into large leaves. Place a generous amount of dressing on each leaf and roll up as for an old-fashioned cigarette. Refrigerate until ready to serve. Broil directly under the flame to brown and heat through. This makes 40 to 50.

Mrs. Max Williams
Dallas, Texas

Swiss Onion Squares

1 egg, well beaten
¾ cup milk
2 cups biscuit mix
2 Tablespoons poppy seeds
2 cups chopped sweet onion
2 Tablespoons butter
1 egg
¾ cup sour cream
½ teaspoon salt
¼ teaspoon pepper
Paprika

Blend egg and milk with biscuit mix and poppy seeds. Turn into greased 9 x 9 inch pan. Fry onions in butter until tender and lightly browned. Spread on dough. Beat egg with sour cream and season with salt and pepper. Spread over onions. Bake at 400 degrees for 25 minutes. Cut into squares, sprinkle with paprika and serve very hot. Serves 12 to 15 for an appetizer. Delicious with roast or steak, also.

Mrs. Jerry Wolff

Sauerkraut Balls
From Gruber's, Cleveland, Ohio.

2 Tablespoons oil, for browning
½ pound ham
½ pound pork
½ pound corned beef
1 onion, chopped
Pinch of parsley
2 cups flour
1 teaspoon dry mustard
1 teaspoon salt
2 cups milk
2 pounds sauerkraut
Flour
1 egg, beaten
Fresh bread crumbs
Shortening for deep frying

Run ham, pork, and beef through a meat grinder. Mix in onion and parsley; fry until brown. Sift two cups flour with mustard and salt; add to meat mixture with 2 cups milk. Cook together until fluffy. Cool, then add sauerkraut and put the entire mixture through food chopper, once and then again, and mix thoroughly. Roll into balls about the size of walnuts. Dredge in flour, dip in beaten egg, roll in bread crumbs and deep fat fry. Serve piping hot. This recipe will yield about twenty-five balls.

Mrs. Dan Moore

Southern Fried Vegetables
Something different, but good.

Cauliflower
Squash
Eggplant
Okra
Salt and Pepper
Flour
Shortening for frying

Prepare squash and eggplant by slicing them very thin and soaking the slices in cold salted water. Drain well on paper towel. You may shake vegetables in flour and salt and pepper, or cornmeal, or pancake mix. Coat well. The okra needs no soaking. Cut in small pieces and fry all in hot shortening as you would chicken. Fry until golden brown and drain. Serve immediately. Very tasty with drinks.

Take a block of cream cheese, cover with: Caviar garnished with lemon slices; Chutney; Guava jelly; Pickapeppa Sauce; or a can of Smoked Oysters. Cheers!

Adrienne's Delight
Great for an afternoon Sherry Party!

12 ounces Philadelphia cream
  cheese
1 stick butter
½ cup sour cream
½ cup sugar
1 envelope plain gelatin
¼ cup cold water
½ cup white raisins
1 cup slivered almonds, toasted
Grated rinds of two lemons
Saltine crackers

Let cream cheese, butter, and sour cream come to room temperature. Cream well and add sugar. Soften envelope of gelatin in 1/4 cup cold water. Dissolve over hot water. Add to cream cheese mixture. Then add raisins, slivered almonds, and lemon rind. Put in one quart mold in refrigerator. When firm unmold and serve with Saltine crackers. This can be used at cocktail parties or as a dessert. Do not substitute for Saltine crackers. You can also freeze this after unmolding it. When ready to use, just thaw. Serves 35.

Mrs. Thermon Smith
Little Rock, Arkansas

Anchovy Paste Spread

2 large packages cream cheese
1 medium onion, grated
2 Tablespoons lemon juice
1/2 tube anchovy paste
2 Tablespoons mayonnaise
Lea & Perrins to taste
Salt and red pepper to taste

Let cream cheese soften at room temperature, add grated onion and remaining ingredients. Blend in a blender until smooth. Mound on a cocktail dish and sprinkle with paprika. Chill. Serve with crackers.

From the files of Mrs. Jack Ratliff

Caper Dip

1- 8 ounce package Philadelphia
  cream cheese
1- 2¾ ounce bottle capers

Beat cheese adding enough caper juice to soften the cheese. Drain off the remaining juice and add the capers, mixing well. Serve with potato chips.

Mrs. Dave Aron

Sardine Paste

1- 8 ounce package cream cheese
1/2 teaspoon salt
1 Tablespoon lemon juice
Black pepper to taste
2 cans sardines, drained
2 Tablespoons dried parlsey
Tabasco to taste
Capers
Parsley to garnish

Cream cheese with salt, lemon juice and pepper. Add sardines and beat in well. Add parsley and Tabasco. Taste for seasonings, adding more lemon juice if desired. Mound or mold; garnish with parsley and capers. Serve with thin toast or Melba rounds.

Mrs. Ed Seymour, Jr.

Schmeerkäas

1- 8 ounce package Philadelphia
  cream cheese
5 Tablespoons Hellman's
  mayonnaise
1½ Tablespoons Lea & Perrins
2 Tablespoons grated onion and
  juice
Garlic salt to taste
1/4 teaspoon Tabasco

With an electric mixer, cream the cheese and add all of the remaining ingredients. This is better if it is prepared ahead and the flavors are allowed to blend. This freezes beautifully. Garnish with parsley and paprika. Serve with potato chips.

Mrs. Kirt Touchstone, Jr

Brandy Cheese Balls

1 pound sharp Cheddar, grated
1/2 pound Roquefort, crumbled
1 pound cream cheese
1 onion, grated
6 Tablespoons Worcestershire
1/4 cup brandy
2 teaspoons Tabasco
1/2 teaspoon celery salt
1/2 teaspoon garlic salt
2 dashes garlic powder
1 cup chopped nuts
1 cup chopped parsley

Let all cheeses reach room temperature. Put cheeses and remaining ingredients in large bowl of mixmaster. Cream thoroughly. Chill several hours. Shape into balls, wrap, refrigerate or freeze. Before serving, roll in chopped pecans and parsley mixed together. These balls will become soft, so do not take out of the refrigerator too long before serving. Recipe may be halved. Make another batch instead of doubling, as you will have too much to beat smoothly.

Mrs. Don Irby

Cheese Balls

1 cup chopped pecans
1 pound Roquefort cheese
2 pounds cream cheese
1 small package processed sharp
    Cheddar, grated
1 onion, minced finely
1 teaspoon Worcestershire
Salt

Set aside half the chopped pecans, add the rest to remaining ingredients and blend well. Divide and shape into three balls. Roll in the reserved pecans and chill. Place on a large plate and surround with crisp crackers. These balls can be frozen.

Mrs. Nat Troy

Cheese Roll

1 pound American cheese, grated
1- 8 ounce package cream cheese
1/2 teaspoon salt
1/4 cup chopped pecans
10 stuffed olives, cut finely
1/8 teaspoon red pepper
1/4 teaspoon sugar
Chili powder
Paprika

Mix all ingredients except the last two. Make cheese roll and roll in chili powder. Sprinkle with paprika. This may be made in a ball or long roll and sliced for crackers. It can also be frozen indefinitely.

Mrs. J. Nolan Harvey

Pimiento Cheese Rolls

1 pound New York State Sharp
  Cheese
1/2 pound pimiento cheese
8 ounce cream cheese
1 onion, grated
2 or 3 cloves garlic, pressed
Paprika

Mix all ingredients with hands. Roll into long, slim rolls about twelve inches long and the diameter the size of a quarter. Roll in paprika and put each roll in wax paper and refrigerate. Serve on crackers. Makes four rolls.

Mrs. Tom Keller
Baton Rouge, Louisiana

Cheese Mold With or Without Caviar

2- 8 ounce packages of Philadelphia cream cheese
8 ounces of Roquefort cheese
1/2 cup mayonnaise
1/4 teaspoon Tabasco
1 garlic bud, pressed
1 small onion, grated
4 teaspoons lemon juice
Caviar, optional

Mix cheeses at room temperature. Use two parts cream cheese to one part Roquefort, according to the size of the party. Mix cheeses with mayonnaise, use more if needed. Add 1/2 teaspoon of salt if caviar is not to be used; it is salty. Add remaining ingredients and blend well. Mold the cheese. Make deep hollow in center of cheese and fill with caviar if you like it and can afford it. Use plain or rye Melba toast or assorted crackers. Serves 15 to 20.

Mrs. DeWitt Milam

Caviar Cheese Ball

2-8 ounce packages cream cheese
1/2 to 1 teaspoon Worcestershire
  sauce
1/2 tube anchovy paste
Salt and pepper to taste
1 jar red caviar

Blend all but caviar well and mold in round bowl. Spread with caviar and serve with potato chips or crackers.

Mrs. Hayden Cutler III
Fort Worth, Texas

Quicky Rotel

1 pound sharp Cheddar cheese
1 can Rotel tomatoes
1 can chili without beans

Cut cheese in large pieces; add Rotel tomatoes and chili. Put over low heat to melt the cheese, stirring occasionally. Serve in a chafing dish with Fritos.

Miss Harriet Swift
Marietta, Georgia

Hot Cheese Dip

2 pounds Velveeta cheese
1 quart mayonnaise
2 medium onions, chopped
3 buttons garlic, crushed
1- 12 ounce can jalapeño peppers

Let cheese come to room temperature. Remove the seeds from the jalapeño peppers. Place the peppers, onion, and garlic in a blender and whirl until blended together. Cut cheese into small blocks and place in a large mixing bowl. Add the mayonnaise and blended mixture and beat until smooth and of dipping consistency. Put in jars and refrigerate. Yields 2 1/2 quarts. Serve with Fritos or tacos. May be served hot or cold.

Mrs. J. Shelby Cage

Jalapeño Pie

1- 7 ounce can jalapeño peppers
1/2 pound sharp cheese, coarsely grated
4 eggs
Salt and red pepper to taste

Drain and seed peppers. Cut into thin lengthwise slivers and line bottom and sides of a 9 inch pie plate. Press grated cheese in plate over peppers. Beat eggs, adding salt and red pepper. Pour over cheese. Bake at 350 degrees for 25 to 30 minutes. After removing from oven, slice into small wedges. Leave pie in plate and pass as finger food.

Mrs. James Altick

Seed jalapeños and coat with beer batter. Fry in deep hot fat. Serve immediately.

Blue Cheese Puffs

1 egg, separated
Dash of salt
1 Tablespoon mayonnaise
Blue cheese spread
16 round crackers

Beat egg yolk, salt, and mayonnaise. Fold in stiffly beaten egg white. Spread crackers with blue cheese; top with meringue. Bake 350 degrees 10 to 15 minutes.

Mrs. Robert Harrison

Cheese Rounds

1 egg
4 ounces cream cheese
1 finely chopped onion
Salt and pepper, to taste
¼ teaspoon dried chives
Party rye rounds
Caraway seeds

Beat egg; add rest of ingredients except seeds. Spread on rye, sprinkle each round with seeds. Freeze for later use. Broil 4 inches from flame before serving.

Mrs. Jerome Heisler
Wilmington, Delaware

Bacon-Cheese Snacks

2 cups grated sharp cheese
1 small can chopped ripe olives
2 Tablespoons chopped onions
1 cup Hellman's mayonnaise
Bacon bits
Rye rounds

Combine all ingredients. Spread on one loaf Pepperidge Party Rye. Sprinkle with bacon bits, *not Bacos*, in a jar. Bake at 300 degrees for 15 to 20 minutes. Can be made ahead and refrigerated or frozen, uncooked. Serve on heated tray or right from oven.

Mrs. Jack Files

Wrap large stuffed olives with bacon; secure with picks. Fry in deep hot fat. Delicious and quick!!

Fried Cheese Grits Party Bites

1 cup quick-cooking grits
1 teaspoon salt
4 cups boiling water
1 full cup extra sharp American
    cheese, finely chopped
1 egg, slightly beaten
Dash red pepper, optional

Cook grits as directed on package. When done, remove from fire and stir in cheese and egg. Continue stirring until cheese is melted. If desired, add red pepper to taste. Grits should have a distinct cheesy flavor. If more cheese is needed to get this desired flavor, add at this point. Stir again until melted. Pour grits into shallow pan or dish. Grits should not be more than one-half inch thick in dish. When completely cool, put into refrigerator for several hours or overnight. When ready to serve, cut grits into bite-size slices. Put into paper bag containing enough flour to coat grits when shaken. Fry in hot deep fat until golden. Drain well and serve at once.

Mrs. Grayson Guthrie

Party Pizza Appetizers

12 pieces bacon
1- 12 ounce bottle chili sauce
1- 8 ounce package grated
    Cheddar cheese
1/2 onion, minced
Oregano to taste
Rye party rounds

Fry bacon until crisp and crumble. Mix all ingredients and heat over low heat until cheese melts. Spread on rye rounds and bake at 400 degrees for 15 minutes or broil until bubbly.

Mrs. Travis Oliver III

Caracus

jar chipped dried beef
stick butter
- No. 2 cans tomatoes
Tablespoons Lea & Perrins
teaspoons chili powder
pound mild cheese, grated
eggs, beaten

Cook beef until softened in butter. Add tomatoes, Lea & Perrins and chili powder. Simmer and add grated cheese and beaten eggs. Stir constantly until cheese is melted and dip is thickened. Serve on crackers or crisp toast. May be used as a hot or cold dip.

Mrs. W. F. Thurman

Beef with Oyster Sauce
Worth the extra effort!

OYSTER SAUCE:

1 pint oysters
3 Tablespoons soy sauce
1 teaspoon beef extract
2 teaspoons bead molasses
2 Tablespoons cornstarch
1½ Tablespoons water

BEEF:

2½ to 3 pounds lean beef roast, diced
1 large onion
1 bunch green onions
3 to 4 cloves garlic
2- 8 ounce cans sliced mushrooms, drained and juice reserved
1 stick butter
3 Tablespoons cornstarch
½ cup mushroom juice
1 can beef broth
Oyster sauce
2 Tablespoons La Choy Brown Gravy
¼ cup Madeira
¼ cup gin
Juice of 1 lemon
2 Tablespoons Worcestershire
2 teaspoons Lawry's Seasoned salt
1 teaspoon Spice Island beef stock base
2 teaspoons lemon-pepper marinade
Tabasco, to taste
Finely minced chives and parsley

Simmer oysters covered with liquor 15 minutes. Blend in blender; return to sauce pan and add remaining ingredients with cornstarch mixed in the water. Simmer uncovered, stirring until thickened.

Beef: Select your piece of beef and smile at your butcher. Have him frost the meat in his freezer, then run it through his slicer as thinly as possible. The meat is then very simple for you to *Dice*. Finely chop the onions, garlic, and 1 can of the mushrooms. Melt butter and sauté meat and vegetables until the meat is no longer pink. Mix cornstarch with 1/2 cup of mushroom juice and add all ingredients except chives and parsley. Simmer about 45 minutes with the cover set askew. Check for seasonings. Serve hot in a chafing dish topped with chives and parsley. Makes two quarts.

Mrs. Don Irby

38

Bourbon Bites

3 pounds hot dogs
1 cup brown sugar
1 cup bourbon
1 cup chili sauce

Skin the hot dogs; cut into bite-size pieces. Combine the remaining ingredients and pour over the hot dogs. Bake, covered, at 325 degrees for 3 hours. Serve hot in a chafing dish. The flavor is better if made a day before needed.

Mrs. Elmer Neill, Jr.
Tallulah, Louisiana

Hot Chili Dip

2 pounds ground chuck
2 large onions, chopped
4 cloves garlic, mashed
1 Tablespoon sugar
1 small bottle Mexene chili powder
2 Tablespoons cumin powder
6 or 8 chili pequins
1 Tablespoon salt or to taste
1 Tablespoon black pepper
2 large cans tomato sauce
4 cups hot water
2 cans Austex hot tamales
2 pound grated sharp cheese
2 bunches green onions, chopped

Put meat and next eight ingredients in a large heavy iron or aluminum pot. Stir until the meat is no longer pink. Add tomato sauce and hot water. Cover the pot and simmer for about three hours. Cool and place in the refrigerator overnight. The next day remove the grease from the top; reheat, add hot tamales, sliced, and cook until disintegrated. Add cheese, reserving 2 cups, and stir until the cheese has melted. Put chili in two oblong flat baking dishes. Sprinkle the remaining cheese on the top and melt the cheese in the oven. Remove from the oven and sprinkle the chopped green onions on top. Serve with king size Fritos. This freezes well, but do so before adding cheese and onion topping. Serves 50.

Mrs. Jack Rogers

Tartare Steak

1 pound lean sirloin or fillet of
   beef, freshly ground
1 egg yolk
4 green onions, finely chopped
1 teaspoon capers
2 anchovies, chopped, optional
Salt and pepper
Hot mustard
Worcestershire sauce
Tabasco
Brown bread
Butter

To be really good, the meat must be lean and freshly ground. Mix the egg yolk, green onions, capers and anchovies with the meat. Add the remaining ingredients to taste. Mix well but do not mash the meat too much. Spread butter on the bread, pumpernickle is great, then spread on the meat. Enjoy it! Serves two for a meal.

Mrs. J. Bennett Johnston, Jr.
Shreveport, Louisiana

Kibby
Raw, Baked, or Fried

2 pounds finely ground lean beef
  or lamb, trimmed from lean
  chuck or round steak
1½ cups finely cracked wheat
1 large onion, ground
Salt and pepper to taste
½ cup ice water

FILLING:
½ pound coarsely ground meat,
  may use trimmings from chuck
  or round steak with exception
  of fascia and not too much suet
½ to 1 cup pine nuts or chopped
  pecans
1 Tablespoon butter
Cinnamon to taste
Salt and pepper to taste

Soak wheat ten to fifteen minutes in cold water. Drain off water and squeeze dry. Add this to the meat, onion, and seasoning. Grind all ingredients together. After grinding, add the 1/2 cup water to soften. Mix well. To serve raw, place on platter and serve with melted butter or olive oil poured over top. To serve baked, use filling ingredients. Sauté all together in skillet. Take half of above raw kibby and spread in greased 8 x 10 inch pan. Dip hand in water to flatten. Spread filling over this and then pat remaining kibby over the filling. Score or cut in triangles with knife. Loosen edges with spatula or spoon. Pour 1/2 cup rendered butter over top*. Bake in 375 degree oven about twenty minutes or until meat is firm. Then brown under broiler. Let set a minute before removing from pan. Serves 8 to 10. For fried kibby, shape raw kibby like footballs by rolling in palms of hand, about 5" long. Make opening at one end and press meat out to form hollow for stuffing. Dip hand in ice water while shaping. Fry in oil until golden brown.

* To render butter, bring butter to a boil and pour off top and discard residue at bottom of pan.

Mrs. Faheam Cannon

PIÑON
(pine nuts)

Filete Guizado

6 pounds round steak, chuck
    roast, sirloin steak, or venison
2 sticks margarine
3 medium onions
2 large bell peppers
Jalapeño juice
3 pods garlic
Flour
1 cup canned tomatoes
2 cans mushrooms
1 cup dry white wine
Bouillon cubes
1/2 cup parsley, chopped
Celery seed
1/4 teaspoon cumin seed
1/4 teaspoon savory
Salt and pepper
1 teaspoon oregano
4 bay leaves
1/4 teaspoon rosemary

Remove all fat, then slice in slivers and sauté meat in one stick margarine melted in large Dutch oven. After red color changes, remove meat from pot and drain, reserving liquid. Melt 3/4 stick margarine in pot, put meat back in and brown. Remove again. Add 2 Tablespoons more of margarine if necessary and saute chopped onions and peppers, crushed garlic pods, and jalapeño juice to taste. Remove vegetables. Add flour to fat and brown. Add drippings from meat to make gravy. Add one cup canned tomatoes including juice, juice from two cans sliced mushrooms, reserving mushrooms, one cup dry white wine and bouillon made with cubes if more liquid is necessary to cover meat and vegetables well. Add rest of ingredients and simmer slowly for two hours. Stir occasionally, adding mushrooms for last hour. Taste for salt and wine, adding more if necessary. Makes large amount. Serve warm in a chafing dish with party rolls.

Mrs. Mike Payne
Eagle Pass, Texas

Roast Fillet

7 to 8 pound fillet of beef
Salt, use plenty
Pepper
Celery salt
Onion salt
2 lemons
2/3 cup A-1 sauce
1/4 cup Worcestershire sauce
1 bottle paprika

Rub each seasoning, except paprika, into entire roast separately. Use more seasoning than you think is necessary. Be sure to get into all crevices. Mix the juice of two lemons, the A-1 sauce, and Worcestershire sauce together. Rub this mixture into the entire roast. If you have any sauce left, save it. Put meat into shallow pan. Coat top, side and ends heavily with paprika. Leave at room temperature for eight to ten hours. It will draw its own juice. Baste with this and any leftover sauce. To cook, pour off sauce. Bake in pre-heated oven at 550 degrees for ten minutes. Then turn down to 450 degrees and bake for eight to ten minutes a pound. Bake uncovered. May use a rib-eye roast.

Mrs. Saul Mintz

Slice rare roast paper-thin. Serve on well-buttered rye bread with a selection of mustards.

Marinated Roast Beef

5 pound boneless beef roast
Salt and pepper

MARINADE:
1 cup red wine vinegar
1⅓ cups olive oil
1 pod garlic
½ teaspoon cracked pepper
¼ teaspoon oregano
2 Tablespoons parsley, minced
1 bay leaf

Salt and pepper roast well. Bake uncovered in 350 degree oven for two hours or until done. Refrigerate until cold. Remove fat and slice as thinly as possible, 1/8 inch if you can talk the butcher into doing it for you. Mix all marinade ingredients and pour over roast. Store three days or more in flat covered container. This is great as hors d'oeuvres, for sandwiches, or in a tossed green salad. Marvelous for leftover roast also.

Mrs. Harry Stone

Flank Steak Hors d'Oeuvres

MARINADE:
½ cup soy sauce
2 teaspoons garlic salt
⅓ cup vegetable oil
⅓ cup sherry

Marinate flank steak, do not tenderize, for 3 or 4 hours in plastic bag; turning often. Charcoal or oven broil 10 minutes on each side for rare. Cool to room temperature, then slice very thin at a 45 degree angle across grain. Roll and fasten with toothpicks for pick-ups or serve with biscuits for party sandwiches.

Mrs. Leonard Kaye

Cocktail Bits

1½ pounds ground round steak
1½ pounds ground pork
1 Tablespoon cumin seed
2 Tablespoons chili powder
½ teaspoon thyme
1 teaspoon garlic powder
Salt and pepper to taste

Combine all ingredients. Shape into tiny balls. Bake 20 minutes at 350 degrees. Place meat balls in a chafing dish and cover with barbecue sauce.

Sweet and Sour Meatballs
Good for large parties.

1 pound ground beef
1½ teaspoons salt
½ teaspoon pepper
1- 5 ounce can water chestnuts,
  sliced finely
1 cup milk
¼ cup flour
½ cup butter
2 Tablespoons cornstarch
½ cup sugar
¼ cup wine vinegar
2 Tablespoons soy sauce, or
  adjust to taste
1 medium green pepper, chopped
  in ½ inch pieces
½ cup celery, chopped in ½
  inch pieces
1 small can pineapple cubes or
  tidbits with juice

Combine beef, seasonings, water chestnuts and milk. Work and form into small balls. Roll in flour and fry in butter over medium heat until brown and well done. Combine remaining ingredients in saucepan and bring to boil. Reduce heat and simmer for three minutes. Pour over meat balls and serve in chafing dish. Serves 20. Can be doubled as many times as needed.

Mrs. Alton Irwin

Chafing Dish Ducks

Ducks
Salt and pepper
Worcestershire
Apple
Onion
Celery
Red wine

Per duck: Clean, wash and season each duck well with salt, pepper and lots of Worcestershire. Stuff each duck with one quarter each apple, onion and celery. Place in roasting pan with 1/4 cup red wine per duck. Cook until duck almost falls off the bone, basting frequently with the drippings and wine in the bottom of the pan. Remove duck and cool. Pull meat from carcass and shred. Check drippings from the pan for seasoning. Add shredded duck to drippings. Serve in chafing dish with party rolls or Melba rounds.

Mrs. John Hunt

Fried Duck

2 ducks
Salt and pepper
2 large onions
1 large bell pepper
2 garlic buds
2 or 3 ribs of celery

Salt and pepper ducks. Stuff with onions, pepper, garlic, and celery. Cover with water. Bring to boil. Turn to low and cook until tender. Let ducks stand in broth until next day in the refrigerator. Next day, take duck off bones. Cut or break breast into small pieces; take thighs, legs, and breast and dip into seasoned flour. Fry in deep, hot fat. I use bacon drippings or Mazola oil. Use rest of duck in cornbread dressing. Fried duck is excellent to serve at cocktail parties with tiny hot biscuits or at a buffet. Serves six.

Mrs. Bruce Brooks

Braunschweiger Paté

1 pound braunschweiger sausage
2 packages Frito Green Onion Dip Mix
1 teaspoon sugar
2 teaspoons water
1 Tablespoon garlic spread
2- 3 ounce packages cream cheese
1 Tablespoon milk
1/8 teaspoon hot pepper sauce

Mash braunschweiger. Combine dip mix, sugar, and water. Add to braunschweiger and blend thoroughly. Form mixture into an igloo shape. Place on serving plate and chill. Melt garlic spread. Whip cream cheese with milk and hot pepper sauce. Blend in melted garlic spread. Spread cream cheese mixture over braunschweiger. Chill. Before serving garnish with parsley. Serve with crackers or Melba rounds.

Mrs. Thomas Zentner

Chicken Liver Paté

1 pound chicken liver
1/2 pound sliced bacon
1 large onion
4 pods garlic
4 bay leaves
1 teaspoon salt
1/4 teaspoon red pepper
2 Tablespoons Lea & Perrins
1/2 teaspoon nutmeg
1 teaspoon mustard
1/8 teaspoon ground cloves

Wash liver; put in a covered pan with cut-up bacon. Add bay leaves, onion, garlic, salt, pepper and Lea & Perrins. Bring this to a boil and cook for twenty minutes in just enough water to cover. When done, discard bay leaves; add remaining ingredients and put in blender, then in molds. This will keep in the refrigerator for a week, and it will also freeze well.

Mrs. Richard Blanchard

Chopped Chicken Livers

1 pound fresh chicken livers
3/4 pound chicken fat
2 large onions, chopped
8 hard boiled eggs
1 medium to small onion, chopped
   very, very finely
1 teaspoon sugar
Salt to taste

Wash chicken livers and let drain on paper towels. Heat chicken fat and sauté chopped onions. Leave onions in skillet and add livers. Lower heat and cook livers until well done, but do not let them get hard. Set to the side and let cool for thirty minutes or longer. Put through meat grinder along with hard boiled eggs. Be sure to add all the drippings through the grinder. Add finely chopped raw onion, sugar and salt. Mix well and set in refrigerator for several hours. If putting in a mold, it is not necessary to grease as the fat in the recipe will prevent it from sticking. Recipe may be halved, doubled, tripled, etc. Well worth the time it takes.

Mrs. Sam Kern
Shaker Heights, Ohio

Scotch Paté

1 pound calf liver
4 strips bacon
1 onion, peeled
4 anchovy fillets
1/2 teaspoon ginger
1 teaspoon marjoram
Tabasco to taste
2 Tablespoons Scotch whiskey
2 teaspoons seasoned salt
1/2 cup flour
1 cup mushroom soup

Grind liver, bacon, onion and anchovies in a meat grinder. Blend in all remaining ingredients. Turn into a buttered loaf pan, 7 x 3 x 2 inches, and set in a shallow pan of hot water. Bake at 275 degrees for 2 hours. Cool; chill in refrigerator without removing from pan. When firmly set, turn out of pan and coat with Quick Aspic for lining molds — see Salad section. Decorate as desired.

Mrs. Ed Seymour, Jr.

Rumaki Hors d'Oeuvres

10 chicken livers
10 slices of bacon
1 flat can of water chestnuts

MARINADE:
½ cup soy sauce
¼ cup honey
½ teaspoon ginger or 1 teaspoon
   garlic for flavor

Mix marinade in 13 x 9 x 1 inch pan. Clean and separate chicken livers in half for bite size pieces. Cut bacon strips in half. Slice water chestnuts into small pieces, three or four slices per nut. Wrap a liver piece and water chestnut in bacon and fasten with toothpick. Place in marinade for four or five hours turning occasionally. Charcoal outside fifteen or twenty minutes or bake on rack over shallow pan in 375 degree oven for about twenty minutes, until bacon is crisp. Turn for even cooking. Recipe may be doubled.

Mrs. Leonard Kaye

Tea Eggs

8 to 10 eggs
3 Tablespoons black tea
1 Tablespoon salt
4 whole cloves star anise or
   4 teaspoons ground anise
2 Tablespoons soy sauce

Place the eggs in cold water to cover; bring to a boil and simmer gently for 12 to 15 minutes. Remove the eggs and reserve the water. Cool the eggs under cold running water for 5 minutes. Roll each egg *gently* to crackle the shell; *do not remove the shell*. Bring the reserved water to a boil. You should have 3 cups; add more water if necessary. Add the tea leaves, salt, anise and the cracked eggs. Simmer, covered, until the eggs turn brown, about 1 hour. Turn off the heat and let the eggs stand, covered, for 2 hours. Drain, cool, and shell. Serve either cut in half, lengthwise or quartered. Serves 8 to 10. The eggs will keep for several days if refrigerated, unshelled, in the liquid they are cooked in.

Hogshead Cheese
Marvelous! Modern method of hogshead cheese.

I. FIRST COOKING:
½ fresh hog jaw
3 to 4 pound pork roast, Boston butt
6 pigs feet
1 onion, chopped
1 stalk celery
2 bay leaves
2 pods garlic
Thyme, salt, pepper and red pepper to taste

II. SECOND COOKING:
1 onion, chopped
4 green onions, chopped
2 stalks celery, chopped
2 or 3 pods garlic
4 Tablespoons Worcestershire sauce
1 Tablespoon lemon juice
Red pepper to taste
Black pepper
1 package gelatin, dissolved in ¼ cup cold water

Boil first seven ingredients with the four seasonings. Let cook until meat falls off bones. Debone and cut off fat and discard. Use skin, meat and all of pigs feet meat and skin. Strain cooled liquid and let grease rise to top. Skim grease. Put meat back into liquid with seasonings for second cooking. Let cook down until not much liquor is left, and it all looks like one mess. Add dissolved gelatin into hot liquid if you want to be sure it jells, but it is usually not necessary to add this. Pour into ungreased pans and let set in refrigerator until firm. Serve on saltine crackers.

Mrs. W.J. Hodge, Jr.

Cocktail Weiners

3 packages weiners
3-12 ounce jars of currant jelly or apple jelly
3-9 ounce jars of mustard

Mix mustard and jelly together and cook over a low fire until dissolved. Cut weiners into bite size pieces and place in mixture. Cook slowly for about two hours. Serve in casserole with toothpicks. Easily prepared ahead of time, then reheated. In order to double, allow one jar mustard and 1 jar jelly to each package of weiners.

Mrs. John Lauve

Grilled Sausages

Cook little pig sausages in dry white wine to cover, simmering them gently for 10 minutes. Drain and put them on small skewers, running the skewer through the sausages the long way. Grill on a hibachi until crisp and brown.

Jalapeño Weiners

30 weiners, cut tiny bit off ends
1 large flat can of jalapeño peppers
1 large sliced onion
Vinegar
Salt

Six weeks before, pack weiners in large mouth glass jars upright, leaving a space in center. Begin placing layers of onion and peppers in jar until center is filled. Add juice from peppers and vinegar until tops of weiners are covered. Add pinch of salt and let stand in refrigerator about six weeks. When ready, slice and serve on crackers.

Mrs. Ronie Flinn
Harlingen, Texas

Bacon Wrapped Dates

1-8 ounce package pitted dates
Bacon

Wrap each date in one third of a strip of bacon and skewer with tooth pick. Bake until bacon is crisp at 350 degrees, 15 to 18 minutes. Drain on paper towels. Serve hot. Makes approximately three dozen.

Mrs. George Ellis

Bacon Crisps

Parmesan cheese
Waverly wafers
Bacon, cut in half

Put heaps of cheese on top of each cracker. Wrap in bacon, no toothpick required. Place on broiler pan rack. No need to turn at all. Bake at 200 degrees for 2 hours. Leave on pan to drain. Eat hot or cold. May be frozen.

Mrs. Charlene Crawley

Piroshki
Delicious with soup or as a hot canape.

PASTRY:
1/2 cup small curd cottage cheese
1/2 cup butter at room
   temperature
1 1/2 cups flour, unsifted
1/2 teaspoon sugar

FILLING:
1/2 pound finely ground beef
1/2 cup minced onions
Butter
2 cooked eggs, finely chopped
1 teaspoon capers
1 teaspoon chives, chopped
1 teaspoon parsley, chopped
Salt and pepper
2 teaspoons sour cream

Drain and cream cottage cheese with butter. Blend with flour and sugar. Form into flattish ball. Wrap in wax paper and place in crisper part of refrigerator overnight. *Filling:* Sauté meat and onion in small amount of butter until meat is light. Add chopped hard-boiled eggs, capers, chives, parsley, salt, and sour cream. Roll dough 1/8 inch thick and cut into 2 1/2 inch squares or smaller. Place a teaspoon of filling on one half corner, fold over other half until edges meet, making a triangle from a square; seal by pressing edges with a fork. Stand triangle on its long side on a baking sheet with sealed edge up. Turn one corner toward you and one away so pastry will remain standing. Bake at 400 degrees until golden brown. May be frozen before baking; partially thaw before baking so centers will cook through. Yields 12 to 18 piroshkis.
Variation: 1 drained can of sardines, mashed with teaspoon minced onion and a teaspoon mayonnaise.

Mrs. Eugene Worthen

Caviar Pie

6 eggs
3-4 ounce jars black caviar
Juice of half a lemon
1/2 pint sour cream
Minced parsley
Paprika

Hard boil and then rice the eggs. Butter a 9 to 10 inch pie plate and make a crust using the eggs. Refrigerate for a day. Put the caviar in a bowl and season with lemon juice; put into the egg crust. Ice the top with sour cream, decorate the edges with minced parsley and sprinkle with paprika. To serve, slice into small wedges, place on individual plates and serve with either toast points or Melba rounds as a first course or hors d'oeuvres. Serves 12.

Mrs. Fred King

Marinate thin slices of cucumber in oil and vinegar dressing. Toast rounds of bread on one side. Lay cucumber slices on untoasted side of bread. Cut a ring of onion to form a rim around the cucumber. Fill the center with caviar seasoned with lemon juice. Sprinkle with grated hard-boiled egg.

Worcestershire Clam Dip

1 cup sour cream
1- 7½ ounce minced clams, drained
1 Tablespoon chopped parsley
2 teaspoons onion powder
2 teaspoons Lea & Perrins
¾ teaspoon lemon juice
⅛ teaspoon salt
Tabasco to taste

Mix all ingredients and chill. May be served with vegetables or crackers.

Clams Casino

½ cup chopped onion
5 Tablespoons butter
2 cans minced clams, drain and reserve juice
6 Tablespoons seasoned bread crumbs
6 Tablespoons dried parsley
7 Tablespoons mayonnaise
Bell pepper, optional
Pimiento, optional

Brown the onions in butter. Add clams, bread crumbs, parsley and mayonnaise. Mix well, adding ½ of the reserved clam juice. Serve warm. If you desire you may add bell peppers and pimientos. Serve on rye rounds or Melba rounds. Serves 6 to 8.

Mrs. Jim Wolff

Hot Clam Dip

2 large packages cream cheese
2 cans minced clams, drained a little
2 Tablespoons Worcestershire sauce or to taste
2 teaspoons lemon juice or to taste
5 or 6 green onions chopped finely, tops included
Parsley, chopped finely
Red pepper to taste

Have cream cheese at room temperature. Combine all ingredients in a double boiler and cook until cheese is melted. This dip is served in a chafing dish with Melba rounds or other crackers. It is better if made ahead so the seasonings can blend. You can substitute 1 can Campbell's Oyster Stew soup and it will have the same flavor as the clams.

Mrs. John Jordan

Crabmeat Mornay

1 stick butter
1 small bunch green onions,
   chopped
1/2 cup finely chopped parsley
2 Tablespoons flour
3/4 pint Half and Half
3/4 pound grated Swiss cheese
Red pepper to taste
Tabasco to taste
Salt to taste
1 pound fresh lump crabmeat
1 Tablespoon dry sherry

In a *heavy* saucepan, melt the butter and sauté the onions and parsley. Blend in flour, cream and cheese until the cheese melts. Add the seasonings except sherry, and gently fold in crabmeat. It is important to continually stir to keep from scorching. Just before serving, blend in dry sherry. This is great served as an hors d'oeuvre in a chafing dish with Melba rounds or in patty shells.

Mrs. Harry Bell

Chafing Dish Spinach and Crab

1 bunch green onions and tops,
   minced
1 clove garlic, crushed
1 stick butter
2 packages frozen chopped
   spinach
1 Tablespoon Parmesan cheese
Salt, pepper and Tabasco to taste
1 pound flaked crabmeat

Sauté the onions and garlic in butter. Cook spinach according to package directions and drain. Add all ingredients to the spinach and season to taste. Serve warm in a chafing dish with crackers.

Mrs. Arthur Brueck

Hot Crab Meat Dip

8 Tablespoons butter
8 Tablespoons flour
3 cups milk
1/4 cup butter
1 small chopped onion
1/2 chopped bell pepper
2 or 3 chopped ribs celery
1 large can sliced mushrooms
1 pound crabmeat
Tabasco to taste
Salt and pepper to taste
Pimientos, optional

Melt the butter in a sauce pan, blend in the flour and add the milk slowly, stirring until the sauce is smooth and thick. If sauce is too thick, add more milk. Sauté in the butter; onion, bell pepper and celery until the vegetables are very soft. Add to the cream sauce. When ready to serve add the mushrooms and crabmeat. Season to taste with Tabasco, salt and pepper.

Mrs. Edel F. Blanks
New Orleans, Louisiana

James' Dip

1 stick butter
¾ cup finely diced celery
1 bunch green onions and tops,
   finely minced
2 cans mushroom soup
2 cans water chestnuts, sliced
2 cans lump crab meat
To taste: Worcestershire sauce,
   salt, pepper and red pepper

Melt the butter and sauté the celery and onions. Add mushroom soup and water chestnuts; stir in crab meat. Add seasonings to taste. Serve hot with Melba rounds.

Mrs. Ralph Brockman

Chafing Dish Dip

2 cans cream of mushroom soup
1 can cream of shrimp soup
1-8 ounce package cream cheese
3 cans small shrimp, drained
   and rinsed
2 cans water chestnuts, sliced
1 pound lump crabmeat
3-8 ounce cans mush
   drained
1 teaspoon Tabasco
2 teaspoons dry mustard
2 teaspoons curry powder
4 Tablespoons Worcestershire
Salt and cayenne to taste

Heat soups; stir in cheese until melted. Add remaining ingredients. Serve hot in a chafing dish with Melba rounds. Serves 75-80.

Mrs. R. L. Vanderpool, Jr.

Crab and Artichoke Antipasto

1- 6 ounce jar marinated artichoke
   hearts
¼ pound crabmeat, flaked
Black or green olives, sliced
Juice of 1 lemon
Garlic salt to taste
Onion salt to taste
Pepper to taste

Cut artichoke hearts into 4 pieces, reserving juice. Mix all ingredients with 1/2 the artichoke juice. Chill. Serve with Melba toast, thin crackers or party rye.

Mrs. Arthur Brueck

Marinated Crab Claws

⅓ cup minced green onions
⅓ cup minced parsley
1 rib celery, minced
1 clove garlic, minced
⅓ cup olive oil
⅓ cup Wishbone salad dressing
2 Tablespoons tarragon vinegar
¼ cup fresh lemon juice
½ cup water
Dash oregano
A-1 Steak Sauce to taste
Worcestershire sauce to taste

Mix all ingredients in a bowl and chill for approximately 8 hours, then add one container of crab claws and marinate for several hours.

Mrs. C. O. Cook, Jr.
Shreveport, Louisiana

Fried Crab Claws

Crab claws
Egg
Self-rising flour

Dip the crab claw in beaten egg, then in self rising flour, back in the egg, and into the flour again. Fry in hot oil until golden brown. Serve with cocktail sauce for dunking.

Chicken drumettes are also great for a cocktail party fried in this manner.

Crab Bacon Roll Ups

1 Tablespoon chopped onion
½ stick butter
1- 6½ ounce can Japanese
   crabmeat
Salt
Red pepper or Tabasco
12 slices bacon

Sauté the onion in butter; remove the onion. Add crab meat and seasonings, tossing the crab meat long enough to absorb all of the butter. Cut the bacon slices in half crosswise and roll about 1 teaspoon of crab meat in each slice, fastening with a toothpick. Place the rolls on an ungreased pan and broil in the oven until the bacon is crisp. Drain well and serve while hot. These may be prepared well in advance and broiled when ready to serve.

Mrs. Emmanuel Teller
Newellton, Louisiana

Hot Crabmeat Canapés

½ pound crabmeat
6 Tablespoons mayonnaise
½ teaspoon salt
½ teaspoon Accent
1 Tablespoon grated onion
1 teaspoon lemon juice or to taste
½ cup freshly grated Parmesan
  cheese
Small rounds of white bread
Paprika

Mix together the crabmeat, mayonnaise, salt, Accent, onion, lemon juice and cheese. Pile the mixture on bread rounds and sprinkle with paprika. Place the rounds under the broiler until they are bubbly and slightly brown. Makes about 3 dozen. These may be prepared ahead of time and kept covered in refrigerator and broiled before serving.

Mrs. Henry Biedenharn, Jr.

Crab and Water Chestnut Canapés

1 pound crabmeat, fresh or
  canned
½ cup water chestnuts, minced
2 Tablespoons soy sauce
½ cup mayonnaise
2 Tablespoons green onion tops,
  minced

Flake crabmeat. Combine with rest of ingredients. Chill and serve with Melba rounds. Makes 3½ dozen canapés.

Mrs. Arthur Brueck

Cocktail Casserole

1- 8 ounce package cream cheese
1 Tablespoon milk
6½ ounces of flaked crabmeat
2 teaspoons minced onions
½ teaspoon horseradish
¼ teaspoon salt
Dash of pepper
1 teaspoon Lea & Perrins
Sliced almonds

Blend all ingredients except almonds; put in an oven proof dish and sprinkle with sliced almonds. Bake for 15 minutes at 375 degrees. Serve with Melba rounds.

Mrs. Richard Blanchard

Cocktail Quiche

Dough for double pie crust
2 cups crabmeat
2 cups coarsely grated Swiss
  cheese
6 eggs
3 cups light cream
1/2 cup dry sherry
1 Tablespoon salt
1 teaspoon nutmeg
1/2 teaspoon white pepper

Prepare favorite pie crust dough and roll in a rectangle to fit a 15½ x 10½ x 1 inch jelly roll pan. Cover bottom with a sheet of wax paper and fill with rice or dried beans and bake at 425 degrees for 5 minutes. Remove, cool, and empty weight. Set aside. Drain crabmeat if necessary, mix with cheese, and set aside. Combine remaining ingredients. Beat well. Place crabmeat in prepared crust, pour egg mixture over all, and bake 15 minutes at 425 degrees. Reduce heat to 325 degrees and bake 20 to 30 minutes, or until knife inserted in center comes out clean. Serve warm, cut in 1 x 2 inch rectangles. Makes about 75 pieces. Recipe may be prepared ahead; except wait until ready to bake before pouring egg mixture over top.

Mrs. Jerry Wolff

Cold Lobster Mousse

1 pound freshly cooked lobster,
  or 1- 12 ounce can of frozen
  lobster
6 large celery ribs
Juice from 1/2 medium onion
1/4 cup water
Juice from 1 lemon
2 Tablespoons unflavored gelatin
1½ cups mayonnaise, homemade
  or add 1 teaspoon Dijon mustard and 1 teaspoon tarragon
  vinegar to Hellman's
  mayonnaise
2/3 cup heavy cream, whipped
Salt and white pepper to taste

Put lobster meat and chopped celery through the finest blade of a meat chopper. Combine with the onion juice. Pour 1/4 cup water and lemon juice in a small pan, sprinkle with gelatin and stir over low heat until gelatin is dissolved. Stir in mayonnaise and fold in whipped cream, adding salt and pepper to taste. Pour into a 1 quart mold. Seal with saran wrap and refrigerate until firm. Do not double this recipe.

Lobster Paté

LOBSTER SEASONINGS:
2 pounds lobster tails to have
   about 3 cups of meat, cut into
   chunks after removing the shells
1/3 cup salt
3 Tablespoons lemon pepper
   marinade
1 onion, halved
2 to 3 celery ribs
1/2 cup white wine
1/2 teaspoon fennel seeds
2 cloves garlic
3 full sprigs of parsley
1 lemon, sliced
3 cloves
1 bay leaf

PATE:
3 to 4 celery ribs
2 green onions
1 teaspoon Worcestershire sauce
Juice of 1 lemon
Mayonnaise to bind
1/2 teaspoon Accent
3/4 teaspoon white pepper
Salt to taste
1 teaspoon Tabasco or to taste
1 Tablespoon Madeira

Boil the lobster tails in water which has been seasoned with the listed ingredients. Remove the cooked meat from the shells. Put the lobster meat, celery and green onions through a food grinder. Add the remaining ingredients and pour into a 3 cup mold. Chill. Be sure to save your stock for other recipes.

Mrs. Don Irby

Lobster Roll

1/2 pound Velvetta cheese
1/4 pound butter
2-6 1/2 ounce cans lobster meat
1 large loaf sliced bread

Melt butter and cheese in a double boiler, stirring to blend. Add lobster meat which has been cut up. Trim crusts from bread, roll very thin with a rolling pin, and spread each slice with lobster mixture. Roll. Wrap in foil and freeze. *To Serve*: slice each roll into 1/2 inch rounds, dip in melted butter, and bake on cookie sheets for about 10 minutes at 350 degrees.

Mrs. Jerome Heisler
Wilmington, Delaware

Oyster Delight

3 jars oysters
3 ribs celery, chopped
1/2 stick butter
2 Tablespoons flour
1 large onion, chopped
1 cup cream or milk
1/2 cup mushrooms, stems and
  pieces
3 sprigs parsley, minced
1 Tablespoon Worcestershire
  sauce
2 teaspoons celery salt
Lemon juice
Tabasco

Cut oysters in small pieces. Chop celery and boil until tender. Melt the butter and blend in flour; add onions. Cook until light brown; add oysters with some of the oyster liquid, the cooked celery, milk and the other ingredients. *Start tasting until it is tangy.* Add Tabasco, lemon juice or more Worcestershire if you desire. *Stir and keep tasting; this must be seasoned to taste.* Cook for 20 minutes over low flame. If not thick enough, add 2 Tablespoons cornstarch mixed with a little cold milk. This makes enough to fill a chafing dish. Serve with Melba rounds.

Mrs. John Wilson

Oysters Dunbar

1 stick butter
1 large onion, chopped finely
1 bunch green onions, chopped
3 toes garlic, mashed
1- 14 ounce can artichoke hearts,
  quartered
3 pints of oysters, quartered
2 cans cream of mushroom soup
3/4 cup parsley flakes or 1/2 cup
  dried parsley
3 Tablespoons Worcestershire
  sauce
1 Tablespoon poultry seasoning
1 teaspoon salt
1/2 teaspoon black pepper
1/2 cup sherry
1- 4 ounce can sliced mushrooms,
  chopped finely
1 small jar pimientos, slivered
1 cup seasoned Italian bread
  crumbs
1/2 to 3/4 cup bread crumbs for
  top; make from French bread,
  preferably

Melt butter, fry onion, green onions and garlic until glazed. Add artichoke hearts and cook for 10 minutes. Strain the oysters, saving the liquid. Cut oysters into quarters or finer depending on the size. Add oysters, liquid and all ingredients except pimientos and bread crumbs. Simmer for 15 minutes; add pimiento and bread crumbs. Additional bread crumbs can be added if the sauce is too thin. Pour into a baking dish, sprinkle with plain bread crumbs. Bake in a 350 degree oven until hot and bubbly. Serve with crackers or in pastry shells. Serves 25 as a dip or 12 in pastry shells.

Mrs. Don Phillips

Oysters Garretson
Serves 50 for a cocktail party

1 gallon oysters
6 bunches green onions
6 bunches parsley
1 pound butter
1/2 cup flour
4 Tablespoons Lea & Perrins
4 Tablespoons lemon juice
Salt to taste

Drain oysters, save liquid and remove all pieces of shell. Chop the green onions and parsley fine and sauté in 2 sticks of butter until tender. In a large iron pot, make a thick roux with 2 sticks of butter and 1/2 cup flour using 2 cups oyster liquor. Add the drained oysters and all the other ingredients. Mix with a *wooden* spoon. Cook slowly, about 15 minutes, then remove to a casserole or chafing dish to keep warm until served. *Do not cover* as oysters should not be watery. The roux should be thick enough to cling to oysters slightly. If the oysters thin the roux too much while cooking, I sometimes have to mix more smooth roux to thicken. Remember this roux is not dark, only medium brown. Half of the recipe is enough for 10 guests served on Holland Rusk for supper with a good salad.

Mrs. Charles Garretson

Oyster Rockefeller Dip
Spinach was not an ingredient in the original Oyster Rockefeller recipe from Antoine's. This is our version.

1 head leaf lettuce
1 head iceberg lettuce
2 bunches parsley
1 bunch celery and tops
2 bunches green onions
1 head of Romaine
8 or 9 pieces of bacon, ground
4 sticks butter
4 dozen oysters
6 cloves garlic
2 Tablespoons anchovy paste
1/2 teaspoon anise seed
3 Tablespoons Worcestershire
  sauce
1/4 teaspoon cayenne pepper
1/2 teaspoon Tabasco
1 teaspoon salt
1 teaspoon Accent
1 teaspoon seasoned salt
1 teaspoon lemon pepper
  marinade
Juice of 2 lemons
Absinthe
3 to 4 egg yolks
1 cup Progresso bread crumbs

Grind all vegetables finely. Sauté bacon until crisp and then remove. Melt the butter with bacon drippings and add the vegetables. Steam for 30 minutes. Grind and add oysters and all seasonings except absinthe, egg yolks and bread crumbs. Let cook for hours, very slowly, stirring occasionally to keep from scorching. Cook until raw taste is gone. It may take 5 to 6 hours. Stir in the bread crumbs and the 3 egg yolks, slightly beaten, to enrich and thicken the sauce. If it is still not thick enough, add the fourth egg yolk, more bread crumbs and check for seasonings. Add absinthe to taste just before serving. This freezes beautifully, but do not add the absinthe until you are ready to serve. Makes 2 quarts.

Mrs. Don Irby
Mrs. Jerry Wolff

Rockefeller Dip

1 pint oysters
2 bunches green onions
2 packages frozen chopped
   spinach
1 pound butter, melted
¼ cup Worcestershire
1 Tablespoon anchovy paste
1 ounce Herbsaint
Salt, pepper, Tabasco to taste
2 teaspoons lemon juice
1 cup Italian breadcrumbs

Drain oysters, reserving liquor. Grind all greens in the blender using 1/2 cup oyster liquor and melted butter for liquid. Place in an enameled or stainless steel pan; add Worcestershire, anchovy paste, Herbsaint, lemon juice, and seasoning. Bring to simmer. Blend or cut oysters into small pieces. Add to spinach mixture and continue to simmer about 1 hour or until raw taste is gone. Check for seasonings. Makes 1 1/2 quarts and may be frozen.

Variation: ROCKEFELLER HORS D'OEUVRES
Omit oysters and lemon juice. Reduce butter to 1 stick and bread crumbs to 1/2 cup. Using canned butterflake biscuits; separate into thin layers, roll dough out thin and put a spoonful of the mixture onto rounds. Fold in half, seal with fork prongs. Bake at 425 degrees until brown. Serve hot. Delicious.

Mrs. Richard Blanchard

Bacon-Oyster Bites

1-5 ounce can smoked oysters,
   drained, and chopped
½ cup herb-seasoned stuffing
   mix
¼ cup water
8 slices bacon, halved, and
   partially cooked

Combine oysters, herb-stuffing mix, and water. Form into balls, using about 1 Tablespoon mixture for each. Wrap a half slice of bacon around each and secure with a toothpick. Place on a rack in a shallow baking pan and cook at 350 degrees for 25 to 30 minutes. These are quick and easy to make. Delicious. Makes 16.

Mrs. Jim Wolff

Oysters Margaret

Raw oysters
Strips of bacon, cut in half
Sliced or halved water chestnuts
Pickapeppa sauce

Wrap strip of bacon around an oyster with a piece of water chestnut in it. Secure with toothpicks. Pour Pickapeppa sauce over the oyster and broil until the bacon is cooked on one side, turn and broil the other side. This is excellent served with drinks.

Mrs. Thomas B. Godfrey, Jr.

Shrimp Butter

1½ pounds shrimp in shell
2 quarts water
½ cup white wine
2 Tablespoons salt
1 box shrimp seasoning
½ onion
1 lemon
⅓ stick butter
½ teaspoon Lawry's seasoned
  salt
½ teaspoon basil
⅛ teaspoon cayenne
Melted butter

Peel and devein shrimp. Boil water with wine, salt, and the shrimp seasoning tied in the bag with onion and 1/2 of the lemon. Squeeze juice of the remaining half into the water. Let water simmer about 30 minutes. Add shrimp and bring to a boil. Remove from heat and let shrimp cool in stock. Drain and blend with butter and all seasonings until mixture is a smooth paste. Pack into a 1/2 pint crock or jar and seal with melted butter. Cover and store in the refrigerator. Butter will keep 2 or 3 weeks sealed.

Mrs. Don Irby

Ara's Shrimp Dip

2- 4½ ounce cans small shrimp
2- 8 ounces cream cheese
½ can of shrimp juice
Juice of 2 lemons
1 Tablespoon grated onion
1 teaspoon pressed garlic
1- 6½ ounce can crabmeat
Tabasco to taste

Drain shrimp and reserve the juice. Cream the cheese and combine with the shrimp juice. Add lemon juice, onion, crabmeat, and half of the shrimp. Add the last of the shrimp and fold in carefully. This is best served from a chafing dish with Ritz crackers but it is also good as a cold dip. It will keep for a week or two in the refrigerator and may also be frozen.

Mrs. Louis L. Peters

Shrimp Dip

½ pint sour cream
1- 8 ounce package cream cheese
½ cup celery
½ cup diced onions
Salt and pepper to taste
Juice of 1 lemon
Red pepper to taste
2 small cans of shrimp

Combine sour cream with cream cheese. Add celery, onions, salt, pepper, lemon juice and red pepper to taste. Mash the shrimp with a fork and add to the cheese mixture. Sprinkle red pepper on top and serve. This recipe will make approximately 1 quart.

Mrs. Pat Garrett
Mrs. Hoye Grafton
Ruston, Louisiana

Dill Shrimp Paté

ASPIC:
½ cup cold tomato juice
2 envelopes unflavored gelatin
1 cup boiling tomato juice
2 cups sour cream
1 Tablespoon dill weed
2 Tablespoons lemon juice
½ teaspoon salt
½ teaspoon Worcestershire
   sauce
2- 5 ounce cans shrimp

Soften gelatin in the cold tomato juice. Place in the container of a blender, add boiling tomato juice and put on low speed until the gelatin is dissolved. Add the remaining ingredients except shrimp. Blend. Add the shrimp and blend until it is chopped. Pour into a 5 cup mold and chill.

Shrimp Paste

1 pound shrimp, cooked
½ bottle catsup
2 Tablespoons Worcestershire
   sauce
1½ sticks butter

Melt butter. Mix all ingredients together. Pack in a mold. Refrigerate until ready to serve on a platter with crackers.

Mrs. Charles Stubbs

Christopher Blake's Shrimp Mousse

6 cups shrimp; cooked, peeled, and deveined
2 cups sour cream
1 pound cream cheese
1 cup mayonnaise
1/2 cup finely minced bell pepper
1/2 cup finely minced celery
1/2 cup finely minced green onion
1/4 cup finely minced pimientos
1/2 cup chili sauce
1/8 teaspoon Tabasco
1 teaspoon salt
1 Tablespoon Worcestershire sauce
2 Tablespoons unflavored gelatin
Juice of 2 lemons
1/4 cup cold water

Boil shrimp in salted water, drain and finely chop. You must have 6 cups of shrimp. Cream together cheese, mayonnaise and sour cream; add all seasonings. Dissolve gelatin in lemon juice and cold water. Heat over water in top of a double boiler for 5 to 10 minutes. Gradually fold into the cheese and seasoning mixture. Add shrimp and blend well. Pour into a 2 quart chilled ring mold. Refrigerate overnight. Unmold and garnish with watercress or parsley. Serve as an hors d'oeuvre or as a main course.

Mrs. R. Dale Phillips
Houston, Texas

Shrimp Balls

1 medium onion
1 medium raw potato
1 1/2 pounds raw shrimp
1 egg
Salt and pepper to taste
Fat for frying

Grind onion, potato and shrimp. Stir in egg, salt and pepper. Batter must be thick. Drop by teaspoons into hot fat and fry until golden.

Mrs. Robert Harrison

Pickled Shrimp

5 pounds shrimp
1 box crab and shrimp boil in a bag
1 large onion sliced thin
2 cups Progresso red wine vinegar
2 jars Progresso Gardiniera with juice
1/3 cup oil

Peel and devein shrimp *before* boiling. In a large soup pot, put enough water to boil the shrimp, add the crab boil, and boil for 20 to 30 minutes *before* adding the shrimp. Add shrimp and cook only long enough for the shrimp to turn pink. *Drain immediately!* Put the *hot* shrimp into a deep bowl and add the remaining ingredients. Refrigerate. Marinate at least 24 hours. Drain before serving. Two, 1 1/2 pound bags of frozen, peeled deveined shrimp, may be used instead of fresh shrimp. Cook the same being careful not to overcook the frozen shrimp as they will shrivel and be tough.

Mrs. Saul Mintz

Shrimp Ceviche

5 pounds raw shrimp, peeled and
  deveined
Juice of 10 limes
1 bunch green onions and tops,
  minced
4 canned jalapeños, seeded and cut
  into strips
¾ cup peanut oil
¼ cup lemon juice
1 cup chopped parsley
½ teaspoon oregano
1 teaspoon tarragon
Salt and pepper to taste
Sliced green olives
3 large tomatoes, peeled and
  seeded

Arrange the raw shrimp in a deep dish and cover with lime juice. Refrigerate for at least 6 to 8 hours. At the end of the marinating period, add all of the remaining ingredients except olives and tomatoes, mixing well. Refrigerate until serving time. Drain and add tomatoes and garnish with olives. Lime juice is preferred although lemon juice may be used since both contain the citric acid that "cooks" the shrimp. Serves 20 to 24 as an appetizer.

Mrs. Sol Courtman

Andy's Creole Shrimp
Great hors d'oeuvre for an outdoor supper.

5 pounds shrimp
1 large bottle Wishbone
  Italian Dressing
1 pound butter
½ cup lemon juice
Worcestershire
Tabasco
Garlic salt

Place unpeeled shrimp in a large baking pan. Pour Wishbone dressing and lemon juice over shrimp; cut sticks of butter into small pieces scattering over shrimp. Sprinkle mixture with seasonings. When melted, this liquid should just about cover the shrimp. Bake at 300 degrees for about an hour, turning frequently. Have plenty of napkins available! Serves 6 to 8.

Mrs. Andy Anders

Minced shrimp, onion juice and mayonnaise served on potato chips or thin sliced toast is quick and easy.

Shrimp Hibachi

1½ pounds raw shrimp
¾ cup salad oil
1 medium onion, grated
2 Tablespoons lemon juice
1 clove garlic, finely chopped
⅛ teaspoon each: oregano, basil
  and ground cloves
½ teaspoon celery seed
½ teaspoon chili powder
½ teaspoon salt

SAUCE:
1 bay leaf
1 clove
1½ cups chili sauce
½ cup tomato juice
½ teaspoon chili powder
1 teaspoon Worcestershire sauce
Dash of Tabasco
1 clove of garlic
¼ cup dry white wine
1 Tablespoon lemon juice

Shell and clean the shrimp, leaving the tail on. Combine the remaining ingredients with shrimp and let stand at least 2 hours. Place on a grill over hot charcoal; broil 5 to 8 minutes, basting occasionally with the marinade. Serve with barbeque sauce. For the sauce, combine the sauce ingredients in a jar. Cover and let stand for several hours before using. One can easily double the amount of shrimp using the same amount of marinade and sauce. It does not hurt to marinate the shrimp a longer time if it is convenient. If using a hibachi for hors d'oeuvres, guests may do their own. Fairly large shrimp work best for this. Serves 8 as an hors d'oeuvres. This recipe was published in a newspaper in the Canal Zone and belongs to Reiko Takada.

Mrs. Ed Long

Shrimp Sizzle

2 pounds shrimp
1 large clove garlic
1 teaspoon salt
3 Tablespoons olive oil
3 Tablespoons melted butter
2 Tablespoons dry sherry
1 Tablespoon lemon juice
2 Tablespoons minced parsley

Peel and devein raw shrimp. Mash pressed garlic and salt; add the remaining ingredients and cover shrimp with the marinade for at least 4 hours. These are great charcoaled on a hibachi or oven broiled. To broil in the oven, lay the shrimp in a single layer in a shallow pan and broil, fairly close to the flame, about 12 to 15 minutes, turning at about 6 minutes. Do not overcook or the shrimp will be tough.

Mrs. Eugene Worthen

Marinate cooked shrimp in oil and vinegar dressing and 3 Tablespoons of brandy to each ½ cup of dressing for one hour. Wrap each shrimp in ½ strip of bacon and secure with a pick. Place shrimp under a preheated broiler until bacon is crisp. Serve immediately.

Janice's Quick, Quick Shrimp Sauce

1 cup ketchup
1 teaspoon garlic salt
1 teaspoon onion salt
5 ribs celery, chopped finely
Juice of 1 lemon
3 teaspoons of Tabasco or to taste

Combine all ingredients well and chill. Serve with boiled shrimp.

Mrs. Parker Parra
Houma, Louisiana

White Sauce for Shrimp

1 cup mayonnaise
½ cup Durkee's salad dressing
2 Tablespoons creole mustard
2 teaspoons grated onion or
  2 Tablespoons chopped
  green onion
2 Tablespoons horseradish
2 Tablespoons Worcestershire
  sauce
Juice of ½ lemon
Tabasco, salt and pepper to taste

Combine all ingredients. Keeps well in the refrigerator.

Mrs. Floyd James
Ruston, Louisiana

Cold Tuna Dip

1- 5 ounce can dark or light
  tuna fish
1 package Italian Good Seasons
  Salad Mix
½ pint sour cream

Drain off all of the oil from the tuna and rinse the tuna well with hot water. Combine all of the ingredients, mixing well. Serve the dip cold. This is better if it is done in advance.

Mrs. Bill Turpin

Pickled Tuna

2 cans solid white tuna, drained
1 large onion, sliced paper thin
1 large lemon, sliced thin
1 jar capers with juice
3 Tablespoons wine vinegar
½ to ¾ cup sour cream

Break drained tuna into large pieces. Mix lightly with onions and lemon rings. Add capers, caper juice, vinegar and sour cream. Toss lightly and refrigerate. This may be prepared a couple of days ahead of time. It is better if refrigerated at least overnight but is not necessary. Serve with party rye bread.

Mrs. Saul Mintz

Tuna Stuffed Jalapeños

Jalapeño peppers, canned
Tuna fish
Finely chopped pecans
Lemon juice
Mashed hard cooked eggs
Mayonnaise to moisten

Early in the day, cut jalapeños lengthwise, remove seeds, wash in cold water and drain. Combine the remaining ingredients, stuff into the jalapeños. Refrigerate. Jalapeños can also be stuffed with cheese spread or with ham spread.

Mrs. James Rivers

Tipsy Fish

½ gallon frozen fish fillets or
  fish steaks
12 ounces beer or enough to cover
  the fish
1 egg, beaten
¼ cup evaporated milk
1½ cups Bisquick
1 teaspoon salt
¾ cup beer

Cut fish fillets into bite size pieces. Place in a container and cover with beer; refrigerate for 24 hours. Make a batter of the egg, milk and sifted Bisquick and salt. Add 3/4 cup fresh beer to the batter ingredients. Dip fish in batter and fry to a golden brown. Serve as appetizers or as a main course. This is good for marlin, fresh tuna, red snapper, grouper or any non-greasy saltwater fish.

Mrs. J.W. Simmons

Dilled Nibbles

½ cup butter
1 package Rice Chex, 6 ounce
   bite size
½ teaspoon salt
2 teaspoons dill weed
1½ ounces Parmesan or Romano
   cheese

Melt butter in a large skillet over low heat. Stir in cereal; toast turning often with a fork until lightly browned. Mix salt, dill weed, and cheese together. Remove cereal from heat; sprinkle with cheese mixture and stir well. Store in tightly covered container.

Mrs. T.M. Sayre
Rayville, Louisiana

Toasted Pecans

12 cups pecan halves
1 stick butter
Salt

Place pecans in a 17 x 12 inch pan in a 250 degree oven. Toast at least 30 minutes to dry and add 1 stick butter, sliced. Let pecans get completely greasy, stirring once or twice. After pecans and butter have mixed well, sprinkle with salt generously and stir very often sprinkling with salt each time as all the salt does not stick to the pecans. Toast pecans one hour or more to desired taste and until butter has been absorbed and pecans are crisp.

Mrs. J.E. Brown
Lake Providence, Louisiana

Pecans Worcestershire

2 teaspoons of butter
⅓ cup Lea & Perrins
2 dashes of Tabasco sauce
Salt to taste
2 cups of large pecan halves

Melt butter, add other ingredients. Remove from heat; add pecans, stir and mix, 5 minutes or more, so that each nut is coated and all sauce is absorbed. Line cookie sheet with paper towels, pour out and spread evenly. Bake at 300 degrees for 15 minutes.

Mrs. Don Phillips

Cheese—Pecan Crisps

½ pound sharp Cheddar cheese
1 stick butter
1 Tablespoon Worcestershire
  sauce
1¼ cups flour
½ teaspoon salt
Dash of red pepper
Dash of Tabasco sauce
1 cup finely chopped pecans

Grate the cheese. Cream butter and cheese and add remaining ingredients. Refrigerate until able to roll into round rolls the size of fifty-cent piece. Put rolls in freezer. May be stored there indefinitely. Take out of freezer and wait a few minutes before slicing into thin rounds. Place on ungreased cookie sheet and bake about 10 minutes at 350 degrees.

Mrs. Tom Zentner

Anchovy Puffs

1 cup flour
1 stick butter
1-3 ounce package cream
  cheese
¼ teaspoon salt
Tube of anchovy paste

Cream flour, butter, cheese, and salt. Chill. Roll dough paper thin. Cut round, about the size of a quarter. Fill each round with anchovy paste. Place another round on top and seal with fork. Bake at 450 degrees about 5 minutes. Freeze unbaked on cookie sheet.

Mrs. Harold McClendon
Bastrop, Louisiana

Krispie Cheese Wafers

Eight ounces of sharp cheese
1 stick oleo
1 cup flour
½ teaspoon salt
1 teaspoon red pepper
1 cup Rice Krispies

Grate cheese and cream with oleo. Sift dry ingredients and add to cheese mixture. Fold in Rice Krispies. Let dough stand in refrigerator overnight. Roll into balls and flatten into small wafers with a fork. Bake on ungreased cookie sheet at 350 degrees for 12 minutes. Makes about six dozen.

Mrs. Richard Blanchard
Mrs. Buck Stewart

Poppy Seed Crisps

1 pie crust stick
½ cup shredded sharp cheese
Lea & Perrins
Cayenne
2 Tablespoons cold water
Melted butter
Poppy seed

Crumble pastry stick; mix with cheese. Sprinkle water, one Tablespoon at a time, until it makes a ball. On lightly floured surface roll very thin in 12 x 10 inch rectangle. Cut in 2 inch squares. Brush with melted butter and sprinkle with poppy seeds. Fold each square into a triangle, brush with more butter and sprinkle with more seeds. Seal edges. Bake on ungreased sheet at 450 degrees about 8 minutes.

Mrs. Dick Etheridge

Blue Cheese Biscuits

1 package refrigerated biscuits
½ cup butter
3 Tablespoons blue cheese, crumbled

Cut biscuit in quarters. Arrange in two 8 inch round baking dishes. Melt together butter and cheese; pour mixture over biscuit pieces, being sure to coat them all. Bake in hot oven, 400 degrees, about 15 minutes or until golden brown. Serve as hot appetizers. Makes 40.

Mrs. B.J. Breard

Hot Cheese Biscuits

1 small jar Kraft Old English cheese spread
½ stick softened butter
½ cup flour
⅛ teaspoon salt

Mash cheese spread and butter; cream well. Add flour and salt. Mix well. Roll into small balls. Chill at least one hour. Put on ungreased cookie sheet. Bake at 450 degrees for 10 minutes. Balls will flatten as they cook. Serve hot. Makes about 3 dozen.

Mrs. Leonard Bunch

Macadamia Cheese Hors d'Oeuvres

¼ cup margarine, softened
1 cup buttermilk biscuit mix
1 egg, slightly beaten
1 cup coarse chopped Macadamia nuts
½ cup shredded Cheddar cheese
Red pepper to taste

Preheat oven to 400 degrees. Blend butter and biscuit mix until it is in coarse crumbs. Stir in egg, nuts, cheese and drop by a teaspoon onto greased cookie sheet. Bake 8 minutes. Makes 48.

Thinly frost each slice of an 8 ounce package of salami with cream cheese seasoned with horseradish and Worcestershire to taste. Restack and frost sides and top. Garnish with sliced olives. Chill several hours. Cut in small wedges to serve. An 8 ounce package of cream cheese will frost three 8 ounce packages of salami.

Mrs. M. F. Courrier
Plaquemine, Louisiana

Sausage Biscuits

8 ounces extra sharp cheese,
    grated
1 pound hot bulk pork sausage
2 cups Bisquick

Combine the three ingredients, work in sausage and cheese well. Drop and shape on ungreased cookie sheet. Bake at 400 degrees until nice and brown. Serve hot. These freeze satisfactorily. Remove from freezer and run in the oven a few minutes.

Mrs. Richard Blanchard

Sausage Rolls

2 cups flour
1/2 teaspoon salt
3 teaspoons baking powder
5 Tablespoons Crisco
2/3 cup milk
1 pound hot sausage

Mix flour, salt, baking powder, Crisco and milk as for biscuits. Divide dough into two pieces. Roll each piece 1/4 inch thick and with knife spread 1/2 of the sausage. Roll as for jelly roll. Place in wax paper and freeze. Makes 2 Sausage Rolls. Will keep indefinitely in freezer. Slice 1/4 inch thick and bake on the rack of your broiler pan at 400 degrees for 30 to 35 minutes or until golden brown. Serve immediately.
For those who don't like hot sausage, you may use mild sausage instead.

Mrs. Paul Lansing
New Orleans, Louisiana

Note: Another idea for sausage rolls is to spread mustard onto rolled out dough before spreading sausage.

Basic Beef Stock

1 pound veal knuckle
1 pound beef knuckle
1 pound marrowbone
6 large carrots, chopped
2 large onions, chopped
Butter
4 ribs celery, sliced
1 or 2 cloves garlic
Bouquet garni: 2 Tablespoons
   chopped parsley stems, ¼ to
   ½ teaspoon thyme, one bay
   leaf, 10 to 12 peppercorns
   tied in cheesecloth.
Salt
¼ pound lean fresh pork
2 pounds lean beef
4 to 5 quarts water

Have the knuckles and marrowbone coarsely chopped or broken by the butcher. Place them in a broiling pan brushed with meat drippings and brown them in the oven. When they are slightly brown, place them in a large saucepan. Brown carrots in butter. Add chopped onion and brown. Add the carrot and onion mixture with the sliced celery and all seasonings to the bones in the saucepan. Cut the meat into 1 to 2 inch chunks, trim fat and brown. Add to the other ingredients. Cover with 4 to 5 quarts cold water and bring slowly to a boil. Remove scum as it accumulates. Simmer for 1 1/2 hours. Add salt and continue to simmer for one hour or until the meat is tender. Correct seasoning and strain the stock through a fine sieve, removing the meat, which may be served as boiled beef or in some other way. Cool and remove the fat from the strained stock. Refrigerate or store in the freezer. This is a perfect beef stock for onion soup, and is also a good base for Espagnol or brown sauce.

Judge Mack E. Barham
New Orleans, Louisiana

Jellied Avocado Soup

A summer delight

1 cup pureed avocado
1 cup sour cream
1 cup canned jellied chicken
　consommé
1 teaspoon lime juice
Grated orange peel

Mix all ingredients. Chill and serve in cold cups. Garnish with watercress leaves.

Mrs. Elton Upshaw, Jr.

Coach House Black Bean Soup

4 cups black beans
Rind and bone of smoked ham
3 bunches green onions
4 bay leaves
1 Tablespoon salt
1 to 2 cloves garlic
$\frac{1}{2}$ teaspoon pepper
3 ribs celery, minced
3 large onions, minced
1 stick butter
$2\frac{1}{2}$ Tablespoons flour
$\frac{1}{2}$ cup parsley, minced
1 can consommé, optional
1 cup Madeira
Lemon slices
Minced parsley

Soak beans overnight. Rinse and drain. Cover with 5 quarts water and boil 1 1/2 hours with ham bone and rind, green onions, bay leaves, salt, pepper and garlic. Sauté onions and celery in butter until soft. Stir in flour and parsley; cook stirring constantly a few minutes until well blended. Add to beans and continue to simmer 6 hours or longer. Add boiling water if necessary so beans remain covered with water. Remove ham bones, rind and bay leaves. Force mixture through fine sieve. Do not use blender as soup will be mealy. After the "soup is sieved" check for seasoning, adding more salt and pepper as desired. If ham bone and rind have not given a rich enough flavor, the can of consommé may be added. Do this before adding additional salt. At serving time, reheat and add 1 cup Madeira, or to taste. After soup is off heat, stir in a lump of soft butter. Garnish soup bowls with a lemon slice sprinkled with a bit of minced parsley. The soup freezes beautifully, but do not add Madeira until just before serving. A first course serving is 1 to 1 1/2 cups. This recipe yields 5 to 6 quarts. Madeira is a basic part of Black Bean Soup and sherry should not be substituted.

Bean Soup

1 large can whole tomatoes
1 small can tomato sauce
1 to 2 large onions, minced
3 pieces garlic, minced
2 to 3 ribs celery, chopped
1 small bell pepper, chopped
Large ham bone, remove fat
1 large package Great Northern
   white beans
1 pound smoked link sausage

Put all ingredients except sausage in an 8 to 10 quart pot filled with water. Add red and black pepper to taste, but no salt. Cook one hour or more; add salt if needed. Cook about 8 hours. Sometime during the day, fry sausage rounds to remove grease. Add to soup. Serve a green salad with Italian dressing and garlic bread. This freezes beautifully, but will need more pepper after thawing.

Mrs. F. M. McGinn
Lafayette, Louisiana

Red Bean and Mock Turtle Soup

$^{1}/_{2}$ pint red beans
$1^{1}/_{2}$ quarts water
Salt to taste
1 onion, chopped
1 Tablespoon butter
1 Tablespoon flour
1 lemon
Garlic powder
Black pepper
Cayenne
1 cup dry sherry or cooking wine
2 hard boiled eggs

Boil the beans until they are tender in the salted water. Mash them through a sieve. Save the water in which they were boiled. Brown the finely chopped onion in butter. Add flour, beans, and bean water; if you do not have enough bean water, add water to equal 1 1/2 quarts. Add the thinly sliced lemon. Be sure you don't get a seed in it. Season highly with garlic, black pepper, and cayenne. Simmer very slowly about an hour. Add sherry and top with finely chopped eggs as you serve. Serves 6.

Mrs. Paul Fink

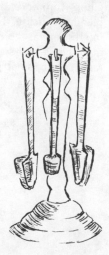

Celery Soup

3 cups finely cut celery, including
    leaves
2 cups chicken stock
2 cups boiling water
¼ cup minced onion
2 Tablespoons butter
3 Tablespoons flour
2 cups milk
1 cup whipping cream
1 teaspoon Accent
Salt
Pepper

Cook celery in stock and water until tender. Rub through a sieve if you wish. Cook onion in butter five minutes but do not brown. Add flour and milk, cooking until thick. Add celery, with the liquid in which it was cooked, cream and seasonings. Serve hot. Makes 8 servings.

Mrs. Stewart E. Meyers, Jr.
Oklahoma City, Oklahoma

Corn Chowder

2 medium potatoes, diced
3 strips bacon, diced
1 cup minced onion
1- No. 2 can cream style corn
1 cup chicken stock
1 tall can evaporated milk
2 cups milk
Salt
Pinch of nutmeg
Chopped parsley

Boil potatoes in small amount of water until they are soft. Do not drain. Fry the bacon very slowly, and when brown and crisp remove from pan. Sauté the onions in the bacon fat until light brown. Add bacon and onions to the potatoes; blend in the corn, stock, and milk. Season with salt and nutmeg. Simmer 5 to 10 minutes. Garnish with parsley. Also delicious with can of drained, minced clams. Serves 6.

Mrs. Jerry Wolff

Gazpacho

2- 1 pound cans Progresso peeled
    tomatoes
½ cucumber, peeled and chopped
4 Tablespoons green pepper,
    chopped
4 Tablespoons salad oil
2 Tablespoons wine vinegar
1 Tablespoon onion, grated
2 cups tomato juice
1 Tablespoon Worcestershire
    sauce
Salt and pepper to taste
4 shakes Tabasco

Chop tomatoes, cucumber and green pepper in blender, quickly. The taste of the seasonings is more interesting as "bits" than pureed. Add remaining ingredients and serve before dinner in chilled demitasse cups or small glasses. Serves 8.

Mrs. Richard Blanchard

Crunchy Gazpacho

1 can tomato soup
1 cup cucumber, thinly sliced
2 Tablespoons onion, minced
2 Tablespoons wine vinegar
Dash of salt
1 cup water
1/2 cup green pepper, minced
2 Tablespoons olive oil
1 clove garlic
Dash cayenne pepper
Lime slices

Combine ingredients. Chill 4 hours. Remove garlic and serve in mugs over ice cubes. Garnish with a slice of lime. Serves 4.

Mrs. William Reed

Minestrone Soup

2 pounds pinto beans, soaked
2 pounds ham hocks, cut up
1 large onion, cubed
1 cup celery, sliced
2 medium carrots, cubed
1/4 head medium cabbage, shredded
2 medium potatoes, cubed
1 teaspoon rosemary
2 Tablespoons salt
1 teaspoon pepper
1 small onion, minced
1 clove garlic, crushed
3 ounces olive oil
3/4 cup noodles

Boil pinto beans and ham hocks in 8 quarts water over low flame for 1 1/2 hours. Add all of the vegetables and spices, except the small onion and garlic. Cook slowly until the vegetables are tender. Sauté onion and garlic in olive oil; add with the noodles to soup about 20 minutes before serving. Serves 12.

Mrs. N. G. Gaston

Onion Soup

4 cups yellow onions, thinly sliced
1/2 stick butter
3 cans bouillon
Salt and pepper

Thinly slice onions. Sauté very slowly in 1/2 stick butter, stirring occasionally, for forty five minutes. Stir in bouillon. Season with salt and pepper to taste. Simmer 1 hour. Serves three to four.

Mrs. George Ellis

Soupe A L' Oignon

24 small white onions
1/2 cup butter
Sugar
6 cups heavy beef stock*
1/4 cup cognac
Salt and cracked pepper
6 to 8 slices French bread,
    toasted
Gruyère cheese, grated

Peel and slice onions thinly. Heat butter in a large saucepan or extra large skillet with a little sugar; add onion rings and cook very gently over low flame, stirring constantly with wooden spoon until an even golden brown. Add beef stock gradually and stir until soup begins to boil. Lower heat, cover pan, and simmer gently for about one hour. Just before serving, add cognac, salt and pepper to taste. Serve in heated tureen or individual serving bowls, each one containing toasted rounds of French bread heaped with Gruyère cheese. I believe the secret to good onion soup is the cooking of the onions very slowly so that they do not burn, but do brown evenly.

Judge Mack E. Barham
New Orleans, Louisiana

* See beef stock recipe.

Potato and Onion Soup

1/4 cup butter
1 yellow onion, sliced
2 leeks or 1 bunch green onions
2 medium red potatoes, peeled
    and sliced
2 quarts water
1 Tablespoon salt
1/4 cup butter
1/2 cup cream
3 Tablespoons chives

In a heavy four quart pan, melt butter and onion until wilted. Add cleaned and sliced leeks or onions, potatoes, water, and salt. Bring to a boil and simmer, partially covered, for 45 minutes or until potatoes are very tender. Remove from heat and cool if you want. Blend the cooked mixture until smooth. Return to the saucepan; add butter, cream and chives. Check for seasonings. Heat, but do not boil or the cream will curdle. Serves 6 to 8.

Variation: To make watercress soup add one bunch of cress and simmer until it is done before blending the soup. Finish as above.

Mrs. Ed Seymour, Jr.

Vichyssoise

2 Tablespoons butter
2 cups green onions, finely
  chopped
3 cups diced white potatoes
2 quarts canned chicken broth
2 cups Half and Half
Salt and pepper to taste

Melt butter, add green onions and simmer until tender. Do not brown. Add potatoes and chicken broth to onions. Cook until potatoes are soft. Let this cool a little, then put it in a blender, 1 to 2 cups at a time. After all is blended, add cream. Heat slowly and add salt and pepper to taste. May be served hot or cold, but it is much better cold. When served cold, sprinkle minced parsley or chives on each portion. This keeps 4 or 5 days in the refrigerator. It tastes better if made a few days before serving. Serves 6 to 8.

Mrs. Ryan Sartor

Vegetable Soup

1- 2½ to 3½ pound chuck roast
1 Tablespoon salt
1 teaspoon pepper
1 large onion, chopped
3 ribs celery, chopped
1 potato
2 small packages frozen mixed
  vegetables
1- 8 ounce can V-8 juice
1- 8 ounce can tomato juice
1 small package frozen cut okra
¼ cup uncooked rice

Put roast in large Dutch oven. Cover with water and add salt. pepper, onion and celery. Cook about three hours until meat is tender. Remove meat and cut in small pieces. Add cup up potato, mixed vegetables, juices, okra, rice and meat to the beef stock. Cook another hour. If it seems to have too much fat on the top, place in the refrigerator and remove the grease that rises to the top.

Mrs. Betty Echols

Vegetable Beef Soup

5 quarts water
1 pound soup meat
1 bunch celery, diced
2 large onions, sliced
2 large carrots, diced
1- 16 ounce can tomatoes, mashed
1- 16 ounce can cream style corn
1 can tomato soup
4 teaspoons salt
1 teaspoon pepper
1 teaspoon celery salt
1 cup rice, uncooked

Simmer soup meat in water for two hours in large covered pan. Add celery, onions, carrots, tomatoes, corn, tomato soup and seasonings. Let this simmer for at least one hour. Add rice and cook thirty minutes more, then test to see if the seasonings suit your taste. This recipe should make six quarts and yield 12 servings. It freezes very well. Great to have on a cold night or to take to a sick friend.

Mrs. W. H. Anders, Jr.

Charlie's Hunters Stew

6 slices bacon, thick sliced
3 pounds boneless beef stew meat
1 pound boneless pork, fresh
3- 1 pound cans tomatoes
1 can Rotel hot tomatoes
3 ribs celery, sliced
6 medium onions, chopped
6 cloves garlic, minced
4 ounces Worcestershire sauce
2 Tablespoons chili powder
2 cups water
Salt to taste
8 small potatoes
1 pound carrots, cut in 1½ inch
   pieces
1- 1 pound can English peas
1- 1 pound can cut green beans
1- 1 pound can whole kernel corn
1 pound cut okra, optional

Using large iron pot, fry bacon until crisp. Remove bacon. Add meat, cut in 1 1/2 inch pieces and brown quickly in very hot fat. Reduce heat, add tomatoes, onions, garlic, celery, 2 cups water, chili powder, Worcestershire sauce and salt to taste. Cover and cook over very low heat until meat is tender, about two hours. Add potatoes and carrots; cook until done. Add peas, beans, corn, and okra. Cook about 10 minutes more. All cooking should be done with lid on the iron pot. Served with hot buttered French bread and assorted pickles, this will serve about 8 hungry men.

Charles Womack

No Peep Stew
Superb!

2 pounds good lean beef
1 cup Irish potatoes
1 cup celery
1 cup onions
1 cup carrots
2 cans Snap-E-Tom Tomato
   Cocktail
2 Tablespoons tapioca
Salt, pepper
Seasonall

Cube and mix together the meat and vegetables. Season to taste with salt, pepper, Seasonall, and any other desired seasonings. Place in a Dutch oven. Dissolve tapioca in the tomato juice and pour over the mixture. Bake 5 hours at 250 degrees. DO NOT PEEP, REPEAT, DO NOT PEEP. Serve with wedges of your favorite cornbread and green salad.

Emmett J. Lee
Farmerville, La.

Chili Con Carne

2 Tablespoons melted shortening
1 medium onion, minced
1 pound ground meat
1/2 teaspoon salt
1/8 teaspoon pepper
2 teaspoons chili powder
1/4 teaspoon cayenne pepper
2 cans tomato soup
1 No. 2 can kidney beans

Sauté onion and meat in shortening until slightly brown. Add remaining ingredients. Simmer for 30 minutes, stirring occasionally. Serve hot with crisp crackers and relishes. This is quick, easy and freezes well.

Mrs. B. F. Pate

Chili Con Carne Cabell

1 pound black beans, cooked
1/4 cup salad oil
2 medium onions, chopped
1 green pepper, chopped
1 clove garlic, chopped
3 pounds lean ground beef
1 small can tomato paste
1 teaspoon celery salt
1 Tablespoon Worcestershire
  sauce
1 teaspoon dry mustard
Cayenne pepper
Cumin seed to taste
3 Tablespoons chili powder
Salt and pepper to taste

Soak beans overnight in plenty of water. Simmer the next day in enough fresh water to cover and 1 Tablespoon salt. When the beans are done, remove from heat but do not drain. Heat the oil in a large heavy casserole and brown the vegetables lightly. Stir in the beef and cook until there is no more red in it. Add the beans, the water in which they were cooked and all of the remaining ingredients. Cover and simmer for about 20 minutes or cover and bake in a 300 degree oven for 25 minutes. Check seasonings before serving. Serves 8 to 10. Red beans may be substituted for black beans or even canned ranch-style pinto beans along with their liquid.

Delicious Chili

1 pound lean ground beef
2 Tablespoons shortening
1 onion, minced
2 pods garlic, crushed
1 No. 2 can tomato juice
1/3 to 1/2 can tomato paste
2 cups water
1 can red beans
Salt, pepper, tabasco, chili
  powder to taste

Salt and pepper the meat and brown in shortening. Add onion and garlic and cook until tender. Blend in remaining ingredients except beans and season to taste. Simmer for 3 hours. Add beans just before serving. Serve piping hot.

Great Grandfather Joe Biedenharn

Ella's Pig Stew

2 pounds pork, cut up like stew
  meat
Bacon grease
1 Tablespoon flour
1 onion, chopped
4 green onions, chopped
1 clove garlic, minced
1 egg yolk
2 Tablespoons vinegar
1 small bottle capers and liquid

Salt and pepper pork and brown in bacon grease; remove. Add flour and make a chocolate brown roux. Add the chopped onions; sauté until tender. Add garlic, pork, and enough water to cover pork. Skim off the excess grease. Cook about 1 1/2 hours and *WATCH*. Beat egg yolk with 2 Tablespoons vinegar. Add capers and juice. Combine with the meat and heat until just before boiling. Serve. Can be made ahead of time without adding egg yolk and vinegar. This must be added just before serving. My grandmother's cook, Ella, made this every Christmas and it was served along with the turkey, dressing, etc. It's very rich and not too good in warm weather. It wouldn't be Christmas without it at my home in New Orleans.

Mrs. Wesley Shafto, Jr.

Chicken Bouillabaisse

3 pounds chicken, cut in serving
  pieces
1 can condensed chicken broth
4 small white onions
1 clove garlic, crushed
1/2 cup celery, chopped
1/3 cup parsley, chopped
1 teaspoon dried thyme
3 Tablespoons olive oil
3 green onions, chopped
2 pounds fresh tomatoes or 1
  pound whole canned tomatoes,
  undrained
Dash of sugar
2 teaspoons salt
1 1/2 cups dry white wine
1/2 teaspoon saffron
6 slices French bread

Wash chicken and remove skin. Combine in 2 quart kettle, 1 cup water, chicken broth, onions, garlic, celery, parsley, and thyme. Bring to boil, reduce heat and simmer 30 minutes. In hot oil in a large skillet, brown chicken and add green onions, cooking for 10 minutes. Peel and chop tomatoes. If using canned tomatoes, break up with a fork, adding pulp and juice to chicken. Cook for 5 minutes. Add chicken and tomato mixture to the kettle, along with sugar, salt, wine, and saffron. Cook over low heat for 30 minutes. Taste for seasonings.

Toast French bread. Place a slice in serving bowl; spoon chicken and soup over bread. Makes 1 1/2 quarts. Serves 6.

Mrs. Jerry Wolff

Bess Burns' Turkey Soup

Leftover turkey and bones
2 Tablespoons parsley flakes
2 Tablespoons onion flakes
1 or 2 Tablespoons Lawry's
  Seasoned Salt
1/2 teaspoon black pepper
1 teaspoon salt
2- 11 ounce cans cream of tomato
  soup
3/4 cup cooked rice

Fill soup pot half full with water. Boil leftover turkey and bones in water for 1 hour. Remove bones and add the rest of the ingredients. Simmer for at least one more hour.

Mrs. Elton Upshaw, Jr.

Courtbouillon

5 pounds red fish
1 cup water
Salt and pepper
GRAVY:
1 cup bacon drippings
1 large onion, chopped
1 sweet pepper, chopped
6 ribs celery, chopped
1 can tomato paste or 6 large
  fresh tomatoes put through a
  ricer
3/4 cup water
1 cup red wine
Salt, black pepper, red pepper,
  and paprika to taste
1/4 cup Lea & Perrins
Small bunch green onions,
  chopped
Small bunch parsley, chopped
6 bay leaves
Good size pinch sweet basil
1/4 teaspoon oregano
2 or 3 cloves garlic
1 teaspoon allspice
1 teaspoon thyme
1 lemon sliced thin

STOCK: Cut the meaty part of red fish into 2 inch squares and set aside. Cook the remaining parts, head, bones, etc. in one cup seasoned water to make stock. I simmer mine on lowest heat for about 2 hours. This can be done the day before. Remove head and bones; reserve stock.

GRAVY: in an iron pot, sauté the onion, sweet pepper and celery in bacon drippings very slowly until very soft and mushy, but not brown. Add the tomato paste, 3/4 cup of water and fish stock. Add the wine and remainder of seasonings. Add garlic and herbs, but not lemon. Cook 2 hours at low temperature. After 1 1/2 hours, add lemon slices and continue cooking for last 1/2 hour. Now add fish and cook for *only* 20 minutes. Let cool and remove lemon. Check seasonings. If bitter, add a good pinch of sugar. This is really better the next day when all the seasonings have had a chance to blend. Serve in bowls over hot rice with a salad and French bread.

Mrs. Wesley Shafto, Jr.

Quick Fish Stock

1 1/2 cups clam juice
1/2 onion, sliced
1 carrot, sliced
1/2 bay leaf
8 parsley sprigs
1 cup water
1 cup dry white wine

Simmer all ingredients uncovered for 30 minutes or until liquid is reduced to 2 cups. Strain through a fine sieve. Correct seasonings. Stock may be refrigerated for a day or frozen for several weeks.

Mrs. Elton Upshaw, Jr.

Shrimp Frank
This is divine!

3 cans mushroom soup
2 soup cans milk
4 green onions and tops, chopped
¼ cup finely chopped celery
Small bud garlic, pressed
Worcestershire sauce
Tabasco
1 small can button mushrooms
1½ pounds raw peeled shrimp
3 Tablespoons dry sherry
Salt and pepper

Stir mushroom soup and milk until smooth on low fire; add finely chopped green onions, celery, and pressed garlic. Season with Worcestershire sauce and Tabasco. Add 1 can small button mushrooms and 1 1/2 pounds raw shrimp. When shrimp are done, add sherry. Season to taste with salt and pepper. Crabmeat may be used instead of shrimp. Serves 8.

George Snellings III

Shrimp Stew

1 pound raw deveined shrimp
Cayenne pepper to taste
Salt to taste
1 large cooking spoon flour
1 large cooking spoon cooking
   oil
1 large onion, chopped finely
1 clove garlic, chopped finely
2 cups water
3 to 4 sprigs parsley, chopped
   fine

Season raw shrimp well with red pepper and salt. Make a dark brown roux with flour and oil. Brown onion and garlic in roux. Add shrimp; when pink, add water and parsley. Cover and simmer for about 45 minutes. More seasoning can be added if desired and more water added if necessary. Serve over rice. Same recipe may be used for crayfish, crabs, and chicken. Serves 4.

Mrs. Parker Parra
Houma, Louisiana

Beulah Count Basse Soup

Butter
1 bunch green onions, chopped
1 can celery soup
1 can water
3 cans cream of shrimp soup
12 ounces crabmeat
Salt and pepper to taste

Sauté green onions, tops and bottoms, in butter. Add to all other ingredients and bring to a boil. Then simmer for 5 minutes.

Mrs. Armand E. Breard

Oyster—Artichoke Soup

1 stick butter
2 bunches green onions
2 garlic cloves
3 cans, 8 to 10 count,
  artichoke hearts
3 Tablespoons flour
4 cans chicken stock
1 teaspoon red pepper flakes
1 teaspoon anise seed
1 teaspoon salt
1 Tablespoon Worcestershire
  sauce
1 quart oysters

In a 4 quart heavy pot, melt butter and sauté chopped green onions and garlic until soft. Wash and drain artichokes; cut each into 4 pieces and add to onions. Sprinkle with flour and stir to coat well. DO NOT BROWN. Add chicken stock, red pepper, anise seed, salt, and Worcestershire. Simmer for about 15 minutes. While mixture cooks, drain oysters, reserve the liquor, and check oysters for shells. To chop oysters put in blender and without removing hand from switch, turn motor on and off twice. Add oysters and oyster liquor to pot; simmer for about 10 minutes. DO NOT BOIL. This soup improves with age. Make it at least 8 hours before serving. Refrigerate; reheat to serve. Keeps well for 2 to 3 days. This is excellent served in mugs for an appetizer. Serves 8 for first course.

Mrs. Sol Courtman

Oyster Stew

2 cups milk
1 cup light cream
1½ Tablespoons flour
1½ teaspoons salt
3 or 4 dashes Tabasco
2 Tablespoons cold water
1 pint oysters with liquor
¼ cup butter
2 Tablespoons minced parsley

Scald milk and cream and set aside, keeping warm. Combine flour, salt, Tabasco sauce, and cold water. Blend to a smooth paste and stir into oysters and their liquor. Add butter and simmer over low heat about 5 minutes or until edges of the oysters curl. Pour scalded milk and cream into oyster mixture. Remove from heat and cover Let the stew stand for 15 minutes to blend flavors. Just before serving, add about 2 Tablespoons parsley. Serves 3 to 4.

Mrs. Levins Thompson

Andouille Sausage, Smoked Turkey and Oyster Gumbo

2 pounds andouille or link pork
   sausage, sliced in 1 to 2 inch
   pieces
Smoked turkey carcass
5 to 6 large onions, chopped
3 cloves garlic, chopped
4 to 5 sprigs parsley, chopped
1 gallon water
3 Tablespoons oil
3 Tablespoons flour
1 pint oysters
Left over turkey
Black pepper
Cayenne
Salt
1 Tablespoon filé

Boil andouille or sausage, turkey carcass, onions, garlic and parsley in the gallon of water about 2 hours. Add water if much evaporates. Make a dark roux with oil and flour. Add oysters and reserved turkey meat to roux, cooking until oysters curl. Add to gumbo and cook on medium heat for another hour. Add seasonings to taste. Then add one Tablespoon of file and simmer for 15 minutes. Serve over rice.

Mrs. Parker Parra
Houma, Louisiana

Green Gumbo
Seasoning is strictly to taste in this recipe.

3 Tablespoons bacon drippings
4 large onions, chopped
2 pounds pork chops, boned and
   cubed
Salt
Seasonall
Garlic powder
Pepper
1 small head cabbage
1 small head lettuce
2 bunches green onions
Celery tops: from at least two
   bunches
1 can spinach
1 package frozen mustard greens
1 package frozen turnip greens

First "you wash your hands". This is a spinoff of the famous Gumbo Zeb of South Louisiana. Melt the bacon drippings in an iron pot and add onions. Cook until well done and tender. Season to taste the boned and cubed pork chops. Add to the above and cook until tender. Chop into small pieces: cabbage, lettuce, green onions; tops and bottoms, and celery tops. Mix these vegetables, toss in the pot with above mixture, and cook until tender. Drain the can of spinach, reserve the liquid, and add to the above along with mustard and turnip greens. Stir mixture and cook slowly until well blended. Use spinach liquid if necessary to prevent mixture from sticking. Serve over hot, fluffy rice. This is not "juicy"; rather, a thick consistency.

Emmett J. Lee, Jr.
Farmerville, Louisiana

First — You make a roux . . .
A heavy pot is a must to make a pretty roux. Mix the flour and oil thoroughly before you start heating the roux. On medium-low heat, stir all over the bottom to be certain nothing sticks. Do not cook the roux fast. As you stir, the roux browns slowly. When the roux reaches the desired color you are ready to add your HOT liquid. Do not add cold liquid because the roux will curdle.

Okra Gumbo

1- 5 pound hen
3 quarts water
¾ cup oil or drippings
2½ pounds okra, cut finely
1 cup onions, chopped
1 cup green onions, chopped
½ cup bell pepper, chopped
½ cup parsley, chopped
1- 1 pound 12 ounce can tomatoes
Salt, pepper, cayenne, Tabasco
   and Worcestershire sauce
Gumbo filé

The day before, boil hen slowly in 3 quarts water that has been seasoned. De-bone and reserve broth, fat removed. In hot fat in large Dutch oven, brown okra, onions, green onions, and bell pepper. Add parsley and tomatoes to the browned vegetables and cook slowly for 15 to 20 minutes, stirring occasionally. Add chicken broth and simmer for 45 minutes. Add chicken and season to taste. Serve over rice and sprinkle on gumbo filé just before serving.

Mrs. William Kelly, Jr.

Turkey Bone Gumbo

Turkey carcass and bones
4 to 5 cloves garlic
2 whole onions
4 to 5 chopped carrots
Tops from bunch of celery
½ bunch parsley
2 rounded teaspoons Spice Island
   chicken stock base
1½ teaspoons cracked pepper
2 to 3 bay leaves
2 large cans Progresso tomatoes
1-8 ounce can Progresso
   tomato sauce
2 cans white shoe-peg corn
1 package butter beans
½ teaspoon thyme
Salt to taste
Garlic salt
MSG
Lemon pepper marinade
1 large package wide noodles

In large 8 to 10 quart pot, cover carcass of turkey and bones with water. Add garlic, onions halved, carrots, celery tops, parsley, chicken stock base, cracked pepper, and bay leaves. Simmer 6 or 7 hours. Remove bones and vegetables; strain broth. Remove meat from bones, mash carrots, and discard the rest. To about 4 quarts of stock, add meat, mashed carrots, tomatoes, tomato sauce, corn, butter beans, thyme, and remaining seasonings. Simmer 45 minutes. Add noodles for the last 15 minutes.

Mrs. Lionel V. Swift
Marietta, Georgia

Easy Gumbo

1½ sticks butter
9 Tablespoons flour
2 cups hot water
4 chicken bouillon cubes
½ cup bell pepper, chopped
2 cups celery, chopped
2 cups green onions with tops,
  chopped
1 cup tomato sauce
1 can stewed tomatoes
2 Tablespoons Pickapeppa sauce
1 bay leaf
2 cloves garlic, chopped
1 can crab claw meat and juice
  from can
Seasoned salt to taste
1½ pounds frozen shrimp,
  cleaned
1 package frozen sliced okra
2 cups parsley, cut finely
Filé powder

In heavy Dutch oven, sauté vegetables, except parsley and okra, in 1/2 stick butter. While this is cooking, brown flour in 1 stick butter in another skillet. Add hot water and chicken bouillon cubes to make a thick gravy. Mix in tomatoes and tomato sauce. Add all to the vegetables in the pot. Add other seasonings, along with the crabmeat and juice. Cook, covered, slowly about 45 minutes. Stir often. Add shrimp, okra and parsley. Let cook about 15 minutes. Let sit on stove, lid on, burner off, until ready to serve, at least an hour. Heat just before serving; taste for salt. Sprinkle filé over the top. Ladle over rice in individual bowls. Garnish with additional parsley. Serves 8.

Mrs. Ben Marshall

Gumbo Supreme

1 cooked whole chicken breast,
  save broth
1 pint boiling water
1 Tablespoon butter
1 Tablespoon flour
1 medium onion, chopped
1 teaspoon minced parsley
1 quart broth
Salt and pepper
1 bay leaf
1 cup cooked shrimp
1 cup crabmeat
1 pint oysters and liquor
1 Tablespoon filé powder
Freshly boiled rice

Boil chicken breast in seasoned water; save the broth. When chicken has cooled, dice, and put to the side. Simmer flour in butter until dark brown; add onions and simmer until lightly browned. Add parsley, then gradually add 1 1/2 quarts liquid, seasonings, and the bay leaf. Stir constantly until smooth and boiling. Add seafood, diced chicken breast, and stir gently. Cook until oysters begin to crinkle. Remove from heat. Carefully sift or sprinkle in file, stirring gently to prevent file from lumping. Pour over rice in individual bowls. Serve at once. This may be frozen, but do not add file or rice if freezing. Serves 4 to 6. This is good, easy, and quick. It has no tomato in it and is different from most gumbo recipes.

Mrs. Buck Stewart

Seafood Gumbo

5 pounds peeled shrimp, cut in
thirds
2 cups okra, sliced thin
1 large white onion, chopped fine
3 cups minced green onions
2 cups celery, chopped fine
½ cup bell pepper, cut finely
2 or 3 garlic pods, mashed
1 cup cooking oil
½ cup flour
2 cans chicken broth
8 cups boiling water
2 Tablespoons salt
1 teaspoon black pepper
⅓ cup catsup
1 Tablespoon Lea & Perrins
1 teaspoon McCormick Seafood
Seasoning, or to taste
Crabmeat: 2 packages frozen
Alaskan King Crab or 2 cans,
fresh or frozen, white lump

First of all, Gumbo should be a two day affair. Peel and cut your shrimp and chop your vegetables one day; cover and refrigerate them. The next day, making the gumbo will be a happy thing. Start with two heavy iron skillets. In one, start the roux by combining *1/2 cup oil* and 1/2 cup flour over a low fire, *KEEP THE FIRE LOW*, and stir constantly. It usually takes an hour and 15 minutes to make roux. Stir it until it becomes brown and flour sort of separates from the grease. At the same time, in the other skillet, put in the other 1/2 cup of oil and sauté the okra and white onions until they are wilted. Add the remaining vegetables with salt and pepper and stir them until they are wilted and soft. When the roux is brown, add it to the vegetables and mix well. Transfer all to a large soup pot. Add the chicken broth, boiling water, half of the peeled shrimp, and all of the seasonings. Let this simmer for about 1 hour. Cook the remaining shrimp in a saucepan with 1/2 cup boiling water and 1 Tablespoon salt until they are pink. Add shrimp and water to the gumbo. Remove from fire. Last of all add the crabmeat, as much or as little, as you want. Serve over rice which has been sprinkled with chopped green onions. Good luck!

Mrs. Ben B. Cobb

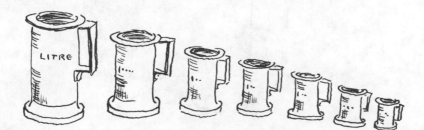

Sallie's Seafood Gumbo

2 pounds raw peeled shrimp,
  reserve heads and peelings
8 small crabs, scalded and cleaned
2 dozen raw oysters, drained,
  liquid reserved
2 pounds fresh okra, thinly sliced
3 large onions, chopped
1 sweet pepper, chopped
4 cloves garlic, pressed
3 Tablespoons shortening
3 Tablespoons flour
1 large can tomatoes
4 bay leaves
Salt and pepper to taste
1 can crabmeat, or fresh lump
  crabmeat
Tabasco sauce, to taste
Worcestershire sauce, to taste

Make a stock out of shrimp heads and peelings; strain and reserve. Fry thinly sliced okra in a little fat until it loses its ropiness. Add chopped onions, sweet pepper, and garlic and cook until soft; remove from pan. Add enough shortening to pan to make three Tablespoons, sprinkle in three Tablespoons flour and cook slowly until roux is dark brown, stirring so it won't burn. Measure shrimp stock and oyster liquid and enough water to make 1 1/2 to 2 quarts. Add tomatoes and liquid slowly to roux, stirring.

Remove claws from crabs and halve the bodies. When gumbo starts to bubble, add crabs, okra mixture, and crushed bay leaves; salt and pepper. Let simmer fifteen minutes and add shrimp and crabmeat. Cover and let simmer one hour. Ten minutes before serving add oysters and sauces. Correct seasonings with salt and pepper. Serve with cooked rice.

Mrs. Wesley Shafto, Jr.

Eggs St. Denis

1 Tablespoon flour
2 or 3 Tablespoons butter
6 green onions, minced
1 rib celery, minced
1 Tablespoon parsley, minced
½ small bell pepper, minced
1 can consommé
¼ cup tomato sauce
1 bay leaf
1 Tablespoon Worcestershire
Salt and pepper to taste
1 pound chicken livers
Drippings
4 slices ham
4 pieces dry toast
Fried eggs

Make a dark brown roux with butter and flour. Sauté onion, celery, parsley and bell pepper until onions are clear. Stir in consommé. Add tomato sauce, bay leaf, Worcestershire, salt and pepper. Simmer for 1/2 hour. Salt and pepper livers lightly and brown quickly in drippings. Remove, drain and chop. Add to the sauce and simmer 20 to 30 minutes or until thick. To serve: Fry sliced ham and place on the dry toast. Top with fried eggs and cover with sauce. Serves 4.

Mrs. C.D. Oakley, Jr.

Eggs Hussarde

MARCHAND de VIN SAUCE:
1/3 cup minced mushrooms
1/2 cup minced green onion
1/2 cup minced onion
1/2 cup minced ham
2 or 3 cloves garlic, pressed
1/2 cup butter
2 Tablespoons flour
Pepper and cayenne, to taste
3/4 cup beef stock
1/2 cup claret
Salt

4 slices Canadian bacon
4 Holland Rusks
4 poached eggs
1 1/2 cups Hollandaise sauce

Lightly sauté vegetables, garlic and ham in the butter until the onion is soft. Stir in flour, pepper, and cayenne. Brown mixture lightly, about 10 minutes, stirring constantly. Blend in stock and claret. Salt to taste, cover and simmer 15 minutes over low heat. Stir occasionally. May be refrigerated if not used immediately. Yields 1 1/2 cups. Grill Canadian bacon and place on rusks. Cover with Marchand de Vin Sauce. Top with soft poached eggs. Ladle Hollandaise sauce and sprinkle with paprika. Serves 4. Can be doubled.

Mrs. Horace Smith

Baked Eggs

1 cup Italian bread crumbs
1/3 cup onion, chopped fine
4 Tablespoons minced parsley
8 scant teaspoons of butter
8 eggs
Salt
Pepper
Paprika

Mix together bread crumbs, onion and parsley. Put a pat of butter into each of eight custard cups and spoon equal amounts of bread crumb mixture over this. Carefully break eggs into each cup and sprinkle with salt, pepper and paprika. Bake in a 350 degree oven for 20 to 25 minutes or until eggs are set as you like them. Serve with buttered toast or English muffins and sausage. Delicious with Hollandaise sauce, too.

Mrs. Norman Guttman
Houston, Texas

Brunch Eggs and Mushrooms

Mushrooms, browned in butter
Eggs
Salt and pepper
Whipping cream
Swiss cheese

Rub custard cups or muffin tins with butter. Place browned-in-butter mushrooms in bottom. Break one egg on top. Sprinkle with salt and pepper. Cover with 2 Tablespoons whipping cream. Sprinkle with grated Swiss cheese. Bake at 325 degrees until eggs are set and bubbling brown.

Mrs. Harry M. Bell

Egg Cups Piquant

⅔ cup mayonnaise
¼ teaspoon salt
Dash of white pepper
1 teaspoon Worcestershire sauce
¼ cup milk
1 cup grated Cheddar cheese
6 eggs

Combine first 4 ingredients. Add milk gradually, stirring until smooth. Add cheese. Cook over low heat until cheese has melted and mixture is thick and smooth, about 5 minutes. Put 2 Tablespoons mixture in bottom of 6 custard cups. Break an egg into each cup. Add another 2 Tablespoons of mixture on top of each. Place in shallow pan. Pour hot water into pan until 1 inch deep. Bake in a 350 degree oven for 25 minutes.

Mrs. Robert Jordan
Lafayette, Louisiana

Egg and Artichoke Casserole
Marvelous for brunch!

1 bunch green onions
2 - 6½ ounce jars marinated
    artichoke hearts
1 clove garlic
4 eggs beaten
8 ounces medium Cheddar,
    grated
6 crackers, rolled

Finely mince onions using half of the tops also. Cut artichokes in thirds and reserve oil. Sauté onions and garlic in the artichoke oil. Combine all ingredients. Bake in a greased 9 x 9 inch pyrex dish at 350 degrees for 40 minutes. Serves 4 as a main dish. This recipe tripled serves 30 for brunch cut in 2 inch squares. It does not have to be kept hot while serving. Prepare a day ahead and refrigerate or freeze. Thaw and rewarm about 15 to 20 minutes in a 350 degree oven.

Mrs. Evelyn Ligon
Baton Rouge, Louisiana

Brookforest Eggs

9 eggs
1½ cups chopped cooked ham
3 Tablespoons chopped green
   pepper
2- 3 ounce cans, sliced
   mushrooms
Sliced American cheese
Salt
Pepper
Paprika

Break 3 eggs into a mixing bowl and beat lightly with a fork. In an ungreased 1 quart casserole, pour enough of the beaten eggs to barely cover the bottom. Sprinkle a thick layer of chopped, cooked ham over that. Add a light layer of chopped green pepper and a thick layer of sliced drained mushrooms. Salt and pepper liberally. Now comes the trick: Take three or four of the unbroken eggs, crack the shell and deposit the eggs, with the yolk unbroken, right on top of the other ingredients. Drop these eggs here and there at random, being careful to keep the yolks intact. Cover the whole thing with slices of American cheese. Use a sharper cheese if you prefer it tangy. Now, start all over, building another layer. Cover that layer with cheese. Sprinkle with paprika, cover and put it in a 275 to 300 degree oven for 2 hours. The way to test it is to stick a good-sized spoon into the middle. If the spoon stands up, it's done. This recipe may be made for any number of people. Allow two eggs per person. If you're having a crowd, you can build five, six, or even seven layers this way. If it is a big casserole, cook it for 2 1/2 hours. The only way to understand or appreciate this dish is to eat it. It is unique. This recipe is delicious served with a fresh green salad or fresh pear halves with a cherry in center; blueberry coffee cake and coffee. Instead of bell peppers and mushrooms, sometimes try using drained artichoke hearts alone with a layer of drained green asparagus spears. Serves 4 or 5.

Mrs. W.M. Harper

The best way to poach eggs! Use a shallow pan or skillet with enough water to cover the eggs. Season the water with salt and 1 Tablespoon white vinegar. Break the eggs, one at a time, into a saucer and slide them into barely boiling water. The eggs will poach to a firm white and a soft yolk in 2 to 3 minutes. Remove the eggs with a slotted spoon. You may do as many eggs as you have room for in the skillet.

Egg Casserole
So simple and delicious for brunch!

2 cups plain toasted croutons
1 cup natural shredded cheese
4 to 6 eggs
2 cups milk
1/2 teaspoon salt
1/2 teaspoon dry mustard
1/8 teaspoon onion powder
Dash of black pepper
6 slices bacon

In bottom of greased 10 x 6 x 1 3/4 inch baking dish combine plain toasted croutons and shredded natural cheese. Combine slightly beaten eggs, milk, salt, dry mustard, onion powder and dash of black pepper. Mix well. Pour over crouton mixture in casserole. Cook 6 slices of bacon until crisp. Drain and crumble. Sprinkle over top. Bake at 325 degrees for 30 to 45 minutes. Can be doubled. Serves 6.

Mrs. R.D. Farr, Jr.

Eggs Florentine

2-10 ounce packages frozen
  chopped spinach, cooked
  according to directions
8 to 10 eggs
1- 10 ounce can cream of celery
  soup
1½ cups shredded process cheese

Line the bottom of a shallow 13 1/2 x 8 3/4 inch baking dish with cooked spinach. Make 8 to 10 indentations in spinach and break an egg into each. Heat soup and 1 cup cheese together. Pour over eggs. Sprinkle remaining 1/2 cup cheese on top. Bake at 350 degrees for 30 minutes. Pretty as well as good! Serves 8 to 10.

Mrs. James Greenbaum

Easy Eggs Sardou

2 packages frozen creamed
  spinach
1 can artichoke bottoms
10 to 12 poached eggs
2 cups Hollandaise sauce
Paprika

Cook spinach according to package direction. Drain artichoke bottoms and warm in salted water. To assemble: on each plate place two artichoke bottoms fill them with spinach, place one poached egg on each and top with a generous amount of Hollandaise. Sprinkle with paprika for color. Serves 5 to 6 depending on the amount of artichoke bottoms in the can.

Mrs. Ed Seymour, Jr.

Baked Deviled Eggs for Brunch

3 cans green asparagus pieces,
  drained
12 hard cooked eggs
3-2¼ ounce cans deviled ham
1 teaspoon dry mustard
½ teaspoon red pepper
2 teaspoons grated onion
6 Tablespoons flour
6 Tablespoons butter
3 cups Half and Half
2 cups grated medium sharp
  Cheddar
1 teaspoon Worcestershire
1 cup buttered bread crumbs

Butter shallow casserole and place asparagus on bottom. Slice eggs lengthwise. Remove yolks. Mash yolks with deviled ham, dry mustard, red pepper and onions. Stuff egg whites with mixture and place on top of asparagus. Make white sauce with butter, flour and Half and Half by melting butter, stirring in flour and gradually add Half and Half. Cook about 5 minutes, stirring constantly. Add cheese and Worcestershire. Stir until melted. Pour over eggs and asparagus. Cover with buttered bread crumbs and bake at 400 degrees for 20 minutes or until brown and bubbly. May be made night before and refrigerated, but place bread crumbs over top just before baking.

Mrs. Sol Courtman

Baked Stuffed Eggs

1 dozen hard boiled eggs
2 cups medium cream sauce
1 package chipped beef
1 teaspoon onion, grated
Salt to taste
White pepper to taste
Parmesan cheese
Paprika

Devil hard boiled eggs. Make a medium cream sauce, adding onion and finely chopped package of chipped beef. Salt and pepper to taste. Place eggs in a flat baking dish and pour sauce over them. Sprinkle generously with Parmesan and enough paprika for color. Bake 20 minutes at 350 degrees. This may be prepared ahead and makes an excellent egg dish for a brunch. Serves 6 to 8.

Mrs. Sol Courtman

Stuffed Eggs

6 eggs
1/3 teaspoon salt
1/4 teaspoon lemon juice
1/4 teaspoon horseradish mustard
5 teaspoons mayonnaise
Few drops of Tabasco
1/4 teaspoon onion juice
Paprika
Parsley, few sprigs

Place eggs in saucepan of cold water. Bring to hard boil and reduce heat slightly. Let boil slowly 15 minutes. Peel under cold running water. Cut eggs lengthwise and remove yolks to bowl. Mash thoroughly with fork. Add mayonnaise and other ingredients. Fill the whites with the mixture. Sprinkle lightly with paprika and garnish with parsley. If the mixture is too dry to spread easily in egg whites, add a little more mayonnaise. If you like a sweet taste add 1/4 teaspoon juice from bottle of sweet pickles instead of lemon juice. Serves 6.

Mrs. Tom Leigh

Egg Croquettes with Mushroom Sauce
Company for the week-end? Prepare ahead!

3 Tablespoons butter
3 Tablespoons flour
3/4 cup milk
1/2 teaspoon salt
Dash of paprika
4 hard-cooked eggs, chopped
1 Tablespoon green onion, minced
1 Tablespoon parsley, minced
1/4 teaspoon Worcestershire
Dash of Tabasco
Cracker crumbs
1 egg, slightly beaten
Deep hot fat

MUSHROOM SAUCE:
2 Tablespoons butter
1/2 pound mushrooms, sliced
2 Tablespoons flour
1 cup chicken broth
1/2 teaspoon lemon juice
Salt and white pepper, to taste
Dash of Worcestershire

Melt butter and add flour. Stir until blended. Blend in milk, salt, and paprika. Stir continually over *low* heat until mixture is very thick and no longer starchy tasting, about 10 minutes. Remove from heat and add hard cooked eggs, onion, parsley and seasonings. Chill. When cold, shape into croquettes. Roll in cracker crumbs; dip in beaten egg and again in the crumbs. Refrigerate overnight. Fry in hot, deep fat until a golden brown, about 2 to 5 minutes. Serve with Mushroom Sauce or Béarnaise is delicious, also. Serves 6.
Mushroom Sauce: Melt butter; add mushrooms and cook about 5 minutes. Blend in flour and add chicken broth gradually. Cook until thickened, stirring constantly. Add seasonings and serve hot. Makes 1 3/4 cups.

To test an egg for freshness: Put it in a bowl of cold water, if it sinks it is fresh.

Scotch Eggs

Hard boiled eggs
Pork sausage
Bread crumbs

Have one egg per person; wrap each peeled egg in sufficient sausage to make a little ball around the egg. Brush with beaten raw egg and roll in bread crumbs. Put in refrigerator and get them cold; will keep overnight. Put an inch of grease in heavy skillet and get it very hot. Place eggs in hot grease and fry until sausage is done, about 15 minutes. Drain off excess grease and cut it in half lengthwise. Serve immediately. Great for a brunch, supper or hors d'oeuvres.

Mrs. George M. Snellings, Jr.
"Cook with Marie Louise"

Dutch Baby

3 eggs
1/2 teaspoon salt
1/2 cup sifted flour
1/2 cup milk
6 Tablespoons melted butter
1/2 lemon
1/4 cup cane syrup*
Confectioners' sugar

*Any syrup can be used. LaCuite is the heaviest, richest cane syrup. The only maker of this syrup I have found is Hudspeth Brothers, Rosa, Louisiana.

Beat eggs in bowl of mixer at medium speed. Gradually add flour and salt blending well. Add milk and blend thoroughly. Spread bottom and sides of a cold Number 8 iron skillet with 3 Tablespoons melted butter. Pour in the batter and bake in a preheated 450 degree oven until crust is brown, about 20 minutes. Mix the juice of 1/2 lemon with remaining 3 Tablespoons butter and add about 1/4 cup syrup. Pour over the cooked product and sprinkle with confectioners' sugar. Serve with crisp bacon and hot coffee. This egg dish is a cross between an omelette and a soufflé. It puffs during the cooking, but falls when served. It may be served with jelly or preserves in place of syrup. Serves 4 to 5.

Judge Mack E. Barham
New Orleans, Louisiana

Fool Proof Omelet

4 eggs, separated
3/4 cup cottage cheese
1/2 teaspoon salt
1/8 teaspoon red and black pepper
1/4 cup milk
3 Tablespoons onion
1 Tablespoon butter
2 Tablespoons light cooking oil

In blender place: egg yolks, cheese, seasonings, milk, onion. Blend until thick and creamy. Fold in stiffly beaten whites. Heat a large heavy 10 or 12 inch skillet, with oil and butter. Do not let it smoke. Slowly cook the omelet until firm. I use an asbestos pad after the initial sizzling has stopped to keep the bottom from burning. When firm, run the pan under the broiler for 5 to 6 minutes until nicely brown. To remove omelet from pan: have platter, all utensils for removing from pan and dinner plate warm. Use thin knife and spatula to carefully help slide onto serving platter. This makes a very showy dish. With a bit of practice it is very simple to do. Recipe may be doubled once. I usually have the guests at the table with the first course. While they are eating, the omelet can be safely left to cook in pan while I have a few minutes with the guests. Then finish the cooking and browning. Serve with or without a sauce. Serves 4 or 5.

Mrs. Burt Sperry

Sour Cream and Ham Omelet

5 egg yolks
1 cup sour cream
1/4 teaspoon salt
5 stiffly beaten egg whites
1 cup finely diced cooked ham
2 Tablespoons butter

Beat egg yolks until thick and lemon colored; beat in half the sour cream and the salt. Fold in egg whites and ham. Heat butter in ten inch skillet; pour in omelet mixture, leveling gently. Cook over low heat until lightly browned on bottom, about 5 minutes. Finish cooking in 325 degree oven until top is golden brown, about 12 minutes. Loosen and slide onto warm plate. Cut into slices; garnish with rest of sour cream. Looks like a pie so serve in wedges.

Mrs. Brent Booker
Dallas, Texas

Omelet pans should be heavy; iron, cast aluminum or tin-lined copper are best. If possible the skillet should never be used for anything else. Never use soap and water, wipe the pan with a paper towel, and the omelet will not stick to the pan.

Scrambled Eggs and Caviar

7 eggs
3 Tablespoons cream
1 Tablespoon chives, snipped
Salt and pepper
1 cup sour cream
1- 2 ounce jar black caviar

Beat eggs with cream, chives, salt and pepper. Scramble in butter until soft. Place on heated serving dish, spoon on sour cream and top with caviar. Serves 6.

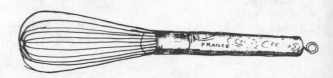

The Garnished Scramble

GARNISH:
1 cup thinly sliced onion
1 cup thinly sliced bell pepper
2 Tablespoons olive oil or cooking oil
1 clove garlic
4 medium tomatoes, peeled, seeded and cut in slivers
Salt and pepper
½ teaspoon oregano
6 to 8 serving slices of ham, ¼ inch thick

EGGS:
10 eggs
½ teaspoon salt
2 Tablespoons cream
½ teaspoon fresh cracked pepper
2 Tablespoons butter
2 Tablespoons chopped parsley

Garnish: Do ahead. Sauté onions and bell pepper in covered skillet until tender, but not brown. Press garlic and stir into vegetables. Lay tomato strips over vegetables and season with salt, pepper and oregano. Refrigerate. Brown ham.

Eggs: Prepare in large ovenproof serving dish, at least 12 inches. Reheat garnish mixture and ham separately while preparing eggs. Beat eggs with salt, pepper and cream until mixed. Melt butter in serving dish and when hot, pour in eggs and stir with fork until just set. Spread vegetables over all. Arrange ham and sprinkle with fresh chopped parsley. Serve immediately. Garnish may be doubled, but prepare eggs in two separate serving dishes. Serves 6 to 8.

Swiss Cheese Fondue

1 pound Swiss cheese, grated
1 clove garlic
3 Tablespoons Kirsch
1 Tablespoon flour
1 cup dry white wine
Salt, pepper, nutmeg
French bread

Dredge 1 pound grated Swiss cheese thoroughly with 1 Tablespoon flour. Bring 1 full cup dry white wine almost to boiling point in baking dish rubbed with garlic. Add cheese slowly, stirring constantly with a fork, until melted. Add salt, pepper, and nutmeg to taste. When the fondue starts to boil, add Kirsch and serve at once. Place over sterno, alcohol or electric plate to keep hot. Have guests dunk cubed French bread into fondue.

Mrs. John Peters
New Orleans, Louisiana

Cheese Soufflé

3 Tablespoons butter
4 Tablespoons flour
1 cup milk
½ teaspoon salt
Speck cayenne pepper
1-3 ounce can Parmesan cheese
4 eggs, separated

Preheat oven to 325 degrees. In double boiler over hot water melt butter; add flour stirring until smooth. Add milk, salt and cayenne. Cook until smooth and thickened, stirring constantly. Add cheese and blend. Beat 4 egg yolks with fork until well blended. Slowly add yolks to cheese sauce. In other bowl beat egg whites with mixer until stiff but not dry. Slowly add cheese sauce mixture into beaten egg whites. Fold until there are no large areas of egg whites. Pour soufflé mixture into greased 1 1/2 quart soufflé dish up to within 1/4 inch of top. With teaspoon make a shallow path 1 inch from edge of soufflé dish all the way around mixture. Set soufflé in center of oven. Bake 45 minutes to 1 hour until golden brown. Good with rolls and salad for brunch or luncheon. Serves 4 to 5.

Mrs. Thomas Peyton

Welsh Rarebit

1 pound sharp cheese, diced
1 teaspoon flour
1 heaping teaspoon dry mustard
1 teaspoon Worcestershire sauce
1 cup warm beer or milk
2 large or 3 small eggs
1 or 2 drops Tabasco sauce
Salt to taste
Dash pepper
1 ounce sherry, if desired

Melt cheese in top of double boiler and blend in flour, stirring constantly. Add seasonings to liquid and well beaten eggs. Blend into cheese and beat with rotary beater until thick. Do not over cook. Add 1 jigger sherry, if desired, before serving. Serve on toast or crackers and top with paprika for festive touch. Serves 4.

Mrs. Charles Womack

Quiche Pastry
For one 9 inch quiche pan

1¼ cups flour
½ cup soft butter
1 egg yolk
1 teaspoon salt
½ teaspoon dry mustard
1 teaspoon paprika
1 Tablespoon ice water

Sift flour, measure and resift into mixing bowl. Make well in the center and add remaining ingredients except ice water. Form a paste and work in the flour. Sprinkle with ice water, toss with fork and form in a ball and chill. This recipe can be doubled for a 12 inch quiche pan. Prebake about 5 or 10 minutes at 450 degrees.
*Line crust with wax paper, fill with rice or beans so pastry will not puff. Chill in freezer about 1 hour before filling.

Mrs. Don Irby

Asparagus Quiche

1½ pounds fresh asparagus or
   2 packages, 10 ounce, frozen
   spears
1 teaspoon salt
8 slices bacon, quartered
½ pound Swiss cheese, grated
4 eggs
1½ cups light cream
⅛ teaspoon nutmeg
⅛ teaspoon salt
Dash of pepper
1 pie crust

Wash asparagus; discard white portion. Scrape ends with vegetable parer. Save 12 of the best spears for decoration. Cut rest of asparagus in 1/2 inch pieces. Cook asparagus in 1 quart of boiling salted water until tender. If using frozen spears, use 1 cup water to 2 boxes of frozen spears. Simmer covered for 5 minutes or until done. Drain and rinse in cold water. Prepare pie crust for 11 inch pie plate. Flute edge. Refrigerate. Preheat oven to 375 degrees. Sauté bacon until crisp and drain. Sprinkle bottom of pie shell with bacon, then cheese, then cut-up asparagus. Beat eggs with cream, nutmeg, salt and pepper until combined. Pour cream mixture into pie shell and arrange asparagus spears on top in spoke fashion. Bake 40 minutes or until puffy and golden. Serve warm. Serves 12.

Quiche Lorraine

2-9 inch pie shells
4 slices bacon, chopped
1 bunch green onions, minced
1 Tablespoon butter
1-4 ounce can sliced mushrooms,
   drained
4 thin slices ham, shredded
½ pound Swiss cheese, grated
4 whole eggs
1½ cups Pet milk
1 clove garlic, pressed
½ teaspoon salt
½ teaspoon dry mustard
Dash of nutmeg
Dash of black pepper

Prebake shells 10 minutes in a 400 degree oven. Fry bacon until crisp. Drain. Sauté onions in the butter. Layer bacon, onions, mushrooms, ham and cheese in the two shells. Combine eggs with the remaining ingredients which have been beaten together well. Pour custard in filled shells and bake in a 350 degree oven 35 minutes or until a knife inserted in the center comes clean. Serves 6 as a main course. For an appetizer, bake in bite size tart shells. When prebaking shells, line with wax paper and fill with rice or dried beans to prevent pastry from puffing. This recipe easily halves if desired.

Mrs. Craig Morgan

Quick Quiche Lorraine

1-10 ounce package frozen
   Stouffer's Welsh Rarebit
3 eggs
¼ teaspoon paprika
5 slices bacon
1-9 inch baked pie shell

Thaw rarebit. Beat eggs well. Add rarebit and pepper. Mix well. Add crumbled crisp bacon. Bake in 350 degree oven for 30 minutes or until the center is set. Let stand at room temperature for 10 minutes before cutting. Serve in wedges. Quiche, asparagus salad and cinnamon sliced apples make a very good and pretty luncheon plate. Shrimp or dried beef are also delicious, used in place of bacon. Serves 5 to 6.

Mrs. Amos Warner
Lawrenceville, N.J.

Swiss Onion Quiche

1-9 inch prebaked pie shell
4 Tablespoons butter
4 onions, sliced thinly
1 teaspoon salt
1 teaspoon cracked pepper
1 cup shredded Gruyere cheese
2 eggs
2 egg yolks
1½ cups Half and Half
⅛ teaspoon nutmeg

Melt butter, add onions, cover and steam until onions are soft. Season with salt and pepper. Drain and arrange the onions in the pastry shell. Sprinkle with grated cheese. Beat the eggs, yolks, cream and nutmeg together and pour into the shell. Bake at 350 degrees for about 30 minutes or until set and puffy. Let set for about 5 minutes before cutting.

Mrs. Dan Sartor

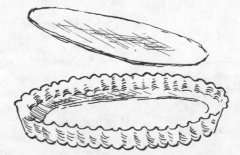

Creary Smith's Famous Bread

2 packages yeast
$1/2$ cup warm water
$2/3$ cup Crisco
2 cups scalded milk
$1/2$ cup sugar
1 Tablespoon salt
1 egg
7 to 9 cups flour

Dissolve yeast in lukewarm water. Melt Crisco; add scalded milk, salt and sugar. Cool to lukewarm. In large bowl of mixer, combine yeast, egg and milk mixture with enough flour to make a soft dough, about 2 to 3 cups. Beat in mixer until dough looks elastic. By hand, add enough flour to make a stiff dough. Knead dough until it is smooth. Put in a greased bowl; turn dough to grease top. With a kitchen fork, punch eight holes in dough, cover and let rise until doubled. Grease three 9 x 5 inch pans. Shape the dough into three loaves. Brush top of dough with melted butter, cover and let rise until doubled. Bake at 350 degrees for about 35 minutes or until done.

Mrs. Elton Upshaw, Jr.

Plaited Homemade Bread

3½ cups milk
6 Tablespoons sugar
2 Tablespoons salt
4 Tablespoons liquid oil
4 packages dry yeast
1 cup warm water
12 cups instant flour such as
  Wondra
Sesame seeds or poppy seeds
1 egg yolk
¼ cup water

Heat milk, sugar, salt and oil just to the point of boiling. Remove from heat and cool. Grease a *large* bowl and dissolve the yeast in the warm water in the bowl. Add the milk mixture to the yeast. The milk must be cool as the hot mixture would make the yeast ineffective. Add 6 cups of flour and blend. Add the remaining 6 cups of flour and mix well. Make a large ball of the dough; cover and let rise for 1 hour. Knead well on a floured surface for about 2 minutes; return to bowl; cover and let rise for another hour. Divide the dough into 4 equal parts. Shape each piece into a long roll, 1 1/2 inches in diameter. Cut each long roll into three pieces, plait them, tucking the ends under. Repeat until four plaited loaves are made. Place on cookie sheets; cover and let rise for 1 hour. Beat 1 egg yolk with 1/4 cup water and brush mixture on loaves. Sprinkle with sesame or poppy seeds. Bake in 425 degree oven for 15 to 20 minutes until golden brown. Serve piping hot. These loaves freeze beautifully after baking.

Mrs. William Mattison

Stovepipe Bread
An easy bread for beginners!

3½ cups sifted flour
1 package dry yeast
½ cup milk
½ cup water
½ cup salad oil
¼ cup sugar
1 teaspoon salt
2 eggs
Butter

Put *1 1/2 cups* of flour into large bowl of mixer. Add yeast and blend at a low speed 1/2 minute. Combine milk, 1/2 cup water, oil, sugar and salt in a small saucepan and heat until just warm. Add to dry ingredients in mixer bowl and beat at low speed until smooth. Add eggs and beat at medium speed until blended. Gradually add 1 cup flour at lowest speed and beat until smooth and well blended. Scrape beaters, remove bowl from mixer and stir in remaining flour with a wooden spoon to make a soft dough. Spoon into 2 well-buttered 1 pound coffee cans. Cover with the plastic lids and let stand in a warm draft-free place. When the dough has risen almost to the top of the cans, remove the lids. Bake in a 375 degree oven for 30 to 35 minutes or until browned. Let cool about 10 minutes in cans before removing to a rack. Makes 2 small loaves. This is better hot than cold. Delicious toasted with jelly.
Variation: Substitute 1 1/2 cups whole wheat flour for 1 1/2 cups of plain flour, 1/4 cup brown sugar in place of sugar to make whole wheat bread.

Mrs. Cecil P. Jarrell

Light Rye Bread

1 package dry yeast
¼ cup water
1 cup water at room temperature
2 Tablespoons honey
2 Tablespoons shortening
2 teaspoons salt
2 to 3 teaspoons caraway seeds
1½ cups rye flour
2 to 2¼ cups sifted white flour

Soften yeast in 1/4 cup warm water. Combine 1 cup water, honey, shortening, salt, caraway seeds, rye flour, *1/2 cup* white flour and the softened yeast. Blend on low speed of electric mixer. Beat 2 minutes at medium speed. Scrape sides and bottom of bowl constantly. By hand, add flour to make a stiff dough. Turn out on floured board and knead until dough is smooth and satiny. Place in a greased bowl, turning once to grease surface. Cover and let rise in a warm place until doubled, about 1 hour. Punch batter down. Spread evenly in a greased 9 1/2 x 5 x 3 inch loaf pan. Cover and let rise in a warm place until doubled about 35 minutes. Bake at 375 degrees for 45 to 50 minutes. Check after about 20 minutes. If the bread is browning too rapidly, cover the top of the loaf loosely with foil.

Dr. Gordon Gates

Cottage Cheese Bread
Good for Italian Dinners

1 package dry yeast
¼ cup warm water
2 teaspoons minced green onion
   tops
1 Tablespoon butter, softened
1 teaspoon salt
1 teaspoon oregano leaves
1 cup small curd cottage cheese
   at room temperature
2 Tablespoons sugar
¼ teaspoon baking powder
1 egg
2 to 2½ cups sifted flour

Soften yeast in warm water. Mix all other ingredients well, except flour. Add yeast mixture and beat well. Gradually add enough flour to make a firm dough. Cover and let rise 1 hour or until doubled in bulk. Punch down and put in well buttered 1 1/2 quart casserole. Let rise 30 minutes or until light. Bake 40 minutes at 350 degrees. Turn out, brush with butter and sprinkle with coarse salt. Serve warm or cold.

Dilly Casserole Bread

1 package dry yeast
¼ cup warm water
1 cup creamed cottage cheese
2 Tablespoons sugar
1 Tablespoon instant minced
   onion
2 teaspoons dill seed
1 Tablespoon butter
¼ teaspoon soda
1 teaspoon salt
1 egg
2¼ cups flour

Soften yeast in warm water. Heat cheese to luke-warm; combine in a mixing bowl with sugar, onion, dill, butter, salt, soda, egg and yeast. Add flour to form soft dough, beating well. Cover, let rise until double in bulk, about 1 hour. Beat down dough. Put in a greased 1 1/2 quart round casserole. Let rise until light, 40 minutes. Bake at 350 degrees until golden brown, 40 to 50 minutes. Brush with melted butter, sprinkle with salt. Serve warm.

Mrs. Robert Curry III

English Muffin Bread

1 package dry yeast
1¼ cups warm water
1 Tablespoon sugar
½ teaspoon salt
1 Tablespoon corn meal
2½ to 3 cups flour

Mix yeast with *1 cup* flour. Heat water, sugar and salt until warm. Mix liquid with flour and yeast until blended. Add the remaining flour 1/2 cup at a time until soft dough is formed. Place in large greased bowl; cover and let rise in a warm place for one hour. Punch the dough down and let rest for 10 minutes. Place dough in a greased casserole sprinkled with 3/4 Tablespoon cornmeal. Sprinkle the top of the bread with the remaining cornmeal. Let rise for one hour. Bake in a 400 degree oven for 45 minutes. If the top browns too quickly, cover with foil.

Mrs. Lestar Martin

Lemon-Peppered Cracklin Bread

1- 13¾ ounce package hot roll
   mix
1 egg
½ cup butter, melted
½ teaspoon onion flakes
1½ teaspoons lemon-pepper
   seasoning
2 cups finely crushed French fried
   pork rinds, cracklings

Prepare hot roll mix with egg as directed on package. Let rise in a warm place for 20 to 30 minutes. Punch down and roll to about a 16 x 13 inch rectangle. Mix the next three ingredients and brush on rectangle, reserving 2 Tablespoons. Sprinkle cracklings on dough, reserving 2 Tablespoons. Roll up the dough tightly and seal. Stretch to about 22 inches in length and coil in a well greased 1½ or 2 quart casserole. Pour reserved butter over top and sprinkle with the reserved cracklings. Let rise in a warm place for 30 minutes or until light. Bake in a moderate oven, 350 degrees, about one hour. Turn out; serve hot or cold.

Savory Casserole Bread

²/₃ cup chopped green onion
  with tops
3 Tablespoons vegetable oil
2 cups biscuit mix
1 cup chopped cooked ham or
  corned beef
2 eggs, slightly beaten
2 cups milk, plain or buttermilk
½ teaspoon prepared mustard
1½ cups grated sharp Cheddar
  cheese
2 Tablespoons sesame seeds
3 Tablespoons melted butter

Sauté onion in 1 Tablespoon oil for about 2 minutes. Combine biscuit mix and ham. Mix remaining oil, eggs, milk, mustard, onions and half the cheese. Add to ham mixture and stir until mixed. Spread in a greased round 10 inch metal pie pan or a 9 inch iron skillet. Sprinkle with remaining cheese and sesame seeds. Pour melted butter over the top. Bake in a moderate oven, 375 degrees, for 35 to 40 minutes. Cut in wedges and serve hot with butter. Serves 8.

Brioche

½ cup milk
½ cup butter at room temperature
⅓ cup sugar
½ teaspoon salt
2 packages yeast
½ cup warm water
1 egg yolk and 3 whole eggs,
  beaten slightly
3½ to 4½ cups flour
Egg wash: beat together 1 egg
  yolk with 2 Tablespoons cream

Scald milk and allow to cool until lukewarm. Cream the butter and sugar in a large bowl in an electric mixer. Add salt. Dissolve yeast in warm water. Add the milk, dissolved yeast, eggs and yolk to the butter and sugar. Add about 2 cups of flour or enough to make a thick batter. Beat for about 10 minutes. Add the remaining flour by hand to make a soft dough. Knead the dough until it is smooth. Put the dough in a greased bowl, turn the greased side up, cover and let rise in a warm place until the dough is doubled in bulk, about 45 minutes. Punch the dough down. To make two large brioches, divide the dough into 2 parts. To form the brioches, use your fingers and squeeze about 1/3 of the dough to separate it almost completely from the rest of the piece. Place dough, large end down, in a well greased brioche pan. Round the smaller portion of dough into a knob and press it firmly into the dough underneath. Be sure the knob is set well into the dough or it will fall over as it rises. Let brioches rise until dough is light. Finger dents remain in the dough. With scissors, snip around knob so that it will keep its shape in baking. Brush with egg wash. Bake in a preheated 400 degree oven for 20 to 25 minutes or until brioches are a deep golden brown. Makes 2 large brioches or 16 individual ones.

Mrs. Leonard Bunch

Buttermilk Brioche

1¼ cups buttermilk
2 eggs
¾ cup butter
5 to 5½ cups flour
⅓ cup sugar
2 teaspoons baking powder
2½ teaspoons salt
2 packages yeast, dry or cake
¼ cup warm water, 105 to 110
  degrees
1 egg yolk
2 Tablespoons cream

One hour ahead of time, set out milk, eggs and butter to reach room temperature. Sift 2 1/2 cups flour, measure and sift again with sugar, baking powder and salt. Sift the remaining flour and measure for later addition. Butter 24 small brioche pans or muffin tins. Dissolve yeast in warm water. Pour buttermilk into a large bowl of electric mixer; add eggs and sifted flour mixture. Blend at low speed and start adding butter, 1 Tablespoon at a time, until well blended. Add dissolved yeast and beat 2 more minutes at medium speed. Stir in remaining 2 1/2 cups flour by hand with a wooden spoon or electric mixer if you have a dough hook attachment. Beat until smooth with mixer or turn out on floured board and knead 5 minutes or until smooth. Divide dough into 2 unequal portions. Form the larger into 24 balls and place in buttered tins. Form smaller portion into 24 pear shaped pieces. Indent larger ball and dip pear shaped knob tip in water and set into indentation. Cover brioches and put in a warm, draft free place to rise, about 45 minutes, or until doubled in bulk. Brush with egg yolk beaten with cream and bake at 350 degrees for 20 to 25 minutes or until brown. Remove from tins and cool.

Ice Box Rolls

1 package dry yeast
1 cup warm water
½ cup shortening
¼ cup sugar
1 egg
1 teaspoon salt
3 cups flour

Dissolve yeast in warm water. Cream shortening with sugar, beat in egg, add yeast mixture and beat until well mixed. Add salt and flour working in until a smooth dough is formed. Place in the refrigerator in a bowl covered with Saran until ready to use. Roll and form rolls. Let rise for 1 1/2 hours. Bake in a 350 degree oven for 15 minutes.

Mrs. Herschel Gentry, Jr.

Egg Washes:

1. Whole egg beaten with 1 teaspoon cream or milk gives a shiny, medium-brown glaze.

2. Egg yolk beaten with 1 teaspoon cream or milk gives the shiniest, brownest glaze.

3. Egg white beaten with 1 teaspoon water gives shine without brownness.

Beer Biscuits
Delicious, try them for dinner tonight.

1½ cups Bisquick
¼ teaspoon salt
½ teaspoon sugar
¾ cup beer

Mix all ingredients. Spoon into 6 buttered muffin cups and bake at 425 degrees for 15 minutes.

Miss Letha Johnson

Quick Biscuits

2 cups self-rising flour
4 Tablespoons mayonnaise
1 cup milk

Mix all ingredients and drop by spoon on a cookie sheet. Extra flour may be worked into the dough and then rolled out and cut. This makes about 20 biscuits. Bake at 450 degrees until the biscuits are golden.

Mrs. Daniel Dupree

Yeast Biscuits

1 cup warm water
1 package yeast
2 Tablespoons sugar
2½ to 3 cups flour
¾ teaspoons baking powder
¼ cup powdered milk
¾ teaspoon salt
½ cup shortening

Dissolve the yeast and sugar in warm water. Sift together the flour, baking powder, powdered milk and salt. Cut the shortening into the dry ingredients; add yeast mix. Stir well until all the flour is moistened. Knead on a lightly floured board. Roll out 1/2 inch thick, cut as for biscuits, brush the tops with melted butter and fold the biscuits. Let rise 40 minutes. Bake at 450 degrees until lightly browned. This dough will keep several days in the refrigerator when covered with wax paper.

Mrs. Alton Irwin

Cornbread

2 Tablespoons melted butter
½ cup minced green onions
1 cup corn meal
½ cup flour
2 teaspoons baking powder
1 Tablespoon sugar
½ teaspoon salt
2 eggs
1 cup milk

Sauté the onions in butter. Do not brown. Mix and sift dry ingredients. Add milk and eggs which have been beaten together with the onions. Pour into a greased baking dish or muffin tins. Bake 20 to 30 minutes at 350 degrees.

Mrs. Russell Bulloch

Hattie's Corn Bread

2 cups white corn meal
1 teaspoon salt
½ teaspoon soda
½ cup flour
1 Tablespoon sugar
2 teaspoons baking powder
1 egg
1¼ cups buttermilk

Mix together the corn meal, salt, soda, flour, sugar and baking powder. Mix together egg and buttermilk and add to the dry ingredients. Use a heavy black iron skillet with just enough grease melted in it to cover the bottom. Pour the corn bread mixture into the skillet and bake in a 425 degree oven for at least 25 minutes. This makes a nice thick cake-like pone of corn bread.

Mrs. Allen Coon

Hot Pepper Corn Bread

1 cup corn meal
1 cup cream corn
1 cup rat cheese, grated
½ cup Wesson oil
½ cup buttermilk
1 teaspoon soda
½ teaspoon salt
2 eggs
3 jalapeño peppers, chopped

Mix all of the ingredients together well. Heat iron skillet with about 1 Tablespoon bacon drippings. Pour drippings out of pan into the bread mixture. Pour mixture into skillet and bake at 400 degrees until crispy brown.

Mrs. Tom King

Corn Pones

1 cup white cornmeal
½ teaspoon salt
¾ cup boiling water
Bacon grease for frying

Combine the cornmeal and salt in a bowl. Pour in the boiling water and beat until the mixture is smooth. Shape the mixture into flat pones. You need approximately an inch depth of grease to fry the pones. Fry on both sides until crisp and golden. Serve with butter or cane syrup. Makes 8 to 12 pones.

Mrs. Ed Seymour, Jr.

Corn Meal Muffins

1 cup scalded milk
1 cup cornmeal
1½ teaspoons salt
3 Tablespoons sugar
¼ cup butter
1 package dry yeast
¼ cup warm water
3 cups flour
1 egg
Butter
Salt
Cornmeal

Pour scalded milk over cornmeal, salt, sugar and butter. Stir until smooth and butter melts. Cool. Soften yeast in warm water. Stir into cornmeal mixture. Add beaten egg. Add flour gradually, beating after each addition. Knead on a floured board until smooth. Shape into a ball and place in a slightly greased container, cover and let rise until doubled, about 2 hours. Punch the dough down and let rest 10 to 15 minutes. Shape the dough and put in greased muffin tins. Brush tops with butter and sprinkle with a mixture of cornmeal that has been salted to taste. Bake at 425 degrees for 15 to 20 minutes. Makes 3 to 4 dozen muffins.

Mrs. Ed Seymour, Jr.

D'Arbonne Hushpuppies

2 cups cornmeal
½ cup flour
1 teaspoon sugar
1 teaspoon salt
2 teaspoons baking powder
½ teaspoon soda
1 cup chopped onion
1 bell pepper, chopped finely
3 chopped jalapeño peppers
½ cup buttermilk
¾ cup water
½ cup melted butter

Mix dry ingredients. Blend in remaining ingredients. Drop with spoon in hot fat, 375 degrees. Makes about 30.

Mrs. Ray Rhymes

Jalapeño Hushpuppies
"The World's Best"

2 cups cornmeal
1 cup flour
2 eggs, beaten
3 teaspoons baking powder
1½ teaspoons salt
1 small can cream style corn
3 jalapeño peppers, chopped
¼ bell pepper, chopped
1 small onion, minced
Buttermilk
Pinch of soda

Mix all ingredients. Use enough buttermilk to make this the consistency of cornbread batter. Test batter by scooping up a portion on a spoon and with your thumb push portion into medium hot grease. THE OBJECT OF THIS RECIPE IS TO HAVE LIGHT, FLUFFY, HUSHPUPPIES. If heavy and do not rise enough, use more baking powder. If hushpuppies are greasy and break apart, add more flour. If you want more tang, add some jalapeno pepper juice.

Bobby Shafto, Jr.

111

Popovers

2 eggs
1 cup milk
1 cup sifted flour
½ teaspoon salt
1 Tablespoon melted butter

Beat all ingredients 1 to 2 minutes. Do not over-beat! Fill 6 or 8 well greased custard cups 1/2 full. Bake in a hot oven, 475 degrees, for 15 minutes. Reduce the heat to 350 degrees and continue baking for 25 to 30 minutes. A few minutes before removing from the oven, prick each popover with a fork to allow the steam to escape. Serve with plenty of butter!

Fluffy Tom Thumb Cakes
Pancakes

1 egg
¾ cup + 2 Tablespoons milk
2 Tablespoons melted shortening
　or salad oil
1 cup enriched flour
½ teaspoon salt
2 Tablespoons baking powder
2 Tablespoons sugar

Combine egg, milk and shortening. Add sifted dry ingredients. Beat until smooth. Bake on ungreased griddle. Pour batter from 1/4 cup measurer or by Tablespoon. Makes 12 small cakes.
No mistake, 2 Tablespoons baking powder is correct.

Mrs. Arthur Emerson

Fly-Off-The-Plate Pancakes

1 cup flour, sifted
¼ teaspoon salt
1 Tablespoon sugar
1 Tablespoon baking powder
1 egg
1 cup milk
2 rounded Tablespoons sour
　cream
2 Tablespoons melted butter,
　cooled

Resift flour with dry ingredients into a mixing bowl. Beat together egg, milk and sour cream. Stir into flour mixture. Add melted butter and beat with a slotted spoon or whisk until smooth. Drop a small spoonful on a hot griddle. If too thick add more milk, 1 Tablespoon at a time. Yields 10 to 12 pancakes. The recipe easily doubles and stores well overnight.

Sourdough Starter

½ cup warm water
1 package yeast
½ cup cooked unseasoned
　mashed potatoes
Flour
Water

Dissolve yeast in the water and mix into mashed potatoes. Put in a jar with a loosened screw lid and sit on counter for 3 days. Stir occasionally. After 3 days, add 1/2 cup flour and 1/2 cup water and let sit for 8 hours. Then add 1 cup flour and 1 cup water. Stir in and let sit for 8 hours. Now you may add 2 cups flour and 2 cups water. Let sit for 8 hours. As you see, it may be doubled every 8 hours. At this point there is enough starter in the jar where it can be used and still leave at least a half cup starter in the jar. Store in the refrigerator and stir occasionally, through the week. Keeps indefinitely. To use any recipe using sourdough it requires a little thinking ahead.

Mrs. Ed Long

Sourdough Hot Cakes and Waffles

2 eggs, separated
½ teaspoon salt
2 cups sourdough starter
2 Tablespoons sugar
1 teaspoon baking soda
2 teaspoons water

FOR WAFFLES:
½ cup melted butter

Beat egg yolks with salt until thick and light. Stir in starter. Beat egg whites until stiff, adding sugar. Fold whites gently into starter mixture. Dissolve baking soda in water and carefully add to the batter. For Waffles: add butter just before adding the soda and water. Prepare on ungreased griddle or waffle iron. To keep your starter going add 1 cup flour and 1 cup water and let it sit out overnight to work.

Mrs. Ed Long

Sourdough French Bread

2 packages dry yeast
1 cup warm water
2 Tablespoons sugar
1½ cups sourdough starter
5 cups flour
2 teaspoons salt

In a large mixing bowl sprinkle yeast over warm water. Let dissolve for 5 minutes. Stir in sugar, sourdough starter and 4 cups flour mixed with salt. Cover bowl with a damp towel. Let rise 1½ hours in a warm place. Turn dough onto a floured board, work in about 1 additional cup flour until dough is no longer sticky. Knead until satiny, about 5 minutes. Shape dough into 1 large or 2 small loaves. Set on a cookie sheet which has been sprinkled with cornmeal. Let rise again in a warm place for 1½ hours. Preheat the oven to 400 degrees. Place a shallow pan of boiling water on the bottom shelf. Brush the tops of the loaves with melted butter or water. Slash the tops of the loaves diagonally with a razor blade so the dough does not fall. Bake 40 to 50 minutes until the crust is medium-dark brown. Set on a rack to cool. Bread may be frozen. Reheat in oven but do not reheat in foil.

Mrs. Paul Lansing
New Orleans, Louisiana

Cinnamon Bubble Bread

Melted butter
Cinnamon sugar

Prepare yeast dough from your favorite roll or bread recipe. Grease a tube pan. Pinch the dough off in balls, about an inch in diameter. Roll balls in melted butter and a mixture of cinnamon and sugar. Place the balls in a hit and miss fashion in the pan until the pan is half full. Allow the bread to rise and bake at 375 degrees until done. To serve, invert on a plate and let each person break off bubbles.

Mrs. Daniel Dupree

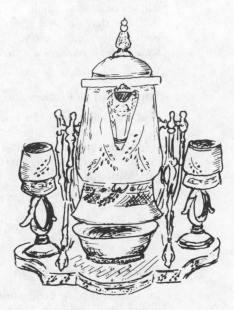

Cinnamon Coffee Ring

2 cups flour
$\frac{1}{2}$ cup sugar
2 packages yeast
2 teaspoons salt
$1\frac{1}{4}$ cups milk
$\frac{1}{4}$ cup butter
2 eggs
3 cups flour
Butter
Sugar
Cinnamon

In a large bowl mix thoroughly 2 cups flour, sugar, yeast and salt. Combine milk and butter in a saucepan and heat until warm. Add to the dry ingredients and beat for 2 minutes at medium speed. Add eggs and beat well. Work in the additional 3 cups flour with a wooden spoon. Knead for 10 minutes until the dough is elastic and smooth. Place in a greased bowl; cover and let rise to double in bulk, about 1 hour. Punch dough down and let rest for 10 minutes. Divide dough into 3 pieces. Roll each piece into a rectangle. Spread with butter, sugar and cinnamon; roll and place in a greased round cake pan. Let rise for 1 hour. Bake in a 350 degree oven for 30 minutes. Makes 3 rings.

Mrs. Lestar Martin

Buttermilk Drop

1 package yeast
¼ cup lukewarm water
1 cup buttermilk
½ cup sugar
¼ cup melted shortening
4 cups sifted self-rising flour
2 eggs, beaten
½ cup finely chopped pecans
Cooking oil
Cinnamon sugar

Soften yeast in warm water. Heat buttermilk until warm. Stir in sugar and melted shortening. Add *two cups* flour and beat well. Add softened yeast, beaten eggs and pecans, mixing well. Add enough flour to make a stiff batter; beat thoroughly. Cover and let rise in a warm place until bubbly, about 1 1/4 hours. When mixture is light, stir down. Heat fat for deep frying to 365 degrees. Drop *small* spoonfuls of batter into hot fat. Fry until golden brown. Drain and roll in cinnamon sugar. Makes 3 1/2 dozen. Delicious for a morning coffee, brunch or special breakfast treat for the family. Serve hot.

Mrs. Pat Garrett

Morning-Call Doughnuts

¾ cup milk
½ cup sugar
½ cup butter
½ teaspoon salt
¼ cup warm water
1 package yeast
1 egg
4 to 4½ cups flour
1 teaspoon nutmeg
Oil for frying

Combine milk, sugar, butter and salt in a saucepan; heat until bubbles appear around the edge of the pan and the butter is melted. Cool to lukewarm. Measure water into a large mixing bowl; sprinkle in the yeast and stir to dissolve. Add lukewarm milk mixture and egg. Beat in *2 cups* flour and nutmeg. Add enough remaining flour to make a soft dough. Turn dough out on a floured board. Knead about 5 minutes or until the dough is smooth and elastic. Put dough into a large greased bowl; turn dough over to bring greased side up. Cover with a damp towel and let rise in a warm place, 85 degrees, about 1 to 1 1/2 hours or until doubled in bulk. Punch the dough down; turn out onto a floured board; knead to distribute the air bubbles. Let rest a few minutes to make rolling easier. Roll out to a 1/4 inch thick rectangle. Cut into 2 1/2 inch squares, cover with a towel and let rise 30 minutes or until doubled. Place enough shortening or oil in a heavy kettle to make a depth of 3 inches. Heat to 375 degrees. Fry doughnuts about 4 minutes, turning once to brown both sides. While warm, shake doughnuts in a paper bag with confectioners' sugar. Makes about 3 dozen doughnuts.

Funnel Cakes
An adaption of the delicious churros served in Spain.

2 beaten eggs
1½ cups milk
2 cups sifted flour
1 teaspoon baking powder
½ teaspoon salt
2 cups cooking oil

In a mixing bowl, combine eggs and milk. Sift together flour, baking powder and salt. Add to the egg mixture; beat smooth with a rotary beater. Test the mixture to see if it flows easily through a funnel: if it is too thick add milk, if it is too thin add flour. Pour cooking oil into an 8 inch skillet and heat to 360 degrees. Covering the bottom opening of a funnel with your finger, pour a generous 1/2 cup of batter into the funnel. Hold the end of the funnel close to the surface of the hot oil. Remove finger and release batter into hot oil in a spiral shape. Fry until golden, about 3 minutes. Using a spatula turn the cake carefully and cook for 1 additional minute. Drain on paper toweling; sprinkle with confectioners' sugar or serve *hot* with syrup. Makes 20 cakes.

Mrs. George M. Snellings III

Golden Puffs

2 cups sifted flour
¼ cup sugar
3 teaspoons baking powder
1 teaspoon salt
1 teaspoon nutmeg
¼ cup Wesson oil
¾ cup milk
1 egg

Sift together flour, sugar, baking powder, salt and nutmeg. Add Wesson oil, milk and egg. Stir with a fork until thoroughly mixed. Drop by teaspoonfuls into deep hot Wesson oil or fat, 375 degrees. If the puffs are too large they will not cook through. The fat cools and the puffs will become grease-soaked if too many puffs are cooked at the same time. Fry until golden brown, about 3 minutes. Drain on absorbent paper and roll in powdered sugar.

Mrs. Tom Keller
Baton Rouge, Louisiana

Poor Knights
Prepare ahead for breakfast.

6 slices day old bread
2 eggs
⅓ cup milk
2 Tablespoons sugar
¼ teaspoon nutmeg
1 teaspoon vanilla
Dry bread crumbs
Butter

Trim crusts from bread and cut in halves or triangles. Place in flat layer in container. Beat eggs, milk and seasonings. Pour over bread. Turn slices several times and refrigerate overnight, or several hours. Roll in dry bread crumbs just before cooking and sauté in butter. Delicious with powdered sugar, syrup or jam.

Cinnamon Nut Coffee Cake

1 cup flour
1/2 cup sugar
2 1/2 teaspoons baking powder
1/2 teaspoon salt
1/2 teaspoon cinnamon
1/2 cup milk
1 egg, beaten
4 Tablespoons melted shortening
1 cup chopped pecans
Cinnamon sugar

Combine first five ingredients. Add milk and well beaten egg; add shortening. Spread on a shallow pan, about 11 x 7 1/2 inches or 9 x 9 inches. Cover thickly with chopped nuts and cinnamon sugar. Bake at 375 degrees for 25 minutes.

Mrs. Eugene Worthen

Sour Cream Coffee Cake

1 package Duncan Hines Butter
   Recipe Golden Cake Mix
1/2 cup sugar
1/2 cup Wesson oil
1-8 ounce carton sour cream
4 eggs
3 Tablespoons light brown sugar
2 teaspoons cinnamon
1/2 cup finely chopped nuts,
   optional
FROSTING:
1 cup confectioners' sugar
1 Tablespoon melted butter
1 Tablespoon milk
1 teaspoon vanilla

Blend the cake mix, sugar, Wesson oil, and sour cream. Add eggs, one at a time, beating well after each, using medium speed. Place half of this batter in a generously greased Bundt pan. A teflon lined pan is ideal. Unsalted shortening, such as Crisco is best for greasing pan; do not use cooking oil, as the oil browns at too low a temperature. Mix brown sugar, cinnamon and nuts together and sprinkle on top of the batter, trying not to let the mixture touch the sides of the pan. Cover with the remainder of the batter and bake at 350 degrees for about 50 minutes. Test with a toothpick to see if the center of the cake is done. Let the cake stand in the pan for 10 minutes before turning out. While the cake is warm, pour the frosting over and let it dribble down the sides. A little more milk may be needed to make it the consistency to pour but too much will make it too thin to stay on the cake.

Mrs. W.L. Alexander

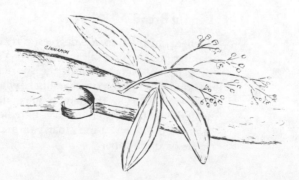

Applesauce Nut Bread

2 cups sifted flour
¾ cup sugar
3 teaspoons baking powder
½ teaspoon baking soda
½ teaspoon salt
½ teaspoon cinnamon
1 egg, beaten
1 cup applesauce
2 Tablespoons melted Crisco
1 cup chopped nuts

Sift together: flour, sugar, baking powder, soda, and cinnamon. Blend in a bowl: egg, applesauce, Crisco and pecans. Pour the applesauce mixture into the dry ingredients and stir just enough to moisten the dry ingredients. Bake in a greased 9 x 5 x 3 inch pan in a moderate oven, 350 degrees, for 45 to 60 minutes. Cool on a cake rack about 20 minutes before removing from pan. This freezes beautifully. The recipe may be doubled. Excellent for a luncheon when using a salad for a main course. Serves 8 to 10.

Mrs. V. A. Wolff
St. Louis, Missouri

Banana Nut Bread

¼ cup shortening
¾ cup sugar
1 egg
2 cups flour
½ teaspoon soda
½ teaspoon baking powder
¼ teaspoon salt
3 Tablespoons sour milk
2 large mashed bananas
½ cup chopped nuts

Cream sugar and shortening. Add egg. Sift dry ingredients together. Add remaining ingredients with dry mixture to sugar and eggs. Pour into a greased 5 x 9 inch loaf pan. Bake 1 hour at 350 degrees. To make sour milk: Mix 1 cup milk with 1 Tablespoon vinegar. Let stand for 15 minutes until it turns to clabber.

Mrs. A.E. Montgomery, Sr.

Lemon Bread

2¾ cups flour
½ teaspoon baking soda
3 teaspoons baking powder
½ teaspoon salt
⅓ cup shortening
1 cup sugar
½ cup wheat germ
3 to 4 Tablespoons grated lemon rind
2 eggs, lightly beaten
½ cup lemon juice
½ cup water

Preheat the oven to 350 degrees. Sift the flour, soda, baking powder and salt into a bowl. With the fingers or a pastry blender, work the shortening in as for making pastry. Stir in the sugar, wheat germ, rind and eggs. Stir in the lemon juice mixed with the water. Mix to moisten the dry ingredients. Turn into a greased 9 x 5 x 3 inch loaf pan and bake for one hour or until done.

Lemon Muffins

1 cup flour
1 teaspoon baking powder
¼ teaspoon salt
½ cup butter
½ cup sugar
2 eggs, separated
3 Tablespoons lemon juice
1 Tablespoon lemon rind
2 Tablespoons sugar
¼ teaspoon cinnamon

Sift together flour, baking powder and salt. Cream butter and sugar, beating until light and fluffy. Beat egg yolks until lemon colored; add to butter mixture, blending well. Add flour mixture alternately with lemon juice. Beat egg whites until stiff; fold into the batter with the lemon peel. Fill lightly greased muffin pan ¾ full. Mix sugar and cinnamon well and sprinkle ½ teaspoon over each muffin. Bake at 375 degrees about 25 minutes. Makes about 10 muffins.

BLUEBERRY

Raleigh House Blueberry Muffins

⅔ cup shortening
1 cup sugar
3 eggs
3 cups flour
3 heaping teaspoons baking powder
1 teaspoon salt
1 cup milk
1 can blueberries, drained

Cream the shortening and sugar until fluffy. Add the eggs, one at a time, beating well after each addition. Sift together the flour, baking powder and salt. Add the dry ingredients alternately with milk. When well blended, add the blueberries. This mixture will keep in the refrigerator for two or three weeks. Bake in greased muffin tins at 375 degrees for 15 to 20 minutes.

Raleigh House Restaurant
Kerrville, Texas

Oatmeal Muffins

1 cup oatmeal
1 cup buttermilk
1 egg
½ cup brown sugar, firmly packed
1 cup flour, ½ cup whole wheat flour may be mixed with ½ cup flour if desired
½ teaspoon salt
½ teaspoon baking soda
1 teaspoon baking powder
½ cup oil

Soak oatmeal in buttermilk for one hour. After the soaking period, add egg and sugar, beating well. Add flour sifted with salt, soda and baking powder. Oil is added last. Divide into greased muffin tins and bake for 15 to 20 minutes at 400 degrees. Makes 1 dozen "great big" muffins or 2 dozen medium ones. These freeze well.

Mrs. T. A. Grant III

Oatmeal Tea Bread

TOPPING:
2 Tablespoons brown sugar
2 Tablespoons chopped pecans
1/4 teaspoon cinnamon

BREAD:
1 1/4 cups sifted flour
3/4 cup sugar
1 teaspoon salt
1 teaspoon baking powder
1 teaspoon baking soda
1/2 teaspoon cinnamon
1/2 teaspoon nutmeg
1 cup quick cooking oats
1/2 cup raisins
1 1/4 cups canned sweetened
   applesauce
1/3 cup Wesson oil
2 large eggs
1/4 cup milk

Prepare topping and set aside. Grease and flour a 9 x 5 x 3 inch loaf pan. In a large mixing bowl sift together dry ingredients. Stir in oats and raisins. Beat applesauce, oil, eggs and milk together. Make a well in the center of the flour mixture; pour applesauce mixture into the well and stir only until dry ingredients are thoroughly moistened. Pour batter into prepared pan and sprinkle with the Topping. Bake in a preheated 350 degree oven until tester comes clean, about 55 to 60 minutes.

Schraftt Nut Bread

1-8 ounce package pitted dates
1 1/2 cups boiling water
2 teaspoons soda
2 1/4 cups flour
1/4 teaspoon baking powder
1 egg, well beaten
1 cup sugar
1/2 teaspoon salt
1 teaspoon melted butter
1 cup nut meats
1 teaspoon vanilla

Combine dates, boiling water and soda and let stand until warm. Mix and sift flour and baking powder. Add eggs, sugar, salt and butter to the flour mixture. Add dates and water in which they stood and then the nut meats and vanilla. Place the batter in a loaf pan which has been greased and lightly floured. Bake in a very slow oven, 275 to 300 degrees for 1 1/4 hours.

Mrs. A. Kemp, R.N.

Fruit Nut Bread

2 1/2 cups sifted flour
2 teaspoons baking powder
1 teaspoon soda
1 teaspoon salt
1 cup sugar
1 cup nuts, chopped
1 cup chopped fruits:
   raisins, citron, pineapple
1 Tablespoon grated orange rind
2 beaten eggs
1 cup milk
1 cup orange juice
1/2 stick butter, melted

Sift dry ingredients together; add fruits, nuts, orange rind. Combine egg, milk, orange juice. Add flour mixture and melted butter. Turn into pans which have been greased, paper lined and greased again. Makes two 8 x 4 x 3 inch loaves. Bake at 350 degrees for 50 to 60 minutes.

Pennsylvania White Nut Bread

¾ cup sugar
2 Tablespoons Wesson oil
1 egg
3 cups sifted flour
3½ teaspoons baking powder
1 teaspoon salt
1½ cups milk
¾ cup chopped nuts

Mix together thoroughly sugar, oil and egg. Sift together flour, baking powder and salt. Add the dry ingredients to the egg alternately with milk. Blend in chopped nuts. Pour into a well greased loaf pan, 9 x 5 x 3. Let it stand 20 minutes before baking at 350 degrees for 60 to 70 minutes. When a toothpick thrust into the center comes out clean the bread is done. Cut with a sharp knife. This is good for sandwiches or for breakfast.

Mrs. Mabel Cole Ratliff

Pumpkin Bread

3 eggs
1½ cups sugar
1½ cups pumpkin
1 cup plus 2 Tablespoons salad oil
1½ teaspoons vanilla
2¼ cups flour
1½ teaspoons baking soda
1½ teaspoons baking powder
1½ teaspoons salt
1½ teaspoons cinnamon
¼ teaspoon cloves
¼ teaspoon ginger
¼ teaspoon nutmeg
¾ cup chopped pecans

Beat eggs and sugar together well. Add pumpkin, oil and vanilla, mixing thoroughly. Sift flour, soda, baking powder, salt and spices. Add to pumpkin mixture and beat. Add pecans. Bake at 350 degrees for one hour in two well greased loaf pans. This freezes well. It is good sliced thin and spread with softened cream cheese for finger sandwiches.

Mrs. George Dean

Raisin Bread

2½ cups whole wheat flour
4 cups white flour
2 Tablespoons baking powder
2 teaspoons salt
1½ cups sugar
3 cups milk
2 eggs, well beaten
4 cups raisins, floured

Sift together dry ingredients. Add the milk, eggs and raisins. Pour into 3 greased bread pans and let stand 15 minutes. Bake at 350 degrees for 45 minutes.

Sweet Banana Bread

2 packages yeast
5½ to 6 cups flour
¾ cup milk
½ cup butter
½ cup sugar
1 teaspoon salt
2 eggs
2 ripe bananas, mashed

Combine yeast and 2 cups flour. Heat together milk, butter, sugar and salt until warm. Add to the dry ingredients; add eggs and bananas. Beat for 3 minutes at high speed. By hand, stir in enough of the remaining flour to make a moderately stiff dough. Knead to smooth the dough, about 5 minutes. Place in a lightly greased bowl, cover and let rise until double in bulk, about 1 hour. Punch down and let rest for 10 minutes. Divide the dough in half and shape into 2 round loaves. Place on a greased baking sheet, make vertical cuts 1/8 inch deep around each loaf at 3/4 inch intervals. Let the dough rise again until double, 30 to 45 minutes. Bake in a 400 degree oven for 30 minutes.

Orange Bread

2 packages dry yeast
½ cup warm water
⅓ cup sugar
¼ cup grated orange rind
1 Tablespoon salt
¼ teaspoon soda
¾ cup milk
¼ cup butter
¾ cup orange juice
2 to 2½ cups flour
Additional flour as needed

In a small bowl soften the yeast in the warm water. In a large mixing bowl combine 1/2 cup sugar, grated orange rind, salt and soda. Heat milk with butter; cool to lukewarm. To the mixture in the large mixing bowl, stir in the milk and melted butter, orange juice and softened yeast. Using a mixer at medium speed, beat in *about* 2 to 2 1/2 cups flour. Beat the soft dough until it looks elastic, at least for 3 to 4 minutes. Cannot beat it too long. *By hand* add enough flour to make a stiff dough. This usually is about 3 cups, but not always. It depends on the flour. I add as much as I can by hand being sure the flour mixes well into the dough. *Then* I put some flour on a bread board and knead it in. Knead the dough until the surface is smooth, about 8 minutes. The dough won't be sticky. Put the dough into a greased bowl and cover with plastic wrap. Let rise in a warm place until it doubles in bulk. Punch dough down. Divide in half. Rest for 5 minutes. Shape into 2 loaves or use in the recipe for Cinnamon Bubble Bread. Bake at 350 degrees for about 35 minutes.

Mrs. Leonard Bunch

Orange Rolls

2 packages dry yeast
1 cup lukewarm water
1 teaspoon salt
1/3 cup sugar
Grated rind of one orange
1/3 cup salad oil
2 eggs
4 cups flour

ORANGE BUTTER:
1/4 cup orange juice concentrate,
   undiluted
1 stick butter
1/2 box powdered sugar
Grated orange rind, optional

Dissolve yeast in lukewarm water. Add salt, sugar, orange rind, salad oil and eggs. Beat well, adding 2 cups flour. Knead the remaining two cups flour into the mixture by hand. Knead until elastic. Let rise until more than doubled in bulk in a greased bowl covered with a cloth. Make into Parkerhouse rolls and let rise again. Bake in greased pans at 375 degrees for 12 to 15 minutes. Makes about 3 dozen small rolls.
ORANGE BUTTER:
Cream orange juice, butter and powdered sugar; grated orange rind may be added if desired. Put into a covered container and spread on warm rolls.

C.D. Oakley, Jr.

Orange Toast

4 Tablespoons soft butter
1 cup sugar
1/2 cup orange juice
Grated rind of two oranges

Mix butter and sugar. Add juice and rind. Spread on hot toast and run under flame to melt the sugar. This is enough mixture for 12 slices of bread.

Basic Crêpe Batter

1 cup cold milk
1 cup cold water
4 eggs
1 teaspoon salt
2 cups sifted flour
4 Tablespoons melted butter

Whirl all ingredients in the blender. Store in the refrigerator several hours. Heat a 6 to 7 inch crêpe pan or iron skillet till a drop of water dances. Grease thoroughly with a piece of salt pork or bacon rind. Pour scant 1/4 cup of batter into the pan and swirl rapidly until batter covers the bottom. Immediately pour off batter that does not adhere. Cook until browned, lift edge and with fingers turn. Cook a few seconds on the other side. It won't be prettily browned but it doesn't matter. Regrease and reheat pan to the smoking point before each crêpe. You may store well wrapped crêpes in the refrigerator with a piece of wax paper between each crêpe. These freeze well so they are worth the little time involved. This recipe is for meat or vegetable crêpes, not desserts. Yields 25 to 30-6 or 7 inch crêpes or 20-8 inch crêpes.

Pimiento Cheese Sandwich Spread

8 ounces sharp Cheddar cheese
1 medium onion
1 teaspoon Lea & Perrins
1- 4 ounce can chopped pimientos
  plus liquid
3 heaping Tablespoons
  mayonnaise
1/4 teaspoon red pepper
1/8 teaspoon salt

In a mixing bowl, grate cheese and onion. Add the remaining ingredients and whip at high speed until light and fluffy. Refrigerate in a 1 pint jar for 24 hours. This is delicious for party sandwiches and to have on hand for snacks.

Mrs. Elton Upshaw, Jr.

Party Pimiento Cheese Spread

2 pounds sharp cheese
1- 7 ounce can pimientos
1/2 bottle Durkee's dressing
1 pint mayonnaise
2 Tablespoons lemon juice
1 teaspoon mustard
1/2 teaspoon Worcestershire
1/2 teaspoon red pepper
3 cloves crushed garlic

Mash pimientos with fork. Add Durkee's, mayonnaise, lemon juice, mustard, Worcestershire, red pepper and garlic. Mix in mixer. Add grated cheese and beat until well mixed and smooth. Makes about 2 quarts and keeps in the refrigerator indefinitely.

Mrs. Tom Keller
Baton Rouge, Louisiana

Cheese Soufflé Sandwiches

1 pound butter
4-5 ounce jars Kraft Old
  English cheese
1 teaspoon Tabasco
1 teaspoon onion powder
1 1/2 teaspoons Lea and
  Perrins sauce
1 teaspoon beau monde seasoning
1 1/2 teaspoons dill weed
2 1/2 loaves thin sliced bread

Soften butter and cheese. Beat with a mixer until fluffy, then add rest of ingredients. Remove crusts from bread. Spread 3 slices with mixture and stack; spread sides and cut into 4 or 6 pieces. Spread cut sides and continue with remaining bread. Place on wax paper and freeze. Then place in plastic bags to store. When ready to use, place on cookie sheet and bake at 325 degrees until done. If thawed, bake for 10 to 15 minutes or until edges are brown. Yields 80 pieces.

Mrs. H. C. Lockridge
Knoxville, Tennessee

Blue Cheese Sandwich Spread

2- 8 ounce packages cream cheese
1- 4 ounce package blue cheese
½ cup finely chopped nuts, more
  if you desire
1 Tablespoon Worcestershire
  sauce
½ teaspoon salt
½ cup salad dressing
Grated onion, optional

Soften the cheeses and mix well. Add the remaining ingredients. Check for seasonings.

Mrs. O.L. Getchell

Ham Salad for Finger Sandwiches

FOR 25:
1 cup ground cooked ham
4 Tablespoons finely minced
  bell pepper
2 teaspoons prepared mustard
4 Tablespoons mayonnaise
2 Tablespoons finely minced
  green onions
2 Tablespoons Worcestershire
  sauce
To taste: Accent, salt and pepper

Mix all ingredients and chill. Bring to room temperature before spreading on buttered bread.

Mrs. Don Irby

Crab Party Sandwiches

1- 7 ounce can crab or 1- 6 ounce
  package crab, frozen
2 Tablespoons finely chopped
  green onion
2 Tablespoons finely chopped dill
  pickle
1 chopped hard-boiled egg
1 teaspoon lemon juice
¼ cup mayonnaise
1 teaspoon prepared mustard
¼ teaspoon salt
Dash of cayenne
2 small loaves sandwich bread

Drain and finely slice crab. Combine all ingredients. Makes 2 dozen party sandwiches.

Shrimp Sandwich Spread

1 pod garlic, minced
1 small onion, minced
2 ribs celery, minced
1 can shrimp
1-8 ounce package cream cheese
Creamy French Dressing
1 teaspoon Lea & Perrins
To taste: red pepper, horseradish
   and mustard

Make sure that all vegetables are finely minced. Mix shrimp with cream cheese and add the minced vegetables and remaining ingredients, using enough French dressing to make this of spreading consistency.

Dr. C.T. Yancey

Tea Sandwiches

2- 4$\frac{1}{2}$ ounce cans shrimp
1 rib celery, chopped fine
1 teaspoon minced green onion
   flakes
1 teaspoon lemon juice
$\frac{3}{4}$ cup mayonnaise
1 jar cocktail onions

Chop shrimp very fine. Add celery, onion flakes and lemon juice. Mix well and blend in mayonnaise. Spread evenly on 1 inch squares of white bread and top with one cocktail onion. This will make 5 dozen.

Mrs. Henry Weaks

French Roll Party Sandwiches

1 large package cream cheese
1 finely chopped sweet pickle
1 teaspoon finely grated onion
1 large can deviled ham
1 Tablespoon finely chopped
   pecans
Worcestershire sauce, to taste
1 package French rolls

Mix all ingredients and set aside. After cooking French rolls, hollow out center section and stuff filling in with an iced teaspoon. Refrigerate for at least 24 hours. Cut into small slices and serve.

Mrs. Andy Anders

FRENCH PASTRY ROLLING PIN

Top Stove Apples

1½ cups sugar
1 cup water
1 teaspoon lemon juice
Few drops red or green coloring,
    if desired
8 apples, peeled and cored

Boil sugar and water in large enough skillet to hold eight apples. Add lemon juice and cake coloring. Cook on low heat until fork tender. Turn apples at least one time. These may be stuffed with candied cherries and chopped pecans; candied cherries and pineapple; or raisins and chopped pecans. Serves 8.

                                    Mrs. Harry Frazer, Sr.

Peaches—spiced, stuffed, brandied—all make a beautiful and appealing accompaniment to meat platters, buffet garnishes, or luncheon fare. Stuffings are easily adapted to various dishes.

Some Suggestions

Fill centers with sour cream and run under the broiler until lightly browned and puffy. Serve cold with a mixture of whipped cream and horseradish; delicious for luncheons. For the holidays; stir a taste of brandy into mincemeat, fill centers, dollop with sour cream and heat until bubbly.

What can beat good Major Grey's Chutney stuffed in the center and warmed just before serving?

Cream cheese, whipped and slightly thinned with cream or fruit juice drained from peaches, is delicious plain or add chopped nuts, cherries, dates, or any of your own ideas. You may like a squeeze of lemon juice if mixing in other sweet fruits.

Baked Orange Cups
Marvelous accompaniment with game.

6 oranges
6 apples, peeled
1 flat can crushed pineapple
1 cup sugar
1/2 stick butter
1 teaspoon vanilla
1/2 cup chopped pecans
1 Tablespoon butter

Cut oranges in half, scoop out pulp and save the shells. Cook pulp with apples, pineapple, sugar and butter until thick and tender. This will take 30 to 40 minutes. Add vanilla to filling and put in orange cups. Mix pecans with 1 Tablespoon of melted butter and sprinkle on top of cups. Bake in a shallow pan with a little water at 325 degrees for 30 minutes.

Mrs. Harold McClendon

Cranberry Conserve

1 pound cranberries
1 cup water
2 cups apple, diced and peeled
1 cup orange, diced and peeled
1/2 cup seedless raisins
3 1/2 cups sugar
Rind of orange, grated
1/2 cup chopped pecans

Wash and pick over cranberries; place in a large saucepan with water. Bring to a boil; simmer 5 minutes until berries pop. Add remaining ingredients, except nuts. Cook about 30 minutes until thick; stir occasionally. Remove from heat; add nuts. Pour into hot sterilized jars. Fill to top and seal at once. Makes 3 pints.

Mrs. Ted Willis
Atlanta, Georgia

Sherried Cranberry Sauce

1 cup sugar
1 cup dry sherry
2 cups fresh cranberries
1/2 cup chopped walnuts

Dissolve sugar in sherry over low heat, stirring constantly. Bring to a boil. Add 2 cups fresh cranberries and cook until berries pop, about eight minutes. Cool and add 1/2 cup chopped walnuts. Put in jars and store in refrigerator. Makes a nice Christmas gift for teachers.

Mrs. John Whatley
Glendale, Arizona

Pear Chutney

4½ pounds hard pears
½ cup bell pepper
1 cup crystallized ginger, diced
1½ pounds seeded raisins
4 cups sugar
3 cups vinegar
½ teaspoon salt
½ teaspoon cinnamon
¼ teaspoon nutmeg
¼ teaspoon cloves
½ teaspoon allspice
6 bay leaves
½ cup Certo

Peel, core and cut pears in small strips. Chop finely. Mix pears, peppers, ginger, raisins, sugar, vinegar, salt and cover with water. Tie spices in cheese cloth and drop into kettle with pears. Simmer until pears are tender and mixture is thick, about 2 hours. Add Certo; then boil hard 1 minute. Pack in hot jars and seal. Makes 8 half pints.

Mrs. DeWitt Milam

Pear Honey

1 quart pears
3 lemons, unpeeled
1 quart sugar

Peel and quarter pears. Seed lemons. Grind pears with lemons. Cook with sugar until mixture is "stiff". Seal in sterilized glasses or jars while the mixture is hot.

Pear Relish

2 quarts ground pears
9 bell peppers
1 red pepper
6 hot small peppers
6 medium onions
1 can pimientos
½ cup salt
4 cups sugar
8 Tablespoons flour
4 Tablespoons ground mustard
1 Tablespoon turmeric
1½ quarts apple cider vinegar

Grind all pears, peppers and onions. Pour the salt over this mixture and let stand 1 hour. Drain off all juices. Sift dry ingredients and stir in cold vinegar. Bring vinegar mixture to a boil and when thickened add ground pear mixture and cut up pimientos. Boil 5 minutes. Bottle in sterile jars while hot and seal.

Mrs. Wesley Shafto

Fresh Basil Jelly
Delicious with lamb or any meat.

1⅓ cups fresh basil leaves, packed
  down
2 cups water
¾ cups vinegar
¼ cup lemon juice
6 cups sugar
5 drops green food coloring
6 Tablespoons Certo

Pick and clean thoroughly a bunch of fresh basil leaves. Boil together in a large pot the water, vinegar and lemon juice. Bruise leaves and add to the boiling liquid. Remove from heat and let steep for ten minutes. Add sugar and coloring. Return to heat and boil, stirring constantly, until sugar dissolves. When syrup is a full rolling boil add Certo. Boil 1/2 minute and remove from heat. Place 2 fresh basil leaves in each sterile jar. Strain jelly into glasses through fine sieve. Cool to room temperature. Clean with a damp cloth upper part of jelly glass and seal with parafin. Yields five 8 ounce glasses.

Mrs. Paul Fink

Test for Jelly

Pectin test for jelly: Since green fruit contains more natural pectin than fully ripe fruit, juice should be tested before making jelly. Nearly ¼ of fruit used should be semi-green. Make a test juice of 1 Tablespoon fruit juice, 1 teaspoon sugar, and 1½ teaspoons Epsom Salts. Put juice into small glass and mix until dissolved, let set 20 minutes, then stir again. If gelatinous particles form, it contains enough pectin; if not, add 1 or 2 Tablespoons of lemon juice for each cup of fruit juice before making jelly. Be sure to pour out your "test" juice.

Hawaiian Hot Pepper Jelly

¾ cup sweet bell peppers
¼ cup hot peppers
6½ cups sugar
1½ cups apple cider vinegar
1 bottle Certo

Discard seeds from peppers, grind separately and retain juice. In measuring peppers, pack solidly in measuring cup and flood with juice. Bring sugar, vinegar and peppers to hard, rolling boil for 10 minutes. Remove from heat; add Certo, stir, pour into clean sterile jars. Makes six glasses.

Note: Oil hands or wear rubber gloves before handling peppers.

This makes a marvelous accompaniment for meats and vegetables or may be served with cheese and crackers.

Mrs. LaMonte Wright
Ruston, Louisiana

Mayhaw Jelly

Juice: Wash berries. It is not necessary to get them perfectly clean. Put in a pot with water about two inches above the level of the berries. Boil until soft, about 25 minutes. Pour them through 3 layers of cheesecloth.

Jelly: Add two cups sugar to three cups juice. Put in large pot and bring to a rapid boil. Cook *about* 20 minutes, until liquid sheets off the spoon. Pour into sterilized glasses and seal with parafin. Repeat process until all juice is used.

If you don't mind cloudy jelly and to make your berries go farther, you may put the pulp from the first batch into a pot, cover with water and boil about fifteen minutes. Pour through the cheesecloth, squeezing cloth to get all the juice and make more jelly from this.

If you do not want to do everything in one day, jelly making can be a two part operation. You can get the juice and put in large jars or covered plastic containers. Then either freeze or refrigerate juice until you are ready to make your jelly.

From the files of
Anna Gray Noe

To prevent discoloration when making jellies, preserves or relishes always use enameled or stainless steel cooking utensils.

Fig Preserves

Figs
Sugar, to cover
1 lemon, sliced

Place figs in pot and cover with sugar. Let sit overnight. The next morning add sliced lemon and cook down until thickened. Pack hot in sterile jars.

Mrs. Sarah Monroe

Alberta's Pear Preserves

5 quarts cup up pears
4½ cups sugar
1 lemon, sliced
10 to 15 cloves

Cover pears with water, add sugar and cook down about 30 minutes over low heat. Add sliced lemon and cloves. Cook uncovered 2 hours over medium heat. Turn up a little and cook 1 hour longer until pears are tender and juice is thickened. Pour into hot sterilized jars and seal.

Mrs. Wesley Shafto, Jr.

Strawberry Butter

1 pint fresh strawberries, or 10
ounces frozen, drained
½ pound unsalted butter
1 cup powdered sugar; if using
frozen berries ½ cup sugar

Put ingredients in blender in order given. Blend until smooth and creamy. If the mixture appears to curdle continue blending until creamy. Chill. Serve with toast, biscuits, muffins, pancakes, or waffles. Makes 2 1/2 cups.

Jezebel Sauce
A delicious condiment with pork or roast beef.

1- 18 ounce jar pineapple preserves
1- 18 ounce jar apple jelly
1 small can dry mustard
1 small jar of horseradish
1 Tablespoon cracked pepper

Combine all ingredients; blend well. Put in jelly jars and refrigerate. This will keep indefinitely.

Mrs. Bill Mattison

June's Mustard Sauce

1 cup mayonnaise
¼ cup mustard
Juice of 1 lemon
2 Tablespoons hot horseradish
2 Tablespoons grated onion
Seasoned salt to taste
Pepper to taste

Mix all ingredients well. This is a delicious sauce for fish, shrimp, crabmeat etc., but is equally good as a spread for ham sandwiches or cold meat of any kind. You may vary it by adding two or three Tablespoons of chopped dill pickle and parsley. This sauce keeps indefinitely and you may double or triple it successfully.

Mrs. Brewer Godfrey

Hot Mustard Sauce

1 cup sugar
1 cup vinegar
½ teaspoon salt
2 cans Coleman's mustard
3 eggs

Blend in mixer or blender. Cook in top of double boiler until thick. Makes 3 baby food jars.

Mrs. Robert Ratille
Alexandria, Louisiana

Relish

6 pounds cabbage
1 cup salt
12 peppers, red or green
6 medium carrots
6 medium onions
2 pounds sugar
3 pints vinegar
1 Tablespoon celery seed
1 Tablespoon mustard seed

Grind cabbage, add salt and let stand 3 hours. Squeeze the brine from the cabbage. Grind peppers, carrots and onions and mix with cabbage. Add sugar, vinegar and spices. This is a cold relish. Pack in hot sterilized jars and seal. Refrigerate after opening. Makes 10 half pints.

Slang Jang

1²/₃ cups chopped ripe tomatoes
1 cup chopped bell pepper
Few hot green peppers, optional
2 cups chopped onions
2 Tablespoons salad oil
¼ cup sugar, less if desired
½ cup vinegar
3 teaspoons Accent
Salt and pepper to taste

Cut vegetables in large pieces and mix oil in first. Add the rest of the ingredients and toss. Put in covered jars.

Owen M. Wright

Hot Pepper Relish

12 large red bell peppers
12 large green peppers
5 to 8 hot peppers
1 pint boiling water
8 medium chopped onions
4 cups white vinegar
2 cups sugar
3 Tablespoons salt

Remove seeds and white membrane from all peppers. Cut up fine. Do Not Grind. Pour 1 pint of boiling water over the pepper mixture and let set 10 minutes; then drain. In large kettle add above peppers, chopped onions, vinegar, salt and sugar. Let cook after it begins to boil for about 15 minutes. Pour into sterilized jars, seal while hot. If you prefer a hotter relish add more hot pepper.

Mrs. DeWitt Milam

Grannie's Sweet Pepper Relish

1 dozen red bell peppers
1 dozen green bell peppers
16 small white onions
1 quart white vinegar
2 Tablespoons mustard seed
2½ cups sugar
2 Tablespoons salt

Grind peppers and onions together with the coarse blade of a food chopper. Cover with boiling water and let stand 10 minutes; drain. Repeat this twice more. Drain well. Combine vinegar with dry ingredients. Pour over pepper mixture and boil 15 minutes. Put in pint jars and seal while hot.

Mrs. Thomas Brakefield

Bread and Butter Pickles

14 medium cucumbers
9 medium onions
2 hot peppers
½ cup salt
5 cups sugar
5 cups vinegar
1½ teaspoons turmeric
2 teaspoons mustard seed
1 teaspoon celery seed
½ teaspoon ground cloves

Slice cucumbers and onions thinly. Layer in a large pot. Cut up peppers over this. Cover with salt. Cover all with ice and let stand 3 hours. Pour off water and add sugar, vinegar and seasonings. Mix well with hands. Let simmer until rinds turn brown. Do *not* let boil. Seal in jars while hot. Makes about 12 pints.

Mrs. W. J. Hodge, Jr.

Green Tomato Pickles

7½ pounds green tomatoes
½ cup salt
5 yellow onions
1 Tablespoon salt
2 cups sugar
2 cups white vinegar
1 Tablespoon mustard seed
1 teaspoon celery seed
1 teaspoon whole black pepper
1 teaspoon ginger
1 teaspoon turmeric
1 teaspoon salt

Slice tomatoes. Put 1/2 cup salt over them and let stand one hour. Slice onions; put 1 Tablespoon of salt over them and let stand one hour. Combine sugar, vinegar and spices that have been put into a cloth bag. Cook until sugar is dissolved. Drain tomatoes and onions in colander; add to vinegar solution. Bring to a boil; remove from heat and seal in sterile jars *immediately*. Especially good on mustard greens.

Mrs. L. N. Pipes
Rayville, Louisiana

Sour to Sweet Pickles

1 quart jar of hamburger dills
2 cups sugar
½ cup tarragon vinegar
2 Tablespoons pickling spice

Drain the pickles and place them in a large bowl. Add sugar and vinegar. Tie the pickling spices in a bag before you add them or you will have a mess! Let set until the sugar melts and put the pickles back in the jar.

Mrs. C. W. Justis
Greeneville, Tennessee

Mustard Pickle Relish

1 gallon green tomatoes, stem
  and quarter to measure
1 bunch celery
1 quart onions
1 large head cabbage
6 red peppers
6 green peppers
6 hot peppers
1 dozen sour pickles
5 cups vinegar
5 cups sugar
1 cup flour
5 to 6 Tablespoons salt
1 small box turmeric
1 small box mustard

Grind all the vegetables coarsely. Add tomatoes and mix together. Pour 3 cups of vinegar over all and bring to a boil. Mix sugar, flour, salt, turmeric and mustard with remaining 2 cups of vinegar; add to vegetables, stirring well to prevent flour from sticking to the bottom of the pot. Continue cooking until vegetables are tender, at least half an hour. Seal in sterile jars. Especially good with roast pork.

Mrs. L. N. Pipes
Rayville, Louisiana

Lazy Woman's Sweet Pickles

1 quart whole sour pickles
3 cups sugar
1 clove garlic
½ teaspoon ground cloves

Pour off liquid from pickles and discard. Slice pickles in 1/4 inch slices and put into large mixing bowl. Add sugar and garlic which has been chopped finely. Add spice; mix and leave at room temperature until sugar is dissolved. Put all back into jar. Seal and refrigerate. After 3 days they are ready to eat.

Mrs. Dick Taylor
Ruston, Louisiana

Modern Caesar Salad

½ cup salad oil
¼ cup red wine vinegar
2 large cloves garlic, cut in half
2 teaspoons Worcestershire sauce
¼ teaspoon salt
Dash pepper
½ cup shredded Parmesan cheese
¼ cup, 1 ounce, crumbled
  Blue cheese
1 medium head romaine, torn in
  bite size pieces, 8 cups
2 cups croutons
1 egg

Dressing: In jar, shake together first 6 ingredients. Chill in refrigerator overnight to blend flavors. Sprinkle cheeses over romaine in salad bowl. Add croutons. Remove garlic halves from dressing. Add egg to dressing. Shake until well blended. Add dressing to salad. Toss. Serves 6 to 8.

Mrs. Harry M. Bell

Dot's Green Salad

Roka Blue Cheese Dressing
Wishbone Italian Dressing
Salad greens
Green onions and tops to taste
Pumpkin seeds
Salad Supreme with Blue Cheese
Salt and pepper to taste

Blend equal parts of dressings together and refrigerate. Fix lettuce as for a tossed salad. Chop several green onions in with it. Set in refrigerator. Just before serving, shake dressing, pour over and toss. Sprinkle liberally with pumpkin seeds. For added flavor add a few shakes of Salad Supreme with Blue Cheese, salt and pepper. Toss again.

Mrs. Elmer Neill, Jr.
Tallulah, Louisiana

Wilted Salad

6 bacon slices
1 large head Boston or leaf
  lettuce
1 medium onion, thinly sliced
1/4 cup vinegar
1 1/2 teaspoons sugar
1/2 teaspoon dry mustard
1/4 teaspoon salt
Dash pepper
2 hard boiled eggs, sliced

In large skillet, fry bacon until crisp. Drain on paper towels. Discard all but 1/4 cup bacon drippings. Tear lettuce into bite size pieces. Crumble bacon and add with onion slices, tossing well. Into bacon drippings in skillet stir remaining ingredients. Heat to boiling, stirring constantly. Remove from heat and add lettuce mixture, tossing until lettuce is slightly wilted and coated with dressing. Return to salad bowl and garnish with hard boiled egg slices. Serves 6.

Oriental Spinach Salad

10 ounces fresh spinach
1- 4 ounce can sliced mushrooms,
  drained or 1/4 pound fresh
2 grapefruit, sectioned and diced
1- 5 ounce can water chestnuts,
  diced
1/4 cup salad oil
2 Tablespoons vinegar
2 Tablespoons grapefruit juice
1 Tablespoon soy sauce
1/4 teaspoon Tabasco
1/4 teaspoon salt
1/4 teaspoon dry mustard
1 teaspoon sugar

Tear spinach in large pieces into large salad bowl. Add drained mushrooms, diced water chestnuts and diced grapefruit. Mix oil, vinegar, grapefruit juice, soy sauce, Tabasco and dry ingredients. Toss with spinach mixture. Serves 6 to 8.

Spinach Crunch

1 pound fresh spinach
8 slices raw bacon
3 teaspoons brown sugar
⅓ cup sliced green onions
Salt
3 Tablespoons vinegar
¼ teaspoon dry mustard

Wash, dry and chill spinach. Tear into bite size bits in salad bowl and just before serving prepare sauce. Dice bacon and fry until crisp. Reduce heat, add sugar, green onions, salt to taste, vinegar and dry mustard. Bring to a boil, remove from heat and pour over spinach. Toss lightly.

Mrs. Robert Curry III

Spinach Salad

6 slices crumbled bacon
2 hard boiled eggs, chopped
1 pound fresh spinach

DRESSING:
½ cup sugar
½ cup vinegar
2 Tablespoons oil
1 Tablespoon chopped green
  onion
1 Tablespoon chopped parsley
1 Tablespoon chives
1 teaspoon Worcestershire sauce
1 teaspoon prepared mustard
Cracked black pepper
1 ice cube

Mix the salad dressing ingredients in a plastic container, shake well and chill. Pour over the spinach, bacon and eggs, seasoning to taste with salt and pepper if desired. Toss well and serve. The dressing keeps well for several days if kept in the refrigerator. Serves 6.

Mrs. Paul Lansing
New Orleans, Louisiana

Slaw

2 cans tomatoes, drained and
  chopped
1 head cabbage, shredded
½ bag carrots, grated
1 bunch celery, chopped
1 onion, chopped
1 bell pepper, chopped
1 pint vinegar
1 pound brown sugar
1 Tablespoon mustard seed
2 teaspoons salt

Combine the first six ingredients in a large bowl. Boil the vinegar, sugar, mustard seed and salt. Pour the liquid over the slaw mixture and refrigerate overnight. Drain and serve on a lettuce leaf as a salad. Makes 1/2 gallon and serves 20. Easily doubles and triples.

Mrs. Glenn Lesley
Greensboro, North Carolina

24 Hour Slaw

1 medium head cabbage,
shredded
2 medium white onions,
sliced into rings
½ cup sugar

DRESSING:
1 teaspoon celery seed
1 teaspoon sugar
1½ teaspoons salt
1 teaspoon dry mustard
1 cup white vinegar
1 cup salad oil

Stir 1/2 cup sugar into cabbage and place half of amount in large bowl. Cover with onion rings. Cover with remaining cabbage. Combine dressing ingredients except oil. Bring to roaring boil. Stir in oil. Bring to boil again. Pour over cabbage and onions. Do not stir. Cover and refrigerate for 24 hours. Keeps indefinitely.

Mrs. Sol Courtman

Creamy Slaw

1 medium cabbage
1 medium white onion
Salt and pepper to taste
¼ cup sugar
1 cup Hellman's mayonnaise
¼ cup white vinegar

Shred cabbage very fine. Slice onion very finely and separate rings. Toss these two together. Salt and pepper to taste. Sprinkle sugar over mixture. Combine mayonnaise and vinegar. Pour over cabbage and onion. Toss. Chill. Serves 8 to 10.

Mrs. Don Giffen

Marinated Kraut
Delicious as a salad or a relish

1 pound can sauerkraut
1 cup chopped bell pepper
1 cup chopped onion
1 small jar chopped pimientos
1 chopped jalapeño pepper,
optional
1 cup sugar
1 cup white vinegar

Drain sauerkraut well and mix with chopped vegetables. Heat sugar and vinegar until boiling and sugar is dissolved. Pour over slaw mixture. Toss thoroughly and cool. Store in a covered bowl in the refrigerator. Keeps well for several days. Wonderful used in Reuben sandwiches.

Mrs. Fred Bennet

Avocado with Tomato Freeze
Beautiful to serve

1 envelope unflavored gelatin
2 Tablespoons water
1 No. 1 can Progresso tomato
   puree or 2 small cans tomato
   paste
1/2 wedge Roquefort cheese
1- 3 ounce package cream cheese
2 heaping Tablespoons
   mayonnaise
1 Tablespoon onion, grated
Juice of 1/2 lemon
1/4 teaspoon salt
2 teaspoons Worcestershire sauce
4 avocados, halved

Soften gelatin in 2 Tablespoons water. Heat puree and stir in gelatin until dissolved. Set aside to cool. Cream cheeses and add mayonnaise. Blend in the tomato-gelatin mixture and the remaining ingredients except avocados. Freeze in trays. Scoop out and serve in peeled avocado halves which have been dipped in lemon juice to keep them from darkening. Serves 8.

Mrs. Lionel V. Swift
Marietta, Georgia

Beet Salad

2 No. 303 cans sliced beets
2 envelopes gelatin
1/2 cup cold water
1/2 cup sugar
1 1/2 teaspoons salt
1/2 cup vinegar
1 1/2 cups celery, minced
1 1/2 cups green onion, minced
2 teaspoons horseradish
1/2 cup India Relish

Drain beets and bring liquid to a boil. Soften gelatin in cold water and add to hot liquid. Add sugar and salt, stir all to dissolve. Blend in vinegar. Set aside to cool to room temperature. Chop beets, celery and onion. Blend in horseradish and India Relish. Combine with gelatin mixture. Pour into a 6 to 8 cup mold. Refrigerate until firm. Serves 8 to 10.

Mrs. J. R. Aycock
Rayville, Louisiana

Herb Tomatoes

6 whole ripe tomatoes
2/3 cup salad oil
1/4 cup vinegar
1 clove minced garlic
1/4 cup snipped parsley
1/4 cup sliced green onions and
   tops
1 teaspoon salt
1/4 teaspoon cracked black
   pepper
1/2 teaspoon dried thyme
Additional minced green onions
   and parsley for garnish

Peel tomatoes; drop in boiling water for a few seconds and peeling is easy. Mix the remaining ingredients. Marinate the whole tomatoes for several hours or overnight in a deep bowl in the refrigerator. To serve: arrange the tomatoes on a serving platter and spoon a small amount of marinade over each tomato and sprinkle with minced green onions and parsley. When tomatoes are not at summer's best, these do well. Serves 6.

Mrs. Bob Hand

Marinated Onion and Tomato Slices

½ teaspoon cracked black
  pepper
½ teaspoon thyme
½ teaspoon oregano
1 teaspoon salt
¼ cup green onion tops
¼ teaspoon garlic powder
⅔ cup Wesson oil
¼ cup Progresso wine vinegar
¼ cup chopped parsley flakes
6 ripe tomatoes, sliced thinly
3 medium onions, sliced thinly

Combine all ingredients except onions and tomatoes in shallow pyrex dish. Add tomato and onion slices and cover. Place in refrigerator overnight or for at least 4 to 6 hours. When ready to serve add more quartered tomatoes. Serves 8.

Mrs. Elton Upshaw, Jr.

Fire and Ice
Great with a steak

2 large purple onions, cut in
  ¼ inch slices
6 large firm tomatoes, peeled
  and quartered
1 bell pepper, cut into strips
¾ cup cider vinegar
¼ cup water
1½ teaspoons celery seed
1½ teaspoons mustard seed
½ teaspoon salt
2 Tablespoons sugar
½ teaspoon cracked black
  pepper

Place onions, tomatoes and bell pepper in a bowl. In saucepan bring all remaining ingredients to boil. Boil 1 minute only. While still hot, pour over vegetables. Chill. Serves 6. Easily doubles.

Mrs. Don Irby

PARSLEY

Red Hot Onions

3 large purple onions
3 Tablespoons Tabasco
3 Tablespoons olive oil
3 Tablespoons red wine vinegar

Slice onions thinly. Pour boiling water over onions and let stand 1 minute, drain. Mix Tabasco, oil and vinegar. Pour over onion rings in a shallow dish. Refrigerate and let stand at least 3 hours. This may be drained to serve. It is a good accompaniment for cold meats, charcoaled steaks and barbecue.

Gene Howard

Pennsylvania Dutch Potato Salad

4 extra large potatoes

BACON DRESSING:
4 slices bacon
2 eggs, beaten lightly
¼ cup sugar or to taste
½ teaspoon salt
¼ cup vinegar
½ cup milk or cream
Chopped onions
2 Tablespoons Miracle Whip

Boil the potatoes in the jackets until they are tender. Peel and cut them into large chunks. *Keep warm!* Fry the bacon until crisp, remove from skillet and reserve drippings. To the beaten eggs add the next four ingredients, mixing well. Add the egg mixture to the bacon drippings and cook over low heat, stirring constantly, until this is a custard consistency. Crumble the bacon and return it to the dressing. Pour the dressing over the potatoes. When cool, add plenty of chopped onions and Miracle Whip. Serves 6 to 8.

Mrs. Mabel Cole Ratliff

Piquant Potato Salad

1½ teaspoons mustard seed
1 teaspoon celery seed
3 Tablespoons vinegar
1½ teaspoons salt
5 cups cooked, diced potatoes
2 or 3 hard boiled eggs, diced
1 bunch green onions, finely
chopped
¾ cup mayonnaise
Chopped pickles, optional

Soak mustard seeds and celery seeds overnight in vinegar. The next day have potatoes and eggs boiled and cooled. Mix all of the ingredients together and serve. Serves 6 to 8.

Mrs. Jim Hurley
Oklahoma City, Oklahoma

Potato Salad with Mustard Mayonnaise

A delicious salad with a divine homemade mayonnaise

3 egg yolks
2 or 3 Tablespoons lemon juice
1½ cups salad oil
½ teaspoon salt
¼ teaspoon dry mustard
3 or 4 Tablespoons Dijon
mustard
6 medium potatoes in jackets
Parsley
Green onions

Warm mixing bowl and beat the devil out of the egg yolks. Add lemon juice and oil very gradually at first. Once mayonnaise starts to make, oil may be added more rapidly. Stir in seasonings and refrigerate. Several hours before serving, boil 6 medium potatoes in salted water until tender. Peel potatoes while warm and slice 1/4 to 1/3 inch thick. While still warm, season with salt, freshly ground pepper, loads of minced parsley and several minced green onions and enough mustard mayonnaise to coat slices lightly. Mix with hands so as not to break up slices too much. Serve at room temperature.

Pasta Salad

1 package vermicelli
1 bunch celery
1 large can pimientos
4 jalapeño peppers, or
  to taste
1 medium onion, grated
1 small bell pepper, optional
2 to 3 cups Kraft Miracle Whip
Salt and pepper to taste

Cook spaghetti according to directions. Drain and cool. Finely chop celery, pimientos and peppers. Grate onion. Add cooled spaghetti, mix and add salad dressing, salt and pepper. Keep in refrigerator covered for 24 hours. It is good when kept 4 or 5 days.

Mrs. George Snellings III

Mexican Salad

10 sliced ripe avocados,
  dipped in lemon juice
1 package cherry tomatoes
5 cans kidney beans, rinsed
  and drained

DRESSING:
2 cartons sour cream
1 small bottle Wishbone
  Italian dressing
Garlic salt
3 Tablespoons chili powder,
Salt and pepper to taste

2 or 3 heads lettuce
1 large package crushed Fritos

Marinate avocados, cherry tomatoes, halved, and kidney beans in sour cream and Wishbone dressing and seasonings for several hours or overnight. Just before serving, add lettuce in bite size pieces and Fritos. This serves about 20 people. Delicious.

Mrs. Jim Geisler
Mrs. J. Alfred Levert II
New Orleans, Louisiana

CAYENNE

Pickled-Black Eyed Peas

2-1 pound cans black-eyed
  peas, drained
1 onion, sliced thinly
½ cup olive oil
¼ cup wine vinegar
2 cloves garlic, mashed
1 Tablespoon Worcestershire
1 teaspoon salt
1 bay leaf
Pepper

Put peas and onions in heat-proof bowl. Combine all other ingredients in a saucepan. Bring to a boil and pour over peas. Refrigerate for several hours. Serves 8.

Mrs. George Ellis

Cold Mirliton Salad

Mirliton recipes are scarce in general cookbooks because the vegetable is so regional. The "Vegetable Pear" as it is also known has found a home in Louisiana, Georgia and South Carolina. The delicate flavored vegetable can be prepared many ways: baked, stewed or stuffed. A cold mirliton salad is enjoyed by all Southerners.

4 small mirlitons
Your favorite French dressing
Whipped cream cheese, optional
Paprika, optional

Cut mirlitons in half; pare and remove center seed. Boil until tender in salted water. Cool and drain. Marinate several hours in French dressing in the refrigerator. Place two halves per serving on crisp lettuce leaves. Company touch: Put a mound of whipped cream cheese in cavities and sprinkle with paprika.

Mrs. Kenneth C. Landry
Baton Rouge, Louisiana

English Pea Salad

2 cans Early June Peas, drained
2 large ribs celery
¾ cup sharp Cheddar
5 green onions
¼ teaspoon cracked black
  pepper
Dash of garlic salt
½ teaspoon salt
½ teaspoon mustard
¾ cup tartar sauce

Finely chop celery and onions. Cube cheese. Mix all ingredients together. This can be served immediately, but it is better if marinated overnight.

Mrs. Harry Stone

Crunchy Vegetable Salad

1 cup oil
1 cup sugar
½ cup vinegar
2 cups cut green beans, drained
2 cups small English peas
1 can water chestnuts, sliced
4 large ribs celery, chopped
  finely
1-4 ounce jar chopped pimientos
Salt to taste
Optional: mushrooms or cocktail onions

Mix oil, sugar and vinegar until blended. Add remaining ingredients and marinate overnight. Do not leave out the water chestnuts for they add a very definite taste to this salad. This keeps well for several days but must be marinated at least 8 hours to be good. Drain and serve as a vegetable or on lettuce as a salad.

Mrs. Jim Lewis

Vegetable Salad

8 to 10 carrots
6 ribs celery
3 cans Blue Lake green beans
2 cans baby beets
2 cans artichoke hearts
1 can olives
4 green onions
French dressing
Seasoned salt

Drop cut up carrots in boiling water. After 5 minutes add cut up celery. Cook 5 minutes more. Drain. Mix all ingredients together and leave overnight. May add asparagus, broccoli, avocado or hard boiled eggs. This is a nice change from tossed green salad. Serves 16.

Mrs. Carrick Inabnett

Cucumbers Vinaigrette

1- 8 ounce bottle Italian style salad dressing
2 Tablespoons lemon juice
1 Tablespoon capers, chopped
¼ teaspoon garlic, crushed
1 teaspoon Worcestershire sauce
2 cucumbers, quartered and sliced
8 Boston lettuce leaves

Mix the first five ingredients well and pour over the cucumbers. Cover and refrigerate for at least 30 minutes. Before serving drain the cucumbers, reserving the marinade. To serve arrange the lettuce on salad plates and pour a small amount of the marinade over and top with cucumbers.

Mrs. DeWitt Milam

The Best Marinated Cucumber Rings

2 large cucumbers, thinly sliced
4- 4 ounce jars pimientos, drained and sliced
⅔ cup vegetable oil
¼ cup white wine vinegar
½ teaspoon salt
2 cups sour cream

Mix together cucumber and pimiento strips. Shake oil, vinegar and salt together. Pour over cucumbers and chill 1 hour. *Drain well.* Just before serving blend with sour cream. Chopped green onion tops may be added while cucumbers are marinating if desired. Serves 12.

Copper Pennies

2 pounds carrots, sliced crosswise
1 small onion, chopped finely
1 medium bell pepper, chopped finely
3 ribs celery, chopped finely
1 cup tomato soup, undiluted
1 cup sugar
¼ cup oil
¾ cup Apple Cider vinegar
1 Tablespoon dry mustard
1 Tablespoon Lea & Perrins
Lettuce

Cook sliced carrots in salted water until fork tender. Add chopped onion, bell pepper and celery to the drained carrots. Set aside. Mix and bring to a boil soup, sugar, oil, vinegar, mustard and Lea & Perrins. Pour this hot mixture over the above vegetables. Refrigerate overnight. Serve on lettuce. Serves 10 to 12.

Miss Lenee Lacey

Marinated Dill Carrots

2 cups carrot sticks
¼ cup Green Goddess dressing
¼ cup Wishbone Italian dressing
¼ teaspoon salt
½ teaspoon pepper
1 teaspoon dill seed
¼ cup grated onion
1 teaspoon parsley flakes

Boil the carrots until tender in salted water. Drain. Mix the remaining ingredients and pour over the cooked carrots. Marinate overnight. Serves 6.

Mrs. Marion Jouett
Shreveport, Louisiana

Dill and Roquefort Green Bean Salad

DILL DRESSING:
1 cup Wesson oil
¼ cup white vinegar
3 Tablespoons lemon juice
½ teaspoon cracked black pepper
¼ teaspoon paprika
½ teaspoon dry mustard
1 or 2 garlic cloves
1 Tablespoon dill seed

2 pounds green beans or 2-1 pound cans
Hamhock
1 onion
Lawry's seasoning salt
Salt and pepper to taste
1 clove garlic

½ pound bacon
1 bunch green onions, chopped
¼ pound Roquefort or blue cheese, crumbled
¼ cup prepared Dill Dressing
¼ cup Hellman's mayonnaise
2 Tablespoons sour cream

The Day Before: Put all the dressing ingredients in a jar and shake well. Refrigerate. Makes 1 1/2 cups. Cook the beans with the seasonings in a small amount of water. When tender, drain and cool. This is *important* for a well flavored salad.

The Day of Serving: Fry bacon until crisp and crumble. Mix the drained beans with onions, 1/2 of the crumbled bacon, and the remaining ingredients. Chill several hours. Garnish the top with the remaining bacon. This can be easily doubled. If you are serving a big crowd, 30 or more, double the amounts in the dill dressing. This is delicious served with bar-b-que or charcoaled meats. Serves 6 to 8.

Mrs. James Tolbert III
Oklahoma City, Oklahoma

Garlic Green Beans

3 cans whole beans
1 cup oil
½ cup vinegar
½ cup sugar
4 to 5 buttons of garlic
To taste: red pepper, black pepper,
   salt

Rinse and drain beans. Mix remaining ingredients and pour over drained beans. Set overnight in refrigerator. Serves 6.

Mrs. Don Stinson

Green Bean Salad

4 medium tomatoes, cut in
   wedges
1 medium onion, sliced
2- 1 pound cans cut green beans
1- 1 pound can cut wax beans
½ cup sliced green pepper

DRESSING:
⅔ cup garlic vinegar
¾ cup sugar
⅓ cup salad oil
1½ teaspoons salt
1 teaspoon pepper

Combine the vegetable ingredients in a bowl. Shake dressing ingredients until well mixed and pour over the vegetables. Chill 24 hours, stirring occasionally. Makes 8 servings.

Mrs. S. O. Henry
Columbia, Louisiana

Artichoke Salad

2 cans beef consommé
1 can water
2 unflavored envelopes of gelatin,
   softened in small amount of
   water
Juice of 2 lemons
Salt, pepper and Tabasco to taste
1 large can artichokes, quartered

Heat consommé and water, add softened gelatin. Add lemon juice and seasoning. Place quartered artichokes in bottom of ring mold or individual molds. Pour consommé mixture into mold and chill. Serve on lettuce with a dash of mayonnaise. Makes about eight individual molds.

Mrs. Rupert Evans
Lake Providence, Louisiana

Avocado Mousse

2 envelopes unflavored gelatin
2 cups cold chicken broth
¼ cup lemon juice
2 Tablespoons red wine vinegar
4 to 6 Tablespoons minced green
   onions
2 or 3 large, very soft avocados
2 teaspoons salt
1 teaspoon Mexican hot sauce or
   Tabasco
⅓ cup mayonnaise
1 cup heavy cream, whipped

Sprinkle gelatin over broth and stir over low heat until melted. Add lemon juice, vinegar and onion. Chill, but not until set. Peel and seed avocados. Beat until smooth and creamy. Measure 2 cups avocado puree. Blend in cold broth mixture and season with salt and hot sauce. Blend in mayonnaise and partially chill. Fold in whipped cream, check seasoning, and pour into 6 cup mold. Chill until firm. The center of the ring mold may be filled with seafood or cherry tomato garnish. Serves 10 to 12.

Mrs. Don Irby

"Green Dream" Congealed Salad

1 package lime jello
1 cup warm water
1 avocado
2- 3 ounce packages cream cheese
½ cup mayonnaise
¾ cup celery, finely chopped
½ large bell pepper, finely
   chopped
½ onion, grated
Salt to taste

Dissolve jello in warm water. Set in refrigerator until partially set. Peel avocado and mash with fork. Blend in cream cheese and mayonnaise with avocado. Mix in celery, bell pepper and grated onion with the avocado mixture. Add salt to taste. Add all to jello, mixing well. Refrigerate. Makes a 1 quart salad mold. Serves 6 to 8.

Mrs. Jesse D. McDonald
Mrs. Norman H. Smith

Broccoli Salad Mold

1 package frozen chopped broccoli
1 can beef consommé
1½ envelopes unflavored gelatin
¼ cup cold water
2 Tablespoons lemon juice
1 Tablespoon garlic flavored
   vinegar
¾ cup mayonnaise

Cook broccoli until almost done. Drain. Heat consommé. Soften gelatin in cold water. Add softened gelatin, lemon juice and vinegar to hot consommé. Stir until gelatin is dissolved. Chill until syrupy. Beat with rotary beater. Add mayonnaise and beat again. Fold in cooked broccoli. Pour into lightly oiled three cup mold. Chill until firm. Six servings.

Mrs. Thomas Holmes, Jr.

Creamy Cucumber Salad Ring

1 package lime jello
¾ cup hot water
2- 3 ounce packages cream cheese
1 cup mayonnaise
1 teaspoon horseradish
¼ teaspoon salt
2 Tablespoons lemon juice
2 cucumbers, skinned and seeded;
  finely chopped or grated to
  equal ¾ cup
½ cup onions, finely sliced

Dissolve jello in hot water. Add cream cheese, mayonnaise, horseradish, and salt. Beat until smooth in mixer. Add lemon juice. Chill about 30 minutes until partially set. Stir in cucumbers and onions. Pour into 1 quart ring mold and chill until firm. Top with mayonnaise when served. Serves 6.

Mrs. Nate Mehl

Cucumber Mousse
Delicious summer salad; Serve with seafood, marinated tomatoes and cucumber slices

5 medium cucumbers
2¼ cups water
2 Tablespoons lemon juice
4 green onions and tops
½ cup parsley leaves, no stems
4 teaspoons Worcestershire
1½ to 2 teaspoons salt
¼ teaspoon pepper
Dash of Accent
Dash of Tabasco
1 cup mayonnaise
3 envelopes unflavored gelatin
1 cup heavy cream

Peel cucumbers, slice in half lengthwise, and with spoon run down the middle to remove seeds. Cook cucumbers in 2 cups of water with lemon juice until tender, about 20 minutes. *Drain well.* Puree in a blender with onions and parsley leaves. Not too long, a few specks of green should be seen. Add the Worcestershire, salt, pepper, a dash of Accent, Tabasco and mayonnaise. Blend. Heat gelatin in 1/4 cup of water until gelatin dissolves. Stir into cucumber mixture and chill until mixture mounds in spoon. Whip cream and fold into mixture. Check for seasoning. Pour into a six cup ring mold and chill overnight. Fill center with additional cucumber slices marinated in French dressing, tomato wedges or with seafood. A well-seasoned salad base that may be used many different ways. Serves 8.

Mrs. Stewart E. Meyers, Jr.
Oklahoma City, Oklahoma

Molded Cucumber Salad

1 small package lime jello
1½ cups hot water
2 Tablespoons vinegar
1 teaspoon salt
1 cup grated cucumber
1 teaspoon onion juice or to
  taste

Mix lime jello with water, vinegar and salt. Add cucumber and onion juice. Mold as desired.

Mrs. William Reed

Molded Vegetable Salad

1 small package lemon jello
2 cups water
1 cup shredded cabbage
1 cup chopped pecans
1 cup chopped celery
1 cup chopped unpeeled red
    apples
1 small bottle stuffed olives

Mix jello with water according to package directions. Mix rest of vegetables together and fill a lightly greased rectangular pyrex dish. Pour jello over vegetables. Chill in refrigerator until firm. Cut in squares and serve on lettuce topped with a dab of mayonnaise. Serves 8.

Mrs. Leonard Bunch

Clarksdale, Mississippi Tomato Aspic

ASPIC:
3 cups tomato juice
1 teaspoon salt
1 teaspoon sugar
1 teaspoon lemon juice
1 teaspoon Worcestershire sauce
Onion juice to taste
Dash of Tabasco
2 envelopes unflavored gelatin
1/2 cup water

VEGETABLES:
1 avocado, chopped
1/2 cup celery, chopped
1/2 cup stuffed olives

CHEESE CENTER:
1 pound cottage cheese
1/2 cup mayonnaise
1/2 cup onion, finely chopped
1/2 cup bell pepper, chopped
1 cucumber, unpeeled, grated and
    drained
Salt and pepper to taste

GARNISH, Optional:
Avocado slices
Artichoke hearts
Durkee's Dressing

Boil tomato juice with seasonings. Steep 10 to 15 minutes. Add gelatin that has been softened in cold water. Stir until gelatin has melted. Cool until mixture begins to thicken.

Prepare vegetables and add to aspic after it has thickened. Pour into ring mold and refrigerate until firm.

Cream cottage cheese with mayonnaise. Add chopped vegetables and season to taste. Fill center of aspic with cheese mixture. Marinate avocado slices and artichoke hearts in Durkee's to garnish, if desired.

Mrs. Mabel Cole Ratliff

Tomato Aspic with Vegetables

3 cups canned tomato juice
1 rib celery
1 small onion, sliced
2 lemon slices
1 small bay leaf
1 teaspoon salt
2½ envelopes unflavored gelatin
⅔ cup cold tomato juice
¼ cup cider vinegar
1 teaspoon salt
1 cup finely shredded cabbage
¼ cup chopped celery
¼ cup grated carrots
¼ cup chopped cucumber
6 chopped green onions
2 teaspoons Worcestershire
2 teaspoons lemon juice
Dash of Tabasco

Combine 3 cups tomato juice with celery rib, onion slices, lemon slices, bay leaf and 1 teaspoon salt. Simmer 10 minutes. Strain. Meanwhile sprinkle gelatin over 2/3 cup tomato juice and vinegar in bowl. When softened, stir in hot tomato juice mixture and stir until gelatin is dissolved. Refrigerate, stirring occasionally, until mixture thickens. Sprinkle additional salt on vegetables and fold them into the gelatin mixture. Pour into individaul molds and refrigerate until firm.

Mrs. Jerry Wolff

Raw Spinach Salad Mold

1- 3 ounce box lemon jello
1 cup boiling water
½ cup cold water
½ cup mayonnaise
1½ Tablespoons vinegar
1 Tablespoon sour cream,
   optional
¼ teaspoon salt
Dash of pepper
1 cup chopped raw spinach
¾ cup cottage cheese, small
   curd
⅓ cup diced celery
1 Tablespoon chopped onion

Dissolve jello in boiling water. Add cold water, mayonnaise, vinegar, salt, pepper and sour cream. Chill until firm. Beat until fluffy and fold in rest of ingredients. Pour into a 4 cup ring mold; chill until firm. Unmold and garnish with parsley and cherry tomatoes. Serves 6 to 8.

Mrs. Gene Worthen

Melon Boats

2 medium cantaloupes, chilled
4 cups seedless grapes
1 cup homemade mayonnaise
1/3 cup frozen orange juice,
  undiluted

Prepare each melon in 6 lengthwise sections, removing seeds and peeling. Heap grapes over and around melon. Combine mayonnaise and juice concentrate. Mix well. Ladle over fruit. Serves 12.

Mrs. Michael Brown
Lake Providence, Louisiana

Fruit Salad

1 large can crushed pineapple
1 cup sugar
1 Tablespoon flour
3 bananas
1 to 2 yellow apples
3 oranges
1 large can Freestone peaches,
  drained
1 large can pears, drained
1- 10 ounce package frozen
  strawberry halves, thawed
  and drained

Heat the pineapple, sugar and flour. Stir until this thickens. Set aside and cool. Slice bananas and dice apples directly into pineapple mixture and mix well. Dice oranges, peaches and pears. Add all with the strawberries and chill. Serves 8.

Mrs. J. L. Davidson
Farmerville, Louisiana

Orange and Avocado Salad

DRESSING:
1/2 cup toasted sesame seed
1 cup sugar
1 teaspoon paprika
1/2 teaspoon dry mustard
1 teaspoon salt
1 teaspoon Worcestershire
1 Tablespoon onion, grated
2 cups Wesson oil

1 cup cider vinegar
Salad greens
Sectioned oranges
Sliced avocados
Purple onion, optional

Toast sesame seeds in a 200 degree oven, watching and stirring frequently. Combine sugar, paprika, mustard, salt, Worcestershire and onion in a bowl and add the oil and vinegar gradually. Transfer to a quart jar, add sesame seeds and refrigerate. Toss with salad greens, sectioned oranges and avocados. Purple onion rings may be added also.

Mrs. Don Irby

Peppered Fruit

1 cucumber
1 large cantaloupe or three cups
　sliced cantaloupe
Fresh chopped parsley
Lettuce

LEMON-PEPPER DRESSING:
$1/2$ cup salad oil
3 Tablespoons fresh lemon juice
$3/4$ teaspoon Dijon mustard
$1/2$ teaspoon salt
$1/2$ teaspoon coarse cracked
　black pepper
$1/4$ teaspoon tarragon or
　rosemary

Peel and thinly slice cucumber and cantaloupe. Mix dressing ingredients, shake well in a jar and pour over fruit. Cover and chill several hours. Toss occassionally. Serve on lettuce leaf, or from a pretty glass bowl, topped with fresh parsley. A delicious change.

Mrs. Jack Brown
Lake Providence, Louisiana

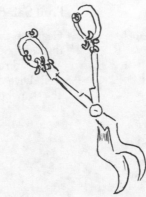

Summer Salad

3 cups sliced peaches, fresh or
　canned; drained
$1^1/2$ cups seedless grapes
Lemon juice

ONION SPICE DRESSING:
$1/2$ cup salad oil
2 Tablespoons wine vinegar
1 Tablespoon lemon juice
1 Tablespoon brown sugar
1 teaspoon salt
$3/4$ teaspoon ground cloves
$1/8$ teaspoon pepper
1 Tablespoon minced green
　onions and tops

Prepare fruit, sprinkle fresh peaches with lemon juice to keep from darkening. Shake together salad dressing ingredients. Gently toss with peaches and grapes. Cover and chill several hours. Serve on lettuce leaf. Serves six. Good with chicken or pork.

Mrs. Jerry Wolff

24 Hour Salad

3 egg yolks beaten
2 Tablespoons sugar
2 Tablespoons vinegar
2 Tablespoons pineapple syrup
1 Tablespoon butter
Dash of salt
2 cups pitted white cherries, drained
2 cups pineapple tidbits, drained
2 oranges, pared and sectioned
2 cups tiny marshmallows
1 cup heavy cream, whipped

Combine first six ingredients in the top of a double boiler. Cook over hot, not boiling water, until thick, stirring constantly. Cool, stir in all fruits and fold in whipped cream. Chill 24 hours. Serves 6 to 8.

Mrs. Fred Petty

Winter Fruit Cup

2 unpeeled red apples
3 medium oranges
1½ cups grapefruit sections
¾ cup packed brown sugar
¼ cup margarine
1 cup sour cream
1 teaspoon vanilla

Core and dice apples, unpeeled. Section oranges. With fork, lightly mix fruits and 1/4 cup brown sugar. Chill. Shortly before serving, combine remaining sugar and margarine in a small saucepan and heat. Stir until margarine is melted and bubbles. Stir in remaining ingredients and serve over the fruits. Serves six.

Mrs. J. E. Brown
Lake Providence, Louisiana

Apricot Salad
Great for a busy day

1 small package Ann Page apricot jello
1 cup hot orange juice
1 cup cold buttermilk

Dissolve jello in hot orange juice. Blend in buttermilk; pour into 4 oiled individual molds or 1 quart mold. Chill until set. Garnish with whole strawberries or sliced bananas that have been dipped in lemon juice to keep from darkening.

Mrs. Leonard Bunch
Mrs. Lovell Hayden III
Mrs. Horace Smith

Apricot—Pineapple Salad

1 large can apricots
1 large can crushed pineapple
2 packages orange jello
2 cups boiling water
1 cup combined apricot and
   pineapple juice
3/4 cup miniature marshmallows

TOPPING:
1/2 cup sugar
3 Tablespoons flour
1 egg slightly beaten
1 cup combined apricot and
   pineapple juice
2 Tablespoons butter
1 cup heavy cream, whipped
3/4 cup grated cheese

Drain and chill apricots and pineapple, dicing apricots and reserving the juices. Dissolve jello in boiling water. Add 1 cup reserved juice, save rest for topping. Chill until slightly congealed. Fold in fruit and marshmallows. Pour into 9 x 11 inch shallow pan. Chill until firm. Spread with topping.

Topping: Combine sugar and flour, blend in egg and juice. Stir over low heat until thickened. Remove from heat, stir in butter, *cool*. Fold in whipped cream and spread over gelatin mixture. Sprinkle with grated cheese. Chill and cut into squares. Serves 10 to 12.

Mrs. Naomi Crawford
Winnfield, Louisiana

Spiced Apricot Mold
Delicious with game, turkey or pork

1-No. 2 1/2 can peeled apricots
1/4 cup vinegar
1 teaspoon whole cloves
4 inches stick cinnamon
1 package orange jello
Jellied cranberry sauce, cut in
   rings

TOPPING:
1 cup sour cream
2 Tablespoons white vinegar
2 Tablespoons sugar
1/2 teaspoon salt

Drain apricots, reserving syrup. Add vinegar and spices to syrup and bring to boil. Add apricots and simmer 10 minutes. Remove apricots and place in individual molds. Strain syrup and measure. Add enough hot water to make 2 cups. Pour over jello and stir until dissolved. Pour over apricots and chill. Unmold over jellied cranberry ring on lettuce leaf. Serve with sour cream topping made by mixing the topping ingredients. Makes 8 servings.

Mrs. Don Isley

Molded Apricot Salad
Men love this!

SALAD:
2 large cans stone free apricots, drain and reserve juices
4 envelopes unflavored gelatin
1 cup cold water
8 teaspoons white vinegar
2 Tablespoons sugar
1 teaspoon salt
1 Tablespoon butter
1 teaspoon prepared mustard
1/2 teaspoon Tabasco
1 pound bag miniature marshmallows
2 pints heavy cream, whipped
2 cups chopped pecans, walnuts or both

PUFFED DRESSING:
1/2 cup sugar
1 teaspoon salt
1 teaspoon Coleman's dry mustard
Vinegar, about 1 1/4 cups, see directions
3 beaten eggs
1/2 pint heavy cream whipped

Drain and mash the apricots or blend lightly. Soften the gelatin in cold water and add the heated juice from the apricots. Dissolve thoroughly. Let chill until partially thickened. In a saucepan heat the mashed apricots, vinegar, sugar, salt, butter, mustard and Tabasco. When hot, add the marshmallows and heat until melted. Cool slightly and add to the gelatin mixture. Cool thoroughly!! When partially set, fold in the whipped cream and nuts. Pour into a slightly greased 8 to 10 cup mold or into individual molds. Keep in the refrigerator for 8 hours or overnight. Unmold onto large serving tray and surround with lettuce leaves.

Dressing: Into a 1 cup measuring cup put the first three ingredients and fill the cup to the brim with vinegar. Pour into a bowl and add 3/4 cup additional vinegar. Stir thoroughly and pour over the beaten eggs. Blend well. Cook in a double boiler until thick. Refrigerate until ready to use. Fold in the whipped cream a small amount at a time just before serving. This will cause the dressing to "puff". Serves 10 to 12.

Mrs. DeWitt Milam

Blueberry Salad

2 small packages blackberry jello
2 cups boiling water
1- 15 ounce can blueberries, drained
1- 8 1/4 ounce can crushed pineapple, drained
1- 8 ounce package cream cheese
1/2 cup sugar
1/2 pint sour cream
1/2 teaspoon vanilla
1/2 cup chopped pecans

Dissolve jello in boiling water. Drain blueberries and pineapple; measure liquid. Add enough water to make 1 cup; add to jello. Stir in blueberries and pineapple. Pour in 2 quart flat pan and refrigerate until set. Combine sugar, sour cream, cream cheese, and vanilla. Spread over jello layer; sprinkle pecans on top. Very sweet and rich, may also be used as a dessert.

Mrs. Elvis Stout

Frosted Cranberry Salad

1-13½ ounce can crushed
    pineapple
2- 3 ounce packages lemon
    flavored gelatin
1- 7 ounce bottle ginger ale
1- 1 pound can jellied cranberry
    sauce
1- 2 ounce package Dream Whip
1- 8 ounce package cream cheese,
    softened
½ cup chopped pecans

Drain pineapple, reserve syrup; add water to make 1 cup, heat to boil. Dissolve gelatin in hot liquid; cool. Gently stir in ginger ale; chill until partially set. Whip cranberry sauce, blend in pineapple and fold in gelatin. Turn into mold; chill until firm. Prepare topping according to direction on package. Blend in creamed cheese with topping; spread over gelatin mold. Sprinkle with pecans. Serves 10 to 12.

Mrs. James Murphy

Quick Cranberry Salad

1 small can crushed pineapple
1- 3 ounce package strawberry
    jello
1 cup boiling water
1- 1 pound can whole cranberry
    sauce
½ cup cold liquid: reserved
    pineapple juice and water to
    make ½ cup
2 teaspoons lemon juice
½ cup chopped nuts, optional
DRESSING:
2 Tablespoons mayonnaise
2 Tablespoons sour cream
½ teaspoon sugar

Drain pineapple, reserving juices. Dissolve jello in hot water. While still warm, stir in cranberry sauce and mix until melted. Stir in 1/2 cup cold liquid, lemon juice, pineapple and nuts, if used. Pour in 1 1/2 quart mold and chill until set. Blend mayonnaise, sour cream and sugar well. Spoon on when serving. Serves 6 to 8.

Miss Harriet Swift
Marietta, Georgia

Special Congealed Salad

2 packages lime jello
2 cups boiling water
1 bottle 7-Up
½ cup miniature marshmallows
2 cups sliced bananas
½ cup nuts, chopped
1 small can crushed pineapple,
    drained

TOPPING:
½ cup sugar
2 Tablespoons butter
2 Tablespoons flour
1 egg
1 cup pineapple juice
½ pint cream, whipped
⅓ cup grated American cheese
3 Tablespoons Parmesean cheese

Dissolve jello in boiling water. Add 7-Up and chill. Add marshmallows, bananas, nuts, and pineapple. Pour into a 13 x 9 inch pan. Chill until firm. *Topping:* mix sugar, butter and flour. Add egg and beat. Add 1 cup pineapple juice and cook until thick. Cool. Fold into whipped cream. Spread on top of jello. Sprinkle with the American cheese, then the Parmesan cheese. Chill. Cut in squares and serve on lettuce. Serves 8. Very good and different.

Mrs. Jerry Callender

Two Layer Salad

LAYER 1:
1 package lemon jello
1 cup cottage cheese
1 cup cream, whipped

LAYER II:
1 package lime jello
1 cup pineapple juice
1 cup crushed pineapple,
   drained
⅓ cup sliced stuffed olives
⅓ cup broken nuts

Layer I: Dissolve lemon jello in 1 cup hot water. After jello has started to set, whip and fold in cottage cheese and whipped cream. Put in mold to set.

Layer II: Dissolve lime jello in boiling pineapple juice. Add crushed pineapple, olives and nuts. After Layer I has set, spread Layer II over Layer I. Put in refrigerator until firm.

Mrs. Robert Curry III

Jellied Ambrosia

1 envelope unflavored gelatin
¼ cup sugar
½ cup boiling water
1¼ cups frozen orange juice,
   diluted
1 Tablespoon lemon juice
1½ cups fresh orange segments
1½ cups banana slices
¼ cup angel flaked coconut
½ cup maraschino cherries,
   halved

Soften gelatin in a little cold water. Add boiling water and sugar and stir until dissolved. Add remaining juices and chill until partially set. Fold in fruits and pour in 1 quart mold. Chill until set. Six servings.

Mrs. Don Irby

Taster's Choice

2 cups favorite fruit juice
1 envelope unflavored gelatin
1½ cups favorite fruit,
   drained
½ to 1 teaspoon lemon juice

Soften the gelatin in 1 cup of the juice. Heat until the gelatin dissolves. Add remaining juice, chill until partly thickened and fold in fruit. Sherry, sauterne or a fruit flavored wine is delicious used as part of the liquid.

Grapefruit Pineapple Congealed Salad

1 large can crushed pineapple
1 large can grapefruit sections
1 large package lemon jello
1/2 cup chopped pecans

Drain fruit in colander, saving juice. Prepare jello according to package instructions, using juice for part of liquid called for. Add fruit and nuts. Refrigerate to set slightly. Put into individaul molds or in a 9 x 13 inch pan to gel. Serve with dollop of mayonnaise and dash of paprika.

Mrs. Jim Altick

Horseradish Salad

1 large box lime jello
1 small box lemon jello
2 cups boiling water
1 large can crushed pineapple,
    undrained
1 small can pimientos
1 large package cream cheese or
    1 carton cottage cheese
3 Tablespoons moist horseradish
1 can sweetened condensed milk
1 cup finely chopped nuts
3 Tablespoons lemon juice
1/4 teaspoon salt

Dissolve jello in boiling water. Add other ingredients. Pour in large rectangle pyrex dish and refrigerate until set. Serves 16.

Dr. Catherine Vaughan

Lime Salad

2 packages lime jello
1 cup water
1- 3 ounce package cream cheese
1/2 cup mayonnaise
1/2 pint whipping cream,
    whipped
2 small cans crushed pineapple,
    undrained
1 cup pecans, finely chopped

DRESSING:
1 cup mayonnaise
1 cup cream, whipped

Dissolve 1 package jello in 1 cup boiling water; cool in refrigerator, then whip in mixer. Cream softened cream cheese and mayonnaise, add to jello and beat slightly. Fold in whipped cream, pineapple and pecans. Stir together well, pour into a 9 x 13 inch pan and set in refrigerator overnight.

Glaze: Follow directions on the other package of lime jello. When it cools pour over the *SET* mixture to form a clear lime top layer.

Dressing: Equal parts of mayonnaise and whipped cream. Garnish with cherries. Serves 10.

Mrs. Tex Kilpatrick

Fruited Cream Salad

1 package orange jello
1 cup boiling water
1 pint vanilla ice cream
1 small jar maraschino cherries,
   drained and cut
1 large can crushed pineapple,
   drained
1 cup chopped pecans

Dissolve jello in boiling water. Add ice cream and stir until melted. Add cherries, pineapple, and pecans. Place in 2 quart mold and refrigerate. Serves 8 to 10.

Mrs. Lestar Martin

Pineapple-Rhubarb Mold

2 cups sliced rhubarb
1/3 cup sugar
1/2 cup water
2 1/2 cups pineapple tidbits
1 package strawberry jello
2 teaspoons lemon juice

Cook fresh rhubarb, sugar and water until just tender, about 5 minutes. Drain, reserve syrup. Drain pineapple, reserve syrup. Combine syrups and add water to make 1 3/4 cups. Heat to boiling; add jello and stir to dissolve. Add lemon juice. Chill until partially set and fold in fruit. Pour in 1 quart mold. Serves 6 to 8.

Mandarin Orange Salad

1 package orange jello
1 cup hot water
Pinch of salt
1/2 envelope plain gelatin
1/4 cup cold water
1/2 can undiluted frozen orange
   juice
1 pint orange sherbet
Small can mandarin oranges

Dissolve jello in hot water. Add salt. Soften un-flavored gelatin in cold water, mix with the jello and hot water to dissolve. Add juice. Whip sherbet with electric mixer. Add gelatin mixture. Blend thoroughly and refrigerate until slightly thick. Stir once during this time. When thickened, add oranges. Mold. Good with sour cream topping. Makes a 1 quart mold.

Mrs. John Lolley

Pineapple Mold

1- No. 2 can crushed pineapple,
   undrained
½ cup sugar
½ cup water
1 large package cream cheese
1 large package lemon jello
1 large can evaporated milk,
   chilled in freezer

Bring first three ingredients to a boil. Remove from heat and blend in cream cheese and jello. Chill. When ice has formed around edge of milk, beat until stiff. Add chilled lemon mixture and beat well. Pour into a 13 x 9 inch pan and chill until firm.

Mrs. Ralph Mantle
Salladasbury, Pa.

Red Raspberry Salad

2 cans frozen red raspberries
1- No. 2 can crushed pineapple
1 can frozen orange juice, thawed
   and undiluted
1 cup boiling water
2 packages red raspberry jello

Thaw and drain raspberries. Drain pineapple. Reserve juices. Add thawed orange juice to drained juice; this would measure 2 1/2 cups. Dissolve jello in boiling water. Add juices and chill until partially set. Add the raspberries and pineapple. Put the mixture in a 1 1/2 to 2 quart mold and chill until set. This is a nice Christmas salad. Serves 10 to 12.

Mrs. V.A. Wolff
St. Louis, Missouri

Pink Fluff
But men love it

1 box raspberry jello
1 cup hot water
1 small can crushed pineapple,
   drained
1 package cream cheese
½ pint whipping cream
1 cup chopped nuts

Dissolve jello in hot water and place in refrigerator. When jello begins to congeal, add well drained pineapple and cream cheese which has been mashed with fork. Whip cream until stiff and stir in nuts. Fold all together and place in a salad mold or individual molds. This salad makes up to be a bright fluffy pink. Serves 8 and doubles easily.

From the files of Mrs. Ruth Lindsey

Strawberry Nut Salad

2 packages strawberry jello
1 cup boiling water
2- 10 ounce packages frozen
  thawed strawberries, undrained
1- 1 pound 4 ounce can crushed
  pineapple, drained
1 cup coarsely chopped walnuts
2 cartons of sour cream

Dissolve jello in water. Add strawberries *with juice*, drained pineapple and nuts. Divide in half. Put 1/2 mixture into pyrex dish, refrigerate until firm. When congealed, spread sour cream over top of this half. Then pour balance of mixture over all.

Mrs. Cecil P. Jarrell

Ed. Note: Mrs. Elizabeth Carrol makes a similar salad, omitting nuts and substituting 2 mashed bananas. It is delicious also.

Frozen Fruit Salad

2- 3 ounce packages cream cheese
1 cup mayonnaise
¼ cup lemon juice
¼ cup granulated sugar
Pinch of salt
2 cups pineapple tidbits, drained
2 cups diced orange sections,
  drained
1 cup snipped maraschino
  cherries
1 cup Royal Anne cherries,
  pitted and halved
1 cup pecans, chopped
3 cups heavy cream
Strawberries

Blend cream cheese, mayonnaise, juice, salt and sugar. Lightly mix with pineapple, oranges, cherries, nuts and 2 cups cream, whipped. Pour in ring mold or bundt pan, cover top tightly and freeze. Thaw, unwrapped, 1 hour in refrigerator. To serve let stand in hot water 2 to 3 minutes. Unmold. To garnish, fill center with 1 cup whipped cream and top with strawberries. This is a beautiful salad and will serve 10 to 12 people.

Mrs. James Aycock

Daiquiri Salad

1- 8 ounce package cream cheese
1 small box egg custard mix
1 can frozen daiquiri mix, thawed
1 medium can crushed pineapple,
  drained
⅓ cup mayonnaise
1 jigger rum
1 envelope Dream Whip
½ cup chopped nuts

Mix all in blender 2 or 3 minutes. Then prepare 1 envelope Dream Whip topping mix according to package directions. Fold Dream Whip and nuts into daiquiri mixture. Place in wax paper lined pyrex dish and freeze at least 3 hours. Serves 9.

Mrs. Bruce Thornton
Houston, Texas

Frosty Strawberry Squares

PART I:
1 cup flour
1/4 cup brown sugar
1/2 cup chopped nuts
1/2 cup melted butter

PART II:
2 egg whites
2/3 cup sugar
1 cup cream, whipped
2 cups sliced fresh strawberries
  or 1 package frozen
  strawberries
2 Tablespoons lemon juice

Part I: Mix all ingredients; spread evenly in shallow baking pan. Bake at 350 degrees for about 20 minutes, stirring occasionally. Let cool and sprinkle 2/3 of crumb mixture in a quart square dish.

Part II: Beat egg whites until stiff peaks form, gradually adding sugar. To this fold in the whipped cream and remaining ingredients. Spoon this over the first mixture of crumbs and smooth out. Top with the remainder of the crumb mixture. Freeze for 6 hours or overnight. Serves 8 to 12, may be used as a salad or dessert.

Mrs. Oscar E. Cloyd, Sr.
Shreveport, Louisiana

Frozen Summer Salad

1 envelope unflavored gelatin
1/4 cup cold water
2/3 cup pineapple syrup
1 cup crushed fresh peaches
1 cup fresh sliced seedless grapes
1 cup pineapple bits, drained
1/3 cup maraschino cherries,
  drained and sliced
1/2 cup mayonnaise
1 cup heavy cream, whipped

Soften gelatin in cold water and dissolve over hot water. Add pineapple syrup. Chill until slightly thickened. Add fruit. Fold in mayonnaise and whipped cream. Freeze. Makes 8 very large servings. This is very attractive in individual molds and served on a lettuce leaf.

Mrs. Charles Hamaker

Georgie's Cranberry Mold

1 tall can cranberry sauce
3 Tablespoons lemon juice
1 cup cream, whipped
1/4 cup mayonnaise
1/4 cup powdered sugar
1/2 cup or more pecans,
  chopped

Whip cranberry sauce and lemon juice together in blender. Place in oiled 9 inch square cake pan and freeze until firm. Then whip 1 cup of whipping cream and blend in mayonnaise, powdered sugar and pecans. Spread over frozen cranberry mixture. Freeze solid. Cut into squares. Let thaw enough to remove from pan. Serve on lettuce leaf with or without mayonnaise topping. Serves 6 to 9, depending on size of squares.

Mrs. Dan Vanderhoeven
Bastrop, Louisiana

Pink Arctic Freeze

2-3 ounce packages cream cheese
2 Tablespoons mayonnaise
2 Tablespoons sugar
1- 1 pound can whole cranberry
  sauce, 2 cups
1- 9 ounce can pineapple tidbits,
  drained
½ cup chopped walnuts
1 cup heavy cream, whipped

Soften cheese; blend in mayonnaise and sugar. Add fruits and nuts. Fold in whipped cream. Pour into 8 1/2 x 4 1/2 x 2 1/2 inch loaf pan. Freeze firm, 6 hours or overnight. To serve, let stand at room temperature about 15 minutes. Turn out on a bed of lettuce; slice. For luncheon, serve with dainty chicken or ham sandwiches or serve with cookies and let it be a bridge dessert. Serves 8 to 10.

Mrs. T.M. Sayre
Rayville, Louisiana

Tropical Ice Salad

4 ripe bananas, mashed
3 cups orange juice
Juice of 1 lemon
½ cup sugar
Small bottle maraschino cherries,
  chopped and drained
1- 10 or 12 ounce can crushed
  pineapple, drained

Mix all ingredients and freeze in 12 custard cups or a 2 quart mold. Before serving, let stand a few minutes at room temperature. Serves 12. This can be doubled.

Mrs. W.H. Anders, Jr.

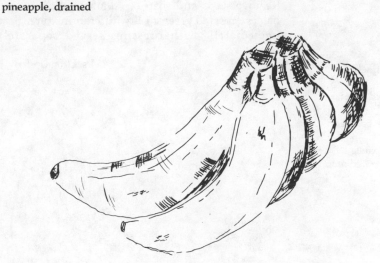

Bouillabaisse Salad

1 lobster tail
½ pound shrimp
1 cup fresh crab meat
1 head Boston lettuce
1 head Romaine
1 bunch watercress
½ cup slivered celery
2 tomatoes, quartered
1 hard boiled egg, chopped
1 Tablespoon chopped chives
1 small onion, sliced thinly

CAVIAR DRESSING:
1 cup sour cream
1 cup mayonnaise
2 Tablespoons horseradish
4 Tablespoons caviar

Prepare seafood to be cooked in seasoned water. Cook until done and shell, devein and dice. Blanche the celery in boiling water for 2 minutes, drain. Chill all well. Mix the dressing. At serving time break the greens into a salad bowl and arrange the seafood, tomatoes and celery on top. Sprinkle the egg, chives and onions on the top. Toss with the caviar dressing. Serves 8 to 10.

Mrs. Harry Bell

Crab Stuffed Avocado

3 Tablespoons olive oil
1 Tablespoon tarragon vinegar
½ pound fresh crab meat
½ cup thinly sliced celery
1 Tablespoon capers, drained
1 Tablespoon chives
2 flat anchovies, cut up,
   optional
2 avocados
Salad greens

DRESSING:
½ cup mayonnaise
1 hard cooked egg, finely
   chopped
1 Tablespoon minced green
   pepper
1 Tablespoon minced stuffed
   olives
1 teaspoon minced parsley
½ teaspoon finely grated onion

In a mixing bowl, with a fork, beat together the oil and vinegar. Add crab meat, celery, capers, chives and anchovies. Cover tightly and chill for several hours.
Dressing: Mix all ingredients together and chill for several hours before serving. Makes ¾ cup. At serving time, cut avocados lengthwise into halves. Remove seeds and strip off skin. Arrange avocado halves on salad greens; fill with crab mixture. Serve immediately with dressing served separately. Serves 4.

Mrs. Elton Upshaw, Jr.

Cucumber and Crab Salad
A Japanese Delicacy

2 cucumbers, thinly sliced
½ cup celery, thinly sliced
  diagonally
½ cup onion, thinly sliced
1- 6 ounce can crab meat
Salt

DRESSING:
½ cup vinegar
½ cup sugar
1 teaspoon soy sauce
Dash of monosodium glutamate

Lightly salt the vegetables and set aside. Mix the dressing ingredients. Add the crab meat to the vegetables. Toss with the dressing and serve immediately. A can of chopped clams may be substituted for the crab meat. This is pretty to stuff into tomato shells.

Mrs. Jim Campbell

West Indies Salad

2 cups crab meat
1 large onion chopped finely
½ cup oil
½ cup vinegar
1 Tablespoon parsley
1 teaspoon Accent
Dash of Tabasco
1 Tablespoon Worcestershire
Salt and pepper to taste
Avocado or tomato slices

Place crab meat in a bowl. Cover with chopped onion. Add seasonings and pour the oil and vinegar over. Toss to mix. Cover and refrigerate for at least 4 hours or overnight. Serve on avocado or tomato slices. Serves 6.

Shrimp Arnaud
A Louisiana speciality

½ or more of a 5¾ ounce
  jar Louisiana Creole Mustard
¾ cup oil
½ cup vinegar
2 Tablespoons paprika, or
  enough to turn the mixture red
6 small green onions and tops,
  finely chopped
⅓ cup chopped parsley
4 teaspoons horseradish
  mustard, optional
3 pounds shrimp, boiled, shelled
 and deveined
Shredded lettuce

Mix all ingredients, except the lettuce, in the order given. Pour over the shrimp and let stand several hours, overnight or longer in the refrigerator. Just before serving, add some shredded lettuce.

Mrs. Clifford M. Strauss

Artichokes Stuffed with Shrimp Salad

4 artichokes
Salt
1 lemon, sliced
2 Tablespoons olive oil

SALAD:
1 cup cooked shrimp
$1/2$ cup chopped celery
1- 5 ounce can water chestnuts,
  drained and chopped finely
2 Tablespoons green onions,
  chopped finely
1 Tablespoon drained capers
$1/2$ cup mayonnaise
$1^1/2$ teaspoons prepared horseradish
Salt, pepper and lemon juice
  to taste

Boil the artichokes in water seasoned with salt, lemon slices and olive oil until the leaves pull off easily, about 45 minutes. Drain and cool. Using a teaspoon scoop out the centers and remove the chokes. Mix the salad ingredients and stuff into the artichokes.

Shrimp in Artichoke Shells

6 large artichokes
Salt
$1/2$ lemon, sliced
1 Tablespoon olive oil
$1/2$ clove garlic
$1/3$ cup mayonnaise
$1/4$ cup sour cream
$1^1/2$ Tablespoons lemon juice
$3/4$ teaspoon grated lemon rind
$1/4$ teaspoon salt
$1/2$ teaspoon dried tarragon
$1/2$ teaspoon Dijon mustard
$1/2$ pound cooked shrimp
6 lemon wedges

Trim artichokes and put in boiling salted water with lemon slices, oil and garlic. Simmer about 45 minutes, until an outer leaf pulls off easily. Drain and cool. Scoop out the center, using a teaspoon to remove the chokes, drain upside down, cover and chill. Mix the mayonnaise, sour cream, lemon juice, lemon rind, salt, tarragon and mustard. Chill. Before serving, put about 2 Tablespoons dressing in the center of each artichoke and top with shrimp. Garnish with lemon wedges.

Basic seafood salads are generally made from 1 cup of seafood, 1 cup of celery and $1/4$ cup mayonnaise. Lemon juice, salt and pepper are used to season as desired. Various additions such as chopped cucumber, chives, capers, parsley and sieved egg create a new interest to old favorites.

Crunchy Tuna Salad

1- 7 ounce can tuna
½ cup finely chopped celery
2 Tablespoons finely chopped
  green onion
1 Tablespoon finely chopped
  radishes
2 Tablespoons mayonnaise
2 teaspoons Worcestershire
2 teaspoons lemon juice
1 teaspoon minced parsley
Salt and pepper to taste

Drain and flake tuna. Mix with celery, onion and radishes. Combine mayonnaise and seasonings and mix. Chill. Delicious for stuffed tomatoes or sandwiches.

Mrs. Jerry Wolff

Crabmeat or Lobster Mousse

1 can tomato soup
3- 3 ounce packages of cream
  cheese
3 Tablespoons unflavored gelatin
1 cup water
¾ cup celery, finely chopped
¾ bell pepper, finely chopped
2 Tablespoons onion, grated
2- 6½ ounce cans lobster or
  crab meat
1 cup mayonnaise
Season highly with salt, Tabasco
  and Lea & Perrins

Mash softened cheese and add soup. Put in double boiler and heat until very hot and cheese melts. Add gelatin which has been softened in water. Refrigerate until mixture begins to congeal. Add remaining ingredients. Pour into a 1 1/2 quart mold that has been greased with mayonnaise or oil.

Mrs. C.M. Strauss

LeHigh Valley Shrimp Mold

1 can tomato soup
1- 8 ounce package cream cheese
2 envelopes unflavored gelatin,
  dissolved in a small amount of
  water
2 pounds shrimp, cooked, peeled,
  deveined, and diced
1 cup diced celery
1 medium onion, diced
Salt and pepper
Dash of Tabasco
1 cup mayonnaise
2 Tablespoons horseradish,
  drained

Heat soup and add cream cheese and stir until cheese is melted. The mixture will be lumpy. Add dissolved gelatin. Stir in the remaining ingredients. Pour into a well greased mold. This recipe will fill a 1 quart mold with a small amount left over. Refrigerate until the mold is set. Unmold by running a sharp knife around the edge of the mold and invert on a large platter. This is a nice party salad. At Christmas it could be molded into a star, tree or ring and decorated with leaves.

Mrs. Mabel Cole Ratliff

Shrimp Supreme
A delightful summer luncheon

1½ cups boiled shrimp
¾ cup minced celery
2 hard boiled eggs, chopped
1 Tablespoon minced pimiento
1 small bottle stuffed green
    olives
1½ teaspoons grated onion
1½ packages unflavored gelatin
Juice of 1 lemon
2 Tablespoons cold water
¾ cup mayonnaise
Salt to taste
Lettuce leaves
Artichoke hearts

Mix first six ingredients together. In the top of a double boiler, dissolve the gelatin mixed with water and lemon juice. Remove from heat and add mayonnaise. Mix well. Pour over salad mixture and salt to taste. Mold in individual molds. Unmold on lettuce leaves and top with an artichoke heart. Serves 6 to 8.

Mrs. Charles Hamaker

Tuna Mousse

2 envelopes unflavored gelatin
½ cup cold water
1 cup mayonnaise
2- 7 ounce cans tuna, drained
½ cup celery, finely diced
¼ cup stuffed olives, chopped
1 Tablespoon chives, finely
    chopped
2 Tablespoons lemon juice
1½ teaspoons horseradish
¼ teaspoon salt
¼ teaspoon paprika
1 cup heavy cream, whipped
Dash of Tabasco

Soften gelatin in cold water; dissolve over boiling water. Stir into mayonnaise. Add remaining ingredients except cream. Mix well. Chill slightly. Fold in whipped cream. Pour into 10 x 6 x 1 inch pan. Chill until firm. Cut into squares and serve on greens. Serve with melon and muffins for a delightful summer luncheon. Serves 8.

Mrs. Don Irby

SALAD DRESSINGS

Oil and Vinegar

1 cup olive oil
¼ cup red wine vinegar
2 teaspoons salt
1 teaspoon white pepper
1 teaspoon Dijon mustard

Combine ingredients and whip with a fork until the mixture thickens.

Mrs. Ed Seymour, Jr.

Oil and Vinegar Variations: omit mustard in above recipe.

For Garlic Dressing:
1 or 2 cloves crushed garlic

For Herb Dressing;
1 teaspoon each: parsley, chives, green peppers, chervil, basil, tarragon

Citrus Fruits:
3 Tablespoons sour cream
1 Tablespoon finely chopped chives

Fruit Salad:
1 Tablespoon Grenadine
½ teaspoon each: grated orange rind, grated lemon rind, Tabasco to taste

Tomato Salad:
2 Tablespoons cottage cheese
2 teaspoons each: chopped sweet pickles, chopped parsley

Roquefort:
2 Tablespoons Roquefort cheese, crumbled

Herb Vinegar
A "Little something" gift

2 quarts red wine vinegar
4 cloves garlic, crushed
½ teaspoon cracked black pepper
1 teaspoon coriander seeds
½ teaspoon fennel seeds
½ teaspoon each thyme, savory
　and oregano
2 bay leaves

Boil vinegar until reduced by one half. Add all seasonings, remove from heat, cover tightly, and let set at room temperature until vinegar is *cold*. Strain into bottles using funnel lined with cheesecloth. Yields 1 quart. May be doubled. Use 1 part of this vinegar to 4 or 5 parts oil for a delicious French dressing. For gift giving—find fancy old bottles, tie onto bottle a note instructing amounts of oil and vinegar to be used.

Mrs. Don Irby

Basic Salad Dressing

Salad oil
½ cup sugar
1 cup vinegar
1 teaspoon salt
Dash red pepper
1 Tablespoon paprika

Stir in some oil with sugar until sugar is coated and dissolves. Add vinegar, salt, pepper and paprika. Store in jar in refrigerator.

Mrs. James Greenbaum

Red French Dressing

1 can tomato soup
½ cup sugar
1 Tablespoon Lea & Perrins
1 Tablespoon salt
1 cup white vinegar
1 teaspoon mustard
1 teaspoon paprika
1 cup vegetable oil
1 large onion, chopped
2 cloves garlic

Mix all ingredients in blender. Keeps well in refrigerator. Makes about 1 quart.

Mrs. Al Irwin

Buttermilk Salad Dressing

1 pint Kraft mayonnaise
1 pint buttermilk
½ teaspoon garlic powder
1 teaspoon onion powder
2 Tablespoons Accent
¾ teaspoon ground pepper
2 teaspoons salt

Mix all ingredients. Let stand in refrigerator 24 hours before using.

Mrs. Horace Smith

Italian Dressing
Just Great!

1 cup chopped onion
1 cup chopped celery
1 cup chopped bell pepper
1 cup chopped green olives
1 cup chopped ripe olives
¾ cup olive oil
½ cup lemon juice
8 to 10 crushed garlic cloves
2 cans anchovy fillets, oil
  included
2-6 ounce jars marinated
  artichoke hearts, oil included
½ teaspoon each: oregano,
  thyme, marjoram, savory
3 leaves rosemary
1 teaspoon capers
½ teaspoon caper juice
½ teaspoon Worcestershire
  sauce

Mix all ingredients together and put in air-tight jar or bowl. Marinate for four days in refrigerator. Add avocado if desired. This would make anything taste good.

Mrs. Harry Stone

Mock Caesar Salad Dressing

½ cup olive oil
1½ Tablespoons white vinegar
1½ Tablespoons wine vinegar
1½ Tablespoons tarragon
  vinegar
1 Tablespoon Lea & Perrins
½ tube or 1 ounce anchovy
  paste
1 clove garlic, pressed
1 hard boiled egg, diced
Cracked black pepper to taste
Parmesan cheese and croutons,
  optional

Add all ingredients except egg, cheese, and croutons. Pour over salad greens. Add chopped egg. Toss.

Mrs. James Greenbaum

Villa Montaña Salad Dressing

1 medium onion, diced
3 medium cloves of garlic
1 Tablespoon salt
¼ teaspoon mustard
¼ teaspoon paprika
⅛ teaspoon pepper
3 Tablespoons sugar
2 cups oil
¾ cups apple cider vinegar
¼ cup water
1 teaspoon parsley, chopped
1 teaspoon celery, chopped

Put all ingredients in the blender and whirl until well blended. This is a most delicious dressing for tossed greens.

The Villa Montaña is a famed posada in Morelia, Mexico. This recipe is an indication of the fine cuisine served by Ray Coté, owner and skilled chef at his "get away from it all haven". Watch for several more recipes he has so kindly allowed us to print in our book.

Homemade Mayonnaise

3 egg yolks
1½ cups of Wesson oil
1½ cups olive oil
Juice of 3 lemons
3 teaspoons salt
¾ teaspoon pepper
¾ teaspoon dry mustard

Beat egg yolks until *thick* and lemon colored. Alternately add the oil and lemon juice, slowly at first. Add the seasonings last, the secret to perfect mayonnaise.

Two ways to bring back curdled mayonnaise:

I. If you have some left-over homemade mayonnaise in the refrigerator it is easy to use this as a base and beat the curdled mayonnaise into this. The curdled mayonnaise should "come back".

II. Take 2 egg yolks and beat them until they are thick and lemon colored. Gradually add a little oil and a little lemon juice to the egg yolks. When this starts to get stiff, add the curdled mayonnaise gradually to this and it will bring it back.

Mrs. George M. Snellings, Jr.
"Cook with Marie Louise"

To make mayonnaise have all ingredients at room temperature. Place the egg yolks in the mixer bowl and BEAT, BEAT, BEAT and beat some more. When the egg yolks are *thick* and very light in color start adding oil DROP BY DROP. Add lemon juice alternately DROP BY DROP. When the mayonnaise "begins to make" you may add the oil more freely. Add all seasonings at the end.

Mayonnaise

Juice of 1 lemon
1 whole egg
1 scant teaspoon salt
1 scant teaspoon paprika
2 level teaspoons prepared
   mustard
2 cups salad oil
1½ to 2 Tablespoons cider
   vinegar

Mix first five ingredients in mixer bowl. Beat at high speed to blend, then slowly add 2 cups salad oil, in about 8 to 10 additions. When finished, cut speed to low and add 1 1/2 to 2 Tablespoons cider vinegar. Makes 1 pint.

Mrs. Charles Bennett

Avocado Dressing

1 ripe avocado, about ½ pound
½ teaspoon chopped green
   onions
½ clove garlic, crushed
¼ cup finally chopped celery
⅛ teaspoon Tabasco
⅛ teaspoon salt
½ cup Italian style salad dressing

In a medium bowl, mash the avocado with a fork. Add onion, garlic, celery, Tabasco and salt. Mix well. Stir in the salad dressing. Refrigerate, covered, at least two hours. At serving time, pour over salad greens and toss lightly.

Blue Cheese Dressing

1- 3 ounce package cream cheese
1 pint Kraft mayonnaise
2½ Tablespoons lemon juice
1 small package Roquefort cheese
1 small package blue cheese
½ small can evaporated milk,
   almost frozen

Blend cream cheese in mixer until smooth, add mayonnaise and mix well. Stir in lemon juice. Crumble in Roquefort and blue cheese. Whip ice cold milk until stiff, fold into first mixture and refrigerate.

Mrs. Davis Bingham

Creamy Roquefort dressing may be easily made by whipping ½ cup cream and folding into 1 cup mayonnaise. Crumble in Roquefort cheese to taste. Chill. Makes about 2 cups.

Roquefort Dressing

2 quarts mayonnaise
8 ounces Roquefort cheese
2 cartons sour cream
3 lemons
1 large onion, chopped
1 handful chopped parsley
3 dashes of Lea & Perrins sauce
Dash of garlic salt
Salt and pepper to taste

Mix mayonnaise and Roquefort and let stand overnight. Use blender and mix all ingredients next day. Keeps well in refrigerator. Makes about 3 1/2 quarts. May be made in half or doubled.

Mrs. Al Irwin

Spring Dressing

3 green onions and tops
1 Tablespoon lemon juice
1/3 bunch parsley
1/2 cup sour cream
1 cup Hellman's mayonnaise
1 pod garlic crushed
3 Tablespoons tarragon vinegar
Salt, pepper, celery salt, and
    Tabasco to taste

Mix all ingredients in blender. Use with tossed greens for a delicious salad.

Mrs. Stephen Nichols

Thousand Island Dressing

3 rounded Tablespoons chili
    sauce
2 hard boiled eggs, chopped
1/2 cup celery, chopped
1 Tablespoon India Relish
1 teaspoon onion juice
3/4 cup mayonnaise
Salt and pepper to taste

Mix ingredients and chill. Serve over lettuce wedges. Serves 4 to 5. This is enough for one large head of lettuce.

Mrs. Miles Sager

Salad Dressing for Potato Salad

3 eggs, beaten
½ cup sugar
¼ teaspoon dry mustard
½ cup vinegar
1 cup coffee cream

After beating eggs real well, add sugar, and mustard. Beat again. Add vinegar and coffee cream. Place all ingredients in double boiler;. cook, stirring occasionally, until mixture thickens. Cool completely. Pour over cooked, sliced potatoes to which chopped onion, celery, salt, and pepper have been added. Serves 4 to 6.

Mrs. V.A. Wolff
St. Louis, Missouri

Quick Aspic for Lining Molds

Give your mousses and molds a shimmering top

2½ cups beef or chicken broth
1 onion
1 egg white, lightly beaten
1 crushed egg shell
1 Tablespoon gelatin

Boil stock, onion and beaten egg white with crushed egg shell for 10 minutes. Let set off heat about 30 minutes. Strain through cheesecloth. Soften gelatin in 1/2 cup cold stock, return to heat to dissolve. Cool slightly. Stir into clarified stock. Pour a *very* thin layer in mold and let chill. Decorate as desired spooning aspic carefully over decorations. Chill. Spoon over one layer more and chill before pouring in mousse or salad mixture. Beautiful for buffets and cocktail parties.

Apple Dressing for Fruit Salads

½ cup Gerber's baby apple sauce
½ cup sour cream
½ cup mayonnaise
1 teaspoon celery seed
2 Tablespoons lemon juice

Blend together. Chill. Delicious with fruit and congealed fruit salads. Double for a crowd.

Mrs. Sol Courtman

Red Currant Dressing

1 cup currant jelly
½ cup mayonnaise
½ cup heavy cream, whipped

With rotary beater, beat currant jelly until soft and smooth. Stir in mayonnaise and then fold in whipped cream. Makes about 2 cups. Excellent for fruit salads.

Mrs. Mabel Cole Ratliff

Sherbet Salad Dressing

2 Tablespoons flour
¼ cup sugar
¼ teaspoon salt
1⅓ cups fresh orange juice
2 Tablespoons fresh lemon juice
2 egg yolks, slightly beaten
1 Tablespoon grated orange peel
3 Tablespoons salad oil
½ pint sherbet: raspberry, orange, pineapple, lemon, or lime

Combine flour, sugar and salt in double boiler. Add orange and lemon juices. Cook, stirring constantly, until mixture thickens. Stir 2 Tablespoons hot mixture into egg yolks. Gradually add yolks to hot mixture. Stir and cook 1 minute. Remove from heat and stir in orange peel and salad oil. Cool and chill. Just before serving, fold in sherbet. Serve at once. Makes 2 cups. Great for your fresh fruit salads.

Mrs. Jerry Wolff

Pineapple Dressing

Grand for frozen fruit salad

2 eggs
4 teaspoons sugar
¼ teaspoon salt
2 Tablespoons flour
Juice of 1 large can of sliced pineapple
1 teaspoon vinegar
½ teaspoon mustard
1 cup heavy cream, whipped

Cook all ingredients, except cream, stirring constantly. When dressing has thickened remove from heat, chill and fold in whipped cream.

Mrs. DeWitt Henry

Garden Collage

3 Tablespoons butter
1 clove garlic, pressed
1 medium onion, chopped
1 bell pepper, chopped
1½ pounds yellow squash or
  2 cups, thinly sliced
2 cups fresh corn, cut from cob
2 tomatoes, peeled and diced
1 teaspoon salt
1 teaspoon Lawry's seasoning
  salt
Pepper to taste
Pinch of sugar
⅓ cup water

In a very large skillet, melt butter and sauté the onion, pepper and garlic until soft. Add squash and cook briefly before stirring in corn, tomatoes and seasonings. Put mixture into a buttered 2 1/2 to 3 quart casserole and add water. Bake covered about 1 hour at 350 degrees. Casserole may be uncovered during the last 30 minutes to reduce the "pot likker". Prepare ahead of time and reheat. Serves 8.

Boiled Artichokes

Artichokes
2 Tablespoons olive oil
1 lemon sliced
3 Tablespoons salt
2 cloves garlic
6 coriander seeds, optional

Trim stems of artichokes and place in a kettle large enough to contain the number used. Cover with water and seasonings. Boil until one of the center leaves pulls out easily. Remove and drain. Remove choke and fill with dressing.

SERVING SUGGESTIONS:

Hot: Herb flavored lemon butter
Hollandaise with crumbled bacon.
Cold: Homemade mayonnaise
Tarragon vinaigrette. See page 232
Mustard mayonnaise
Stuffed with your favorite seafood salad

Artichoke Casserole

3 artichokes
1 large onion, chopped
1 stick butter
1 can mushroom soup
1 can mushrooms, drained
½ cup buttered bread crumbs
Lemon slices

Boil artichokes in seasoned water. Scrape meat from leaves and cup up the heart. Sauté onion in butter. Add mushrooms and soup. Blend in all artichoke meat. Put in a baking dish. Top with buttered bread crumbs and lemon slices. Bake 45 minutes in a 350 degree oven. Serves 6. This freezes well. It is also good as a dip with Melba rounds.

Mrs. George M. Snellings III

Artichokes and Spinach

1 package chopped spinach
4 artichokes
1 clove garlic, pressed
Oil and vinegar dressing
2 Tablespoons butter
2 Tablespoons flour
1 cup Half and Half
½ cup Parmesan cheese
Salt and pepper
Additional Parmesan cheese

Cook spinach, drain and set aside. Boil artichokes in water seasoned with garlic and salt until tender. Scrape meaty part from leaves and reserve. Marinate bottoms in dressing. Make a rich cream sauce with butter, flour, and cream. Add 1/2 cup Parmesan cheese or to taste. Add cooked spinach and meaty part scraped from leaves. Check for seasonings. Place bottoms in a greased casserole. Cover with the spinach mixture and sprinkle with cheese. Bake in a 350 degree oven until cheese is brown.

Mrs. Wesley Shafto, Jr.

Artichoke Bottoms en Brochette

12 medium size fresh mushrooms
12 artichoke bottoms, canned
  or fresh, pre-cooked
¼ cup butter
Nutmeg
Salt
Pepper
½ cup olive oil
¼ teaspoon salt
1 large garlic clove, crushed

Peel mushroom caps and snap off stems. Sauté mushrooms and artichoke bottoms in butter for 5 minutes. Drain and season with salt, pepper and a pinch of nutmeg. Fill six skewers alternately with 2 mushrooms and 2 artichoke bottoms. Roll each skewer in olive oil that has been seasoned with the salt and garlic. Broil each for 5 minutes, turning often. Serve very hot.

Stuffed Italian Artichokes

4 large artichokes

STUFFING:
1 cup Progresso bread crumbs
6 ounces grated Parmesan cheese
1 small can rolled anchovies,
  finely chopped, optional
4 cloves garlic, mashed
4 to 5 ounces olive oil

Trim tops of artichoke leaves to remove pointed tips. Soak artichokes in salted water about 15 minutes. Drain. Mix the stuffing ingredients well. Fill the artichoke leaves with stuffing. Stand stuffed artichokes on a rack in the bottom of a Dutch oven. Put a small amount of water in the container, but do not let the water touch the artichokes. Cover and steam slowly, *adding* several drops of imported olive oil over stuffing about every 15 minutes. Continue to steam until artichokes are done when the leaves pull out easily, almost one hour. The secret to this recipe is in the use of the olive oil. *Do not use too much!*

Mrs. Dave Aron

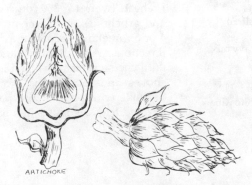

ARTICHOKE

Artichokes Italiano

1 large can artichoke hearts,
 20 to 24 count, drained
1 can flavored bread crumbs
1 medium bottle olive oil
6 to 8 cloves garlic, chopped
l large can Parmesan cheese
1 cup water

Place artichoke hearts in a casserole dish. Mix the next 4 ingredients and pour over the artichokes. Cover with the water. Bake in a moderate oven, 375 degrees, about 30 minutes or until browned. Serves 4 to 6. Cheese and garlic may be toned down to suit individual taste.

Mrs. Howard John

Spinach Soufflé Stuffed Artichokes

1 can artichoke bottoms, drained
French dressing
1 package Stouffer's spinach
 souffle, thawed
2 Tablespoons fine bread crumbs
2 teaspoons melted butter

Marinate artichokes overnight in French dressing. Drain. Place bottoms cut side up, slightly apart in a shallow casserole. Fill with the thawed spinach soufflé. Mix bread crumbs with butter and sprinkle lightly over soufflé. Bake uncovered in a 400 degree oven for 20 minutes. Serves 6 to 8.

Mrs. Charles Stubbs

Mushroom—Artichoke Velvet

2 cans artichoke hearts
1- 6 ounce can B & B sliced
 mushrooms
1 envelope chicken gravy mix
Dash of thyme
Dash of marjoram
4 ounces Swiss cheese
2 Tablespoons dry white wine
Bread crumbs
Paprika
Parsley flakes

Preheat oven to 350 degrees. Drain mushrooms and artichokes and layer in a 1 quart casserole or 4 or 5 ramekins. Prepare gravy according to package directions. Add thyme, marjoram and cheese. Stir until cheese is melted. Blend in wine. Pour over artichokes and mushrooms. Top with bread crumbs. Sprinkle with paprika and parsley flakes. Bake uncovered for 25 minutes in a 350 degree oven. Serves 4 to 6.

Mrs. James Altick

Artichokes Sauté

4 Tablespoons oil
1 onion, sliced thinly
1 carrot, diced
1 can artichokes or 1 package
    frozen, thawed
Salt
Pepper
1 cup chicken broth
½ teaspoon lemon juice
½ teaspoon rosemary

Sauté onion, carrot and 1/4 teaspoon salt for a few minutes in oil. Add artichokes and 1/2 teaspoon salt and cook until onion is soft. Add the remaining ingredients and cook about 5 minutes. Serves 3 or 4.

Lt. Col. Rebecca Parks
Waverly, Tennessee

Scalloped Artichokes

1 small onion, chopped
¾ green pepper, chopped
5 Tablespoons butter
2 cans artichoke hearts, drained
⅛ teaspoon each: sweet basil
    and thyme
¼ teaspoon salt
Dash of Tabasco
1 egg
1 cup sour cream
10 crackers

Cook onion and green pepper in the butter until the onion is clear. Add drained artichoke hearts and seasonings, mixing well. Place in a 2 quart casserole. Beat egg slightly and combine with sour cream. Crumble 5 crackers over artichoke mixture. Pour sour cream over artichokes and crumble remaining crackers on top. Bake at 375 degrees about 20 minutes. Serves 6.

Mrs. W.J. Hodge, Jr.

Artichoke Fritters

2-9 ounce packages artichoke
    hearts
1½ cups flour
3 egg yolks
Salt and pepper to taste
Tabasco to taste
¼ teaspoon nutmeg
1¼ cups milk
¾ teaspoon baking powder
Oil for frying

Cook artichokes according to package directions; drain well. Place flour in a bowl and add egg yolks, seasonings and 1 cup milk. Stir in baking powder. If batter is too thick add additional milk. Coat artichokes with batter and fry until golden brown. Drain and serve hot. Serves 6 to 8.

Asparagus

Nothing surpasses fresh spring asparagus served simply with lemon butter and a sprinkling of buttered bread crumbs if desired.

Wash fresh asparagus well and scrape the tough outer layer from the stalks with a potato peeler.

Tie in bundles and plunge into 6 or 8 quarts boiling water, seasoned with 1 1/2 teaspoons salt per quart or part bouillon cubes. Boil rapidly 12 or 15 minutes, just until fork tender.

Serve immediately with butter, Hollandaise, or any vegetable sauce desired.

To serve cold, rinse in cold water immediately and drain. Delicious in the summer topped with a sweetened mustard-mayonnaise or marinated in a vinaigrette and topped with sieved egg.

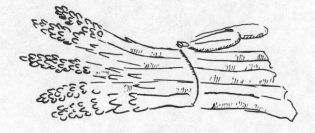

Hot Asparagus Bowl

2 Tablespoons lemon juice
2 Tablespoons melted butter
Dash of Worcestershire
Salt and pepper to taste
Juice from asparagus
1 can whole green asparagus

Combine lemon juice, butter, Worcestershire, salt, pepper and juice from asparagus. Simmer about 5 minutes. Pour over asparagus. Serves 4.

Mrs. James Rivers

Asparagus Caesar

2 cans asparagus spears or parboiled fresh asparagus
1/4 pound butter, melted
3 Tablespoons lemon juice
Paprika
1/2 cup grated Parmesan cheese

Drain asparagus, rinse with cold water and drain again. Drizzle on butter and lemon juice. Sprinkle with paprika and cheese. Place in hot oven, 425 degrees, for 15 minutes until asparagus spears are crispy; or run under broiler to heat and crisp just before serving.

Mrs. Pat Shoemaker
Oklahoma City, Oklahoma

Asparagus Casserole

2 cans asparagus
2 eggs, hard boiled
1 can mushroom soup
1 Tablespoon liquid from
    asparagus
1/2 teaspoon celery salt
Salt and pepper
1 Tablespoon butter
1 1/3 cups grated cheese
Crumbled Ritz crackers

Drain asparagus reserving a small amount of liquid. Butter a 1 quart casserole and arrange half of the asparagus on the bottom. Cover with the sliced eggs. Heat soup with the seasonings; pour half over the eggs and sprinkle with 2/3 cup of cheese. Repeat with asparagus, soup and cheese. Top with crumbled crackers. Bake in a 350 degree oven until brown and bubbly. Serves 6.

Mrs. Paul Tennis
Mrs. Ansel Smith

Asparagus and Shrimp Casserole
Some expected ingredients and some surprises

2 large cans asparagus spears
2 boiled eggs, sliced
1 small can water chestnuts,
    sliced
1 small can mushroom stems
    and pieces
1 small can sliced ripe olives
1 large can small shrimp
1 cup grated cheese
1 can mushroom soup
1/2 can water
10 or 12 crushed crackers
1 can onion rings

Butter a 1 1/2 quart pyrex casserole. Place a layer of asparagus, eggs, chestnuts, mushrooms, olives, shrimp, and cheese in this order. Dilute soup with 1/2 can water and pour 1/2 of this on first layer. Repeat the layers. Top with cracker crumbs. Cook for 30 minutes at 350 degrees. Place onion rings on top and brown for about 2 or 3 minutes.

Mrs. Allen Coon

Scalloped Asparagus with Artichokes

1-14 ounce can cut green
    asparagus, drained
1-14 ounce can artichokes,
    drained and juice reserved
2-4 ounce cans mushrooms,
    drained
4 Tablespoons butter, heaping
4 Tablespoons flour, heaping
2 cups milk
1/2 cup artichoke juice
Salt and pepper to taste
1 teaspoon Accent
1/4 pound cheese, grated

Place asparagus, halved artichokes and mushrooms into layers in a casserole. Melt butter and blend in flour; slowly add milk and artichoke juice, stirring to make a heavy cream sauce. Add salt, pepper, Accent and half of the grated cheese to the cream sauce. Pour over vegetables. Top with the remaining cheese. Bake for 25 minutes in a 350 degree oven. Serves 6.

Mrs. Carey J. Ellis, Jr.
Rayville, Louisiana

185

Seasoned Beans—Fresh or Canned

Ham hocks
1 to 2 Tablespoons bacon
    drippings
2 teaspoons Lawry's seasoning
    salt
1 teaspoon salt
1 clove garlic, optional
1 to 2 teaspoons sugar
1 large onion, quartered or finely
    chopped if desired
Cracked black pepper
Slivered bell pepper also adds
    excellent seasoning
2 pounds fresh green beans

The secret to those good ole summer fresh green beans is good seasoning and not overcooking. Fill a large pot with water and add remaining ingredients. Bring to a boil, reduce heat and simmer 30 to 45 minutes. Add beans, cook until tender; remove from heat, check for salt, and let beans cool in seasoned water. Reheat before serving. Remove garlic and onion if desired. For canned beans; drain, rinse with cold water several times and cook 20 to 30 minutes in seasoned water.

String Beans Excellenté

1 medium onion, minced
3 Tablespoons bacon grease
1- No. 2 can string beans,
    drained
½ cup chili sauce
1 teaspoon salt
Dash of pepper

Combine onion and bacon drippings in a saucepan; let simmer on very low heat until onions are tender. Add drained beans, chili sauce, salt and pepper. Cook about 30 minutes.

Bean Bundles

2 cans vertical packed green beans
½ pound bacon

SAUCE:
3 Tablespoons butter
3 Tablespoons tarragon vinegar
½ teaspoon salt
1 teaspoon paprika
1 Tablespoon fresh parsley,
    chopped
1 teaspoon onion juice

Drain beans. Divide into bundles of approximately 5 beans each. Cut 1 slice of bacon in half; wrap around beans and secure with a toothpick. Broil on a rack until the bacon is cooked.
Sauce: Combine butter, vinegar, salt, paprika, parsley and onion juice; simmer until hot. Pour over the cooked bean bundles and serve. Beans and sauce may be done ahead of time and refrigerated. Broil bean bundles and reheat sauce at serving time. Serves 8.

Mrs. Eugene Worthen

Green Beans Supreme

2 cans French style green beans
Salt pork
1 medium onion, chopped finely
2 Tablespoons butter
1 teaspoon MSG
1 teaspoon salt
2 teaspoons soy sauce
⅛ teaspoon Tabasco
2 Tablespoons Worcestershire
1 can mushroom soup
1-5 ounce can water chestnuts,
    sliced and drained
¾ pound sharp Cheddar cheese,
    grated
1 can fried onion rings

Cook beans and juice with salt pork. Drain beans. Sauté onion in butter. Add seasonings and soup. In a 1 1/2 quart casserole layer beans, chestnuts, sauce and cheese. Repeat the layers. Bake at 350 degrees for about 30 minutes or until hot and bubbly. Top with onion rings and heat 10 more minutes. Serves 6 to 8.

Mrs. D.L. Gibbs

Dill Bean Casserole

2-16 ounce cans Blue Lake
    whole beans
¼ cup bacon fat
1¼ teaspoons dill seed

SAUCE:
5 Tablespoons butter
5 Tablespoons flour
2½ cups bean juice, add milk if
    needed
3 Tablespoons grated onion
1 teaspoon cracked pepper
2½ teaspoons Accent
Tabasco to taste
Cracker crumbs

Boil beans, bacon fat and dill seed together for 45 minutes. Let the beans cool in the stock. Drain the beans; reserve the juice.
Sauce: Melt the butter and blend in flour, add bean juice, grated onion and seasonings. Place beans in a casserole and cover with the sauce. Sprinkle the top with cracker crumbs. Bake 30 minutes at 350 degrees. Serves 8. This recipe may be made a day ahead.

Mrs. Michael Cage

Green Bean Casserole

3 cans string beans, drained
Garlic salt to taste
1 carton sour cream
1 can mushroom soup
8 ounces Velvetta cheese
24 crackers, crushed and
    buttered

Put beans in the bottom of a 6 x 12 inch baking dish. Sprinkle with garlic salt. Mix soup and sour cream; pour over beans. Slice cheese and place on top. Cover with buttered cracker crumbs. Bake uncovered at 375 degrees until hot, about 30 minutes. Serves 8 generously.

Mrs. Steve Nichols

Butter Beans

2 pounds small butter beans
2 Tablespoons bacon drippings
1 teaspoon Lawry's seasoning salt
1 onion, halved
Pepper to taste
1 clove of garlic, optional
1 teaspoon salt

SAUCE:
2 Tablespoons butter
6 green onions, chopped
1 Tablespoon flour
1 cup liquid from beans
¼ teaspoon paprika
Salt and pepper to taste

Cook fresh beans with drippings and seasonings in a small amount of water until tender. Remove the onion; drain beans and reserve 1 cup of the cooking liquid.
Sauce: Melt the butter in a saucepan and sauté the green onions briefly. Stir in the flour until smooth and add the cooking liquid. Stir until thickened. Add beans, paprika, salt and pepper to taste. If dried beans are used double the amount of sauce. Frozen baby limas may also be used but be sure to cook in the seasoned water for the amount of time specified on the package. Serves 4 to 6.

Butter Bean Casserole

1 can green butter beans
2 beef bouillon cubes
1 medium onion, chopped finely
Dash of Worcestershire
½ teaspoon Accent
1 Tablespoon bacon drippings, optional
½ cup mild cheese, cut in thin slices
½ cup chopped pecans
Bread crumbs
Butter

Drain beans and reserve liquid. Dissolve bouillon cubes in the reserved heated liquid; add onion, dash of Worcestershire, Accent and bacon drippings. Butter a one quart casserole. Alternate layers of beans, cheese and pecans. Repeat. Pour onion mixture over each layer. Cover with crumbs and dot with butter. Bake in a 350 degree oven about 35 minutes. Serves 6 to 8.

Mrs. Thyra Holt

Succotash
An old-fashioned favorite

1 pound fresh butter beans
Salt meat
Onion
Garlic
4 ears of corn
½ stick butter
Half and Half

Cook the butter beans in water seasoned with salt meat, onion and garlic until done. Drain the beans and reserve liquor. Cut the corn off the cob into a heavy skillet containing melted butter. Add the beans. Pour cream and enough of the bean liquor into the skillet to barely cover the succotash. Season with salt and pepper to taste. Simmer slowly 15 to 20 minutes until the corn is tender.

Mrs. Wesley Shafto, Jr.

Lima Bean Casserole

2 cups dried lima beans
1 teaspoon salt
1/2 to 1 pound ground meat
1/2 cup onion rings
1 clove crushed garlic
1 teaspoon red pepper
2 Tablespoons fat
2 cups tomatoes
1 Tablespoon chili powder
1/2 cup grated sharp cheese

Cook beans for 1 hour beginning with cold water. Add salt the last half hour. Drain and reserve 1 to 2 cups liquid. Brown beef, onion, garlic and pepper in fat. Add tomatoes, chili powder, lima beans and cheese. Put in a greased baking dish. Add enough of the reserved liquid to barely cover beans. Bake in a 350 degree oven for 1 hour.

Mrs. W. J. Hodge, Jr.

Limas in Cream Sauce
Quite easy and delicious.

1- 10 ounce package frozen
 Fordhook lima beans
1/2 teaspoon Accent
1/2 teaspoon Lawry's seasoned
 salt
Cracked black pepper
3/4 cup Half and Half

Place frozen beans in a buttered 1 quart covered casserole. Sprinkle with salt, Accent and heavily with cracked pepper. Pour cream over the beans. Bake, covered at 350 degrees, stirring after 20 minutes. Reduce oven to 300 degrees and bake 20 minutes longer or until tender. Do not let cream boil as it will curdle.

White Beans
As a salad or a vegetable

1 pound tiny white navy beans
2 quarts water
2 cups chopped onion ·
1 thick slice salt meat
1/2 cup bell pepper, chopped
Hot peppers to taste
2 pods of garlic, pressed
1 bunch green onion tops,
 chopped fine
1/4 cup parsley, chopped
Salt to taste

Pick and wash the beans; soak overnight. Drain and rinse. Put beans into a pot with water and onions. Bring to a boil, cover, lower heat and simmer. When the beans have simmered for 30 minutes put the meat in. If the meat is salty, parboil before adding. The meat may salt the beans without having to add any salt. When the beans begin to get tender add the bell pepper, hot pepper and garlic. Add more water if needed. About 10 minutes before beans are done, add green onion tops and parsley. It usually takes several hours or more. This dish freezes well and is good served hot or cold with pork and a cooked fruit.

Mrs. O.H. Junot
New Iberia, Louisiana

Key West Black Beans
For all you Black Bean lovers, these are the best!

1 pound black beans
1 quart cold water
6 cloves garlic, minced
2 bell peppers, slivered
2 large onions, minced
⅔ cup olive oil
2 bay leaves
1 teaspoon salt
1 Tablespoon vinegar
1 Tablespoon sugar
Cooked white rice

Soak beans overnight. Rinse. Cover with cold water and boil 1 hour. Add remaining ingredients except vinegar and sugar. Cook slowly 4 hours or until beans begin to thicken. Add vinegar and sugar just before serving. These beans are best if cooked the day ahead. Serve on rice with smoked pork chops, ham or sausage. Serves 8.

Ray Coté
Villa Montaña
Morelia, Mexico

Red Beans and Rice
Bayou country favorite

2 cups red beans
1 onion, diced
2 cloves garlic
2 teaspoons seasoning salt
Bay leaf
Pinch of sugar
Red pepper to taste
Ham hocks
Cooked rice

Wash beans, soak overnight and drain. Cover beans and all ingredients with cold water. Bring to boil, reduce heat and simmer until done. Serve over rice. Large link smoked sausage, added the last 30 minutes gives delicious seasoning and makes a complete meal with hot fluffy rice and tossed salad. Serves 6.

Easy Red Beans and Rice

2- 15 ounce cans Van Camps New
  Orleans Style kidney beans
3 slices of bacon
1 large chopped onion
½ cup chopped celery
1 small chopped bell pepper
2 Tablespoons parsley
⅓ cup green onion tops
2 Tablespoons catsup
1½ teaspoons Lea & Perrins
1- 2 ounce jar pimiento, chopped
1- 8 ounce can tomato sauce
1 or 2 teaspoons chili powder

Fry bacon and crumble into kidney beans. In bacon drippings, sauté vegetables. Cook until well wilted but not brown, stirring frequently. Add beans and remaining ingredients. Cover and simmer about 30 minutes. Serve over rice. Good with cornbread. Kolbase Polish sausage, cut into 1 inch sections and prepared according to directions on package, may be added at the end of the heating period. Fresh fruit salad goes well with this or fruit may be used as a dessert.

Mrs. Pascal Norris

Suzanne's Beans

4 slices bacon
2 onions, chopped
1 cup bell pepper, chopped
1 cup parsley, chopped
1 cup celery, chopped
2 cloves garlic, pressed
2 large cans pork and beans
1 can Rotel tomatoes
1 can pimiento, chopped
1 Tablespoon prepared mustard
1 teaspoon chili powder
Salt and pepper to taste

Fry the bacon strips crisp, remove from drippings and set aside. Sauté all of the fresh vegetables in the bacon drippings until tender. Add beans, tomatoes, pimientos, seasonings and crumbled bacon. Place in a casserole or bean pot and bake at 300 degrees for 1 1/2 hours. Serves 10 to 12.

Mrs. Jerry Wolff

Baked Beans Milamo
Just great for a "gathering"

3 - 20 ounce cans pork and beans
3 large onions, chopped
1 bunch fresh green onions,
    chopped
3 bell peppers, chopped
2 hot peppers, chopped
6 ribs celery, chopped
2 heaping Tablespoons mustard
2 heaping Tablespoons brown
    sugar, syrup or molasses
1 can applesauce or 2 large apples
    peeled, cored and chopped
1 can Progresso tomato paste
¾ cup tomato juice
1 pound sharp cheese, cubed
Seasoned salt and pepper to taste
Ham cubes, optional
Bacon strips

If time permits, all of the ingredients may be placed in a casserole or bean pot and topped with bacon strips. Cook for 4 hours at 300 degrees. *To hasten cooking time:* sauté all of the fresh vegetables in seasoned fat; add all the remaining ingredients and cook at 300 degrees for 2 hours. Do not cook too dry as the juices will thicken some when removed from the oven. I hope you will like them. Serves 12 to 15.

Mrs. DeWitt Milam

Harvard Beets

2 cups canned sliced or diced
  beets, drain and reserve the
  juice
2 Tablespoons sugar
1 Tablespoon cornstarch
1/4 teaspoon salt
1/4 cup vinegar
1/3 cup beet liquid
2 Tablespoons butter

In a saucepan combine the sugar, cornstarch and salt. Stir in the beet liquid and vinegar. Add the butter and cook, stirring constantly, until the mixture thickens. Add the beets and heat. Serves 4 to 6.

Mrs. DeWitt Milam

Pickled Beets

1 No. 2 can sliced beets
Vinegar
6 cloves
1 Tablespoon sugar
1 slice lemon
1 small onion, thinly sliced

Drain beets. Cover with vinegar. Add cloves, sugar and lemon. Bring to a boil and remove from heat. Separate onions into rings. Add to beets. Chill until serving time.

Mrs. Ed Seymour, Jr.

Broccoli Mold with Almonds
A beautiful ring for a buffet filled with sautéed mushrooms

2-10 ounce packages chopped
  broccoli
3 Tablespoons butter
3 Tablespoons flour
1/4 cup chicken broth
1 cup sour cream
1/3 cup minced green onions,
  tops and all
3 eggs
3/4 cup grated Swiss cheese
1/2 cup slivered toasted almonds
1 teaspoon salt
1/2 teaspoon pepper
1/2 to 1 teaspoon nutmeg

Cook broccoli in 1 cup salted water until barely tender. Drain thoroughly. Chop finely. Don't use your blender, you'll have baby food. Heat butter in a skillet and blend in flour, add chicken broth and sour cream gradually. Stir in green onions and cook over low heat, stirring until thick and blended. Beat eggs lightly and stir into hot sauce. Cook 1 minute stirring constantly; blend in cheese until melted. Add broccoli, almonds, and seasonings; adding more salt and pepper if desired. Oil a 1 quart ring mold or 8- 5 ounce custard cups. Spoon in mixture. Bake at 350 degrees in a hot water bath for about 50 minutes for the ring and 30 minutes for the custard cups or until a knife inserted is clean. Marvelous to do ahead and freeze. May be placed in the oven frozen, but increase baking time about 30 minutes.

Mrs. Don Irby

Broccoli with Rice

1 stick butter
1 onion, chopped
1 rib celery, chopped
1 package frozen chopped
   broccoli
1 can cream of chicken soup
1 cup grated cheese
   or 1 small jar Cheese Whiz
1 1/2 cups cooked rice
Tabasco
Salt and pepper to taste
Bread crumbs

In a large skillet saute the onions and celery in butter until the vegetables are clear. Cook broccoli according to the package directions; drain well. Mix broccoli with soup and cheese; add to celery and onions. Stir in rice; season and mix well. Put into a greased casserole and top with bread crumbs. Bake at 350 degrees for 45 minutes. This can be mixed ahead and frozen. Serves 6.

Mrs. Armand E. Breard

Creamed Broccoli Pudding

2 packages chopped broccoli
1 cup Miracle Whip
1 cup sharp Cheddar cheese,
   grated
2 slightly beaten eggs
1 cup cream of celery soup
2 Tablespoons minced onions
Butter
Cracker crumbs

Cook broccoli according to package directions and drain well. Make a mixture of Miracle Whip, cheese, eggs, soup and onions. Add the broccoli and mix well. Pour into a well greased casserole. Dot with butter and top with cracker crumbs. Bake in a 350 degree oven for 45 minutes. This dish can be kept frozen up to three months. Serves 10.

Mrs. W. T. Armstrong

Party Broccoli Casserole

1 large onion, chopped
1 stick butter
4 packages broccoli spears
1 cup cream of mushroom soup
1 1/2 rolls garlic cheese
1 teaspoon MSG
1 large can mushrooms, drained
1/2 cup bread crumbs made from
   Pepperidge Farm Stuffing

Sauté onions in butter. *Briefly* parboil broccoli according to package directions. Drain. Melt cheese in mushroom soup; add MSG, drained mushrooms and sautéed onions. Alternate layers of broccoli spears and sauce in a lightly buttered casserole. Sprinkle bread crumbs over the top and bake until bubbly in a 300 degree oven. Serves 12 to 14.

Mrs. Elton Upshaw, Jr.

Broccoli au Gratin
An excellent low calorie recipe.

1 box frozen chopped broccoli
1 cup dry cottage cheese
2 eggs, slightly beaten
¼ teaspoon salt
1 teaspoon seasoned salt
¼ teaspoon pepper
¼ teaspoon steak sauce
1 teaspoon instant minced onion
4 Tablespoons butter, melted
¼ cup soft bread crumbs

Cook and drain broccoli. Mix with all ingredients except butter and bread crumbs. Stir in 2 Tablespoons butter and put in a small shallow baking dish or pie pan. Mix remaining butter and bread crumbs; sprinkle on the top. Bake for 30 minutes at 350 degrees. This may easily be doubled. Serves 4 to 6.

Mrs. Clark Boyce

Broccoli-Spaghetti Bake
Marvelous accompaniment with any Italian meat dish

3 bunches green onions and tops, chopped
1 stick butter
3 packages chopped broccoli
Salt and pepper
1-7 ounce package spaghetti
1 cup cream
6 to 8 slices American cheese

Cook onions in butter for 5 minutes; add broccoli, cover and cook until just barely tender. Season with salt and pepper to taste. Grease oblong shallow dish. Place cooked spaghetti on bottom. Spread broccoli and onions on top. Pour cream over all and top with cheese. Bake at 375 degrees for 30 minutes. This may be prepared a day ahead, but if so, do not place cheese on top until ready to bake. Serves 10.

Mrs. Jimmy Woods

Broccoli Soufflé

1 package chopped broccoli
3 Tablespoons butter
3 Tablespoons flour
1 cup milk
1 teaspoon salt
½ teaspoon white pepper
1 Tablespoon lemon juice
1 Tablespoon onion, finely minced
4 eggs, separated
MUSHROOM SAUCE:
2 Tablespoons butter
2 Tablespoons flour
1 cup milk
1 small can sliced mushrooms, drained
½ cup cheese, grated

Cook broccoli according to package directions reducing cooking time to leave broccoli slightly crisp. Drain and *finely* chop. Melt butter, blend in flour and gradually add milk. Cook over medium heat, stirring until mixture thickens. Add salt, lemon juice, white pepper, onion and broccoli. Beat egg yolks until thick and stir into broccoli mixture. Check for seasonings. Fold in stiffly beaten egg whites. Pour into a 1-1/2 quart soufflé dish and bake 40 minutes at 350 degrees. Serve at once topped with mushroom sauce. Serves 6 to 8.
Sauce: Make white sauce of butter, flour and milk. Add mushrooms and cheese. Stir until melted; season to taste with salt and pepper.

Brussels Sprouts

2-10 ounce packages Brussels
   sprouts
1 stick butter
Salt, Accent and pepper to taste
½ cup grated Swiss cheese
½ cup Parmesan cheese

Thaw the Brussels sprouts just enough to separate them. Parboil the sprouts in 1 cup salted water for 3 or 4 minutes. Rinse in cold water and drain. Grease a casserole heavily with 2 Tablespoons of butter. Melt the remaining butter. Arrange the Brussels sprouts in the casserole. Sprinkle with seasonings to taste and pour half of the melted butter over all. Cover loosely and bake for 10 minutes at 350 degrees. Remove the casserole from the oven and increase oven temperature to 425 degrees. Toss the Brussels sprouts with the grated cheeses, coating the sprouts well. Pour on the remaining butter and return to the oven, uncovered, for 10 minutes or until the cheese is nicely browned. Serves 6.

Savory Brussels Sprouts

2 packages Brussels sprouts
2 chicken bouillon cubes
2 Tablespoons butter
½ cup sliced almonds
1 can cream of chicken soup
⅛ teaspoon thyme, crushed
1 small jar chopped pimientos
Black pepper

Cook Brussels sprouts as directed on package adding bouillon cubes. Drain. Saute almonds in butter; stir in the soup and blend well. Add pimientos, black pepper and thyme. Pour over drained Brussels sprouts and serve. To prepare ahead, place Brussels sprouts in casserole, cover with sauce, and heat at 350 degrees at serving time. Serves 6.

Mrs. Morris Phillips

Skillet Cabbage

4 cups shredded cabbage
1 green pepper, shredded
2 cups diced celery
2 large onions, sliced thinly
2 tomatoes, chopped
¼ cup bacon fat
2 teaspoons sugar
1 teaspoon Accent
Salt and pepper to taste

Combine ingredients in large skillet. Cover. Cook over medium heat for 15 minutes or longer, if needed. Serves 6.

Lt. Col. Rebecca Parks
Waverly, Tennessee

Cabbage Supreme

1 medium cabbage
¾ stick butter
1 large onion, chopped
2 ribs celery, chopped
½ pound grated mild Cheddar
  cheese
1 cup bread crumbs
Celery seed, demitasse spoonful
½ cup milk
Seasoning salt to taste
Black and red pepper to taste

Shred cabbage and boil in salted water until tender. While cabbage is boiling, sauté onion and celery in butter until they are clear. Add cheese, bread crumbs, celery seed and milk to sauteed onions and celery. Drain cabbage. Add to mixture and season. Put in greased 1 1/2 quart casserole. Bake in 350 degree oven until warm. Serves 6.

Mrs. W. J. Hodge, Jr.

Cabbage Casserole

1 large cabbage, chopped
2 onions, chopped
3 cloves of garlic, minced
Cooking oil
1 stick butter
7 slices bread, soaked in enough
  milk to moisten bread well
1 pint cream
5 slices grated American cheese
Salt and red pepper to taste
Italian bread crumbs

Parboil cabbage in salted water. Drain thoroughly and set aside. Sauté the onions and garlic in enough cooking oil to moisten the vegetables. Add the cabbage to the onions. Add butter, moistened bread, cream and cheese. Stir well and season to taste. Pour half of the mixture into a casserole and top with Italian bread crumbs; cover with remaining cabbage mixture and top with additional crumbs. Bake at 350 degrees about 30 minutes or until brown.

Mrs. Roy Kelly

Chinese Cabbage Casserole

1 medium head cabbage, chopped
1 cup celery, chopped
1 cup bell pepper, chopped
1 cup onion chopped, may use
  some green onion
1 can Chinese vegetables
1 can sliced mushrooms
1 can water chestnuts, sliced
Butter

SAUCE:
3 Tablespoons butter
3 Tablespoons flour
1½ cups milk or
  1 can cream of mushroom soup
½ pound sharp cheese, grated
Dash of Tabasco
1 teaspoon Accent
Chinese noodles

Boil cabbage in a small amount of salted water for five minutes and drain. Sauté all vegetables except cabbage in butter. Butter a baking dish and layer cabbage, then vegetables, repeating until all are used. Pour cream sauce over all and top with Chinese noodles.
Sauce: Make a cream sauce and stir in cheese until melted. Add seasonings.

Mrs. Fred Fudickar, Jr.

Carrots au Sucre

These are excellent.

2 pounds carrots
¼ cup butter
1 cup sugar
1 teaspoon salt

Scrape carrots; cut into thin strips or rounds. Put all in a heavy covered skillet. Cover and cook very slowly, shaking pan frequently, 30 to 40 minutes or until tender. Uncover pan as little as possible so steam will not escape. Serves 8 to 10.

Buttery Grated Carrots

2 pounds carrots
1 Tablespoon salad oil
¼ teaspoon finely chopped garlic
½ teaspoon salt
⅛ teaspoon pepper
2 Tablespoons water
¼ cup butter

Peel carrots and grate on medium grater. Place in a skillet with tight-fitting cover. Toss with oil, garlic, salt, pepper and 2 Tablespoons water. Cook covered over medium heat, stirring occasionally, 10 to 15 minutes or until tender. Remove from heat and toss with butter.

Brandied Carrots

2 bunches carrots, scraped and
    sliced thinly
½ cup butter, melted
¾ teaspoon sugar
½ teaspoon salt
¼ cup brandy

Parboil carrots for 10 minutes or until slightly tender. Place in a large casserole in a thin layer. Combine melted butter, sugar, salt and brandy. Pour over carrots. Cover casserole and bake 30 minutes in 325 degree oven. Serves 8.

Mrs. Ed Seymour, Jr.

Super Carrots

2 Tablespoons chopped onion
1 Tablespoon chopped parsley
2 Tablespoons butter
8 medium carrots, cut in 1½ inch pieces
1 can consommé
Dash nutmeg

In a saucepan, cook onion and parsley in butter, 5 minutes. Add carrots, consommé and nutmeg. Cover and cook over medium heat for 25 minutes. Uncover and cook 20 more minutes until carrots are tender.

Mrs. Herbert Mayo

Carrot Fritters

1 bunch carrots
1 egg
1 Tablespoon sugar
3 Tablespoons flour
Salt and pepper to taste
1 teaspoon baking powder
Shortening for deep frying

Scrape and boil the carrots until they are tender. Cream carrots, egg and sugar together; add flour and baking powder. Pick batter up in a spoon and drop into shortening that is hot enough to brown them instantly! Drain on a paper towel and serve immediately. This recipe can easily be doubled or tripled. Serves 6 to 8.

Miss Mary F. Buckner

Corn Fritters

4 ears corn
1 egg yolk
Self-rising flour
Salt and pepper
1 teaspoon sugar
Oil
1 teaspoon bacon grease, optional

Grate corn in a bowl and stir in flour to make a thick batter. Salt and pepper well, adding 1 teaspoon sugar. Drop batter by a Tablespoon into hot oil with 1 teaspoon of bacon grease added for flavor. Fry until golden brown. Flip over and fry on the other side.

Mrs. Wesley Shafto, Jr.

Roast Corn
A summer favorite

1/2 cup butter
2 Tablespoons finely chopped
 chives
2 Tablespoons chopped parsley
Salt and pepper
8 ears of corn

Melt butter with chives and parsley. Brush corn with butter mixture, salt and pepper. Roast in husks over hot coals turning frequently or wrap in foil and bake at 400 degrees for 30 minutes.

Corn Mango

1/4 cup butter
1/4 cup flour
2/3 cup milk
3 eggs, separated
1 can whole yellow corn, drained
1 1/2 cups sharp cheese, grated
1/4 cup ground bell pepper
Salt and pepper to taste

Melt butter and stir in flour. Add milk and well beaten egg yolks and cook until thick. Mix in drained corn, cheese and bell pepper. Season to taste with salt and pepper. Fold in stiffly beaten egg whites. Place in a buttered 2 quart casserole. Bake 35 to 45 minutes at 350 degrees. Serves 4 to 6.

Mrs. Jerry Wolff

Corn Pudding

2- No. 2 cans cream corn, 5 cups
1 stick butter, melted
1 Tablespoon flour
2 Tablespoons sugar
1/2 teaspoon salt
4 eggs, beaten
1 cup milk

Mix all together and put in a casserole to bake. May be made ahead of time and refrigerated until ready to cook. Bake at 350 degrees for 50 minutes or until knife inserted is clean.

Mrs. Jack Rodgers

Helly Hot

3 slices bacon
1 cup sliced okra
1 large onion, finely chopped
1 cup chopped celery
6 tomatoes
1 bell pepper
1 hot pepper
Salt and pepper
1 pint cream corn

Fry the bacon and set aside. Seal the edges of okra in the hot bacon fat. Add onions and celery. Sauté until waxy looking but not brown; add finely chopped tomatoes, bell pepper and hot pepper. Cook all together until tomatoes are well done, then add the pint of cream corn and cook 20 minutes more. Before serving crumble in the bacon. Very good cold or hot.

Mrs. Briscoe Trousdale, Sr.

Ratatouille

2 pounds zucchini
2 pounds eggplant, peeled
1/3 cup butter
3 green peppers, thinly sliced
2 onions, sliced
3 cloves garlic
2 pounds tomatoes
Salt and pepper
Basil
Thyme
Bay Leaf

Cut the unpeeled zucchini and eggplant into 1/2 inch slices and sauté in the butter a few at a time, several minutes on each side. Remove and drain. In the same skillet stir the green peppers, onions and garlic. Cook for 10 minutes. Remove and discard garlic. Add the tomatoes that have been peeled, seeded and sliced. Layer eggplant, zucchini and half of the tomato mixture, season with salt, pepper and herbs. Repeat, ending with tomato sauce and seasonings. Bake covered for about 1 hour in a 350 degree oven. This is a great hot vegetable or serve cold as a salad or hors d'oeuvre.

Mrs. Dan Sartor

Eggplant Parmegiana in Fresh Tomato Sauce

SAUCE:
3 onions, chopped
2 to 3 cloves garlic, pressed
1/4 cup olive oil
3 teaspoons salt
1 Tablespoon sugar
1 teaspoon oregano
1 teaspoon basil
1/2 teaspoon anise seed
8 large ripe tomatoes
   peeled, seeded and chopped
3/4 cup chicken stock
1/4 cup white wine
2 Tablespoons parsley, chopped

EGGPLANT:
2 medium eggplants or 1 large
   eggplant
2 eggs, well beaten
1 cup Progresso bread crumbs
1/2 cup olive oil
1 heaping cup Parmesan cheese
1/2 pound Mozzarella cheese,
   grated or sliced

Sauce: Sauté onions and garlic in oil. Add seasonings, liquid and tomatoes. Simmer 25 to 30 minutes. Add chopped parsley and simmer 5 more minutes.
Eggplant: Peel and slice eggplant. Dip in salted ice water; pat dry, salt and let drain 15 to 20 minutes. Dip in beaten eggs then bread crumbs and brown in hot oil. Layer eggplant, sauce and cheese in a casserole. Repeat layers. Dot with butter. Bake 30 minutes in 350 degree oven. The size of the casserole depends on the size of the eggplants used. Make ahead, refrigerate and bake before serving.

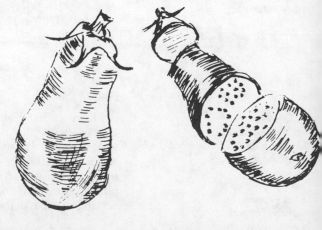

New Orleans Eggplant

2 medium eggplants
1 large onion
1/2 sweet pepper
1/2 bunch green onions
2 cloves garlic
Bacon drippings
2 Tablespoons minced parsley
3 to 4 slices of bread, soaked in
    water
1 pound shrimp, boiled and peeled
1 small piece of ham, ground
1 or 2 eggs
1/2 teaspoon sugar
Salt and pepper to taste
Bread crumbs

Boil eggplants until fork tender. Cool. Chop onions, peppers, and green onions finely; sauté in bacon drippings with garlic, do not brown. Scoop out eggplant pulp carefully so as not to damage skin. Add pulp to onion mixture and simmer 20 minutes. Stir in minced parsley and simmer about 5 minutes. Take off heat. Squeeze bread dry and mix in well. Add chopped up shrimp and ground ham. Blend in one or two eggs to bind, sugar, salt and pepper to taste. Stir in a few bread crumbs if needed. Stuff shells, sprinkle with bread crumbs and dot with butter. Bake at 350 degrees for 45 minutes.

Mrs. J. M. deBen
New Orleans, Louisiana

Sherried Eggplant

5 slices bread
1 large eggplant or 2 small
1 heaping Tablespoon salt
2 quarts of water
1 pound of headless shrimp or
    1 large can tuna fish
2 medium onions, chopped
Bacon fat
Butter
2 bay leaves
Salt and pepper
Dash of thyme
Tabasco to taste
3/4 cup evaporated milk
1 can chicken broth
1/4 pound grated American cheese
Sherry to taste

Toast the bread, then place in a slow oven until the slices have dried out for several hours. Make fine toast crumbs. Peel the eggplant and cut into small cubes. Soak in a brine solution made with the salt and water. The eggplant will float, so weight it down with a lid. After 30 to 45 minutes, pour off the salt water and let the eggplant soak in plain water until ready to use. Remove the shells and devein shrimp. Simmer the shells in water to cover. Sauté the onions slowly in bacon fat and a small amount of butter. Add seasonings. Drain the eggplant well and add to the onions; cook until soft, slightly browned and reduced to half. Add the shrimp and stir until the shrimp are slightly fried. Add most of the toast crumbs, the evaporated milk and at least 1/2 cup of the liquid in which the shells have been simmered. Add the grated cheese, salt, pepper and sherry to taste. Stir over low heat until the mixture has thickened but is still soft enough to allow for baking. Sprinkle remaining crumbs over the top and bake in a 350 degree oven until bubbly and brown. If you substitute tuna fish for the shrimp, use chicken broth in place of liquid from the shrimp shells. Dry golden toast crumbs made in your oven are the key to the success of the dish. Serves 6.

Mrs. Paul Tennis

Texas Stuffed Eggplant

1 eggplant
½ cup bell pepper, chopped
3 Tablespoons minced onion
1 cup chopped ripe olives
¾ cup grated cheese
1 cup Pepperidge Farm seasoned
  stuffing
1 teaspoon salt
½ teaspoon pepper
1 Tablespoon butter
Paprika
1 Tablespoon minced parsley

Parboil the eggplant 20 minutes or until tender. Cool. Halve and scoop out the pulp leaving shells intact. Mash the pulp and add remaining ingredients, reserving a small amount of crumbs and cheese for the topping. Refill the shells. Dot with butter. Top with reserved crumbs, cheese, paprika and minced parsley. Bake in a 325 degree oven for 30 minutes. Serves 2. This may also be baked without the shell in a greased casserole and will serve 4.

Mrs. George M. Snellings III

Eggplant Casserole

3 eggplants
1 cup green onions, chopped
1 cup white onion, chopped
1 stick butter
1 clove garlic, pressed
½ cup parsley, chopped
1 teaspoon thyme
Salt to taste
Red pepper to taste
3 eggs
2 cups bread moistened with water
  and squeezed dry
1 pound boiled shrimp, peeled
1 pound crabmeat
Bread crumbs

Peel and dice eggplants. Boil in salted water until tender. Drain. Sauté onions, garlic and parsley in butter for about 5 minutes. Add eggplant, thyme, salt and pepper. Work in squeezed bread and slightly beaten eggs. Fold in shrimp and crabmeat. Remove from heat. Place in a buttered casserole and top with bread crumbs, butter and parsley. Bake at 350 degrees for 20 to 30 minutes. Serves 6.

Mrs. George M. Snellings III

Meat-Stuffed Eggplant

1 eggplant
2 Tablespoons butter
1 onion, chopped
1 rib celery, chopped
1 garlic clove, pressed
½ pound ground chuck
1 can tomatoes, chopped
½ bell pepper, chopped
Salt and pepper to taste
1 bay leaf
½ cup bread crumbs
½ cup cheese, grated

Halve eggplant lengthwise. Scoop out the pulp, chop, salt and set aside to drain. Parboil the eggplant shells for 5 minutes. Remove from the water and place in a greased baking dish. Sauté the onion, celery and garlic in butter; add meat and cook until brown, stirring. Add tomatoes, green pepper, eggplant, bay leaf, salt and pepper to taste. Simmer for 30 minutes. Mix in bread crumbs and check for seasonings. Stuff eggplant shells with the mixture and top with cheese. Bake in a 350 degree oven for 30 minutes. A little leftover shrimp or crabmeat can be added just before stuffing. Serves 2.

Mrs. Joe Montgomery

Eggplant Soufflé

2 medium size eggplants
2 Tablespoons butter
2 Tablespoons flour
1 cup milk
1 cup grated Cheddar cheese
1 Tablespoon catsup
1 Tablespoon grated onion
2 eggs, separated
Salt and pepper to taste

Peel and boil eggplant until tender. Mash well. Melt butter, add flour and stir in milk slowly until thickened. Add grated cheese, catsup, onion and beaten egg yolks. Blend in mashed eggplant. Season to taste with salt and pepper. Fold in stiffly beaten egg whites and check for seasoning. Bake in a buttered soufflé dish 1 hour at 350 degrees. Serve immediately.

Mrs. Rupert Campbell
Shreveport, Louisiana

Stuffed Mirlitons
Truly a Louisiana dish

4 mirlitons
1 large onion
2 green onions and tops
1/3 cup butter
1/2 cup seasoned crumbs or herb
   stuffing mix
2 cans of shrimp
Accent
Salt and pepper
Tabasco

Boil mirlitons until fork tender. Drain, cool and cut in half. Remove seed and scrape out the pulp, leaving skin intact. Mince 1 large onion. Sauté along with finely sliced green onions and tops in butter. Add the mirliton pulp and simmer until mixture is well blended and tender but not too dry. Add crumbs and shrimp that have been drained but not rinsed. Stir to blend and season to taste. Lightly stuff the skins. Sprinkle top with seasoned crumbs and dot with butter. Bake at 350 degrees until hot and crumbs are slightly brown. This mixture can be baked in ramekins if you don't wish to fool with the skins. They are delicate and tear easily. These freeze well. Serves 8.

Mrs. Dan Sartor

Scalloped Cucumbers

3 Tablespoons butter
3 Tablespoons flour
1 cup milk
1/2 teaspoon dried chives
1/2 teaspoon salt
2 large thin cucumbers
3/4 cup bread crumbs
1 cup cream
Paprika

Make a white sauce of butter, flour, milk and seasonings. Wash cucumbers and score with a fork. Slice thinly. In a buttered 1 quart casserole layer cucumbers, white sauce, and bread crumbs. Salt and pepper each layer. Repeat layers saving 1/4 cup bread crumbs. Pour the cream over the mixture. Sprinkle with bread crumbs and paprika. Bake 20 minutes at 350 degrees. Serves 4 to 6.

Mrs. Jim Altick

Pepper Grits

½ cup grits
2½ cups water
1 teaspoon salt
2 rolls jalapeño cheese, grated
2 cups Cheddar cheese, grated
4 eggs, beaten
¼ teaspoon garlic powder,
  optional

Stir grits into boiling salted water. Cover and cook slowly 25 to 30 minutes. Add all cheese except 3/4 cup and stir until melted. Blend a small amount of grits into beaten eggs, then stir eggs into grits. Add garlic powder if used. Pour into a greased two quart casserole, sprinkle with remaining cheese and bake 20 minutes at 350 degrees. Serves 8 to 10.

Gourmet Hominy Bake
A delicious dish to serve with charcoaled foods

2-1 pound, 13 ounce cans
  white hominy
2-4 ounce cans green chilies,
  minced
Salt and cracked pepper to taste
Butter
Sour cream
½ cup heavy cream
1 cup shredded Monterrey Jack
  cheese

Drain and rinse the hominy. Generously butter a 2 1/2 to 3 quart casserole. Layer the ingredients in the following order: hominy, green chilies, season with salt and pepper, dot with sour cream and butter. Repeat the layers, ending with a layer of hominy. Dot the top with butter and pour the cream over all. Sprinkle with cheese. Bake at 350 degrees for 25 to 30 minutes. Serve piping hot.

Old-Fashioned Macaroni and Cheese Bake

1 cup macaroni
1 cup grated cheese
2 eggs
⅔ cup milk
½ teaspoon salt
¼ teaspoon paprika
Cayenne to taste
Dry bread crumbs
Butter
Additional grated cheese

Parboil macaroni in salted water. Drain. In a buttered casserole layer macaroni and 1 cup grated cheese. Beat eggs, milk and seasonings well. Pour over layered macaroni and cheese. Sprinkle with bread crumbs, dot with butter and top with additional grated cheese. Bake at 350 degrees for 20 minutes or until knife inserted in the middle comes clean. Serves 4.

Macaroni Casserole
Roquefort cheese adds a zest

1 box small elbow macaroni
1 pound sharp cheese, grated
1 can mushroom soup
1 small can mushrooms and juice
1 cup mayonnaise
¼ cup chopped onions
¼ cup chopped green pepper
3 Tablespoons melted butter
1 small package Roquefort cheese
1½ cups cracker crumbs

Prepare macaroni according to package directions. Rinse and drain. Mix thoroughly with the next six ingredients. Place in a 1½ to 2 quart casserole. Melt butter and Roquefort cheese together. Combine with cracker crumbs; sprinkle over macaroni. Bake at 350 degrees for 30 minutes. Serves 8 to 10. This recipe freezes well.

Mrs. Naomi Crawford
Winnfield, Louisiana

Italian Macaroni and Cheese

1- 8 ounce package elbow
   macaroni
4 Tablespoons butter
2 Tablespoons flour
3 cups milk
1 cup Mozzarella cheese, diced
½ cup Parmesan cheese, grated
½ cup Cheddar cheese, grated
1 teaspoon onion, grated
1 Tablespoon A-1 Sauce
1 teaspoon salt
Pepper to taste

Prepare macaroni according to package directions. Rinse and drain. Make a cream sauce with butter, flour and milk. Blend in remaining ingredients, stirring until cheeses melt. Remove from heat and combine with the macaroni. Put into a buttered casserole and bake at 350 degrees for about 30 minutes. Serves 8.

Mrs. Dan Sartor

Bess' Noodles

4 Tablespoons butter
1 small onion, chopped
1 medium can mushrooms,
   drained and juice reserved
2 cans consommé
1- 10 ounce package noodles
1 cup slivered almonds

Sauté onion and mushrooms in 2 Tablespoons of butter. Add consomme and mushroom juice. Bring to a boil, add noodles and cook until liquid is absorbed. Sauté almonds in remaining butter and mix into noodles. Serves 8 to 10.

Mrs. Sol Courtman

Noodle Soufflé

1- 10 ounce package thin noodles
3 eggs, separated
½ cup melted butter
2 teaspoons sugar
1 pound creamed cottage cheese
1 cup sour cream
Salt and pepper to taste

Cook noodles according to package directions and drain. Beat egg yolks, add melted butter and sugar. Stir in cheese, cream and noodles. Fold in stiffly beaten egg whites. Add salt and pepper to taste. Place in a buttered 2 quart casserole. Dot with butter. Bake 45 minutes at 375 degrees. Serves 10 to 12.

Mrs. Lionel Greenbaum
Shaker Heights, Ohio

Mushrooms Sous Cloche
A Delicious Appetizer

6 Tablespoons soft butter
1 Tablespoon chopped parsley
2 teaspoons lemon juice
½ teaspoon salt
¼ teaspoon dried chervil
Dash of pepper
4-½ inch thick slices French
  bread, toasted
1¼ pounds fresh mushrooms,
  stems trimmed to ½ inch
½ cup heavy cream
Sherry to taste

Preheat oven to 375 degrees. Cream butter with chopped parsley, lemon juice, salt, chervil and pepper. Use 1/2 of the mixture to spread on toast slices. Place slices, buttered side up, in individual ramekins or small casseroles. Mound mushrooms over toast and spread with remaining butter mixture. Drizzle with cream. Cover with an ovenproof glass "bell" or a cover. Bake 20 minutes or until mushrooms are just tender. Pour a little sherry over each and serve at once. The dish can be prepared ahead of time except for baking. Serves 4. It can be doubled.

Mrs. James Godfrey
New Orleans, Louisiana

Mushroom Soufflé

24 large mushrooms
1 small onion, finely diced
¾ cup butter
2 Tablespoons flour
1 cup chicken broth
4 eggs, separated
½ teaspoon salt
¼ cup Parmesan cheese

Wash, dry, and detach stems; do not peel the mushrooms. Chop stems and 6 whole mushrooms; sauté with the onion in 4 Tablespoons of butter. Make a cream sauce of 2 Tablespoons butter, the flour and broth. Add the sautéed mixture. Cool. Beat egg yolks and blend into the creamed mushrooms and onion. Season with salt to taste. Stiffly beat egg whites and fold into mixture. Place whole mushrooms in a buttered casserole, hollow side up. Brush with butter. Pour soufflé over the mushrooms. Sprinkle with Parmesan cheese. Bake at 350 degrees until puffed and brown. Serves 6 to 8.

Mrs. Elton Upshaw, Jr.

Mushroom Ramekins

2 pints fresh mushrooms
2 Tablespoons butter, more if
  needed
1 cup sour cream
2 Tablespoons chopped chives
3 Tablespoons minced bacon

Sauté mushrooms in butter until tender. Add sour cream and chives; stir to coat. Fill small ramekins with mushrooms and sour cream. Sprinkle with bacon. Pretty served on toast also.

Mrs. Wesley Shafto, Jr.

Champignons Derbigny
A Beautiful Luncheon

1 pound fresh mushrooms
3 Tablespoons butter
½ teaspoon salt
1 teaspoon onion salt
Dash of pepper
2 Tablespoons white wine
2 Tablespoons dry sherry
¾ cup sour cream
1 Tablespoon minced chives
Toast points or English muffins

Wash and dry mushrooms. Slice. Sauté in butter for 4 minutes. Add salt, onion salt, pepper, wine and sherry. Sauté for one minute. Reduce heat; add sour cream and chives. Heat thoroughly. Do not let boil. Serve on toast points or toasted, sliced English muffins. This is delicious and so easy. Serves 4.

Mrs. James Godfrey
New Orleans, Louisiana

Mushroom Pie

1-8 inch baked pie crust
3 Tablespoons flour
3 Tablespoons real butter
1 cup light cream
1 pound fresh mushrooms, sliced
2 Tablespoons butter
1 clove garlic, pressed
2 or 3 minced shallots
2 egg yolks
1 Tablespoon light cream
Salt and pepper to taste
2 Tablespoons white wine
½ cup grated Swiss cheese

Make a very thick cream sauce of flour, butter and cream. Cool. In a *stainless* or *enameled* skillet, sauté the sliced mushrooms in the 2 Tablespoons of butter with garlic and shallots. *Drain off any excess liquid.* Add mushrooms to cream sauce, plus the egg yolks beaten with 1 Tablespoon cream. Blend in salt, pepper and wine. Check for seasoning. Pour mixture into crust and top with cheese. Bake at 350 degrees until hot, from 10 to 20 minutes. Serve with any meat, fowl or fish. Can be made ahead and put in the pie shell just before baking.

Mrs. Clark Boyce

A beautiful garnish for a serving tray is sautéed mushrooms. They are easily prepared ahead of time or at the last minute. Using ½ pound of mushrooms; toss a few at a time in 2 Tablespoons of butter and 1 Tablespoon of oil over high heat for 4 or 5 minutes until lightly browned and shiny. DO NOT OVERCOOK as they will lose their juices. Minced chives sautéed with the mushrooms are a flavorful addition.

Pat's Parmesan Mushrooms

12 medium mushrooms
2 Tablespoons olive oil
¼ cup chopped onion
2 cloves garlic, chopped
⅓ cup seasoned bread crumbs
3 Tablespoons Parmesan cheese
⅛ teaspoon oregano
½ teaspoon salt
1 Tablespoon parsley, chopped
2 Tablespoons olive oil

Wash mushrooms, break off stems and remove a little meat to make a deeper cavity for the stuffing. Chop stems and scraped meat. Sauté onions, garlic and chopped mushrooms in the oil. Combine remaining ingredients except additional oil with the sautéed mixture. Pile into mushroom caps. Place mushrooms in a casserole greased with additional oil. Bake at 400 degrees for 15 to 20 minutes. Delicious as a meat accompaniment or hors d'oeuvres.

Mrs. James R. Wolff

Freezer Stuffed Mushrooms

8-3 to 4 inch mushrooms with
stems
2 Tablespoons butter
¼ pound bulk sausage
2 ribs celery, chopped
½ cup finely chopped onion
1 teaspoon Lea & Perrins
½ teaspoon lemon juice
Dash of Accent
½ teaspoon dry mustard
2 Tablespoons finely minced
parsley
1 cup bread crumbs; made from
Pepperidge Farm herb stuffing
1 cup strong beef stock; use Spice
Islands beef broth base
2 Tablespoons melted butter

Wash mushrooms and pat dry. Remove stems and scoop out a thin layer of each mushroom. Chop stems finely. If mushroom stems have been broken off, buy a few extra as you should have 6 Tablespoons chopped mushroom stems. Melt 2 Tablespoons butter and brown the sausage. Add vegetables and sauté. Remove from heat and stir in seasonings, parsley, and bread crumbs. Slowly add enough broth for a good stuffing consistency. Brush caps all over with melted butter. Place on broiling pan, rounded side up and broil 1 minute in a preheated broiler. Remove and stuff. Place on a flat pan and freeze until firm. Pack in plastic bag or container and return to freezer. To serve; partially thaw, dot with butter and broil 4 to 5 minutes until lightly browned and heated through. A beautiful accompaniment for roast or turkey. Serves 8.

Mrs. Jim Hurley
Oklahoma City, Oklahoma

Fried Okra

Okra
Salt and pepper
Cornmeal

Wash and cut okra in 1 inch pieces or use very small whole okra. Salt and pepper liberally. Shake the okra in cornmeal which has been seasoned. Fry in deep fat until golden and crisp. Drain and serve with a meal or as snacks.

Mrs. Roy Champagne
Lafayette, Louisiana

Okra-Bacon Casserole

1½ pounds tender okra
3 fresh tomatoes, chopped
1 onion, chopped
½ bell pepper, chopped
Salt and pepper, to taste
5 strips bacon

Slice okra into thin rounds. Grease a 2 1/2 quart casserole. Place layers of okra, tomatoes, salt, pepper, onion and bell pepper. Repeat layers. Lay bacon, overlapping, on the top. Bake at 350 degrees for one hour. Serves 6 to 8.

Mrs. Robert Curry III

Okra Evangeline
A delicious recipe from the bayou

1 pound fresh okra, sliced
1 stick butter
½ cup finely chopped onion
½ cup shredded ham, grate on
   coarse blade
1 clove garlic
Salt and pepper
Accent to taste
1 cup cooked rice
4 large tomatoes

Smother okra in the butter with onion, ham and seasonings. Hollow out the tomatoes while cooking okra. When cooked through, add rice and tomato pulp. Check for seasoning. Stuff tomatoes and bake 10 minutes at 400 degrees. Serves 4. In those long winter months when tomatoes are not at their best, stir in about 3 to 4 canned tomatoes, chopped and partially drained. This makes a delicious casserole.

Baked Onions

Medium white onions, 1 per
person
Salt
Pepper
Soy sauce
Butter

Remove the outer shell from onions and place each on a foil square. Score the onions two-thirds deep. Salt and pepper generously. Pour soy sauce over the onions and top with butter. Wrap well in foil and bake in a 350 to 375 degree oven for 1 hour or until tender. The onions make their own sauce and take the place of a baked potato.

Mrs. J.E. Brown
Lake Providence, Louisiana

French-Fried Onions

4 yellow onions
Milk
Flour
Oil for frying
Salt and pepper

Peel and cut the onions into ½ inch slices and separate into rings. Dip each onion ring in milk and then in flour. Fry in deep fat, 380 degrees, until browned and crisp. Drain the onions and season to taste with salt and pepper. Serves 4.

Stuffed Onions

8 medium onions
¼ cup butter
½ pound sausage
1¼ cups soft bread crumbs
⅓ cup light cream
¼ cup chopped parsley
¼ teaspoon thyme
Salt and pepper to taste
1 cup beef stock
½ cup dry white wine
Chopped parsley

Scoop out the centers of 8 peeled onions leaving a 1/4 inch thick shell. Chop the centers to equal 1 1/2 cups. Blanch the cases for 5 minutes and turn upside down to drain. In a skillet sauté the chopped onion in 1/4 cup of butter until it is lightly colored. Add the sausage meat, crumbled, and cook a few minutes. Stir in 1 1/4 cups bread crumbs, which have been soaked in the light cream. Simmer for about 5 minutes and add parsley, thyme, salt and pepper. Fill the shells lightly with stuffing and arrange in a buttered shallow dish. Pour the stock and wine around them. Bring to a boil on top of the stove and then bake in a 350 degree oven, basting several times for 45 minutes. Transfer the onions to a serving dish. Reduce the juices by half, pour over the onions and sprinkle with chopped parsley. Serves 8.

Mrs. Dan Sartor

Scalloped Onions

5 or 6 large yellow onions
1 stick butter
2 Tablespoons flour
1 teaspoon salt
1/2 teaspoon pepper
1/2 to 1 teaspoon dry mustard
1 cup milk
8 ounces grated cheese
Crumbs from Peppridge Farm
  herb stuffing
Butter for topping

Thinly slice onions to equal about 4 cups. Sauté in 1/2 stick of butter. In a saucepan melt remaining 1/2 stick of butter and stir in flour and seasonings. Slowly stir in milk and grated cheese. Cook slowly until cheese is melted. In a 1 quart baking dish alternate layers of onions and sauce. Sprinkle top with crumbs and dot with butter. Bake at 400 degrees for 20 minutes. Serves 6.

Mrs. George Snellings III

Tarte à l'Oignon—Belgian Onion Pie

1-8 inch baked pie shell
1/2 pound butter, real, please
3 large yellow onions, cut into
  half moons
3 Tablespoons flour
1/4 cup milk, warmed
1/4 cup cream, warmed
Pinch of nutmeg
2 eggs, at room temperature
Salt
Tabasco
A handful of freshly grated Parmesan and Romano

Preheat oven to 425 degrees. Prepare French Pastry Crust in the pastry section using 1/2 of the recipe and onion soup for the liquid. Bake for 10 minutes, then turn heat to 375 degrees and bake for five minutes more. Set shell aside. *Prepare Filling:* Select a skillet with a lid. Melt butter until it foams. Sauté onions in the butter until they are transparent. Cover; cook the onions until they are limp and just start to color. Stir to color the onions the least bit on all sides. Through a sifter, sprinkle the flour over the onions, stirring constantly to prevent lumps. Gradually add the warmed milk and cream. Stir to a smooth paste. The mixture should be the consistency of mashed potatoes. Remove from the fire. Beat eggs well and blend in. Add salt and pepper to taste. Add the cheeses and mix well. Preheat oven to 400 degrees. Pour mixture into the prebaked pie shell. Bake for 30 to 40 minutes, until the center is set and top is a delicate straw color. Preparation may be completed ahead, but do not put onion filling in the crust until baking time.

211

Quick and Easy Hot Peas

1 can cream of mushroom soup
1 roll Kraft garlic cheese
$^1/_2$ teaspoon red pepper
Salt to taste
2 cans LeSueur peas, drained

Heat the soup. Add the cheese and stir until melted. Season to taste and add drained peas. Serves 8.

Mrs. Joe Dixon

Company Peas

2-17 ounce cans small
  English peas
1 can cream of mushroom soup
$^1/_2$ cup sharp cheese, grated
1 can shrimp, washed and drained
$^1/_2$ can water chestnuts, sliced
1 Tablespoon Worcestershire
1 Tablespoon sherry, optional

Drain the peas, reserving 1/4 of the liquid. Mix all ingredients in a saucepan. Cook until cheese melts. Simple but good. Serves 8.

Mrs. Bill Wilson

Sweet Pea Sallie
The snapper—currant jelly

$^1/_3$ stick of butter
3 Tablespoons currant jelly
1 Tablespoon sugar
2 cans LeSueur peas
Salt and cracked pepper

Melt butter, currant jelly and sugar in a double boiler. Heat the peas gently; drain off part of the liquid. Add peas and remaining liquid to the jelly mixture. Season with salt and pepper. Keep warm in the double boiler. Serves 8. Excellent accompaniment for rib roast and Yorkshire Puffs.

Mrs. Harry Bell

Green Peas Bonne Femme
The flavor is marvelous

4 cups shelled peas
2 large lettuce leaves
$^1/_2$ pound fresh mushrooms
8 green onions
4 Tablespoons butter
1 cup consommé
$1^1/_2$ teaspoons salt
$^1/_4$ teaspoon pepper
$^1/_2$ teaspoon nutmeg
$^1/_4$ teaspoon marjoram
1 teaspoon sugar
3 or 4 sprigs parsley

Line a 1 1/2 quart deep casserole with lettuce leaves. Sauté sliced mushrooms and finely chopped onions in butter. Remove from heat, add peas and toss. Place in lettuce lined casserole. Heat consommé and add seasonings. Pour over peas, top with sprigs of parsley, cover and refrigerate several hours. Preheat oven 375 degrees and bake covered for 50 to 60 minutes or until peas are tender. Uncover; discard parsley and lettuce, stir and serve. Frozen peas and canned mushrooms may be substituted in this recipe, but the fresh ingredients are so delicious. Also 1/4 cup of sherry may be substituted for 1/4 cup of consommé.

Mrs. Lee Kennedy
Oklahoma City, Oklahoma

New Year's Luck Peas and Jowls

1 pound dried black-eyed peas
½ pound smoked hog jowl
1 large onion, chopped
Red pepper to taste
Dash of mace
3 cloves garlic
Salt to taste

Wash peas and cover with water; soak overnight. Cook jowl in water until tender. Add peas, onions, red pepper, mace and garlic; cook slowly about two hours. Remove jowl, slice and brown in oven. Season peas with salt. Arrange slices of the meat over the bowl of peas.

Mrs. M. A. Cooper
Rayville, Louisiana

Old-Fashioned Pea Delight

2 cups fresh or frozen purple-hull peas or black-eyed peas
3 strips bacon
2 Tablespoons finely chopped mushrooms
2 Tablespoons chopped bell pepper
2 Tablespoons finely chopped onion
¾ cup canned tomatoes, cut into small pieces
¼ cup tomato paste
¼ teaspoon black pepper
¼ teaspoon chili powder
½ teaspoon salt

Cook peas in seasoned water. Drain. Fry bacon crisp. Use drippings to sauté bell pepper, onions and mushrooms. Add sautéed mixture, crumbled bacon, tomatoes, tomato paste and spices to cooked peas. Serve hot to 6 or 8.

Mrs. Dick Taylor
Ruston, Louisiana

Stuffed Sweet Peppers

4 sweet peppers
1 large onion
$1/2$ sweet pepper
1 rib celery
$1/2$ bunch shallots
2 cloves garlic
2 Tablespoons butter
2 Tablespoons chopped parsley
$1/2$ pound ground beef
1 carrot, grated
2 or 3 slices of bread
1 or 2 eggs as needed
$1/2$ teaspoon sugar
Salt and pepper
Bread crumbs

Parboil 4 peppers about 3 minutes. Cut in half and cool. Finely chop remaining pepper and vegetables. Sauté onion, sweet pepper, celery, shallots and garlic in 2 Tablespoons butter or bacon drippings until soft. Add parsley and ground meat. Cook until meat is brown. Remove from heat. Add grated carrot, bread squeezed in water and 1 egg. Mix; add sugar, salt and pepper to taste. Add the remaining egg if mixture is too stiff. Fill pepper shells. Cover with bread crumbs, dot with butter and bake 30 to 40 minutes at 350 degrees.

Mrs. J. M. de Ben
New Orleans, Louisiana

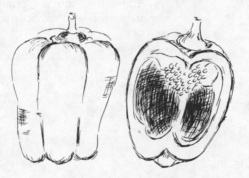

Piperies Yemistes
Peppers stuffed with meat and rice

10 to 12 medium green peppers
2 teaspoons salt
$1/2$ cup butter
1 onion, finely chopped
1 clove garlic, crushed
$1 1/2$ pounds minced meat, not
   mincemeat
$1/2$ cup rice
Chopped parsley
2 tomatoes, peeled and chopped
Salt and pepper
1 cup soft bread crumbs
Melted butter
$1 1/2$ cups tomato juice

Cut off a slice at stem end of peppers and reserve. Seed and wash shells. Parboil in salted water for 5 minutes. Drain. Heat butter in a frying pan and sauté onion until soft. Add garlic and minced meat, stirring with a fork. Mix in rice, 2 or 3 Tablespoons of chopped parsley, tomatoes, salt and pepper. Simmer for 5 minutes. Fill peppers and top with cut off slices. Place in a baking dish. Toss the crumbs with the melted butter and sprinkle over the top of the peppers. Pour the tomato juice in the baking dish around the peppers. Bake in a moderate, 350 degree, oven for about one hour.

Mrs. Kenneth A. Garrison

Spring Potatoes

1½ pounds small new potatoes
1½ Tablespoons chopped green
  onion
⅓ cup chopped cucumbers
2 Tablespoons sliced radishes
1 teaspoon salt
Pepper to taste
½ cup sour cream
2 Tablespoons chopped green
  pepper

Scrape potatoes and boil in lightly salted water until tender. Drain and keep warm. Combine the remaining ingredients and heat, but do not boil. Pour sauce over hot potatoes just before serving. Serves 4.

Mrs. Lionel V. Swift
Marietta, Georgia

Potato Quenelles

6 new potatoes
1 Tablespoon butter, melted
½ large onion, minced
1 Tablespoon minced parsley
2 eggs, separated
Salt and pepper to taste
Seasoned bread crumbs
Deep fat for frying

Boil the peeled potatoes. Mash and add the butter, onion, parsley and well beaten egg yolks. Season with salt and pepper. Roll into medium sized balls, set out to dry on paper towels *all day long!* When ready to fry, dip the balls into lightly beaten egg whites and roll in bread crumbs. Fry in deep hot fat but not too hot because the quenelles tend to fall apart. These are hard to make, but they are well worth the trouble it takes to do them. These have to be made with *small fresh new potatoes.* This recipe will not work if the potatoes are watery. Serves 4.

Mrs. C.D. Oakley, Jr.

Jalapeño Potatoes

4 medium red potatoes
1 small bell pepper, slivered
1 small can pimientos
Salt and pepper to taste
½ stick butter
1 Tablespoon flour
1 cup milk
½ roll garlic cheese
½ roll jalapeño cheese

Boil potatoes in the jackets in salted water until tender, but not falling apart. When cool enough to handle, peel, slice and layer in a buttered casserole with slivered bell pepper and pimiento. Salt and pepper each layer. Melt butter in a saucepan, add flour and stir until well blended. Gradually add milk, stirring constantly. Add cheeses which have been cubed or grated and cook until melted. Pour over the potatoes and bake at 350 degrees about 45 minutes to 1 hour. Serves 6 to 8. A whole roll of either cheese may be used but the combination is delicious.

Mashed Potatoes-Oak Ridge Style

8 medium potatoes
1/4 pound butter
1 wedge blue cheese
Half & Half
Salt and pepper to taste

Peel and boil potatoes until tender. Drain and place in a large bowl with butter and cheese. Whip with just enough Half and Half for potatoes to form peaks. Add salt and pepper to taste. *Variations:* Instead of using blue cheese, add grated onion, bacon or other flavors desired. Serves 10.

Allen Barham

Potatoes Stuffed with Crabmeat

10 medium baking potatoes
2 sticks butter
1 cup Half and Half
1 1/2 teaspoons salt
1 1/2 teaspoons white pepper
3/4 cup green onions and tops, chopped finely
2- 6 1/2 ounce cans crabmeat
1 cup mild cheese, grated

Scrub potatoes well and bake in a 450 degree oven until thoroughly done. Cut the potatoes lengthwise, scoop out the pulp and mash with butter, cream, salt and pepper. Mix thoroughly! Add onions and crabmeat. Fill the reserved shells with the mixture and top with the grated cheese. Bake at 350 degrees for 15 to 20 minutes or until the cheese is melted. This may be made ahead of time and baked later. These also freeze beautifully. Serves 10.

Mrs. Jerry Wolff

Special Twice Baked Potatoes

4 white Idaho potatoes
1 chopped onion
1 stick butter
1/8 teaspoon red pepper
2 teaspoons salt
1/4 teaspoon black pepper
1 cup shredded sharp cheese
Milk

Scrub potatoes, dry and pierce. Bake at 450 degrees for about 1 hour on rack without foil. Melt butter and sauté onion until clear and tender. Halve potatoes lengthwise. Scoop out the pulp leaving shells in tact. Mash potatoes; add red pepper, salt, black pepper, butter, onion and cheese. Beat in enough milk for fluffy consistency. Fill 6 to 8 of the shells. Pile high and score tops with a fork. Bake in hot oven until tops are lightly brown. Serves 6 to 8.

Mrs. W. M. McElroy, Jr.

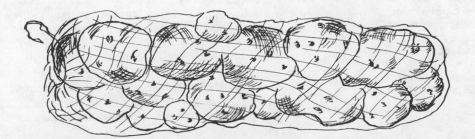

Grand Potatoes
A showy dish Men love it.

4 medium Irish potatoes, ground
Grated cheddar cheese
Salt and pepper to taste
Cream

In a flat buttered baking dish, layer the ingredients in the following order: potatoes, grated cheese, salt and pepper. Repeat ending with cheese. Pour enough cream over the layers to almost reach the top of the casserole. Do not fill this too full or it will boil over. Bake at 350 degrees until the casserole is hot, reduce the oven heat to 250 degrees. Bake for 3 hours. This is great with barbecued chicken or steak.

Mrs. Paul Lansing
New Orleans, Louisiana

Party Potatoes au Gratin
Great for freezer

6 cups cubed cooked potatoes
1 stick butter
¼ cup sliced green onions
½ cup chopped green pepper
¼ cup chopped pimiento, undrained
2 teaspoons salt
¼ teaspoon pepper
1 Tablespoon parsley flakes
1 teaspoon paprika
6 Tablespoons flour
4 cups of milk
½ pound shredded sharp cheese

In melted butter sauté onions, green pepper, and pimientos about 1 minute. Add seasonings and flour. Blend in milk, stirring until thickened. Add potatoes and 1 cup cheese. Stir until cheese is melted. Pour into a 3 quart, flat, casserole. Spread remaining cheese on top. Bake in a 350 degree oven 30 to 45 minutes or until bubbly. Makes 10 to 12 servings. Make ahead and refrigerate before baking. Freezes perfectly.

Mrs. Dixie White
New Orleans, Louisiana

Swiss Scalloped Potatoes

1½ cups shredded Swiss cheese
½ cup sliced green onions with tops
1 Tablespoon dill weed
2 Tablespoons butter
2 Tablespoons flour
1 teaspoon salt
1 cup milk
1 cup sour cream
6 to 7 cups cooked, peeled, thinly sliced potatoes, about 4 large potatoes
¼ cup fine dry bread crumbs
¼ cup butter, melted

In a small bowl, toss together one cup Swiss cheese, onions and dill; set aside. In a 1 quart saucepan, melt butter; stir in flour and salt. Gradually stir in milk. Cook over medium heat, stirring constantly until thickened. Cook two additional minutes. Remove from heat and stir in the sour cream. In a shallow, three-quart buttered baking dish, layer 1/3 of potatoes, 1/2 Swiss cheese mixture, and 1/2 of sour cream mixture. Repeat, making the top layer with last 1/3 of the potatoes. Combine 1/2 cup of Swiss cheese, bread crumbs and melted butter. Sprinkle over top of casserole. Bake in preheated oven at 350 degrees for 30 to 35 minutes. Serves 8 to 10. Three cups diced ham can be included in layering to make this a meat-vegetable dish.

Mrs. Don Phillips

Sweet Potato Shells
Beautiful for a buffet

5 oranges, unpeeled
¼ cup firmly packed brown sugar
½ cup brandy
¼ cup light cream
¼ cup melted butter
1 teaspoon salt
4 cups mashed cooked sweet
  potatoes
Marshmallows, optional

Grate peel from 1 orange. Halve remaining four oranges. Scoop out pulp to yield 2 cups of drained fruit. Sprinkle orange pulp with brown sugar and set aside. Heat brandy, cream, butter and salt together. Mix all ingredients and stuff into the orange shells. Top with marshmallows if desired. This may also be prepared in a casserole. Bake 350 degrees for 30 minutes.

Bourbon Sweet Potatoes

6 sweet potatoes
2 cups light brown sugar
1 stick butter
½ cup bourbon

Boil sweet potatoes in jackets until partially done. Peel and cut into large chunks. Put one layer of potatoes into a buttered casserole and cover with 1 cup of sugar and dot with 1/2 stick butter. Repeat. Pour bourbon over all and bake about 30 to 45 minutes at 350 degrees until brown and bubbly.

Mrs. Charles Searcy

Ambrosia Sweet Potato Bake
For a holiday feast

6 or 7 cups sliced sweet potatoes
  cooked or canned
½ lemon, sliced
½ orange, sliced
1 cup crushed pineapple
½ cup brown sugar
½ cup melted butter
½ teaspoon salt
½ cup shredded coconut
Maraschino cherries for garnish

Alternate potatoes with lemon and orange slices in a buttered 11 1/2 x 7 1/2 x 1 1/2 inch baking dish. Combine pineapple, sugar, butter, and salt. Pour over all, sprinkle with coconut, and garnish with cherries. Bake 30 minutes at 350 degrees. Serves 8 to 10.

Aunt E's Sweet Potatoes Supreme

1- 1 pound can Trappey's Yams
  in heavy syrup
1 stick butter
2 eggs
1½ cups sugar
3 Tablespoons flour
1 small can evaporated milk
1 teaspoon lemon extract
1 teaspoon vanilla

Cover and simmer potatoes in syrup at least 1 hour. Drain. Whip potatoes and butter until fluffy. Add remaining ingredients and continue whipping until fluffy again. Put in a greased 1 quart casserole; bake at 375 degrees for 1 hour. You may use an 8 inch pie plate with crust. If used as pie, whipped cream is a delicious topping.

Mrs. Elton Upshaw, Jr.
Mrs. Paul Dean

Sweet Potato Casserole
Simply delicious

3 cups sweet potatoes,
   about 4 good-sized ones
1/2 cup sugar
1/2 cup butter
2 eggs, beaten
1 teaspoon vanilla
1/3 cup milk

TOPPING:
1/3 cup melted butter
1 cup light brown sugar
1/2 cup flour
1 cup chopped pecans

Boil and mash potatoes. Mix in sugar, butter, eggs, vanilla and milk. Put in 13 x 9 inch baking dish. *Topping:* Melt butter and mix in remaining ingredients. Sprinkle on top of potato mixture. Bake 25 minutes at 350 degrees. Serves 10 to 12.

Mrs. C. D. Hamaker
Bastrop, Louisiana

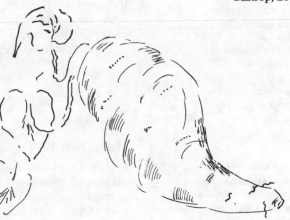

Rice O'Brien

1 cup white rice
2 cups rich chicken broth
1 teaspoon Lawry's seasoned salt
1/4 cup butter
1/2 cup slivered green pepper
1/2 cup chopped green onions,
     tops and all
3 Tablespoons diced pimiento

Cook rice in broth with seasoned salt. Drain. Melt butter, sauté vegetables and rice until onion and pepper are tender crisp. Toss in pimientos with a fork and serve.

Chili Rice

3 cups sour cream
1/2 cup chopped green sweet
   chilies
1/2 cup chopped green hot chilies
Salt and pepper to taste
3 cups cooked rice
3/4 pound Monterey Jack Cheese,
   cut into strips
1/2 cup grated Cheddar cheese

Mix sour cream, chilies, salt and pepper. Add cooked rice. Butter a 2 quart casserole. Place half of the rice mixture in the bottom of the dish, top with half of the Monterey Jack cheese. Repeat. Sprinkle the grated cheese on top. Bake at 350 degrees for about 25 minutes or until the cheese is melted and bubbly. Serves 6 to 8. More or less chilies may be used as desired. This is a wonderful make-ahead recipe and can be frozen.

Mrs. Bob Powell

Cajun Dirty Rice
Need we say more!

2 chicken livers
6 gizzards
1/2 cup chicken fat or oil
1/2 pound ground meat
1 large onion, chopped
1 bell pepper, chopped
3 ribs celery, chopped
2 cloves garlic, minced
1/4 teaspoon red pepper
1 to 2 teaspoons salt
2 bay leaves
1/2 teaspoon thyme
2 cups water
2 cups uncooked rice
4 green onions, chopped
1/4 cup parsley, chopped

Boil chicken livers and gizzards until done. Sauté ground meat in oil, breaking into small pieces, until brown. Add onion, bell pepper and celery to meat. Cook until vegetables are transparent but not brown. Put chopped chicken livers and gizzards through the blender. Add to the meat mixture with the seasonings and 2 cups of water. Simmer for 30 minutes, remove the bay leaves and set aside. Boil rice as usual and when done, mix with the heated dressing. Add chopped green onions and parsley. Remove from heat for 10 minutes before serving. This freezes well.

Mrs. Stan Mintz

Mae's Dirty Rice

1 package chicken necks
1 1/4 pounds chicken livers
3/4 pound chicken gizzards
1 1/2 cups minced green onions
2 white onions
6 large ribs celery
1 large bell pepper
1/2 cup fresh parsley
2 cups rice
1 stick butter
Salt
Pepper
Seasoned salt
Garlic powder, optional

Boil necks in salted water to make broth. Discard necks and reserve at least 2 1/2 cups of broth. Boil livers and gizzards. Drain. Mash the livers and set aside. Finely mince all vegetables and the gizzards. The more finely these ingredients are minced, the better the recipe. Do not grind the vegetables as they become too watery. Cook rice as usual. Saute all chopped vegetables in the butter until very soft. Mix rice and giblets into the sauteed vegetables. Cook and stir adding about 2 1/2 cups of reservéd broth to moisten mixture. Season with salt, pepper and optional garlic. Continue cooking and stirring about 30 minutes. Place in a baking dish and reheat when ready to serve. Definitely best when made the day before and refrigerated. A marvelous freezer dish also. Serves 12 to 15.

Mrs. Nat Troy

Rice Casserole

1 cup rice
1 cup parsley, finely chopped
1/2 pound sharp cheese, grated
1 medium onion, chopped
1 clove garlic, minced
2 cups milk
2 eggs
1/4 cup olive oil
1 teaspoon salt
1/2 teaspoon pepper

Partially cook rice. Rinse and drain. Add remaining ingredients and mix well. Check for seasonings. Bake 1 hour at 350 degrees in a buttered casserole. Serves 6 to 8.

Mrs. Morris Phillips

Green Rice

2 cups raw rice
2/3 cup bell pepper, chopped
1/3 cup parsley, minced
1 cup green onions and tops, minced
1/4 cup cooking oil
1 1/2 Tablespoons Worcestershire
1 teaspoon salt
1/4 teaspoon red pepper
4 cups bouillon or chicken stock

Mix all ingredients. Bake without stirring in a tightly covered 2 quart casserole for 45 minutes at 350 degrees or longer until the rice is no longer soupy. Remove the cover and toss with a fork as seasonings come to the top. This needs no gravy. May be frozen after baking. Serves 12.

Mrs. F.M. McGinn
Lafayette, Louisiana
Mrs. Doyle Hamilton

Mamie Eisenhower's Green Rice

1 cup raw rice
1/2 package frozen chopped spinach
1 cup finely chopped onion
2 Tablespoons butter
3/4 cup grated Parmesan cheese
Salt
Pepper

Cook rice in boiling, salted water. Cook spinach according to package directions and drain well. Sauté onions in butter. Reserve 3 Tablespoons of cheese for the topping. Layer in oven proof casserole: rice, spinach, onions, cheese and liberal amounts of salt and pepper. Repeat about three times or until all is used. Sprinkle the top of casserole with the reserved cheese. Bake 20 to 30 minutes at 350 degrees. Serves 6 to 8.

Mrs. James Altick

Sausage and Rice Royal

1/2 pound smoked link sausage
1 small onion, chopped
1 rib celery, chopped
1 small bell pepper, chopped
2 cups water
1 teaspoon salt
1 cup rice
1 green onion and top, chopped

Cut sausage into 1/2 inch rounds. Fry over low fire in skillet until slightly browned. Drain sausage on paper towels. Sauté onion, celery and bell pepper in the drippings until wilted. Add water and salt; bring to a boil for 2 minutes. Remove from fire; add sausage, raw rice and green onion. Pour all into a greased casserole with a tight fitting lid. Bake at 375 degrees for 30 minutes. Turn oven to 350 degrees for 45 minutes more. Serves 6 to 8.

Mrs. Lestar Martin

Chinese Style Rice

1 cup white long grain rice
1 large white onion
2 ribs celery
1 can water chestnuts
4 Tablespoons butter
Soy sauce to taste
Bell pepper
Green onion tops

This recipe does not take long to prepare and is good with duck or game. Wash and cook 1 cup of rice in salted water. Drain. Sauté chopped onion, finely chopped celery, and diced water chestnuts in butter. Stir in rice, soy sauce, salt and pepper to taste. Keep warm in a double boiler. Serve in a bowl garnished with lots of finely chopped green onion tops and thinly sliced bell pepper. Serves 6.

Mrs. John Jordan

Editor's note: To get a great flavor you will use a lot of soy sauce, perhaps 4 to 6 Tablespoons or more.

Wild Rice
Pretty to serve in a chafing dish as a game accompaniment

²/₃ pound sausage
1 minced small onion
4 green onions, minced
1-8 ounce can mushrooms, drained
8 ounces wild rice, precooked
¹/₃ cup cream
1¹/₃ cups chicken broth
Toasted almonds

Brown the sausage breaking with a fork to crumble. Stir in onions and mushrooms; sauté until soft. Add precooked wild rice with chicken broth. Simmer to reduce broth. Blend in cream and heat thoroughly. Sprinkle almonds on top and serve at once.

Wild Rice and Sausage Casserole

1 pound sausage
1 pound sliced mushrooms, drained
1 cup chopped onions
2 cups Uncle Ben's wild rice mix
¹/₃ cup toasted, slivered almonds

SAUCE:
¹/₄ cup flour
¹/₂ cup heavy cream
2¹/₂ cups condensed chicken broth
1 teaspoon pepper
Generous pinch of oregano, thyme, and marjoram

Sauté sausage, breaking into small pieces. Remove sausage. In drippings, sauté drained mushrooms and chopped onions. Return sausage to the skillet. Meanwhile, back at the range, in boiling salted water, cook washed rice for 10 to 12 minutes. Drain.
Sauce: Mix flour with cream until smooth. Add condensed chicken broth and cook until thick. Blend in seasonings. Combine all ingredients in a two quart casserole. Bake 25 to 30 minutes at 350 degrees. Sprinkle toasted almonds over top before serving. If made ahead, add more broth before baking. Serves 12. Delicious with game.

Mrs. Jim Geisler

Wild Rice and Shrimp

1 can cream of mushroom soup
2 Tablespoons chopped green
pepper
2 Tablespoons chopped onion
2 Tablespoons melted butter
1 Tablespoon lemon juice
2 cups cooked wild rice
½ teaspoon Worcestershire sauce
½ teaspoon dry mustard
¼ teaspoon pepper
½ cup cheese, cubed
½ pound uncooked shrimp,
peeled and deveined

Mix all of the ingredients together thoroughly. Pour into a greased 1 1/2 quart casserole and bake for 30 to 35 minutes at 375 degrees. Serves 8 to 10.

Mrs. Clark Boyce

Wild Rice and Mushroom Dressing

2 cups cooked wild rice
2 cups cooked white rice
4 strips bacon
1 medium onion, chopped
½ teaspoon thyme
1 bay leaf
2 Tablespoons finely minced
parsley
1 large can sliced mushrooms and
liquid
Salt and pepper to taste
¼ to ½ cup chicken broth

Cook rices according to package directions. Sauté bacon until crisp; remove and crumble. Sauté onion in bacon drippings until soft and yellow. Add remaining ingredients using enough chicken broth for a moist dressing. Season with salt and pepper. Bake 30 minutes at 325 degrees. Excellent with turkey, ducks and other game birds. Freezes well. Serves 8.

Mrs. Don Phillips

The trouble with spinach—

2 pounds fresh spinach
1 clove garlic, halved
Lawry's seasoned salt
1 strip bacon
1 Tablespoon butter
Cracked black pepper
Vinegar

—is overcooking. Wash the spinach leaves well. Shake slightly from the last rinse and put into a heavy skillet with a lid. Add the garlic, bacon, butter and a generous amount of seasoned salt to the skillet. Cover. Cook until sizzling; toss to distribute butter and seasonings. Recover and in 3 or 4 minutes test for doneness. It should be just tender, not overcooked. Remove from heat, toss with black pepper and 1 to 2 teaspoons of vinegar. Serve immediately. Sliced hard-boiled eggs are a delicious garnish.

Mrs. Don Irby

Spinach Nests

4 Tablespoons butter
2 packages frozen chopped
  spinach, thawed
3/4 cup Ricotta or cottage cheese
2 eggs, beaten
6 Tablespoons flour
3/4 cup Parmesan cheese
1/2 teaspoon salt
1/2 teaspoon pepper
Pinch of nutmeg
4 Tablespoons melted butter

Melt butter in a large stainless steel skillet. Add defrosted spinach and cook, stirring until the moisture has almost boiled out and the spinach begins to stick to the skillet. Add the Ricotta cheese, stirring until it blends. Transfer the contents to a large bowl and mix in eggs, flour, 1/4 cup of Parmesan, salt, pepper and nutmeg. Place in greased ramekins and top with remaining 1/2 cup Parmesan. Drizzle the melted butter over the top. Bake at 350 degrees until hot, about 20 to 30 minutes.

Mrs. Ed Seymour, Jr.

Spinach Casserole

2-10 ounce packages chopped
  spinach
1-6 ounce can mushroom
  crowns
6 Tablespoons butter
1 Tablespoon flour
1/2 cup milk
1/2 teaspoon salt
Pinch of dry mustard
Dash of red pepper
1 medium size can mushroom
  pieces
1-1 pound can artichoke bottoms

SOUR CREAM SAUCE:
1/2 cup sour cream
1/2 cup mayonnaise
2 Tablespoons lemon juice

Cook spinach according to directions, drain and mash. Sauté mushroom crowns in butter; remove and set aside. Add flour to melted butter and cook until bubbly. Blend in milk and stir until smooth. Add seasonings, mushroom pieces and spinach. Put artichokes on the bottom of a buttered casserole and cover with spinach mixture.
Sour Cream Sauce: Mix ingredients and pour over spinach. Arrange mushroom crowns over all. Heat through. Serves 6 to 8.

Mrs. Loretta Rivers

Spanakopeeta
Greek Spinach-Cheese Casserole

1 package chopped spinach,
  thawed
3 beaten eggs
6 Tablespoons flour
2 cups cottage cheese
2 cups Cheddar cheese, grated
1 teaspoon salt
Pepper to taste

Beat the eggs and flour until smooth. Mix the rest of the ingredients and check for seasonings. Bake uncovered in a 2 quart casserole for an hour at 350 degrees. Let stand a few minutes before serving. Serves 6 generously.

Mrs. Eugene Worthen

Mexican Spinach

4 Tablespoons butter
1/2 cup chopped onion
2 cups tomato puree
2 Tablespoons lemon juice
1 to 2 Tablespoons chili
  powder
1 pod garlic, minced
1 teaspoon salt
1/8 teaspoon pepper
1 package frozen spinach, thawed
1/2 cup grated cheese

Melt the butter and sauté the onions until golden. Add tomato purée, lemon juice and seasonings. Simmer for 5 minutes. Add spinach and pour into a 1 quart casserole. Top with cheese and bake for 20 minutes at 350 degrees. This recipe may be doubled or tripled. It may be frozen without the cheese on the top. Serves 6.

Mrs. Clark Boyce

Spinach Manade

4 boxes leaf spinach
12 small white boiling onions
2 teaspoons oregano
2 teaspoons basil
1 stick butter
1 cup grated sharp cheese
3 or 4 strips of bacon

Prepare spinach and onions separately by boiling in salted water. Drain. Season the spinach with 1 teaspoon each of the herbs and 1/2 stick of butter. Spread in a large flat casserole. Arrange the onions on top of the spinach and sprinkle with remaining herbs, salt and pepper. Dot generously with butter and cover with grated cheese. Top with bacon and bake in a 350 degree oven for 30 minutes or until bacon is crisp.

Mrs. H. A. Genung

Herbed Spinach Bake

1- 10 ounce package frozen
  spinach
1 cup cooked rice
1 cup shredded sharp American
  cheese
2 slightly beaten eggs
2 Tablespoons softened butter
1/3 cup milk
2 Tablespoons chopped onion
1/2 teaspoon Worcestershire sauce
1 teaspoon salt
1/4 teaspoon rosemary, crushed

Cook spinach according to directions and drain. Mix together with all other ingredients. Pour mixture into a 10 x 16 x 1 1/2 inch baking dish. Bake in a moderate oven, 350 degrees, about 25 minutes or until a knife inserted half way between center and edge comes out clean. Cut into squares.

Mrs. Jim Geisler

Spinach à la Sophia

4 boxes chopped spinach
1 stick butter
1 large onion, chopped
1 cup Half and Half
3 hard-boiled eggs, chopped
Chicken or shrimp, optional
2 cans mushroom soup
1/2 pound sharp cheese, grated
Paprika

Defrost the spinach and *drain well* to remove all moisture. Sauté the onion in butter. Combine the onion, spinach and cream in a casserole. Mix well and *do not stir again!* Place the chopped eggs over the spinach mixture and cover with the mushroom soup. Top with the grated cheese and sprinkle with paprika. Bake at 375 degrees for 40 minutes. Before serving, stir to mix all ingredients. Flavors mingle when this is prepared a day ahead. *Variation:* A delicious main dish casserole may be made by adding chicken or shrimp when you add the eggs.

Mrs. Edel Blanks, Jr.

Spinach Soufflé Mold
It doesn't fall!

3 packages frozen leaf spinach
1 large onion minced
4 Tablespoons butter
1 teaspoon salt
1/4 teaspoon garlic powder,
    optional
Pepper
1/2 teaspoon nutmeg
1 1/2 cups milk
3 Tablespoons butter
8 eggs, beaten, 7 if very large
1 cup bread crumbs
1 cup grated Swiss cheese

Thaw, drain, and squeeze spinach as dry as possible. Chop until almost puréed. In a large stainless steel or enameled pan cook onion in butter until tender and stir in the spinach. Add seasonings, cover and cook slowly about five minutes until spinach is done. Stir in milk and additional butter; add eggs slowly, stirring constantly. Blend in bread crumbs and cheese. Taste for seasoning. Butter a six-cup mold and line the bottom with wax paper. This may be refrigerated or frozen at this point. Bake in a hot water bath for 50 minutes or until knife inserted is clean at 325 degrees. If frozen, allow 1 1/2 hours. Unmold onto a warm serving platter and top with hollandaise or your favorite vegetable sauce. Serves 8.

Squash Casserole

12 medium yellow squash
1 bunch green onions, sliced
2 Tablespoons butter
1 can cream of celery soup
2 whole eggs
1/3 cup bread crumbs
1/4 teaspoon garlic powder
Pinch of basil
1 Tablespoon Worcestershire
1 teaspoon salt
Grated cheese
Bread or cracker crumbs
Butter

Cook squash in salted water until tender. Drain and break up, but do not mash. Brown green onions in butter and stir into the celery soup. Add eggs, bread crumbs and seasonings. Combine the soup mixture with the squash. Put into a buttered casserole and cover with the grated cheese and additional bread crumbs. Dot with butter. Cook at 375 degrees for 45 minutes. Serves 8 to 10.

Mrs. Floyd James
Ruston, Louisiana

Stuffed Squash

5 medium yellow squash
1 pound ground round
1/2 cup finely chopped onion
1 rib celery, finely chopped
1/4 cup Progresso Bread Crumbs
2 to 3 Tablespoons Parmesan
  cheese
Salt and pepper to taste
1-8 ounce can tomato sauce with
  mushrooms
Parmesan cheese

Boil squash in salted water until easily pierced with a fork. Cool, split lengthwise and scoop out pulp. Save the pulp. Sauté the meat with onions and celery. Add squash pulp, bread crumbs, 2 to 3 Tablespoons of Parmesan cheese and season to taste with salt and pepper. Stuff shells with the dressing. Put in an oven-proof dish. Pour tomato sauce over squash. Sprinkle with Parmesan cheese. Bake at 350 degrees about 35 to 40 minutes. This can be made early in the day. Good as a meat or vegetable.

Mrs. Leonard Bunch

Zucchini Parmesan

5 small zucchini squash, thinly
  sliced
3 Tablespoons butter
1/2 teaspoon salt
Dash of pepper
2 Tablespoons grated Parmesan
  cheese

Put zucchini, butter and seasonings in a skillet. Cover and cook slowly 8 to 10 minutes, less if you prefer "tender-crisp" texture. Uncover; cook, turning slices about 5 to 8 minutes more. Sprinkle with cheese and toss. Serves 4.

Mrs. Charles Womack

Savory Squash Casserole

1/2 cup butter
4 cups thinly sliced zucchini
4 cups thinly sliced yellow squash
1/2 cup red bottled barbecue sauce
1/2 cup soft bread crumbs
1/4 cup grated Parmesan cheese

In a large covered skillet sauté zucchini in 1/4 cup butter, stirring frequently, 7 to 10 minutes or until slices are transparent. Set aside. In the remaining butter, sauté yellow squash. Return the zucchini to the pan. Pour barbecue sauce over the vegetables and toss until coated. Heat and place in a shallow oven-proof dish. Sprinkle with bread crumbs and Parmesan cheese. Broil 5 inches from heat for 1 or 2 minutes until the crumbs are golden brown. Serves 6 to 8.

Cushaw

Cushaw
Cinnamon
Nutmeg
Sugar
Butter

Peel cushaw and boil in salted water until tender. Drain and mash. Season to taste with cinnamon, nutmeg, sugar and butter. Place in buttered casserole and heat until brown.

Mrs. Ed Seymour, Jr.

Skillet Tomatoes
Delicious for peak of the season—

4 large ripe firm tomatoes
1 teaspoon butter
1 to 2 teaspoons sugar
1 clove garlic, pressed
1 Tablespoon parsley, minced
1 Tablespoon vinegar
2 Tablespoons olive oil
1 teaspoon salt

Halve tomatoes. Melt butter in a skillet and place tomatoes cut side down. Fry for a few minutes until golden brown. Turn over, add seasonings, cover tightly and simmer until tender, 15 to 20 minutes. Great with a steak.

Mrs. Lionel V. Swift
Marietta, Georgia

Buffet Tomatoes
So pretty for a dinner party

12 tomatoes
2 packages frozen chopped
  spinach
2 large onions, chopped
1/4 cup parsley, chopped
6 ribs celery, chopped
1 large green pepper, chopped
4 carrots, chopped
6 Tablespoons butter, melted
1 1/2 cups seasoned bread crumbs
2/3 cup milk
2 eggs, beaten
Salt and pepper to taste
Parmesan cheese

Cut a thin slice from the top of tomatoes and scoop out seeds and pulp. Salt shells and invert to drain for 15 minutes. Cook spinach in salted water. Sauté the onions, celery, parsley, pepper and carrots in butter until onion is brown. Add drained spinach to vegetables. Stir in bread crumbs, milk and eggs. Salt and pepper to taste. Pack mixture in tomatoes and sprinkle with grated Parmesan cheese. Place in a buttered baking dish and bake at 400 degrees for 20 minutes. They are delicious and may be prepared the day before. Do try these! Serves 12.

Mrs. Jerry H. Wolff

Mushroom Stuffed Tomatoes

6 tomatoes
1 pint fresh mushrooms
2 Tablespoons butter
½ cup sour cream
2 egg yolks, beaten
¼ cup bread crumbs
1 teaspoon salt
Dash of pepper
Pinch of thyme
1 Tablespoon melted butter
3 Tablespoons bread crumbs

Cut stem end from tomatoes; scoop out pulp. Salt the insides of the shells and invert to drain. Mince the pulp; measure 1 cup and set aside. Sauté the mushrooms in butter until tender. Combine sour cream and egg yolks. Add to mushrooms with tomato pulp; mix well. Stir in 1/4 cup bread crumbs, salt, pepper and thyme. Cook and stir until mixture thickens and boils. Check for seasoning. Place tomato shells in 10 x 6 x 1 1/2 inch baking dish. Spoon mixture into tomatoes. Combine melted butter and 3 Tablespoons bread crumbs; sprinkle on top of the tomatoes. Bake in a 375 degree oven for 25 minutes. Serves 6.

Mrs. Lestar Martin

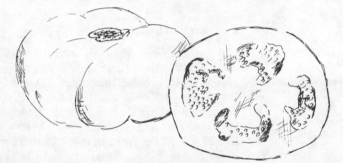

Tomato Timbales

8 medium tomatoes

BROCCOLI FILLING:
1 package frozen chopped broccoli
   or spinach
2 Tablespoons minced onion
¼ cup butter
½ cup flour
½ teaspoon sweet basil
¼ teaspoon nutmeg
½ cup chicken broth
½ cup sherry
½ teaspoon salt
⅛ teaspoon pepper

Chill 8 tomatoes until very cold. Dip into boiling water; remove skins. Slice 1/4 inch off the top and discard. Scoop out pulp; discard. Drain tomatoes thoroughly. Place each tomato in a greased 6 ounce custard cup. Salt inside of tomato. Stuff with broccoli filling. Arrange cups in a pan of hot water. Bake at 350 degrees for 25 minutes.

Broccoli Filling: Cook 1 package frozen chopped broccoli in boiling salted water until tender crisp, drain. Sauté minced onion in butter until soft. Remove from heat. Stir in flour, sweet basil and nutmeg. Cook paste, stirring, for 3 minutes. *Do Not Brown.* Gradually add chicken broth and sherry. Cook 3 minutes, stirring constantly. Add broccoli, salt and pepper. Check for seasoning. Cook until hot. If tomatoes are large, you will have to double broccoli filling. Serves 8. One cup chicken broth may be used, if desired, rather than 1/2 cup chicken broth and 1/2 cup sherry.

Mrs. Wesley Shafto, Jr.

Baked Tomato Rockefeller

12 thick slices of tomatoes
2 packages chopped spinach or
  2 packages creamed spinach
1 cup seasoned bread crumbs
1 cup plain bread crumbs
6 chopped green onions
6 eggs, slightly beaten
¾ cup melted butter
¼ cup Parmesan cheese
¼ teaspoon Worcestershire
½ teaspoon fresh garlic, minced
1 teaspoon salt
½ teaspoon black pepper
1 teaspoon thyme
1 teaspoon Accent
¼ teaspoon Tabasco

Cook spinach according to directions. Add remaining ingredients except sliced tomatoes. Arrange tomatoes in a single layer in a buttered baking dish. Mound spinach topping on the tomato slices. Bake at 350 degrees for about 15 minutes. The topping freezes well. Delicious with all meats, especially beef. The topping may be spread thinner to cover more tomato slices.

Mrs. Stan Mintz
Mrs. F. M. McGinn
Lafayette, Louisiana

Tomato Stack-Ups

3 large tomatoes
Salt
4 ounces Swiss cheese, shredded
1-10 ounce package chopped
  broccoli
¼ cup chopped green onion and
  tops

Cut tomatoes into slices 3/4 inch thick and sprinkle each lightly with salt. Set aside 2 Tablespoons of the cheese. Cook broccoli and drain. Combine remaining cheese and onion with broccoli. Place tomato slices on a baking sheet. Spoon the broccoli mixture on tomatoes and sprinkle with reserved cheese. Broil 7 to 8 inches from heat for 10 to 12 minutes or until cheese bubbles and tomato slices are hot. Serves 6.

Mrs. Lestar Martin

Stuffed Tomatoes with Rice
Tomatoes Yemistes me Rizi—Greek recipe

10 to 12 medium tomatoes
4 Tablespoons sugar
Salt
1¼ cups olive oil
1 large onion, chopped
1 cup rice, slightly parboiled
½ cup hot water
½ cup currants, optional
2 Tablespoons pine nuts, optional
2 Tablespoons chopped mint or
  parsley
Salt and pepper to taste
Dry bread crumbs

Wash tomatoes and cut a thin slice from the stem end. These must be saved and used later as lids. Scoop out the pulp, drain and chop. Sprinkle the insides with salt and 1 Tablespoon sugar; invert and drain. Heat 1/2 cup olive oil and sauté the onions until soft. Stir in the rice, and cook for a few minutes. Add half the tomato pulp, hot water, currants, pine nuts, mint or parsley, remaining sugar, salt and pepper. Cover and cook 10 minutes. Fill tomatoes with mixture, leaving room for the rice to swell; replace the lid and arrange in a shallow baking dish. Force the remaining pulp through a sieve and pour into the pan. Pour 1 Tablespoon oil over *each* tomato and sprinkle with bread crumbs. Bake in a 350 degree oven for 1 1/2 hours. Serve hot or cold.

Mrs. Kenneth A. Garrison

Tasty Turnips

4 medium turnips
1½ teaspoons sugar
1½ teaspoons salt
½ teaspoon pepper
½ to ¾ stick butter
Sugar to taste
Salt and pepper to taste

Peel and dice turnips. Boil with sugar, salt, and pepper until tender. Rinse and set aside in a colander to drain *thoroughly*. Melt butter; add to turnips and mash. Season to taste with more sugar, salt and pepper. Butter is the secret to this recipe!

Mrs. Jim Rivers

Turnip and Potato Casserole

2 cups quartered potatoes
2 cups quartered turnips
1 teaspoon salt
½ teaspoon pepper
4 Tablespoons butter
½ cup grated Cheddar cheese

Cook potatoes and turnips in boiling salted water until tender; drain. Mash, adding salt, pepper and butter. Spoon mixture into a 1 quart buttered casserole, top with cheese and bake at 300 degrees until cheese is melted, about 20 minutes. Serves 4 to 6.

Turnip and Cheese Bake
Cook those greens—but save the turnips for this!

1½ pounds turnips, pared and
  sliced, 4 cups
2 Tablespoons butter
2 Tablespoons flour
½ teaspoon salt
Pepper to taste
1 cup milk
½ cup shredded sharp cheese
Snipped parsley
Paprika

Cook turnips in boiling salted water until tender; drain. In a saucepan melt butter. Blend in flour, salt and a dash of pepper. Add milk; stir until thickened. Reduce heat, stir in cheese until melted. Combine cheese sauce and turnips; turn into a 1 quart casserole. Cover and bake in 350 degree oven for 15 to 20 minutes. Sprinkle with parsley and paprika. Serves 6.

Mrs. Jerry Wolff

Tarragon Vinaigrette

½ cup tarragon vinegar
¼ cup olive oil
4 teaspoons sugar
1 teaspoon tarragon

Combine all ingredients and shake well. Let stand. Use with fresh boiled artichokes or to marinate any fresh vegetable.

Nut Butter for Fresh Green Vegetables

½ stick butter
1 teaspoon grated onion
1 teaspoon lemon juice
½ teaspoon grated lemon peel
¼ cup chopped pecans or
    almonds

Melt butter. Add remaining ingredients. Mix well and pour over vegetable of your choice.

Seasoned Butter for Vegetables

8 Tablespoons butter
4 Tablespoons fresh bread crumbs
½ teaspoon dry mustard
2 Tablespoons parsley, chopped
Grated rind of 1 lemon
1 teaspoon of herbs if desired:
    oregano, thyme, chervil, etc.

Melt butter, add bread crumbs and dry mustard. Brown well. Add parsley, lemon rind and herb seasoning of your choice. Pour over or toss with any green vegetable. Yields about 1/2 cup.

Mock Hollandaise Sauce

1 stick butter, melted
2 egg yolks
Juice of 1 lemon
Tabasco
Cayenne pepper
Paprika
Salt

In a small deep bowl beat the egg yolks until thick and lemon colored. Add the melted butter slowly at first, as for mayonnaise. When you have used all of the butter, season this to your own taste. This can be used immediately for the best results, reheated over hot water or kept in the ice box.

Mrs. Ed Seymour, Jr.

Blender Hollandaise Sauce
Never Fails!

4 egg yolks
2½ Tablespoons lemon juice
½ teaspoon salt
Dash of red pepper
½ pound butter

Put egg yolks, lemon juice, salt and pepper in blender top and set in a pan of warm water for about 10 minutes. Heat butter slowly to the hot bubbly stage. Put egg yolk mixture into the blender and turn on, covered, then immediately uncover and add hot butter in a steady stream. Serve immediately. Makes 1 1/4 cups sauce. To keep, store in refrigerator. Good for vegetables and eggs.

Mrs. Harry L. Stone

Hollandaise Sauce

4 egg yolks
1½ Tablespoons lemon juice
½ pound butter, melted
¼ teaspoon salt
Red pepper to taste

In top of double boiler, beat egg yolks. Add lemon juice. Cook slowly on low heat. Do not allow water in the bottom of the pan to come to a boil. Add melted butter a little at a time, stirring constantly with a wooden spoon. Add salt and pepper. Cook until thickened. Makes 1 cup.

Mrs. John Kelso, Jr.

Mushroom Sauce

¼ cup butter
1 pound fresh or canned
mushrooms, sliced
⅓ cup butter
1 teaspoon onion juice
4 Tablespoons flour
Salt
Pepper
2 cups milk
1 Tablespoon vermouth or
sherry, optional

Sauté mushrooms in 1/4 cup butter. Lightly brown 1/3 cup butter, do not burn, and add onion juice, flour, salt and pepper and continue to make a medium brown roux. Slowly stir in milk and wine. Add mushrooms and continue to cook until thickened.

Cheesy Mornay Sauce
Good and Creamy

¼ pound butter
1 cup flour
4 cups milk
2 pounds Velveeta cheese, cubed
1 can beer

Melt butter, add flour and cook until bubbly. Add milk. Stir and cook until smooth. Bring to a boil for one minute. Put cheese into the sauce. Beat on medium speed for 15 minutes, adding beer a little at a time to the desired consistency. This sauce is very good served over sliced turkey, chicken, broccoli or cauliflower. Can be stored in the refrigerator for later use. Serves approximately 6 to 8.

Mrs. Dick Ethridge

A Great Mornay Sauce
Delicious with broccoli, spinach mold or asparagus tips

2 Tablespoons butter
2 Tablespoons flour
⅔ cup chicken stock
⅓ cup vermouth
¼ cup grated Swiss cheese
Salt
Pepper

Make a light roux of butter and flour. Combine chicken stock and vermouth. Slowly blend this mixture into the roux. Stir and cook until mixture thickens. Add cheese and continue stirring until completely melted. Season to taste.

Pineapple Soufflé

3 eggs
2½ cups crushed pineapple
2 Tablespoons sugar
3 Tablespoons flour
1½ Tablespoons butter, melted
1½ Tablespoons lemon juice
Pinch of salt

Beat eggs until light. Add remaining ingredients. Pour into a buttered baking dish and bake at 350 degrees for 45 minutes to 1 hour, or until the consistency of soft rice pudding. Serve with ham or fried chicken.

Mrs. Wesley Shafto, Jr.

Bananas on the Half Shell

6 bananas
¼ cup lemon juice or enough to sprinkle over bananas
6 Tablespoons brown sugar
Butter
¼ to ⅓ cup rum

Do not peel bananas but slit them in half. Place in a baking dish with cut side up. Sprinkle with lemon juice and brown sugar; dot with butter. Let set for half an hour. Pour rum over the bananas and put under broiler for 10 to 15 minutes. Baste once or twice and serve when bubbling hot as a meat accompaniment. Delicious with ham, Shrimp Creole, or any spicy entree.

Mrs. Stewart Meyers, Jr.
Oklahoma City, Oklahoma

Orange Spiced Peaches

1- 1 pound 13 ounce can peach halves
1 teaspoon whole cloves
6 inches of stick cinnamon
10 whole allspice
⅓ cup vinegar
½ cup sugar
1 orange, sliced

Drain peaches reserving 1/2 cup syrup. Put spices in a small piece of cheesecloth. In a saucepan, combine the reserved peach syrup, vinegar, sugar, orange slices, peaches and spice bag. Heat to boiling. Simmer, uncovered, 5 minutes. Cover and let cool to room temperature. Remove the spice bag. Serve peach halves on top of sliced oranges. Good served warm or cold.

Mrs. Henry Guerriero

Glazed Oranges

2 cups sugar
1 cup water
2 Tablespoons lemon juice
3 or 4 large seedless oranges

Combine sugar, water and lemon juice in a large skillet. Bring to a boil on low heat and simmer for 5 minutes. Wash oranges and cut into fairly thick unpeeled slices. Poach the orange slices gently in the syrup, turning at least once, until the skins of the oranges are transparent. Cool in the syrup, but drain just before serving. A flavor variation may be achieved by adding a few whole cloves or a small piece of dried ginger root to the syrup. Place a whole clove or a candied cranberry in the center of each slice, if desired.

Mrs. Elmer Neill, Jr.
Tallulah, Louisiana

Glazed Apple Rings

6 large firm apples
2 cups sugar
1½ cups water or cranberry juice
¼ cup lemon juice
2 pieces stick cinnamon, if desired
2 or 3 whole cloves, if desired

Wash and core apples; slice, unpeeled, into fairly thick slices. Place in large flat baking pan and cover with remaining ingredients which have been boiled together for 5 minutes. Bake apple slices at 275 to 300 degrees until apples are transparent, basting occasionally with syrup. These slices may be prepared in large quantities and frozen for later use. Pack into plastic containers with a double fold of waxed paper between the layers. They may also be served as dessert with vanilla ice cream or a boiled custard.

Mrs. Elmer Neill, Jr.
Tallulah, Louisiana

Lucy's Curried Fruit Bake
Yummy!

1- No. 2½ can Fruits for Salad
1 cup black pitted cherries
½ cup maraschino cherries
½ cup brown sugar
2 Tablespoons cornstarch
1 Tablespoon curry powder
2 bananas
½ cup butter, melted

Cut and drain fruit, except bananas, for several hours or overnight. Combine sugar, cornstarch and curry powder. Peel and cut bananas into salad size pieces. Mix with other fruit. Add melted butter to fruit, and sprinkle with sugar mixture. Mix fruit very lightly. Turn into a buttered casserole. Bake 40 minutes at 350 degrees. Serve hot with baked ham, chicken or any kind of meat. This recipe is easily doubled. Serves 8 to 10.

Camp Waldemar
by
Mrs. Doyle Hamilton

Hot Sherried Fruit Casserole

1 medium can sliced pineapple
1 medium can peach halves
1 medium can pear halves
1 medium can apricot halves, optional
1 jar apple rings

SAUCE:
1 stick butter
2 heaping Tablespoons flour
½ cup light brown sugar
1 cup sherry

Drain fruit and arrange in layers in a 2 quart casserole; place apple rings on top. Cook sauce in a double boiler until thick and smooth. Pour hot sauce over fruit. Cover and refrigerate overnight or several days. Bake uncovered at 350 degrees for 30 minutes, or until hot and bubbly. This recipe is easily doubled.

Mrs. R.L. Davis
Mrs. Claude Earnest

Hot Fruit Casserole
A delicious Thanksgiving treat with turkey or may be used for brunches

1-28 ounce can peach halves
1-28 ounce can peach slices
1-28 ounce can pear halves
1-15¼ ounce can pineapple chunks
1-1 pound, 1 ounce can apricot halves
1-1 pound, 1 ounce jar Kadota figs or figs packed in light syrup
1-1 pound can pitted dark cherries
2 cans slivered toasted almonds
3 to 4 bananas
Lemon juice
6 dozen almond macaroons
Brown sugar
Butter
⅓ cup banana liqueur or Cointreau

The day before, drain fruit *dry*. Crumble macaroons, but leave in small pieces; you do not want fine crumbs. The day of serving: slice bananas and sprinkle with lemon juice to keep them from turning brown. Mix all fruits together. Layer half the fruit and macaroons in a 2 quart casserole. Sprinkle liberally with brown sugar, almonds, and dot with butter. Repeat. Pour banana liqueur over top. Bake at 300 degrees for 20 to 30 minutes or until hot and bubbly. This amount will make enough to serve 20 people and will fill 2 casseroles. More liqueur may be needed. This recipe may be doubled for a large party or cut in half for family size. The macaroons may be purchased at a bakery and are about the size of a silver dollar. If you buy larger ones, cut down to 3 or 4 dozen macaroons.

Mrs. Saul Mintz

Roast

TYPES OF ROAST
Prime Rib
Sirloin Tip
Rump Roast
Eye of Round

INGREDIENTS
Salt and pepper to taste
Worcestershire sauce
Garlic
Chopped onions
Chopped celery
Chopped parsley
Chopped green onions

Rub the roast with a mixture of salt, pepper and Worcestershire sauce. Stick a few cloves of garlic into the roast. Put the oven on "broil" and cook the roast for a total cooking time of 20 minutes. Remove the roast and place a double handful of the vegetables on top. Replace the roast in the oven, uncovered, and reduce the oven heat to 350 degrees. Add 1/4 cup water. Let the total cooking time elapse. Cook the roast for 12 minutes per pound plus 12 minutes. If the roast is over 4 pounds, add 10 minutes; over 5 pounds add 15 minutes; very large roast such as 7 or 8 pounds, add 18 to 20 minutes.

Mrs. George M. Snellings, Jr.
"Cook with Marie Louise"

Traditional Yorkshire Pudding

The roast placed on the rack above the pudding is the traditional method of preparation, as was the cooking of the pudding in the pan with the roast. In Yorkshire, the pudding was served before the meat course as a rich pudding, but we find it delicious served with the roast as a starch. Serve the pudding in the dish in which it baked, cut into squares. It may also be made in muffin tins filled about 5/8 full.

2 eggs, at room temperature
1 cup milk
1 cup flour
Dash of salt
Drippings from prime rib roast

Have *milk* and *eggs* at room temperature. Beat eggs until fluffy, add milk and beat in flour and salt until light and bubbly. When roast is almost done, remove about 5 or 6 Tablespoons of drippings from the pan. Pour drippings in an 8 inch square pan and place in hot oven. Beat pudding again and pour immediately into hot drippings. Bake in a preheated 450 degree oven for 15 minutes. Reduce heat to 350 degrees and bake 10 minutes longer. During the last 10 minute baking period, remove roast, place on a rack above pudding, and let the meat juices drip from roast onto top of the pudding. You will have a puffy and well-browned pudding. Serve immediately as it will fall after about five minutes. Serves 4. Easily doubles.

Mrs. R.M. Troy

Note: Line oven with foil for easier clean up!

Rib Eye Roast—Pink in the Middle

8 to 9 pounds rib eye roast
Cracked black pepper
Salt

Rub the rib eye all over with pepper and place it in a shallow pan. Preheat the oven to 500 degrees. When the oven is hot, put the roast in the oven and close the door. *Do not* open the door for 2 hours and then the roast is ready to serve. The roast should be cooked 5 minutes a pound at 500 degrees and then the heat should be turned off. If the roast weighs 8 pounds you cook the roast 40 minutes and turn the oven off. From the time you start the roast until it is ready to slice the time is 2 hours. Pour part of the fat out of the pan and add some water and salt for a delicious natural gravy. The roast will be pink in the middle every time. You may want to cook your roast for 6 minutes per pound if you do not like it quite as pink.

McVae Oliver via Allen Barham

Stuffed Tenderloin

4 Tablespoons beef marrow or
  butter
2 green onions, finely chopped
1 can sliced mushrooms
1 clove garlic, pressed
4 to 5 sprigs of fresh parsley,
  chopped
1 whole fillet of beef
3 Tablespoons blue cheese
Melted butter

In the marrow, sauté the onion, mushrooms, garlic and parsley, Slit the tenderloin and add the vegetables. Spread the blue cheese over the stuffing. Close the slit with toothpick or with No. 8 thread. Brush the fillet with melted butter and broil on the barbeque pit until the desired degree of doneness is obtained. May also be oven broiled.

Mrs. Charles Cicero

Aunt Doris' Roast Burgundy

5 to 6 pound eye of round or top
  round roast
Smoked garlic salt, Safeway brand
Salt and pepper to taste
Cracked black pepper
Burgundy wine
Water

Sprinkle the roast with salt, pepper and garlic salt. Cover the roast thoroughly with cracked pepper so that every centimeter of the roast is covered. Take your fist and use it like a hammer and pound the seasonings into the roast. Place the roast in an uncovered Dutch oven and cook it for 1 hour at 350 degrees. For the next hour, at 15 minute intervals, pour 1/2 cup of Burgundy on the meat until half of the fifth of Burgundy is used. When you remove the meat from the oven, add 1/2 cup of water to the gravy which is ready for you to use. The total cooking time is two hours for a 6 pound roast. It will be black on the outside and red in the center. If you prefer very rare meat, cut down on the cooking time in the last 1/2 hour.

Mrs. Elton Upshaw, Jr.

Beef Wellington
A most elegant dinner

PASTRY:
3 cups flour
1 cup butter, room temperature
½ cup ice water, approximately

DUXELLES:
1 pound mushrooms, finely
   chopped
8 green onions and tops, finely
   chopped
1 clove garlic, finely minced
1 stick butter
¼ cup parsley, finely chopped
Pâté de foie gras

TENDERLOIN:
3 to 3½ pounds beef tenderloin
4 Tablespoons butter
½ cup Madeira wine

SAUCE:
1 cup beef broth
½ cup Madeira wine
1 Tablespoon cornstarch
Salt and pepper to taste
2 to 3 truffles, optional
1 egg yolk
Water

The Day Before: Prepare the pastry or you can make your own puff paste. It is fun, if you are so inclined. Refrigerate the pastry. *Duxelles:* Cook the mushrooms, onions and garlic in butter very slowly, stirring occasionally until all moisture has disappeared. The mixture should almost be a paste. Stir in the parsley and let the duxelle cool. Refrigerate overnight. The next day, before using, let it come to room temperature. *Morning of Serving Day:* Tie the end of the tenderloin under to make it a uniform size. Melt the butter in a pan large enough to hold the meat. Braise the meat on top of the stove, basting with Madeira, turning frequently, about 30 minutes. Remove the meat and cool, but *do not refrigerate.* *Sauce:* Pour the butter-Madeira basting mixture into a saucepan and add beef broth. Heat and add the cornstarch which has been dissolved in the Madeira. Stir over low heat until the sauce has thickened. Season to taste with salt and pepper. Add the chopped truffles if desired. *About one hour before serving:* Roll out the pastry to about 1/4 inch thick between sheets of waxed paper. This should be a rectangular shape large enough to envelope the tenderloin. Mix the pâté de foie gras with the duxelles and spread one side of the pastry, leaving a 1 inch strip uncovered on one edge and both ends. Center the tenderloin on the pastry and wrap the sides over, uncovered edge last. Tuck in the ends and seal with water. Put the tenderloin, seam side down, on a baking sheet. Slash or prick the dough in a pretty pattern or decorate it with fancy shapes cut from dough scraps. Brush the top with the egg yolk mixed with a little water. Bake for 40 minutes at 350 degrees or until the pastry is nicely browned. Pass the sauce. So much of the preparation is done ahead that this is not really difficult at all. It is quite impressive. Serves 8.

Mrs. Don Irby

Beef Bordelaise

3 pounds boneless sirloin strip,
  one piece
Pepper to taste
1/2 cup finely chopped green
  onions
2 Tablespoons flour
2 Tablespoons pan drippings
1 cup beef broth
1 cup dry red wine
1/2 teaspoon cornstarch
1 Tablespoon water
1 Tablespoon softened butter

Have the meat at room temperature. Preheat the oven to 500 degrees. Sprinkle the beef liberally with pepper. Place on a rack in a shallow roasting pan. Roast at 500 degrees for 20 minutes, reduce the heat to 400 degrees and roast for 15 minutes more for rare; 22 minutes for medium; and 25 for well done meat. For a strip weighing more, judge about 5 minutes more per pound for rare and etcetera. While the steak is cooking, chop the green onions. Drain off 2 Tablespoons drippings from the bottom of the pan and make a roux of the drippings and flour. Stir in the broth, add green onions and wine. Remove from the heat. When the steak is done, remove and keep warm. Drain off all but 1 Tablespoon fat and stir in the gravy mixture, scraping the pan. Boil 10 minutes until slightly reduced. Lower heat. Add cornstarch mixed with water, stirring a minute or two until slightly thickened. Remove from heat and blend in the butter. Place some of the sauce on a heated platter, place sirloin on top and slice. Serve the remaining sauce separately. Serves 6.

Sauerbraten

4 to 6 pounds beef, round or rump
Salt and pepper
1 1/2 Tablespoons pickling spice
1 onion, sliced
2 Tablespoons sugar
1 cup water
1 cup white vinegar
1/2 cup sugar
12 to 16 ginger snaps
1/4 cup hot water
1/2 cup raisins
Blanched almonds, optional

Place beef in a large glass or crockery container and sprinkle salt, pepper, pickling spices and sliced onion over meat. Add about 2 Tablespoons sugar to about 1 cup of water and 1 cup of vinegar. Cover. Let stand in the refrigerator for 4 to 5 days. Put meat in a large kettle to cook. Add all of the vinegar, water, spices, onion and cook covered until the meat is just barely tender. Take the meat out of the liquid. Cool liquid and strain to remove all of the spices and onion. Return the strained liquid to the heat in a large container. In a small iron skillet, caramelize 1/2 cup sugar and pour into the liquid. In a small bowl, put the ginger snaps and pour 1/4 cup hot water over them and stir until they are of a gravy consistency. Add this to the liquid and stir until smooth. Remove all the fat and skin from the cooked meat and cut into 2 inch slices. Add raisins to the liquid and cook about 5 minutes. Add the meat and cook in the gravy or liquid for about 30 to 40 minutes on a low heat. Almonds may be added. This should serve 8 to 10 people. Mashed potatoes or potato dumplings are very good with this meat.

Mrs. V. A. Wolff
St. Louis, Missouri

Sandy's Specials
A Delicious Po' boy Sandwich

Individual French bread loaves or
   rolls
1 top round roast

MARCHAND DE VIN SAUCE:
6 small green onions, diced
4 Tablespoons butter
¾ cup dry red wine
1 cup Franco-American
   brown gravy
Dash of lemon juice
2 large cans sliced mushrooms,
   drained

Brown rolls lightly and split in half. Cook roast according to your favorite method, rare or medium rare, but season with salt, pepper and bar-b-que seasoning. When roast is done, allow to cool and slice paper thin.

MARCHAND DE VIN SAUCE:
Sauté green onions in butter until soft. Add red wine and cook rapidly to reduce the liquid to one half its original volume. Add brown gravy and lemon juice. Add mushrooms. Pile a generous amount of sliced roast on bottom half of each loaf; spoon sauce on top of meat and cover with top half of loaf. Serve immediately. This is great with slaw and sliced dill pickles.

Nat Troy

Steak au Poivre

2 pounds sirloin steak
2 Tablespoons cracked black
   pepper, more if desired
½ cup butter
½ cup oil
¼ cup hot consommé
½ cup Madeira
½ cup parsley, finely chopped

Press cracked pepper into both sides of the meat. Use more pepper if necessary as the steak should be completely black from the pepper. Brown the steak quickly in butter and oil. Lower the heat and continue to cook until the desired degree of doneness is reached. Remove the steak and keep warm. Pour off the excess oil and stir in the hot consommé, Madeira and parsley. Check for seasonings as this may need salt. Heat the sauce and serve over the steak. Serves 4.

Steak Dianne

4- 10 ounce sirloin steaks, well
   trimmed and about 1 inch thick
Salt and pepper to taste
2 Tablespoons butter
8 green onions and tops, finely
   chopped or 1 cup finely
   chopped onion
16 fresh mushroom caps
2 teaspoons Worcestershire sauce
4 ounces Brandy
Watercress for garnishing

Salt and pepper the steaks to taste. Preheat the skillet of a chafing dish until it is hot enough to sizzle a drop of water. Add butter enough to prevent steaks from sticking. Brown the steaks quickly. Cook over medium heat, turning often, about 6 minutes, or until the desired degree of doneness is reached. Add the remaining ingredients. Cook for 2 minutes. To ignite, pull the pan to the edge of the flame and tilt slightly away from you or light it with a match. Slide the pan back and forth while blazing to blend the sauce well When the flame is about extinguished, remove the steaks to heated plates and spoon the sauce over the steaks. Garnish with watercress and serve with baked potatoes or wild rice. Serves 4.

Mrs. L. E. Hayden III

Marinated Steak

3 or 4 garlic pieces
½ bottle soy sauce
½ bottle concentrated lime juice
Accent to taste
3 inch thick top round steak
Black pepper
Salt

Squeeze garlic and mix all ingredients except steak and pepper in a shallow pan. Pepper the steak liberally and place in pan. Turn often and let stand several hours or overnight in the refrigerator. Charcoal broil the steak basting with remaining marinade until the desired degree of doneness is reached. Salt the steak after it is done. This is delicious with baked tomatoes.

Mrs. F. M. McGinn
Lafayette, Louisiana

Baked Steak

1 sirloin steak, 3 inches thick
½ teaspoon salt
¼ teaspoon pepper
1 garlic clove
1 cup Heinz catsup
3 Tablespoons Worcestershire
  sauce
½ cup butter
1 Tablespoon lemon juice
1 onion, thinly sliced

Place meat in a shallow pan and broil on one side only. Season the browned side with salt, pepper and garlic. Turn and season the raw side the same way. Melt the catsup, Worcestershire, butter and lemon juice in a small saucepan and pour over the raw side of the steak and top with onion. Bake uncovered at 350 degrees for 1 1/2 hours for medium doneness.

Mrs. Davis Bingham

Baked Steak with Spaghetti

2 to 2½ inch steak, sirloin
  or tenderloin
2 to 3 Tablespoons shortening
Salt and pepper
1 large sliced onion
1 to 2 tomatoes, sliced
1 bell pepper, sliced, optional
Bacon
SAUCE:
2 Tablespoons butter
1 cup sliced onions
1 cup diced celery
2 heaping Tablespoons flour
1 can tomato paste
1 can water
Salt and pepper to taste
1 can English peas, drained
1 can sliced mushrooms, drained
Cooked spaghetti
Pimiento stuffed olives

Melt shortening in a baking pan. Salt and pepper the steak and sear on both sides. You can do this on top of the stove; it need not be brown. Put a layer of onions, tomatoes, bell pepper and bacon strips. Bake in a 300 degree oven about 1 hour or until the steak is done. While steak is cooking, make the tomato sauce and keep warm. Melt the butter, glaze the celery and onions, add flour and brown. Add tomato paste and water. Season to taste. Cover and let simmer over low heat for 1/2 hour. The sauce is ready when the celery is tender. Add the peas and mushrooms. To serve, put meat on a platter. Top with alternating layers of sauce and spaghetti. Decorate with stuffed olives. Serves 8.

Mrs. James Greenbaum

Pepper Steak

2 pounds round steak
Salt
¼ teaspoon pepper
¼ cup flour
¼ cup cooking oil
1- 1 pound can tomatoes
1¾ cups water
1 Tablespoon beef stock base or
    bouillon cube
½ cup chopped onion
1 clove garlic, minced
1½ teaspoons Lea & Perrins
2 large green peppers, cut in
    strips

Cut steak into 1/2 inch strips and lightly salt. Mix 1/2 teaspoon salt and the pepper with 1/4 cup flour. Dredge meat and brown in hot oil. Set aside remaining seasoned flour. Drain tomatoes, reserving liquid. Add tomato liquid, water, beef stock base, onion and garlic to the meat in skillet. Cover and simmer 1 1/4 hours. Add green pepper strips, Lea and Perrins and simmer 5 minutes more. Finally, blend in tomatoes and reserved flour and simmer about 5 minutes. Delicious with noodles or rice. Serves 6.

Mrs. John Stephens
Metarie, Louisiana

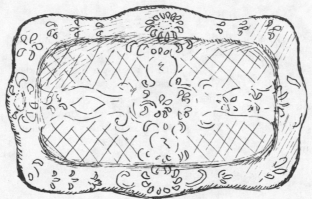

Stuffed Flank Steak Burgundy

2 pounds flank steak, tenderized
4 cups soft white bread crumbs
½ cup melted bacon fat
1 small onion, minced
1 teaspoon poultry seasoning
Salt and pepper, to taste
¼ cup water
Seasoned flour
½ stick butter
¼ cup water
1 can cream of mushroom soup
½ cup water
1 cup Burgundy

Place the steak out flat on a bread board. Combine the crumbs, fat, onion, poultry seasoning, salt, pepper and 1/4 cup water to make a dressing. Mix well. Spread the dressing on top of the steak and roll, jelly roll style. Secure with string or toothpicks. In a large electric skillet heat the butter. Roll the meat-roll in seasoned flour and brown on all sides. Add approximately 1/4 cup warm water, cover and lower heat. When meat is tender and ready to serve, add the soup, water and wine. Cook for 15 minutes until the soup is well blended. This makes an excellent gravy. This takes about two hours cooking, it may be necessary to add a little warm water to keep the meat from sticking to the bottom of the pan. Serves 6 generously.

Mrs. V. A. Wolff
St. Louis, Missouri

Boeuf Bourguignonne

THE ONIONS:
½ pound lean salt pork, cut into strips 1½ inches long and ¼ inch in diameter
1 quart water
1 Tablespoon butter
18 to 24 peeled white onions, about 1 inch in diameter

THE MUSHROOMS:
3 Tablespoons butter
¾ pound fresh mushrooms, sliced if large

THE BEEF:
3 pounds lean boneless beef rump, cut into 2 inch chunks
Bouquet garni made of 4 parsley sprigs and 1 bay leaf tied together
2 Tablespoons finely chopped shallots
¼ cup finely chopped carrots
3 Tablespoons flour
1 cup hot beef stock, fresh or canned
2 cups red Burgundy
1 Tablespoon tomato paste
1 teaspoon finely chopped garlic
1 teaspoon thyme
1 teaspoon salt
Cracked black pepper
2 Tablespoons parsley, finely chopped

Preheat the oven to 350 degrees. To remove the excess salt, the salt pork should be blanched by simmering it in 1 quart water for 5 minutes. Drain it on paper towels and pat dry. In a heavy skillet, melt the butter and brown the pork pieces until crisp and golden brown. Remove with a slotted spoon and set aside to drain on paper towels. In the rendered fat left in the skillet, brown onions lightly over moderately high heat, shaking the pan occasionally to roll them around and color them as evenly as possible. Transfer the onions to a shallow baking dish large enough to hold them in one layer. Sprinkle them with 3 Tablespoons of the pork fat. Reserve the rest of the fat. Bake the onions uncovered for 30 minutes or until they are barely tender when pierced with the tip of a sharp knife. Remove from the oven and set aside.

Melt the butter in an enameled or stainless steel skillet and when foam subsides, sauté the mushrooms for 2 or 3 minutes, tossing and turning them frequently until they are slightly soft. Add to the onions and set aside.

Preheat the oven to 350 degrees. Brown the meat on all sides in the rendered pork fat over moderately high heat. When brown, place in a heavy 4 to 6 quart flameproof casserole. When all of the meat is browned bury the bouquet garni in the meat in the casserole. Add the chopped shallots and carrots to the fat remaining in the skillet. Cook over low heat until they are lightly colored. Stir in the flour and cook, stirring constantly, until the flour begins to brown lightly. Remove from heat, let cool a minute and pour in the beef stock, beating vigorously with a wire whisk. Blend in the wine and tomato paste and bring to a boil, whisking constantly as the sauce thickens. Mix in garlic, thyme, sautéed pork strips, salt and pepper. Pour sauce over beef and toss gently to moisten. Add more wine or beef stock if sauce does not almost cover meat. Bake in lower oven, 2 to 3 hours until it is fork tender. Gently stir onion, mushrooms, and their cooking juices into the beef mixture in casserole. The dish may be prepared the day before and reheated before serving. To serve, remove bouquet garni, skim fat, and taste for seasonings. Sprinkle with parsley and serve from casserole.

Mrs. Wesley S. Shafto, Jr.

Beef Burgundy Casserole

3 pounds round steak, cubed
1 can tomatoes
5 carrots, halved or quartered
2 onions, quartered
1- 8 ounce can mushrooms,
   drained
2 ribs celery, chopped
1 can beef consommé
Salt and pepper to taste
1/2 cup Burgundy
Noodles
Parsley to garnish

Brown the meat in a skillet without fat. Place in a large casserole and add vegetables, consommé, Burgundy and seasonings. Cover and bake at 350 degrees for 2 hours. Serve with noodles and garnish the top with parsley. Serves 8.

Mrs. Lestar Martin

Beef Stroganoff

2 1/2 to 3 pounds of beef sirloin or
   tender from steak, cut into strips
   1/2 inch thick
Salt and pepper to taste
1 stick butter
4 to 6 green onions, white part
   only, chopped
5 Tablespoons flour
1 beef bouillon cube dissolved
   in 1 cup hot water
1 can beef consommé
1 teaspoon Dijon mustard
1-6 ounce can of mushrooms
1/3 cup sauterne wine
1/3 cup sour cream

Remove all fat from the beef. Cut the beef into 2 inch strips across the grain of the meat. Salt and pepper the strips. Heat the butter in a Dutch oven and brown the beef, turning frequently to brown evenly. Set the meat aside and cook the onions until they are transparent. Set the onions aside. Add the flour to the drippings and mix well. Return the meat and onions to the Dutch oven, add beef bouillon cube, water and beef consommé. Stir the mixture until it is smooth. Add mustard, cover and cook very slowly for 1 hour or until the meat is tender. Add the undrained mushrooms, sauterne and sour cream. Serve over rice or noodles. Serves 6.

Mrs. Fred Bennett

Stroganoff Piquant

2 pounds sirloin, cut in
   1/2 inch cubes
Salt and pepper to taste
1/3 cup flour
6 Tablespoons shortening
2 medium onions, chopped
2- 4 ounce cans sliced mushrooms,
   drained
2 cloves garlic, minced
1 can condensed tomato soup
1 soup can of water
2 Tablespoons Worcestershire
   sauce
1 teaspoon Tabasco
1 green pepper, chopped
1 cup sour cream

Cut the meat in cubes, salt and pepper and dredge in flour. Brown the meat in hot shortening and remove from the skillet. Sauté the onions, mushrooms and garlic until the onions are transparent. Discard the excess shortening. Combine the soup, water, sauces and green pepper. Put all of the ingredients back into the skillet and cover. Cook on high heat until hot and steaming. Reduce heat to simmer for 30 or 40 minutes until the meat is tender. Stir often adding more salt and pepper if needed. When the meat is tender add some of the hot mixture to the sour cream and then add all to the skillet mixture. Serve over steamed rice. This is good the second day warmed over. If freezing, do so before adding the sour cream. Serves 6.

Mrs. Morris Phillips

Company Hash

2 cups left over meat, sliced thin
  and in small strips
6 Tablespoons olive oil
6 Tablespoons flour
2 medium onions, finely chopped
1 cup celery, finely chopped
4 cloves garlic, minced
1-10 ounce can Franco-American
  beef gravy
1/2 teaspoon Worcestershire sauce
1 teaspoon Accent
1 teaspoon oregano
1/2 teaspoon thyme
1 bay leaf
1 Tablespoon soy sauce
1-3 ounce can mushrooms
1/2 cup Claret wine
4 carrots, sliced, parboiled
4 potatoes, chopped, parboiled
1/2 cup Claret

Make a dark roux using the oil and flour. Sauté the onion, celery and garlic until they are clear. Add the rest of the ingredients, including the meat, and simmer for 30 minutes. While the meat mixture is cooking, parboil carrots and potatoes. Add to the meat mixture after 30 minutes. Cook for 5 minutes and add the additional 1/2 cup Claret. Cook for 5 additional minutes. This may be served over rice, noodles or toast. Serves 6.

Ed Seymour, Jr.

Bess Burns' Hash

1 cup or more of leftover roast
  and its gravy
1/2 cup flour
1/4 cup bacon drippings
2 Tablespoons parsley flakes
1 small white onion, chopped
1/4 cup bell pepper, optional
2 teaspoons salt
1/2 teaspoon garlic salt
1/2 teaspoon pepper
1/2 teaspoon Lawry's seasoning
  salt

Slice the left over roast very fine and with the grain. Using a black iron skillet, brown the flour in the bacon drippings until the roux is dark. Add 2 cups of water and all of the seasonings. When this comes to a boil add the meat and leftover gravy. Simmer and cook for at least 2 hours, stirring occasionally. Serve over Uncle Ben's rice or just plain bread with a green salad. Serves a family of 6.

Mrs. Elton Upshaw, Jr.

Shish Kabobs

3½ pounds lean meat,
   cut in cubes
SAUCE:
1½ cups wine vinegar
1⅓ cups salad oil
1 teaspoon salt
1 teaspoon pepper
1 Tablespoon rosemary
1 Tablespoon thyme
1 teaspoon dry mustard
½ teaspoon Worcestershire sauce
2 cloves garlic, chopped
⅓ cup soy sauce
VEGETABLES:
12 small whole onions, parboiled
   if desired
12 large button mushrooms
2 bell peppers, cut into large
   pieces

Marinate the meat in a sauce made of the sauce ingredients overnight in the refrigerator. Place on skewers in the following order: meat, onion, mushroom, meat, bell pepper slice, meat, onion, mushroom, meat, bell pepper and meat. This will make approximately 6 to 8 kabobs. Cook on charcoal grill, turning frequently until the meat is done. Baste with the remaining marinade.

Mrs. Charles Hamaker

Pineapple-Beef Kabobs

3 pounds beef
1- 20 ounce can pineapple chunks
⅓ cup cider vinegar
⅓ cup catsup
½ cup brown sugar
1 teaspoon salt
1 teaspoon ginger
2 Tablespoons soy sauce
18 cherry tomatoes
1- 16 ounce can small white onions
2 large bell peppers, cubed

Cut beef in 1 1/2 inch cubes. Drain pineapple; add water to syrup to make 1 cup. Combine with cider vinegar, catsup, brown sugar, salt, ginger, and soy sauce. Pour over meat and marinate 2 to 4 hours in the refrigerator. Thread beef cubes on skewers, alternating with vegetables and pineapple. Place each filled skewer in aluminum foil and spoon on remaining marinade. Seal each foil bundle and place on the grill about 3 inches above very hot coals. Grill to desired doneness, turning several times.

Mrs. Henry Hinkle, Jr.

Note: Double marinade, thicken remaining liquid after preparing Kabobs for a delicious sauce.

Veal Birds

Veal cutlets, cut in approximately
5 by 2 inch pieces
Equal number thinly sliced ham
pieces
Chopped green onion
Chopped celery
Salt and pepper to taste
Garlic powder
Milk
Egg
Flour

Cover each veal piece with ham pieces, onion, celery and the seasonings Roll, pin-wheel fashion as tightly as possible. Secure with toothpicks, closing ends if possible. Chicken fry the veal birds by mixing egg with milk and dipping each bird in this, then in flour. The flour may be seasoned with salt and pepper if desired. Fry in an iron skillet with a minimum amount of grease until they are dark brown. If desired make a cream gravy as you would after any chicken-fried recipe. Add extra chopped celery and onion to the gravy and pour over the veal birds at serving time.

Mrs. O. P. Lowery, Jr.
Rayville, Louisiana

Veal Roll-Ups

1 package herb-seasoned stuffing
1 cup hot water
1/2 cup chopped carrots
1/4 cup snipped parsley
1/2 cup butter, melted
8 veal cutlets
1/4 cup flour
1/4 cup butter
1 cup chicken broth

OPTIONAL SAUCE:
1 can condensed Cheddar cheese
soup
1/3 cup milk
Worcestershire sauce
Red pepper

Combine the stuffing with hot water, carrots, parsley and butter. Spread about 3 Tablespoons of mixture on each cutlet, roll up jelly-roll fashion and secure with toothpicks. Coat each roll in flour and brown in butter. Arrange rolls in a 2 quart casserole, add the chicken broth, cover and bake in a 350 degree oven for 45 minutes. Extra stuffing may be placed in the dish and baked also. The optional cheese sauce may be ladled over each bird as it is served. To make the sauce, blend all of the sauce ingredients, seasoning to taste, and heat.

Mrs. James Altick

To rub the surface of veal roasts or cutlets generously with fat before cooking will produce a fine brown color and meat will remain very juicy.

Curried Veal

1 cup onion, chopped
2 medium cored, peeled, sliced
   apples
6 Tablespoons butter
3 cups diced cooked veal
1 Tablespoon curry powder
2 teaspoons flour
1 cup veal stock or chicken broth
3 Tablespoons lemon juice
Salt and pepper to taste
Steamed rice
Hard-boiled eggs, chopped
Chopped peanuts
Chutney

Sauté the onions and apples in 4 Tablespoons butter until tender. Remove and set aside. Add remaining 2 Tablespoons butter and brown the veal slightly. Remove from the pan and set aside. Add curry powder and flour. Blend in the veal stock or chicken broth slowly, stirring until smooth. Return onions, apples and meat; simmer until the flavors have blended. Add lemon juice, salt and pepper to the gravy. Serve over steamed rice with eggs, peanuts, Chutney or any of your favorite condiments.

Mrs. Stan Mintz

Veal Scaloppine in Wine

2 pounds veal steak
Salt and pepper to taste
Flour
6 Tablespoons safflower oil
6 Tablespoons butter
1 cup chicken broth, 2 bouillon
   cubes dissolved in 1 cup hot
   water may be substituted
½ cup dry white wine
Fresh parsley, chopped

Pound the veal steak until it is thin and cut it into 8 scallops. Salt and pepper the scallops lightly and dredge in flour. Use two skillets with 3 Tablespoons each of oil and butter in each skillet. Fry the veal quickly. Add chicken broth and half of the wine in equal parts to each skillet. Cover and simmer for 10 minutes. Transfer the meat to a platter. To the liquid left in one skillet add the remaining wine and pour over the meat. Garnish with fresh parsley. This may be prepared for later use by postponing simmering and reserving 1/4 cup of wine. Store in the refrigerator until just before serving time, then simmer and add the remaining wine.

Mrs. Joseph Cecil Brown, Jr.

Baked Brisket

2 onions, sliced
Paprika
Lawry's seasoned salt
1 brisket of beef
1 Pepsi-Cola, 10 to 12 ounces

Slice the onions, put in the bottom of a roaster. Sprinkle with paprika and Lawry's salt. Place the brisket, fat side up, on top of the onions and sprinkle more paprika and Lawry's salt on top. Place in a 450 to 500 degree oven uncovered for 1/2 hour. Pour a bottle of Pepsi over the roast and reduce the oven heat to 325 degrees. Cover with foil and bake until fork tender about 2 1/2 to 3 1/2 hours, depending on size of brisket. Baste occasionally adding more Pepsi if needed.

Mrs. Robert Deutsch
Shaker Heights, Ohio

Smoked Brisket

4 to 6 pounds whole brisket
1 bottle liquid smoke
Salt
Garlic salt
Celery salt
2 onions chopped
Worcestershire
6 ounce bottle Kraft Barbecue
    Sauce

Pour liquid smoke over whole brisket. Liberally season with salts and cover with chopped onion. Cover and refrigerate overnight. Before cooking, pour off the liquid smoke and douse with Worcestershire. Cover with foil and bake at 275 degrees for 5 hours. Uncover, pour the barbeque sauce over and bake 1 more hour. Delicious!! Great for other roasts also.

Mrs. Jim Folk
Mrs. Malcom Sevier
Tallulah, Louisiana

Beef Brisket and Soup

3 to 4 pounds boneless beef brisket
1 Tablespoon salt
1 bay leaf
1 teaspoon oregano
1 Tablespoon black pepper
1 Tablespoon parsley
1 Tablespoon Season-all
1/2 teaspoon thyme
1 teaspoon garlic salt
1 onion, chopped
1 clove garlic, cut
2 ribs celery, chopped

FOR SOUP:
Elbow macaroni
1 can tomato paste, optional

Cover the brisket with water that has been seasoned with the next 11 ingredients. Bring all to a rolling boil and cook, covered until it falls apart or is tender. Add more water if needed during the cooking time, 2 to 3 hours. *For soup:* remove the brisket and add the elbow macaroni to the water and 1 can of tomato paste if desired. Serve the brisket with a sauce of catsup and horseradish to taste.

Mrs. Tom Keller
Baton Rouge, Louisiana

Corned Beef

3 to 4 pounds corned beef brisket
  or round
1 onion, quartered
2 ribs celery and tops
1 bay leaf
1 teaspoon Lawry's seasoning salt
4 whole cloves
3 or 4 cloves garlic
1 carrot
1 teaspoon brown sugar
1 teaspoon cracked pepper

Cover meat with cold water and seasonings. Bring to a boil, reduce heat and simmer about 3 hours or until meat is tender. Test. When fork easily pierces as with a baked potato, the meat is done. Overcooking dries meat and prevents you from slicing well. For a boiled dinner, remove meat, and boil cabbage, new potatoes, carrots and such in the beef stock. After boiling, the brisket may also be rubbed with mustard and brown sugar and baked in the oven about 30 minutes at 350 degrees or until glazed.

Corned Beef Po' Boys

3 cups finely shredded cabbage
½ cup finely chopped celery
1 Tablespoon finely chopped
  onion
¼ cup mayonnaise
¼ teaspoon crushed red pepper
1 teaspoon salt
1 small clove garlic, pressed
4 small loaves French bread,
  Gigots
Soft butter
Mustard
½ pound cornbeef
Tomato slices
Lettuce leaves

An hour or two before serving, or longer, mix together cabbage, celery, onion, mayonnaise, red pepper, salt and garlic. Refrigerate. Just before serving: warm beef, spread bread with butter, and toast. Spread toast with mustard, layer cornbeef, cabbage, tomatoes and lettuce. Delicious!

PACKARD MOTOR LUNCHEON KIT 19

Morning Casserole

1½ pounds lean ground meat
2 medium onions, chopped
1 clove garlic, minced
1 cup finely chopped celery
1 chicken bouillon cube
1 teaspoon salt
1 teaspoon seasoned salt
½ teaspoon MSG
½ teaspoon bell pepper, finely
   chopped
½ teaspoon basil
1 can tomato soup
1- 3 ounce can chopped
   mushrooms, undrained
8 ounce package of noodles,
   cooked and drained
Parmesan cheese
Paprika

Brown the meat until the redness is gone. Add onions, garlic and celery, sautéing until soft. Add the remaining ingredients except noodles, Parmesan and paprika. Simmer for 15 minutes or more. To assemble place a layer of noodles in a greased shallow 3 quart casserole, top with half of the meat mixture and repeat the layers. Top heavily with Parmesan and sprinkle with paprika for color. Prepare ahead of time. Bake at 350 degrees for 30 minutes before serving.

New Casserole Dish

2 pounds ground meat
1 Tablespoon oil
2 bunches shallots, chopped
¼ cup celery, chopped
¼ cup parsley, chopped
½ cup bell pepper, chopped
1 medium can mushrooms
2 Tablespoons beef stock base
1 package Lawry's Brown Gravy
   Mix
2 cups water
10 ounce package of noodles
1 Tablespoon butter
1 large can ripe olives, sliced
1 pound Cheddar cheese, grated

Brown meat in oil, then add onions, celery, parsley, and bell pepper. Cook until softened. Mix beef stock base and gravy mix with water and add with the mushrooms to meat mixture. Cook noodles, drain, lightly butter and toss in sliced olives. Add grated cheese, reserving about 1 1/2 cups for topping. Mix all together and turn into two 2 quart casseroles. Top with cheese. Bake in a 350 degree oven until cheese is melted and the dish is heated through. Freezes and reheats beautifully.

Mrs. Roy Kelly

Cherokee Casserole
Great, well flavored, busy day meal

1 pound ground beef
¾ cup chopped onion
1½ teaspoons salt
Pepper to taste
½ bay leaf
⅛ teaspoon oregano
⅛ teaspoon thyme
⅛ teaspoon garlic powder
2 cups tomatoes
1 can mushroom soup
1 cup Minute Rice
6 stuffed olives, sliced
2 to 3 slices cheese, cut in strips

Brown the meat and add onions. Cook over medium heat until the onion is tender. Stir in the seasonings, tomatoes, soup, rice and half of the olives. Simmer for 5 minutes, stirring occasionally. Spoon into a baking dish and top with cheese strips. Broil until the cheese is melted and decorate the casserole with the remaining olive slices. Black olives may be substituted for the green olives. Serves 4 to 6.

Mrs. Jim Campbell

Beef Bonaparte

Salt
1 pound ground beef
1- 16 ounce can tomatoes, drained
　　and reserve juice
1- 8 ounce can tomato sauce
2 teaspoons garlic juice
2 teaspoons sugar
2 teaspoons salt
Cracked black pepper and
Tabasco to taste
1 bay leaf, optional
1- 5 ounce package of thin egg
　　noodles
1- 3 ounce package Philadelphia
　　cream cheese
6 green onions, chopped
1 recipe homemade sour cream or
　　1 cup commercial sour cream
1 cup grated Cheddar cheese
1 package Mozzarella cheese

Early in the day or the day before: Sprinkle the bottom of an iron skillet with salt and heat the skillet to brown the beef. When browned, drain well and add the tomatoes. Brown the tomatoes lightly and add the reserved juices and tomato sauce. Season with garlic juice, sugar, salt and Tabasco. Stir and lower heat to simmer. Sprinkle with cracked pepper, and add the bay leaf which has been snipped in two. Let simmer for 30 minutes. Cook the noodles, drain and combine with cream cheese, chopped green onions and sour cream. Grease a 9 x 12 inch glass baking dish and alternately layer noodle mixture, meat mixture and grated cheese. Bake covered in a 350 degree oven for 20 minutes. When you are ready to serve, reheat the casserole covered for 30 minutes or longer if it is very cold. Uncover and place strips of Mozzarella cheese across the top. Bake for 5 minutes longer or until the cheese has melted. Freezes well. Serves 6.

Mrs. John Pere

Cabbage Rolls

1/2 pound ground chuck or lamb
1/2 cup raw rice
1/2 to 3/4 teaspoon cinnamon
1 1/2 teaspoons salt
1/2 teaspoon pepper
1/2 can tomato paste
1 teaspoon lemon juice
1 whole cabbage

Mix meat, raw rice, cinnamon, salt, pepper and tomato paste together. Remove the leaves from a medium size cabbage and parboil the leaves until they are limp. Drain and cut the hard core from the leaves. Put enough meat mixture on each leaf to make a nice roll. Tuck the sides of the leaves in and roll into a long narrow roll. Put the rolls into a boiler lined with cabbage leaves, cover with water, add lemon juice and a small amount of tomato paste. Cover and cook on top of the stove until the rice is done, approximately 30 minutes. This same meat mixture may be used to stuff small yellow squash. Hollow out the squash and fill with the meat. Cook the same as the cabbage.

Mrs. M. A. Bodron

Stuffed Cabbage

BEEF MIXTURE:
1 large cabbage
1 pound ground beef
2 Tablespoons raw Minute Rice
4 heaping Tablespoons chopped
   onion
Salt and pepper to taste
1 cup water

SAUCE MIXTURE:
2- 1 pound cans tomatoes
1- 15 ounce can tomato sauce
Juice of 2 lemons
7 heaping Tablespoons brown
   sugar
1 can tomato paste with 3 cans
   of water

Put cabbage head in boiling water to soften the leaves. Separate the leaves and drain them well. Mix all the ingredients for meat mixture. Roll a small amount of meat into loose small balls. Put a ball into cabbage leaf and fold the leaf over the meat, sealing all 4 sides as for an envelope. Place the rolled leaf into an oblong baking pan. Continue rolling mixture in leaves until the mixture is all used. Place all of the rolled leaves as close together as possible. Shred large pieces of cabbage over this. Mix sauce ingredients well and pour over the cabbage mixture. Cover pan with foil and bake at 325 degrees for about 4 hours. Baste and add extra water if needed. This is better if it is made ahead.

Mrs. Harold Greenbaum
Hollywood, Florida

Grasse Hamburgers
When the teen-agers arrive

MEAT:
4 pounds ground meat
4 eggs
1 can tomato soup
1/2 cup catsup
1/4 cup Worcestershire sauce
Salt and pepper to taste

SAUCE:
4 cups chopped onions
2 cups chopped celery
1 large can tomato juice
1/2 cup Worcestershire sauce
1/4 cup mustard
Salt and pepper to taste

Mix the ingredients in the given order to the ground meat. Make into patties. Place the patties on a broiler pan and cook for 10 to 12 minutes at 350 degrees. Broil them for about 1 to 2 minutes until they are brown.

SAUCE:
Add the chopped onions and celery to tomato juice. Let it cook slowly for about 2 hours. Add the Worcestershire sauce, mustard and salt and pepper and cook for 15 additional minutes. Using an earthenware crock, place alternate layers of hamburgers and sauce until all of them are used. This can be placed in the refrigerator and used the next day. It may also be frozen. Makes approximately 20 to 25 patties. When serving, put a small amount of sauce on a bun instead of using the usual condiments.

From the files of William Grasse

Pork Roast

3 pound boneless pork roast
Salt and pepper
Sage
2 cloves garlic
Butter
1 onion, sliced
1 carrot, sliced
Sprig of parsley
1 bay leaf
1/2 cup strong beef stock,
    canned bouillon or use stock
    with a beef cube

Rub the roast with salt, pepper and sage and stud with slivers of one clove of garlic. Let the seasonings penetrate for several hours at room temperature or in the refrigerator overnight. Dry the meat. Trim the fat and render it in a Dutch oven or covered heavy casserole just large enough to hold the roast. Brown the roast well and remove it. Pour out the fat and add butter if the fat has burned. Sauté the vegetables and the other clove of garlic slowly about 5 minutes. Return the meat, add the bay leaf, cover and cook at 325 degrees about 2 hours or 30 minutes per pound. Baste the roast several times during roasting. Remove the meat. Add the stock and simmer several minutes. Skim off the fat and mash the vegetables into the juices. Boil rapidly to thicken, strain and serve.

Marinated Pork Roast
Must be started a day ahead . . .

1/2 cup soy sauce
1/2 cup dry sherry
2 cloves garlic
1 Tablespoon dry mustard
1 teaspoon ginger
1 teaspoon thyme
1-4 to 5 pound rolled pork roast
    or 1/4 to 1/2 of a pork loin roast

Make a marinade of the first six ingredients. Put the roast in a plastic bag and pour the marinade over it. Close the bag and refrigerate overnight. Remove the meat from the marinade. Roast uncovered at 325 degrees for 2 1/2 to 3 hours. Baste occasionally during the last hour of cooking with the reserved marinade. This tastes entirely different from the usual pork roast. Approximately 10 servings.

Mrs. Richard Blanchard

Sweet 'n Sour Pork Roast

1 boneless pork roast
Salt
Pepper
Rosemary

BASTING SAUCE:
1/4 cup honey
1/2 cup catsup
1/2 cup soy sauce
3 cloves of garlic, pressed

Salt and pepper the roast generously. Use rosemary sparingly. Bake the roast for 30 minutes per pound at 350 degrees. About 30 to 45 minutes before the roast is done, start basting frequently with the basting sauce. Serve extra sauce in a gravy boat. The sauce is also good on barbequed pork chops; be careful because it burns. The amount of people the recipe will served depends on the size of the roast. I always allow 1/2 pound per person.

Mrs. Ed Seymour, Jr.

Pork Tenders

Flour
6 to 8 pork tenderloins
1 cup chopped onion
1 clove garlic
1 teaspoon ground ginger
1 large can applesauce
1/2 cup "Haute" Sauterne
1/2 cup soy sauce

Flour and brown the pork tenders and onions, garlic and ginger. Mix the applesauce, sauterne and soy sauce. Pour over the tenderloins. Put all in a baking dish and cook for 1 hour at 350 degrees. Serves 4. Halved butterfly pork chops may be used if pork tenderloins are unavailable.

Mrs. Oliver Vreeland

Pork Chops with Fresh Tomatoes

6 pork chops, 1 inch thick
Salt
2 Tablespoons butter
1 cup minced onion
1 Tablespoon flour
1 1/2 cups chopped, peeled
   tomatoes
1/4 teaspoon salt
1/2 teaspoon pepper
1 teaspoon brown sugar
1/4 teaspoon thyme
1 large garlic clove, mashed
1 can beef broth and white wine to
   make 1 1/2 cups or all broth
1 to 2 Tablespoons tomato paste,
   Progresso or Contadina

Season the pork chops with salt. Trim the fat and render in a large covered skillet or casserole. Brown the chops, remove and set aside. Pour out the fat, add the butter and onions. Cover and cook slowly until the onions are quite limp. Stir in the flour and cook, stirring until smooth. Stir in the tomatoes and other seasonings except salt. Cover and cook slowly about 5 minutes. Stir in liquids, all bouillon may be used if desired, and simmer for a few minutes. Add salt, stir and check for seasonings. Add tomato paste to deepen the flavor and color. Arrange the chops in a skillet or casserole and baste with the sauce. This dish may be prepared ahead and final baking done before serving. Cover the skillet and simmer about 35 to 40 minutes or cover the casserole and bake at 325 degrees about 35 to 45 minutes. Skim the sauce and boil down to thicken. Check seasonings, pour over chops and serve. If canned tomatoes are used, drain and chop. Serves 6.

Mrs. Paul Reimer
Lawton, Oklahoma

Baked Pork Chops

3 Tablespoons salad oil
6 lean pork chops
1 1/2 cups raw rice
Salt to taste
6 large onion slices
6 lemon slices
6 Tablespoons chili sauce
3 cups tomato juice
1/2 teaspoon Tabasco

In a Dutch oven, heat the oil, add the pork chops and brown them on both sides. Remove the chops and drain off all but 4 Tablespoons of the fat. Stir in the raw rice, coating all the grains with fat. Arrange the chops on top and sprinkle with salt. Place a slice of onion, a slice of lemon and a spoonful of chili sauce on each chop. Add the tomato juice and Tabasco, cover closely and bake the chops until they are tender, about one hour in a 325 degree oven.

Mrs. Ben W. Sturdivant
Glendora, Mississippi

Family Pork Chops

Salt and pepper to taste
6 pork chops
Onion slices
3/4 cup catsup
1 cup water
2 Tablespoons Worcestershire
   sauce
2 Tablespoons vinegar
2 Tablespoons brown sugar
1 teaspoon paprika
1 teaspoon chili powder

Salt and pepper the chops and place them in a shallow baking dish. Top each chop with an onion slice. Make a sauce of the remaining ingredients and pour over the chops, cover and bake at 300 to 325 degrees for about 1 1/2 hours. Uncover for the last 20 minutes. Serves 6. The sauce can be made up and kept on hand. It may be used on chicken, meat loaf, spareribs or stew meat. The gravy is good on rice.

Mrs. Elvis Stout

Stuffed Pork Chops

6 pork chops, 2 inches thick,
   with pocket cut in side
1 small onion, chopped fine
6 green onions, tops and bottoms,
   chopped fine
1 rib celery, chopped fine
2 to 3 Tablespoons shortening
8 slices bread
15 soda crackers
2 eggs, beaten
1 Tablespoon chopped parsley
Salt and pepper to taste
Flour
Shortening

Sauté both types of onions and celery in shortening until tender. Soak bread and crackers in water. Squeeze out the excess water. Add bread and crackers to celery and onions. Cook over medium heat, stirring constantly until the mixture is firm but still moist, about 5 minutes. Remove from the stove and cool. Add the beaten eggs, parsley, salt and pepper to taste. Stuff the pockets of the pork chops with the dressing. Salt and pepper both sides of the chops and dredge them lightly in flour. Fry the chops in hot shortening until they are brown. Remove from the skillet. Drain off excess fat from the skillet and add water to make a thin gravy. Replace the chops in the gravy. Bake at 350 degrees uncovered until done, about one hour.

Mrs. Dave Aron

Charcoaled Pork Chops

6 loin pork chops, 1 to 1¼ inches
  thick
Lemon pepper marinade
Salt
MSG
Black pepper
Worcestershire sauce

Prepare charcoal fire using enough charcoal to provide a hot fire and sufficient to cook all six chops together. Allow chops to come to room temperature and sprinkle lemon pepper, salt, MSG, and black pepper to taste on each chop. Allow chops to set at room temperature for 30 to 40 minutes after seasoning. When all coals are red and flaming add several small pieces of presoaked hickory chips and put chops on hot fire. Sear chops well, about 1 1/2 to 2 minutes each side, then baste with Worcestershire. Close top of grill so smoke will choke out fire. Open every two minutes to turn chops and baste with Worcestershire. Total cooking time, including searing time, should be 11 to 12 minutes.

John Kelso, Jr.

Hong Kong Pork Chops

8 loin pork chops, 1 to 2 inches
  thick
Salt
Hot oil
1 onion, sliced
¼ cup soy sauce
¼ cup sherry or orange juice
2 Tablespoons lemon juice
1-4 ounce can sliced mushrooms
½ teaspoon ground ginger
¼ teaspoon garlic powder
½ green pepper, sliced
1 can water chestnuts, sliced
1 lemon, sliced
Steamed rice

Season the chops well with salt; brown on both sides in hot oil. Drain off the excess fat. Cover the chops with onion slices. Combine soy sauce, wine or orange juice, lemon juice, mushrooms, ginger and garlic powder. Pour over the chops. In a 11 x 17 x 2 inch pan bake the chops, covered, at 350 degrees for 40 minutes. Add green pepper, chestnuts and lemon slices; bake uncovered 15 minutes longer. Serve over steamed rice.

Mildred Swift

Smoked Ribs—Shafto Style

Five or six slabs of pork ribs
Salt
Pepper
Hickory wood chips
Favorite barbeque sauce

Have butcher remove top strip of back bone from ribs, if not already done. Build medium fire at one end of your charcoaler. Top with hickory chips. These may be soaked in water, if desired, to keep them from burning down so fast. Salt and pepper ribs well. Pork ribs have enough fat to baste themselves. Place at far end of grill, not over fire. Turn and swap around about every 1 1/2 hours. Total cooking time will be 4 to 6 hours. The longer the better for tenderness, but meat should not be falling off the bone. Charcoal and hickory may have to be added a little at a time during cooking period. After ribs are done, cut apart, and serve with your favorite sauce. Bobby's favorite sauce is Ted Allen's "Barbeque Sauce for Smoked Meats" found in the sauce section. If you have ribs left over, wrap well in foil and freeze, reheat over charcoal fire or in oven. Broilers are also delicious prepared this way. Rub with Wesson Oil, salt and pepper. Smoke 2 1/2 hours.

The Bobby Shaftos'

Spunky Spareribs

4 pounds spareribs
Salt and pepper to taste
1- 6 ounce can frozen orange
 juice, undiluted
1¹₂ teaspoons Worcestershire
 sauce
¹₂ teaspoon garlic salt
¹₈ teaspoon pepper

Salt and pepper the ribs and place them, meaty side down, in a shallow pan. Roast in 450 degree oven for 30 minutes. Drain off the fat, turn the ribs and roast 30 additional minutes. Drain again. Combine remaining ingredients and brush the mixture on the ribs. Reduce the oven heat to 350 degrees. Cover the ribs and roast for one hour or until tender, basting occasionally with the sauce. Very different. Serves 4.

Mrs. Jerry Wolff

Corn Dogs

⅔ cup corn meal
1 cup flour
1½ teaspoons baking powder
1 teaspoons salt
1 egg, slightly beaten
2 teaspoons oil
¾ cup milk
1 pound wieners, boiled first
Shortening for deep frying

Combine the dry ingredients. Combine the egg and oil with the milk. Add to the dry ingredients and mix well. Insert wooden skewers into the wieners; cover the wieners with the corn meal mixture and fry in deep shortening until golden brown. Serve with mustard or chili sauce. Children are very fond of these and like the leftover mixture dropped by a spoonful into hot shortening to make a "puff-ball."

Mrs. M. A. Bodron, Jr.

Jambalaya

¹₂ pound bacon
2 cooking spoons flour
2 cooking spoons oil or use the
 bacon drippings if desired
1 pound diced ham
¹₂ pound salt meat, chopped in
 1 to 2 inch pieces
1 pound pork sausage, chopped in
 1 to 2 inch pieces
4 medium onions, chopped
3 cloves garlic, minced
¹₂ can Rotel tomatoes
8 to 12 ounce jar of oysters and
 their juices
1 cup raw rice
2¹₂ cups water

Fry bacon and set aside. Make a roux of flour and oil until the roux is dark brown. In a separate skillet place the ham, bacon, salt meat, sausage, onions and garlic. Brown them about 15 to 20 minutes. Drain well and add to the roux. Add the tomatoes and oysters with oyster liquor. Simmer about 15 minutes and add rice and water. Cover and cook for 15 to 20 minutes or until the rice is cooked with the sauce. This is a meal in itself. The seasonings in the ingredients should be sufficient but additional seasonings can be added if you desire.

Mrs. Parker Parra
Houma, Louisiana

Ham

Smoked ham
Red and black pepper
4 ribs of celery
1 onion
2 bay leaves
1 Tablespoon pickling spice
Garlic
Brown sugar
Cloves

Soak plain smoked ham overnight in cold water or for at least 3 hours. Add fresh water in a pot large enough to hold the ham and all of the seasonings to taste. Simmer the ham: 12 pound ham for 3 hours, 16 pound ham for 4 hours. Let the ham cool off in the water. Remove the ham and skin it. Score the fat on the ham crossways and rub with brown sugar and stud it with cloves. Bake at 400 degrees for 30 minutes. This ham is hard to beat and it never dries out. It is always juicy.

Mrs. George M. Snellings, Jr.
"Cook with Marie Louise"

Villa Montaña Baked Ham

Villa Montaña's most popular dish . . . delicious and different!

Pre-cooked, boned ham; such as
    a Cure 81
Whole cloves
1½ cups brown sugar
2 cups pineapple juice
1 Tablespoon mustard
2 cups fresh or canned diced
    pineapple
Ginger ale

Stud the ham with cloves. Mix in blender the sugar, pineapple juice, diced pineapple and mustard. Place ham on a low rack in roasting pan. Pour pineapple mixture over ham. Bake for one hour at 350 degrees. Reduce heat to 300 degrees and cook for 2 hours. As juice in pan boils down, add ginger ale. *Baste ham every 15 minutes*, adding ginger ale as needed. Slice and cover with pan drippings before serving. I always remove ham from the rack for the last 30 minutes of cooking and place directly in the sauce in the bottom of the roasting pan. This, plus the frequent basting, gives that *extra* special flavor.

Ray Coté
Villa Montaña
Morelia, Mexico

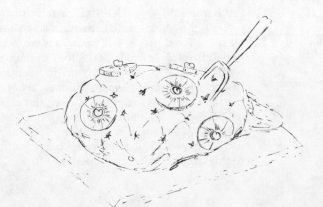

Savory Stuffed Ham

10 to 12 pound ham, boned
3 Tablespoons shortening
1 cup celery, minced
1 cup shallots, minced
1 cup bell pepper, minced
1/2 cup pecans, minced
1/2 cup parsley, minced
Salt to taste
Tabasco, to taste
Herbs of your choice: marjoram,
    cumin, savory and etc. to taste
1 package frozen chopped spinach,
    thawed and undrained
1 cup cooked rice
1/2 cup mushrooms, coarsely
    chopped
1 cup mixed dried fruit, coarsely
    chopped
2 or 3 cans beer
Cloves
Blackberry jelly
Dark brown sugar

Have the butcher bone the ham and take off the rind. Save for other seasoning purposes. In 3 Tablespoons shortening smother celery, shallots, bell pepper, pecans, parsley and seasonings. When the mixture is soft, but not brown, add the spinach and blend well, stirring constantly. Add cooked rice, mushrooms and chopped fruits, again stirring until the mixture is blended, but not cutting up the mushrooms. Set aside and reserve. Wipe ham well inside and out. Stuff dressing into cavity and tie securely in several places, if necessary. Place in a 350 degree oven, bake 20 minutes to a pound, planning so the ham will be done about 20 minutes before serving time. Pour a can of beer over the ham and baste from time to time with the mixture of beer and drippings. Add more beer gradually to make up for evaporation. Forty minutes before the ham is done take the pan from the oven, stud the fat side with cloves, brush with jelly and hand-pack the sugar over the top, to glaze the ham. Baste with the beer-jelly-fat drippings as before. Serve hot or cold. Strain fat from pan drippings before serving with the meat. Serves 20 to 25.

Mrs. Edel Blanks, Jr.

Smoked Ham

6 to 8 pound cooked ham,
    bone in
1 part brown sugar
1 part lemon juice
1 part dark molasses
2 cans diced or crushed
    pineapple, with juice

Smoke ham on grill away from coals for 1 to 1½ hours. Remove and wrap in foil to prevent drying. Return to grill, still on opposite end from coals for another 2 to 3 hours. Unwrap again and score top and sides deeply. Pour mixture of sugar, lemon juice and molasses over ham and rewrap. Return to grill for ½ hour. Ham should be cooked by this time. Unwrap once more and surround ham with pineapple, pouring juice over top. Wrap and heat 15 minutes, just enough for pineapple to heat but not wilt.

Robert Lewis Wroten

Stuffed Ham

This is a recipe of Mrs. Walter T. Williams, my grandmother, of Vicksburg, Mississippi. It is one of the specialities of the Old Southern Tea Room in Vicksburg which is a favorite tourist spot. It is noted for its typical old Southern dishes.

1 whole ham
Pineapple juice

DRESSING:
1 bell pepper, chopped
1 large onion, chopped
3 ribs celery, chopped
1/2 stick of butter
2 cups of bread crumbs
2 Tablespoons vinegar
1 Tablespoon sage
2 Tablespoons brown sugar
1 1/2 teaspoons dry mustard
1/2 teaspoon red pepper
1/2 teaspoon black pepper
1 teaspoon celery seed
2 eggs, beaten
Ham or beef broth

Pour pineapple juice over the ham and bake the ham at 325 to 350 degrees for 15 minutes per pound. The last 30 minutes remove the ham and stuff with the dressing. If you are using a ham with a bone in it, split the ham on the bottom side and carefully remove the bone. Fill the cavity with dressing; tie the ham together with cord. If you desire to, you may ice the outside of the ham with dressing. Bake for 30 minutes additional at 350 degrees. If you are using a party ham or a canned ham, bake the ham as usual and then ice the outside with the dressing and decorate it with pineapple and cherries. Make a roll of the dressing and bake it and the ham about 30 minutes at 350 degrees. Slice the dressing and serve with the ham. *Dressing:* Sauté the chopped vegetables in the butter until they are tender and combine with the bread crumbs. Add all of the seasonings. Add the beaten eggs and enough broth to make this a nice dressing consistency.

Mrs. Elmer Neill, Jr.
Tallulah, Louisiana

Patsy Hayes' Ham

2 raw ham steaks, 1 inch thick
3/4 cup dark brown sugar
Coleman's dry mustard
1 can sliced pineapple or 1 can
  fruit for salad

Cover the top side of ham slices with a scant amount of mustard and all of the brown sugar. Place one slice of the ham on a baking pan, sugared side up, and cover with half of the drained fruit. Put the second slice of ham on top of the first and top with the remaining fruit. Bake ham, covered, in a moderate oven, 350 degrees, for 1 1/2 to 2 hours. Slice across and serve. This may be eaten cold if desired. Always score the edges of the ham to prevent the ham from curling. Serves 6 to 8.

Mrs. C. D. Oakley, Sr.

Grilled Surprise Sandwiches

Butter
Roquefort cheese
Boiled ham
Swiss cheese
Whole wheat bread
1 egg mixed with 2 Tablespoons
  milk

To assemble the sandwiches: butter the bread, spread with Roquefort, top with boiled ham and then sliced Swiss cheese. Finish the sandwich with another slice of buttered bread. Dip the sandwich in the egg and milk mixture and grill in a buttered skillet until the sandwich is golden and the cheeses are melted.

Mrs. Ed Seymour, Jr.

Ham Loaf

1½ pound ground ham
1 pound ground lean pork
1 cup cracker meal or dried bread
  crumbs
1 cup milk
2 eggs beaten

SAUCE:
½ cup brown sugar
⅓ cup vinegar
1 cup water
Reese Ham Fruit Glaze

Preheat the oven to 325 degrees. Combine ham, pork, cracker meal, milk, eggs and mix well. Mold into a loaf in a 9 1/2 x 5 1/4 x 2 3/4 inch loaf pan. Mix the brown sugar, vinegar and water and pour over and around the loaf. Cover with heavy foil and bake at 325 degrees for 2 1/2 hours. When done, discard the liquid and glaze the ham loaf with Reese Ham Glaze and return the loaf to the oven for 10 to 15 more minutes. Serves 8 to 10. Good served hot with hot sherried fruit or good sliced cold for sandwiches.

Mrs. Claude B. Earnest

Ham Crêpes

12 Basic Crêpes
CREPES FILLING:
2½ Tablespoons butter
¾ teaspoon salt
2½ Tablespoons flour
2 cups cream
½ cup shredded Swiss cheese
1 Tablespoon chopped parsley
12 slices boiled ham

In a sauce pan, melt the butter and stir in the flour and salt. Add the cream gradually, stirring until smooth and thick. Add the cheese and stir until it is melted. Add the parsley, check the seasonings. On each crêpe, center a ham slice and spoon about 2 Tablespoons of sauce over the ham. Roll two ends of ham to center, fold the crêpes over the ham. Place crêpes in a baking pan, cover and bake for 15 minutes at 400 degrees. Serves 6.

Mrs. Lestar Martin

Ham Puffs

Delightful luncheon! Serve with a good green salad, white wine and a fruit dessert

6 Pepperidge Farm Puff Pastry Shells
4 Tablespoons butter
1 onion, finely chopped
1 bunch green onions, finely chopped
1½ cups cooked ham, finely chopped
½ cup Italian black olives, chopped
½ teaspoon salt
½ teaspoon Tabasco
¼ cup parsley
2 egg yolks
½ cup heavy cream
1 Tablespoon Madeira
Melted butter

Prepare pastry shells according to the package directions. Save the tops to be used later as caps Melt the butter and sauté the onions until golden. Add the ham and olives and mix well. Season with salt and Tabasco and add the parsley. Remove from heat and cool slightly. Mix the egg yolks and heavy cream. Stir into the ham mixture and cook over very low heat until thickened. Do not let it boil. Add the Madeira. Fill the pastry shells with the ham mixture and replace the tops, brush with melted butter and heat about 15 minutes at 350 degrees. Serves 6. All may be prepared the day before serving, but do not fill the shells until just before baking. Have shells at room temperature and reheat the filling until warm.

Mrs. Harold Woods, Jr.

Ham Casserole

2 Tablespoons butter
2-8 ounce cans Hunt's tomato sauce
1 clove garlic, minced
1 Tablespoon sugar
1 teaspoon each salt and pepper
2 pounds ham, cut into cubes
1-8 ounce package medium or wide noodles
8 ounces cream cheese, softened
1 cup sour cream
6 green onions and tops
1 cup grated sharp Cheddar cheese

Grease a 2 quart casserole. Heat butter in a large skillet. Stir in the tomato sauce, garlic, sugar, salt and pepper. Mix in the ham pieces. Cover and simmer for about 1 hour. Cook the noodles, drain and rinse. Beat the cream cheese until smooth and add the sour cream. Add the onions. Spoon the noodles into the casserole. Cover with the cream cheese mixture. Spoon the tomato and ham mixture over cream cheese mixture and top with grated cheese. For a drier casserole, put it in layers. Bake at 350 degrees for 30 minutes. Serves 6 to 8.

Mrs. Carrick Inabnett

Leg of Lamb

Leg of lamb
Salt and pepper
1 small jar prepared mustard
Flour
Garlic, optional
Worcestershire sauce

Generously salt and pepper lamb. Smear mustard all over the lamb. Sprinkle a little flour over all. Place a few pieces of garlic on the roast if desired. Sprinkle with Worcestershire. Roast uncovered at 325 degrees until it reaches the desired degree of doneness, about 20 minutes a pound for a pink roast. Remove from pan to a heated platter and make gravy by adding a little flour and water to the drippings in the pan. Season with additional salt and pepper.

Mrs. Dan Sartor

Butterfly Lamb

4 to 6 pounds leg of lamb
1/2 teaspoon oregano
1/2 teaspoon beau monde
1/4 teaspoon lemon peel
1/4 teaspoon garlic powder
1/2 teaspoon fine herbs
1/2 teaspoon season-all
1/2 teaspoon chopped parsley
1/2 bay leaf broken
1/4 cup olive oil

Have the butcher bone and butterfly the leg of lamb. Rub the seasonings into the meat and rub in the oil. Let the roast marinate at least one hour before broiling. Put it 8 inches from the heat for 40 minutes, fat side up; turn and cook for 10 minutes. Slice and serve.

Mrs. Clifford M. Strauss

Grilled Leg of Lamb with Onions

1- 4 to 6 pound leg of lamb
6 whole yellow onions
1 cup peanut oil
2 cups red wine
6 cloves garlic, cut in pieces
2 teaspoons cracked pepper
2 teaspoons salt
Juice of 1 lemon
1 teaspoon dried tarragon
1/2 teaspoon basil

Have butcher bone and butterfly the leg of lamb, removing as much fat and tendon as possible. Before marinating, pick over meat removing any fat the butcher might have missed. Leaving the meat flat, place in a pan large enough to accommodate the meat, marinade and whole onions. Peel medium size onions and prick all over with tine of fork to allow marinade absorption. Place in pan with the meat. Mix marinade ingredients and pour over the meat and onions. Marinate at least 6 hours in a cool place or overnight in the refrigerator. Turn often. Lamb should be grilled in the same manner as a steak. For rare, cook 8 minutes on each side. Onions should be placed on grill before meat in order to brown well. Serves 4 to 6.

Joe Baum
New York City, New York

267

Lamb with Brown Sauce

I had lamb at Ernie's in San Francisco and this is a sauce I have tried to copy from there.

Fillets of lamb, 2 inches thick
  or rolled out lamb chops
2 large cans Franco-American
  Mushroom Gravy
1 cup dry white or red wine
4 ounces brandy
1 Tablespoon A-1 steak sauce
1 teaspoon freshly ground pepper
1 teaspoon Tabasco, optional
1 or 2 large cans mushrooms
  stems and pieces
Salt to taste

Bake the lamb in the oven until it is pink in the middle and spoon lots of sauce over each serving. Allow two fillets per person. To make the sauce mix all of the remaining ingredients and heat. You may have to add a little more brandy or wine to get the taste that you really want. I have served this to people who did not like lamb and now they have changed their minds about eating the same.

Allen Barham

Spring Pan Broil

8 loin lamb chops, ¾ to 1 inch
  thick
1 Tablespoon oil
1 Tablespoon butter
1 large clove garlic, halved
Salt and pepper
½ stick butter
½ lemon, juiced
1 Tablespoon Worcestershire
2 Tablespoons minced parsley

Trim fat from chops. Heat oil and butter. Sauté garlic. Over medium high heat sear chops and broil turning often until juices run pink, not red, when pricked with a fork. Remove, salt and pepper. Salting after cooking helps retain juices. Pour off cooking fat. In hot skillet add lemon juice and scrape bottom of pan. Return to heat, add butter, Worcestershire and fresh parsley. Stir until blended. Serve with sautéed fresh mushrooms and tiny boiled and butter glazed onions. Serves 4.

Mrs. Don Irby

Lamb and Potato Hot Pot

6 round or shoulder lamb chops,
  as lean as possible
¼ cup flour
2 teaspoons salt
½ teaspoon pepper
3 Tablespoons butter
1- 10½ ounce can chicken broth
1 generous sprinkle garlic powder
¼ teaspoon marjoram
¼ teaspoon crushed bay leaf
3 teaspoons A-1 steak sauce
3 large onions, sliced
6 carrots, pared and sliced
3 to 4 large potatoes, pared and
  sliced

Trim the fat from the meat and melt in a large skillet. Salt meat, then mix flour, salt and pepper. Coat meat with the flour mixture and reserve the remaining flour. Brown the chops in butter and remove them from the skillet. If there is not 2 Tablespoons of fat remaining add 2 Tablespoons of butter. Stir in the remaining flour. Gradually add the stock and other seasonings, stirring until smooth. Simmer for a few minutes and remove from heat. In a 3 1/2 quart, buttered casserole, layer half of the onion slices and half of the carrots. Place the lamb on top and cover with half of the sliced potatoes and the remaining onions. Layer the rest of the potatoes and carrots. Bake for 1 1/2 hours at 350 degrees covered. Uncover and bake an additional 30 minutes.

Cannelloni

MEAT FILLING:
4 cloves garlic
1 medium onion
2 Tablespoons butter
2 Tablespoons olive oil
1 pound ground round steak
1 package chopped spinach, thawed
2 chicken livers, chopped
5 Tablespoons Parmesan cheese, grated
1/2 teaspoon oregano
Salt and pepper to taste
2 Tablespoons cream
2 eggs, beaten
1 package macaroni for stuffing, cooked and drained

CREAM SAUCE:
4 Tablespoons butter
4 Tablespoons flour
1 cup milk
1 cup heavy cream
1 teaspoon salt
White pepper to taste

TOMATO SAUCE:
2 Tablespoons olive oil
1 small onion
2- 1 pound cans Progresso tomatoes
3 Tablespoons tomato paste
1 teaspoon basil
1 teaspoon sugar
1/2 teaspoon salt
Black pepper to taste

3 Tablespoons Parmesan cheese, grated
Butter

Blend garlic and onion in the blender. You may use a small amount of water if you need it to make your blender work. Add the onions and garlic to heated butter and olive oil and cook for about five minutes. Add the meat and brown it well. Add the spinach and cook until almost all of the moisture is out of the spinach-meat mixture. Add the chopped chicken livers and seasonings. Cool and add eggs which have been beaten with cream. Stuff the macaroni tubes with the mixture.

Melt the butter and add flour. Cook for 2 minutes and add milk and cream, stirring constantly until thick. Add the seasonings.

Blend the onion in a blender and add to heated olive oil. You may have to use a small amount of water to make your blender work. Blend the tomatoes and add to the onion mixture. Add tomato paste and seasonings; simmer partially covered for 30 minutes.

To assemble the casserole, glaze the bottom of a pyrex dish with tomato sauce. Put in one layer all of the stuffed macaroni, cover with the cream sauce and top with tomato sauce. Sprinkle with about 3 Tablespoons Parmesan cheese and dot with butter. Cook in a 350 degree oven until bubbly and brown the top under the broiler. Serves 6 to 8.

Mrs. Ed Seymour, Jr.

Sicilian Moussaka

1 pound ground lamb
5 Tablespoons olive oil
1 large eggplant, unpeeled and
    sliced into ¼ inch rounds
1 large onion, thinly sliced
1 large green pepper, sliced
2 cups cooked tomatoes
2 teaspoons oregano
1 teaspoon lemon pepper
2 teaspoons salt
4 eggs, slightly beaten

Preheat the oven to 350 degrees. Sauté the lamb in 1 Tablespoon of oil until it is no longer pink. Beginning with the eggplant, arrange all ingredients, except the eggs, in alternate layers in a 2 quart casserole. Sprinkle each layer with some of the seasonings and drizzle a little olive oil over it. Pour the eggs over the mixture. Bake in the oven for 1 hour.

Mrs. Michael Brown
Lake Providence, Louisiana

Near-East Lamb Stew

2 Tablespoons flour
1 Tablespoon seasoned salt
Seasoned pepper
4 pounds lamb stew meat
¼ cup salad oil
2 medium onions, chopped
2 cloves garlic, minced
½ teaspoon thyme
1 cup water
4 medium tomatoes, cut into
    wedges
2 green peppers, cut into squares
1 medium eggplant, cut into 1 inch
    chunks
1½ teaspoons seasoned salt

On waxed paper, combine flour with salt and pepper. Coat the lamb and set aside. In a Dutch oven brown the lamb in hot oil. Add the onions and garlic and brown a few minutes longer. Sprinkle with thyme and add 1 cup water. Simmer covered for 1 1/2 hours until lamb is almost tender. Stir occasionally. If necessary, add a little more water during cooking. Add tomatoes, green peppers and eggplant; sprinkle with seasoned salt and cook 15 minutes longer or until the vegetables are tender. Serves 6.

Mrs. T. M. Sayre
Rayville, Louisiana

Lamb Shish Kabobs

2 pounds boneless lamb
¼ cup fresh lemon juice
½ cup good olive oil
1 teaspoon salt
½ teaspoon oregano
1 large onion, sliced
3 cloves garlic, pressed
2 bunches finely chopped parsley
10 to 15 large bay leaves
Cherry tomatoes
Lemon wedges
Boiled onions
Bell pepper, cut in chunks

Trim all fat from lamb and cut in 2 inch cubes. In a large bowl, big enough to hold lamb, beat lemon juice, olive oil, salt and oregano. Add the onions, garlic, parsley, bay leaves and lamb. Toss thoroughly with your hands. Marinate at room temperature 6 hours or overnight in the refrigerator. String lamb on 4 skewers alternating with tomatoes, lemon wedges, onions and bell pepper chunks. Grill kabobs 3 inches from heat over white coals on the grill, or in the oven broiler set at the highest point. Grill 10 minutes, turning several times. Lamb should be pink in the middle. Serves 4.

Lasagne

1 clove garlic, minced
1 medium onion, chopped
1/2 cup celery, chopped
1/2 bell pepper, chopped
1 1/2 pounds ground meat
Olive oil
1 can tomato paste
2 tomato paste cans water
1 large can tomatoes
4 teaspoons oregano
2 teaspoons basil
1/2 teaspoon salt
Pepper to taste
1/2 teaspoon sugar
3/4 package Lasagne noodles,
  cooked and drained
2 cartons sour cream
3- 8 ounce packages Mozzarella
  cheese

Brown garlic, onion, celery, green pepper and meat in olive oil. Add tomato paste, water, tomatoes, seasonings and sugar. Simmer for 2 to 3 hours. Layer in a large baking dish as follows: noodles, sour cream, sauce and Mozzarella. Repeat to make two layers. Bake at 350 degrees for 45 minutes. Serves 8. This freezes well. If you desire, the sauce may be made a day before serving and refrigerated.

Mrs. George Dean

Peppy Lasagne

1 pound bulk Italian sausage
1/2 cup onion, chopped
1/2 cup celery, chopped
1/2 cup carrots, chopped
1- 16 ounce can tomatoes
1- 6 ounce can tomato paste
1 teaspoon salt
1/2 teaspoon oregano
1/4 teaspoon pepper
10 ounces Lasagne noodles
3 cups Ricotta cheese
1 cup Parmesan cheese, grated
2 beaten eggs
2 Tablespoons parsley
1/4 teaspoon pepper
16 ounces Mozzarella cheese,
  sliced

In skillet, cook sausage, onion, celery and carrots until meat is lightly browned. Drain off excess fat. Stir in tomatoes, tomato paste, salt, oregano, and the first 1/4 teaspoon of pepper. Simmer, uncovered, 30 minutes, stirring occasionally. Cook lasagne according to package directions. Combine Ricotta, Parmesan, eggs, parsley, and the remaining pepper. Place half the noodles in a greased 13 1/2 x 8 3/4 x 1 3/4 inch baking dish. Spread with half the cheese filling, half the Mozzarella and half the meat sauce. Repeat layers. Bake, uncovered, in a 375 degree oven for 30 minutes. Let stand 10 to 15 minutes before serving. Cut into squares to serve. Serves 10 to 12.

Note: A mixture of ground chuck and pork sausage may be substituted if desired.

The key to good "pasta" is to immerse them so gradually into boiling water as not to disturb the boiling point. One half pound of pasta calls for about 2 quarts of water seasoned with 2 teaspoons of salt and a little oil. The boiling point is maintained throughout until the pasta is done.

"What is done?" This is a matter of taste. Overcooking should be avoided, especially if it is to be reheated in sauce. When done: drain in a strainer and rinse with cold water. Reheat over hot water.

Eggplant Parmegiana with Meat

SAUCE:
2 Tablespoons olive oil
1 medium onion, chopped
2 cloves garlic, pressed
1½ pounds ground round steak
2 teaspoons salt
1- 1 pound can Progresso
    tomatoes
1- 6 ounce can tomato paste
2 teaspoons oregano
1 teaspoon basil
¼ teaspoon pepper
1 Tablespoon brown sugar
1 cup chicken stock or 1 teaspoon
    Spice Island Chicken Stock base
    to 1 cup hot water

EGGPLANT:
2 medium eggplants, slender
    in shape
2 eggs slightly beaten
1 cup Progresso bread crumbs
½ cup olive oil
1 heaping cup Parmesan cheese
½ pound Mozzarella cheese,
    sliced or grated

Sauté the onion, garlic, salt and meat in olive oil until the meat is no longer pink. Add the remaining ingredients and simmer, uncovered, for 30 to 40 minutes until most of the juice is absorbed but not dry.

While the sauce is simmering, peel and slice the eggplant into 1/2 to 3/4 inch slices, depending on the size of the eggplant. The eggplant is cut to make a single layer in the bottom of a large oblong pyrex casserole. Dip the eggplant in salted ice water, pat dry, salt again and let drain on paper towels for 15 to 20 minutes. Beat the eggs slightly, dip the eggplant slices in egg, bread crumbs and brown in olive oil. Drain. Arrange the eggplant slices in a single layer in a casserole, top with sauce, then Parmesan cheese and Mozzarella. Bake at 350 degrees for 30 minutes. Serves 6 to 8. This may be prepared early in the day, refrigerated and baked before serving. The sauce also makes a good spaghetti sauce and freezes well.

Mrs. Don Irby

Baked Manicotti

Salsa di Pomodori
1-8 ounce box manicotti
    shells

FILLING:
2 pounds Ricotta cheese
1-8 ounce package Mozzarella
    cheese, grated
⅓ cup Parmesan cheese
2 eggs
1 Tablespoon parsley, chopped
1 teaspoon salt
¼ teaspoon pepper

2 Tablespoons Parmesan cheese,
    grated

Make Salsa di Pomodori
Boil manicotti shells according to package directions. Set aside.

In a large bowl, combine Ricotta, Mozzarella, ⅓ cup Parmesan, eggs, the chopped parsley, salt and pepper; beat with a wooden spoon until well blended.

Stuff each shell with the cheese mixture. Spoon some sauce in the bottom of a large baking dish. Place shells in a single layer. Cover with remaining sauce; sprinkle with Parmesan cheese. Bake, uncovered, 30 minutes at 350 degrees until bubbly. Serves 8.

Mock Ravioli

MEAT SAUCE:
2 pounds ground meat
2 onions, chopped
1 clove garlic, chopped
1- 10$^1\!/_2$ ounce can El Chico Hot
　　Sauce
1 can tomato sauce
1$^1\!/_2$ cups water
$^1\!/_2$ cup mushrooms
$^1\!/_2$ teaspoon Italian herbs
Salt and pepper to taste

VEGETABLE LAYER:
$^1\!/_2$ cup salad oil
1 package frozen chopped spinach,
　　cooked and drained
1 cup bread crumbs
$^1\!/_2$ cup chopped parsley
1 garlic clove, minced
1 scant teaspoon sage
1 teaspoon salt
4 eggs, beaten

PASTA:
1 pound butterfly or bow
　　macaroni
$^1\!/_2$ cup grated cheese

Brown meat, onions and garlic. Add the rest of the ingredients and simmer for about 2 hours.

Mix all of the vegetable ingredients well.

Cook the macaroni according to package directions and drain. Place a layer of cooled pasta in an oiled casserole, then a layer of spinach mixture, then meat. Repeat for 3 layers ending with pasta. Top with grated cheese. Bake 40 minutes at 350 degrees. Serves 8 to 10.

Mrs. Eugene Worthen

Salsa di Pomodori
"Tomato Sauce"

$^1\!/_4$ cup olive oil
1 cup minced onion
1 clove garlic, crushed
1-2 pound, 3 ounce can Italian
　　tomatoes, undrained
1 can tomato paste
2 sprigs parsley
1 Tablespoon salt
2 teaspoons sugar
1 teaspoon oregano
$^1\!/_2$ teaspoon basil
$^1\!/_4$ teaspoon pepper
1$^1\!/_2$ cups water

In hot oil, sauté onion and garlic until golden brown. Add the remaining ingredients along with 1$^1\!/_2$ cups water. Mix well, mashing the tomatoes with a fork. Bring to a boil. Reduce heat; simmer, covered, stirring occasionally for 1 hour.

Italian Spaghetti Sauce

2 Tablespoons olive oil
4 cloves garlic, minced
1 green pepper, chopped
1 small white onion, chopped
1 pound fresh mushrooms
1 pound ground round steak
1 pound sausage meat
1 quart can Italian plum tomatoes
2- 6 ounce cans tomato paste
2 Tablespoons parsley, minced
1 teaspoon oregano
1 Tablespoon salt
1 teaspoon pepper
¾ cup red wine

Heat oil in heavy skillet and in it cook garlic, green pepper, onion and mushrooms until tender. Cook sausage meat until lightly browned, breaking it up with a fork. Drain. Add ground round and sausage meat to vegetable mixture, cooking until meat is no longer pink. Blend in the remaining ingredients and simmer for about 2 hours. Add the wine while cooking. Serve over spaghetti with hot French bread, green salad and a good Italian chianti. Serves 8.

Mrs. Paul Lansing
New Orleans, Louisiana

Spaghetti and Meat Balls

MEAT BALLS:
2 pounds lean ground round
½ pound ground pork
4 eggs
2 cups grated Italian cheese
1½ cups dry French bread, rolled
    fine
1 chopped onion
2 cloves garlic, pressed
½ bunch fresh parsley, minced
½ cup milk, or more to hold
    mixture
1½ Tablespoons catsup
Salt and pepper to taste
Olive oil

SAUCE:
1 onion, minced
1 clove garlic, pressed
1 Tablespoon olive oil
2 cans tomato paste
1½ to 2-quarts water
Salt and pepper, to taste
1 teaspoon sugar
1 Tablespoon sweet basil
1 Tablespoon oregano

Toss all ingredients lightly. Shape into balls and brown in olive oil. Set aside.

In heavy pot cook onion and garlic until soft in the olive oil. Add all ingredients and mix well. Add browned meat balls and simmer for one hour or longer until sauce thickens. Serve over cooked spaghetti. Serves 6 to 8.

Mrs. Stan Mintz

Herbed Spaghetti

4 to 6 cloves garlic, mashed
3 Tablespoons olive oil
½ cup butter, melted
1 cup fresh herbs: chives, parsley, dill, green onion tops, chopped
Salt
1 pound thin spaghetti, cooked

Sauté the garlic in oil until golden. Remove from heat and add butter and herbs. Season with salt to taste. Toss the spaghetti lightly with the herb mixture. Serve immediately. Serves 6.

Summer Spaghetti

2 pounds very ripe tomatoes
1 small onion, finely minced
1 clove garlic, minced
2 Tablespoons finely minced fresh parsley
½ teaspoon basil
¼ cup olive oil
Tarragon wine vinegar
Salt and pepper to taste
1 pound spaghetti
Freshly grated Parmesan cheese

Peel and dice the tomatoes. Add the onions, garlic, parsley, basil and olive oil to the tomatoes and season to taste with vinegar and salt and pepper. Set aside. Boil the spaghetti until al dente and drain. Toss the hot spaghetti with the tomato mixture. Serve immediately topped with cheese. The tomato mixture may be prepared ahead but if it is refrigerated bring it back to room temperature before mixing with the hot spaghetti. Serves 4 to 6.

White Clam Sauce for Vermicelli

2 cloves garlic, halved
⅔ cup olive oil
1 cup bottled clam juice
¼ teaspoon salt
Fresh cracked pepper
½ teaspoon oregano
2- 7½ ounce cans minced clams
½ cup parsley
½ cup minced green onion tops
1 pound vermicelli, cooked
Freshly grated Parmesan

Sauté garlic in oil, mashing to extract juice. Add clam juice, salt, pepper and oregano; simmer 5 minutes. Add clams with juice, stir in well and cook uncovered about 8 to 10 minutes so liquid will reduce a little. Mix in parsley and onion tops. Toss ½ of the sauce with vermicelli and top with the rest of the sauce and freshly grated Parmesan. Delicious served with stuffed artichokes for an entrée.

TORTILLAS:
1 cup Bisquick
¼ cup water
Corn meal

ENCHILADA MIXTURE:
1 large onion, chopped
1 pound ground chuck
1 can chili without beans
½ teaspoon salt
Pepper to taste
1 teaspoon chili powder
Red pepper, optional
½ pound grated cheese
Additional chopped onion
1 can El Paso Enchilada
  sauce, optional

Enchiladas

Tortillas:
Mix all of the ingredients together and knead about 1 minute on a corn meal floured board. Pinch off a ball and pat out to desired thickness. Do not make them too thin because they will be brittle when cooled. Bake on an ungreased sheet until light brown. Makes 8.
Enchilada mixture:
Sauté the onion and ground meat until the meat is browned and the onions are tender. Add the chili and seasonings. On each tortilla put a small amount of meat mixture, cheese and onion. Roll up and place in a baking dish. Pour the remaining meat sauce on top, more onion and top with cheese. Bake at 350 degrees until the cheese melts. If the sauce seems too dry or there is not enough to cover the tortillas, use a can of El Paso Enchilada Sauce.

Mrs. Elvis Stout

Tacos

2 large onions, chopped
1 clove garlic, minced
2 Tablespoons bacon grease
3½ pounds ground meat
2 cans kidney beans, mashed
3 cans enchilada sauce
2 Tablespoons Mexene chili
  powder
Salt to taste
1 large can of tortillas or
  packaged taco shells
Shredded lettuce
Durkee's salad dressing
Grated cheese
Chopped onion

In a large skillet or Dutch oven, brown the onions and garlic in bacon grease. Add the meat and continue browning. Add the mashed beans to meat and stir. Add two cans of enchilada sauce, reserve the third to be added later if the mixture becomes too stiff. Stir in the chili powder and salt. Simmer for 1 1/2 to 2 hours. It should turn a dark red. Prepare the tortillas according to directions on the can. Put a small amount of filling into a taco shell, top with shredded lettuce mixed with Durkee's, grated cheese and onion. The filling freezes well. It makes a large amount that should serve 16 to 20. This is a meal in itself.

Mrs. Pat Garrett

Mexican Tamale Pie

1 pound ground chuck
1 clove garlic, finely chopped
2 onions, chopped
1- 14½ ounce can tomatoes
1- 6 ounce can Snap-E-Tom
  tomato cocktail (or spicy
  tomato juice)
3 Tablespoons chili powder,
  or to taste
1 teaspoon cumin
Salt to taste
Red pepper to taste

MAKE A STIFF MUSH

2 cups corn meal
1 teaspoon salt
1 cup liquid from meat mixture
3 cups water

¾ cups grated cheese
Fritoes

Brown meat, garlic and onions in bacon grease. Add tomatoes and Snap-E-Tom (or spicy tomato juice). Dissolve chili powder in a little water and add with cumin. Stir over medium fire for 15 minutes. Drain liquid and save. In another pan bring to boil 1 cup liquid from meat mixture and 3 cups of water. Add meal. Cook stirring constantly until thick. Line greased glass casserole with layer of mush. Pour in meat mixture, cover top with balance of mush. Sprinkle top with grated cheddar cheese and bake for 45 minutes at 350 degrees or moderate oven. Have top covered. For last 5 minutes remove cover and sprinkle top with Fritoes if desired. Serves 6 to 8. Doubles easily.

Mrs. J. L. Adams

Tamale Pie

3 large onions, chopped
2 pounds ground meat
2 Tablespoons drippings
3 cans condensed tomato soup
1 Tablespoon salt
1 teaspoon black pepper
1 teaspoon cayenne pepper
3 pods garlic, minced
3 Tablespoons chili powder
1½ cups ripe olives, halved
1-12 ounce can whole kernal
  corn
2 cans Black Label Ranch Style
  Beans

CORNBREAD BATTER:

½ cup flour
1 teaspoon salt
1 teaspoon baking powder
½ teaspoon soda
¾ cup corn meal
1 cup buttermilk
1 beaten egg
2 Tablespoons salad oil

Brown onion and meat in hot fat. Add the remaining ingredients and pour into two, 2 quart greased casseroles and cover. Bake at 325 degrees for 1 1/4 hours. Stir and spread with corn bread batter and bake uncovered at 425 degrees for 25 minutes. Serves 10 to 12.

Batter: Sift all of the dry ingredients and add to the corn meal, mixing well. Add buttermilk, egg and salad oil. May be doubled for a large crowd.

Mrs. Jerry Gregg
Sterlington, Louisiana

Chop Suey

2 pounds beef, slivered or 2 cups
   left-over roast
Salt and pepper
3 cups diced onion
2 cups diced celery
3 Tablespoons oil
2 Tablespoons flour
2 or 3 Tablespoons soy sauce
2 cups beef broth or part left-over
   gravy
1 Tablespoon brown sugar
3 Tablespoons Bead Molasses,
   do not substitute
1 medium can mushrooms
1 can bean sprouts
1 can Chinese mixed vegetables
1 can Chow Mein Noodles

Sauté meat in a little oil to brown well if not using left over roast. Remove meat and saute onions and celery in 3 Tablespoons oil until glazed. Stir in flour. Return meat, add soy sauce, stock, and gravy, if used, brown sugar and molasses. Simmer about 30 minutes or until meat is tender. Just before serving heat all vegetables, drain, and add to the meat mixture. Serve topped with heated noodles on rice. A 4 to 5 pound boiled hen may be used in this recipe also. Be sure you have a well-seasoned broth. Serves 8.

Mrs. Saul Mintz

Chinese Casserole

1 pound sliced fillet of beef
1/4 cup cooking oil
3/4 cup diced celery
1 small can mushrooms
1 large onion, chopped
2 cans mushroom soup
1/2 cup water chestnuts,
   sliced
Salt and pepper to taste

Sauté the meat until lightly brown. Remove from the pan and set aside. Sauté celery, mushrooms and onion until soft. Return the meat and mix in the remaining ingredients. Simmer until heated through. Salt and pepper to taste. Serve over rice or Chinese noodles.

Mrs. Charles Cicero

Beef Teriyaki

2 pounds sirloin, round or
   chuck steak

MARINADE:
1/2 cup Kikkoman soy sauce
1/4 cup white wine
2 cloves garlic, crushed
2 Tablespoons sugar
Small piece fresh ginger the
   size of a garlic pod or 1 Tablespoon ground ginger

Cut meat 1/2 inch thick in serving pieces. Marinate in soy sauce mixture at room temperature for at least one hour. This can be broiled in the oven, but is even better cooked over charcoal. Serves 4.

Mrs. A. C. Warner
Trenton, New Jersey

MEAT SAUCES

Barbecue Marinade

¼ cup vegetable oil
¼ cup bourbon or dry sherry
2 Tablespoons soy sauce
1 teaspoon Worcestershire
1 teaspoon garlic powder
Several twists of the peppermill

Combine all ingredients in a polyethylene bag. Add the meat, tie securely and place in a pan in case the bag breaks. If used to marinate roasts, place in the refrigerator for one or two days; if steaks, allow at least four hours; if fish or chicken, at least two hours. Turn bag several times during marinating time.

Mrs. Harry Bell

Superb Barbecue Sauce

¼ cup vinegar
½ cup water
2 Tablespoons sugar
1 Tablespoon prepared mustard
½ teaspoon pepper
1½ teaspoons salt
¼ teaspoon cayenne pepper
1 thick slice of lemon
1 sliced onion
¼ cup butter
½ cup catsup
2 Tablespoons Lea & Perrins
1½ teaspoons liquid or powdered
  smoke, optional

In a sauce pan, mix all ingredients except the catsup, Lea & Perrins and smoke. Simmer uncovered for 20 minutes. Add the remaining ingredients and bring to a boil. Serve hot. Use for charcoaling ribs, chicken or lamb. Use also as a basting sauce. Makes 1 3/4 cups. Doubles or triples easily.

Mrs. Don McBride
Mt. View, Oklahoma

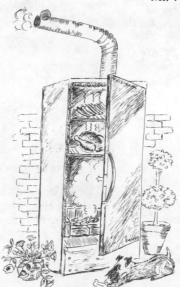

Bar-B-Que Sauce for Smoked Meats

1 onion, finely chopped
2 Tablespoons oil
2- 5 ounce bottles Worcestershire
2 regular size bottles catsup
1 lemon sliced
2 pods garlic, halved
1 bay leaf

Sauté onions in oil until soft. Simmer all remaining ingredients with onions. Serve with smoked meats. This sauce is not to be used for basting.

Ted Allen

Barbecue Steak Sauce

1 stick butter
1- 5 ounce bottle A-1 Sauce
2 Tablespoons Lea & Perrins
Juice of 1 lemon

Melt the butter and add the remaining ingredients. Stir well. It is not necessary to simmer this.

Mrs. Dave Aron

Blue Cheese Steak Sauce

¼ pound butter
¼ pound blue cheese
2 Tablespoons chives or chopped
    shallots

Blend all ingredients together over low heat, do not boil. Cover the steak with a lot of freshly ground pepper and spoon lots of the hot sauce over the steak.

Allen Barham

Steak Sauce

1 stick butter
1 bunch green onions, chopped
1 Tablespoon flour
4 Tablespoons B-V "The Beefer-
    Upper"
½ bottle Chablis Blanc

Melt butter. Sauté onion and add flour, stirring until brown. Stir in "Beefer-Upper", add wine and bubble a few minutes. Serve immediately.

Miss Jennifer Frazer

Hot Mustard Sauce

3 teaspoons dry mustard
2 Tablespoons brown sugar
1 Tablespoon flour
¼ cup wine vinegar
¼ cup boiling water
Yellow food coloring

Blend mustard and sugar together. Add remaining ingredients. Cook over slow heat, stirring constantly for 3 or 4 minutes or until sauce thickens. Delicious for ham or smoked meats.

Mrs. Travis Oliver III

Lemon-Butter-Sauterne Steak Sauce

2 sticks butter
2 Tablespoons lemon juice
3 Tablespoons sauterne
3 Tablespoons Lea and Perrins
½ Tablespoon garlic powder
½ Tablespoon cracked pepper
½ Tablespoon salt

Melt butter in sauce pan over medium heat and add other ingredients. Baste on steaks prior to charcoaling or broiling. Use remaining sauce to pour over meat as soon as removed from fire. Salt to taste. Ample sauce for 8 rib eyes or strips and also enough for 2 large sirloins. Extra sauce may be refrigerated.

Mrs. Elton Upshaw, Jr.

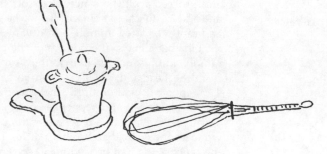

Bordelaise Sauce

1 cup Burgundy wine
1 small bunch green onions, chopped
1 cup thickened beef gravy left over from roast
1 bouillon cube

Cook the Burgundy and onions until the liquid is reduced by half. Strain and add this to the gravy to which the bouillon cube has been added. Cook in a double boiler, uncovered, over simmering water for two hours. Do not return the sauce to direct heat. This makes approximately 1 1/2 cups of sauce which is great over beef cooked on the grill. Also delicious over meat in a chafing dish.

Mrs. M. A. Bodron, Jr.

Béarnaise Sauce

2 egg yolks
1 stick butter, real please!
,1½ teaspoons tarragon vinegar
¼ teaspoon salt
1½ teaspoons lemon juice
½ teaspoon parsley flakes

Put egg yolks in a cup and place the cup in a pan of warm water. Beat with wire whisk. Gradually add large pieces of butter to the egg yolks, melting each piece before adding more butter. When all of the butter is melted take the cup out of the water and add the vinegar, lemon juice, salt and parsley flakes. Serve at room temperature with meat fondue, fish, or over most vegetables. This cannot be reheated as the butter and the eggs separate. Makes approximately 1 cup.

Mrs. Ernest E. Bruce, Jr.

Marchand de Vin Sauce
From the finest rib-eye to a ground round pattie!

5 to 6 Tablespoons softened butter
3 Tablespoons minced green
   onions
½ cup dry red wine
Salt and pepper
2 to 3 Tablespoons parsley

Pan broil the steak using 1 Tablespoon oil and 1 Tablespoon butter to desired doneness. Remove to a hot platter and keep warm. Salt and pepper to taste and proceed with the sauce. Pour off the drippings and add 1 Tablespoon butter. Stir in the green onions and sauté for a few minutes. Add wine, scraping up the bits that cling to the bottom of the pan, and boil rapidly until sauce is like a thin syrup. Remove from the heat and rapidly stir in softened butter a Tablespoon at a time until thickened. Add parsley and check for salt and pepper seasoning. Spoon over warm meat. This takes a very few minutes and does wonders for even that broiled pattie. The secret of the sauce is the pan broiled meat, so if you are preparing for 6 to 8 use two skillets: First put butter and onion mixture in each one, then wine in each, scraping one skillet out and into the other. Continue as above, doubling the amount of butter as needed to thicken the sauce, i.e., 8 to 10 Tablespoons.

Duckling Madeira

1 Long Island Duckling
Lawry's seasoning salt
Salt and pepper
1/2 stick butter
1 onion, sliced
1 clove garlic, halved
1 can black cherries
1/2 cup Madeira
1 1/2 teaspoons flour
1 1/2 teaspoons butter

Quarter duckling and season with salts and pepper. Melt butter in large heavy covered pot or roaster. Brown duck well. Remove duck, add onions and garlic; sauté until soft. Drain the cherries, reserving the juice. Return duck to pan; add 1/2 cup cherry juice and Madeira. Cover the pot and braise the duckling for 30 minutes or until tender. Remove duckling and keep warm. Strain the sauce, removing excess fat from the liquid. Make a paste of the flour and butter and stir in the sauce until smooth. Add the drained cherries and heat. To serve: place the duck on a serving platter and surround with the cherries and spoon the sauce over sparingly. Pass the remaining sauce. Serves 4.

Mrs. T. O. Bancroft, Jr.

Athenian Chicken

2 fryers, quartered
2 Tablespoons salt
1 Tablespoon white pepper
Flour
½ cup butter
Juice of 5 lemons
2 quarts chicken stock
¼ cup chicken stock base
½ teaspoon oregano leaves
½ teaspoon garlic powder
½ cup flour
6 to 8 potatoes

After fryers have been quartered, season, roll in flour and fry in butter or oil until browned. Mix remaining ingredients and bring to boil; thicken to sauce consistency with 1/2 cup flour. Lay chicken in shallow greased pan; pour sauce over chicken. Bake at 400 degrees for 40 minutes, covered. Quarter potatoes, fry in butter, place in the same pan with the chicken if there is room. If not, place in another pan, cover with sauce, cover the pan and bake the same time and temperature.

Tony James
Chef, Ramada Inn
Monroe, Louisiana

Barbecued Chicken

1 fryer, cut in pieces
6 Tablespoons catsup
2 Tablespoons vinegar
2 Tablespoons lemon juice
4 Tablespoons Lea & Perrins
4 Tablespoons water
4 Tablespoons butter
6 Tablespoons sugar
2 teaspoons salt
1½ teaspoons chili powder
2 teaspoons paprika
2 teaspoons mustard
½ teaspoon red pepper

Combine all ingredients for sauce and pour over the frying chicken. Bake in a covered casserole at 350 degrees for 1 1/2 hours. Serves 4 to 6.

Mrs. Jim Dennis

Burgundy Chicken

1 large fryer or equivalent, such
  as 2½ pounds breasts
Salt and paprika
Lawry's seasoned pepper
Garlic powder, not garlic salt
⅓ to ½ cup dehydrated onion
1 teaspoon curry powder
¾ cup Burgundy wine
1 chicken bouillon cube dissolved
  in 1 cup hot water
1- 4 ounce can sliced mushrooms

Preheat oven 350 degrees. Generously cover all sides of uncooked chicken pieces with salt, garlic powder, paprika and Lawry's seasoned pepper. Layer in Dutch oven with dehydrated onion sprinkled throughout. Stir curry powder with Burgundy, mix with bouillon and pour in with chicken. Place in oven, uncovered, for approximately 15 minutes. Add mushrooms, cover and cook until very tender, approximately 45 minutes. Add remaining 1/4 cup Burgundy before serving. Recipe may easily be tripled, but it is not necessary to triple the liquid. Serve the gravy over brown rice.

Mrs. O. P. Lowery, Jr.
Rayville, Louisiana

Cajun Chicken

2 fryers, disjointed or 10 to 12
  chicken breasts
Butter or oil for browning
1 cup flour
1 1/4 cups butter
3 medium onions, chopped
3 bell peppers, chopped
1/2 bunch celery, chopped
5 cups hot water
1 bay leaf
2 teaspoons Worcestershire
3 dashes hot sauce
1/4 teaspoon poultry seasoning
Salt and pepper to taste
1-12 ounce can mushrooms

Salt and pepper chicken. Brown lightly in butter or oil. Remove from fire and drain. In a large Dutch oven make a roux of flour and butter, stirring constantly, until it turns a rich brown. Add chopped vegetables to the roux and stir until slightly softened. Slowly add hot water, stirring constantly. Add the chicken and seasonings. Cover and simmer about 1 hour. Stir occasionally to prevent sticking. Add mushrooms the last 10 minutes. Serve over rice. All the more delicious if made the night before.

Mrs. Robert Cudd III

Chicken Continental

3 or 4 pounds frying size chickens,
  cut up
1/3 cup seasoned flour
1/4 cup shortening
1 can cream of chicken soup
2 1/2 Tablespoons grated onion
Dash of pepper
1/2 teaspoon celery flakes
1/2 teaspoon paprika
1 teaspoon salt
1 Tablespoon minced parsley
1/8 teaspoon thyme
1 1/3 cups water
1 1/3 cups Minute Rice or partially
  cooked white or brown rice
Paprika

Roll chicken in seasoned flour and sauté in shortening until tender. Combine soup, onion and seasonings in a saucepan, gradually add water and blend thoroughly. Bring to a boil, stirring constantly. Reserve 1/3 cup of the soup mixture. Pour the remaining soup over Minute Rice in a shallow casserole. Stir just to moisten all of the rice. Top with chicken and the remaining soup. Cover and bake at 350 degrees for 20 to 25 minutes. Sprinkle with paprika.

Mrs. Ansel Smith
Mrs. Naomi E. Crawford
Winnfield, Louisiana

Note: The brown rice gives a rich nutty flavor and is a nice change.

Chicken Jerusalem

1 chicken, disjointed
Salt and pepper to taste
½ stick butter
4 artichoke hearts, halved
¾ pound mushrooms
⅓ cup sherry
1 Tablespoon lemon juice
1 cup heavy cream
1½ Tablespoons chopped chives
¾ cup sour cream

Salt and pepper chicken and brown in butter. Add mushrooms and artichoke hearts. Add the sherry and lemon juice; cover and cook for 15 minutes until the wine is reduced. Stir in the cream and chives and warm about 5 minutes. Remove chicken to serving platter. Whip the sour cream and stir into the sauce in the skillet. Pour over the chicken. Serves 4.

Doro's Restaurant
San Francisco, California

Coq au Vin
A do ahead. The flavors mingle all the more.

2 fryers
Seasoning salt
4 slices bacon, diced
¼ cup butter
2 cloves garlic
24 small boiling onions
1 pound mushrooms, halved
¼ cup brandy
1½ cups red wine
1 rib celery, finely diced
4 small carrots, grated
¼ cup chopped parsley
½ teaspoon thyme
1 bay leaf
1 teaspoon salt
½ teaspoon pepper
2 Tablespoons butter
2 Tablespoons flour
1 can consommé

Cut chickens in serving pieces, pat dry, salt with seasoning salt. In a large heavy casserole fry bacon until crisp, remove and set aside. Add butter and crushed garlic, sauté for a few minutes. Have butter and bacon drippings HOT and brown chicken pieces quickly, a few at a time. Return all chicken to the casserole; add bacon, onions and mushrooms. Heat brandy briefly, pour over chicken, ignite and let burn off. Pour in wine and all seasonings. Mix butter, flour and consommé together and add to casserole. Bring all to a simmer and cook covered 30 minutes. Remove chicken, onions, and mushrooms; set aside. Bring sauce to a boil and boil rapidly until sauce is reduced by half, about 2 1/2 cups. It will thicken and lightly coat spoon. Return the chicken, onions and mushrooms. Cool and refrigerate. One hour before serving bring to room temperature. Reheat at 300 degrees about 30 to 45 minutes or until chicken is hot through. Do not overcook the chicken. Garnish the top with fresh chopped parsley.

This is particularly good with small boiled new potatoes tossed in butter, parsley and cracked pepper. Serves 8.

Mrs. Don Irby

Chicken Baked in Sour Cream

1- 3 pound chicken
2 teaspoons Accent
1 stick butter
1 small onion, minced
3 Tablespoons flour
1 cup chicken broth
1 teaspoon paprika
1/2 teaspoon grated lemon rind
1 cup sour cream
Salt and pepper to taste
2 Tablespoons sherry
2 Tablespoons parsley

Cut chicken into serving pieces. Sprinkle with Accent and let stand 15 minutes. Melt butter in a skillet, brown chicken slowly on all sides; place in a casserole. Add onion to skillet drippings and sauté gently five minutes. Blend in flour until smooth. Add broth; cook, stirring constantly, until mixture thickens and boils. Add paprika, lemon rind, sour cream, salt and pepper. Pour gravy over chicken. Cover and bake at 350 degrees 45 minutes. Place chicken on a serving platter. Add sherry and parsley to the gravy and pour over chicken. Serves 4. May be made ahead of time and refrigerated.

Mrs. Steve Nichols

Chicken with Duck Sauce
Quick and easy, sweet and sour

2-3 pound broilers, cut up
1-8 ounce bottle Russian dressing
2 envelopes onion soup mix
1-8 ounce jar apricot jam

Put chicken pieces in an open roasting pan. Mix all other ingredients together and spread over chicken. Bake uncovered at 300 degrees for 2 hours. Serves 4.

Amy Vanderbilt

Seven Boy Indian Curry
Great and different for all who love curry!

3 to 4 pound fryer
1 cup minced green onion
1/2 cup minced white onion
2 1/2 Tablespoons ground coriander
1 Tablespoon ground tumeric
2 1/2 teaspoons ground cumin
1 teaspoon ginger
3/4 teaspoon black pepper
3/4 teaspoon red pepper
2 cloves garlic, pressed
2 Tablespoons cider vinegar
1 Tablespoon salad oil
2 bay leaves
1 stick cinnamon
1/4 cup oil
2 1/2 teaspoons salt
1 teaspoon brown sugar
1 cup hot water
2 Tablespoons flour

Have chicken ready-to-cook and cut in serving pieces. Pat dry. Make a paste of onions, coriander, turmeric, cumin, ginger, peppers, garlic, vinegar and 1 Tablespoon of oil. Rub and pat mixture over all surfaces of chicken pieces. Place in a covered container and marinate 24 hours. About 1 hour before serving, heat oil with bay leaves, cinnamon and salt in a Dutch oven or large covered skillet. Brown chicken well on all sides. Add brown sugar and 1 cup of hot water; cover and simmer until chicken is tender, about 30 minutes. Remove chicken, stir in flour to thicken sauce slightly, return chicken to pot and set off heat to mellow. Serve hot with rice, cooked in chicken broth with a little curry added. Serves 6. Serve with Seven "Boys" or condiments. The "drums" of chicken wings prepared this way make a great hors d'oeuvre served hot or cold.

Mrs. Don Irby

Curried Chicken

Five or six pound hen
3 ribs celery
¼ green pepper, chopped
2 onions, chopped
2 Tablespoons butter
1 cup broth
2 cans condensed tomato soup, undiluted
3 to 4 teaspoons curry powder
Tabasco, to taste
Salt to taste
1 cup heavy cream

Cover hen with water in a large pot with lid. Season with celery and tops, salt and pepper. Cover and simmer for 2 hours. Cool and remove meat from the bones. Cut into bite size pieces. Save broth. Sauté green pepper and onions in butter for 15 minutes. Add 1 cup broth and simmer for another 15 minutes. Add tomato soup and curry powder. Simmer about 15 minutes. Add chicken to sauce. Put all in the top of a double boiler, partially cover, and simmer for 1-1/4 hours, stirring often. Check for seasoning. Use Tabasco carefully as curry powder is hot. Before serving stir in heavy cream. Serve on rice mounds. Pass condiments. Serves 6.

Note: Shrimp can be used in place of the chicken. Use about 1/2 of the broth in recipe so sauce will not be too watery. Use a small part of the shrimp for long simmering and reduce the 1-1/4 hours to 45 minutes. This is for seasoning, as shrimp shrivel up when cooked too long. Do not use lid unless the sauce looks too dry. Add the rest of the shrimp just long enough to cook them before serving. Sauce should be doubled and 5 pounds cleaned raw shrimp used. Serves 10 to 12. Prepare recipe for chicken or shrimp the day before; do not add the cream or final addition of shrimp until just before serving. Reheat in a double boiler or improvise one.

Mrs. Jack Peat
Madison, Connecticut

Curry Sambals

Grated fresh coconut
Chopped bacon
Minced green onion
Chopped peanuts
Banana wedges
Riced egg
Chutney
Chopped pickles
Chopped green peppers

Chopped almonds
Chopped pistachio nuts
Raisins
Freshly chopped mint
Freshly grated ginger
Mango chunks
Chopped fresh hot peppers
Chopped dates

Chicken 'n Dumplings

1 fryer, cut into pieces
1 medium onion
2 ribs celery
Salt and pepper to taste
1 cup flour
¼ teaspoon salt
⅛ teaspoon baking powder
1 Tablespoon shortening
1 egg yolk
¼ cup broth or milk
1 egg, hard-boiled

Boil the chicken in water seasoned with onion, celery, salt and pepper. To make the dumplings, mix flour, salt, and baking powder and shortening together. Add egg yolk and mix well. Add 1/4 cup broth or milk to make a dough. Roll the dough thinly on a floured surface and cut into squares. Lay the squares on waxed paper for 30 minutes or more to dry out. Remove the chicken from the stock, bring the stock to a boil and drop the dumplings in. You may add a small amount of milk or hard-boiled egg to the broth. Return the chicken to the pot, cover and let cook for approximately 5 minutes or until the dumplings are tender. Serves 4 to 6.

Mrs. J.E. Brown
Lake Providence, Louisiana

Plantation Chicken Pie

1- 3 pound chicken
1 green pepper, chopped
1 garlic bud, chopped
1 sweet red pepper, chopped
2 Tablespoons vinegar
1 chopped onion
½ cup dry sherry
1 Tablespoon sugar
2 cans tomato sauce
Salt and pepper to taste
Dash of paprika
1 cup small peas
1 cup whole green olives
2 eggs, hard-boiled

CRUST:
6 cups flour
1 Tablespoon baking powder
1 Tablespoon salt
4 eggs
1 cup shortening, melted
2 ounces sherry
¼ pound butter
2 Tablespoons water

Cook chicken whole in salted boiling water until tender. Cool, remove from bones. Dice in small pieces. Make a sauce by sautéing the green pepper, garlic, red pepper, vinegar, onion, sherry, sugar, tomatoes, salt, pepper and paprika for 20 minutes. Add chicken and drained peas. Line a large *baking* dish with crust. Put in the chicken mixture, olives and sliced hard-boiled eggs. Cover with a top crust brushed with melted butter. Bake for 1 hour at 250 degrees.

Crust: Sift dry ingredients. Make a well in the flour mixture and drop in the eggs, shortening, sherry and butter softened with water. Knead, making a smooth, soft dough. Let the dough stand for 2 hours in a cool place, not in refrigerator. Knead again and roll out. If dough is too stiff add a little butter. This pie may be prepared on Saturday and reheated on Sunday. The secret is in the crust. It does not get soggy.

Mrs. S.A. Collins

Chicken Breasts in Sour Cream

1 package chipped dried beef,
  finely chopped
6 chicken breasts, boned, skinned
  and split
6 slices bacon
2 cartons sour cream
2 cans mushroom soup

Place chopped dried beef in the bottom of a casserole. Wrap the chicken with bacon and arrange on the beef. Mix the soup and sour cream. Pour over the chicken. Bake at 275 degrees for 2 1/2 or 3 hours. Serve the gravy over the chicken with rice as a side dish.

A can of celery soup may be substituted for 1 of the cans of soup.

Mrs. R. D. Farr, Jr.

Artichoke and Chicken Sauté

8 chicken breast halves, boned
1 stick butter
¼ cup flour
3 chicken bouillon cubes
2½ cups water
1- 4 ounce can mushrooms
1- 15 ounce can artichoke
  bottoms, quartered
½ teaspoon Lea & Perrins
Salt and white pepper, to taste
2 Tablespoons sherry

Prepare chicken and season with salt. Melt butter in large skillet and brown chicken on all sides. Remove and set aside. Add flour to pan drippings and cook 2 minutes. Dissolve bouillon cubes in water and add to the flour mixture. Stir until thickened. Add mushrooms, artichokes, chicken and seasonings except sherry. Cover and cook for 20 minutes, spooning sauce over chicken occasionally. Add sherry a few minutes before serving. Delicious with yellow rice. Serves 8.

Mrs. Ed Seymour, Jr.

Chicken Breasts with Artichoke Hearts

12 chicken breast halves, boned
2-14 ounce cans artichoke hearts
Mushrooms, optional
2-10½ ounce cans cream of
  chicken soup
½ cup white wine
Salt and red pepper to taste
1 cup Pepperidge Farm herb-
  seasoned stuffing
½ stick butter

Rinse artichoke hearts and drain well. Sliced or whole mushrooms may be added too. Place in a buttered 3 quart pyrex dish. Add soup and wine. Season to taste with salt and pepper. Push chicken breasts partially into the mixture, leaving parts exposed to brown while cooking. Cover with the stuffing and dot with butter. This may be prepared and frozen until ready to bake. Cover with foil and bake for 45 minutes at 350 degrees. Remove foil and continue baking until brown and chicken appears to be done, approximately 30 minutes. This may be left in a warm oven until serving time. Serves 8 generously.

This recipe may be halved but do not double it. Just make two casseroles instead.

Mrs. Walter L. Hastings

Baked Chicken Breasts

2 cups Progresso bread crumbs
8 chicken breast halves, skinned
Salt and pepper
4 beaten eggs
2 cups milk
½ teaspoon garlic powder
1 Tablespoon Worcestershire
  sauce
¼ teaspoon mace
½ cup green onions and tops
1½ cups Mozzarella cheese,
  grated
½ cup green stuffed olives,
  chopped

Preheat the oven to 325 degrees. Cover the bottom of a flat 13 x 9 inch casserole with half of the bread crumbs. Season the chicken breasts and lay on top of the crumbs. Mix eggs, milk, garlic powder, Worcestershire sauce, mace and green onions. Pour over the chicken. Cover with foil and bake for 40 minutes. Uncover and sprinkle with remaining bread crumbs, cheese and olives. Keep uncovered and bake for another 30 minutes. Serves 6.

Mrs. Sol Courtman

Chicken Breasts Supreme

6 whole chicken breasts, halved
  and skinned
¼ cup flour
2½ teaspoons salt
1 teaspoon paprika
¼ cup butter
¼ cup water
2 teaspoons cornstarch
1½ cups Half & Half
¼ cup sherry
1 teaspoon lemon peel
1 Tablespoon lemon juice
1 cup Swiss cheese, grated
½ cup parsley, chopped

Up to 1 week before serving if you want to freeze this: If not do it the day of serving:
Coat the chicken with the flour, salt and paprika. Lightly brown the chicken in hot butter. Add 1/4 cup water and simmer the chicken, covered, for 30 minutes or until almost tender. Remove the chicken and set aside. Mix cornstarch and 1/4 cup Half & Half, stir into the drippings and cook, stirring over low heat. Gradually stir in the remaining Half & Half, sherry, lemon peel and lemon juice. Continue cooking, stirring, until sauce is smooth and thickened. Place the chicken breasts in a large oblong dish, freezer-to-oven type if you plan to freeze this, and pour the sauce over the chicken. Freeze, covered, at this point. To cook frozen chicken, defrost for 4 hours or until almost thawed but still cold. Bake covered in a 350 degree oven about 35 minutes or until sauce is bubbly. Uncover and sprinkle with cheese and bake until the cheese is melted. Sprinkle with parsley. Serves 12.

Mrs. Nat Troy
Mrs. DeWitt Milam
Mrs. Jack McBee

Chicken Cordon Bleu
Delicious and easy to prepare a day ahead

6 chicken breast halves
Garlic salt
Salt
1/3 cup flour
1 teaspoon salt
1/4 teaspoon pepper
1 stick butter
1/2 medium onion, chopped,
    about 6 Tablespoons
4 Tablespoons vermouth or dry
    white wine
6 thin slices ham
12 thin slices Swiss cheese
1 cup chicken stock
2 Tablespoons vermouth or dry
    white wine
1 Tablespoon cornstarch
4 egg yolks
1/2 cup heavy cream

Sprinkle chicken breasts with garlic salt and salt. Toss breasts in a paper sack with flour and additional salt and pepper. Melt butter and sauté breasts with chopped onion and vermouth until golden. Remove and let cool. Carefully remove bone and insert ham and one piece of cheese. Return breasts to ovenproof skillet and top with remaining pieces of cheese. Refrigerate.

One hour before serving, remove the chicken from the ice box and let chicken reach room temperature. Pour 1/4 cup chicken stock in skillet. Bake uncovered for 15 minutes at 350 degrees. Transfer to a serving dish and KEEP WARM.

Add additional wine or vermouth to skillet and raise to high heat, scraping the bits from the bottom of the pan. Reduce heat and stir in the cornstarch, which has dissolved in 1/2 cup chicken broth. Beat egg yolks and cream together. Stir in a little of the hot liquid and then stir the eggs and cream into the hot mixture in the skillet. Simmer, stirring constantly, until the sauce is smooth. Adjust seasonings with salt and pepper to taste. Add the remaining stock if necessary to thin the sauce. Spoon a little of the sauce over the breasts and pass the rest. This may be doubled.

Mrs. Don Irby

Chicken Deluxe

1 cup flour
3 teaspoons salt
1/4 teaspoon pepper
2 teaspoons paprika
6 chicken breast halves
1/4 cup butter
1/4 cup cooking oil
3 cups celery, cut in bite size
    pieces
1 can cream of chicken soup
1/2 cup Half & Half
2 Tablespoons pimiento, chopped
1 cup American cheese, grated
1 cup bread crumbs
2 Tablespoons melted butter
1/2 cup slivered almonds

Combine flour, salt, pepper and paprika. Roll the chicken breasts in mixture and brown in the butter and oil. Place celery in the bottom of a greased 3 quart casserole. Place chicken breasts on top of celery. Combine soup, cream, pimiento and cheese and pour over the chicken. Top with buttered bread crumbs and almonds. Bake for 45 minutes at 350 degrees. This may be prepared ahead and stored in the refrigerator. Let it reach room temperature before cooking. Serves 4 to 6.

If serving men, cook more.

Mrs. Jerry Gregg

Martha's Chicken Breasts

6 boned chicken breast halves
6 small pieces cooked ham,
  boiled ham may be used
½ cup Durkee's
1 can cream of chicken soup

Place the ham on the chicken and roll up. Hold this in place with toothpicks. Place in a shallow pyrex dish and cover with Durkee's and soup mixed together. Cover the baking dish with foil and bake at 350 degrees for 2 hours. Serves 6.
For men, plan more breasts.

Mrs. Bill Reed

Deviled Chicken

5 pounds chicken breasts
1 medium onion, sliced
2 ribs celery
1 bell pepper
4 Tablespoons flour
6 Tablespoons butter
1 medium onion, chopped
2 Tablespoons bell pepper,
  chopped
2 Tablespoons parsley, chopped
4 cups chicken stock
1 small can mushrooms
Salt and pepper to taste

Boil the first four ingredients in water that has been salted and peppered to taste. Remove the chicken from the water, cool it and cut it into bite size pieces. Save the stock. Make a dark roux of flour and butter. Sauté the onion, bell pepper and parsley in the roux until they are wilted. Slowly add the chicken stock and cook until thick. Add the chicken and mushrooms and check seasonings. Cook over low heat until the seasoning is thoroughly cooked-in. Serve over Holland Rusk or in pastry shells. This is also delicious as a filling for chicken pie. Serves 8.

Mrs. E. J. Seymour, Sr.

Chicken Geraldine

1- 9 ounce package frozen artichoke hearts
1 teaspoon salt
4 whole chicken breasts, boned
Pepper
8 slices lean bacon
4 Tablespoons sweet vermouth
1 cup chopped canned tomatoes,
  drained
1 cup sharp cheese, shredded

Thaw the artichoke hearts, sprinkle with 1/2 teaspoon salt and arrange them on the bottom of a flat pyrex baking dish. Place chicken breasts, skin side up, on top of the artichokes, seasoning lightly with pepper. Lay bacon slices close together on top of the chicken and spoon vermouth over all. Roast in a 350 degree oven about one hour, draining fat as necessary during that time. Combine tomatoes, cheese and the remaining 1/2 teaspoon salt. Spoon over the chicken 15 minutes before serving, adding more vermouth if desired. Brown under the broiler for a few minutes if the chicken is not already brown. This can easily be doubled or tripled. Serves 4.

Mrs. Landry Ducote

Chicken Breast Magnifique

8 chicken breast halves
1/2 cup butter
1 cup sliced mushrooms
2 cans cream of chicken soup
1 cup water to thin, as needed
Garlic to taste
Pinch of thyme
Pinch of rosemary
2/3 cup light cream
Toasted almonds

Brown chicken well in butter; remove from skillet. Brown mushrooms, stir in soup, garlic and seasonings. Return chicken breasts to the skillet. Cover; cook over low heat for 45 minutes stirring occasionally. Add water as it thickens. Blend in cream and heat slowly. Serve over white or wild rice or a combination of the two. Garnish with toasted almonds. Serves 8.

Mrs. James Aycock

Chicken Supremes

6 whole chicken breasts
2 cups sour cream
1/4 cup lemon juice
4 teaspoons Worcestershire sauce
4 teaspoons celery salt
2 teaspoons paprika
4 cloves garlic
4 teaspoons salt
1/2 teaspoon pepper
1 3/4 cups bread crumbs
1 cup butter, melted
1/3 cup parsley, chopped

Halve and debone chicken breasts, makes 12 pieces. Wipe well. Combine next eight ingredients. Marinate the breasts overnight in sour cream mixture. Remove and roll in the bread crumbs. Pour 1/2 cup of the melted butter over the breasts and bake in a large oblong baking dish for 30 minutes at 325 degrees. Pour remaining 1/2 cup butter over the breasts and let cook another 15 minutes. Sprinkle the parsley over chicken before serving. Serves 12.

Mrs. Don Stinson

Chicken Parmesan

1 1/2 cups Italian Progresso bread crumbs
1/2 cup Parmesan cheese
1 teaspoon salt
1 teaspoon pepper
6 chicken breasts or 3 whole breasts, deboned
2 sticks butter

Combine bread crumbs, cheese, salt and pepper. Dip the chicken breasts in the melted butter and then in the bread crumbs being careful to coat the breasts heavily. Place the breasts, skin side up in a baking dish and bake in a 350 degree oven for 45 minutes to 1 hour, uncovered. Do not turn the chicken.

The chicken breasts can be prepared the day before and refrigerated, then baked. This freezes well, before or after baking. To reheat after thawed bake in a 325 degree oven until hot.

The recipe is very popular with men and children, both of whom can usually eat more than one! It is quite good with a savory rice dish.

Mrs. William Mattison
Mrs. F. M. McGinn
Lafayette, Louisiana

Rolled Chicken Surprise

2 Tablespoons butter
1/4 cup onion, chopped
1/4 cup celery, chopped
2 Tablespoons flour
1/3 cup light cream
1/4 teaspoon salt
Cayenne pepper to taste
1 cup shredded Cheddar cheese
6 whole chicken breasts, boned
Salt and pepper to taste
Flour
2 eggs, slightly beaten
1 1/2 cups cracker crumbs

Sauté onion and celery in butter. Blend in flour; stir in cream and add salt and pepper. Cook, stirring, until mixture becomes very thick. Add cheese and cook over low heat until cheese is melted. Check for seasoning.

Pour mixture into a pie plate and chill thoroughly. Cut the firm cheese mixture into six portions and shape into short sticks.

Remove the skin from the chicken breasts. Place each piece of chicken between two pieces of plastic wrap and pound thin with a mallet. Sprinkle the meat with salt. Place a cheese stick on each piece of chicken breast. Tucking in sides, roll as for jelly roll and fasten with toothpicks. Dust each chicken roll with flour, dip in eggs and roll in crumbs. Fry the rolls in deep fat at 375 degrees for 5 minutes or until golden brown. Place rolls in a shallow baking dish and bake at 350 degrees for 30 minutes. Serves 6.

Mrs. William Ledoux

Chicken Kiev
A treat you will never forget!!

8 double or 16 single chicken
   breasts
Lemon pepper marinade
Salt to taste
1/2 pound butter
Lemon juice
Fresh parsley, chopped
2 eggs beaten with 2 Tablespoons
   milk
Bread crumbs

Debone each chicken breast. One double chicken breast will make 2 rolls. Pound each chicken breast between sheets of waxed paper with a meat cleaver or rolling pin until it is thin. Sprinkle each breast with pepper and salt to taste. Mix the butter, lemon juice to taste and parsley together and then form them into balls of about 1 inch in diameter. Place one ball in the center of each fillet. Roll the meat over the butter ball, tuck the ends in and secure with toothpicks. Dip each roll in milk and egg mixture and then roll in bread crumbs. You may make your own bread crumbs by toasting one loaf of bread on both sides, let it harden and roll into crumbs. Fry each roll in hot deep fat until they are golden. When cut open the butter will pour out. Serves 8. These may be frozen after frying and heated in a 350 degree oven before serving.

Mrs. Scottie Evans
Shreveport, Louisiana

Baked Chicken Casserole
Unexpected company or a quick Sunday Supper

1-5 ounce can Swanson's diced chicken
1 can cream of chicken soup
1 cup celery, diced
3 hard-boiled eggs, diced
1/2 cup almonds, chopped fine
3/4 cup mayonnaise
2 teaspoons onion, chopped
1 medium package potato chips, crushed

Mix all ingredients together, reserving 1/4 of potato chips. Pour into a greased baking dish. Top with the remaining potato chips and bake for 15 minutes at 450 degrees. Serves 4 to 6.

Mrs. Jim Campbell

Chicken and Artichoke Casserole

1-3 pound fryer and 2 or 3 extra breast halves
1 cup butter
1/2 cup flour
3 1/2 cups sweet milk
3 ounces Gruyère or Swiss cheese
1/8 pound sharp Cheddar cheese
1 Tablespoon Accent
2 cloves garlic, pressed
1/2 Tablespoon red pepper
2 large cans button mushrooms, drained
2 large cans artichoke hearts, drained

Boil chicken in seasoned water. Remove skin and bones and cut meat into large pieces. Set aside. Melt butter, stir in flour until blended. Slowly add milk and stir until the sauce is smooth. Add cheeses, cut into small pieces or grated, and seasonings. Stir until cheese melts and sauce bubbles. Add chicken to the sauce. Add mushrooms and artichoke hearts. Check for seasonings. Put the combined mixture in a casserole and bake 30 minutes at 350 degrees. Lobster, crab or shrimp may be substituted for chicken. This is good served with buttered noodles. Serves 12.

Mrs. Rupert Evans
Lake Providence, Louisiana

Chicken Rice Casserole

10 or 11 chicken breasts
9 cups water
3 packages dry Lipton Chicken Noodle Soup Mix
2 cups raw rice
1 pound hot sausage
1 bell pepper, chopped
1 large onion, chopped
1 cup celery, chopped
Salt to taste
Curry powder to taste
2 cans mushroom soup, undiluted
1/2 cup blanched almonds, toasted in melted butter

Debone raw breasts and cut into small pieces. Set aside. To boiling water add soup mix and rice; boil for 9 minutes in an uncovered pot. Fry the sausage, remove from the skillet and drain. In the sausage drippings, brown the bell pepper, onion and celery. Add this and the sausage to the soup mix, seasoning to taste with salt and curry powder. Add mushroom soup and chicken pieces. Place mixture in casseroles and bake for 45 minutes at 350 degrees. Top with blanched toasted almonds and bake 15 additional minutes. Serves 16. This may be prepared and frozen, thawed and baked.

Mrs. Daniel Dupree

Chicken and Asparagus Casserole Ole
A Good Company Dish

6 whole chicken breasts
1 medium onion, chopped
½ cup butter
1- 8 ounce can mushrooms
1 can cream of mushroom soup
1 can cream of chicken soup
1- 5⅓ ounce can Pet milk
½ pound sharp cheese, grated
¼ teaspoon Tabasco
2 teaspoons soy sauce
1 teaspoon salt
½ teaspoon pepper
1 teaspoon Accent
2 Tablespoons pimiento, chopped
2 cans green tip asparagus
½ cup slivered almonds

Boil chicken breasts in seasoned water until tender. Cool, debone and tear into bite size pieces. Set aside. Sauté onion in butter and add remaining ingredients, except asparagus and almonds. Simmer sauce until the cheese melts. To assemble; place a layer of chicken in a large casserole, a layer of asparagus and a layer of sauce. Repeat layers ending with sauce. Top with almonds. Bake at 350 degrees until bubbly. Do not add liquid even if it looks dry. If large breasts are used this will serve 12. It also freezes well.

Mrs. William Durrett

Chicken Eggplant Casserole

1 chicken
2 medium eggplants
2 medium onions, chopped
2 or 3 ribs celery, chopped
3 medium bell peppers, chopped
1 teaspoon parsley flakes
1 Tablespoon shortening
½ teaspoon sugar
Salt and pepper to taste
1 stale bun, crumbled
18 Ritz crackers, crumbled
1 stick butter, melted
2 cups chicken stock
2 eggs
Additional Ritz crackers, crumbled

Cook chicken in seasoned water until tender. Cut into bite sized pieces and reserve the chicken stock. Peel the eggplant and cut into 1 1/2 inch slices. Put in a bowl and sprinkle generously with salt. Let stand about 1 1/2 hours. Wash the eggplant and press most of the seeds out. Wash again to get the salt out. Simmer in a little water until tender. Sauté the onions, celery and pepper in 1 Tablespoon of shortening. Add the drained eggplant, sugar, salt, pepper and parsley flakes. Cook until well mixed. Crumble the bun and crackers together and pour the melted butter over them. Add to the eggplant mixture along with the chicken. Put in a casserole and make knife openings in the top; pour over the top the stock that has been beaten with the eggs. Top with additional cracker crumbs. Bake in a 350 degree oven until thoroughly hot and bubbly.

Mrs. M. A. Cooper
Rayville, Louisiana

Chicken Sauterne

3 whole chicken breasts or
  6 halved chicken breasts
1 teaspoon salt
1 package frozen peas and onions
1 pound small mushrooms
2 Tablespoons butter
3 Tablespoons butter
3 Tablespoons flour
1 Tablespoon instant minced
  onion
½ teaspoon salt
½ teaspoon celery salt
½ teaspoon paprika
½ teaspoon dried oregano
½ teaspoon Worcestershire sauce
¼ teaspoon Tabasco
1 cup chicken broth
½ cup sauterne wine
1 cup light cream

Simmer chicken breasts in water seasoned with 1 teaspoon salt, covered, until tender. Remove skin and bones, leaving chicken in large pieces. Reserve 1 cup broth.
Cook the package of frozen peas and onions according to package directions. Sauté mushrooms in 2 Tablespoons of butter and remove from the skillet. In the same skillet, melt the remaining 3 Tablespoons butter, stir in the flour and seasonings. Stir in the chicken broth and wine. Cook, stirring, over low heat until sauce is thickened. Cool slightly. Stir in the cream, mushrooms, peas and onions with chicken. Reheat but do not boil. Serve on hot, fluffy rice. Serves 6.

Mrs. Thomas Zentner

Chicken Crunch

½ cup chicken broth or milk
2 cans cream of mushroom soup
4 cups diced cooked chicken
¼ cup onion, minced
1 cup celery, diced
1 can water chestnuts, sliced
1- 3 ounce can Chow Mein
  noodles
⅓ cup toasted almonds

Blend broth into soup in a 2 quart casserole. Mix in remaining ingredients except almonds. Bake in a slow oven, 325 degrees, for 40 minutes. Just before serving sprinkle with almonds. You may omit the chestnuts and use 1 1/2 cups chopped celery. Serves 4.

Mrs. Jerry Gregg

Chicken Noodle Casserole

1- 6 ounce package noodles
1 can cream of chicken soup
1- 5⅓ ounce can evaporated milk
¼ teaspoon salt
1 cup Cheddar cheese, shredded
3 cups diced cooked chicken
1 cup diced celery
¼ cup diced pimiento
1 cup slivered almonds, toasted
Buttered bread crumbs

Cook noodles according to package directions and drain. Place half of noodles in each of two small greased casseroles. Combine soup, milk and salt; heat, stirring constantly. Add cheese and stir until melted. Add chicken, celery, pimiento and half of almonds. Pour over noodles. Top with bread crumbs and the remaining almonds. Bake uncovered at 400 degrees for about 20 minutes.

Mrs. Joe Montgomery

Chicken Spectacular

3 cups cooked chicken
1 package Uncle Ben's
   Combination Wild and White
   Rice, cooked
1 can cream of celery soup
1 medium jar sliced pimientos
1 medium onion, chopped
2 cups French style green beans,
   drained
1 cup Hellman's mayonnaise
1 can water chestnuts, diced
Salt and pepper, to taste

Mix all ingredients. Pour into a 2 1/2 or 3 quart casserole. Bake 25 to 30 minutes at 350 degrees. Serves 16. To freeze do not cook prior to freezing.

Mrs. John Smith
Mrs. Naomi E. Crawford
Winnfield, Louisiana

Tetrazzini

3 to 4 pound hen
1 onion
1 bay leaf
2 ribs celery and tops
Salt and pepper
¼ pound butter
1 bunch green onions, minced
½ cup bell pepper, minced
¼ pound mushrooms, minced or
   1 large can mushrooms,
   chopped
¼ cup parsley, minced
½ cup celery, minced
1 clove garlic, pressed
1 cup cream
1 cup stock
2 Tablespoons white wine or
   sherry
1 Tablespoon lemon juice
2 Tablespoons flour
2 Tablespoons butter
1- 7 ounce package vermicelli
¾ cup grated Parmesan

Boil hen until tender with onion, bay leaf, celery, salt and pepper. Remove; cool, strain stock and reserve. Cut chicken in bite-size pieces and set aside. Sauté all vegetables and garlic in butter until soft. Add chicken, cream, stock, lemon juice and wine. Season to taste with salt and pepper and cook slowly over low heat, until heated through. Make a paste of additional butter and flour. Blend in and stir until smooth and thickened. Cook vermicelli al dente in boiling stock. Drain and spread on bottom of a shallow buttered casserole. Pour chicken mixture over and sprinkle with Parmesan. Bake 20 minutes at 350 degrees. Serves 6 to 8. May prepare ahead and refrigerate until serving time. Increase baking time a little.

Mrs. Don Irby

Easy Chicken Tetrazzini

1-4 pound hen
½ stick butter
1 large can mushrooms
1 Tablespoon parsley flakes
2 cans cream of chicken soup
½ pint sour cream
Salt
Pepper
12 ounces spaghetti
Parmesan cheese

Boil hen in seasoned water. Cool, debone and cut into bite size pieces. Melt butter in a large skillet and add drained mushrooms. Sauté 10 minutes. Add parsley flakes and chicken. Cover and let sit for 10 minutes. Add the cream of chicken soup and sour cream. Break spaghetti into bite size pieces and cook as directed on package or in the left over chicken stock. Drain and cool. Combine with chicken mixture and place in a buttered casserole. Sprinkle with cheese and bake uncovered in a 300 degree oven until hot.

Chinese Chicken Spaghetti

1 hen
2 large bell peppers, chopped
2 large onions, chopped
1 bunch celery, chopped
1 can pimientos, chopped
1 can whole mushrooms
Chicken stock
1 package spaghetti
Salt
Pepper
Accent
Soy Sauce

Cook hen in seasoned water and leave in broth to cool. Debone hen when cooled and reserve stock. Cut meat into bite size pieces. Cook the bell pepper, onions and celery in 1 cup of chicken stock. Cook the spaghetti in rest of chicken stock until tender. You will find you absorb all of the stock. Toss all together and add the pimientos and mushrooms. Season to taste with salt, pepper and Accent. This is a very good and different chicken spaghetti. Pass soy sauce. Serves 8 to 10.

Mrs. George Snellings III

Lexington Chicken Spaghetti for 50

4 hens, approximately 5 pounds
  each
16 to 20 cups water
Celery
Onions
Salt and pepper to taste
8 onions, chopped
2 bunches celery, chopped
4 bell peppers, chopped
8 buttons garlic, chopped
4 cans tomato sauce
8 cans tomato paste
1¾ cups Worcestershire
1⅓ bottles catsup
4 teaspoons black pepper
Salt to taste
20 cups broth
4 pounds spaghetti

Boil hens in water seasoned with celery, onions, salt and pepper to taste using 4 to 5 cups of water for each hen. Remove meat from bones. Save broth and fat. Sauté onions, celery, bell pepper and garlic in chicken fat until soft. Add tomato sauce, tomato paste, Worcestershire sauce, catsup, pepper, salt to taste and 20 cups broth. Simmer for one hour and add chicken. Boil the spaghetti in a separate container for 8 to 12 minutes in salted water. Drain and add to the sauce. This may be kept in the refrigerator overnight. Use additional broth to moisten the spaghetti if necessary. To heat in an electric roaster allow several hours at 325 degrees using additional broth as needed. Stir well from bottom while heating to keep from sticking. Serves 50.

King Ranch Chicken
A Mexican party must!

3 to 4 pound hen
1 onion
1 or 2 ribs celery
Salt and pepper
1 onion, chopped
1 large bell pepper, chopped
1 can mushroom soup
1 can cream of chicken soup
1/2 pound Cheddar, grated
Chili powder
Garlic salt
1 package frozen tortillas
1 can Rotel Tomatoes and Chilies, undrained

Boil hen until tender in water seasoned with onion, celery, salt and pepper. Cut chicken into bite size pieces and reserve all stock. Chop onion and bell pepper, combine soups and grate cheese. Just before putting casserole together, soak the frozen tortillas in boiling chicken stock until wilted. Start layering casserole in a 9 x 12 inch baking dish in this order: Tortillas "dripping with stock", chicken, onion, bell pepper, sprinkling to taste with chili powder and garlic salt, soup mixture and cheese. Repeat the layers, being sure the tortillas are ozzing with the stock. Cover the casserole with the Rotel tomatoes and all the juice. Juices in the casserole should be about half of the depth of the dish, if not add a little more stock. May be made and frozen several days ahead, but always make at least one day ahead and refrigerate so that the flavors will blend. Bake casserole uncovered at 375 degrees for 30 minutes. Serves 8 to 10. Secret: a well seasoned stock.

Mrs. Mike Cage
Mrs. John Lolley

Cream Sauce for Chicken
A delicious base which may be served in many various ways.

1 stick butter
1/2 cup flour
2 egg yolks
1 cup milk
1/2 cup chicken broth
1/2 cup cream
3 Tablespoons butter
6 green onions, finely chopped
3 or 4 ribs of celery, finely chopped
1/4 bell pepper, finely chopped
Salt and pepper to taste

OPTIONAL:
Pimiento, drained
Mushrooms, drained
2 or 3 Tablespoons sherry

2 cups chicken
6 patty shells

Melt butter, stir in flour until smooth. Beat egg yolks with milk, chicken broth and cream and add to first mixture. Stir until quite thick. Sauté the green onions, celery and pepper in 3 Tablespoons of butter. Add to cream sauce and season with salt and pepper. Add optional ingredients if desired. Stir in chicken. Heat thoroughly and fill patty shells.

Mrs. Floyd James
Ruston, Louisiana

Fletcher's Chicken Livers

3 or 4 medium size white onions
10 or 12 chicken livers
3 large strips bacon
¼ to ½ cup sherry, or to
taste
Salt and pepper to taste

Slice the onions 1/4 inch thick and arrange in a flat baking dish, 3 quart size or larger. On top of each onion, place 1 chicken liver and salt lightly. Cut strips of bacon in 4 pieces, if bacon comes in smaller strips, use enough for each onion and liver to be covered. Salt and pepper generously. Pour sherry over all. Bake, uncovered, in a moderate oven, 350 degrees. Baste occasionally with pan drippings, until bacon begins to crisp, about 45 minutes. Take up with a spatula and serve as a main meat dish. This recipe was made up by my husband as a good way to use chicken livers when chickens have been used for a barbeque. Serves 4.

Mrs. Fletcher Ashcraft

Cornish Hens Bordelaise

8 Cornish hens, about 1 pound
each
Lawry's seasoning salt
Salt
Pepper
Butter
1 large onion, cut into 8 pieces
1 rib celery, cut into 8 pieces
Paprika
¼ cup melted butter

SAUCE:
½ teaspoon thyme
1 bay leaf
1 cup Madeira wine
1 cup boiling water
3 teaspoons Spice Islands Chicken
Stock base
1½ Tablespoons cornstarch
2 teaspoons sugar, or to taste
1 medium onion, finely chopped

Wash and dry hens. Sprinkle with seasonings and rub with butter inside and out. Place a small piece of onion and celery in each. Tie the legs together and sprinkle with paprika. Roast uncovered about one hour at 425 degrees basting with the melted butter. *Sauce:* In a small bowl combine thyme, bayleaf and wine; set aside. Dissolve stock base in 1 cup boiling water, mix in cornstarch and sugar. Set aside. When birds are done remove to a heated platter and keep warm. Pour off 1/2 cup hot drippings into small skillet. Sauté the onion until soft. Stir in the cornstarch mixture and bring to a boil. Reduce heat. Stir in wine and simmer for 5 minutes. Strain sauce into a gravy boat. Serve with a wild rice dish. Serves 8.

Mrs. E. Rupert Campbell
Shreveport, Louisiana

Marie Louise's Turkey and Gravy

*This is the best way we have found that will
make the juiciest and most flavorful turkey
that you have ever cooked! Editor's Note.*

1 turkey
Dry mustard
Worcestershire sauce
Olive oil
Salt and pepper
Vinegar
1 onion, cut in half
Celery
Parsley
Bacon
Butter
2 cups chicken stock

GRAVY:
Turkey giblets
4 to 5 cups water
2 ribs celery
1 onion
Salt and pepper
1 Tablespoon oil or butter
1 Tablespoon flour
1 onion, chopped
1 rib celery
Chopped parsley
Bay leaf
Salt and pepper to taste
2 cups giblet stock

If you buy a frozen turkey, be sure that the turkey is well thawed. A few hours before you propose to cook it, the day before if possible, rub the turkey well inside and out with a paste which you make up of dry mustard, Worcestershire sauce, olive oil, salt, pepper and a little vinegar in the proportions to make it into a soft paste. Rub the bird well inside and out with this, then place inside it a whole onion cut in half, a couple of pieces of celery and a little parsley. Across the breast of the turkey lay 2 pieces of bacon and in the little crevice between the drumstick and the body of the turkey stick hunks of butter, about a stick of butter all together. Soak a dishtowel or cheesecloth in olive oil and lay it over the turkey and put it in an uncovered roaster. To this you can add about one to two cups of stock in the roaster, or if you have any gravy left, that is fine too. In cooking the turkey, you cook it according to the following scale using a 300 degree oven:

7 to 10 pounds 30 minutes per pound
10 to 15 pounds 20 minutes per pound
15 to 18 pounds 18 minutes per pound
18 to 20 pounds 15 minutes per pound
20 to 23 pounds 13 minutes per pound

You may baste the turkey only once or twice during the course of cooking. This browns the turkey beautifully and makes it completely tender when you eat it.

Gravy: While the turkey is cooking, take the neck and giblets and cook them all in about 4 to 5 cups of water with celery, onion, salt and pepper and let them boil until they are thoroughly done. In the meantime, you take a Tablespoon of oil or butter and one Tablespoon of flour and make a roux by browning the flour. Add one chopped onion, 1 piece of chopped celery, some chopped parsley, a bay leaf, salt and pepper to taste. Sauté this until soft and add the stock to this roux. Let it simmer down to make the gravy for the turkey. This can be increased to make as much gravy as you desire. Add the giblets, which have been chopped, to the gravy.

Turkey Chop Suey

1- 1 pound can bean sprouts
½ cup onion, sliced thinly
2 Tablespoons butter
2 cups diced turkey
1 cup celery, sliced
1 can water chestnuts, sliced
½ cup chicken broth
2 Tablespoons cornstarch
¼ teaspoon salt
¼ teaspoon MSG
¼ cup water
2 Tablespoons soy sauce
½ cup slivered toasted almonds,
   optional

Drain bean sprouts and reserve liquid. Cook onion in butter until tender but not brown. Add turkey, celery, water chestnuts, broth and bean sprout liquid. Heat to boiling. Combine cornstarch, seasonings, water and soy sauce. Stir into turkey mixture and cook stirring constantly until thick. Add bean sprouts and heat. Serve on hot rice or Chinese noodles. Sprinkle with almonds and pass extra soy sauce. Serves 6.

Mrs. George Purvis
Rayville, Louisiana

Mrs. Ben W. Sturdivant of Glendora, Mississippi adds 1 can of drained pineapple chunks and 1 can of drained mushrooms.

Turkey Leftover Surprise

1- 6 ounce package Uncle Ben's
   Wild Rice
2 Tablespoons butter
1 pound bulk sausage
3 cups leftover turkey, chopped
2 cans mushroom soup
1 can button mushrooms

Cook rice according to package directions, adding 2 Tablespoons butter. Sauté sausage and drain. Layer ingredients twice in this order: sausage, turkey, rice, soup and ending with mushrooms. Bake in a 400 degree oven until lightly brown, about 20 minutes. Chicken may be used in lieu of turkey. Serves 6 with green salad and garlic bread accompaniment.

Mrs. Elton Upshaw, Jr.
Mrs. Henry Weaks

Guacamole Topped Turkey

1 medium sized avocado
1/8 teaspoon salt
1/8 teaspoon pepper
1/8 teaspoon onion powder
Dash of cayenne pepper
2 teaspoons lemon juice
1/4 teaspoon Tabasco
1/4 cup sour cream
1 Tablespoon mayonnaise
12 slices cooked turkey roast
6 sautéed toast rounds
Parsley
Tomato wedges

Cut avocado in half. Remove seed and mash the pulp. Combine with the remaining ingredients except turkey. Check for seasoning. Place the seed in the spread to prevent discoloration while chilling. Serve mounded on top of 2 turkey slices, which have been placed over toast. Garnish with parsley and tomato wedges. This makes great po boy's too! Serves 6.

Mrs. Elton Upshaw, Jr.

Grilled Turkey Sandwich

1 cup coarsely ground cooked
　turkey or chicken
1/2 cup toasted nuts, chopped fine
1 teaspoon grated onion
2/3 cup mayonnaise
1/4 cup chopped mixed sweet
　pickles
1/2 teaspoon salt

Combine all ingredients. Cover and chill for several hours or overnight. Spread bread generously with filling. Spread outside of sandwich with butter. Grill on both sides under the broiler. This makes a good filling for party sandwiches.

Mrs. Henry Guerriero

Easy Turkey Dressing

1/2 onion
1/2 bunch green onions
1 small bell pepper
3 ribs celery
1 or 2 sticks butter
1/2 pound bulk sausage, optional
1 package Pepperidge Farm corn
　bread and herb stuffing
2 cups well seasoned chicken
　stock
1 egg, slightly beaten
1 cup minced parsley
Salt and pepper
Worcestershire
Tabasco

Finely chop all vegetables and sauté all but parsley, in butter and sausage. If omitting sausage, use two sticks butter. Empty dressing mix into large bowl. Add stock; if you have none prepare from Spice Islands Stock Base. Toss in vegetables, egg, fresh parsley and seasonings. Stuff cavity of turkey just before roasting. Bake remaining dressing in pan or stuff in parboiled hollowed onions about 30 minutes, adding a little more stock if necessary to prevent dryness.

Bess Burns' Cornbread Dressing

1 black iron skillet of cornbread,
    any recipe
½ bell pepper, chopped
3 celery ribs, chopped
1 bunch green onions, chopped
1 medium onion, chopped
1 pound Bryan's sausage
4 chicken bouillon cubes, dis-
    solved in 1 cup boiling water
1 can Morton's chicken broth
1 cup chicken fat or butter
4 eggs
1 teaspoon Lawry's seasoning
    salt
⅛ teaspoon cayenne pepper
¼ teaspoon pepper
Salt to taste
1 pint oysters, drained
1 package Pepperidge Farm
    dressing mix

Make cornbread ahead of time by your favorite recipe in your iron skillet. Sauté bell pepper, celery, and onions with the sausage. Melt 4 chicken bouillon cubes in the boiling water. Add chicken broth and chicken fat or butter. Pour all the ingredients into a large Dutch oven with the crumbled cornbread. Add the remaining ingredients. Bake in a 450 degree oven, about 1 to 1-1/2 hours, until the crust is brown on top. This will serve 12 amply.

Mrs. Elton Upshaw, Jr.

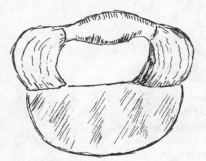

Oyster Dressing

3 large onions, chopped fine
1 bell pepper, chopped fine
1 bunch green onions, chopped
4 ribs celery, chopped fine
Bacon drippings or margarine to
    sauté vegetables
3 cloves garlic, pressed
½ bunch parsley chopped
Salt to taste
Pepper to taste
½ teaspoon sugar
6 dozen oysters
1 loaf week-old French bread
2 or 3 eggs

Finely chop onions, bell pepper, green onions and celery. Sauté in bacon drippings until tender. Add garlic, parsley, salt, pepper, sugar and simmer until wilted. In a separate pan, heat oysters in their juice and let simmer until the edges curl. Remove and cut into pieces. Break the bread into small pieces and soak them in the hot oyster liquid. Squeeze out the excess liquid. Add to the vegetable mixture. Stir in the chopped oysters. Add the eggs, starting with two, and mix well. Check for seasonings, adding more salt and pepper if desired. Bake at 350 degrees in a casserole until browned and crusty, about 45 minutes.

Mrs. J. M. deBen
New Orleans, Louisiana

Potpourri Dressing

Livers and gizzards
1 onion, minced
1 rib celery, finely chopped
2 Tablespoons parsley
2 Tablespoons shortening
3 cups cold cooked rice
2 cups cold cornbread crumbs
3 dozen oysters with liquor
2 eggs
1 Tablespoon melted butter
1 teaspoon salt
½ teaspoon pepper
1 cup chopped pecans

Boil giblets in water to cover until they are tender enough to chop. Reserve liquid. Brown onion, giblets, parsley and celery in hot shortening. To this add the rice, cornbread and oysters, chopped or whole, and gradually add the oyster liquor and liquid from boiling the giblets. Add beaten eggs, melted butter, salt, pepper and pecans. Fill the turkey cavity loosely with the mixture and bake the remaining dressing in a baking dish at 350 degrees until brown.

Mrs. E. C. Rowan

Geneva's Matzo Balls

5 matzos
2 cups cool water
1 Tablespoon chicken fat or
   butter
½ onion, chopped fine
2 ribs celery, chopped fine
2 eggs
Salt and pepper to taste
2 Tablespoons parsley, chopped
¼ cup, approximately, matzo
   meal

Break matzos into pieces and soak in about 2 cups cool water until fluffy, about 15 to 30 minutes. Drain and squeeze dry. Heat fat in a skillet and sauté onion and celery. Add the soaked matzos, stirring occasionally and cook until the mixture leaves the skillet clean. Let this mixture get cold. Add eggs, salt, pepper, parsley and matzo meal. Let stand for several hours to swell. Shape into balls not quite an inch in diameter; test one by dropping into boiling lightly salted water. If it falls apart, add more meal. Cook by dropping the balls into soup, roast or chicken gravy, cover and cook until they rise to the top, about 15 minutes.

Tips: Stir the matzo balls with a fork rather than a spoon for lightness. Mixture or balls can be made the day before and refrigerated.

Do not roll the balls too tightly.

This can be frozen cooked or uncooked but uncooked does best.

This recipe can be doubled, tripled, quadrupled ad infinitum, but onions and celery are added to taste.

Mrs. Clifford Strauss

NOTES

Oysters DeSiard
"on the shell"

1 Tablespoon butter
1 Tablespoon flour
1 bunch green onions
$\frac{1}{2}$ cup chicken broth
$\frac{1}{2}$ cup minced shrimp
$\frac{1}{3}$ cup minced mushrooms
1 egg yolk
$\frac{1}{3}$ cup white wine
1 Tablespoon lemon juice
$\frac{3}{4}$ teaspoon Worcestershire
$\frac{1}{4}$ teaspoon Accent
Salt, pepper and Tabasco to
  taste
$\frac{1}{2}$ cup bread crumbs
$\frac{3}{4}$ cup grated Parmesan cheese
Paprika
1 dozen oysters on the half shell

Make a medium roux with butter and flour. Stir in green onions and simmer until soft. Blend in chicken broth stirring continually. Add shrimp and mushrooms, simmer about 5 minutes until mushrooms soften. Beat egg yolk with wine. Blend in a little of the hot mixture and stir all back into sauce. Add lemon juice, Worcestershire, Accent, salt, pepper and Tabasco to taste. Simmer 15 minutes or so. Combine bread crumbs, cheese and paprika to color slightly. Set aside. Place oysters on a bed of rock salt in large pan. Bake in a preheated 350 degree oven 6 to 8 minutes. Remove and drain. Return oysters to shells, top with sauce and cover with crumb mixture. Bake about 12 minutes until hot and bubbly. This recipe easily doubles if preparing more oysters. Serve with lemon wedges.

Mrs. J. M. deBen
New Orleans, Louisiana

Deviled Oysters on the Shell

4 Tablespoons melted butter
3 Tablespoons grated Parmesan
½ cup seasoned bread crumbs
1 clove garlic, pressed
2 Tablespoons chopped parsley
Dash of Tabasco
1 to 1½ dozen oysters

Mix all ingredients. Place drained oysters on shells in a large baking pan covered with rock salt. Cover with mix and bake 15 to 20 minutes in a preheated 350 degree oven.

C. McVea Oliver

Oysters Rockefeller
*Personal taste is the secret of this recipe.
Amounts of seasonings given are to be adjusted
to your taste, more or less.*

2 packages chopped spinach
1 cup finely chopped celery
¾ cup green onions and tops
½ head finely chopped lettuce
½ cup parsley, minced
¾ stick butter
¼ cup olive oil
¼ cup water
1 teaspoon salt
1 teaspoon pepper
Dash of Tabasco
1 lemon, juiced
2 Tablespoons Worcestershire
1 teaspoon Tabasco
2 ounce tube anchovy paste
½ cup parsley, minced
¼ cup bread crumbs
2 Tablespoons cream
Absinthe or anise to taste,
     optional
4 dozen oysters on the
     half shell

Simmer for several hours spinach, celery, green onions, lettuce and 1/2 cup parsley in butter, oil and 1/4 cup water, salt, pepper and Tabasco. When vegetables taste done, blend in seasonings using almost whole tube of anchovy paste and additional parsley. Simmer a short while longer and blend in bread crumbs and cream. Adjust seasoning. Refrigerate or freeze. If using absinthe do not add until ready to use. Place oyster shells on a bed of rock salt in large roasting pans. Put in a preheated 400 degree oven to heat shells. Remove from oven, place drained oysters in shells and top with Rockefeller sauce. Bake 15 minutes at 400 degrees and 5 minutes under broiler.

Mrs. William D. Brown
Lake Providence, Louisiana

Oysters Mosca

2 cups Progresso Bread Crumbs
1 Tablespoon crushed red pepper
2 lemons, juiced
¾ cup olive oil
1 clove garlic, pressed
3 Tablespoons chopped parsley
1 cup Parmesan cheese
Salt to taste
1 quart oysters, drained

Combine all ingredients except oysters. Place oysters in a baking dish, ramekins or shells. Top with mixture. Bake at 350 degrees until oysters curl and then place under the broiler until slightly browned.

Mrs. Louis Kusin

Oyster Casserole

1 cup chopped celery
1 cup chopped onions
1 cup cracker crumbs
1 pint cream sauce made with
  butter, flour and milk
Dash of Tabasco
1 quart oysters, drained
Red and black pepper
Salt to taste

Cook celery and onions in small amount of salted water until just tender. Place a layer of cracker crumbs in bottom of casserole. Start making layers of ingredients; first spoon in seasoned cream sauce, then celery and onions, dash of red and black pepper and salt to taste. Add some oysters. Repeat layers until all layers are used. Place crumbs on top and dot generously with butter, enough to season through the casserole. Bake at 350 degrees about 30 to 40 minutes. Serve while hot. Serves 6.

Mrs. D. E. Burchett
Benton, Louisiana

Deviled Oysters

4 Tablespoons bacon grease
1 cup green onions, chopped fine
1 cup celery, minced
5 to 6 slices bread, toasted medium
  brown
2 Tablespoons bacon grease
1 pint drained oysters, 2 cups,
  save juice
Juice of ½ lemon
1 Tablespoon Worcestershire
  sauce
Salt and pepper
Butter
Cracker crumbs

Sauté onions and celery in bacon grease. Wet toasted bread, squeeze dry, break into pieces, and drop in skillet. Add 2 more Tablespoons bacon drippings. Brown slowly, stirring constantly, 45 minutes. Add more bacon drippings as you go along if needed. Drop in oysters. Chop up oysters with spoon and knife as you continue to stir, 30 minutes. Add lemon juice, Worcestershire sauce, salt and pepper. Stir. Pour some oyster juice in this mixture. Cover tightly, simmer slowly, stirring every so often. Then add a lump of butter. Put in individual shells. Top with cracker crumbs. Put in a 350 degree oven until crumbs are brown. Serves 6. Can be used as a dip rather than a main course. May be prepared and frozen before baking.

Mrs. Armand E. Breard

311

Baked Oysters

1 pint oysters, drained
½ stick butter
½ lemon, juiced
Worcestershire to taste
Tabasco to taste
Salt and pepper
1 Tablespoon cream
Unseasoned bread crumbs
4 chopped green onions
¼ cup minced parsley

Drain oysters well and lay in a well buttered 8 inch pie pan, individual ramekins or shells. Make sauce of butter, lemon juice, Worcestershire and Tabasco. Salt and pepper oysters well. Sprinkle with cream. Pour sauce over and sprinkle with bread crumbs. Cover heavily with minced green onions and parsley. Bake 30 minutes in a 350 degree oven.

Mrs. Wesley Shafto, Jr.

Oyster Loaf

1 loaf French bread
1 stick butter
1 clove crushed garlic
1 Tablespoon parsley
1 pint drained oysters
2 cups vegetable oil
1 cup corn meal
 SAUCE:
1 cup ketchup
2 Tablespoons horseradish
1 Tablespoon lemon juice
1 teaspoon Worcestershire sauce
Dash Tabasco sauce
2 dill pickles sliced thinly

Slice top of bread lengthwise and hollow out. Brush inside with melted butter, garlic, and parsley. Toast in a 300 degree oven about 25 minutes. Meanwhile, mix sauce and set aside. Dredge oysters in corn meal and fry in hot oil just until brown. Drain and salt. Place oysters in warm toasted loaf. Spoon sauce over, and top with pickles. Replace top of bread and slice in serving portions. Serves 4. You can make individual loaves.

Mrs. George M. Snellings III

Oyster Patties

2 dozen oysters, 1 pint jar, save
    liquid
3 Tablespoons flour
3 Tablespoons bacon drippings,
    butter or Crisco
2 onions, finely chopped
2 ribs celery, finely chopped
½ sweet pepper, finely chopped
4 shallots, finely chopped
1 clove garlic, chopped or minced
6 to 8 parsley sprigs, finely
    chopped
Salt and pepper to taste
Pepperidge Farm frozen patty
    shells

Make a very dark roux with flour and drippings. Add onions, celery, sweet pepper, shallots, garlic, and parsley to roux. Cover and simmer 1 hour or longer. Add oyster liquor; be sure to strain liquid to get out all pieces of shell. Cook until thick, then add oysters and cook for about 15 to 20 minutes. This will make enough for 4 patty shells. May be made the day before, but do not put in the patty shells until ready to serve. To make enough to fill 6 patty shells, use 4 Tablespoons of flour and 4 Tablespoons of drippings to make roux. Add extra oysters but do not add more liquid, as oysters will create juice of their own.

Mrs. Milton deBen
New Orleans, Louisiana

Oysters St. Pierre

3 dozen oysters
1 Tablespoon flour
1 Tablespoon butter
1 cup milk
2 egg yolks, beaten
1 small can mushrooms
½ onion, chopped
Green onion tops, chopped
Salt and pepper to taste
Bread crumbs
Parsley, minced

Boil oysters in their juices until they are puffy. Remove and chop. Work the flour and butter together. Put milk in the top of a double boiler. As it comes to a boil, stir in the flour and butter; blend in the beaten egg yolks, mushrooms, onions and seasonings. Add the oysters. This may be put in a casserole or individual shells. Sprinkle with bread or cracker crumbs and minced parsley. Bake at 350 degrees for about 5 or 10 minutes. Serves 5 to 6.

Mrs. Custer Primos

Oysters and Artichokes

12 artichokes
1½ sticks butter
5 Tablespoons flour
½ cup green onions, chopped fine
½ cup parsley, chopped fine
2 cloves garlic, pressed
1 teaspoon Accent
Pinch of thyme
Red pepper to taste
1 Tablespoon lemon juice
Seasoned salt to taste
1½ cups oyster liquor, add
  chicken broth to make amount
6 dozen oysters
1 teaspoon absinthe
Paprika
Lemon slices

Boil the artichokes in salted water until they are tender. Remove, invert them and drain well. Remove the bottoms from the artichokes and reserve them. With a spoon, scrape the soft pulp from each leaf and reserve it. Discard the leaves. You may want to save a few leaves for garnishing the finished dish. Make a dark roux with the butter and flour. Add the onions, parsley and garlic and sauté in the roux until the vegetables are soft. Add the seasonings and the oyster liquor to the above and cook about 20 minutes until the sauce is smooth and thick. Push the leaf scrapings through a sieve to be certain that all of the stringy parts are out of the scrapings! Add the leaf scrapings and the oysters to the mixture and cook until the oysters are curled. Add the absinthe and check for seasonings. To serve, place the reserved artichoke bottoms in individual ramekins, spoon the sauce over the bottoms, sprinkle with paprika and top with a lemon slice. Brown in the oven or under the broiler. After the ramekins are browned, you may stick a few of the reserved artichoke leaves around the edge of the dish for dunking the sauce. Serves 12.

Mrs. Ed Seymour, Jr.

Oyster Rockefeller Casserole

1 quart raw oysters
1 stick butter
1 rib celery, finely chopped
1 medium onion, finely chopped
1/2 cup parsley, finely chopped
1 box frozen chopped spinach,
    thawed and drained
1/4 teaspoon anise seed
1/4 cup Lea & Perrins sauce
1/2 cup bread crumbs
Salt, pepper and cayenne to taste
1 cup sharp cheese, grated
Bread crumbs

Drain oysters. Melt butter and sauté celery. Add onions, parsley, spinach, anise seed, Lea and Perrins, bread crumbs, salt, pepper and cayenne. Grease a shallow casserole. Arrange oysters in one layer only. Cover with Rockefeller mixture as thick as desired. Bake in 450 degree oven for 30 minutes. Remove and sprinkle with grated cheese and a very thin layer of bread crumbs. Return to oven for 10 minutes until slightly brown.

Mrs. Henry Hammonds

Escargots

24 snails and shells
1/3 pound butter
2 cloves garlic, crushed
1 teaspoon chopped parsley
1 teaspoon salt
1 1/2 teaspoons chopped green
    onions
Pepper to taste

Cream butter and stir in all the other ingredients. Put a little butter mixture in each shell and put a snail in each one. Cover the snails with the remaining butter mixture. Bake at 450 degrees until butter begins to bubble and turn brown. Serve at once.

Mrs. John Kelso, Jr.

Boiled Shrimp

1 lemon, sliced or cut into wedges
1 onion, diced
1 package crab boil
1 cup salt
1 gallon water
5 pounds shrimp

Put lemon and onions into bag with crab boil. Add salt and the bag of seasonings to water. Bring to boil. Add shrimp and bring back to boil. Cook 5 minutes. Remove from heat and let stand 10 to 15 minutes. Remove shrimp and drain. Perfect shrimp everytime.

Mrs. Dan Sartor

Shrimp Sauté

2 pounds raw shrimp, shelled
1 stick butter
2 cloves garlic, minced
Juice of 1 lemon
Salt
Cracked pepper
Dash of Worcestershire
1/3 cup minced parsley
1 or 2 Tablespoons chives,
   minced, optional

Prepare shrimp. Melt butter and sauté garlic. Add shrimp, lemon juice, salt, pepper, and a dash of Worcestershire. Sauté slowly, tossing, until shrimp turn pink. Turn heat on high to cook off any liquid shrimp have given off. *Do not overcook.* Toss in parsley and minced chives at the last minute just to heat through. Fresh shrimp or fresh frozen shrimp should be used, not frozen prepared shrimp, as they will toughen.

Mrs. Don Irby

Manale's Bar-B-Qued Shrimp

1 pound shrimp
Olive oil
Cracked black pepper
Salt
Lemon juice
Tabasco
Lea & Perrins
Butter

Place whole shrimp, keep shells on, in single layer in oven proof dish. Drizzle olive oil on top of shrimp. Pepper shrimp until they are black; when you think you have enough pepper, add more. Add lots of salt, lemon juice, Tabasco and Lea and Perrins. Remember you are seasoning through the shells. Cut up butter on top of shrimp and broil until shrimp are cooked, 15 to 20 minutes. Be sure and taste to see if they are done. Serve these with newspaper on the table and lots of napkins. Have French bread to sop up the oil and encourage guests to eat the shells, as well, if river shrimp are used. With cold beer and green salad, you have the makings of a great informal party.
Base the amount of shrimp on the number of guests.

Mrs. George Snellings III
Mrs. Jerry Wolff

Beer Batter Fried Shrimp

2 pounds shrimp, shelled
1- 12 ounce can beer
1 cup flour
1 Tablespoon salt
1 Tablespoon paprika
Red pepper to taste

Prepare raw fresh shrimp. Pour beer into a mixing bowl. Sift dry ingredients into the beer and beat with a wire whisk until frothy. While using, whisk lightly from time to time. Batter may be used immediately or stored in the refrigerator several days. This is also a great light crisp batter for frying vegetables, chicken or game.

Steamed Shrimp

FINELY MINCE:
1 cup green onions
1 cup white onions
1 cup celery
1 cup bell pepper
1/4 cup parsley
1 or 2 cloves garlic
1/2 cup oil
5 pounds shrimp in shells
Salt
Red pepper

Sauté all minced vegetables in oil. Cover and cook until reduced to 1/3 original volume, stirring often so it doesn't stick. Wash shrimp and drain on paper towels, do not peel. Sprinkle shrimp heavily on both sides with salt and red pepper. Add to vegetable mixture, cover and steam until done, 20 to 30 minutes. Serve warm with salad and French bread. Incidentally this gravy and leftover shrimp make great shrimp stew.

Mrs. Harry Stone

Shrimp and Wild Rice

1/2 cup thinly sliced onion
1/4 cup thinly sliced green peppers
1/2 cup fresh mushrooms, sliced
   thin
1/4 cup butter
1 Tablespoon Worcestershire
   sauce
A few drops Tabasco
2 cups cooked wild rice
1 pound cooked and shelled
   shrimp
2 Tablespoons flour
2 Tablespoons butter
2 cups chicken broth

Sauté the onion, green peppers and mushrooms in butter until soft. Add the seasonings, rice and shrimp to the vegetables. In a separate saucepan, melt butter and blend in flour. Add chicken broth slowly and stir constantly until the sauce is smooth; add to the shrimp mixture. Place in a buttered casserole and bake at 300 degrees until thoroughly heated.

Mrs. Harry Bell

Company Shrimp Casserole

2 to 3 pounds shrimp, cooked,
  peeled and cleaned
1 cup rice, cooked
1 cup sharp cheese, grated
1 can mushroom soup
½ cup chopped green pepper
½ cup chopped green onion
½ cup chopped celery
1 stick butter
8 lemons, sliced very thin

Mix first four ingredients together. Sauté green peppers, green onions, and celery in butter. Add to shrimp mixture. Put in long flat casserole and completely cover top with sliced lemons. Cook covered about 20 minutes at 375 degrees. May be frozen ahead. Serves 6.

Delicious served with salad, French bread and dessert.

Mrs. Carrick Inabnett

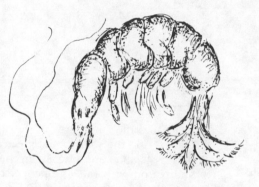

Shrimp Casserole

¼ cup chopped green pepper
3 Tablespoons butter
2 Tablespoons flour
1 can mushroom soup
1 cup milk
Dash pepper
1¾ cups Cheddar cheese, grated
2 cups shrimp, cooked and
  deveined and cut in bites
Bread crumbs
Paprika

Sauté chopped green pepper in the butter. Stir in flour. Combine soup, milk and pepper. Stir into the flour mixture. Cook until smooth and thickened, stirring constantly. Add cheese and shrimp. Pour into a buttered 1 quart casserole. Top with bread crumbs and sprinkle with paprika. Bake at 375 degrees for 30 minutes. Serves 6.

This may be made thinner by the addition of 1/2 cup milk and then served over rice.

Mrs. Dick Ethridge

Shrimp Orleans

¼ cup butter
¼ cup olive oil
½ cup flour
1 cup or bunch green onions
1 can whole peeled tomatoes,
    drained, reserve ½ cup juice
Salt to taste
Red and black pepper to taste
2 pounds boiled shrimp
2 cups sour cream
¼ cup dry white wine
¼ cup Parmesan cheese,
    freshly grated
2 Tablespoons capers
Toast or pastry shells

Melt butter in iron skillet and add olive oil and flour. Brown slowly on medium heat until dark or darker than caramel. Using blender, combine green onions and tomatoes with salt and pepper to make purée. Transfer roux to a heavy Dutch oven and add tomato mixture. Allow 20 minutes or more to simmer. Stir occasionally. Add all remaining ingredients and cook only for a minute or so. Stir to mix uniformly and correct seasonings. Cook just long enough to heat thoroughly. The 1/2 cup reserved juice is to make the mixture to your desired consistency, and for reheating also. It tends to thicken some when left standing. I have frozen this for a short time and found it successful. Serve on toast or pastry rame-kins. Serves 6 to 8.

Mrs. Roy Kelly

Shrimp Croquettes

⅓ cup minced onion
2 cloves of garlic, minced
3 Tablespoons olive oil
½ cup finely chopped fresh
    tomato
⅓ cup minced green pepper
⅓ cup chopped parsley
¼ teaspoon oregano
Salt and pepper to taste
3 slices dry bread, crusts removed
1¼ cups milk
2 Tablespoons butter
¼ cup flour
2 cups diced cooked shrimp
Bread crumbs
2 eggs beaten with 1 Tablespoon
    milk
Deep shortening for frying

Sauté the onion and garlic in the oil in a skillet until tender. Add the tomato and green pepper and cook until vegetables are soft. Stir in the parsley, oregano and season with salt and pepper to taste. Remove from the heat and set aside. Soak the bread in 1/2 cup milk until the bread is soft. Squeeze dry and add to the onion mixture. Melt the butter in a saucepan and stir in the flour to make a light roux. Cook for 2 minutes and slowly add the remaining milk. Cook slowly until the sauce is smooth and thick. Add the sauce to the onion mixture. Add the shrimp and salt and pepper to taste. Chill the mixture and form into croquettes. Roll the croquettes in bread crumbs, dip into egg and milk and them roll in bread crumbs again. If you are not ready to fry the croquettes place them in the refrigerator. Deep fry in shortening, about 375 degrees until they are golden brown. Drain on absorbent paper. Serves 4 to 6. A cream sauce may be served over the croquettes or you may serve them with your favorite tartare sauce.

Shrimp in Sour Cream

½ stick butter
1 small bunch green onions
1 pound cooked shrimp
1- 4 ounce can sliced mushrooms
1 Tablespoon flour
Salt and pepper to taste
8 ounce carton sour cream
Milk, optional
Rice

Finely mince green onions and sauté in butter. Add shrimp and cook briefly with onions. Drain mushrooms and blend in the flour with the juice. Stir juice and mushrooms into the shrimp mixture, stirring until thickened. Season with salt and cracked pepper. Just before serving add sour cream and heat, *do not boil.* Serve over rice. Thin slightly with milk if needed. May also be used as a dip, unthinned. Serves 4, for a main dish.

Mrs. Roy Johns

Shrimp Curry For A Crowd
About 25 to 30

10 pounds shrimp, shelled, cleaned
   and boiled in salted water
1½ cups butter
⅓ cup flour
2½ cups chopped onion
2 cloves garlic
6 Tablespoons chopped celery
1½ teaspoons salt
3 Tablespoons curry powder
3 cups chicken broth
3 cups milk
3 cups Half and Half
6 Tablespoons Madeira or to
   taste
Rice

Prepare shrimp. Melt butter and stir in flour, sauté vegetables, but do not let brown. Add salt and curry. Stir in liquids and let *simmer* over low heat 30 minutes. Add shrimp and Madeira. Let heat through; check for seasoning. Let set overnight and reheat *very slowly* so it will not curdle. Serve over hot rice with curry condiments and broiled bananas.

Curry of Shrimp

⅓ cup of butter
3 Tablespoons flour
1 to 2 Tablespoons curry powder
   or to taste
½ teaspoon salt
¼ teaspoon paprika
Dash of nutmeg
2 cups light cream
3 cups cleaned, cooked shrimp
1 to 2 teaspoons ginger
1 Tablespoon lemon juice
Dash of Worcestershire
Salt to taste

BAKED RICE:
1 cup rice
2 Tablespoons butter
1 teaspoon salt
2¼ cups water

Melt butter; blend in flour, curry powder, paprika, salt and nutmeg. Add cream gradually, cooking until it thickens, stirring constantly. Blend in remaining ingredients. Serve with Baked Rice and condiments. Serves 4.

Baked Rice: Combine all ingredients in a 6 cup baking dish. Cover. Bake in a preheated 350 degree oven 1 hour or until rice is tender and liquid is absorbed.

Mrs. Ben W. Sturdivant
Due West Plantation
Glendora, Mississippi

Shrimp Etouffée

6 Tablespoons butter
3 Tablespoons flour
1 cup chopped onion
6 green onions and tops, chopped
½ cup chopped bell pepper
½ cup chopped celery
2 cups water
3 pounds shrimp, peeled and
  deveined
¼ cup chopped parsley
Salt and pepper to taste
1 small bay leaf
Tabasco to taste
Rice

In a skillet, melt the butter and stir in the flour. Cook, stirring constantly, until this is a rich brown. Add the vegetables and cook until tender. Stir in the water, shrimp, parsley and seasonings. Simmer uncovered for 20 minutes or until the shrimp are done. Serve over hot rice. Serves 4 to 6.

Mrs. Ed Seymour, Jr.

Senator Allen J. Ellender's Louisiana Shrimp Creole
or a delicious variation for Jambalaya

5 Tablespoons fat, vegetable oil
  or bacon drippings
3 rounded Tablespoons flour
2 pounds onions, minced
3 ribs celery, minced
1 medium bell pepper, minced
1 lemon; use grated rind then
  remove white pulpy membrane
  and chop rest of lemon
3 cloves garlic, pressed
A few dashes each: Worcestershire, Tabasco, thyme and
  McCormick "Season All"
2 bay leaves
2 cans tomato paste
3 pounds peeled raw shrimp
Salt to taste

To the fat, add flour and brown, stirring constantly to make a *dark* roux. Add the onions and fry slowly until well browned and reduced to pulp. Add the rest of the ingredients at one time, except shrimp. Continue to cook slowly for at least 30 to 45 minutes or longer. About 20 minutes before serving, add shrimp and cook for 15 to 20 minutes. Serve with rice. Serves 12.

Note: For an especially well flavored dish, prepare and let cool so flavors blend. Reheat slowly before serving.

Senator Ellender prepared many creole dishes from this sauce omitting the tomato paste and shrimp. For *Jambalaya*, he added 1/2 can tomato *sauce* to the basic recipe and then: 3 pints oysters added and simmered 10 minutes, then 3 cups of rice added with fresh green onion tops and snipped parsley, about a handful mixed together. If you feel you do not have 6 cups of liquid in the pot, add enough water to equal 6 cups. Stir and mix thoroughly until mixture comes to a boil. Cover tightly and lower heat to simmer. Cook for about 25 minutes. Do not remove the lid. Test rice to be sure it is done thoroughly at the end of the 25 minutes cooking period.

Howard's Boiled Crawfish

30 pounds crawfish
15 gallons water
3 cans red pepper
2 cans black pepper
8 pounds table salt
2 or 3 dozen lemons
1 dozen onions
½ box bay leaf
1- 4 ounce bottle Liquid Crawfish Boil
4 bags Crawfish or Shrimp boil

Wash crawfish with fresh water. Purge them in salt water. Drain. Add seasonings to fresh water and let boil to increase the flavor. Add crawfish and make sure they are covered with 3 to 5 inches water. Bring water back to a boil and keep boiling for 13 to 15 minutes. Let steep in water for added flavor. Crawfish may be served hot or cold. When making more than one cooking add to the above water 1/2 bottle liquid crawfish boil or 2 to 3 bags shrimp boil and salt and pepper. Should count on 5 pounds live crawfish per person. Drop red potatoes left in jackets, into water after removing crawfish. The most delicious potatoes to make a meal—

Mrs. Jerry H. Wolff

Crawfish Etouffée for 12

5 pounds peeled and deveined crawfish and the fat
2 bunches green onions, chopped
1 chopped large onion
¼ chopped bell pepper
2 ribs celery, chopped
4 Tablespoons olive oil
1 stick butter
1 can chicken broth
2 Tablespoons cornstarch

Cook the vegetables in olive oil and butter until limp and transparent. Add the peeled crawfish and the crawfish fat; cook for 10 minutes. Add chicken broth and thicken to suit your taste using 2 Tablespoons cornstarch that has been mixed with a small amount of water to start with. If crawfish fat is not available you may use a teaspoon of tomato paste for color. You do not want a tomato taste just the color.

Mrs. Roy Kelly

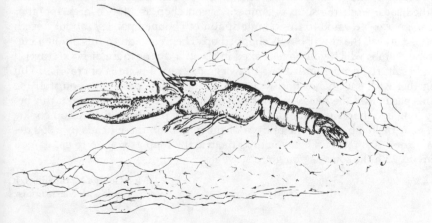

Marie Louise's Crayfish Bisque
The finest . . .

Editor's note: After you have caught, bought, or come by those delicious spring delicacies and decided to venture into the making of this fine bisque, your needed ingredients will be:

Onions	Butter	Eggs
Celery	Flour	Crayfish
Parsley	Garlic	Lots of salt
Bay Leaf	Whole red pepper	Vinegar
Lemons	Tomato paste	Bacon grease
Green onions	Toasted bread crumbs	

Read carefully as the method is the importance of any good recipe and this does produce a fine bisque.

This is a unit measure for making crayfish bisque for about 2 1/2 pounds of crayfish. I am well aware of the fact that this would make no soup to speak of, but it is simply to give you a proportion measure along with the method, and then you can decide whether you wish to use it for 10, 20, 30, or 100 pounds of crayfish, as you wish. First of all you have to clean your crayfish very, very well, putting a great deal of salt and a little vinegar in the water. Remove and *retain* all the fat while cleaning. Boil them in sufficient water with plenty of salt and other seasoning, such as bay leaf, whole onion, a couple of ribs of celery and some parsley, a piece of lemon and some whole red pepper. When they are boiled, I peel the crayfish, keeping the heads separate to stuff, and put the shells back into the water and cook to get my stock. Then, get about 1 quart of stock for every 2 1/2 pounds of crayfish. To make the soup, you fry one onion to the above amount of crayfish, chopped fine in 3 Tablespoons butter and 3 Tablespoon flour. When this is good and brown, you may add a little paprika for color if you wish. Now add 1/2 cup of chopped green onions, 1 good Tablespoon of chopped parsley, 1 rib of celery, chopped, 2 bay leaves, salt, red pepper to taste and the fat which you got out of the crayfish heads in cleaning them. This simmers for an hour or more and if you find you do not have any color that you like in the soup, you can add a Tablespoon of tomato paste. For the stuffing for the heads, while the soup is simmering, you chop and fry 1 large spoon of onion in bacon grease. Now add to this a large spoon of chopped parsley about 2 teeth of garlic chopped and all the crayfish tails chopped up. Then you add to this about 1 cup of toasted bread crumbs which you have soaked in about a cup or more of your crayfish stock. Then add salt, red pepper and about 1 raw egg to every 3 pounds of crayfish. You work this together with your hands until you make it into a fine paste and you stuff the heads with this paste. Roll the heads in flour or you can fry them in butter, but this becomes a very long and involved situation. I find it better to put them in rows on cookie sheets which have melted butter in the bottom of them and run these heads in a 350 degree oven for a good 20 minutes. Then you drop them in the soup as you go to eat it. You just heat them up with the soup as you go to serve it.

Mrs. George M. Snellings, Jr.
"Cook with Marie Louise"

Crab Searcy

Parsley to taste
1 or 2 green onions and tops,
    chopped
1 button garlic, crushed or garlic
    salt
1 rib celery, chopped
²/₃ green pepper, chopped
¹/₃ stick butter
3 hamburger buns
Cream or 1 small can PET milk
1 pound crab meat, fresh or
    canned
Red pepper or Tabasco

Sauté parsley, onion, garlic, celery and green pepper in butter till clear. Pour cream or Pet milk over 1 1/2 buns and let soften and add to butter and vegetables stirring in well. Add crab meat and place in buttered casserole. This should be about the consistency of dressing. Toast remaining buns with butter; grate and sprinkle on top. Cook at 350 degrees about 30 minutes or until brown on top. Serve with a bowl of Dill Sauce Searcy. Recipe is located with the Seafood Sauces. Serves 6 to 8.

Mrs. Charles Searcy

Galatoire's Luncheon for Four
need we say more—

6 whole fresh artichokes
1 sliced lemon
6 Tablespoons salt
1 stick butter
¹/₂ pound fresh mushrooms,
    sliced
2 teaspoons fresh lemon juice
1 cup green onions and tops,
    minced
4 Tablespoons minced parsley
1 clove garlic, minced
1 pound fresh lump crabmeat
1 Tablespoon fresh lemon juice
Salt and white pepper to taste
Accent
Lemon wedges

This is an approximate version of a favorite luncheon entrée served in one of New Orleans finest restaurants. We hope you enjoy it.

Boil artichokes in water to cover with 1 lemon sliced and 6 Tablespoons of salt. When tender; drain, cool and discard all but the bottoms and a few leaves. Cut the bottoms in 1/8's and set aside. Melt 2 *Tablespoons* of butter in a large heavy skillet. Sauté mushrooms, *slowly*, with 2 teaspoons lemon juice until any liquid has evaporated, about 15 to 20 minutes. Add remaining butter to the skillet and sauté 1/2 cup onions, 2 Tablespoons parsley and garlic until soft. Mix in artichoke bottoms. *Very carefully*, with rubber spatula fold and toss in crabmeat so as not to break up lumps. Add remaining lemon juice, salt, pepper and Accent to taste. Heat through adding remaining 1/2 cup onions and remaining parsley. Serve immediately on luncheon plate with lemon wedges and garnish with leaves. Fresh green salad, French bread and a nice little chablis, complete a scrumptious luncheon.

Crab Mornay Florentine

3 packages frozen leaf spinach
1 clove garlic
2 Tablespoons grated onion
6 Tablespoons butter
4 Tablespoons flour
3 cups milk
1 cup Swiss cheese, grated
1 cup light cream
2 teaspoons lemon juice
Pinch of garlic powder
Dash of nutmeg
Salt and cayenne to taste
2 pounds crabmeat
1 cup fresh bread crumbs

Cook spinach with whole garlic and grated onion. Drain, remove garlic, and finely chop the spinach. Transfer to a buttered 2 quart flat baking dish or 8 ovenproof shells. Preheat broiler. Melt 4 Tablespoons butter in saucepan, stir in 4 Tablespoons flour until smooth. Gradually add milk, stirring constantly until smooth and thickened. Add cheese along with cream and seasonings. Cook over low heat until thick, about 10 minutes. Remove from heat and carefully fold in crabmeat. Pour mixture over spinach, sprinkle with bread crumbs and dot with remaining butter. Broil about 5 minutes or until browned. Serves 8. *Brunch suggestion.* Layer hard boiled eggs, halved, on spinach; then top with sauce.

Mrs. George M. Snellings III

Crab Roll
Delicious for luncheon or light supper

2 Tablespoons mayonnaise
1 Tablespoon prepared mustard
1 egg
1 teaspoon salt
1 teaspoon Worcestershire
Dash of garlic powder
Tabasco, to taste
White pepper to taste
2 or 3 green onions, minced
2 Tablespoons parsley
3 Tablespoons cracker meal
1 pound crabmeat

PASTRY:
1½ cups flour
½ cup shortening
1 teaspoon salt
½ teaspoon sugar
Ice water to bind

SAUCE:
1 can mushroom soup
2 Tablespoons vermouth
1 Tablespoon lemon juice

Combine mayonnaise, mustard, egg and seasonings. Blend well. Add this mixture to parsley, green onions, cracker meal and crabmeat, tossing lightly. Check for seasoning. Prepare pastry and roll in a 12 x 8 x 1/4 inch thick rectangle. Put crab mixture in the middle, bring sides together, folding over to seal crabmeat in. Fold over each end. Put in baking pan and bake in hot oven 375 degrees until pastry is crisp and brown, about 25 minutes. Serve with Mushroom Sauce. Serves 6 to 8.

Fried Soft-Shell Crabs

Soft shell crabs
Salt and pepper
Buttermilk
Seasoned bread crumbs, meal
  or flour
Deep fat

To prepare soft shell crabs, lift up the pointed ends of the soft shell and remove the spongy fingers. Cut off the face, pull off the apron and remove the spongy stuff under it. Wash in cold water and wipe dry. Season with salt and pepper. Dip in buttermilk and then in seasoned crumbs or flour. Fry about 7 minutes on each side in hot grease. Serve on toast with tartare sauce and lemon wedges.

Seafood Casserole

1 medium bell pepper, chopped
  fine
1 medium onion, chopped fine
1 cup celery, chopped fine
1 can fancy crabmeat
1 can claw crabmeat
2- 5 ounce cans shrimp
½ teaspoon salt
Red and black pepper to taste
1 Tablespoon Worcestershire
  sauce
1 cup mayonnaise
1 cup sour cream
¾ cup raw rice, cooked and
  drained
Bread crumbs

Mix all the ingredients together and put in casserole and sprinkle top with bread crumbs. Bake in 350 degree oven for 30 minutes.

Mrs. J. L. Adams

Hot Seafood Salad

4 Tablespoons chopped green
  pepper
2 Tablespoons chopped green
  onion
1 cup chopped celery
1 cup crab meat
1 cup cooked shrimp
1 cup cold cooked rice
1 package cooked, frozen English
  peas
½ teaspoon salt
½ teaspoon Lea & Perrins
½ teaspoon pepper
1 cup mayonnaise
1 medium size bag potato chips

Mix all together, except potato chips. Put into casserole, cover with crushed potato chips. Cook 30 minutes at 325 degrees. Serves 6.

Good with congealed grapefruit and avocado salad, hot rolls, relish plate and lemon pie.

Mrs. James Brown
Ruston, Louisiana

Seafood Crêpe Pie
Prepare 8 to 10 eight inch crêpes. See Basic Crêpe Recipe

FILLING:

4 cups prepared seafood; crab, lobster, shrimp or a combination
½ stick butter
1 clove garlic, pressed
½ cup green onions, minced
½ cup water chestnuts, minced
¼ cup Madeira
1 teaspoon salt
⅛ teaspoon cayenne
½ teaspoon dry mustard
¼ teaspoon nutmeg
½ cup parsley, minced

SAUCE:

4 Tablespoons butter
4 Tablespoons flour
2 cups fish stock or clam juice
½ cup milk
1 cup grated Gruyère or mild Swiss, 4 ounces
1 cup heavy cream
½ teaspoon salt
½ teaspoon Lawry's Seasoning Salt
Pinch of garlic powder
Cayenne to taste
¼ teaspoon saffron
1 Tablespoon lemon juice
1 Tablespoon vermouth
1 Tablespoon Madeira
1 cup remaining seafood
1 Tablespoon minced chives

Filling: Melt butter, sauté garlic and onions until soft, but not browned. Add water chestnuts and 3 cups seafood. Cook for 2 minutes. Add wine and seasonings; toss over moderate heat until liquid almost evaporates. Stir in parsley and set aside.

Sauce: Melt butter for sauce, stir in flour until smooth and gradually add stock. Stir over low heat until thick and smooth. Add milk, cheese, cream, salts, cayenne and garlic powder. Dissolve saffron in vermouth and add with lemon juice and Madeira. Carefully stir in 1 cup remaining seafood and chives. Check for seasoning.

Pie: Stir 1/2 cup of sauce into the filling. In a buttered 9 inch pie plate, layer crêpes and filling, beginning and ending with the crêpes. Wrap and store overnight or freeze. Store remaining sauce. If frozen let thaw 1 hour before baking. Pour 1 cup of sauce over pie and bake 30 minutes in a 350 degree oven or 1 hour if pie has been frozen. Cut in pie shaped wedges "à table" and pass remaining sauce.

Mrs. Don Irby

Lobster Pilaff

12 small lobster tails
Butter
Garlic
1 cup minced green onions and
  tops
½ cup butter
2 cups rice
4 cups chicken stock
Salt to taste
½ cup minced bell pepper
½ cup chopped pimiento,
  optional
2 heaping Tablespoons minced
  parsley
Paprika

Prepare lobster tails: Thaw, remove membranes and brush tails generously with melted butter. Wrap each tail in foil with a sliver of garlic.
Make Pilaff: Sauté *1/4 cup* of onions in the butter and add rice. Stir until the rice is transparent and add 2 cups chicken stock. Cook, stirring frequently and add additional stock as liquid is absorbed. Cook abour 45 to 60 minutes. Stir in salt to taste, additional onion and other vegetables. Bake the lobster tails for 15 minutes in a preheated 450 degree oven. Remove the foil when done, discard garlic and *pour the juices over the rice* and sprinkle with paprika. Serve the tails atop the rice bed. Serves 6.

Stuffed Crêpes for Twelve

A divine dinner or luncheon—

Prepare 24 crêpes: See Basic Crêpe Recipe

FILLING:
1 stick butter
½ cup green onions, minced
2 pounds fresh lump crabmeat
½ cup vermouth
Salt and white pepper to taste
Dash of garlic powder, optional

SAUCE:
⅔ cup vermouth
¼ cup cornstarch
¼ cup milk
4 cups heavy cream
Salt and white pepper to taste
2½ cups grated Swiss cheese,
  the more the better
Butter

Filling: Melt butter in a large skillet. Stir in minced green onion, then crab. Toss *lightly* and cook a few minutes. Add salt and pepper to taste and garlic if used. Add vermouth and boil rapidly until liquid is almost evaporated. Scrape into a bowl and set aside.
Sauce: Add vermouth to the same skillet and boil rapidly until reduced to 2 Tablespoons. Remove from heat and stir in cornstarch and milk which have been mixed together. Return to low heat and add cream slowly with salt and pepper. Cook several minutes until slightly thickened. Stir in *1 1/2* cups grated cheese and cook until melted and well blended. Check seasoning.
Filled Crêpe: Blend 1/2 of the sauce with the crabmeat and check for seasoning again. Don't eat all this, tasting. Put a large spoonful on each crêpe and roll. Place seam side down in a buttered dish. This recipe will fill two large rectangular pyrex dishes. Spoon remaining sauce over crêpes and sprinkle with remaining cheese. Dot with butter. Refrigerate. Remove from the refrigerator 30 minutes before baking. Bake 20 minutes at 400 degrees until hot and bubbly. A little tossed salad, a little white wine, a dining pleasure. This may be frozen.

Mrs. Don Irby

Seafood Cream Sauce for Patty Shells

½ bunch chopped green onion
4 ounces sliced mushrooms
1 stick butter
¼ cup salad oil
1 cup flour
1 pint hot milk
2 cups clam juice, shrimp stock,
  or oyster liquor
1 cup sherry
Salt, pepper, cayenne to taste
¼ teaspoon dry mustard
¼ teaspoon curry powder
2 Tablespoons parsley, minced
2 egg yolks
¼ cup lemon juice
Seafood: 1 pound fresh crabmeat,
       1 pint boiled shrimp,
       1 pint fresh oysters
Parsley for garnish

In a stainless steel or enameled pan, sauté the onions and mushrooms until the onions are clear in the butter and oil. Blend in the flour. Cook about 2 minutes, stirring constantly. Do not brown. Gradually add hot milk, seafood liquid, sherry and seasonings. This may be prepared ahead to this point. Just before serving, carefully heat, do not let boil at any time. Add beaten eggs by stirring a little of the hot sauce into yolks and returning all to the sauce. Carefully blend in lemon juice and seafood with a wooden spoon. Heat through or until oysters curl. Serve at once in patty shells, over toast or noodles; garnished with minced parsley. Serves 6.

Mrs. Burt Sperry

Lobster Thermidor

6 large live lobsters or large
  frozen lobster tails
2 cloves garlic, chopped
1 onion, chopped
½ cup salt
2 teaspoons pepper
¾ cup butter, plus 3 level
  Tablespoons butter
½ cup flour
1½ cups light cream
9 canned mushrooms, cut up
½ teaspoon Dijon mustard
3 Tablespoons chopped fresh
  parsley
1 cup sherry
3 dashes paprika
Parmesan cheese

Put lobsters or tails to boil for 30 minutes in a pot of water seasoned with the garlic, onion, salt and pepper. Let cool. Remove from the pot. Remove the meat from tails. Dice; set aside and reserve the shells. Melt 3/4 cup butter in a pot, add the flour, and stir until smooth. Add the cream, stirring until the sauce is thick. Take off the heat and set aside. Sauté the lobster meat and mushrooms in the 3 Tablespoons butter for 5 minutes. Add the lobster meat, mushrooms, mustard and parsley to the cream sauce. Stir for 5 minutes, then add the sherry and blend in well. Add paprika, then place the mixture in the lobster shells. Sprinkle with Parmesan cheese; put in a 450 degree oven and bake for 15 minutes. Serves 6.

Mrs. Paul Tennis

To Fry That Catch

Bass D'Arbonne
May be used with salt water fish as well as any fresh water fish.

Milk
Flour
Salt
Pepper
Cream
Cracker crumbs or
   corn meal
Peanut Oil

Soak fillets in milk for about 45 minutes. Season flour with salt and pepper. Dip fillets in flour, then whole cream and roll in crumbs. Let dry about 30 minutes, the breading will stay on better. Fry in shallow hot oil until golden in color, drain on paper towels, serve with tartare sauce and lemon wedges.

Mrs. Foster Wallace

Buttermilk Batter
A simple light method for any type fish.

Buttermilk
Self-rising flour
Salt
Pepper
Wesson Oil

Soak fish 30 minutes or so in buttermilk. Season flour well with salt and pepper. Start heating deep fat. This is the secret to any good fried fish. When the grease reaches 350 to 375 degrees on a grease thermometer, your grease is ready. Dip fish in seasoned flour, drop in a *few* at a time and fry until crisp. Serve with tartare sauce, or a meunière sauce.

Bobby Shafto

Jimmy Owens' Fried Fish
For a delicious and different fish fry—

Fish, whole or fillets
Salt
Pepper
Mustard, small jar
Worcestershire
Cornmeal
Chopped green onions
Thinly sliced onion rings

Season fish inside and out thoroughly with salt and pepper. Dip in mixture of mustard diluted with enough Worcestershire to make a thin paste. Shake in cornmeal seasoned with salt, red and black pepper. Fry in very hot grease until done, *but do not overcook.* As fish is done, drain and cover with chopped onions and onion rings. Continue making layers of fish and onions. No onion or mustard flavor is prominent and these will be the best fish you ever ate!

Mrs. F. M. McGinn
Lafayette, Louisiana

Flounder

2 large flounder
½ lemon, sliced thin
1 stick butter, melted
¾ Tablespoon poultry seasoning
Salt and pepper
Juice of 1 large lemon
1 Tablespoon parsley, minced
3 green onions, diced, tops and
    bottoms

Score flounder. Lay lemon slices into the slits. Melt butter. Add poultry seasoning, salt, pepper, lemon juice, parsley, and diced onions. Broil flounder in center of oven, basting with sauce. Broil about 20 minutes or until fish is done. Fish should be moist, but flaky when done.

Mrs. George Snellings III

Poisson Jourdain

1 stick butter
½ cup lemon juice
1 beef bouillon cube dissolved in 2
    Tablespoons water
½ teaspoon Angostura bitters
6 fish fillets, trout excellent
Finely crushed bread crumbs
Corn oil

Mix sauce ingredients ahead. Clean fish fillets and dry. Coat lightly with bread crumbs. Brown in a skillet with *just enough* oil to keep fish from sticking. Remove to serving dish and keep warm. Bring sauce to a boil and pour over fish. Garnish with lemon slices and parsley.

Mrs. James Godfrey
New Orleans, Louisiana

Snapper Creole

1- 3 or 4 pound red snapper
1 large chopped onion
½ cup chopped celery
1 chopped bell pepper
½ cup bacon drippings
1 small can tomatoes, mashed
1 can tomato sauce
½ cup water or fish stock
½ cup dry red wine
2 Tablespoons Worcestershire
    sauce
1 Tablespoon chopped parsley
2 bay leaves
Pinch of basil
¼ teaspoon oregano
2 cloves minced garlic
Salt and pepper to taste
Tabasco to taste
¼ teaspoon MSG

Clean snapper well inside and out. Remove head and boil in a little seasoned water to get the fish stock. In a heavy pot, saute the onions, celery and bell pepper in bacon drippings until they are wilted. Add tomatoes, tomato sauce and fish stock. Add the remaining ingredients and simmer, covered, for at least an hour. Taste the sauce and adjust the seasonings. Season the fish with salt and pepper, dot it with butter and sprinkle it with flour. Slit the underside of the fish so that the seasoning will penetrate. Put the fish in a greased baking dish. Bake 400 degrees for 15 minutes; pour the sauce over it. Bake in a 350 degree oven about 40 minutes or until the fish is done, adding a little water to the pan if necessary. Baste the fish frequently. Garnish with lemon slices. Serves 6.

Mrs. T. M. Sayre
Rayville, Louisiana

Fish Fillets in Sour Cream

1 pound fish fillets or steaks
Salt and pepper to taste
Pinch red pepper or dash of
   Tabasco
1 cup sour cream
2 Tablespoons dill pickle,
   finely chopped
2 Tablespoons onion, minced or
   grated
2 Tablespoons green pepper,
   chopped
1 Tablespoon parsley, chopped
1 Tablespoon lemon juice
¼ teaspoon dry mustard
¼ teaspoon sweet basil
Paprika, Hungarian sweet, if
   available

Arrange fish in a well buttered baking dish. Sprinkle with salt and pepper. Combine remaining ingredients except paprika and mix until blended. Spread on fish. Sprinkle liberally with paprika, cover and bake at 325 degrees for 45 to 60 minutes, depending on thickness of fish. Fish should flake when tested with a fork. Serves 4.

Mrs. Don Phillips

Fish with Chablis

8 small whole fish: trout, bass, etc.
6 Tablespoons butter
1 large onion, grated
4 mushrooms, diced
1½ cups fresh bread crumbs
3 Tablespoons parsley, minced
2¼ cups chablis
½ teaspoon salt
Cayenne pepper
Buttermilk
Flour
4 Tablespoons butter
4 Tablespoons cooking oil
½ lemon, juiced
1 Tablespoon brown sugar
½ teaspoon salt
Pepper

Four larger fish may be used and halved after cooking to produce 8 servings. These are pan broiled so keep the size in mind. Clean, leaving whole, slit and remove part of bone if desired. Melt butter and brown grated onion, reserving 2 Tablespoons, and mushrooms. Stir in bread crumbs, 2 Tablespoons parsley and 1/4 cup chablis. Salt and pepper to taste. Lightly stuff fish, being careful not to pack too heavily. Secure with a toothpick. Dip in buttermilk, roll in flour and brown *slowly* in butter and oil. If you are using the larger fish which are thicker, cover during first half of the cooking time so fish will cook through. Then uncover. Turn only once. Remove and keep warm. Add remaining 2 cups chablis, 2 Tablespoons grated onion, sugar, lemon juice, salt and pepper to the skillet. Turn heat high, bring to a boil and cook until the sauce is reduced by one half. Check for seasoning. Spoon over fish and serve. These may be prepared ahead of time, refrigerated, and then set out 1 hour before cooking to reach room temperature. Serves 8. A marvelous and easy stuffed fish.

331

Stuffed Fish

1- 2 or 3 pound fish, snapper or
  flounder, etc.
1 cup of Minute Rice
1 can of consommé
1 small can of ripe olives
1 Tablespoon minced onion
1 large can of small shrimp
1 large can of white crabmeat
2 Tablespoons Worcestershire
  sauce
1/2 teaspoon Tabasco
Salt and pepper to taste
1 stick butter
2 lemons

If you are purchasing your fish at a local market you should ask them to take all the bones out but leave the fish head on for decorative purposes. Mix all of the remaining ingredients except butter and lemon. Line a pan with enough foil to fold over the fish and close tightly. Stuff the fish with the stuffing and place in the pan. Cover with melted butter and lemon juice. Tightly close foil and bake at 350 degrees for 45 minutes. Fold back the foil and cook for 10 to 15 more minutes until the fish is a golden color. Serve with spiced peaches and garlic bread.

Mrs. Allen Coon

Stuffed Gulf Coast Flounder
An elegant entrée

1 medium size onion, minced
  finely
8 Tablespoons butter
2 ribs celery, diced finely
1/4 green pepper, chopped
  finely
1 dozen fresh shrimp, chopped
1 small can chopped mushrooms
1/2 pound crabmeat
Pinch of thyme leaves
1 small bay leaf
1 Tablespoon Worcestershire
  sauce
1/4 pound almonds, browned and
  chopped finely
1/2 cup cream
Bread crumbs
Salt and pepper
3 ounces sherry or white wine,
  plus 1/2 ounce for basting
2 fresh flounders, 2 to 21/2 pounds
  each, or 4 small ones, not frozen
2 Tablespoons cooking oil
Juice of 1/2 lemon

Sauté the finely chopped onion in 4 Tablespoons of butter until the onion is soft and brown; add celery and pepper and sauté 2 or 3 minutes longer. Add shrimp and mushrooms with their liquor, sautéing until the shrimp are pink. Then add crabmeat, thyme, bay leaf, Worcestershire sauce, almonds, cream and enough bread crumbs to hold the whole thing together or to stretch the dressing to desired proportions, according to variation in fish size. Salt and pepper to taste. Add the sherry or white wine. Slit tops of fish and stuff. Close the slits with the aid of small skewers and lace up. Heat 2 generous Tablespoons cooking oil along with a large lump, at least 2 Tablespoons, of butter in a broiler pan and place the fish in the pan. Broil the fish *slowly* under a *low* flame, spooning a bit of butter over them from time to time as they cook. As the fish begin to brown, add a jigger of sherry or white wine to the broiler pan to increase basting liquid and keep the fish moist. When the fish is golden brown, it will be cooked through. Serve on individual plates or on a serving platter garnished with lemon slices and parsley. Spoon the sauce from the pan over the fish, and sprinkle with juice from 1/2 lemon. Serves 4.
Note: Use real butter as butter substitutes are not good in fish sauces.

Mrs. Paul Tennis

Trout Fillets

Bass or trout fillets
Salt and pepper
1 egg, beaten
Old London bread crumbs
1 stick butter
Fresh lemon juice

Salt and pepper bass or trout fillets. Dip in egg, roll in bread crumbs and pan fry in butter in skillet over medium heat. When golden brown, remove to platter and squeeze lots of fresh lemon juice over all.

Mrs. Bill Husted

Trout Amandine

2 pounds fish fillets
2 eggs
1/2 cup milk
1 teaspoon salt
1/2 teaspoon pepper
1/2 cup pancake flour
2- 6 ounce packages slivered almonds, toasted
1/2 stick butter, melted
1/2 lemon, juiced

Have fillets cleaned and prepared. Beat eggs well. Add milk, salt, pepper and 3 Tablespoons flour. Dip fish in the batter and set aside about 30 minutes. Sprinkle remaining flour on separated fish. Deep fry at 375 degrees. Toast almonds in oven until brown. Add almonds to melted butter and lemon juice. Serve over warm fried fish. Serves 8. This also makes a good fried shrimp batter.

Mrs. Richard Blanchard

Bonne Trout

6 fillets of fish, trout or red snapper
4 to 5 minced green onions
6 large mushroom caps, sliced
2 dozen shrimp, shelled and deveined
3/4 cup dry white wine
1 cup fish broth
Dash of Accent
1/2 teaspoon salt
White pepper to taste
1 cup Hollandaise sauce
1 cup heavy cream
1 Tablespoon melted butter
2 Tablespoons flour
7 Tablespoons butter
1 egg yolk
Juice of 1/2 lemon
Tabasco to taste
2 Tablespoons dry white wine

In a large buttered skillet, place onion, fish, mushroom caps and shrimp. Add wine, fish broth, Accent, salt and pepper. Cover the skillet and poach the fish gently for about 10 minutes or until it is done. Remove the fish, mushrooms and shrimp; set aside and *keep warm*. Reduce the poaching liquid to 1/2 cup over high heat. While this is cooking make 1 cup of your favorite Hollandaise sauce. When the poaching liquid is reduced, cool; add the cream and bring it to a simmer. Blend in *1 Tablespoon* melted butter and the flour until smooth. Stirring constantly, cook the sauce until it is smooth and thickened. Combine the Hollandaise with this sauce and swirl in 7 Tablespoons butter, one Tablespoon at a time, until all is mixed well. Blend in the egg yolk, lemon juice, Tabasco and 2 Tablespoons wine. Place the fish on a serving platter, arrange the mushrooms and shrimp over it and top with the sauce. Serve immediately. Serves 6.

Mrs. Ed Seymour, Jr.

Fish Casserole

Bass fillets, enough to cover bottom of flat 2 quart casserole
Milk, enough to cover fish
Flour
1 stick butter
1 bell pepper, diced
5 or 6 green onions, diced
2 cans shrimp soup
1 small can shrimp, deveined
1 can mushrooms, sliced; save juice
Juice of 1 lemon
1/3 cup sherry
Salt
Red pepper
Worcestershire

Soak fish, bass especially good, fillets in milk 2 to 3 hours. Dip in flour and brown in butter. Put into baking dish. Brown bell pepper and onion in butter until limp. Add shrimp soup, can of shrimp, mushrooms and 1/3 of mushroom juice, juice of lemon, sherry, salt, red pepper and Worcestershire to taste. Pour over fillets and bake 350 degrees for 30 to 40 minutes. Serves 6 generous portions.

Mrs. Ralph Brockman

Grant's Grenouilles

Frog legs
Salt

BATTER:
2 cups buttermilk
3 beaten eggs
Few dashes Tabasco
3 shakes Worcestershire
Few shakes of garlic salt
Salt to taste
Lots of pepper
Self-rising flour

Salt frog legs. Set aside. Mix batter ingredients. Dip legs, roll in flour and fry in moderately hot deep fat until golden. If grease is too hot the batter will burn.

Tommy Grant

Salmon Croquettes

1- 15 ounce can pink salmon,
   drain and save juice
1 egg
½ cup flour
Pepper to taste
½ cup chopped green onion
½ teaspoon Worcestershire or
   to taste
¼ cup salmon juice
1 heaping teaspoon baking
   powder
Deep shortening for frying

Mix salmon and egg with fork. Add 1/2 cup sifted flour and stir. Mixture will be thick. Add pepper, onions and Worcestershire. In the 1/4 cup salmon juice, put the baking powder and beat with fork until it foams. Pour this into salmon mixture and mix with fork. Drop by small spoonsful into deep hot shortening. Be sure and cook within 15 minutes of mixing. Very light and lacy. Serves 4 to 6.

Mrs. Joe Wheeler

Salmon or Tuna Ring Mold

2 beaten eggs
2 cups salmon or tuna or a devilish
   mixture, drained and flaked
2 teaspoons salt or seasoning salt
½ teaspoon pepper
1 heaping teaspoon paprika
1½ Tablespoons Worcestershire
   sauce
Dash of Tabasco
1 cup chopped onion
2 chopped ribs celery
1¾ cups milk
1 cup Quaker oatmeal, quick or
   old-fashioned

CHEESE SAUCE:
½ pound processed cheese, cut
   into cubes
½ cup milk

Combine all ingredients thoroughly; place in a buttered casserole or a greased, aluminum foil lined, 8 inch ring mold. Bake in a 350 degree oven for 50 to 60 minutes or until set. Serve with cheese sauce or Milam's Tomato Sauce. Serves 6 to 8. A green vegetable such as broccoli may be served in the center of the mold and the cheese sauce poured over all.
SAUCE:
Mix cheese and milk in double boiler over low heat until the cheese melts.

Mrs. DeWitt Milam

Milam's Tomato Sauce

½ cup tomato paste
1 cup water
2 ribs celery, chopped fine
1 onion, chopped fine
1 can tomato soup
½ can milk
1 Tablespoon Lea & Perrins
1 Tablespoon lemon juice
½ teaspoon mustard
Salt and pepper to taste
1 Tablespoon butter
¼ pound sharp cheese, cubed

Cook tomato paste, water, celery and onion over low heat for about 15 minutes or until tender. Add the remaining ingredients and simmer until well mixed and piping hot. If double the amount of sauce is needed, add 1 can of cream of celery soup and 1/2 can of milk. This gives a good taste and not too much tomato or celery flavor.

Mrs. DeWitt Milam

Toasted Salmon Sandwiches

1- 16 ounce can salmon
¼ cup minced green onions
Juice of ½ lemon
Pinch of salt and pepper
12 white bread slices
⅓ cup butter, melted
1 can mushroom soup
4 eggs
2 cups milk

Preheat oven to 325 degrees. Flake salmon and toss with green onions, lemon juice, salt and pepper. Brush one side of bread with melted butter and arrange 6 slices, buttered side up, in one layer in a well buttered 13 x 9 inch baking dish. Arrange salmon mixture on top and place rest of bread over salmon, buttered side up. In a medium bowl beat soup, eggs and milk until well blended. Slowly pour over and around bread. Bake 30 to 45 minutes or until knife inserted in custard portion comes out clean. Serve at once. Makes 6 to 8 servings.

Miss Harriet Swift
Marietta, Georgia

Fresh Tuna with Tomato Sauce

2 pounds tuna fish
Salt and pepper
4 Tablespoons olive oil
1 Tablespoon chopped parsley
1 clove garlic
1 small onion, sliced
½ can tomato paste
2 cups hot water

If you are so lucky as to have fresh tuna have fish sliced 1 1/2 inches thick. Wash and dry; sprinkle with salt and pepper. Heat oil in skillet; cook onion, garlic and parsley 5 minutes until soft. Blend tomato paste in 2 cups hot water; add to mixture in the skillet; cover; simmer 20 minutes, stirring occasionally. Add fish; cover; cook 15 minutes or until tender. Serve very hot. This amount can be doubled but you may need more tomato paste. This is very similar to the way it's fixed on Martinique Island. Serves 4.

Mrs. Ben Marshall

Hot Tuna Sandwiches

½-4 ounce can chopped mushrooms
1-7 ounce can white tuna fish
½-10½ ounce can mushroom soup
4 hard boiled eggs, chopped
1-4½ ounce can ripe olives, chopped
2 Tablespoons salad dressing
½ teaspoon onion salt
Butter
Bread

SAUCE:
2 cups white sauce
½-10½ ounce can mushroom soup
½-4 ounce can chopped mushrooms
Grated cheese

Mix all filling ingredients except butter together. Butter bread and spread with the above mixture. Make triple decker sandwiches. Wrap the sandwiches in waxed paper and refrigerate for at least an hour. Brush each sandwich with melted butter and place on a cookie sheet. Bake for 25 minutes in a 350 degree oven.

SAUCE:
Make a sauce using white sauce and the remaining mushroom soup and mushrooms. Top the sandwiches with sauce and sprinkle with grated cheese. Serve the sandwiches hot.

Mrs. Amos Warner
Lawrenceville, N.J.

SEAFOOD SAUCES

Tartare Sauce

1 cup homemade mayonnaise
  with olive oil base
1 teaspoon dry mustard
1 Tablespoon grated onion
2 Tablespoons minced parsley
1 clove garlic, pressed
2 Tablespoons minced dill pickle
2 Tablespoons drained capers
1 Tablespoon minced green onions

Combine all ingredients. Let mellow 30 minutes or so. The ingredients can be used with a commercial mayonnaise, but the homemade makes this especially delicious.

Mrs. Wesley Shafto, Jr.

Dill Sauce Searcy

1 cup mayonnaise
A little green onion with tops,
  chopped finely
6 or 8 dill pickle slices,
  chopped finely
A little parsley, minced
Lea & Perrins
Tabasco
About 1 teaspoon green pepper,
  chopped very finely

Combine all ingredients. I thin this with a little dill juice into which I have sliced onions and let set in the refrigerator to use in salads.

Mrs. Charles Searcy

Maître d'Hôtel Sauce
Delicious with broiled fish!

1 Tablespoon butter
1 Tablespoon flour
Juice of ½ lemon
1 Tablespoon chopped parsley
½ can consommé
½ can water
1 egg yolk, well beaten
Salt and pepper to taste

Place butter in the top of a double boiler. Blend in flour. Add juice of lemon, parsley, consommé and water. Let boil 15 minutes. Remove from stove and *cool*. Add well beaten egg yolk. Season to taste with salt and pepper. May be stored in the refrigerator for days. Serves 8.

This sauce is also delicious to use with button mushrooms and served in ramekins.

Mrs. C. D. Oakley, Sr.

NOTES

Hunter's Choice

Doves or quail, 2 per serving
Salt
Pepper
2 or 3 bacon strips
½ stick butter
½ lemon, juiced
1 Tablespoon Worcestershire
    or to taste
Toast points

Season each bird well with salt and pepper. Barely cover bottom of a large heavy skillet with water. Place birds and cover with a *tight* fitting lid. A flat lid is preferable with a brick set on top. Steam birds 8 to 10 minutes. Remove birds, pour off liquid. Fry bacon; remove and brown bird in drippings. Pour grease off and stir in butter, lemon juice and Worcestershire. Serve birds with sauce over toast points.

Bobby Shafto, Jr.

Proper Cleaning and Storing Are Basic
Ingredients of Any Good Game Recipe

As most of the "main course" dishes of meat, fowl, or fish which we prepare involve "store bought" main ingredients, it is understandable that it is not natural for us to devote a great deal of time and attention to the care of game from the time it is reduced to the bag or creel until the time that it is served upon the table. However, I believe that at least half of the game dishes which do not turn out satisfactorily are from improper cleaning or freezing methods, not so much from lack of a proper recipe or culinary ability on the part of the cook.

First, with regard to freezing, I believe that freezing game in water wherever possible will add considerably to the freezer life of the game, and this certainly includes fish. Quart milk cartons or plastic freezer containers are ideally suited to the purpose. Heavy-duty plastic sacks are all right for filleted fish, chunks of boneless meat, and the like, but unsatisfactory for fish with fins on and birds and things of this nature because the projecting fins or limbs will more often than not puncture the sacks before the water is frozen. I have found that ducks will do quite well without being frozen in water, but I believe that they should be double wrapped in heavy-duty aluminum foil with no parts of the bird protruding, or wrapped several times in Saran Wrap or other similar material and then wrapped once in heavy-duty aluminum foil. Venison and other meat will keep well if wrapped first in butcher paper and then in heavy freezer paper. Saltwater fish will retain their natural moisture and also will endure more storage time if frozen with the scales left on the fish. When the scales are left on, these fish can be stored individually simply by wrapping each one in four or five coverings of Saran Wrap. They can then be "stacked like cord wood" and afford the added convenience of allowing exactly as many as are desired for the table to be remove from the freezer at a time.

Sometimes all of us have game cleaned by someone other than ourselves, but I have often said that the very best taken care of game to go in the freezer is always the game I clean myself. When others clean our game, we should not take it for granted that they have done an entirely satisfactory job, for many times our assumptions in this regard will prove incorrect. When someone else cleans my ducks, for instance, I find that nine out of ten times they leave the lights in the cavity. These are the birds' lungs and are in recessed areas far up in the cavity on either side of the bird's backbone, and they can be removed by inserting the index and middle finger and going all the way to the front of the cavity and then drawing the fingers back hard against the areas immediately adjacent to the top of the backbone. Also, I seldom find that the cavities have been properly rinsed. With many birds I find that the crops, or craws, have not been removed or cleaned and still contain vegetable matter which can sour during the freezing process and greatly damage the flavor of the bird. All game should be rinsed so thoroughly prior to freezing that the water runs clean.

Obviously, different types of game have different characteristics and different requirements so far as handling is concerned, and I will, therefore, now mention a few specifics with regard to individual types of game which apply only to these particular types.

VENISON: I think venison is probably the most misunderstood and mishandled table game, particularly, of course, on the part of nonhunters who are the recipients of donated meat. This being so, I have made special efforts to improve the quality of the meat by proper handling prior to cooking.

First, on field dressing deer, unless the head is to be saved for a mount it is a good idea to split the deer's brisket all the way up to the top of its neck. When the deer has been gutted it should be picked up by the head and tail and held upside down and allowed to drain thoroughly, or in a case where there is no one to help and the deer is too heavy for one person to pick it up, the head should be lifted up high off the ground and the remaining blood and other matter allowed to run out of the back end of the open pelvic arch thoroughly. Great care should be taken to see that the bladder, stomach and intestines are not punctured when the gutting is done, as spillage from these organs taints the meat. Of course, with a "gut-shot" deer, about all that can be done is to hose out the carcass thoroughly as soon as water is available. Further, hair, sticks, leaves and other debris should be kept out of the carcass. It is also a good idea to prop the cavity open with a cut green stick in order to allow the deer to properly "cool out". Depending upon the weather, it is possible not to eviscerate a deer for a couple of hours after killing it if it is not gut-shot. A gut-shot deer should be cleaned out immediately. It is not indispensable to skin a deer soon after killing it, and in fact the deer can be skinned as long as a week or ten days after it has been killed without adversely affecting the meat. Temperature is a big factor here. Generally speaking, it is advisable to go ahead and skin a deer as soon as it is convenient to do so. A deer can be butchered fairly promptly after killing it, but if it is possible to do so the whole deer, or the two halves, or the four quarters, should be allowed to hang in a cooler for five to ten days to permit aging of the meat. This is the same idea underlying aged beef, and the aging process does improve the flavor.

Too many people just take their deer to a processing plant and leave instructions for the deer to be "cut and wrapped", and this usually results in a few roasts, some round steaks, some chops, some stew meat, and some ground hamburger type meat. A deer can produce as great a variety of cuts as a steer, and some thought should be given to individual preferences for cuts of meat. For instance, I have just about gone entirely away from putting up any deer meat with "bone in", preferring the boneless cuts. For example, take the ham of a deer. This can be trimmed and left whole for a whole ham roast, or it can be cut into round steaks of any desired thickness, it can be made into boneless roasts, with the eye of the round the most desirable boneless roast coming from the ham, or all of the muscles can be boned out from the ham and trimmed and then cut into small chunks for stew or fondue or for making of cutlets which are really excellent. If the butcher is not told differently, your backstrap, rib eyes and tenderloins, will probably come out as small steaks with bones, like chops or T-bones, and whereas these are fine, the boned out rib eyes and tenderloins are to my way of thinking much better. These are the choicest pieces of meat from the deer, and can quite easily be boned out into long flat boneless roasts. Also, these boned out and trimmed backstraps can be sliced into small steaks of about three-eighths inch thickness and these are excellent as "breakfast steaks". This trimming is very important in handling deer meat. Most processing plants only make a half way effort in this direction, and it is very important that all of the fascia be trimmed from the muscles.

WATERFOWL: As I have previously said, ducks and geese should be rinsed thoroughly so that before they are put up the water runs clean. Birds with excessive pinfeathers should be skinned, and a good thing to do with these is simply to bone out the breasts and mark them separately. By the end of the season, there will probably be a good enough accumulation of boned out breasts to make a meal or two of these, and they can be delicious prepared in a number of ways. Also, ducks which have to be skinned because of excessive pinfeathers can be used in gumbo or dishes where they are cooked in gravy in a Dutch oven. The biggest loss from skinning a bird is flavor and moisture, and these problems are avoided when the skinned birds are prepared in either of the above ways. The heart, liver and gizzard should be saved for dicing to be used in gravy or dirty rice. The gizzard from geese is especially good, but it should be remembered that gizzards must be cleaned, and this should be done prior to freezing them. Cleaning is a simple matter of notching the gizzard with a knife, slitting it open, and thoroughly washing all of the sand and silt out. The pocket tissue can be removed or left intact, but the gizzard should be thoroughly cleaned.

SNIPE, QUAIL AND DOVES: Many people "breast" their doves, because there are usually quite a number of them in the bag and this is such a swift procedure. I have always felt that it is worth the extra time to pick doves, because they are so much more moist and flavorful with the skin on. Also, the legs are only a scanty bite but sufficiently tasty to be preserved. Snipe and quail should be skinned because the skins are so fragile that picking is virtually impossible, as the skins will tear and split. For this reason, snipe can just as well be breasted rather than purely picked or skinned. Quail are among the most notorious offenders in so far as needing to be eviscerated soon and thoroughly washed prior to freezing. Failure on these counts will result in the bird having a strong odor when they are thawed out, and although it may be debatable whether the flavor is impaired, it cannot be argued that this condition can take some of the joy out of cooking the partridges. I recommend soaking quail in cool water and either baking soda or salt for about one hour prior to freezing. This will draw out any remaining blood and eviscera.

SQUIRRELS: Here, as with deer, it is important that trash be kept out of the cavity and hair off of the skinned body of the squirrel. The flanks of squirrel should be trimmed away, as they are of no nutritive value and, in the case of sow squirrels, have mammary residue attached.

The places where shot have entered the squirrel should be crisscrossed slightly with a knife, or the bruised mass cut out, to remove clotted blood. Squirrels have musk glands, and these are found under the forearm pits and as a white kernel in back of the knees or hind legs which can be seen when the hind legs are stretched slightly. These glands should be cut out. When the squirrel has been thus taken care of, it should be placed in cool water, after having been thoroughly rinsed, with salt or baking soda, for a half an hour to an hour to allow all the blood to be drawn out. This will also cause the squirrel to whiten and the meat will be more attractive. After this, and another rinsing, I prefer to quarter the squirrels.

I have only touched on the principal types of game encountered in the South and usually found on the table in the homes of those of us who are wont to take to the woods and the fields in the Fall and Winter of the year; but the idea is the important thing. The extra efforts in care and freezing of game are well worthwhile in terms of satisfaction as to the condition of the meat in the freezer and improved results with the meat on the table.

One last word, and most important, do not keep any fish in the freezer over six months and no game over a year. Sure, occasionally you may eat two year old ducks that are great; but as they say "The exception proves the rule", and it's a pious idea to clean the freezer out completely from one season's game to the next.

George M. Snellings III

Doves

6 doves
1½ sticks melted butter
1 Tablespoon Worcestershire
   sauce
1 teaspoon garlic salt
⅓ cup Maderia
1 cup chopped mushrooms
Salt and pepper to taste
⅓ cup flour

Season doves and brown on all sides in melted butter in large iron skillet. After doves are brown, add remaining ingredients except flour; cover and cook until tender. Remove doves from skillet; add ⅓ cup flour, forming a roux. Place doves on toast points and top with sauce. Allow 2 doves per person.

Mrs. Jerry Wolff

Roasted Dove

Any number of doves
Olive oil
Curry powder
Dry mustard
Celery salt
Garlic salt
Salt
Pepper
Chicken broth made with stock
   base or bouillon cube
2 Tablespoons Worcestershire
Juice of one orange
Juice of one lemon

Roll each dove in enough olive oil to get them well greased. Sprinkle small amounts of curry powder, dry mustard, celery salt, garlic salt, salt and pepper over each one. Put doves in a covered roaster or Dutch oven in a single layer with a small amount of chicken broth or water and cook 1 1/2 hours in a 250 degree oven. Add Worcestershire sauce and juice of orange and lemon. Cook for 10 to 15 minutes longer uncovered or until tender and brown.

Mrs. T. A. Grant III

Tender Doves

Doves: just the breast
Onions
Celery
Salt and pepper

SAUCE:
1 stick butter, melted
Juice of 1 lemon
1 teaspoon salt
1 teaspoon pepper
3 Tablespoons Lea & Perrins

Boil the dove breasts in water with quartered onions, celery stalks, salt and pepper until tender and done. Drain.
Arrange breasts in a shallow baking dish, skin side up. Cover. This can be done the day before. Refrigerate. Before broiling, have doves at room temperature. Make the sauce. Put the doves under the broiler and baste frequently with the heated sauce. The doves should broil about 5 to 10 minutes until golden brown. Put pan low in the oven so that the doves will not brown too quickly. Before serving, pour the remaining sauce over the doves. At least three breasts are needed for each adult.

Bill Mattison

Barbecued Doves

Doves cooked in this manner need to be cooked forty minutes to one hour after the coals have whitened, or if you have a smoker arrangement, they can be smoked. In this case it will take about an hour and a half to two hours and fifteen minutes to get thoroughly done. If cooked directly over the coals, they will be done when the bacon is done and the doves are more or less golden brown, and if cooked by a smoker will be done when they are thoroughly tender and a light golden brown. The doves should be thoroughly cleaned and rinsed prior to marinating. The directions that follow will be the same for one dozen to two dozen doves, and if more or less doves are used marinade will have to be increased or decreased accordingly. The doves should be marinated in the following ingredients at least all day before cooking in the evening, and twenty-four hours of marination is perfectly all right. The ingredients for the marinade follow:

2 cups vegetable oil
¼ cup Worcestershire sauce
¼ cup vinegar
2 Tablespoons salt
1 Tablespoon cracked black pepper
5 or 6 generous dashes Tabasco sauce
Juice of 4 lemons
3 or 4 Tablespoons of commercial barbeque sauce
Garlic to taste if desired
Bacon

Prior to cooking remove doves from marinade and wrap each dove in half slice of bacon. Skewer doves on shish kabob skewer, or if none is available, fix the bacon to the dove with a toothpick. Baste with marinade occasionally while cooking and just before doves are done, warm remaining marinade slightly. When doves are done place same on platter for serving and cover with remaining marinade.

George M. Snellings III

Doves or Quail with Shallots and Mushrooms

8 to 10 shallots, chopped finely
8 Tablespoons butter
1-4 ounce can sliced mushrooms
1 teaspoon salt
½ teaspoon black pepper
1 teaspoon Worcestershire sauce
Dash of Tabasco
½ teaspoon dried thyme
¼ cup olive oil
1 clove garlic, finely chopped
12 doves or quail, dredged in flour
⅓ cup cognac
½ cup flour or ¼ cup flour and one envelope brown gravy mix
1-10½ ounce can chicken broth
1 Tablespoon currant jelly
1 cup Burgundy wine

Sauté the shallots in 4 Tablespoons butter. Add mushrooms and seasonings. In a Dutch oven or roasting pot, heat the olive oil and 4 Tablespoons butter. Add the garlic and birds and turn until browned on all sides. Flame with cognac. When flame dies down, remove birds. Add flour and gravy mix, working into good paste. Pour in chicken broth, jelly and wine. Stir until well blended and gravy thickens. Add shallot-mushroom mixture and cook five minutes, stirring constantly. Return birds to cooker and bake covered 1 1/2 to 2 hours at 325 degrees. Serves 4 to 6.

Mrs. Don Phillips

Grilled Quail or Dove

Birds, 2 per serving
Salt and pepper
Bacon

Using the rotisserie basket of a charcoal grill, lay strips of bacon on one side. Season birds and arrange close together over bacon. Top with additional bacon strips and clamp basket closed. Cook 20 to 30 minutes over hot coals. A clamp basket with a handle may be used also. Turn frequently. Delicious flavor and so easy!

Bobby Shafto, Jr.

Smothered Quail

6 quail or 12 doves
6 Tablespoons butter
3 Tablespoons flour
2 cups chicken broth
1/2 cup sherry
Salt and pepper to taste
Cooked rice

Season quail or dove with salt and pepper. Brown in a heavy skillet in 6 Tablespoons butter. Remove quail to baking dish. Add flour to butter in skillet and stir well. Slowly add chicken broth, sherry, salt and pepper to taste. Blend well and pour over quail. Cover baking dish and bake at 350 degrees for 1 hour or until done. Serve with cooked rice. Doves may be used also. Serves 6.

Mrs. Jerry Wolff

Quail Shafto

Quail
Wesson Oil
Salt
Pepper
1/2 strip bacon per bird
1 stick butter
1 Tablespoon Worcestershire
1/2 lemon, juiced

Plan 2 quail per person. Clean, wash thoroughly and pat dry. About 1 hour before roasting, rub each quail well with the oil. Season with salt and pepper inside and out. Wrap bacon strip over breast and secure with a toothpick through the bird. Set aside to come to room temperature. Melt butter, adding Worcestershire and lemon juice for basting. Preheat oven to 400 degrees. Place quail on a rack in an open pan. Baste. Roast 15 minutes at 400 degrees. Baste. Increase oven to 425 degrees and bake 10 minutes more. Remove from oven, place on serving platter and pour drippings from the bottom of the pan over all. Serve immediately.

The roasting time is of great importance to produce very tender and juicy bit of bird. Don't overcook.

Bobby Shafto, Jr.

Ducks Au Sang
You won't believe how easy this is!

2 wild ducks
1 medium onion, minced
4 to 6 green onions, minced
½ cup good red wine
10 whole black peppercorns
1 bay leaf
½ teaspoon thyme
1 clove garlic
2 Tablespoons butter
1 teaspoon flour
Lawry's seasoning salt to taste
Garlic salt to taste
Pepper to taste
Small pieces of onion
Small pieces of celery
3 Tablespoons butter
Holland Rusk or toast rounds
Parsley
Consommé

This recipe is based on 4 servings but if your ducks are small prepare 3 ducks for larger meat portions. Have the ducks clean and ready to roast.

Ahead of time finely mince onions and place in saucepan with wine, peppercorns, bay leaf, thyme and garlic. Simmer over low heat about 20 or 30 minutes until mixture is reduced by half. Stir in butter and flour until smooth. Press and strain through a sieve. You should have 1/4 cup of liquid. Discard onion mixture.

About 45 minutes before serving rub ducks with seasoning salt and garlic salt and pepper, inside and out. Stuff the cavities with small pieces of onion and celery.

Heat oven to 475 degrees. Place ducks in a heated shallow pan in the oven and dry roast 15 minutes per pound!!! Small wild ducks will be removed from the oven in 15 or 20 minutes. A larger 2 or 2 1/2 pound mallard will be removed after 25 or 30 minutes. The secret of the recipe is a rare duck so do not overcook!!!

While the ducks are roasting sauté Holland Rusk or toast rounds in melted butter. Set aside and keep warm.

Remove the ducks from the oven and let set, in the pan, 5 or 10 minutes. Remove the legs to be served on the side of the plate. *Slice all the remaining meat thinly off the carcass while over the roasting pan to retain all of the juices.* Place the sliced meat on the toast rounds and *keep warm.* Into the retained juices, stir in the strained wine mixture, salt and pepper to taste. Heat slowly, do not let boil or it will curdle. If you do not have enough juices to make sauce for 4 servings add a small amount of consommé or broth. When the sauce is well heated, remove from heat, swirl in 1 Tablespoon butter and parsley and spoon over the duck and toast.

This is truly the finest duck you will ever eat. After the meat is sliced the juices are in the sauce and the redness of the meat is gone if you are squeamish.

You may add a small amount of consommé or broth to stretch the sauce; wine may be used but will need to cook a little longer to burn off the overpowering taste.

Mrs. Don Irby

Baked Wild Duck—Smokey Flavor
Try this for a different tasting bird

Any number of wild ducks
Salt and pepper to taste
Dry red wine
Charcoal
2½ pounds hickory chips, soaked
in water

Place the charcoal at one end of the barbeque pit. Light the pit and let the charcoal burn until well coated with gray ash. Salt and pepper the ducks and place them on the grill at the end away from the fire. Put the hickory chips over the charcoal and put the lid down. Smoke the ducks 30 to 45 minutes, depending on the size of the ducks. Roll each duck up in foil adding 2 ounces of wine per duck. Bake at 275 degrees, breast side down, for 3 hours.

Allen Barham

Ducks or Doves

4 ducks
Celery
Bell pepper
Onion
Salt and pepper
Bacon drippings
1- 10 ounce bottle Lea & Perrins
1¼ cups water
4 Tablespoons catsup
Juice of 1 lemon
1 whole lemon, sliced
1 bay leaf
1 teaspoon dry mustard
1 cup cooking sherry

Stuff ducks with a piece of celery, onion, and bell pepper. Salt and pepper well inside and out. Brown the ducks in bacon drippings. Pour off the bacon drippings and make the sauce in the same container using the remaining ingredients. Add the ducks; cover and cook slowly, basting every 30 minutes for 4 to 5 hours. Cook on top of the stove. Use remaining sauce as gravy. Serves 8.

Mrs. Mike Herrington

Ducks in Olive Gravy

4 ducks
3 kitchen spoons oil
3 kitchen spoons flour
1½ cups chopped bell pepper
1½ cups chopped celery
4 large onions, chopped
3 cloves garlic, pressed
1 cup sherry
3 bay leaves
½ teaspoon thyme
¼ cup minced parsley
Tabasco to taste
Salt and pepper to taste
3 to 4 cups water
1 small bottle green olives, sliced

Brown ducks in a 500 degree oven. Make dark roux with oil and flour. Add vegetables and wilt. Blend in other seasonings and stir in 3 to 4 cups of water. Pour all over ducks. Bake at 350 degrees until tender, about 2 1/2 hours. Stir in the sliced olives during the last 30 minutes of cooking.

Mrs. Jim Folk
Tallulah, Louisiana

Creole Duck

5 ducks, cut up for frying
Salt and pepper
2½ Tablespoons shortening
5 onions, chopped
2 teaspoons bell pepper, chopped
5 cloves
2 square inches of ham, cut into
  small pieces
2½ teaspoons herb bouquet
2½ wine glasses claret wine
1 large can mushrooms
Flour to thicken gravy

Salt and pepper ducks and fry in shortening in large roaster. Remove the ducks and sauté the onion and bell pepper until soft. Add the ducks and the remaining ingredients, except the mushrooms, to the roaster. Cover and cook until tender, about 2 to 2½ hours. Thicken gravy with a paste of flour mixed with water. Correct the seasonings, add the mushrooms and serve.

Mrs. Elmer Neill, Jr.
Tallulah, Louisiana

Duck Breasts

3 ducks
6 Tablespoons bacon fat
3 Tablespoons flour
1 onion, chopped
1 bell pepper, chopped
2 ribs celery, chopped
¼ cup Worcestershire sauce
¼ cup red wine
¼ cup Pickapeppa sauce
2 bay leaves
Garlic salt
Seasoned salt
Pepper
4 cups water

Pull skin off the breast area of the duck. Then cut the breast sections off the duck. Clean the breasts and pat dry. In a heavy skillet, make a roux using 3 Tablespoons bacon fat and 3 Tablespoons flour. Meanwhile, brown duck breasts in remaining 3 Tablespoons bacon fat and set aside. To the roux, add onion, bell pepper and celery. Cook slightly. Add Worcestershire, wine, water, bay leaves, seasonings and duck breasts. Simmer for about 2 hours. Adjust seasonings if necessary. Serve over wild rice, or a long grain, wild rice mixture. Serves 4.

Mrs. Bob Kennedy

Note: The remainder of the duck is great for gumbo.

Glazed Duck

Duck
Salt and pepper
Flour
1½ cups water
½ orange
4 apricots
2 Tablespoons frozen concentrated orange juice
2 strips bacon
1 cup orange wine
1 cup chopped onion
½ cup chopped celery
¼ cup chopped parsley

Salt, pepper, flour duck and fry in Dutch oven about 15 minutes until brown all over. Remove duck and make a gravy with flour and drippings. Stuff cavity of duck with orange half and arrange the 4 apricots and 2 Tablespoons frozen concentrated orange juice over the duck's breast. Cover with 2 strips bacon. Return duck to Dutch oven and gravy and add 1 cup orange wine or just any wine you might have on hand. Sprinkle 1 cup chopped onion, 1/2 cup chopped celery, 1/4 cup chopped parsley over the duck. Cover and bake at 300 degrees 2 to 3 hours until tender. Baste every 40 minutes. When the leg sticks tender, your duck is just right.

Mrs. George M. Snellings III

Lil's Stewed Duck
A spicy bit of game

I.
8 wild ducks, 6 if very large
Salt and pepper
Garlic salt
Cinnamon
Allspice
Flour to dust
½ cup olive oil

II.
3 chopped onions
3 chopped ribs celery
Small garlic clove, crushed
¼ cup seedless raisins, optional
2 Tablespoons flour
4 cups hot water

III.
½ Tablespoon sage
½ Tablespoon salt
½ Tablespoon pepper
1 teaspoon Lea & Perrins
Dash of Tabasco
Sprinkle of allspice
Sprinkle of cinnamon
Sprinkle of powdered cloves
1 Tablespoon sugar
1 bay leaf
½ Tablespoon thyme
1 small piece chopped bell pepper
1 cup canned apple sauce
½ cup orange juice
Piece of orange rind
½ Tablespoon marjoram
½ cup chopped ripe olives
¼ cup canned coconut
¼ cup pecans
½ Tablespoon rosemary
¼ cup wine
1 small can mushrooms
1 Tablespoon Parmesan cheese
1 Tablespoon butter
½ teaspoon Accent
Small quantity browned sausage
Parsley, chopped

Cut ducks into small pieces as you do a chicken. If ducks are small, quarter them. Wash thoroughly and dry with a cloth.

Season duck meat with the spices. Flour well.

Put olive oil in a heavy skillet. Heat and add ducks, browning well on all sides. Remove, reserving oil.

In same oil cook onions, celery, garlic and raisins until wilted. Remove and save oil.

Make a roux in oil by adding 2 Tablespoons flour and brown but do not burn.

Add cooked onions, celery, garlic and raisins to roux. Stirring well, add about 4 cups hot water. Add all the seasonings except the parsley. Add browned duck. Correct seasonings to your taste after this has cooked for a while. Simmer over low heat, covered for 1 1/2 hours. Watch well and stir occasionally. Before serving add fresh chopped parsley to the gravy.

Stew can be made a day ahead. Cool to room temperature and store in refrigerator in same pot. Reheat slowly, stirring often.

To serve, place duck pieces on warmed deep china platter and put gravy in a large china bowl. Use your soup tureen if you have one. Put duck and gravy both in it. Serve with rice and a green salad, French bread and white wine, cup custard for dessert. This recipe can be doubled. Serves 12 to 16. The preparing time is about 2 hours.

Mrs. Ben Marshall

349

Duck Salad or Duck Glacé

6 mallard ducks
5 celery ribs, chopped
1 bell pepper, chopped
3 green onions, chopped
1 Tablespoon lemon or lime juice
Hellman's mayonnaise
Salt and pepper to taste

Cook the ducks any way you desire but be sure that they are done enough to debone. Remove all bones and skin and run the meat through a food grinder. Chop all vegetables very fine and add to the ground duck. Add the lemon or lime juice and enough mayonnaise to make the meat mix and mold easily. Add salt and pepper to taste. This can be served on leaves of lettuce as a salad or molded into a glacé for cocktail parties. This is ideal for the housewife that doesn't know what to do with all those "horrible old wild ducks" filling up the deep freeze.

Allen Barham

Duck Gumbo

6 or 8 ducks
1 cup salad oil
1 scant cup flour
2 bunches green onions, chopped
4 large onions, chopped
1 bunch celery
2 bunches parsley
26 cups hot water
2 Tablespoons salt
Red pepper to taste
Green onions, chopped
Parsley, chopped
Filé powder

In a heavy iron skillet brown the ducks without oil after you have salted and peppered them. In a hot Westinghouse roaster combine the oil and flour and brown until it is dark. Set the oven about 350 degrees and stir often. This takes about 1 1/2 hours. After the roux is made add the chopped greens, salt and pepper. Cook until the vegetables are tender. Add the hot water slowly, stirring until smooth. Add the duck, breast down. Cover the roaster and adjust the heat to 300 degrees. This depends on your roaster. The gumbo should simmer, not boil. For large ducks the cooking time is about 3 hours, smaller ones will be done sooner. When done, remove the ducks, bone them, cut the meat into large pieces and return to the soup. When ready to serve, add fresh chopped green onion, parsley and filé. This serves 18 and freezes well.

Mrs. Stewart Scott

Wild Turkey

1 wild turkey
Salt and pepper
1 onion, chopped
1 bell pepper, chopped
1 cup celery, chopped
Butter

Truly the king of game birds! Not only in size but in the skill with which he eludes the most crafty hunter. It is an especially rare treat to cook!!

Wash bird thoroughly and wipe dry. Salt and pepper the outside of the bird and inside of the cavity. Fill the cavity with coarsely chopped onion, bell pepper and celery. Cover the entire bird with a liberal coating of butter.

Pad the wing tips, tail and leg ends with double folds of aluminum foil to prevent the puncturing of foil wrapper. Tear off sufficient amount of heavy duty aluminum foil and cover the entire bird loosely. Place the foil on a large shallow pan, set the bird in the center and bring the long ends of the foil over the breast of the bird, folding together loosely. Turn up the foil at each end in a single fold at least 4 inches from the outer edge of the foil. The wrapping should not be completely air tight but should prevent the drippings from running out.

Roast the bird in a hot oven, preheated to 450 degrees according to the following table:

7 to 9 pounds 2 to 2½ hours
10 to 13 pounds 2¾ to 3 hours
14 to 17 pounds 3 to 3¼ hours
18 to 21 pounds 3¼ to 3½ hours

About 45 minutes before you expect the bird to be done, open the foil wrapper and fold back in pan fashion. Check for tenderness of the meat by pressing the thigh with your fingers protected by a paper towel.

Return the bird to the oven to finish browning, basting frequently.

Serve with wild rice dressing.

Mrs. Elmer Neill, Jr.
Tallulah, Louisiana

Dry Fry Venison

Loin or any lean part venison,
   tender or young
Pet milk
Flour
Salt
Pepper

Cut venison in 3 inch by 1/4 to 1/2 inch strips, trimmed of fat. Soak in Pet milk 30 minutes. Then put seasoned flour with lots of pepper in bag and shake. Fry in deep hot grease 5 minutes or until meat floats and is good and brown. Drain. Salt at this time, not before, as it makes meat tough.

Dr. Dan Keith

Venison Roast, Tensas Style
Not a "quickie" but worth the effort

10 pound venison roast

MARINADE:
1 quart vinegar
1 quart water
1 Tablespoon red pepper
1 Tablespoon black pepper
1 Tablespoon salt
3 cloves garlic, chopped
3 bay leaves
1 teaspoon cloves
1 teaspoon allspice
1 teaspoon mustard seed
1 teaspoon thyme

PREPARATION:
1/2 pound salt meat, cut into
   strips
1 medium onion, cut in strips
12 strips of celery
1/2 cup sour cream
1/2 cup currant jelly
1 Tablespoon brandy

Mix marinade ingredients and pour over meat in a bowl which can be covered. Place in the refrigerator and turn several times during a 12 hour, or longer, period. Before roasting, punch at least 10 holes in the roast with a sharp knife. Insert the salt meat, onion strips and celery strips. Insert a meat thermometer. Roast at 325 to 350 degrees as for a beef roast. Baste frequently with the remaining marinade and meat drippings. When roast is done add sour cream, jelly, and brandy to the skimmed meat drippings for a truly delicious gravy.

Mrs. J. W. Cummins

Venison Backstrap

1 venison backstrap
Salt
Pepper
Flour
Butter

Slice meat paper thin; slices better when partially frozen. Salt, pepper and flour. Then on a chopping block, hack the meat thoroughly with a knife. Brown meat quickly in butter in heavy skillet. Take out of skillet and place on paper towel to drain. Make a brown gravy in skillet and put meat in gravy. Cover and simmer in gravy 30 minutes to an hour. Bake big camp size biscuits. Split biscuits and put on plate. Serve the venison and gravy over biscuits.

Mrs. Elmer Neill, Jr.
Tallulah, Louisiana

Venison Roast

A good cut of game, properly cleaned, butchered and cared for is delicious prepared as a good cut of beef.

Venison leg or any roast cut
Lemon peel
Garlic slivers
Salt and pepper
Butter
2 or 3 bacon strips
2 ribs celery
1 bell pepper
1 small onion
4 Tablespoons drippings
4 Tablespoons flour
1 cup water
1 cup red wine

Have meat at room temperature. Pierce roast and stud with peel and garlic slivers. Rub well with salt and pepper. Dot with butter and lay bacon strips over meat. Place in roasting pan and surround with cut up pieces of vegetables. Put a little water in the bottom of the pan. Roast at 350 degrees, 20 minutes per pound for rare; or 22 minutes for medium. After placing roast in the oven, make a dark roux using flour and drippings. Add water and wine slowly, stirring until thickened. Add gravy to the bottom of the roasting pan after about an hour of the roasting time has elapsed.

Mrs. Wesley Shafto, Jr.

Venison Burgers

2½ pounds ground venison
½ cup minced onion
1 clove garlic, minced
4 Tablespoons chopped parsley
⅔ cup dry red wine
2 Tablespoons soy sauce
Salt and pepper to taste

Mix all ingredients; form into thick patties. Cook on grill or broil in oven, ten minutes on each side. Serve on buns. Serves 8 to 10.

Mrs. Jack Brown
Lake Providence, Louisiana

Squirrel Mulligan

2 squirrels
Flour
Drippings
Salt and pepper
1 onion, chopped
3 ribs celery, diced
1 Tablespoon parsley, minced
4 cloves garlic, minced
1-1 pound can tomatoes
1 bay leaf
1 crushed red pepper or
   cayenne to taste
1 medium can corn
1-10 ounce box frozen butter
   beans
2 potatoes, large dice

Soak squirrels overnight in salted water with a little vinegar added. Quarter squirrels, salt, pepper, flour and fry until golden in drippings, about 3 Tablespoons. Add onions, parsley, celery and garlic; sauté until clear. Blend in 1 pint of water and add tomatoes and bay leaf. Return squirrels to the pot and salt and pepper well adding crushed pepper or cayenne. Cook until the squirrel is tender. Add vegetables last and simmer until done. If the squirrel is done before the vegetables, remove so it will not fall to pieces. Reheat separately in a double boiler. Squirrel in one, sauce in another.

Mrs. C. D. Oakley, Jr.

Mulligan Stew

4 ducks, quartered, or equal
  amount doves or deer meat,
  cleaned
Salt and pepper to taste
Flour
2 bay leaves
2 large pods garlic, cut finely
2 Tablespoons dehydrated parsley
½ teaspoon thyme
2 large onions, chopped finely
1 green pepper, chopped finely
1½ cups celery, chopped finely
  and including leaves
½ cup green onion tops, chopped
  finely
1 large can mushrooms, ends and
  pieces
Shortening

Dry, salt, pepper, and flour meat generously. Brown in shortening. Place in large iron pot and barely cover with water. Add bay leaves, garlic, parsley, thyme, onion, green pepper, celery, green onions, and mushrooms. It is imperative that all added ingredients be chopped very fine so they will cook away. Cook slowly until meat is tender but not cooked to pieces. Some water may be added in very small amounts while cooking if stew seems too thick. Serve over rice with butter-toasted French bread and a light wine. Start looking for a place to lie down. The sinking spell is only a few minutes away.

Mrs. C.O. Cook, Jr.
Shreveport, Louisiana

Moose Leg Roast

6 pound haunch roast from hind
  leg
¼ cup butter
4 or 5 sprigs parsley, minced
½ teaspoon dried savory
½ teaspoon dried tarragon
10 to 12 juniper berries
Flour
Salt and pepper
1 cup red wine or equal parts
  wine and game stock
1 cup game stock or beef broth
¼ cup red wine
1 Tablespoon brandy
1½ Tablespoons roux

Melt butter without browning; add herbs and cook together several minutes. Place roast, seasoned with salt and pepper and lightly sprinkled with flour in roasting pan. Pour over savory butter and place in oven which has been preheated to 450 degrees. After 20 minutes, reduce heat to 325 degrees; add wine and stock, cover and roast 25 minutes per pound, basting frequently. When roast is tender, remove to a heated platter and keep warm while you prepare the sauce. Add 1 cup game stock to the juices in the roasting pan, set over flame and stir briskly to loosen the crusty bits in the pan. Strain through a sieve into a small saucepan, add 1/4 cup red wine, 1 Tablespoon brandy, and 1 1/2 Tablespoons roux. Stir briskly until sauce is smooth and thickened. Check for seasoning. Allow to simmer a few minutes and pour into preheated serving boat.

Mrs. Elmer Neill, Jr.
Tallulah, Louisiana

Grand Champion Sponge Cake

1 ¼ cups sifted all purpose flour
1 cup sugar
½ teaspoon baking powder
½ teaspoon salt
6 egg whites
1 teaspoon cream of tartar
½ cup sugar
6 egg yolks
¼ cup water
1 teaspoon vanilla

Sift together flour, 1 cup sugar, baking powder and salt. In large mixing bowl beat egg whites until frothy. Add cream of tartar. Gradually beat in ½ cup sugar a little at a time. Beat until whites form stiff, not dry, peaks. In a small bowl combine egg yolks, water, vanilla and sifted dry ingredients. Beat at medium high speed 4 minutes until mixture is light and fluffy. Fold yolk mixture gently into beaten egg whites. Turn into ungreased 10 inch angel food pan. Bake at 350 degrees for about 45 minutes. Invert pan to cool at once. Serves 12 generously.

Mrs. V. A. Wolff
St. Louis, Missouri

CAKE BAKING TIPS

BEFORE YOU BEGIN:
Preheat the oven, prepare the cake pan and measure all the ingredients. Allow all the ingredients to come to room temperature.

OVEN TEMPERATURE:
Be sure that the temperature of your oven is correct if your cake is to rise properly. An oven thermometer can be purchased at grocery stores and variety stores.

PREPARING THE CAKE PAN:
Most recipes tell you how the cake is to be prepared. A bundt pan is usually greased thoroughly with shortening. Cakepans are usually greased with a thin film of shortening or butter and sprinkled with flour. The flour should cover the entire bottom and sides. Turn the pans over and thump bottom to remove excess flour.

FLOUR:
Measure flour accurately. This is essential! To measure, sift flour into a measuring cup until it overflows. Level off excess flour even with the rim of the cup, using a knife or something with a flat edge. DO NOT tap or press down the flour. Always use plain flour unless cake flour or some other specific kind is called for in the recipe.

BLENDING FLOUR:
If flour and liquid are to be added to a cake batter, you should always add them alternately, beginning and ending with the sifted flour. Do not beat your cake when adding flour, but fold or stir in flour carefully.

BUTTER AND SUGAR:
Many recipes direct that butter and sugar be creamed. This may be done with an electric mixer or by hand. Be sure to start with the butter at room temperature. Beat at moderate speed until mixture is light, fluffy and a pale ivory color.

EGGS:
Eggs should be added, or beaten and added, as directed by the recipe. Most recipes intend the eggs to be of medium size.

BAKING:
Unless otherwise instructed, cakes should be baked on the center rack of your oven. Do not allow the pans to touch each other or the sides of the oven. Do not bake layers on separate racks, one over the other. When baking 3 layer cakes, divide the oven racks evenly. Arrange pans so one is not directly on top of the other allowing for full circulation of heat.

Cakes may be tested for doneness with a clean broom straw, or a cake tester inserted in the center of the cake after ¾ of the baking time has passed. If it comes out clean, the cake is done. Do not over-bake.

If glass pan is used. reduce oven temperature 25 degrees.

REMOVING CAKE FROM PAN:
Allow the cake to sit in its pan for about five minutes before removing it to a cake rack to cool unless the recipe instructs differently. To remove the cake from the pan, run the blade of a thin knife all around between the pan and the cake. Place rack on top of pan and gently invert. Lift pan from cake and allow to cool completely before icing or storing.

STORING:
Cakes that have been baked and thoroughly cooled may be stored, uniced, for several days in an airtight container or wrapped securely and frozen.

Grandmother's Angel Food Cake

1½ cups sugar
1 cup Swans Down Cake flour
1½ cups egg whites
Pinch of salt
¾ teaspoon cream of tartar
1 teaspoon vanilla
1 teaspoon lemon flavoring

Sift flour and sugar before measuring, then sift flour and sugar together 6 or 8 times. Beat egg whites by hand, do not use an electric mixer. When frothy, add salt and cream of tartar and continue beating until you can turn the bowl you are beating them in upside down. Fold in flour mixture a little at a time. Add flavorings. Put in an ungreased angel food cake pan. Start in a cold oven, gradually increasing temperature to 350 degrees. Bake about 45 minutes. When done, turn pan upside down and let it remain in this position until cool. Remove from pan and ice with your favorite icing.

Mrs. John Ensminger

Butter and Egg Cake

½ pound butter
2 cups sugar
5 eggs
2 cups flour, sifted
1 teaspoon vanilla
1 cup pecans, chopped
1 or 2 Tablespoons flour

Cream butter and sugar well. Add 1 egg and a small part of flour, beating mixture constantly. Continue alternating flour and eggs until all ingredients are used and well mixed into batter. Add vanilla. Dredge nuts in 1 or 2 Tablespoons of flour and mix into batter. Pour into a greased and floured tube or bundt pan. Bake 1 hour at 350 degrees. Cool cake slightly before removing from pan.

Mrs. Jennings Wilkins
Mrs. Thomas Brakefield

Gold Ice Box Torte

9 egg yolks
1½ cups sugar
¾ cup water
2¼ teaspoons baking powder
2¼ cups cake flour
1 teaspoon vanilla
Dash of salt

ICING:
1 pint heavy cream
1 small can Hershey chocolate
  syrup
Chopped almonds

Beat egg yolks well, then add sugar and water. Add vanilla. Sift flour, baking powder and salt together; add to mixture. Grease and flour three 9 inch layer pans. Bake at 375 degrees for 12 to 15 minutes. Layers will be thin. After cake is cool, cut each layer in half.

ICING:
Beat cream until thick. Fold in chocolate syrup. Spread between layers and outside of cake. Sprinkle with chopped almonds. Refrigerate overnight.

Mrs. Sam Rubin, Jr.

Vanilla Wafer Cake

2 sticks butter
2 cups sugar
6 eggs
1-12 ounce box vanilla wafers,
   crushed
½ cup milk
1-7 ounce package flaked coconut
1 cup pecans, chopped

Cream butter and sugar. Add eggs one at a time, beating after each addition. Add crushed wafers and milk. Mix in coconut and pecans. Bake in a well greased tube pan at 275 degrees for 2 hours or until done.

Mrs. William Ledoux

Buche de Noël

CAKE:
6 eggs
¾ cup sugar
⅓ cup unsweetened cocoa
1 teaspoon vanilla extract
½ teaspoon almond extract
Confectioners' sugar

FILLING:
1 cup heavy cream
¼ cup sifted powdered sugar
1 teaspoon vanilla extract
1 teaspoon almond extract

ICING:
⅔ cup sugar
⅛ teaspoon cream of tartar
⅓ cup water
5 egg yolks
1 cup soft butter
3 ounces unsweetened chocolate,
   melted

CAKE: Separate eggs and let whites warm to room temperature. Preheat oven to 375 degrees. Lightly grease bottom of a 15½ x 10½ x 1 inch jelly-roll pan; then line with wax paper. Beat egg whites until soft peaks form and gradually beat in ¼ cup sugar, beating until stiff peaks form. Meringue will be shiny and moist. Beat egg yolks at high speed with remaining sugar until thick and lemon colored, about 5 minutes. At low speed, beat in cocoa and extracts just until combined. With rubber spatula, fold egg yolk mixture into egg whites just until combined. Turn into the prepared pan, spread evenly, and bake 12 to 14 minutes or just until surface springs back when gently pressed with fingertip. Test at 12 minutes so you will not overcook. Have ready a clean damp towel, covered with a dry towel which has been dusted with powdered sugar. Turn cake out onto sugar, peel off wax paper, and trim crisp edges quickly. Starting with long edge, roll up cake, jelly-roll fashion. Place seam side down on rack 30 minutes to cool. Meanwhile whip cream with flavorings. Gently unroll cake, remove towel, spread with filling and reroll. ICING: Combine sugar, cream of tartar and water in a saucepan. Place over low heat and stir until sugar is dissolved. Raise heat and boil without stirring until syrup reaches 238 degrees or soft ball stage. While syrup is cooking beat egg yolks until they are fluffy. Pour hot syrup in a thin stream in yolks, beating constantly. As the mixture cools it will become thick and light. Continue to beat for a few more minutes. Set aside to cool. Beat in softened butter. Add the melted chocolate to the butter cream. If the butter cream is too soft to hold its shape, it may be chilled for a few minutes. Spread on roll. Store in the refrigerator. Serves 8 to 10.

Mrs. Don Irby

Old Fashioned White Birthday Cake

1 cup butter, softened
2 cups sugar
3½ cups cake flour
½ teaspoon salt
3½ teaspoons baking powder
1 cup milk
1 teaspoon vanilla extract
1 teaspoon almond extract
7 or 8 egg whites
⅛ teaspoon salt

Cream butter and sugar. Sift cake flour before measuring. Resift twice with the salt and baking powder. Add flour mixture, alternating with milk. Beat smooth after each addition. Add vanilla and almond extract. Beat egg whites until stiff but not dry. Add ⅛ teaspoon salt to beaten whites. Fold egg whites lightly into cake batter. Pour batter into a greased 9 inch tube pan. Bake at 325 degrees for 1 hour or until cake tests done. Ice with seven minute icing.

Mrs. T. M. Sayre
Rayville, Louisiana

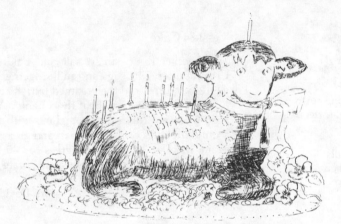

Italian Cream Cake

1 stick butter
½ cup Wesson oil
2 cups sugar
5 eggs, separated
1 cup buttermilk
1 teaspoon baking soda
2 cups flour
1 teaspoon vanilla
1 cup shredded coconut
½ cup nuts, chopped

ICING:
1-8 ounce package cream cheese, softened
1 stick butter, softened
1 teaspoon vanilla
1 box powdered sugar
½ cup nuts, chopped fine

Cream butter, oil and sugar. Add egg yolks one at a time, beating after each addition. Stir baking soda into buttermilk. Add sifted flour into batter, alternating with buttermilk mixture. Add vanilla, coconut and chopped nuts. Beat egg whites and fold into mixture. Pour into a greased and floured 9 x 13 inch cake pan for a sheet cake or three 8 or 9 inch layer pans. Bake at 325 degrees for 45 minutes. Cool and ice.

ICING:
Beat cream cheese and butter. Add vanilla, powdered sugar and nuts. Continue to beat until of spreading consistency.

Mrs. W. J. Hodge Jr.
Mrs. William Reed
Mrs. Hoye Grafton
Ruston, Louisiana

Snippé Kake

A Norwegian Cake

4 eggs
1 cup sugar
½ cup butter, melted
1 cup flour
1 teaspoon baking powder
1 teaspoon almond extract
¼ cup whole currants
¼ cup almonds or other
  nuts, chopped fine
Powdered sugar

Combine eggs with sugar and beat until light and lemon colored. Add melted butter. Sift flour and baking powder together. Add to batter. Add flavoring. Spread thin on a greased cookie sheet. Sprinkle top with whole currants and chopped nuts. Bake 10 to 15 minutes at 375 degrees. Cut into desired size pieces while hot and dust with powdered sugar.

Mrs. Faheam Cannon

Lessie's Cake

2 cups cake flour
1¼ cups sugar
½ teaspoon salt
3 teaspoons baking powder
1¼ sticks butter, softened
3 eggs
¾ cup milk
2 teaspoons vanilla
2 teaspoons orange extract
⅓ teaspoon mace

Sift together flour, sugar, salt and baking powder. Cream butter. Mix eggs and milk together. Alternate a little at a time into the creamed butter, the egg mixture and flour mixture. Beat thoroughly. Add flavorings. Grease a tube cake pan. Line with wax paper around the sides of the tube pan and grease and flour again. Bake at 300 to 325 degrees for 40 to 45 minutes. Serving suggestion: pour a chocolate glaze icing over the cooled cake.

Mrs. David Garrett, Jr.

Oatmeal Cake

1½ cups boiling water
1 cup quick cooking oatmeal
1½ cups flour
1 teaspoon cinnamon
1 teaspoon baking soda
½ teaspoon salt
1 cup brown sugar
1 cup white sugar
2 eggs
½ cup salad oil

TOPPING:
1 cup brown sugar
½ cup evaporated milk
1 stick butter
1 teaspoon vanilla
½ cup nuts, chopped
1 can coconut

Pour boiling water over oatmeal and let stand while preparing the following: sift together flour, cinnamon, baking soda and salt; add these dry ingredients to sugars, eggs and oil; then add oatmeal. Mix well. Pour into a greased and floured bundt pan. Bake at 350 degrees for 30 to 40 minutes.

TOPPING:
Dissolve the sugar in milk. Add butter and cook. Stir almost constantly until mixture boils and becomes thick. Take from heat and add vanilla, nuts and coconut. Pour over cake while hot.

Mrs. Lestar Martin

Pound Cake

1 cup butter
2 cups sugar
4 eggs
1 teaspoon vanilla
1 teaspoon almond extract
1 teaspoon lemon extract
3 cups cake flour
½ cup milk

Cream butter and sugar until fluffy. Add eggs one at a time, beating after each addition. Add vanilla, almond and lemon extract. Fold in flour and milk alternately. Bake in a greased bundt pan at 325 degrees for about 1 hour or until cake tests done.

Mrs. Dan Sartor

Chocolate Pound Cake

1 cup butter
½ cup Crisco
3 cups sugar
5 eggs
3 cups sifted flour
½ teaspoon baking powder
½ teaspoon salt
4 Tablespoons cocoa
1 cup milk
1 Tablespoon vanilla

Cream together butter, Crisco and sugar. Add eggs one at a time. Sift together flour, baking powder, salt and cocoa. Add alternately with milk. Add vanilla. Pour into a greased and floured tube pan. Bake at 325 degrees for 80 minutes or until it tests done. If you omit the cocoa, this recipe makes a delicious yellow pound cake. This cake freezes well.

Mrs. Glenn Lesley
Greensboro, North Carolina

Caramel Pecan Cake

½ cup butter
3 cups sugar
1 Tablespoon fresh lemon juice
6 large eggs
1-8 ounce carton sour cream
¼ teaspoon baking soda
3 heaping cups cake flour
½ teaspoon salt
1 teaspoon almond flavoring
1 teaspoon vanilla

ICING:
2½ cups sugar
1 egg, beaten
1 stick butter
¾ cup evaporated milk
1 teaspoon vanilla
¼ teaspoon almond flavoring
Dash of salt
Chopped pecans or toasted
  almonds

Cream butter, add sugar and fresh lemon juice. Cream until light and fluffy. Add eggs, one at a time, mixing well after each addition. Combine baking soda to sour cream; sift flour twice with salt. Turn mixer onto low speed and alternately add sour cream and flour to batter. Add flavorings. Pour batter into a greased and floured bundt or tube pan and bake at 325 degrees for 1½ hours.

ICING:

In a heavy saucepan, mix 2 cups sugar, beaten egg, butter and milk. Put on a low fire and let come to a slow boil. In a small black iron skillet, melt remaining ½ cup sugar and let cook until brown and runny. Add this to the sugar mixture and continue to cook until the temperature reaches the soft ball stage, 238 degrees. You must cook this slowly to prevent the milk from scorching. Remove from fire and let cool slightly; then add salt and flavorings. Beat until icing reaches a spreading consistency. Ice on cooled cake. Sprinkle top with chopped nuts.

Mrs. Fred Millsaps

Pineapple Pound Cake

3 sticks butter
1½ boxes powdered sugar, sifted
6 eggs
1 teaspoon vanilla
1 teaspoon lemon juice
1 powdered sugar box filled with sifted flour
1 No. 2 can crushed pineapple, very well drained, reserve juice

GLAZE:
2 cups powdered sugar, sifted
8 Tablespoons pineapple juice

Preheat oven to 325 degrees. Cream butter and sugar. *It is best to measure first box when sifting to judge the ½ box accurately.* Add eggs one at a time, beating well after each addition. Blend in vanilla and lemon juice. Add all the flour, *sifted until level into the box,* beat until well mixed. Blend in pineapple, which has been drained several hours or overnight, if possible. Grease tube cake pan and bake at 325 degrees for 1½ hours or until cake tester comes out clean. Mix glaze ingredients well and pour on cake while still slightly warm.

Mrs. R. D. Kellogg

Coconut Pound Cake

6 eggs, separated
1 cup shortening
½ cup butter
3 cups sugar
½ teaspoon almond extract
½ teaspoon coconut extract
3 cups sifted cake flour
1 cup milk
2 cups canned flaked coconut

Preheat oven to 300 degrees. Separate eggs. Set egg whites aside and allow to return to room temperature. Beat egg yolks with shortening and butter at high speed until well blended. Gradually add sugar, beating until light and fluffy. Add extracts and beat. At low speed, beat in flour, about ¼ at a time, alternating with milk, about ⅓ at a time. Begin and end with flour. Add coconut and beat. Beat egg whites until stiff peaks form. Gently fold whites into batter. Pour into a greased 10 inch tube pan. Bake for 2 hours or until cake tester inserted near center of cake comes out clean. Cool in pan on wire rack 10 to 15 minutes. Remove from pan. This cake has a nice macaroon-like top. It slices better the day after it is made. It may also be stored in the refrigerator for several days.

Mrs. Thomas Zentner

Rum-Coconut Pound Cake

2 sticks butter
½ cup shortening
3 cups sugar
5 eggs
1 teaspoon coconut flavoring
¼ cup rum
3 cups flour, sifted
½ teaspoon baking powder
1 cup milk

ICING:
1 cup sugar
½ cup water
1 teaspoon almond extract

Cream butter, shortening and sugar. Add eggs, one at a time, beating well after each addition. Add flavoring and rum. Sift the flour three more times adding baking powder. Fold the flour in alternately with milk. Bake at 325 degrees for 1½ hours or until it tests done in a greased and floured tube pan. Let the cake cool in the pan and remove it before spooning on the glaze. Bring icing ingredients to a boil and spoon on cold cake.

Mrs. R. B. Stroud

Apricot Brandy Cake

1 cup butter
or
1/2 cup butter and 1/2 cup
   margarine
3 cups sugar
6 eggs
3 cups flour
1/2 teaspoon salt
1/4 teaspoon baking soda
1 cup sour cream
1/2 cup apricot brandy
1 teaspoon vanilla
1/2 teaspoon rum extract
1/2 teaspoon lemon extract
1/4 teaspoon almond extract

Cream together butter and sugar. Add eggs one at a time. Sift flour, salt and baking soda together. Mix sour cream, apricot brandy and all extracts together. Now alternately add sour cream mixture and flour mixture into creamed butter and sugar. Pour into a greased and floured angel food cake pan. Bake at 325 degrees for 70 minutes or until done.

Mrs. T. B. Godfrey, Jr.

Bourbon Pound Cake

1 pound butter
3 cups sugar
8 eggs, separated
3 cups flour, sifted
2 teaspoons vanilla
1 teaspoon butter flavoring
2 teaspoons almond flavoring
4 Tablespoons bourbon
1 cup nuts, chopped

Cream butter and sugar together until fluffy. Add egg yolks and beat well. Mix in sifted flour, flavorings and bourbon. Beat egg whites until stiff. Fold into batter. Prepare a tube pan. Do not use bundt pan. Grease well the bottom of the pan. Cut a circle of wax paper and fit into bottom. Grease wax paper. Sprinkle bottom of pan with 1/2 cup nuts, add batter and sprinkle remaining 1/2 cup of nuts on top. Bake at 325 degrees 1 1/2 to 2 hours or until brown. To prevent top of cake from cracking open, cover with foil the last 30 minutes of cooking.

Mrs. Dick Taylor
Ruston, Louisiana

Rum Cake

2 sticks butter
2 cups sugar
6 eggs
2 cups plus 3 Tablespoons
   sifted flour
1/8 teaspoon salt
1/4 cup rum

RUM SAUCE:
1 1/2 cups sugar
1/4 cup water
2 Tablespoons white corn syrup
1/2 cup rum

Cream butter then blend with sugar. Add eggs one at a time, beating well after each addition. Add flour and salt all at once. Blend in rum. Bake in a 2 quart loaf pan or tube pan for 1 hour and 45 minutes at 300 degrees.

SAUCE:
Bring sugar, water and syrup to a boil. Remove from heat and add rum. Pour over cake while still warm.

Mrs. Alton Irwin

Con's Chocolate Cake

2 cups sugar
½ cup Crisco
2 eggs
1 teaspoon baking soda
½ cup buttermilk
3 heaping Tablespoons cocoa
2 cups flour
1 teaspoon vanilla
1 cup boiling water

Cream sugar and shortening. Add eggs and beat well. Put baking soda into buttermilk and stir well. Add to sugar mixture. Sift flour and cocoa together and add to batter, mixing well. Add vanilla and boiling water. Bake in a greased 9 x 13 inch pan at 350 degrees for 35 to 40 minutes. If you want a large sheet cake, use a greased 11 x 16 inch pan and bake at 400 degrees for 10 to 15 minutes. When completely cool, frost with Chocolate Fudge Icing or icing of your choice.

Mrs. George Purvis
Rayville, Louisiana

Devil's Food Cake with Caramel Frosting

1 cup butter
2 cups sugar
3 squares bitter chocolate, melted
5 eggs, separated
2½ cups cake flour, sifted
½ teaspoon salt
1 cup buttermilk
1 teaspoon vanilla
1 teaspoon baking soda
1 teaspoon boiling water

ICING:
1 pint cream
1 stick butter
½ cup light Karo syrup
3 cups, minus 2 Tablespoons sugar

Cream butter. Add sugar gradually and continue to beat until well creamed. Add melted chocolate and mix well. Add egg yolks and beat mixture thoroughly. Sift flour with salt and add alternately with buttermilk into mixture. Stir in vanilla. Dissolve baking soda in boiling water and blend into batter. Beat egg whites until stiff and fold into batter. Pour into three 9 inch well greased and floured cake pans. Bake at 375 degrees for 20 minutes.

ICING:
Mix cream, butter and Karo in a small saucepan. *Set over low heat.* Melt sugar in black iron skillet over low heat until brown and runny. Add to cream mixture and cook until soft ball forms in water. Remove from heat and beat until spreading consistency.

Mrs. Fred Bennett

DeLuxe Chocolate Ice Box Cake

Delicate, delicious and traditional party fare

SPONGE CAKE:
3 eggs, separated
1 cup sugar, scant
4 Tablespoons cold water
1 cup flour
½ teaspoon salt
1 teaspoon baking powder
1 teaspoon vanilla

CHOCOLATE MIXTURE:
4 squares bitter chocolate
1 stick butter
4 egg yolks
1 cup sugar
4 stiffly beaten egg whites

CREAM MIXTURE:
2 cartons heavy cream
Sugar
Vanilla

Prepare sponge cake ahead and freeze. Beat yolks and sugar until very light. Add cold water. Fold in flour, salt and baking powder which have been sifted together. Fold in egg whites and vanilla carefully. Bake at 325 degrees for 30 minutes in a 9 inch square ungreased, wax paper lined pan. Sponge cake should be inverted between two racks and completely cooled before removing. Freeze.

Chocolate Mixture: Melt chocolate and butter. Beat egg yolks with sugar, blend in cooled chocolate mixture and fold in stiffly beaten egg whites. Refrigerate briefly if not thick enough to spread.

Layering cake: Cut thawed sponge cake in half, vertically, having two loaves. Using a sharp knife cut one loaf into as many thin layers as possible. Whip 1 carton of cream flavored with sugar and vanilla to taste. Starting with the bottom layer spread a thin layer of the chocolate mixture on it and top with a layer of cake. Spread whipped cream on that layer and top with next layer of cake. Build up layers alternating chocolate filling and whipped cream ending with top piece of cake. Treat other loaf similarly; refrigerate. When ready to serve ice with the other carton of whipped cream. Quite simple when you make your sponge cake ahead and freeze it. The sponge cake easily doubles to have ready to prepare at any time.

Mrs. Wesley Shafto, Sr.

Feathery Fudge Cake

2/3 cup butter, softened
1¾ cups sugar
2 eggs
1 teaspoon vanilla
2½ -1 ounce squares unsweetened
   chocolate, melted
2½ cups cake flour, sifted
1¼ teaspoons baking soda
½ teaspoon salt
1¼ cups ice water

Cream together butter, sugar, eggs and vanilla until fluffy; beat 5 minutes at high speed of mixer, scraping bowl occasionally. Blend in cooled chocolate. Sift together flour, baking soda and salt; add to creamed mixture alternately with ice water. Begin and end with flour mixture. Beat after each addition. Bake in 2 paper lined 9 inch round pans at 350 degrees for 30 to 35 minutes.

Mrs. Ed W. Stinson, Jr.

Chocolate Chip Cake

1-7 ounce package dates
1 cup boiling water
1 teaspoon baking soda
½ cup butter
½ cup Crisco
1 cup sugar
2 eggs, beaten
1 teaspoon vanilla
2 Tablespoons cocoa
1¾ cups flour
½ teaspoon salt
1-6 ounce package chocolate
   chips
1 cup pecans, chopped

Chop dates fine. Place in a bowl and cover with boiling water. Stir in baking soda and let stand until cool. Cream together butter, Crisco and sugar. Add beaten eggs, vanilla and cocoa. Sift together flour and salt. Alternately stir in flour mixture and date mixture. Pour into a greased 13 x 9 inch pan. Sprinkle top with chocolate chips and pecans. Bake for 35 minutes at 350 degrees.

Mrs. H. Werner Wolf

Chocolate Skillet Cake

½ cup cold water
½ cup cocoa
1½ cups sifted flour
½ teaspoon salt
1 teaspoon soda
1¼ cups packed brown sugar
½ cup Crisco
3 eggs
½ cup buttermilk
1 teaspoon vanilla
10 Hershey Bars, small

Add water to cocoa and beat. Sift flour, salt and baking soda into bowl. Add sugar, Crisco, eggs and ¼ cup buttermilk. Beat for 3 minutes. Add vanilla, remaining ¼ cup buttermilk and cocoa mixture. Beat for 2 minutes. Pour into a 10 inch greased skillet. Break 5 Hershey Bars into pieces and place on top of batter. Cover skillet with a tight lid or tightly fitting foil. Bake 350 degrees for 1 hour. When done and while still hot, repeat Hershey topping with remaining 5 bars. This is best served hot.

Mrs. Herbert E. Smith, Jr.
Mrs. Walter L. Hastings
Mrs. Clark Boyce

Crazy Chocolate Cake

3 cups flour
2 cups sugar
2 teaspoons baking soda
1 teaspoon salt
½ cup cocoa
¾ cup oil
1 teaspoon vanilla
2 Tablespoons vinegar
2 cups water

Sift into an ungreased 9 x 13 inch pan the flour, sugar, baking soda, salt and cocoa. Add oil, vinegar and vanilla. Pour water over entire ingredients. Mix with a fork until smooth. Bake at 350 degrees for 20 to 25 minutes. Cool. Ice in pan with favorite frosting.

Mrs. David Garrett, Jr.

Hershey Bar Cake

1-10 ounce Hershey Bar
1 cup butter
2 cups sugar
4 eggs
1 cup buttermilk
½ teaspoon baking soda
2½ cups cake flour
1-5½ ounce can Hershey
   chocolate syrup
1 teaspoon vanilla
Powdered sugar

Melt chocolate bar in top of double boiler. Cream together butter and sugar. Add eggs, one at a time, beating well after each addition. Stir baking soda into buttermilk. Alternately add buttermilk and flour into creamed butter mixture. Add melted chocolate bar, chocolate syrup and vanilla. Pour into a greased and floured tube pan, not a bundt pan. Bake for 70 minutes at 350 degrees. Cool and sprinkle with powdered sugar.

Mrs. W. J. Hodge, Jr.
Mrs. Charles Siess, Jr.
Houston, Texas

Coca-Cola Cake

2 cups flour
2 cups sugar
2 sticks butter
1 cup Coca-Cola
3 Tablespoons cocoa
½ cup buttermilk
2 eggs, beaten
1 teaspoon baking soda
1 teaspoon vanilla
2 cups miniature marshmallows

ICING:
1 stick butter
6 Tablespoons Coca-Cola
1 box powdered sugar
1 teaspoon vanilla
3 Tablespoons cocoa
1 cup toasted pecans or almonds
   or both

Combine flour and sugar, mixing well. Heat butter, Coca-Cola, cocoa and bring to a boiling point. Pour over flour and sugar. Add buttermilk, eggs, baking soda and vanilla. Mix well. Then add marshmallows and pour into a 9 x 13 inch greased cake pan. Bake for 30 to 35 minutes at 350 degrees. The marshmallows will rise to the top during the baking.

ICING:
Cream butter. Add remaining ingredients and beat well. Pour over cake while still in the pan. This cake will keep for days if left in the pan in which it was cooked.

Mrs. B. F. Pate
Mrs. Herbert Mayo

Mrs. Kaplan's Chocolate Cake

2 sticks butter, softened
2 cups sugar
4 squares Baker's semi-sweet
 chocolate, melted
5 eggs
2 cups buttermilk
3½ cups flour, sifted 3 times
2 teaspoons baking soda
2 teaspoons vanilla

ICING:
1½ sticks butter, softened
3 Tablespoons cocoa
1½ boxes powdered sugar
4 to 5 Tablespoons milk

Cream together butter and sugar until light and fluffy. Add melted chocolate. Add eggs, one at a time, beating well after each addition. Alternately add flour and 1¼ cups buttermilk. This can be done by dividing the flour into 3 parts. Stir baking soda into the remaining ¾ cup buttermilk. Gently fold buttermilk into batter. Add vanilla. Pour batter into three greased and floured 9 inch cake pans. Place in a *cold* oven. Bake for 20 minutes at 300 degrees; then bake at 325 degrees for 15 minutes; then bake 10 minutes more at 350 degrees. Ice when cold.

ICING:
Cream butter. Add cocoa and powdered sugar. Continue beating and add milk slowly until icing reaches desired consistency for spreading. Put a generous amount of icing between layers, then cover top and sides.

Mrs. David Kaplan

Milky Way Cake

8-1¾ ounce Milky Ways
3 sticks butter
2 cups sugar
4 eggs, well beaten
2½ cups flour
¼ teaspoon baking soda
1¼ cups buttermilk
1 teaspoon vanilla
1 cup pecans, chopped
Powdered sugar

ICING:
2½ cups sugar
1 cup evaporated milk
1 stick butter
1 cup marshmallow cream
1-6 ounce package chocolate
 chips
1 cup pecans, chopped

Melt Milky Ways with 1 stick butter. Remove from fire and let cool. Cream remaining 2 sticks butter with sugar. Add beaten eggs and cooled chocolate mixture. Sift flour and baking soda together. Alternately add flour and buttermilk to the batter, blending well. Add vanilla and nuts. Grease and dust with powdered sugar three 9 inch cake pans. Bake at 325 degrees for 30 to 45 minutes.

ICING:
Combine sugar and evaporated milk. Cook to a soft ball stage. Remove from heat and add butter, marshmallow cream and chocolate chips, stirring until all have melted. Add pecans.

Mrs. A. N. Briggle
Dallas, Texas

Heavenly Hash Cake

2 sticks butter
4 Tablespoons cocoa
2 cups sugar
4 eggs
2 cups pecans, chopped
2 Tablespoons vanilla
1 1/2 cups self-rising flour

ICING:
1 bag marshmallows, cut in half,
   not jet-puffed or miniature
1 box powdered sugar
4 Tablespoons cocoa
4 Tablespoons butter, melted
1/2 cup evaporated milk or water

Melt butter. Add cocoa and mix well. Add rest of ingredients in order given. *Stir*, do not beat. Pour into a greased and floured 13 x 9 inch pan. Bake at 350 degrees for 25 to 35 minutes. Do not remove from pan when done.

ICING:
Cut marshmallows and have ready before the cake is done. As soon as you remove cake from the oven place marshmallows, cut side down, on top, cramming them as close together as possible. The marshmallows will begin to melt from the heat of the cake. Now combine the icing ingredients together and beat until smooth. Pour over the top of the marshmallows. Let set before cutting into squares.

Mrs. Saul A. Mintz

Mocha Cake
A French Genoise

6 large eggs
1 cup sugar
1 cup flour, sifted
1/2 cup unsalted butter, melted
1 teaspoon vanilla

SIMPLE SYRUP:
1 cup sugar
1/2 cup water

MOCHA CREAM:
3 sticks butter, softened
1 1/2 cups sifted powdered sugar
2 egg yolks, slightly beaten
2 teaspoons vanilla
1 Tablespoon instant powdered
   coffee
1 teaspoon water
1-5 ounce can roasted
   almonds, diced

Allow eggs to return to room temperature before starting cake. Beat eggs and sugar at high speed in electric mixer 10 to 15 minutes; they will triple in bulk and look like whipped cream. Sift flour, 1/4 cup at a time, over egg mixture, gently folding each addition by hand. Add the cooled melted butter and vanilla, again folding in very carefully. Pour batter into three 8 inch greased and floured pans. Bake at 350 degrees for 15 to 20 minutes or until cakes tests done. Turn out of pans at once and cool on wire racks. Brush cooled cakes with warm simple syrup.

SYRUP:
Combine sugar and water and bring to boil, only. Set aside until slightly cooled.

MOCHA CREAM:
Cream butter until light and fluffy. Gradually add sugar, then beat in egg yolks. Dissolve coffee in water and vanilla then add to icing mixture. Frost between layers, tops and sides of cakes. Pat diced nuts on sides of iced cake. Refrigerate. Cake is better if allowed to mellow a day or two before serving. If you prefer a chocolate cake instead of a yellow cake, substitute 1/2 cup cocoa with 1/2 cup flour, rather than using 1 cup flour. Be sure and sift cocoa and flour together before using.

Mrs. Don Irby

Fresh Apple Cake

4½ cups raw apples, chopped
Lemon juice
1½ cups salad oil
2 cups sugar
2 large eggs
2½ cups all purpose flour
1 teaspoon salt
1 teaspoon baking soda
2 teaspoons baking powder
2 teaspoons vanilla
1½ cups pecans, chopped

FROSTING:
1 stick butter
⅛ teaspoon salt
2 Tablespoons milk
1 cup dark brown sugar, firmly
   packed
Small amount of powdered sugar

Prepare apples. Put a little lemon juice over them; set aside and cover. Add sugar and eggs to oil; mix well at low speed until creamy and smooth. Sift flour and measure. Sift again with salt, soda and baking powder. Add flour mixture to creamed mixture a little at a time. Fold in well after each addition. Add vanilla. When batter is stiff, remove beaters and finish mixing by hand. Fold in apples and nuts. Bake in a 9 x 13 inch pan for 55 minutes to 1 hour at 350 degrees.

FROSTING:
Combine butter, salt, milk and brown sugar in saucepan. Heat and stir until smooth. Remove from fire. Add powdered sugar and continue stirring until spreading consistency.

Mrs. Wesley Shafto, Sr.

APPLE CORE --- BALTIMORE!

Soused Apple Hill Cake

4 cups baking apples; peeled,
   cored and chopped
6 Tablespoons brandy
2 cups flour
2 teaspoons cinnamon
2 teaspoons baking soda
1 teaspoon nutmeg
1 teaspoon salt
¼ teaspoon ground cloves
2 cups sugar
½ cup salad oil
2 eggs
1 cup walnuts, coarsely chopped
1 cup raisins, coarsely chopped
Heavy cream, whipped

Put chopped apples into a bowl and pour as much brandy over them as they will absorb. Sift together flour, cinnamon, baking soda, nutmeg, salt and cloves. Toss flour mixture into soaked apples. Beat together sugar, oil and eggs. Combine with the flour and apple mixture. Stir batter well. Add walnuts and raisins. Pour into a greased 9 x 13 inch baking pan. Bake at 325 degrees for 1 hour or until done. Serve warm or cold, topped with whipped cream. A delicious way to serve left over cake is to break cake into chunks and layer in parfait glasses with whipped cream. Serves 12.

Mrs. Jerry Wolff

Fig Cake

3 eggs
2 cups sugar
1 cup Wesson oil
2 cups flour
1 cup buttermilk
1 teaspoon baking soda
1 cup drained chopped
  fig preserves
1 teaspoon cinnamon
1 teaspoon cloves
1 teaspoon salt

Beat eggs. Add sugar and cream whipping until light and fluffy. Add oil. Stir baking soda into buttermilk. Alternately add flour and buttermilk mixture into batter. Add remaining ingredients. Pour into a greased tube pan and bake at 350 degrees for 70 minutes or until tests done.

Mrs. W. J. Hodge, Jr.

Lemon Nut Cake

1 pound butter, softened
2 cups sugar
5 eggs
4 cups flour
1 teaspoon baking powder
2 ounces lemon extract
4 cups pecans, chopped
1 package white raisins

Cream together butter and sugar. Add eggs one at a time, beating well after each addition. Sift dry ingredients together. Measure ¾ cup of flour and add to nuts and raisins. Dredge well. Now alternately add remaining flour and extract to butter mixture. Fold in nuts and raisins. Pour into a greased and floured bundt pan or loaf pans. Bake at 275 to 300 degree oven for 1 hour or more, depending on size of pan. This cake freezes well.

Mrs. Ray Martin
Delhi, Louisiana

Fresh Coconut Cake

1 cup real butter
2 cups sugar
4 egg yolks
1½ teaspoons vanilla
2⅔ cups cake flour
1½ teaspoons baking powder
½ teaspoon salt
½ cup coconut milk
½ cup milk
4 egg whites

ICING:
2 egg whites
1½ cups sugar
5 Tablespoons cold water
Pinch of cream of tartar
1½ teaspoons white Karo
1 teaspoon vanilla
Freshly grated coconut

Cream butter and sugar until light and creamy. Beat in egg yolks one at a time. Add vanilla. Sift cake flour before measuring. Resift with baking powder and salt. Combine milk and coconut milk. Add the sifted ingredients to the butter mixture, in about 3 parts, alternately with the liquid mixture. Beat egg whites until stiff and fold in lightly by hand into the batter. Pour into 3 greased 9 inch layer pans. Bake for 30 minutes at 350 degrees. Remove layers from pans before completely cool.

ICING:
Combine all ingredients except vanilla and grated coconut in top of double boiler. Blend well. Then place over rapidly boiling water and beat constantly with electric or rotary beater for 6 minutes. Remove from fire and add vanilla. Spread between layers sparingly and sprinkle with freshly grated coconut. Secure layers with toothpicks. Ice whole cake and garnish with coconut.

Mrs. Tim Allen

Plum Cake

2 cups self-rising flour
2 cups sugar
1 teaspoon cinnamon
1 teaspoon nutmeg
2 jars plum with tapioca, baby
food
1 cup Wesson oil
3 eggs, beaten
2 cups pecans, chopped

TOPPING:
½ stick butter
1 cup powdered sugar
Juice of 1 lemon
Grated rind of 1 lemon

Mix together flour, sugar and spices. Add plums, oil and beaten eggs. Add nuts. Just mix this cake, do not beat. Bake at 350 degrees for about 1 hour in a greased and floured tube pan. An angel food pan works well.

TOPPING:
Melt butter. Mix together with rest of ingredients. Pour half of this on cake before taking out of pan. Remove cake from pan and pour remaining half over the top of cake.

Mildred Swift

Date Loaf Cake

1 pound pitted dates, chopped
2 teaspoons baking soda
2 cups boiling water
2 cups sugar
2 Tablespoons butter or Crisco
2 eggs, beaten
2½ cups all purpose flour
1 teaspoon cinnamon
½ teaspoon allspice
1 cup nuts, chopped
Whipped cream, optional

Chop dates with sharp knife or cut with scissors. Put into a large bowl. Sprinkle soda over dates and pour boiling water over mixture. Stir well and set aside. Mix sugar and butter together. Add beaten eggs. Alternately add sifted flour and date mixture, beating after each addition. Add spices and nuts. Bake in a 300 degree oven for 1 hour or until done. Use tube pan or loaf pans. May be served with a spoon of whipped cream on each slice. This is very good at Christmas.

Mrs. M. A. Bodron, Jr.

Banana Cake

2 cups sugar
1½ cups salad oil
3 eggs
4 bananas
3 cups flour
1 teaspoon cinnamon
1 teaspoon nutmeg
½ teaspoon salt
2 teaspoons baking soda
1 cup pecans, chopped

FROSTING:
1 stick butter, softened
1-8 ounce package cream cheese,
softened
1 box powdered sugar
1 teaspoon vanilla

Mix sugar and salad oil until well blended. Add eggs one at a time, beating between each addition. Break up bananas in chunks and add to batter. Sift flour, measure; add cinnamon, nutmeg, salt, soda and sift again. Add slowly to the batter and continue beating. Fold in pecans. Grease and flour an angel food or bundt pan. Bake for 1 hour at 350 degrees. Let cool for 30 minutes before removing from pan. Frost cake when cold. This cake may be frozen before frosting.

FROSTING:
Cream together butter and cream cheese. Add powdered sugar and vanilla and continue beating until of spreading consistency.

Mrs. Jerry Webster

Carrot Cake

2 cups flour
2 cups sugar
2 teaspoons baking powder
2 teaspoons baking soda
2/3 teaspoon cinnamon
1 teaspoon salt
4 eggs
1½ cups Wesson oil
3 cups carrots, grated
½ cup nuts, chopped

FROSTING:
1-8 ounce package cream cheese
½ stick butter
1 box powdered sugar

Mix together all dry ingredients. Beat eggs and add oil. Combine dry ingredients with egg mixture. Add carrots and nuts. Pour into 3 greased 9 inch layer pans. Bake at 300 degrees for 45 minutes or at 350 degrees for 25 to 30 minutes.

FROSTING:
Cream together cream cheese and butter. Add sugar and beat well. Frost lightly between layers then ice sides and top.

Mrs. Prent Castle
St. Joseph, Louisiana

Sweet Potato Surprise Cake

1½ cups cooking oil
2 cups sugar
4 eggs, separated
4 Tablespoons hot water
2½ cups sifted cake flour
3 teaspoons baking powder
¼ teaspoon salt
1 teaspoon ground cinnamon
1 teaspoon ground nutmeg
1½ cups finely grated
   raw sweet potatoes
1 cup pecans, chopped
1 teaspoon vanilla

FROSTING:
1-13 ounce can evaporated milk
1 cup sugar
1 stick butter
3 egg yolks
1 teaspoon vanilla
1½ cups flaked coconut

Combine oil and sugar, beating until smooth. Add egg yolks one at a time and beat. Add hot water. Sift together all dry ingredients and add to batter. Stir in potatoes, nuts and vanilla. Beat. Beat egg whites stiffly and fold into mixture. Bake in 3 greased 8 inch cake pans at 350 degrees for 25 to 30 minutes. Cool and frost.

FROSTING:
Combine milk, sugar, butter, egg yolks and vanilla in saucepan. Cook over medium heat for 12 minutes, stirring constantly until mixture thickens. Remove from heat and add coconut. Beat by hand until cool and of spreading consistency.

Mrs. Jerry Gregg

Pork Sausage Cake

1 cup raisins, chopped
1 cup water off raisins
½ pound pork sausage, uncooked
2 cups light brown sugar
1 teaspoon soda
1 teaspoon cinnamon
1 teaspoon baking powder
2½ cups flour
1 cup nuts, chopped finely

PENUCHE ICING:
½ cup butter
1 cup brown sugar, packed
¼ cup milk
1¾ to 2 cups sifted confectioners' sugar

Cover raisins with water and cook for 20 minutes. Mix all other ingredients, except water. Add water from raisins. Bake in two lightly greased and floured round 9 inch cake pans at 350 degrees for about 45 minutes. When cake is cool, ice with Penuche icing. Will freeze nicely. Serves 8 to 10.

ICING:
Melt butter in saucepan. Add brown sugar. Boil over low heat for 2 minutes, stirring constantly. Add milk and bring to a boil. Cool to lukewarm and gradually add confectioners' sugar. Place pan in ice water and stir until spreading consistency.

Mrs. Cora Feathers
Memphis, Tennessee

Sauerkraut Cake

⅔ cup butter
1½ cups sugar
3 eggs
1 teaspoon vanilla
2¼ cups flour
½ cup cocoa
1 teaspoon baking powder
1 teaspoon baking soda
¼ teaspoon salt
1 cup water
⅔ cup sauerkraut, drained

Cream sugar and butter; beat eggs and vanilla together and add to creamed mixture. Sift dry ingredients together and add alternately with water to creamed mixture. Rinse sauerkraut, drain and chop. Stir into batter. Pour into two 8 inch pans or one 9 by 13 inch pan, lightly greased and floured. Bake for 30 to 40 minutes at 350 degrees. Ice with desired icing and fill with Mocha whipped cream.

Mrs. Cora Feathers
Memphis, Tennessee

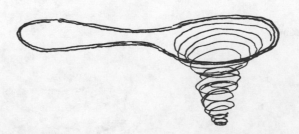

English Christmas Cake

1¾ cups coarsely chopped
   candied cherries
1¾ cups coarsely chopped
   candied pineapple
3 cups broken pecans
1 pound white raisins
6 Tablespoons brandy
1 cup butter
2¼ cups sugar
6 eggs
4 cups sifted flour
1½ teaspoons salt
½ teaspoon baking powder
1½ teaspoons cinnamon
1 teaspoon nutmeg

FROSTING:
2-8 ounce cans almond paste
2 egg whites
1¾ cups powdered sugar
⅛ teaspoon cream of tartar
Marzipan candy fruits

Line a 10 inch tube pan with aluminum foil. Mix the fruits, nuts and ¼ cup brandy together and let stand while measuring remaining ingredients. Stir once or twice. Cream the butter, add the sugar and beat until light and fluffy. Mix in the eggs, one at a time, beating well after each. Sift the flour with the remaining dry ingredients, then divide in half. Stir half the flour into the egg mixture along with the remaining 2 Tablespoons of brandy. Stir the other half of the flour into the fruits and nuts. When they are well coated, mix them into the batter. Pour the batter into the tube pan and bake for 3 hours and 45 minutes, or until done, in a slow oven, 275 degrees. Place a pan of water in the bottom of the oven to keep the cake moist. Cool cake for 5 minutes; remove from pan. When completely cool, wrap in a brandy soaked cheesecloth for several weeks; however, this cake cuts very well after only 2 days.

FROSTING:
Soften the almond paste with your hands. Sprinkle a board with confectioners' sugar and roll out the paste until you have a long strip. Measure the depth of your cake and cut this strip to fit. Brush the sides of the cake with 1 slightly beaten egg white and shape the strip of almond paste to the sides. When the sides are covered, brush the seams with egg white. Work the remaining paste into a ball and roll it to fit the top of the cake. Use the bottom of your tube pan as a pattern. Brush the top of the cake with egg white, fit the almond paste circle in place and brush the seams with egg white also. Beat the remaining 1 egg white with the cream of tartar until frothy. Gradually add the sugar, beating until very thick. Frost the cake smoothly and allow to dry over night. Garnish with marzipan fruits.

Mrs. Dan Sartor

Lemon Pecan Fruit Cake

4½ cups flour
1 pound candied cherries
1 pound mixed fruit
1 quart chopped pecans
1 pound butter
2¼ cups sugar
6 eggs
1-2 ounce bottle pure
   lemon extract

Mix flour with fruit and nuts. Cream butter and sugar. Add eggs one at a time. Blend in lemon extract. Stir creamed mixture into floured fruit. Bake in a large tube pan at 275 degrees over a pan of water for two hours or until done when tested with a straw.

Mrs. F. N. Steele

Agnes' Christmas Cake
*A very special white fruit cake for
the holiday season*

Favorite white cake batter using
juice from 2 large coconuts

FRUIT FOR BATTER:
1 cup dates, chopped
1 cup nuts, chopped
1 bottle Maraschino cherries,
  diced
1 teaspoon orange rind

FROSTING:
4 oranges, juiced and strained
4 cups sugar
1 teaspoon grated orange rind
2 teaspoons lemon juice
2 large coconuts, grated
Whipped cream, optional

Have all fruits and nuts prepared for the cake and
frosting before beginning this recipe.

Puncture coconuts and let drain. Use milk from coconuts in making white cake batter. Add the dates,
nuts, cherries and 1 teaspoon of orange rind to cake
batter. Pour into 3 greased and floured 8 or 9 inch
cake pans. While cakes are baking, prepare fruits for
frosting.

FROSTING:
Mix orange juice, lemon juice, orange rind and
sugar. Let boil for 5 minutes. Mix in grated coconut
and let boil 10 minutes longer, stirring constantly.
Ice between each layer and on top of cake while cake
layers are still warm. Sides of cake may be frosted
with unsweetened whipped cream. Store in refrigerator and serve next day.

Mrs. Edward Poore
Williamston, South Carolina

Japanese Fruit Cake

1 cup butter
2 cups sugar
4 eggs
1 teaspoon vanilla
3 cups cake flour
2 teaspoons baking powder
Dash of salt
1 cup milk

TO MAKE DARK LAYERS ADD:
1 teaspoon cinnamon
1 teaspoon allspice
1/2 teaspoon ground cloves
1 cup raisins, chopped
1 cup nuts, chopped

FILLING:
Juice of 2 lemons
Grated rind from 2 lemons
1 medium coconut, grated
2 cups sugar
1 cup boiling water
3 Tablespoons cornstarch
  dissolved in a little water

Cream butter and sugar. Add eggs one at a time,
beating between additions. Add vanilla. Sift baking
powder and salt into flour. Add flour and milk
alternately. This batter can make two dark and two
light layers, or two dark and one light layer. Divide
batter accordingly and add ingredients for the dark
layers. Paper line and grease 8 inch square pans.
Bake 20 to 25 minutes at 350 degrees.

FILLING:
Put all ingredients except cornstarch into pan and
bring to boil. Add starch mixture and cook until
thickened. Cool and spread. Filling may be used
between layers and over cake or just between layers
and cake may be iced with 7-Minute frosting.

Mrs. W. O. Colvin
and
Mrs. C. D. Case
Atlanta, Georgia

Walnut Torte
A very special dessert for special occasions

12 eggs, separated
2 cups ground walnuts
3 Tablespoons cocoa
2 cups sugar
1 teaspoon vanilla

ICING:
4 Tablespoons drip coffee
1½ cups water
1 cup sugar
½ pound butter, softened
3 egg yolks
2 Tablespoons cocoa
Ground walnuts, optional

Separate eggs and set aside to reach room temperature. Grind nuts finely in blender. Mix nuts with cocoa and set aside. Prepare three 9 inch pans: grease, line with wax paper, then grease and lightly flour over paper. Beat egg yolks until light and lemon colored. Add sugar very slowly, 2 Tablespoons at a time, beating constantly. Add vanilla and beat well. Beat egg whites until stiff but not dry. Place beaten whites on top of batter. Over this put walnut and cocoa mixture. Carefully cut and fold all together. Pour batter into pans and bake at 300 degrees for 30 minutes without opening door. When done, invert pans on cake rack and cool before removing from pans. The cakes will settle after removing from the oven. If well wrapped, these cakes can be kept in the refrigerator for at least two weeks.

ICING:
Make strong drip coffee with the 4 Tablespoons of coffee and 1½ cups of water. In a small saucepan, place sugar and 1 cup of the coffee. Simmer slowly until this is the consistency of honey, reaching a temperature of about 225 degrees. In another bowl, put softened butter and add egg yolks, one at a time, beating well after each addition. Add cocoa, alternating with cooled coffee syrup. This should be of spreading consistency. If too soft, put in the refrigerator for 10 minutes. Spread thinly between layers, on top and on sides of torte. Sprinkle with ground nuts.

The coffee syrup takes quite a while to simmer and reach proper consistency. Make ahead and let simmer while making and baking cake. Use a candy thermometer for perfect results.

Mrs. Dick Young

Quick Banana Cake

1 box white cake mix
2 whole eggs
½ cup water
1 cup mashed bananas

ICING:
½ cup butter, softened
1 Tablespoon shortening
4 cups confectioners' sugar,
   1 box
¼ cup evaporated milk
1 cup ground nuts

Combine cake mix with eggs, water and bananas. Beat for 5 minutes at medium speed. Bake in two 9 inch prepared pans at 350 degrees for 25 to 30 minutes or until done.

ICING:
Put all icing ingredients in mixer and beat until thoroughly mixed and of spreading consistency.

Mrs. Dan Sartor

Coffee Royal Cake

1 small box yellow cake mix
1 small box chocolate cake mix

FILLING AND TOPPING:
1½ cups heavy cream
3 Tablespoons instant coffee
⅓ cup sugar
1-11 ounce jar raspberry
   preserves
1 cup heavy cream
Shaved chocolate

Prepare each cake mix according to package directions. Bake in 9 inch cake pans. Cool and split each layer crosswise, forming two chocolate and two yellow layers.

FILLING AND TOPPING:
Combine heavy cream with instant coffee and sugar. Chill thoroughly, including bowl. Whip cream until stiff. Place one yellow layer on serving plate. Spread with half of raspberry preserves, then with ⅓ of coffee filling. Place one chocolate layer on top; spread with ⅓ coffee filling. Follow with second yellow layer cake, remaining raspberry preserves and coffee filling. Now top with second chocolate layer cake. Garnish with whipped cream and shaved chocolate. Keep refrigerated until ready to serve.

Mrs. Ed Brown

Cherry Crunch

1 can dark sweet cherries, pitted
1 box Ann Page butter pecan
   cake mix
1/2 stick butter, melted

Grease an oblong pyrex dish. Pour in cherries, undrained. Sprinkle the cake mix over cherries. Spoon melted butter over cake mix. Bake in a 350 degree oven for 30 to 40 minutes or until slightly brown. Serve warm with ice cream or sweetened whipped cream.

Canned sliced apples may be used instead of cherries.

Mrs. E. N. Jackson

Good Luck White Cake

1 box Duncan Hines white
   cake mix
1/2 cup sugar
3/4 cup buttery Wesson oil
1/4 teaspoon almond flavoring
4 eggs
1-8 ounce carton sour cream
1 teaspoon vanilla

Put cake mix into mixing bowl. Add remaining ingredients in order given and beat well on high speed of mixer. Grease and flour two 9 inch pans. Divide batter in half and pour into pans. Bake at 350 to 375 degrees for 20 to 25 minutes. Do not overcook. When done, cool for 5 minutes in the pan. Turn out and ice with seven minute icing and fresh coconut.

Mrs. Floyd James
Ruston, Louisiana

Lemon Bars

1 package lemon cake mix
1/2 cup butter, melted
1 egg, slightly beaten
1 package lemon frosting mix
1-8 ounce package cream
   cheese, softened
2 eggs

Combine cake mix, butter and 1 egg; mix with forks until moist. Put into a 9 x 13 inch pan. Grease bottom of pan only. Blend frosting mix into cream cheese. Reserve 1/2 cup of cheese and frosting mix. Add 2 eggs to remaining frosting mix and beat 3 to 5 minutes. Spread over cake. Bake at 350 degrees for 30 to 40 minutes. Cool. Spread top with reserved frosting mix.

Mrs. Jim Geisler

Sherry Loaf Cake
Quick Dessert

1 package yellow cake mix
1 package instant vanilla
   pudding
4 eggs
3/4 cup cooking oil
3/4 cup sherry
1 teaspoon nutmeg, optional

Mix all ingredients. Beat 5 minutes. Bake in a greased tube pan at 350 degrees for 45 minutes or until tester comes out clean.

Mrs. Alton Irwin

Viennese Torte

1-6 ounce package semi-sweet
  chocolate pieces
½ cup butter
¼ cup boiling water
4 slightly beaten egg yolks
2 Tablespoons confectioners'
  sugar
1 teaspoon vanilla or 1 jigger
  brandy
1-12 ounce store bought
  pound cake

In heavy saucepan, heat chocolate, butter and water over medium heat, stirring until blended. Cool slightly. Add egg yolks, sugar and flavoring. Stir until smooth. Chill until mixture is of spreading consistency, about 45 minutes. Slice cake horizontally in 6 layers. Cake will slice easily if frozen first. Spread chocolate filling between layers, then frost top and sides. Chill at least 45 minutes before serving. Cut in ¼ inch slices. This cake freezes beautifully.

Mrs. Sol Courtman

Quick Rum Cake

1 cup pecans, chopped
1 package yellow cake mix
1 package French vanilla
  instant pudding
½ cup water
½ cup Wesson oil
½ cup rum
4 eggs

SAUCE:
1 stick butter
1 cup sugar
¼ cup water
2 ounces rum

Sprinkle chopped pecans on bottom of greased tube or bundt pan. Mix together cake mix, pudding, water, Wesson oil and rum. Beat in eggs one at a time. Pour batter into pan and bake 1 hour at 325 degrees. Let cool.

SAUCE:
Boil butter, sugar, water and rum together in saucepan. Pour over cake while in pan. This will soak into cake. Let cake completely cool before removing from pan. This freezes beautifully.

Mrs. Leonard Bunch
Mrs. Ken Abington
Lake Village, Arkansas

Spring Glow Angel Cake

1 box angel food cake mix
1-4 ounce package vanilla
  pudding
2 cups milk
1 No. 2 can peach pie filling
1 cup heavy cream, whipped

Prepare cake mix according to directions. Bake in a 10 inch tube pan. Cool and remove from pan. Slice entire top from cake, about one inch down. Hollow center out, leaving an inch base and sides. Prepare pudding as directed, using 2 cups milk. When pudding has cooled, add half of pie filling and blend well. Spoon mixture into the cavity of the cake. Replace the top. Fold remaining pie filling into whipped cream and frost the cake. Chill and serve.

Mrs. Horace Smith

Strawberry Cake

1 box white cake mix
1 small box strawberry Jello
¾ cup Wesson oil
¾ cup milk
4 eggs, separated
1 cup shredded coconut
1 cup pecans, chopped
2 cups strawberries, halved

FROSTING:
½ stick margarine, softened
1 box powdered sugar
½ strawberry mixture

Combine cake mix and Jello. Mix together by hand. Add oil, milk and egg yolks; beat just enough to mix. In a separate bowl mix coconut, nuts and strawberries. Put half of this mixture in batter; reserving the remaining half for frosting. Beat egg whites until stiff but not dry. Fold into batter. Pour into three 8 or 9 inch greased and floured cake pans. Bake 20 to 25 minutes at 350 degrees.

FROSTING:
Cream margarine. Stir in powdered sugar. Add remaining half of strawberry mixture and beat well. Ice cooled cake.

Mrs. Joe Wheeler

FROSTING

Angel Food Cake Topping

1 pint whipping cream,
  whipped
6 Heath bars, crushed in
  blender
½ cup Hershey syrup

Add crushed Heath bars to whipping cream. Add syrup. Cut cake in three layers. Fill and ice cake.

Mrs. Dan Sartor

Raw Apple Icing for Spice Cake

1 raw apple, sliced
1 cup sugar
1 egg white
Juice of ½ lemon

Put all of the ingredients in a bowl and beat, starting on low speed and increasing speed until mixture is thick enough to spread.

Mrs. R. M. Kobs
Mt. View, Oklahoma

Chocolate Fudge Icing

1 stick butter
2 cups sugar
1-5⅓ ounce can Pet milk
1-6 ounce package chocolate
  chips
12 marshmallows
1 teaspoon vanilla

Combine butter, sugar and Pet milk in saucepan and bring to a boil. Cook for 5 minutes. Remove from stove and add remaining ingredients. Beat until spreading consistency.

Mrs. Dan Sartor

Creamy Chocolate Glaze

6 ounces unsweetened chocolate
1½ cups heavy cream
2 cups sugar
½ cup water
2 Tablespoons corn syrup
2 eggs slightly beaten
2 Tablespoons vanilla

Combine chocolate, cream, sugar, water and corn syrup. Stir over low heat until chocolate is melted and sugar is dissolved. Raise heat a little and cook without stirring for about 5 minutes, or until mixture is thick enough so that a bit, dropped into a glass of cold water, forms a soft ball. Stir 2 or 3 Tablespoons hot chocolate into beaten eggs. Pour egg mixture back into remaining chocolate, stirring briskly. Replace over low heat and cook a few more minutes or until chocolate is a little thicker. Stir constantly. Remove from heat. Add vanilla. Cool slightly before pouring over cake. This frosting stays shiny and cuts easily even after many days. It will make enough chocolate glaze for the top and sides of a 9 inch, 2 layer cake. This is also a delicious cake filling. Half the recipe and cool completely before filling the cake.

Paula Peck via Mrs. Sol Courtman

Seven Minute White Icing

2 unbeaten egg whites
1½ cups sugar
5 Tablespoons cold water
¼ teaspoon cream of tartar
1½ teaspoons light corn syrup
1 teaspoon vanilla

Combine all ingredients except vanilla in top of a double boiler. Cook over rapidly boiling water for 7 minutes, beating constantly. Remove from heat and add vanilla. Continue beating until correct consistency to spread. This makes enough icing for a 2 layer cake.

Mrs. Jack Taylor
Mrs. Ed W. Stinson, Jr.

Seven Minute Icing

1½ cups sugar
2 egg whites
5 Tablespoons water
Pinch of cream of tartar
6 large marshmallows or 60
  small ones

Put all ingredients into top of a double boiler over simmering water. Cook, beating constantly with an electric mixer at high speed for about 7 minutes or until icing becomes stiff and glossy. Remove from heat and add vanilla. This holds up very well, even in damp weather.

Mrs. J. Y. Abraugh
Rayville, Louisiana

Tennessee Icing
If you don't have a dime, a pinch will do

4 egg whites
2½ cups granulated sugar
1 cup water
Cream of tartar, enough
  to cover a dime

Beat egg whites until stiff, gradually adding ½ cup sugar. Combine remaining 2 cups of sugar with water, cooking mixture until it spins and makes a thread when lifted by a spoon. Set beater on slow and pour hot syrup in a steady stream into egg whites. Beat just enough to blend. Add cream of tartar. Put mixture into top of double boiler and cover. Steam mixture over simmering water from 14 to 17 minutes. If undecided when icing is done, lift some of the icing with a spoon and dump on top of cake; icing will keep its shape if done. This icing will amply fill and cover a 2 layer cake. Never add fruit or nuts to icing; however, flavoring may be added but is not necessary.

Mrs. C. D. Oakley, Sr.

Broiled Coconut Icing

¾ cup coconut
¾ cup light brown sugar
½ teaspoon salt
⅓ cup butter
2 Tablespoons milk

Before removing cake from pan, combine frosting ingredients and cook, stirring constantly, until sugar melts. Spread on top of warm cake. Return to 375 degree oven for 10 to 12 minutes until topping is lightly browned. Makes frosting for a 9 inch square cake.

Mrs. Prentice Norred

French Apple Pie

Pastry for a 9 inch pie shell
1/3 cup sugar
2 Tablespoons flour
1 cup milk
3 egg yolks
1 Tablespoon butter
1 teaspoon vanilla
2 pounds tart apples
1 Tablespoon lemon juice
2 Tablespoons butter
2 Tablespoons sugar
1/4 teaspoon nutmeg
3/4 cup apricot preserves
1 egg yolk

Combine sugar and flour in a small saucepan. Slowly add milk and bring to a boil, stirring constantly. Reduce heat and simmer until thickened, about 1 minute. Beat the 3 egg yolks in a small bowl and add a little of the hot mixture. Stir back into saucepan, beating well. Cook until slightly thickened. Stir in 1 Tablespoon butter and vanilla. Pour into bowl and set aside to cool. Pare apples and slice. Sprinkle with lemon juice. In a skillet melt 2 Tablespoons butter with sugar and nutmeg. Add apple slices and sauté about 5 minutes until partially cooked. In another saucepan, heat preserves just until melted. Turn the custard filling into the pie shell, arrange apples on top and spread with preserves. Make a lattice design on top and brush strips with egg yolk mixed with a little water. Bake for 35 to 40 minutes at 425 degrees on the bottom shelf of the oven.

Mrs. James R. Wolff

385

Banana Pie Supreme
Superior

6 Tablespoons cake flour
⅔ cup sugar
¼ teaspoon salt
1¾ cups milk
2 egg yolks, slightly beaten
1¼ teaspoons vanilla
½ cup cream, whipped
3 bananas
½ lemon
1 baked 9 inch pie shell
1 Tablespoon grated orange rind
Whipped cream

Mix together flour, sugar, and salt in the top of double boiler. Add milk and cook over hot water, stirring constantly, until mixture thickens. Cook 15 minutes longer, stirring occasionally. Pour small amount of mixture over egg yolks, beating vigorously; return to double boiler, and cook 2 minutes longer stirring constantly. Remove from fire. Cool. Add vanilla. Chill. Fold in whipped cream. Layer cream filling and sliced bananas, sprinkled with lemon juice, in the pie shell. Garnish with whipped cream and grated orange rind.

Mrs. Harry Frazer, Jr.

Cherry Ice Box Pie
Makes 2 at one time

1 No. 2 or 3 can sour Bing
  cherries
1 can Eagle Brand milk
¼ cup lemon juice
½ teaspoon almond extract
1 cup pecans, chopped
1 pint whipping cream
4 Tablespoons sugar
2-8 inch graham cracker crusts

Thoroughly drain cherries. Add lemon juice and almond extract to condensed milk. Stir. Add cherries and nuts to milk mixture. Whip cream separately adding sugar slowly; then fold whipped cream into milk mixture. Pour mixture into 2 pie crusts. Chill over night.

Mrs. Fred Huenefeld, Jr.

Coconut Cream Chiffon Pie

1 Tablespoon gelatin
¼ cup cold water
3 eggs, separated
½ cup sugar
¼ teaspoon salt
1 teaspoon vanilla
1 cup milk, scalded
2 cups cream, whipped
1-10 inch baked pie crust
¾ cup coconut

Sprinkle gelatin in cold water. Combine egg yolks, sugar, salt, and vanilla. Add to hot milk. Cook in a double boiler until mixture coats spoon. Add gelatin to hot mixture; stir until dissolved. Chill until syrupy. Fold in stiffly beaten egg whites and 1 cup whipped cream. Pour into a crust-lined pan and chill. Top pie with remainder of whipped cream and sprinkle with coconut.

Mrs. Buck Stewart

Editor's note: Additional coconut may be added to the cream filling.

Coconut Custard Ice Box Pie

1 Tablespoon butter
8 Tablespoons flour
2/3 cup sugar
1/4 teaspoon salt
2 egg yolks
2 cups milk
1 Tablespoon vanilla
2 egg whites, well beaten
3/4 cup shredded coconut
1 pint cream, whipped
Coconut for garnish
1-9 inch baked pie shell

Melt butter; add flour, sugar, salt, well beaten egg yolks and milk. Cook over hot water until thick, stirring constantly. Add vanilla and pour hot custard over well beaten egg whites. Add shredded coconut and put in a baked pie shell. Top with a pint of whipped cream and sprinkle top with coconut. Place in the refrigerator several hours or overnight before serving.

Mrs. Charles Donnelly
Alexandria, Louisiana

French Coconut Pie
Just Yummy

Unbaked 9 inch pie shell
3 eggs
1 1/2 cups sugar
1 teaspoon vanilla
1/2 cup melted butter
1 cup coconut

Brush a little egg white on the unbaked pie shell and bake at 400 degrees about 1 minute. This prevents a soggy crust. Beat eggs slightly; add other ingredients. Pour into pie shell and bake at 400 degrees 10 minutes; 375 degrees 15 minutes; at 350 degrees 15 to 20 minutes.

Lemon Cheese Pie

1 baked 9 inch pie shell
1-8 ounce package Philadelphia
  cream cheese
2 eggs, unbeaten
1/2 cup sugar
2 to 4 Tablespoons lemon juice
1/2 pint whipping cream
2 Tablespoons confectioners'
  sugar
1 teaspoon vanilla

Soften cheese and whip until fluffy. Add eggs, one at a time, beating after each. Blend in sugar and juice. Pour in the baked shell. Bake at 350 degrees for 15 to 20 minutes until slightly firm. Chill and top with whipping cream, whipped with sugar and vanilla. *Note:* 2 Tablespoons lemon juice gives a light lemon flavor, 4 Tablespoons is tart.

Mrs. Bob Kennedy

Lemon Chiffon Pie

4 eggs, separated
1/2 teaspoon salt
Juice of 3 lemons
2 teaspoons grated lemon peel
1/2 cup sugar
1 Tablespoon gelatin
1/4 cup cold water
1/2 cup sugar
1 cup heavy cream, whipped
1-9 inch graham cracker crust

Beat egg yolks slightly, add 1/2 cup sugar, salt, juice and peel. Cook over hot water until thick, about 5 minutes. Remove from heat. Soak gelatin in cold water and add to the egg yolk mixture. Stir to dissolve and cool. Beat egg whites until stiff adding 1/2 cup sugar. Fold into cooked mixture. Fold 1/2 cup whipped cream into filling. Pile lightly into crust. Swirl remaining whipped cream on top of pie around edges. May be further garnished with raspberries or other fruit.

Mrs. James Altick

Old Fashioned Lemon Meringue Pie

1 1/2 cups water
1 1/2 cups sugar
4 Tablespoons butter
1/2 teaspoon salt
1/3 cup cornstarch
4 eggs, separated
1/4 cup lemon juice
2 Tablespoons lemon rind
9 inch baked pie shell

MERINGUE:
2/3 cup egg whites
1/4 teaspoon salt
1/4 teaspoon cream of tartar
2/3 cup sugar

Combine sugar, salt, 1 cup of water and butter. Heat until sugar is dissolved. Blend cornstarch with 1/2 cup of cold water and add slowly to the hot mixture. Cook on low heat until clear, about 8 minutes. Beat egg yolks and add slowly, cook 3 minutes, stirring continually. Remove from heat and add lemon juice and rind. Cool. Pour in a baked pie shell. Set aside. *Meringue:* Beat egg whites until foamy, add salt and cream of tartar. Continue beating and add sugar gradually until stiff peaks form. Pile on the lemon filling, sealing edges. Brown in a 375 degree oven for 10 to 15 minutes.

Mrs. Jim Geisler

Orange Chiffon Pie

1-9 inch baked pastry shell
  or meringue shell
1 envelope Knox gelatin
1 cup sugar
¾ cup orange juice
2 teaspoons lemon juice
4 eggs, separated
½ teaspoon cream of tartar
1 teaspoon grated lemon rind
1 can orange sections
Whipped cream

Combine gelatin, ½ cup sugar, juices and slightly beaten yolks. Cook in a double boiler until it coats a spoon. Cool. Chill until creamy. Beat egg whites and cream of tartar until fluffy, gradually add remaining ½ cup of sugar. Fold in gelatin mixture and rind. Pour into crust. Garnish with orange sections and whipped cream. May be made the day before using. Store in the refrigerator.

Pineapple Chiffon Pie

1-9 inch baked pie shell
1½ Tablespoons unflavored
  gelatin
½ cup cold water
1 No. 1 can crushed pineapple,
  undrained
¾ cup sugar
1 Tablespoon lemon juice
½ teaspoon salt
3 egg yolks
3 egg whites
¾ cup heavy cream, whipped

Sprinkle the gelatin over the cold water. Let set for five minutes. Heat the pineapple, ½ cup sugar, lemon juice and salt. Add the gelatin and stir until it is dissolved. Stir the hot mixture into slightly beaten egg yolks, mixing well. Chill. Beat the egg whites until soft peaks form. Gradually add the remaining ¼ cup sugar and beat until stiff peaks form. Whip the cream and fold into the egg whites. Stir the cooled pineapple mixture. Gently fold the cream and egg white mixture into the pineapple. Pile into the cooled pie shell. Chill until set. Top with additional whipped cream, if desired.

Mrs. T. M. Sayre
Rayville, Louisiana

Crunchy Peach Cobbler

Pastry for double crust pie
5 cups sliced peaches
1 cup sugar
¼ cup water
3 Tablespoons flour
¼ cup sugar
⅛ teaspoon salt
½ teaspoon almond flavoring
Butter

Roll half of the pastry very thin and line a 2 inch deep baking dish. Roll and cut the other half into strips. Bake half the strips in a 375 degree oven until brown. Put fruit, 1 cup sugar and water in a saucepan and cook until fruit is soft. Mix flour, sugar and salt; add to fruit. Cook stirring until slightly thick. Stir in flavoring and cooked pastry strips. Spoon in the crust-lined dish, dot with butter, and cover with uncooked strips. Bake at 400 degrees until brown. 6 to 8 servings.

Mrs. Joe Montgomery

Peach Glaze Pie

1 quart sliced fresh peaches,
  drained
¾ cup water
1 cup sugar
3 Tablespoons cornstarch
1 Tablespoon lemon juice
1 Tablespoon butter
⅛ teaspoon salt
Baked 9 inch pie shell
Whipped cream

Mash 1 cup of the peaches. Add water and cook four minutes. Mix sugar and cornstarch; add to the fruit mixture. Cook until thick and clear. Add lemon juice, butter and salt. Let cool. Arrange remaining fruit in the cooled pie shell. Pour cooled glaze over fruit. Chill. Top with whipped cream and a few peach slices when ready to serve.

Mrs. T. A. Calloway
Bosco, Louisiana

Editor's note: Vanilla is also a good flavoring for a peach pie.

Elegant Strawberry Pie

CRUST:
1 cup flour
¼ cup brown sugar
½ cup chopped nuts,
  pecans or walnuts
½ cup soft butter

FILLING:
2 egg whites
1½ cups fresh strawberries,
  crushed
1 cup sugar
2 Tablespoons lemon juice
1 cup heavy cream, whipped

Crust: Cream together all ingredients. Put into the bottoms of two 9 inch pie pans. Cook in a 350 degree oven 20 minutes. Crumbs should be slightly brown. Reserve ⅓ cup of the crumbs for sprinkling on top of the pies. *Filling*: Place all ingredients except cream in a large bowl; beat until stiff peaks form. This takes about 30 minutes. Fold in whipped cream. Divide between pans and sprinkle reserve crumbs on top. Freeze. To serve, cut directly from freezer. 2 cups of fresh peaches are a delicious substitute.

Mrs. Amos Warner
Lawrenceville, N.J.

Louisiana Fresh Strawberry Pie

1 quart fresh strawberries
¾ cup water
3 Tablespoons cornstarch
1 cup sugar
1 teaspoon lemon juice
1 cup cream, whipped
1-9 inch pastry shell

Line a baked pastry shell with fresh strawberries. Reserve about 1 cup of the berries for glaze. Simmer 1 cup of berries and ¾ cup water for 3 to 4 minutes. Combine cornstarch and sugar. Add this to berries along with lemon juice. Cook this mixture until thickened and clear. Pour over the berries in shell and chill in the refrigerator. Top with whipped cream.

Mrs. Bishop Johnston III

Anne's Strawberry Pie

Juice of two lemons
1 can condensed milk
2 egg yolks
1 teaspoon vanilla
2 egg whites, beaten stiff
1 pint fresh strawberries, sliced
1 baked 10 inch pie shell
½ pint cream, whipped

Stir condensed milk into lemon juice. Add egg yolks and vanilla. Fold in stiffly beaten egg whites and berries. Pour into the baked shell and bake for 10 to 15 minutes in 275 degree oven. Chill. Top with whipped cream.

Mrs. Bill Wilson

Strawberry 7-Up Pie

1 pint fresh strawberries, frozen berries should be thawed and drained
1 cup sugar
3 Tablespoons cornstarch
1 small bottle 7-Up
Red food coloring
1 carton heavy cream
1-9 inch baked pie shell

Wash and slice the fresh berries. Cook sugar, cornstarch 7-Up and coloring until thick. *Cool*. Add sliced strawberries and pour into baked pie shell. Top with whipped cream. Chill.

Mrs. Jim Dennis

Strawberry Glazed Pie
A Delightful Surprise

1 baked 9 inch pastry shell
1-8 ounce package cream cheese, softened
2 or 3 Tablespoons milk or sour cream
½ cup sugar
1 Tablespoon lemon juice
½ teaspoon lemon rind, grated
2 cartons fresh strawberries, 4 cups, washed and hulled
1 cup sugar
3 Tablespoons cornstarch
Whipped cream

Whip softened cream cheese with milk or sour cream, sugar, lemon juice and rind until very light and fluffy. Spread in the bottom of the pastry shell. Slice about one cup of strawberries over the cream cheese in the shell. Place remaining berries in the blender and whirl. Remove, mix with 1 cup of sugar and set aside 30 minutes. Blend in cornstarch and cook until thick and clear. Mash through colander to remove any lumps. Pour strawberry mixture over sliced strawberries. Chill. Garnish with whipped cream.

Mrs. Wesley Shafto, Jr.

Fruit Cobbler

1 stick butter
1 cup sugar
1 cup flour
1 teaspoon baking powder
1 cup milk
1 cup drained fruit,
   fresh or canned

Melt butter in a 1 quart pyrex dish. Add sugar, flour and baking powder; mix well. Slowly stir in milk and add fruit, mixing gently. Bake in a 350 degree oven for 1 hour. Top with ice cream or whipped cream. Serves 6.

Mrs. Lestar Martin

Fruit Pie

2-8 inch graham cracker
   pie shells
1 can condensed milk
½ cup lemon juice
1 No. 3 can sliced peaches
1-11 ounce can mandarin
   orange slices
1-8½ ounce can crushed
   pineapple
1-9 ounce can Cool Whip
1 cup chopped pecans,
   optional
1 cup coconut, optional

Drain fruits well, this is important. In a large bowl put condensed milk; add lemon juice and stir until well mixed. Add fruits to the milk mixture. Mix. Fold in Cool Whip. Add pecans and coconut, if using these, or sprinkle on top of the pies after pouring it in the crusts.

Mildred Swift

Mincemeat Pie
A Thanksgiving Treat

1⅔ cups mincemeat
¾ cup chopped apples
¾ cup raisins
1 cup whole cherry preserves
4 Tablespoons lemon juice
⅔ cup sugar
½ stick butter, cut up
Whipped cream
Sherry

Combine all ingredients, pour into the unbaked pie shells, top with crust; bake at 400 degrees for 40 to 50 minutes. Serve with whipped cream flavored with sherry. Makes two 8 inch pies or 1 deep 10 inch pie.

Mrs. Jack Taylor

The Best Pecan Pie

1 stick butter
1 cup light Karo
1 cup sugar
3 large eggs, beaten
½ teaspoon lemon juice
1 teaspoon vanilla
1 dash of salt
1 cup chopped pecans
8 or 9 inch unbaked pie shell

Brown butter in saucepan until it is golden brown, *do not burn*; let cool. In separate bowl add ingredients in order listed; stir. Blend in browned butter well. Pour in unbaked pie shell and bake at 425 degrees for 10 minutes, then lower to 325 degrees for 40 minutes.

Mrs. Russell Bulloch

Rich Pumpkin Pie

3 eggs, slightly beaten
1 cup evaporated milk
1 cup sugar
1 cup pumpkin
1/8 teaspoon salt
1 stick butter, melted
1/2 teaspoon cinnamon
1/2 teaspoon nutmeg
1/2 teaspoon allspice
1/2 pint heavy cream
English walnuts

Cream eggs, milk and sugar. Add remaining ingredients, and mix in well. Pour into an unbaked 8 inch pie shell and bake at 400 degrees for 40 minutes or until a silver knife inserted in the center comes out clean. Cool. Have edge of crust crimped high, as this is a very generous filling. Whip cream and spread over the cooled pie. Shave English walnuts over top. This is a delicious pie. It does not have too much pumpkin, more like a spicy custard pie.

Mrs. Henry Guerriero

Gourmet Pumpkin Pie

Pastry dough for 1-9
  inch pie shell
1/4 cup chopped pecans
1-30 ounce can pumpkin or
  3 2/3 cups fresh cooked
  pumpkin
1 egg
1 can sweetened condensed
  milk

STREUSEL TOPPING:
1/2 cup brown sugar, packed
1/4 cup flour
1/4 cup chopped pecans
1/4 cup firm butter
1/2 teaspoon cinnamon

Heat oven to 375 degrees. When making pie shell, measure chopped pecans in with flour and salt in bowl. Blend egg, pumpkin and condensed milk and pour mixture into pie shell. *Streusel Topping*: Mix all ingredients with a fork until crumbly. Sprinkle streusel on pie and bake 50 to 55 minutes or until knife inserted in center comes out clean. Cool. Chill. This is good, especially for people who don't like pumpkin pie.

Sweet Potato Pie
Good and Lemony

1½ cups mashed sweet
  potatoes
1 stick butter, melted
1½ cups sugar
3 Tablespoons flour
2 eggs
⅔ cup evaporated milk
1 teaspoon lemon extract
1 teaspoon vanilla

Combine all ingredients and pour into a 9 inch unbaked pie shell. Bake at 375 degrees. Test with silver knife after 45 minutes.

Mrs. Paul Dean

Louisiana Yam Pie
Old Fashioned and Spicy

1½ cups cooked sweet
  potatoes
½ cup sugar
1 teaspoon cinnamon
1 teaspoon allspice
½ teaspoon salt
3 eggs
1 cup milk
2 Tablespoons butter
9 inch unbaked pastry shell

Mash sweet potatoes until free of lumps. Add sugar, cinnamon, allspice and salt. Beat eggs, add to mixture and cream well. Blend milk and butter; mix well. Pour into pastry shell. Bake 40 to 45 minutes at 350 degrees.

Mrs. S. O. Henry, Jr.
Columbia, Louisiana

Amber Pie

¾ cup mayhaw jelly or
  any other tart jelly
½ cup sugar
3 Tablespoons flour
Pinch of salt
1¼ cups buttermilk
4 eggs, separated
3 Tablespoons butter
¼ teaspoon cream of tartar
¼ teaspoon salt
½ cup sugar
1-9 inch baked pie shell

Combine jelly, sugar, flour, salt, buttermilk and egg yolks in the top of a double boiler. Cook until thick. Add butter. Put in a browned pie shell. Beat the egg whites until foamy, add salt and cream of tartar. Continue beating and add sugar gradually until stiff peaks form. Pile on the top of the pie filling, sealing edges. Brown in a 375 degree oven for 10 to 15 minutes or until golden.

Mrs. Ed Seymour, Jr.

Raleigh House Buttermilk Pie

1 stick butter
2 cups sugar
3 eggs
2 rounded Tablespoons flour
1 cup buttermilk
Dash of nutmeg
1 teaspoon vanilla
Unbaked 9 inch pie shell

Have butter at room temperature and cream with sugar. Add the eggs and flour, mixing well. Stir in buttermilk, nutmeg and vanilla. Pour into the pie shell and bake at 350 degrees for 45 minutes. These pies freeze well.

Raleigh House
Kerrville, Texas

Chess Pie

5 egg yolks
1¾ cups sugar
1 Tablespoon meal, heaping
1 Tablespoon flour, heaping
½ cup butter, melted
1 cup milk
2 teaspoons vanilla
Unbaked pie shell

Beat egg yolks with 1 cup of sugar until light. In another bowl mix remaining ¾ cup of sugar with flour and meal. Add melted butter; mix well, add milk. Combine two mixtures and flavor with vanilla. Pour into the unbaked pastry and bake in moderate oven, 350 degrees, until the filling is set. Shake pie gently; center should be firm.

Mrs. L. N. Pipes
Rayville, Louisiana

Caramel Pie

STEP I:
1 cup sugar
½ cup boiling water

STEP II:
2 Tablespoons butter
5 Tablespoons flour
¼ teaspoon salt
½ cup milk
3 egg yolks, slightly beaten
1-9 inch baked pie shell

STEP III:
3 egg whites
Pinch of cream of tartar
½ cup sugar

Step I:
In heavy iron skillet stir sugar until it melts and turns golden brown. *Turn Heat Off.* Add boiling water and stir until dissolved. You may have to turn heat on low briefly for this. Set the caramel syrup aside.

Step II:
In saucepan melt the butter. *Turn Off Heat.* Stir flour and salt into butter mixing thoroughly. Add ¼ cup milk and stir. Turn heat to *Low* and add remaining milk and caramel syrup, *Stirring Constantly.* Cook until thick. Add about one half of this mixture slowly to slightly beaten yolks. Add yolks to remaining caramel mixture. Cook one minute and pour into the baked pie shell. Top with meringue.

Step III:
Beat egg whites with cream of tartar until foamy. Add sugar, very slowly, beating until egg whites are stiff. Put over warm filling and bake at 400 degrees until lightly browned.

Mrs. C. A. Petrus

Chocolate Pie

3 eggs
1 cup sugar
1/3 cup cocoa
1/3 cup flour
4 Tablespoons butter
2 cups milk
2 teaspoons vanilla
1-9 inch baked pie crust
Whipped cream

Place all ingredients in an enameled or stainless steel 2 quart pot. Beat with a wire whisk. Cook over low heat, stirring occasionally, scraping sides and bottom to avoid sticking. Cook until thickened, about 30 minutes. Pour into the baked pie shell and refrigerate for several hours or overnight before cutting. Top with whipped cream that has been sweetened to taste.

Mrs. Ben Marshall

German Sweet Chocolate Pie
Coffee and chocolate in a nutty meringue crust—irresistible.

CRUST:
4 egg whites, room temperature
1/4 teaspoon cream of tartar
1/8 teaspoon salt
1 cup sugar
1/2 teaspoon vanilla
1/2 cup finely chopped walnuts

FILLING:
2-8 ounce packages German's sweet chocolate
6 Tablespoons water
2 teaspoons vanilla
1 teaspoon instant coffee
2 cups heavy cream, whipped

Preheat oven to 275 degrees. Combine egg whites with cream of tartar and salt. Beat until foamy. Add sugar *gradually* while beating until meringue makes very stiff glossy peaks. Fold in vanilla and nuts. Spread over bottom and sides of a well-greased 9 inch pie plate. Bake 50 minutes. Turn off oven and let cool without removing. *Filling:* Place chocolate and water in a saucepan over low heat. Stir until chocolate has melted. Add coffee. Cool and add vanilla. Fold mixture into whipped cream and pile into cooled meringue crust. Chill at least two hours before serving.

Mrs. Sol Johnston
San Antonio, Texas

Chocolate Chiffon Pie

1-9 inch baked pie shell
1 envelope gelatin
¼ cup cold water
½ cup water
1 teaspoon instant coffee
2 squares unsweetened chocolate
3 eggs, separated
1 cup sugar
¼ teaspoon salt
1 teaspoon vanilla
Whipped cream

Soften gelatin in ¼ cup cold water. In a saucepan, combine ½ cup water, coffee and chocolate. Stir over low heat until blended. Remove from heat; add gelatin and stir until dissolved. Beat egg yolks until thick and lemon colored; gradually beat in ½ cup sugar; add salt and vanilla. Blend into chocolate mixture. Chill until partially set. Beat egg whites with remaining ½ cup sugar. Fold into chocolate filling. Pile in the baked pie crust and chill until firm. May be served with whipped cream on top.

Mrs. T. M. Sayre
Rayville, Louisiana

Fudge Pie

1 cup sugar
1 stick butter, melted
2 eggs
½ cup flour
Dash of salt
5 Tablespoons cocoa
1 teaspoon vanilla
½ cup chopped pecans
Whipped cream

Mix sugar and melted butter. Beat until creamy. Add whole eggs, flour, salt, cocoa, and vanilla. *Beat well.* Stir in pecans. Bake in a greased 8 inch pie pan for 30 minutes at 300 degrees. Test until a toothpick comes out clean. Serve with whipped cream or ice cream.

Mrs. Sam Brown

Hawaiian Chocolate Pie

1-9 inch baked pie shell
1 No. 1 can crushed pineapple
1⅓ cups sugar
½ cup flour
½ teaspoon salt
3 cups milk
3 egg yolks, slightly beaten
2 Tablespoons butter
2 teaspoons vanilla
2 squares unsweetened
  chocolate, melted
¾ cup nuts, chopped
  finely
Whipped cream, optional

Drain pineapple and set aside. Combine sugar, flour and salt in a heavy saucepan. Gradually add milk. Blend well. Bring to a boil, stirring constantly; cook over medium heat until thick. Blend a little of the hot mixture into the egg yolks. Return the mixture to the saucepan and cook for 1 minute, stirring constantly. Blend in the butter and vanilla. Divide in half. Stir the drained pineapple into one portion. Cover and cool to lukewarm. Blend the chocolate into the second portion. Cover and cool to lukewarm. Sprinkle half of the nuts over the cool, baked pie shell. Spoon in half of the chocolate mixture. Cover with the pineapple mixture and then with the remaining chocolate mixture. Top with remaining nuts. Chill. Top with whipped cream if desired.

Mrs. Davis Bingham

Chocolate Pecan Pie

2 squares unsweetened
  chocolate
2 Tablespoons butter
3 large eggs
½ cup sugar
¾ cup dark corn syrup
⅔ cup chopped nuts

Melt chocolate and butter together. Beat eggs and add the remaining ingredients except nuts. Add melted chocolate mixture to batter. Stir in nuts. Pour into an 8 or 9 inch buttered pie plate. Bake 40 to 50 minutes at 375 degrees.

Mrs. Walter Koch

French Silk Chocolate Pie

CRUST:
1 cup flour
¼ cup powdered sugar
1 stick butter

FILLING:
¾ cup butter
¾ plus ⅓ cup sugar
2 squares Baker's chocolate
1 teaspoon vanilla
3 eggs
Whipped cream

Crust: Mix all ingredients together and press in a 12 inch pie plate. Cook at 400 degrees 10 to 12 minutes or until light brown. *Filling*: Cream butter and sugar. Blend in melted, cooled chocolate and vanilla. Add eggs one at a time, beating *5 minutes or longer*, after each addition at medium speed. Pour into the cooled crust and refrigerate until set. When served, top with a dab of whipped cream on each slice if desired.

Mrs. W. J. Hodge, Jr.

Pie in the Sky

1-9 inch baked pie shell

MERINGUE:
2 egg whites
¼ teaspoon salt
½ teaspoon vinegar
¼ teaspoon cinnamon
½ cup sugar

FILLING:
1 small package semi-sweet
  chocolate morsels
2 egg yolks
¼ cup hot water
¼ teaspoon cinnamon
¼ cup sugar
1 cup whipping cream

Meringue: Beat egg whites together with salt and vinegar. Add cinnamon and sugar gradually. Beat until stiff but not dry. Spread meringue over bottom and sides of baked pastry shell. Bake in a 325 degree oven 12 to 15 minutes until lightly browned. Cool. *Filling:* Melt chocolate morsels over hot, not boiling water. Blend 2 egg yolks beaten with hot water into the melted chocolate until smooth. Spread 3 Tablespoons of the chocolate mixture over cooled meringue. Chill remaining chocolate mixture until it begins to thicken. Whip 1 cup cream until it begins to get light and gradually add cinnamon and sugar. Continue whipping until thick. Spread ½ of the whipped cream mixture over chocolate layer in the pie shell. Fold chilled chocolate mixture into remaining whipped cream. Spread over whipped cream in the pie shell. Chill at least four hours before serving.

Mrs. Minnie Bougton

Old Fashion Black Bottom Pie

CRUST:
1½ cups vanilla wafers
5 Tablespoons melted butter

CUSTARD:
2 cups Half and Half
½ cup sugar
1¼ teaspoons cornstarch
4 eggs, separated
1 Tablespoon gelatin soaked
   in 3 Tablespoons cold water
1¼ melted chocolate squares
1 teaspoon vanilla
½ cup sugar
¼ teaspoon cream of tartar
Rum or bourbon
Whipped cream
Bitter chocolate, grated

Crust: Crush vanilla wafers and add butter. Press in the bottom of an oblong cake pan, 6 x 11 inches, and bake until crisp. Cool. *Custard*: Scald cream. Mix cornstarch and sugar; add beaten egg yolks and mix well. Slowly add scalded cream. Cook in a double boiler until thickened. Add softened gelatin. Mix a little hot custard with gelatin first. Divide the custard; to one portion add melted chocolate and vanilla. Beat this vigorously until smooth and chocolate is well blended. Add remaining custard to 4 stiffly beaten egg whites that have had ½ cup sugar and ¼ teaspoon cream of tartar beaten into them. Add rum or bourbon to taste. Spread chocolate custard over crust. Set in ice box for a few minutes. Top with other custard. Chill until set. Before serving, cover with whipped cream and grate bitter chocolate sparingly over the top. Serve in squares.

Mrs. J. E. Brown
Lake Providence, Louisiana

Brandy Alexander Pie

1-9 inch crumb crust,
   graham, zwieback, chocolate
   wafer
1 envelope unflavored gelatin
½ cup cold water
⅔ cup sugar
Pinch of salt
3 eggs, separated
¼ cup cognac
¼ cup crème de cocoa
1 cup heavy cream whipped for
   topping

In saucepan stir gelatin, water, ⅓ cup sugar, salt and slightly beaten egg yolks. Heat over low heat stirring until gelatin dissolves and mixture is slightly thickened. *Do not boil.* Remove from heat, add cognac and crème de cocoa. Chill until mixture starts to mound. Beat egg whites until stiff but not dry with remaining ⅓ cup sugar. Fold into thickened mixture. Fold in one cup of whipped cream. Turn into crust and chill. Garnish with remaining cream.

Mrs. Ray Harkins
San Antonio, Texas

Daiquiri Pie
Beautiful and different

1 envelope unflavored gelatin
1½ cups sugar
½ teaspoon salt
4 egg yolks
½ cup lemon juice
2 Tablespoons lime juice
1 teaspoon grated lemon peel
6 drops green food color
½ cup light rum
4 egg whites
½ cup heavy cream, whipped
1-9 inch baked pie shell

In the top of a double boiler, combine gelatin with 1 cup sugar and the salt. In a small bowl, beat egg yolks with lemon and lime juices just until combined. Stir into gelatin mixture. Cook over boiling water, stirring constantly, until gelatin is dissolved and mixture is thickened, 10 to 12 minutes. Remove from water; stir in lemon peel, food coloring, and rum. Set in a bowl filled with ice cubes and water. Cool, stirring occasionally, until mixture is thick and mounds when it is dropped from a spoon, about 30 minutes. In a large bowl, beat egg whites until soft peaks form. Gradually add remaining sugar, 2 Tablespoons at a time, beating well until stiff peaks form. Fold gelatin mixture and whipped cream into egg whites just until combined. Turn half of mixture into baked pie shell. Refrigerate along with the rest of the mixture, 20 minutes. Spoon rest of chilled mixture in center of pie, mounding high. Refrigerate until firm, 4 hours or overnight. If desired, decorate with whipped cream and grated chocolate before serving. Makes 8 servings.

Marble Top Chocolate Rum Pie

½ cup sugar
1 envelope gelatin
Dash of salt
1 cup milk
2 beaten egg yolks
1-6 ounce package semi-sweet
  chocolate bits
⅓ cup dark rum
2 egg whites
¼ cup sugar
1 cup heavy cream
2 Tablespoons powdered sugar
1 teaspoon vanilla

Combine ½ cup sugar, gelatin and salt. Stir in milk and egg yolks. Cook in double boiler until slightly thick. Remove from heat and add chocolate. Stir until melted. Add rum. Chill until partially set. Beat egg whites until soft peaks form. Fold into chocolate mixture. Whip cream with enough sugar to sweeten. Add the vanilla. Layer one half of the chocolate mixture into a graham cracker crumb crust to which you may add ¼ cup ground pecans, if you desire; spread two-thirds of the whipping cream over the layer of chocolate. Top with the remaining chocolate and ending with the remainder of the whipped cream. Swirl the top to marble. Chill until firm. I use a spring form pan for this, but a pie plate may be used.

Mrs. Michael Gregory
Memphis, Tennessee

Grasshopper Pie

CRUST:
2 Tablespoons melted butter
14 crushed Hydrox wafers

FILLING:
24 marshmallows
½ cup milk
4 Tablespoons green crème de menthe
2 Tablespoons white crème de cacao
1 cup cream, whipped

Combine butter and wafers and press in pie plate. *Filling: Melt marshmallows in milk. Add crème de menthe and crème de cacao. Chill. Fold in whipped cream. Pour into shell, freeze; serve frozen.*

Mrs. George T. Walker

Frozen Chocolate Rum Pie

CRUST:
1 package 11¼ ounce pie crust mix
1½ cups finely chopped walnuts
½ cup light brown sugar, firmly packed
2 squares unsweetened chocolate, coarsely grated
2 teaspoons vanilla extract

FILLING:
4 eggs
1⅓ cups sugar
¼ teaspoon salt
2 envelopes unflavored gelatin
⅔ cup light or golden rum
4 cups heavy cream, may use Cool Whip, but be careful in measuring as Cool Whip is pre-whipped.
1⅓ cups confectioners' sugar

GARNISH:
Whipped cream
Chocolate curls

Crust: Preheat oven to 375 degrees. Line 2-9 inch pie plates with foil letting foil rise ¼ inch above rim of plates to contain the generous filling. Combine pie crust mix, nuts, brown sugar, and chocolate; stir in 2 Tablespoons water and the vanilla. Press into foil-lined plates. Bake 15 minutes or until lightly browned and cool completely on wire racks. *Filling*: In large bowl beat eggs with granulated sugar and salt until they are well combined. Set bowl over a pan of boiling water; continue beating at high speed until mixture is very thick, 6 to 8 minutes. Remove bowl from water; cool in the refrigerator, about 20 minutes stirring occasionally. Soften gelatin in rum. Dissolve over hot water; cool to room temperature. Gradually beat gelatin into cooled egg mixture until well blended. Chill briefly. Whip cream with confectioners' sugar just until stiff; fold in egg-gelatin mixture until well combined. Refrigerate until mixture is stiff enough to mound into the pie shells. Freeze until firm, 4 to 5 hours. Before serving, garnish and let stand at room temperature about 10 minutes or until soft enough to cut.

Mrs. Henry Guerriero

Rum Cream Pie

3 egg yolks
½ cup sugar
⅛ teaspoon salt
¾ Tablespoon Knox gelatin
¼ cup water
¼ cup dark rum
2 cups whipped cream
1 bar semi-sweet chocolate,
  shaved

In a double boiler cook egg yolks, salt and sugar until thick. Add gelatin which has been soaked in ¼ cup water. Let cool. Fold in rum and 1 cup whipped cream. Pour into an 8 inch graham cracker crust. Top with the remaining whipped cream and shaved semi-sweet chocolate. May be made the day before using.

Mrs. Don Phillips

Chocolate Ice Cream Pie

4 egg whites
½ teaspoon cream of tartar
1 cup sugar
½ pint heavy cream
1 cup Hershey's Fudge Sauce
½ teaspoon peppermint
  flavoring
1 quart vanilla ice cream

Beat egg whites until frothy with cream of tartar. Slowly add sugar, beating until stiff. Spread the meringue in a big buttered pie plate. Bake at 300 degrees for 50 minutes. Cool. Whip cream slowly; fold in Fudge Sauce and peppermint flavoring. Soften ice cream. Spread in the meringue shell. Cover with chocolate whipped cream. Keep in freezer 24 hours before serving.

Mrs. Edwin Pries
Newellton, Louisiana

Pontchartrain Ice Cream Pie

1-10 inch baked pie shell
1 quart vanilla ice cream
1 quart coffee ice cream
5 egg whites
1 teaspoon vanilla extract
½ cup sugar

SAUCE:
2-6 ounce packages sweet
  chocolate bits
2 squares unsweetened
  chocolate
¾ cup light cream
½ cup sugar

Soften ice cream and spread in the pie shell. Freeze. Beat whites and vanilla until soft peaks form. Add 2 Tablespoons of sugar at a time and beat until stiff. Spread over frozen ice cream. Broil 5 to 6 inches from heat until golden brown. Return to freezer. In the top of a double boiler stir sugar and chocolate with ½ cup cream until thick. Remove from heat and gradually beat in remaining cream. Makes 2 cups sauce. Serve pie in wedges with chocolate sauce.

Mrs. Wesley Shafto, Jr.

Frozen Lemon Pie

4 egg yolks
1 can sweetened condensed
  milk
1-6 ounce can frozen lemonade
  or juice of 4 lemons
1 cup cream, whipped
4 egg whites, stiffly beaten
8 or 9 inch almond flavored
  graham cracker crust
Whipped cream

Beat egg yolks. Add milk, and undiluted lemonade or lemon juice. Place in the refrigerator while whipping cream and beating egg whites. Fold cream and beaten egg whites into lemon mixture. Spoon into graham cracker crust, cover, and freeze overnight. Serve topped with whipped cream. Yield: 6 to 8 servings.

Mrs. John Ensminger

Lemon Ice Cream Pie
Quick and easy

2-8 inch graham cracker
  crusts
1 half gallon vanilla
  ice cream
1-6 ounce can frozen
  lemonade
Graham cracker crumbs

Soften lemonade and ice cream. Beat together until creamy. Pour in graham cracker crust and freeze until serving time. Sprinkle top with graham cracker crumbs.

Mrs. Jim Dennis

Flaky Pastry

3 cups sifted flour
1 teaspoon salt
1 cup shortening
1 egg
6 Tablespoons water

Sift flour with salt. Cut shortening into flour. Beat the egg with 5 Tablespoons of water. Add to flour mixture. Use remainder of water, if necessary. Makes 3 pie shells.

Mrs. Jim Wolff

Nanny's Good and Easy Pastry

1 PIE CRUST:
1 cup sifted flour
¼ heaping teaspoon salt
1 pinch of sugar, a must for
   good pastry crust
⅓ cup shortening
3 Tablespoons cold water

DOUBLE CRUST:
1½ cups sifted flour
½ heaping teaspoon salt
Big pinch of sugar
½ cup shortening
4 to 5 Tablespoons cold water

Sift flour, salt and sugar. Cut in shortening. Sprinkle water over different parts and toss quickly with a fork until particles stick together. Roll and shape in pie plate. Prick and cover bottom with rice if you cook ahead of time. Bake at 350 degrees until white-golden, about 25 minutes.

Mrs. Elton Upshaw, Jr.

French Pastry Shells

2 cups oatmeal
1 cup flour
1 cup powdered sugar
1 teaspoon salt
¾ cup butter
1 egg, beaten
1 teaspoon vanilla

Mix dry ingredients well. Cut butter into mixture until crumbly. Stir in egg and vanilla. Shape mixture into two flat rounds. Wrap each and chill. Roll chilled dough ⅛ inch thick on a lightly floured board. Cut dough to fit small pastry pans or to fit muffin tins. Bake in a 375 degree oven for 8 minutes. Makes 36 pastry shells. Fill with favorite filling, fruit or cream.

Mrs. Lestar Martin

French Pie Dough
Delicious for use with any pie or
vegetable filling

2 cups triple sifted flour
Pinch of salt
*Spices to taste to compliment filling
¼ pound butter
¼ cup chilled liquid

*Grated lemon rind and a pinch of sugar for a lemon pie. Cinnamon added for an apple pie, and apple juice as the liquid: Use onion soup when making a crust for an onion pie, etc.

Triple sift flour again with salt and spices. Blend ½ of the butter into flour with a pastry blender until it looks like coarse meal. Cut remaining butter in until it looks like coarse peas. Sprinkle liquid over the dough from the tip of a spoon, trying to moisten as much dough as possible with as little liquid as possible. Mix lightly with a fork. As soon as dough sticks together when pinched between two fingers, it is ready. Dip a cloth in cold water, wring out well and tuck it over dough in bowl. Refrigerate ½ hour before rolling out on a lightly floured board.

Oil Pastry Crust

1 cup sifted flour
¾ teaspoon salt
¼ cup oil
2 Tablespoons cold water

Mix ingredients together and roll between two layers of waxed paper. Makes a single crust.

Mrs. Russell Bulloch

NOTES

Pargoud Plantation Christmas Ambrosia

6 oranges
1½ cups sugar
½ cup freshly grated coconut
½ cup sherry wine
Maraschino cherries

Peel and divide oranges into sections. Arrange a layer of orange sections in the bottom of a glass dish. Sprinkle generously with sugar and coconut. Repeat until all ingredients are used. Pour sherry over all. Looks beautiful served in a cut-glass bowl. Add maraschino cherries for color.

Mrs. Mabel Cole Ratliff

Apple Dumplings

1 recipe for a double pie crust
6 apples
1 Tablespoon butter
½ cup sugar
1½ teaspoons cinnamon

SYRUP:
1 cup sugar
2 cups water
½ teaspoon cinnamon
4 Tablespoons butter

Wash and core apples. Leave whole and unpeeled. Mix butter, sugar and cinnamon. Sprinkle evenly into the cavity of the 6 apples. Roll pastry and cut in squares large enough to cover apples. Wrap apples and seal. Boil syrup ingredients for 3 minutes. Arrange apples in shallow pan, pour syrup over all and place in preheated 500 degree oven for 5 to 7 minutes. Reduce heat to 325 degrees and bake 35 to 40 minutes.

Mrs. E. S. Eby

Jay's Bananas Foster

½ stick butter
6 heaping Tablespoons brown sugar
4 bananas
1 Tablespoon banana liqueur, overflow a bit
1 Tablespoon light rum
2 Tablespoons brandy
Ice cream

Mix butter and brown sugar in skillet. Cook over medium heat until sugar is melted. Slice bananas in halves or quarters and add to butter mixture cooking until tender. Add liqueur and stir. Sprinkle rum and brandy over top. Ignite. Spoon gently a few times. Serve warm over vanilla ice cream. Serves 6.

Jay Biedenharn

Strawberries Romanoff

1 quart vanilla ice cream
1 pint whipping cream, whipped
Juice of 2 lemons
½ cup Cointreau
¼ cup rum
Sugared berries

Whip ice cream slightly and fold in whipped cream. Add lemon juice and liqueurs. Freeze in plastic containers. Heap slightly sugared berries over this to serve. Have plates cold. Drain frozen berries if used and do not sugar. Quick, easy and delicious.

Mrs. Wilbur Marsh
Dallas, Texas

Margaret's Banana Pudding

3 Tablespoons flour
1 cup sugar
Dash of salt
6 Tablespoons water
3 egg yolks
3 cups of whole milk
1 stick of butter
1 teaspoon vanilla
6 large bananas
1- 16 ounce package of vanilla
  wafers
3 egg whites
6 Tablespoons sugar

Mix in the saucepan of a double boiler the following: flour, sugar, salt; add water to make a smooth paste in bottom of pan. Then add egg yolks and milk which have been well mixed. Place over simmering water and stir constantly until the mixture thickens and comes to a boil. Remove from heat and add butter and vanilla. Pour in a 2 quart pyrex that has been buttered and layered with the bananas and vanilla wafers. Beat egg whites until soft peaks form. Gradually beat in the sugar and continue to beat until stiff peaks form. Spread over the pudding and bake at 350 degrees until golden. Very good, pretty, and easy. This makes a very large amount. It could serve 10 to 12.

Mrs. Elton Upshaw, Jr.

Date Pudding

1 pound pitted dates, snipped
1/2 cup water
1/2 cup sugar
2 Tablespoons flour
1 teaspoon baking powder
2 egg yolks
2 egg whites, beaten
1 teaspoon vanilla
1/2 cup nuts, if desired
Whipped cream

Heat dates and water until soft and blended. Use more water if needed. Remove from heat and add sugar, flour, baking powder and egg yolks. Stir in vanilla and nuts. Then fold in beaten egg whites. Grease a 9 x 9 inch pan and bake at 325 degrees for 30 to 40 minutes or until toothpick comes clean. Serve warm, cut into squares and top with whipped cream.

Mrs. Milton Rosenfeld
Houston, Texas

Hawaiian Layer Pudding

1-12 ounce box vanilla wafers
5 Tablespoons melted butter
1/2 cup softened butter
2 cups confectioners' sugar
3 eggs, beaten
1/2 teaspoon vanilla
1 cup chopped nuts
2 cups drained pineapple
1 pint whipping cream
1/2 teaspoon vanilla
1/8 teaspoon salt
1 Tablespoon sugar
Cherries

Roll wafers into fine crumbs. Combine 1/2 crumbs with 5 Tablespoons melted butter. Turn into 15 x 9 x 2 inch pan and press over the bottom. Cream together softened butter and confectioners' sugar. Add beaten eggs and vanilla. Mix well. Spread over crumbs. Sprinkle with one cup of chopped nuts. Over nuts spread layer of drained pineapple. Beat whipping cream until thick. Stir in 1/2 teaspoon vanilla, salt and remaining sugar. Spread over pineapple. Sprinkle top with remaining crumbs. Place in refrigerator for at least 12 hours. Cut in squares and garnish with cherries. Serves 16.

Mrs. Daniel Dupree

Boiled Custard

1 quart milk
¼ cup sugar
Dash of salt
4 eggs
2 teaspoons vanilla

Scald milk in the top of a double boiler. Blend sugar, salt and the slightly beaten eggs. Pour some of the milk into the egg mixture. Pour all of the egg and milk mixture into the double boiler. Cook stirring constantly until it is thick enough to coat a spoon. Remove from the heat and add vanilla. Strain to remove any lumps and chill. Serve in a glass with a dollop of whipped cream on top.

Father William Baldridge
Rayville, Louisiana

Mother's Cup Custard

1 cup sugar
3 large eggs
1⅔ cups evaporated milk
¼ cup hot water
1 teaspoon vanilla
½ teaspoon nutmeg

For rich custard with caramel sauce: Put one teaspoon sugar, from the 1 cup sugar in the recipe, into each of 8 pyrex 5 ounce baking cups. Put on a cookie sheet in a 350 degree oven to melt sugar until slightly brown. Take out and cool to lukewarm. Beat eggs, stir in milk and other ingredients with a wooden spoon. Let sit a while for bubbles to disappear. Pour slowly into individual cups. Put cups in an oblong large baking pan. Pour warm water to come about 3/4 inch up on cups. Cook 45 minutes in a moderate oven, 350 degrees. Cool cups on a wire rack or wooden counter. Refrigerate. To serve, turn out on a small dessert plate. Let sauce drip over top and sides. The recipe can be doubled. If two pans are needed to bake custard, put second pan in another oven for best results. Serves 8.

Mrs. Ben F. Marshall

Lemon Custard Cups

1 cup sugar
2 Tablespoons salad oil
⅛ teaspoon salt
¼ cup sifted flour
2 teaspoons grated lemon peel
⅓ cup lemon juice
1½ cups scalded milk, cooled
    until lukewarm
3 egg yolks, beaten
3 egg whites, beaten stiff

Combine sugar, oil, salt and flour. Add lemon peel and juice. Stir milk into egg yolks. Add to lemon mixture. Fold in egg whites. Pour into 8 ungreased custard cups or a 1 quart casserole. Set in pan of warm water and bake in slow oven, 325 degrees, for 40 minutes or until set when tested with a knife. Serve warm or chilled, unmolded, and with sweetened whipped cream on top. If you wish to chill, cover with foil or plastic while still warm. Serves 8.

Mrs. Jerry Wolff

Floating Island

6 egg yolks
½ cup sugar
3 cups milk, scalded
1 Tablespoon vanilla or rum to taste
6 egg whites
2 Tablespoons sugar
1 cup milk
½ cup sugar, optional

Custard may be prepared ahead, but meringues should be prepared only an hour or two before serving as they tend to disintegrate somewhat after poaching. Beat egg yolks with sugar, scald milk and add a little to the egg yolks. Stir back into milk and cook over hot water in a double boiler until it coats a silver spoon. Cool and stir in flavoring. Refrigerate, covered. Whip egg whites until frothy. Gradually beat in 2 Tablespoons sugar. Heat one cup of milk in skillet till bubbles appear around edges. Drop meringues by large spoonfuls on top of milk. Poach for a minute or two. Remove with slotted spoon. Store briefly in the refrigerator. If desired melt sugar in a black iron skillet until caramel syrup. Drizzle over meringues. Always a favorite dessert as it is light and compliments any meal. Serves 8.

Mrs. George Snellings III

Caramel Custard Mold

If it's a dog's day, you may forget caramelizing if you wish.

1 cup sugar
6½ cups milk
9 eggs
5 egg yolks
1½ cups sugar
¾ teaspoon salt
1 teaspoon almond extract
1 teaspoon vanilla
Boiling water
¾ cup heavy cream

Place 1 cup sugar in black iron skillet, set over high heat and watch! When it begins to melt, tilt pan back and forth to keep sugar moving. When sugar is melted and light brown, quickly pour into a 2 1/2 quart ovenproof soufflé dish. In large kettle scald milk. Beat eggs and egg yolks with 1 1/2 cups sugar. Add about half of the scalded milk to the egg yolks. Pour all back into the remaining milk and mix well. Add the extracts and salt. Pour into the carameled soufflé dish. Place in pan, a roaster works well, and fill to within 1/2 inch of the top of the dish with boiling water. Bake in a preheated oven at 325 degrees for 1 hour and 10 minutes or until knife comes clean. Cool on wire rack and refrigerate. To serve, have cream whipped and set aside. Run spatula around dish, place serving platter over custard and invert. Spoon off 1/4 cup caramel syrup and fold into the cream which has been whipped.

A Poof

6 egg whites
3 Tablespoons powdered sugar
1 envelope gelatin
1 teaspoon vanilla
1 cup whipping cream, whipped
  with 1 Tablespoon sugar
Fresh fruit

Beat egg whites until foamy. Add alternately the powdered sugar and gelatin that has been dissolved in a little hot water, then cooled. Beat until stiff peaks are formed, adding vanilla last. Pour the mixture into a wet ring mold. Refrigerate until firm. Turn out on a platter and cover with sweetened whipped cream. Fill center with fresh fruits or berries. This is a very light non-filling dessert, perfect after a rich meal.

Mrs. Ed Seymour, Jr.

Pavolova

A favorite dessert in Australia-usually served with a topping of passion fruit

6 egg whites
12 Tablespoons sugar
2 teaspoons vanilla
2 teaspoons vinegar

Topping:
1 pint heavy cream, whipped,
  sweetened to taste
Sliced fresh fruit of own choice,
  such as peaches or strawberries

Beat egg whites until stiff. Gradually add sugar while beating. Fold in vanilla and vinegar. Lightly grease a cookie sheet and cover with brown paper or wax paper. Mound egg whites on paper and shape into a large circle, keeping it approximately 2½ to 3 inches thick and about 8 or 9 inches round. Bake in a low oven, 200 degrees, for 1 hour. Turn off heat at the end of the hour and allow meringue to remain in oven for an additional hour. Do not shorten time. Remove from oven and peel paper off bottom. Place on a flat cake plate. Center may fall slightly after cooling. When ready to serve, ice top and sides with whipped cream. Decorate top with sliced fresh fruit or berries. This dessert is different from a meringue because the center does not "dry out" but has a consistency more like marshmallow. Recipe may be prepared a day before and kept covered until ready to ice and serve. Keep in refrigerator after icing. Serves 6 to 8.

Mrs. Ralph Simpson

MERINGUES: *These elegant desserts are easy to make and can be filled with such a variety of good things. Beat 2 EGG WHITES with a PINCH OF SALT until foamy. Add 1 TEASPOON OF LEMON JUICE and beat until stiff. Gradually add 1/2 CUP OF SUGAR and beat until meringue is stiff and glossy. On heavy brown paper on a large cookie sheet spoon heaping Tablespoons of meringue to form 6 mounds three inches apart. With the back of a spoon shape the center of each mound into a shell. Bake at 275 degrees for 60 minutes. Turn off heat and let stand in the oven until cool. Carefully peel off paper and store in tins. Fill with ice cream and sauce or fresh fruit; any fresh fruit with whipped cream; lemon jelly with whipped cream or just use your imagination.*

Chocolate Mousse

4 ounces German's chocolate or
    semi-sweet
4 egg yolks
½ stick butter, softened
Dash of salt
1 teaspoon vanilla
Dash of peppermint, optional
4 egg whites
6 Tablespoons sugar

Put chocolate into a saucepan. Cover with 2 inches of very hot tap water. Cover with a lid. Let stand about 5 minutes or until chocolate is soft enough to stick your finger through. When chocolate is soft, but not dissolved, drain off water. Don't worry that some water clings to chocolate.

Add the yolks. Stir with a whisk and cook over very low heat until thick. Remove from heat. Add the butter, salt, vanilla and peppermint. Mix well. Cool, but don't let it get cold. Beat egg whites. Gradually add sugar. Beat until stiff. Beat a "gob" of whites into the chocolate, mixing it in well. Fold remainder of whites into chocolate. Pour into a compote or individual serving dishes. Cover with transparent wrap and refrigerate until ready to serve. Serves 6.

Mrs. Don Stinson

Pot de Crème

½ pound semi-sweet chocolate
½ cup sugar
¼ cup water
5 eggs, separated
1 teaspoon vanilla
Milk, if needed
½ pint whipping cream

Melt together in top of double boiler, chocolate, sugar and water. Stir until smooth and thoroughly blended. Remove pan from heat to a pan of cold water. Cool over the cold water. Stir occasionally until cool. Add well beaten egg yolks and vanilla. The mixture should be semi-fluid. If too firm, add 4 or 5 Tablespoons of tepid milk. Beat 5 egg whites until stiff. Fold in chocolate mixture gently but thoroughly. Pour mousse into individual Pot de Crème cups or demi-tasse cups and chill for at least 6 hours. Top with thick cream whipped or unwhipped. Serves 8 to 10, depending on size of cups.

Mrs. Charles Stubbs

Cold Lemon Soufflé

1 envelope unflavored gelatin
¼ cup cold water
¾ cup cold milk
4 egg yolks
½ cup sugar
½ cup lemon juice
3 Tablespoons grated lemon rind
1 cup heavy cream
7 egg whites
Dry cake crumbs

Fold over lengthwise a long strip of aluminum foil and oil it on one side. Secure foil neatly around a 1 quart soufflé dish, oiled side in, making a collar standing 3 inches above the top. Sprinkle gelatin over water to soften. Heat the milk in top of a double boiler. Beat egg yolks with the sugar until they are light and lemon colored. Pour the hot milk over the egg mixture, beating constantly. Return mixture to the top of double boiler and add gelatin. Cook mixture over hot water, whisking constantly, until it is thick and creamy, being careful it does not boil. Remove pan from heat, allow mixture to cool. This is important to preserve the freshness of the lemon. Add lemon juice and rind. Refrigerate mixture until it begins to thicken, but do not let it set solid. Whip cream until it is thick but not stiff and fold into lemon custard mixture. Refrigerate until it is just beginning to set. Beat egg whites until they are stiff but not dry. Fold gently into mixture with a rubber spatula. Spoon soufflé into prepared dish and chill at least 3 hours or longer. Remove collar before serving and pat dry cake crumbs over the side.

Mrs. Don Stinson

Coffee Soufflé

2 envelopes unflavored gelatin
½ cup sugar
3 cups freshly brewed boiling coffee
2 egg whites
¼ cup sugar
2 cups heavy cream, whipped or 4 cups whipped topping

Stir gelatin and sugar together well. Pour coffee over and stir to dissolve. Chill until slightly thickened. Meanwhile, beat egg whites until foamy, then continue beating and add sugar gradually until meringue forms stiff peaks. Whip cream or prepare topping. Fold the meringue and whipped cream into the thickened gelatin mixture and pour into a 2 quart soufflé dish. Chill until firm, at least 3 hours. Serves 8 to 10.

Mrs. Fred Huenefeld

Chocolate Soufflé

2 envelopes unflavored gelatin
2 cups milk
1 cup sugar
¼ teaspoon salt
4 eggs, separated
2-6 ounce packages semi-sweet
   chocolate pieces
2 teaspoons vanilla
2 cups heavy cream, whipped

Sprinkle gelatin over milk in medium saucepan. Add ½ cup sugar, salt, egg yolks and chocolate pieces. Stir until thoroughly mixed. Place over low heat, stirring until gelatin is dissolved and chocolate is melted. Remove from heat and stir in vanilla. Chill until mixture mounds. Beat egg whites with remaining ½ cup sugar until stiff. Fold into chocolate mixture with whipped cream. Put a collar on a 1 ½ or 2 quart soufflé dish and carefully pour in mixture. Chill. Serves 12.

Mrs. Richard Blanchard

Hot Chocolate Soufflé

3 Tablespoons butter
3 Tablespoons flour
1 cup milk
½ cup sugar
3 squares bitter chocolate
Dash of salt
5 beaten egg yolks
7 egg whites
Vanilla

Melt butter and mix with flour in the top of a double boiler. Cook a moment. Add milk, stirring constantly, until mixture is rich and creamy. Stir in sugar until dissolved. Blend in chocolate which has been broken into bits. The mixture will appear grainy for a while. Keep stirring until smooth. Take from fire, add a dash of salt and beat for a minute. Allow it to cool a bit, then add beaten egg yolks; beat until smooth. Beat egg whites until stiff. When the chocolate is really cool, take a large spoonful of white and fold vigorously in the chocolate mixture until it appears slightly foamy. Dribble this sauce over the egg whites and fold thoroughly and carefully with vanilla. Slide into a buttered and sugared 2 quart soufflé dish and bake at 300 degrees for 30 minutes.

Mrs. Dick Culpepper

"Crêpes for dessert" and your reputation as a cook is made forever. The serving may be as simple or elaborate as you wish—from a crêpe sprinkled with lemon, rolled and dusted with confectioners' sugar to "crêpes flambe". Recipes for more elaborate fillings and sauces may be found in many cookbooks. However, excellent quick and easy fillings may be made from flavored whipped cream, a thick custard or canned pie fillings. Top the rolled crêpes with your favorite sauce. The dessert will be as delicious as the crêpe. With a little practice your crêpes will be perfect—light, delicate and paper thin.

Dessert Crêpes

8 Tablespoons butter
½ cup cold water
¼ cup milk
2 eggs plus 2 additional egg
    yolks
¾ cup unsifted all purpose flour
1 Tablespoon sugar
1 teaspoon freshly grated lemon
    peel
¼ teaspoon salt

First clarify the butter by melting it in a small, heavy saucepan or skillet over low heat, skimming off the surface foam. Spoon the clear butter into a bowl, and discard the milky solids at the bottom of the pan. Make the batter for the crêpes. Combine flour, eggs, milk, water, salt, sugar, 2 Tablespoons of clarified butter and lemon peel in a blender jar and blend at high speed for a few seconds. Turn off, scrape down sides of jar and blend again for 40 seconds. Cover and let batter rest for 2 hours in refrigerator.

To cook crêpes: Combine 3 Tablespoons clarified butter with 1 Tablespoon vegetable oil. Heat a 5 inch crêpe pan or heavy skillet over high heat until a drop of water flicked into it evaporates instantly. With a pastry brush, lightly grease the bottom and sides of the pan with a little of the melted butter and oil combination. With a small ladle pour about 2 Tablespoons of batter into the pan and tip the pan so that the batter quickly covers the bottom; the batter should cling to the pan and begin to firm up almost immediately. The finished crêpe ought to be paper thin. Cook the crêpes a minute or so until browned. Turn over and cook the other side a minute longer. Slide the crêpes onto a plate. Brush skillet again with butter and oil and proceed with the rest of the crêpes. Makes 12 crêpes.

Crêpes may be made hours or even days ahead and kept layered with wax paper separations and tightly covered in the refrigerator or freezer. Let them return to room temperature before separating them.

Crêpes Soufflées au Citron
As divine as it sounds

3 Tablespoons unsalted butter
5 level Tablespoons sifted all
   purpose flour
½ cup hot milk
3 egg yolks
4 Tablespoons sugar
3 Tablespoons strained fresh
   lemon juice
1 Tablespoon freshly grated lemon
   peel
3 egg whites
Salt
12 dessert crêpes

Preheat oven to 400 degrees. In a heavy saucepan, melt 3 Tablespoons butter over low heat. Stir in the flour, then cook, stirring, for 1 to 2 minutes. Remove from the heat and let cool for a moment. Beat in the milk vigorously to blend roux and liquid. Cook, stirring constantly, until the mixture boils and thickens. Immediately scoop into a large bowl and beat in the egg yolks, one at a time. Add 3 Tablespoons of the sugar, the lemon juice and peel, stirring thoroughly until all the ingredients are combined. In a separate bowl, beat the egg whites and a pinch of salt; gradually add the remaining 1 Tablespoon of sugar and beat until the whites form stiff peaks. With a rubber spatula, stir an overflowing Tablespoon of egg white into the lemon soufflé base; then lightly fold in the rest of the egg whites. Carefully separate the crêpes and lay them speckled side up on wax paper. Place 1 Tablespoon of lemon soufflé mixture on the top half of each crêpe and gently lift the lower half up over it. Then lightly fold the crêpes into quarters to make small triangles. Arrange the crêpes side by side in a large, shallow, buttered baking dish. Sprinkle each crêpe with a little sugar, then bake them on the middle shelf of the oven for 10 minutes or until they have puffed up and sugar has melted to a light glaze. Serve at once on heated platter or plates. If made ahead, cover crêpes with Saran wrap and keep in refrigerator. Allow to get to room temperature before baking. Serves 6 with two crêpes per serving.

Apple Crêpes with Roquefort Cheese

2 pounds cooking apples
2 Tablespoons butter
1 Tablespoon sugar
¼ pound Roquefort cheese
¼ pound cream cheese
1 or 2 Tablespoons cream
12 prepared crêpes
Butter
Sour cream

Peel and thinly slice apples. Sauté in melted butter, sprinkled with sugar until browned but not soft. Cream cheeses with cream and spread over surface of crêpes. Put 1 or 2 Tablespoons of apples on each crepe and fold into envelopes. Place in a buttered dish, dot with butter and bake at 400 degrees for 15 minutes. Serve with sour cream.

Mrs. Ed Seymour, Jr.

Strawberries Fitzgerald

12 dessert crêpes
2 pints fresh strawberries
2/3 cup sugar, or to taste

CRÊPE FILLING:
6 ounces cream cheese
6 Tablespoons sour cream
2 Tablespoons cream

SAUCE:
1/2 cup sugar
1/2 stick butter
1 ounce Kirsch
1 ounce strawberry liqueur,
    optional
2 ounces warmed rum

Prepare crêpes ahead of time. Wash and slice strawberries. Add sugar to sweeten. Set aside. Whip filling ingredients until fluffy. Refrigerate, but set out well before serving to reach room temperature. Spoon a generous amount of filling on the edge of each crêpe and roll. Arrange 2 crêpes per serving on 6 dessert plates. Place strawberries and all ingredients for sauce in a chafing dish, except rum. Let cook until sugar and butter thicken mixture very slightly. Pour over warm rum and ignite. Spoon carefully until flame dies and ladle over crêpes.

Mrs. William D. Brown

Cherry Crêpes

Prepare 16 dessert crêpes

FILLING:
1 cup sugar
1/4 cup flour
1 cup milk
2 eggs plus 2 egg yolks
3 Tablespoons butter
2 teaspoons vanilla
1/4 teaspoon almond extract
1/2 cup slivered toasted almonds

SAUCE:
2- 10 ounce cans frozen cherries,
    thawed
2 Tablespoons cornstarch
4 Tablespoons rum
2 Tablespoons Kirsch
1/2 teaspoon grated lemon peel
1 Tablespoon lemon juice
1/2 stick butter
Sugar to taste, optional
2 ounces of warm brandy or rum
    to flame, optional

Filling: Combine sugar and flour in a heavy saucepan; stir in milk and cook stirring until thick. Cook two more minutes. Beat eggs with yolks. Stir a little of the hot mixture into the eggs, then stir all back into hot mixture and continue cooking until thickened. Remove from heat and beat until smooth. Add the rest of the ingredients. Cover with wax paper and cool. *To serve:* Spread 1 heaping Tablespoon of filling on each crêpe and roll. Arrange in a well-buttered baking dish; brush with melted butter, sprinkle with sugar, and bake at 350 degrees 20 minutes or until bubbly and heated through. Heat cherries with cornstarch, stirring until slightly thickened. Add remaining ingredients and simmer 15 to 20 minutes. When crêpes are hot, arrange on a dessert plate and top with sauce. All can be prepared ahead and crêpes baked just before serving. If you wish to flame, heat the sauce in a chafing dish at the table, pour on warm liquor and ignite. Spoon gently until flame dies. Ladle onto arranged crêpes on plate.

Apricot Torte

MERINGUE:
3 egg whites
¾ cup sugar
½ teaspoon vinegar
½ teaspoon vanilla
½ cup graham cracker crumbs
½ cup shredded coconut
1 cup chopped nuts

FILLING:
2 cups drained stewed apricots
Sugar to taste
1 cup cream, whipped
1 Tablespoon sugar

Meringue: Beat egg whites until soft peaks form. Gradually add sugar, vinegar and vanilla, beating until stiff peaks form. Mix crumbs, coconut and nuts together. Fold into the egg white mixture. Oil bottom and sides of 9 inch pie plate. Spoon meringue onto pie plate, gently sloping around edges to form shell. Bake at 300 degrees for 30 minutes. Turn off oven and leave torte in oven to cool and dry. *Filling:* Add sugar to taste to drained apricots and whip lightly with a fork. Spread over torte. Top with whipped cream sweetened with 1 Tablespoon of sugar. Refrigerate for 2 or 3 hours. Very rich.

Mrs. Davis Bingham

Lemon Ice Box Torte

1 cup chocolate wafer crumbs
6 Tablespoons sugar
3 Tablespoons butter, melted
2 eggs, separated
1 cup Eagle Brand milk
1 Tablespoon grated lemon rind
½ cup fresh lemon juice
½ teaspoon almond flavoring

Combine crumbs, 2 Tablespoons each of sugar and butter. Reserve about 2 Tablespoons of crumb mixture for top and press remainder in the bottom of a 9 x 9 inch pan. Chill. Beat egg yolks, add milk, lemon rind, juice and flavoring. Cook on low heat until thick. Cool. Beat egg whites until frothy and gradually add remaining 4 Tablespoons of sugar beating until stiff peaks form. Fold into cooled lemon mixture. Pour into prepared pan. Sprinkle with reserved crumbs. Freeze. Serves 6 to 8. Remove from freezer about 5 minutes before serving.

Mrs. Victor Mitchell

Cracker Torte

3 egg whites
1 teaspoon cream of tartar
1 cup sugar
1 teaspoon vanilla
1 cup pecans
16 saltine crackers, crumbled
2 Tablespoons pineapple preserves
½ pint whipping cream
1 package frozen coconut

Beat egg whites until dry. Add tartar, sugar, and vanilla. Then add pecans and crumbled crackers. Bake in a 9 x 9 inch ungreased pan for 20 minutes in a 375 degree oven. When cold, spread with 2 Tablespoons of pineapple preserves and top with whipped cream. Sprinkle coconut over the torte. Chill. This can be frozen for several weeks to use when unexpected company drops in!

Mrs. W. F. Thurman

Swedish Pineapple Cream

1/2 cup butter
1 1/2 cups powdered sugar
2 eggs, separated
1/2 teaspoon lemon extract
3/4 cup pineapple, well drained
1 cup sour cream
8 ladyfingers

Cream butter and add powdered sugar. Add 2 egg yolks one at a time and beat well. Add lemon extract, pineapple, and 1 cup sour cream. Fold in stiffly beaten egg whites. Split 8 lady fingers. Put half in 9 x 6 x 2 inch pan. Pile the pineapple mixture on this and top with remaining lady fingers. Chill. Serves 8. This freezes well. Thaw before serving. It does not keep well after thawing.

Mrs. T. A. Grant III

Charlotte Russe

1/2 cup water
2 envelopes Knox plain gelatin
3 egg yolks
1 cup sugar
Pinch of salt
1 3/4 cups scalded milk
1 teaspoon sherry extract
1 teaspoon vanilla
Sherry, about 1/4 cup
3 egg whites
1 pint heavy cream
1 box Pepperidge Farm ladyfingers

Lightly butter a spring form pan and line with split ladyfingers. Soften gelatin in water while making custard. Scald milk. Beat egg yolks with sugar and a pinch of salt, stir in milk. Place all in double boiler over simmering water. Cook until it coats the spoon then pour immediately over gelatin and stir until dissolved. Cool. When it begins to set, blend in flavorings and sherry which together total 1/4 cup. Beat egg whites with a pinch of salt until stiff. Whip cream. Fold all three together and refrigerate until slightly thickened. Pour in prepared pan and refrigerate until set.

Mrs. Wharton Brown

Chocolate Charlotte Russe

1 envelope unflavored gelatin
2 Tablespoons cold water
3- 1 ounce squares unsweetened
chocolate
1/2 cup water
4 eggs, separated
1/2 cup sugar
1 teaspoon vanilla
Dash of salt
1/2 teaspoon cream of tartar
1/4 cup sugar
1 cup heavy cream, whipped
1/2 cup chopped pecans
18 double ladyfingers, split

Soften gelatin in 2 Tablespoons cold water. Melt chocolate in 1/2 cup of water over low heat, stirring constantly. Remove from heat; add softened gelatin, and stir to dissolve. Beat egg yolks until thick and lemon colored. Gradually beat in 1/2 cup sugar; add vanilla and a dash of salt. Blend in the chocolate mixture. Cool, then stir until smooth. Beat egg whites and cream of tartar to soft peaks. Gradually add remaining sugar, beating to stiff peaks. Fold into chocolate mixture. Fold in whipped cream and nuts. Set aside about 10 ladyfingers for center layer. Line bottom and sides of an 8 inch spring form pan. Fill with half the mixture. Layer reserved ladyfingers and fill with remaining chocolate mixture. Chill 8 hours or overnight. Serves 8 to 10.

Mrs. Ralph Brockman

Chocolate Ice Box Cake

2 sticks unsalted butter, softened
1 cup sugar, sifted
4 eggs, separated
4 ounces bitter chocolate, melted
1 teaspoon vanilla
1/2 teaspoon almond extract
1 dozen ladyfingers
1 dozen almond macaroons,
    crumbled
1/2 pint heavy cream, whipped

Cream softened butter with sifted sugar. Add well beaten yolks, and beat well. Add melted chocolate and flavorings. Beat egg whites until stiff. Fold whites into chocolate mixture. Line sides of spring mold with halves of ladyfingers. Crumble remainder of ladyfingers into bottom of mold. Layer crumbled macaroons on top of crumbled ladyfingers. Pour in chocolate mixture. Refrigerate until set. Cover top with whipped cream. Can be made a day or two ahead of time, but do not garnish with whipped cream until ready to serve.

Mrs. H. W. Greene

Angel Food and German Chocolate Refrigerator Cake

2 cakes German's Sweet Chocolate,
    1/2 pound
4 Tablespoons boiling water
6 eggs, separated
1 teaspoon vanilla
1-10 inch angel food cake
1/2 pint whipping cream

In double boiler melt chocolate with the water. Cool slightly. Beat egg yolks and add chocolate, vanilla, and stiffly beaten whites. Pour over angel food cake broken into about 1 inch pieces. Pack into 9 inch, waxed paper lined spring form pan. Refrigerate several hours. Remove rim and turn out as you would a cake, remove wax paper and "ice" with whipped cream. This chocolate filling may also be used with ladyfingers in parfait glasses.

Mrs. Clifford M. Strauss

Chocolate Spring Cake

1 large package chocolate chips
2 Tablespoons sugar
3 eggs, separated
1 1/2 cups heavy cream, whipped
1 angel food cake
Whipped cream for garnish

Melt chocolate in double boiler, add sugar and beaten egg yolks. Cool. Fold in stiffly beaten egg whites and add whipped cream. Break cake into large pieces and layer into spring mold with chocolate mixture. Chill for 24 hours. Unmold and garnish with whipped cream.

Mrs. Edel Blanks, Jr.

Charlotte Cake

1 medium angel food cake
1/2 pound butter, not oleo
2 cups confectioners' sugar,
  sifted
3 egg yolks
1/4 cup bourbon
Dash of salt
1 cup chopped pecans

Cream butter and confectioners' sugar, add egg yolks, salt, and bourbon; then fold in pecans. Slice cake into three layers. It is best to use a loaf-type cake that is not too fresh from the oven to prevent tearing. Ice layers generously, securing with a few toothpicks. Ice outside of cake thickly, enclose with foil or in a cake box, and refrigerate at least 12 hours. This recipe may be doubled, tripled, etc. I always make a generous amount as I like lots of icing.

Hints: Bourbon may be increased if desired; at Christmas it's nice with more of a bourbon flavor.

Mrs. Robert D. Wood

Tipsy Parson

1 angel food cake
3 cups milk
2 inch vanilla bean
6 egg yolks
2/3 cup sugar
1 Tablespoon flour
Sherry
3 cups toasted slivered almonds
3 cups heavy cream, whipped

Prepare favorite angel food cake flavored with vanilla and almond extract. *Make custard:* Scald milk with vanilla bean, remove from heat and let stand 10 minutes. In a bowl beat egg yolks until they are light, gradually beat in sugar until smooth and creamy. Stir in flour. Pour some of the scalded milk slowly over egg mixture stirring constantly. Return all to heavy pan and cook over low heat, stirring constantly, until it coats the back of a silver spoon. Stir with whisk and refrigerate. *To assemble:* slice cake into 3 layers. Place bottom slice in shallow bowl larger than cake so there will be adequate room for the custard sauce. Sprinkle the layer generously with sherry and chopped toasted almonds, top with custard. Repeat layering of cake, sherry, almonds and custard. Sprinkle top layer with sherry. Spread top and sides with whipped cream. Sprinkle remaining almonds on top and pat on sides. Pour remaining custard around cake in bowl and when serving, *generously* spoon on custard. It makes the dessert!

Mrs. Don Irby

Angel Food Lemonade Cake
Quick, easy and delicious

½ gallon vanilla ice cream
1 small can lemonade
10 inch angel food cake or loaf
    angel food cake
Strawberries, sweetened to
    taste

Soften ice cream, add can of lemonade and stir in until well mixed. Slice cake in 2 or 3 layers. Spread with ice cream in between layers. Ice with remainder of ice cream mixture. Serve immediately topped with strawberries or return to freezer. Let set out 10 to 15 minutes before serving.

Mrs. John Ensminger

Orange Delight

1 envelope Knox gelatin
½ cup cold water
⅔ cup sugar
⅛ teaspoon salt
1-6 ounce can frozen orange
    juice
1 pint heavy cream, whipped
1-14 ounce angel food cake

GARNISH:

½ pint whipping cream, whipped
1-11 ounce can mandarin oranges
¼ pound green grapes

Dissolve gelatin in 1/2 cup cold water in saucepan. Stir over low heat until dissolved. Add sugar and salt; stir until dissolved. Remove from heat. Add thawed orange juice. Refrigerate until thick and fold in whipped cream. Remove crust from angel food cake and break into bite size pieces. Spoon layer of orange mixture in 2 1/2 quart bowl which has been lightly greased with Wesson oil. Place layer of cake pieces over orange mixture. Make 4 layers of cream and 3 layers of cake. Refrigerate overnight. Unmold and frost with whipped cream. Arrange orange slices and grapes in decorative manner on top. Serves 8 to 10.

Mrs. John Cole

Jelly Roll Dessert

3 or 4 small jelly rolls
1-3 ounce package raspberry jello
1½ cups hot water
1 package frozen raspberries,
    thawed and undrained
½ pint heavy cream, whipped

Cut jelly rolls in 1/2 inch slices. Line the sides and bottom of a 9 inch spring form pan with slices. Set aside. Mix jello with hot water. Cool to thicken, but not set. Fold in frozen raspberries with juice and whipped cream. Pour in prepared spring form pan. Refrigerate until set. If desired, garnish top with more whipped cream. Remove sides from pan when serving. You see the slices of jelly roll surrounded by the pink dessert. Elegant to serve "at the table."

Mrs. Ernest Strauss

Cottage Cheese Cake

CRUST:
1/2 cup butter
2 cups Zwieback crumbs
3/4 cup sugar
1 teaspoon cinnamon

CAKE:
2-12 ounce cartons creamed
   cottage cheese
4 eggs
1 cup sugar
1 cup Half and Half
1/4 teaspoon lemon rind
3 Tablespoons lemon juice
1/4 teaspoon salt
4 Tablespoons flour

Crust: Melt butter and mix in the rest of the ingredients. Reserve 3/4 cup of mixture for topping. Press into a 9 inch spring form pan covering bottom and sides.

Filling: Press cottage cheese through a sieve and set aside. Beat the eggs well, adding sugar gradually. Blend in remaining ingredients in the order given. Stir in cottage cheese. Pour in crust lined pan, sprinkle with crumbs and bake at 350 degrees for 1 hour and 15 minutes. Remove sides from pan after cake has cooled.

Mrs. Ernest Strauss

Raleigh House Cheese Cake
Rich and Yummy!

CHEESE CAKE:
9 inch graham cracker crust
12 ounces cream cheese
1/2 cup sugar
1/2 teaspoon vanilla
2 eggs

TOPPING:
1 1/2 cups sour cream
2 Tablespoons sugar
1/2 teaspoon vanilla

Have ingredients at room temperature. Beat at a moderate speed until smooth. Pour into graham cracker crust and bake at 325 degrees for 20 minutes. Let cool 15 minutes. Mix topping ingredients together well with rubber spatula. Spread over cheesecake. Return to the oven for 5 minutes. Let cool and put in refrigerator. So easy, to be so delicious.

Blueberry Cheese Cake

CRUST:
2 cups graham cracker crumbs
1/2 stick butter, melted
1/2 cup sugar

FILLING:
6 eggs, room temperature
2 cups sugar
2- 8 ounce packages cream cheese,
   room temperature
1 can Blueberry Pie Filling

Mix all ingredients for crust. Lightly pack in the bottom of a spring form pan. Set aside. Beat eggs; add sugar slowly, then blend in cream cheese. Pour over crust. Bake at 375 degrees until lightly browned on top, about 35 minutes. Cool. Pour pie filling over the top of the cake and refrigerate.

Mrs. Fredric King

Cheesecake with Strawberries and Apricot Glaze

CRUST:
4 Tablespoons butter, softened
½ box Zwieback

FILLING:
4-8 ounce packages cream cheese, softened
4 eggs
1¾ cups sugar
Rind and juice of 1 lemon
Fresh hulled strawberries

APRICOT GLAZE:
1-10 ounce jar apricot jam
¼ cup sugar
¼ cup water
1 Tablespoon rum or fruit brandy

Crust:
Crumble Zwieback into small crumbs; mix with softened butter. Butter a spring form pan. Cover sides and bottom of pan with crumbs. Refrigerate.

Filling:
Have cheese and eggs at room temperature. Mix all ingredients together except strawberries. Beat with an electric mixer until smooth. Pour into prepared spring form pan. Bake in a 325 degree oven for 1 1/2 to 2 hours or until cake is firm. Cool in pan on cake rack.

Glaze:
Combine apricot jam, sugar and water in small saucepan. Stir over low heat until well mixed. Strain through a sieve and discard pulp. Cool, then stir in brandy or rum. Place cooled cake on serving platter and remove side of spring form pan. Cover top with whole, hulled strawberries. Spoon glaze over top and sides of cake. Refrigerate.

Mrs. George Ellis

Chocolate Cheesecake

CRUMB CRUST:
1¼ cups chocolate wafer crumbs,
¼ cup melted butter
2 Tablespoons granulated sugar
¼ teaspoon cinnamon or nutmeg

CHEESE FILLING:
⅓ cup sifted flour
Pinch baking soda
¼ teaspoon salt
2-4 ounce packages German or sweet chocolate
3 large eggs
¾ cup granulated sugar
3-3 ounce packages cream cheese
2 cups heavy whipping cream
1 teaspoon vanilla
1 Tablespoon sifted confectioners' sugar
½ jigger crème de cocoa

Crust: Combine ingredients and press into bottom of greased 9 inch spring form pan.

Filling: Sift together the flour, soda and salt; return to sifter; set aside. In the top of a double boiler, melt chocolate, stirring occasionally. Remove from heat to cool slightly. In a small mixing bowl beat eggs until thickened and lemon colored. Beat in sugar 1 Tablespoon at a time; mixture will be very thick and ivory. Without washing beater, in a large mixing bowl, beat cream cheese until soft and fluffy; add *1-1/4 cups* of unwhipped cream and vanilla; beat until smooth and of whipped cream consistency. Add slightly cooled melted chocolate and beat gently to blend. With a rubber spatula, fold in egg mixture; sift in flour mixture folding it in as you do so. Turn into prepared pan. Bake in preheated 325 degree oven 1 hour and 15 minutes. Cool. Top of cheese cake will crack. Remove sides of pan; cover and chill. Before serving, bring cheesecake to room temperature if you like. Whip the remaining 3/4 cup cream adding powdered sugar and crème de cocoa. Spread whipped cream over cheesecake. Serves 8 to 10.

Mrs. Don Phillips

Simple Bread Pudding
A family dessert

1 stick butter
4 pieces bread, toasted
2 cups milk
3 eggs
1 cup sugar
Cinnamon
Nutmeg

Melt butter in a 6 x 12 inch pyrex dish. Toast bread until brown on both sides. Break into rather large pieces in the pyrex dish. Scald milk and add to eggs beaten with sugar. Add this mixture to toast and butter in dish. Sprinkle generously with cinnamon and nutmeg. Put dish in a pan of boiling water and bake for 35 minutes at 350 degrees. When knife inserted comes out clean, remove from oven.

Mrs. Nell Bennett

Spiced Bread Pudding for 6

3 cups cubed bread or stale cake
½ cup raisins
½ cup chopped nuts, optional
3 Tablespoons butter
¼ teaspoon each: nutmeg, mace, corriander
2 Tablespoons grated lemon peel
5 eggs
4 cups milk
1½ cups sugar
1 teaspoon vanilla
¼ teaspoon almond extract

ORANGE SAUCE:
½ cup sugar
6 Tablespoons cornstarch
2 eggs
2 teaspoons butter
2 cups orange juice
2 teaspoons almond extract
½ cup brandy or sherry
Grated rind of 2 lemons or oranges

Put bread, raisins, and nuts in large rectangular baking dish. Dot with butter. Sprinkle on spices and rind. Mix all thoroughly. Beat eggs till frothy; add milk and sugar with flavorings. Pour over bread mixture. Put in a pan of hot water as for a custard and bake at 300 degrees for about 30 minutes or until firm. Serve warm with Orange Sauce or cream.
Orange Sauce: In the top of a double boiler mix sugar, cornstarch, beaten eggs and butter. Add orange juice. Stir until thickened and fairly clear over hot water. Remove from fire and add flavoring, brandy, and grated rind. Correct seasonings, serve warm. May be prepared ahead. Use an enamel or pyrex pan and stir with a wooden spoon.

Mrs. Burt Sperry

426

Ginger Bread

½ cup butter
½ cup sugar
1 egg
½ cup dark cane syrup
½ teaspoon soda
1½ cups flour
½ teaspoon ginger
1 teaspoon cinnamon
½ cup buttermilk

Cream butter and sugar and add egg. Beat syrup and soda until it foams and add to first mixture. Sift the flour and spices. Add alternately with the buttermilk. Line the bottom of a greased 8 x 8 inch pan with wax paper. Grease paper. Bake at 350 degrees for about 30 minutes or until tester comes clean when removed.

Mrs. H. A. Mangham
Rayville, Louisiana

Lemon Tart

1 stick butter
⅔ cup sugar
6 eggs beaten
1-6 ounce can frozen lemonade
Tart shells, 12 large or 16 small
1 carton heavy cream, whipped

Melt butter in double boiler. Add sugar and remove from stove. Add beaten eggs and can of lemonade. Put back over water and cook until thick. Pour in tart shells, cool, and top with whipped cream.

Mrs. William H. Reed

Lemon Jelly
A delicious tart filling

3 eggs
1 cup sugar
1 heaping Tablespoon cornstarch
Juice of 3 lemons
Rind of 2 lemons
2 Tablespoons butter

Beat eggs and add sugar mixed with cornstarch gradually. Add the lemon juice and rind. More lemon juice can be added if the lemons are small. Cook in the top of a double boiler until very thick, stirring constantly. Add butter and cool. This is a delicious lemon filling for 3 dozen 1 inch tart shells or a 9 inch pie shell. I also use it to frost a yellow cake or fill a jelly roll.

Mrs. J. Y. Abraugh
Rayville, Louisiana

Peach Cheese Tarts

Prebaked tart shells
1-8 ounce package cream cheese
1 can condensed milk
⅓ cup lemon juice
1 teaspoon vanilla
3 to 4 fresh peaches
½ cup apricot preserves
2 Tablespoons sugar
Whipped cream

Whip cheese, add condensed milk. Whip again. Stir in lemon juice and continue beating until thickened. Pour into the tart shells and chill. Slice peaches and place in shells. Melt preserves with sugar. When sugar is dissolved pour glaze over peaches. Top with whipped cream.

Mrs. W. J. Hodge, Jr.

Egg Nog Mousse

2 cups milk
²⁄₃ cup sugar; divided
3 eggs, separated
2 cups heavy cream
4 Tablespoons bourbon
½ pint whipping cream
1 Tablespoon sherry

Combine milk, 1/3 cup sugar, and egg yolks in double boiler. Cook until the mixture coats the back of a spoon. Remove from heat and cool. Beat 3 whites until stiff, but not dry, with remaining 1/3 cup sugar. Beat 2 cups cream and add bourbon. Fold all ingredients together and freeze in refrigerator trays or a 2 quart mold. Serve with whipped cream flavored with sherry. Serves 8. Pretty to fold in candied fruit or cherries during holiday season.

Mrs. L. V. Swift
Marietta, Georgia

Maple Mousse Parfait

8 egg yolks
1½ cups pure maple syrup
½ teaspoon salt
1 quart heavy cream

Beat egg yolks until very light. Bring syrup to a boil and very slowly add to egg yolks and salt. Put in a double boiler or pan of hot water and cook until the thickness of cream. Chill. Beat heavy cream until slightly thick. Slowly pour cold egg and syrup mixture into cream beating until well blended. Pour into cans, such as large juice concentrate type, or 18 parfait glasses and seal tightly with Saran wrap. Freeze. Take out about 5 minutes before serving. Slice or pass parfait glasses. A delicious frozen cream and very rich. Real maple syrup is the secret and should not be substituted unless absolutely necessary. The recipe may be halved, serving 6 to 8 and frozen in an airtight container.

From the files of
Mrs. E. L. Neville

Frozen Mousse Grand Marnier

MOUSSE:
2 egg whites
Salt
6 Tablespoons sugar
1 cup heavy cream
¼ cup Grand Marnier

BERRY SAUCE:
1-10 ounce package frozen
  berries
Grand Marnier

Beat egg whites with a pinch of salt until softly peaked. Gradually add 4 Tablespoons sugar and beat until meringue is stiff and shiny. Whip cream until stiff and add remaining 2 Tablespoons of sugar. Gently blend Grand Marnier into cream and fold in egg whites. Turn into a 1 quart mold or individual molds. Freeze. Serve with Berry Sauce. Serves 4 to 6. Easily doubles or triples.
SAUCE:
Defrost berries just enough to drain excess juice. Pureé in blender. Strain and add Grand Marnier to taste.

Mrs. Ray Harkins
San Antonio, Texas

Frozen Apricot Cream

¾ stick butter
2½ ounce package slivered
  almonds
1½ cups vanilla wafer crumbs
1 quart vanilla ice cream, softened
10 ounce jar apricot preserves

Melt 3/4 stick butter in a 9 x 9 inch pan in a 350 degree oven. Add almonds to melted butter and cook until toasted a golden brown. With a slotted spoon, lift almonds out of butter and drain on paper towels. Add vanilla wafer crumbs to butter in pan and mix until coated. Then press to make crust. Next add a layer of vanilla ice cream, sprinkle half of almonds on top and then put entire jar of preserves over this. Top with another layer of vanilla ice cream. Sprinkle with remaining toasted almonds. Freeze. Serves 6 to 8.

Mrs. Charles Hamaker

Lemon Angel Frost

2 egg whites
½ cup sugar
2 egg yolks
1 teaspoon grated lemon rind
¼ cup fresh lemon juice
1 cup heavy cream, whipped

Beat egg whites until soft peaks form. Gradually add sugar and whip until stiff. Set aside. Beat egg yolks until thick and lemon colored. Fold into egg whites with lemon juice and rind. Fold in whipped cream and freeze. This is also a delicious topping, chilled and served over slices of angel food cake. Makes 1 quart.

Mrs. J. K. Haley
Mt. View, Oklahoma

Creole Cream Cheese

1 small can evaporated milk
2 cartons Creole Cream Cheese,
  not Philadelphia
1 pint buttermilk
1 cup sugar
1 teaspoon vanilla
1 beaten egg white

Chill evaporated milk, then whip. Make sure cream cheese is ripe; that is, if it is very fresh and liquidy when bought, store in the refrigerator for a few days until it solidifies. If it is still too juicy, drain. Ice cream will be icy instead of smooth and creamy if cheese is watery. Mix all ingredients together well and fold in beaten egg white. Put in 2 ice trays and freeze until mushy. Take it out, put in a large bowl and whip it with the electric mixer. Return to freezer and freeze until firm. When firm, cover with wax paper so ice crystals won't form. Makes 2 quarts.

Mrs. J. M. deBen
New Orleans, Louisiana

Hattie's Frozen Cheese Cake

1 cup sugar
1- 8 ounce package cream cheese
3 eggs, separated
1 Tablespoon vanilla
1 pint heavy cream
Graham cracker crumbs

Cream sugar and cream cheese. Add egg yolks and vanilla. Beat well. Whip heavy cream and egg whites separately and fold both into cheese mixture. Sprinkle graham cracker crumbs in large rectangular baking dish. Pour cheese mixture over and sprinkle with graham cracker crumbs. Freeze. To serve, allow about 15 minutes to soften. Serves 10 to 12.

Mrs. E. J. Seymour, Sr.

Chocolate Dessert

1 cup vanilla wafer crumbs
2 squares bitter chocolate
2/3 cup butter
2 cups powdered sugar, sifted
1 cup chopped pecans
1 teaspoon vanilla
2 Tablespoons water
2 stiffly beaten egg whites
1/2 gallon butter pecan ice
  cream

Spread cookie crumbs on bottom of a 13 x 9 inch cake pan. Melt chocolate in butter and cool. Stir in powdered sugar, chopped pecans, vanilla and water. Fold in egg whites. Spread this mixture on top of the cookie crumbs. Freeze for 2 hours. Soften 1/2 gallon butter pecan ice cream and spread on top. Refreeze and cut in squares to serve.

Mrs. Grant C. Boardman

Russian Mint Pies
Very rich, yummy for "just a bite of dessert"

1 cup butter
2 cups sifted powdered sugar
4 squares unsweetened chocolate, melted
4 eggs
1 teaspoon peppermint
2 teaspoons vanilla
18 vanilla wafers
1 cup heavy cream, whipped
Chopped nuts
Maraschino cherries
18 cupcake papers

Cream butter and sugar. Blend in melted chocolate. Add eggs and beat well, then blend in flavorings. Put a vanilla wafer into cupcake papers. Fill with chocolate mixture 3/4 full. Place a dollop of whipped cream on top, sprinkle with nuts and top with half a cherry. Freeze in muffin tins to keep shape. Store in plastic bags after frozen. Serve frozen to 18.

Mrs. Mack Walker

Frozen Fruit Torte

CRUST:
1½ cups vanilla wafer crumbs
¼ cup butter, melted

FILLING:
¼ cup butter
1½ cups powdered sugar, sifted
2 eggs
Fresh fruit
½ pint whipping cream
1 teaspoon sugar
½ cup salted nuts, chopped
½ cup vanilla wafer crumbs

Crust: Mix wafer crumbs and melted butter. Pat on the bottom of a 9 x 9 inch glass dish. Chill 10 minutes. *Filling:* Cream butter and sugar; add eggs one at a time, beating well after each. Spread over crust. Top with fresh fruit. Whip cream with sugar. Spread on top of fruit and sprinkle with nuts and then crumbs. Freeze overnight.

Mrs. Sam Rubin

Joan's Frozen Surprise

½ gallon vanilla ice cream
1 cup chopped pecans
1 cup chopped chocolate chips
4 quarts sherbet, different flavors
1 pint heavy cream, whipped

Soften vanilla ice cream. Stir in nuts and chocolate chips. Spread vanilla mixture 1 inch deep in an angel food cake pan. Closely arrange balls of sherbet, alternating colors on top of vanilla mixture. Continue layering vanilla mixture and sherbet balls ending with vanilla mixture. Freeze solid. Remove from pan onto serving plate. Frost with whipped cream. Return to freezer until solid. Remove about 15 minutes before serving. Slice as a cake. Serves 12.

Mrs. Fredric King

Strawberry Angel Delight

CRUST:
½ cup flour
¼ cup brown sugar
¼ cup butter, softened
⅓ cup chopped pecans

FILLING:
2 Tablespoons lemon juice
1-7 ounce jar Kraft marshmallow creme
1-16 ounce package frozen Strawberries
1 cup heavy cream

Crust: Combine flour and sugar; cut in butter and add nuts. Press into an 8 inch spring form pan. Bake at 350 degrees for 20 minutes. Cool.
Filling: Gradually mix lemon juice with marshmallow creme. Stir in strawberries. Whip cream and fold into strawberry mixture. Pour into crust-lined pan and freeze. Serves 8 to 12.

Mrs. John Ensminger

Bisque Tortoni

1½ cups almond macaroon
   crumbs
3 cups heavy cream
3 egg whites
¾ cup confectioners' sugar
6 Tablespoons good sherry

Crumble macaroons in advance. Dry out overnight. Toast until dry, and crumble finely. Do not use gummy centers if any remain. If any macaroons are left over, they may be frozen. Whip cream with sugar. Beat egg whites separately. Fold together whip cream, egg whites, and sherry. Add macaroon crumbs, reserving 1/4 cup to sprinkle on top. Pour into a loaf pan and smooth evenly. Sprinkle macaroons on top, cover with foil and freeze. When ready to serve, cut in squares. This is a delicious dessert.

Mrs. C. D. Oakley, Sr.

Tortoni

¼ cup almonds, chopped and
   toasted
¼ cup toasted coconut
1 pint vanilla ice cream
¼ cup raisins
1¼ teaspoons rum extract
6 cherries

Mix almonds and coconut. Mash vanilla ice cream a little, just to soften. Add raisins, rum extract and a little more than 1/4 cup of the almond coconut mixture. Spoon into paper or foil muffin cups. These will hold their shape better if they are put in a muffin pan and frozen immediately. Do not let ice cream soften too much. Top with remaining coconut and almonds and a cherry. Serves 6.

Mrs. Dan Sartor

Perfect Refrigerator Ice Cream

CUSTARD:
3 cups milk
⅔ cup sugar
½ teaspoon salt
4 egg yolks

BOILED MIXTURE:
⅔ cup sugar
½ cup water
4 Tablespoons corn syrup
4 egg whites
2 teaspoons vanilla

Custard: Cook milk, salt and sugar over hot water until sugar dissolves. Beat egg yolks. Pour first mixture over yolks, stirring. Return to double boiler. Cook until mixture coats a spoon. Cool, then pour into freezing tray of refrigerator. Freeze to mushy consistency without stirring.
Boiled mixture: Cook sugar, water and corn syrup to 236 degrees or until it spins a thread. Beat egg whites until stiff. Add sugar syrup gradually, beating constantly. Blend in vanilla and cool. Beat partially frozen custard until smooth in mixmaster. Fold in boiled mixture. Put in freezing tray of refrigerator and cover. This will not get icy. Makes about 2 quarts.

Mrs. Thomas M. Keller
Baton Rouge, Louisiana

Caramel Pecan Ice Cream

14 Kraft vanilla caramels
½ cup milk
1 cup small marshmallows
1 cup cream, whipped
½ cup chopped pecans

Melt caramels, milk and marshmallows in top of double boiler. Cool. Fold into whipped cream and add chopped pecans. Mix and freeze in plastic container or ice cube trays. Stir occasionally. Serves 5. May be doubled or tripled.

Mrs. Walter Hastings

Peppermint Ice Cream

2 cups milk
1 pound peppermint candy
1 pint whipping cream

Melt candy in milk. Cool. Whip cream, fold into candy mixture. Freeze in refrigerator freezer. Stir twice. A special dessert served in meringue shells and topped with crushed peppermint. Serves 6.

Mrs. George Ellis

Refrigerator Fruit Sherbet

6 bananas, mashed
2 cups sugar
1 large can apricots, cut up
1- No. 2 can crushed pineapple
3 lemons, juiced
2 small cans frozen orange juice
2 orange juice cans of water

Combine all ingredients well. Pour in refrigerator trays or other container and place in deep freeze until solid. Coconut may be added for a true frozen ambrosia. To serve, fill parfait glasses with sherbet and pour gingerale to fill the glass. Serves 20.

Peggy Strong Folds

Note: A scoop or two served in sherbet glasses with 1 or 2 teaspoons of cognac is a delicious finale.

Fresh Grapefruit Sherbet

Dessert or beautiful to serve on a luncheon plate with fresh fruit and finger sandwiches.

2 cups sugar
1 cup water
2 egg whites
2 Tablespoons sugar
1½ teaspoons grated grapefruit peel
1¾ cup fresh grapefruit juice *
¼ cup fresh lemon juice

Grate and juice grapefruit. Steep peel in boiling water and drain. Set aside. Boil water and sugar until it spins a long thread. Meanwhile in a large mixing bowl beat egg whites to a soft peak and gradually add 2 Tablespoons of sugar, beating until stiff peaks form. Beating continually, add hot syrup in a thick steady stream and beat until thick and glossy. Gradually add rind and juices. Pour into shallow pan and freeze until slushy. Turn into a chilled bowl and beat until very smooth and fluffy. Return to freezer and freeze until solid, stirring through occasionally. Makes 1 ½ quarts.*2 large grapefruit should produce needed amounts.*

Mrs. Don Irby

Holiday Bombe

2 pints pistachio ice cream
2 pints chocolate, or other favorite
  flavor
1/4 cup chopped raisins
1/4 cup chopped mixed candied
  fruit
2 teaspoons rum
1 pint vanilla
1 1/2 cups heavy cream
1/4 cup powdered sugar

Chill a 2-1/2 quart bowl. Soften pistachio ice cream slightly. Line bowl with plastic film or foil and with the back of a large spoon press first layer of bombe over the interior of the bowl. Return to freezer and freeze until firm. Soften second flavor and repeat, pressing ice cream onto pistachio flavor. Return to freezer until firm. Mix raisins, fruit and rum. Let stand about 30 minutes. Soften vanilla ice cream and mix in fruits. Fill center of the bombe with this mixture. Freeze until firm. Whip cream with sugar. Turn bombe out on a sheet of foil. Decorate with whipped cream, freeze. After frozen, wrap well in foil and return to freezer. Let soften 30 minutes in the refrigerator before serving. Cut bombe at the table. Serves 18 to 20. This recipe may be easily halved, using a 1-1/4 quart mold or bowl to serve 10.

Basic Vanilla Ice Cream

8 cups Half and Half
1 1/2 cups sugar
3 Tablespoons vanilla

Stir cream with sugar and vanilla for a few minutes to dissolve the sugar. Pour the mixture into the freezer can and freeze according to freezer directions. *A good rule:* Alternate layers of cracked ice and rock salt in the proportions of 1 cup salt to 6 cups ice. When ice cream is frozen, remove dasher, press the ice cream down and cover the can lightly. Drain off the salt water, return the can to the freezer, and repack it with ice and salt until ready to serve. If you like a richer ice cream you may use 8 cups of heavy cream in place of the Half and Half.

Mrs. Dan Sartor

D' Orr's French Vanilla Ice Cream
For a three quart electric freezer

6 large eggs, beaten
1⅔ cups Pet evaporated milk
1 quart whole milk
3 cups sugar
1 slight pinch salt
3 Tablespoons vanilla or 2
  Tablespoons vanilla and 1
  Tablespoon lemon extract
3 cups whipping cream

Put beaten eggs, both kinds of milk, sugar and salt in a stainless steel or enameled 4 quart pan. Cook until it boils for one minute, stirring constantly with wooden spoon. Pour into freezer can and allow to cool. After cooling add extracts and cream to make 2 1/2 quarts. Freeze in ordinary manner. Remove dasher, place foil over top of can, put lid back on. Pack in ice and salt. Cover with newspaper and let sit for at least an hour. Makes 15 servings. Custard may be made and left overnight in the refrigerator. Cover well so as not to pick up any other odor. Home-made ice creams are better if eaten the same day. When placed in the refrigerator freezer it becomes too hard and loses its texture which is the secret of good home-made ice cream.

Mrs. Ben F. Marshall

Rich Vanilla Ice Cream
Old-fashioned cooked custard

12 whole eggs
4 cups sugar
4 quarts whole milk
1 pint whipping cream
2 Tablespoons flour
Pinch of salt
2 to 3 teaspoons vanilla

Beat eggs until light and fluffy. Beat in sugar. Add milk and cream, reserving some of the liquid to mix with flour. Mix flour with reserved milk forming a smooth paste. Add to the custard mixture along with the salt. Cook over low fire stirring constantly. Continue to cook until it begins to thicken and coats spoon. Remove from fire and add vanilla. Allow to cool, then pour into an electric ice cream freezer. Makes 1 1/2 gallons.

Mrs. James Greenbaum

Brown Sugar Ice Cream

4 whole eggs
1 pound of dark brown sugar
½ cup white sugar
2 Tablespoons cornstarch
1 quart milk, scalded
1 quart of Half and Half or milk
½ pint of whipping cream

Beat eggs and add sugars and cornstarch. Add scalded milk and cook, stirring constantly until it coats the spoon heavily. Let cool and then add the rest of the milk and cream. This fills a 1 gallon freezer.

Mrs. Randy Ewing

Coffee Ice Cream
A superior ice cream

3 cups light cream
3 cups heavy cream
6 egg yolks
1⅓ cups sugar
⅓ cup instant coffee
2 Tablespoons hot water
1 teaspoon vanilla

Scald creams in the top of a large double boiler. Beat egg yolks until light and add sugar gradually, beating continually. Pour the hot cream into the egg mixture and return to the top of the double boiler. Cook over hot water, stirring constantly, until custard coats a spoon. Remove from heat. Dissolve coffee powder in hot water and stir into custard with the vanilla. Chill thoroughly. Freeze in a hand cranked or electric ice cream freezer. Serve in bowls and offer Kahlua or coconut syrup for topping. Makes 2 1/2 quarts. Serves 12.

Mrs. Don Irby

Chocolate Ice Cream

2 ounces chocolate
2 cups milk
1 cup sugar
⅛ teaspoon salt
1½ teaspoons vanilla
1 cup cream, whipped
1 cup Half and Half cream
7 cups milk

In the top of a double boiler over hot water, melt the chocolate in the milk. Stir in sugar and salt. Remove from heat and whip with whisk until cool and fluffy. Add vanilla. Fold in whipped cream and add Half and Half. Put all into a one gallon freezer container and store in the refrigerator overnight to produce a smoother texture. It also enhances the flavor. When ready to freeze, add about 7 cups of milk to fill container 3/4 full. Freeze. Remove dasher after frozen, cover, and repack in ice and salt for a couple of hours to ripen.

Mrs. T. A. Calloway
Bosco, Louisiana

Fudge Almond Ice Cream

2 large packages chocolate
  pudding
1 large can Pet milk
6 eggs, separated
3/4 cup sugar
1-10 1/2 ounce package
  marshmallows
1 package toasted almonds

Cook pudding according to package directions. Stir in Pet milk, beaten egg yolks, sugar and marshmallows. Continue to cook until marshmallows have dissolved. Let cool. Beat egg whites until stiff, add toasted almonds, and fold into chocolate mixture. Freeze in electric ice cream freezer. Makes one gallon.

Mrs. T. B. Godfrey, Jr.

Lotus Cream

1 quart milk
2 Tablespoons sugar
2 lemons, sliced very thin
Juice of 3 lemons
2 cups sugar
Pinch of salt
1 pint whipping cream

Freeze 1 quart milk and 2 Tablespoons sugar until it is a mush in a pan in the refrigerator freezer. Slice lemons very, very thin. Add to juice, remaining sugar, and salt; let stand for 2 hours. Combine partially frozen milk and lemon mixture. Whip cream and add to mixture. Freeze in electric or crank style freezer.

Mrs. Claude Earnest

Peach Ice Cream
Delicious and stays wonderfully creamy in your deep freeze

6 large very ripe peaches
1 cup sugar
4 eggs
3 cups sugar
2 quarts milk
1 quart whipping cream
1 1/2 Tablespoons vanilla

Peel, cut and mash peaches with potato masher. Stir in 1 cup sugar and set aside. Beat eggs in a large bowl; add sugar and mix well. Heat 1 quart of milk to scalding point and add to egg mixture, beating constantly. Pour into the freezer container and blend in the other quart of milk. Beat the whipping cream, not too stiff, and fold into mixture in the container with the peaches and vanilla. Freeze in a large electric freezer. The recipe may be halved if using a 1 gallon freezer. Pretty to serve in meringue shells, garnished with fresh peach slices.

Mrs. T. A. Grant III

Fruit Ice Cream

Juice of 3 oranges
Juice of 3 lemons
3 bananas, chopped
2 pints fresh strawberries
　or two packages frozen
2 cups sugar
2 cups milk
4 eggs, beaten
1/2 pint whipping cream
1 pint Half and Half

Combine all ingredients, slightly crushing strawberries. Mix well and freeze in a gallon ice cream freezer.

Mrs. Al Smith
Overland Park, Kansas

Tangy Apricot Sherbet

Juice of 6 lemons
Juice of 6 oranges or 12 ounce
　can of frozen concentrated
　juice
4 cups water
1 cup sugar
2-16 ounce cans apricot halves
1/2 pint of light cream
1/2 pint whipping cream

Combine juice of lemons and oranges with water and sugar. Put apricots in the blender unless you wish larger pieces in your sherbet. If so, cut in bite sizes. Add to juice mixture. Stir in all cream until well mixed. Freeze in a one gallon ice cream freezer. I double this recipe for my 1 1/2 gallon freezer. This makes a delightful summer dessert for a party. Serve in scalloped orange cups.

Mrs. Doyle Hamilton

Mint Sherbet
Monroe's famous sherbet

6 Tablespoons mint leaves
6 oranges, juiced
2 lemons, juiced
grated rind of 1 lemon
2 cups sugar
2 cups water
green food coloring, optional
1 stiffly beaten egg white
1/2 pint heavy cream

Soak chopped mint leaves in the orange and lemon juices along with the grated lemon rind for at least 30 minutes. Boil the sugar and water for 5 minutes, without stirring. Pour the hot mixture into the fruit juices. When cold, strain. Add a few drops of food coloring, if desired. Add the egg white and cream. Freeze in an electric or hand freezer.

Mrs. R. C. Sparks

Orange-Lemon Sherbet

1 large can frozen orange juice
1 small can frozen lemonade
3 cups sugar
1 pint whipping cream
1 1/2 quarts whole milk

Do not dilute juices. Combine ingredients, freeze and pack. Makes 3 quarts.

Mrs. Jack Davis

Chocolate Fondue
A great "sweet" for your cocktail parties

2 Tablespoons honey or light corn
  syrup
1/2 cup Half and Half
1-9 ounce bar chocolate
1/4 cup finely chopped toasted
  almonds, optional
1 teaspoon vanilla
2 Tablespoons Cointreau

Heat honey and Half and Half over hot water in a double boiler. Add chocolate broken in pieces. Heat stirring until the chocolate is melted and the mixture is smooth. Blend in vanilla and Cointreau, adding almonds if desired. Serve in a fondue pot with very low heat or the chocolate will scorch. Makes 1½ cups of sauce. This is very good with small pieces of cake, apples, bananas, cantaloupe, pineapple, strawberries, oranges, or marshmallows to dip. Easily doubles or triples.

Lemon Fondue
Marvelous for Coffees, "Afternoon Affairs" or just a refreshing dessert

1 cup sugar
1/2 cup cornstarch
1/2 teaspoon salt
4 cups water
2 Tablespoons grated lemon rind
1/2 cup lemon juice
8 Tablespoons butter

Combine sugar, cornstarch and salt in saucepan. Gradually mix in water. Stir over medium heat until mixture thickens and reaches a boil. Boil one minute more. Reduce heat and add remaining ingredients. Stir until well blended. Serve warm in a fondue pot or chafing dish. Spear fresh fruit, gingerbread, or bite size meringues in fondue.

Wallace's Gingerbread Sauce

2 cups sugar
1 cup Carnation milk
1 Tablespoon butter
1 Tablespoon lemon rind

Put sugar and milk in double boiler. Cook until the sugar is dissolved and mixture is well blended and creamy. Add butter and rind. Pour over warm gingerbread while sauce is warm. This will keep several weeks in the refrigerator. Serves 10 to 12.

Mrs. Tom Munholland

Sabayon Sauce

1 egg yolk
2 Tablespoons sugar
4 to 6 Tablespoons brandy or
  sauterne
Grated rind of 1 lemon
Dash of salt
Nutmeg, optional

This is a basic recipe for 1 person. Multiply quantities of yolks and sugar by number of guests. Add brandy and flavoring to your taste. Beat egg yolks and sugar together thoroughly. Place in double boiler over hot, not boiling water. As temperature rises, add brandy or sauterne. Stir constantly until thick and lemon colored. Remove from heat and stir in flavorings. Cool. Serve over any fresh fruit or pound cake. The trick is to beat the egg and wine over warm but not boiling water, or it will curdle.

Mrs. Burt Sperry

Hot Rum Sauce

½ cup butter
1 cup brown sugar
1 teaspoon flour
½ cup boiling water
⅓ to ½ cup rum

Place butter, brown sugar and flour in sauce pan. Blend thoroughly and add boiling water. Cook over low heat until mixture thickens and is clear. Remove from heat. Stir in rum. Serve over ice cream or bread pudding. Serves 8.

Mrs. Tom Peyton

Hot Brandy Sauce

½ pound butter
2 eggs
1 cup dark brown sugar
2 lemons, grated and juiced
½ cup brandy or bourbon

Place all ingredients in upper part of double boiler over boiling water. Beat with rotary beater about 5 minutes or until it thickens. Serve over cake.

Mrs. Bachman Lee

Praline Sundae Sauce

1½ cups light brown sugar
⅔ cup white Karo
4 Tablespoons butter
1 small can evaporated milk

Mix the first three ingredients and heat to boiling point. Remove from stove and cool. When luke warm, add evaporated milk. Blend well. Store in jars in the refrigerator. Delicious on ice cream with pecans sprinkled over the top. Keeps quite a long time. The recipe makes about 1½ cups and may easily be doubled or tripled for little thoughtful gifts.

Mrs. William Mattison

Hot Fudge Sauce for Ice Cream

4 heaping Tablespoons cocoa
¾ cup sugar
½ cup milk, or little more
⅓ stick butter

Mix cocoa and sugar together, stir in the milk and cook over low heat. Blend in butter. Continue to cook until you reach desired consistency. Recipe makes 1 cup and may be doubled or tripled. Store in the refrigerator. This even freezes beautifully.

Mrs. James Greenbaum

Hot Fudge Sauce

1 stick butter
4 squares unsweetened chocolate
　or 12 Tablespoons cocoa
3 cups sugar
½ teaspoon salt
1 large can evaporated milk

Melt butter in top of double boiler; drop in chocolate and stir until melted. Add sugar, a little at a time, stirring well until all sugar has been added. Add salt. Slowly stir in evaporated milk. After all milk has been added, let cook over hot water until all the sugar is completely dissolved, stirring occasionally. This is delicious over hot cake or ice cream. It keeps in the refrigerator for a long time and may be reheated for ice cream.

Mrs. Alton Irwin

Chocolate Almond Sauce

3-1 ounce squares un-
　sweetened chocolate
1¾ cups Half and Half
1 cup sugar
¼ cup flour
¼ teaspoon salt
1 Tablespoon butter
1 teaspoon vanilla
½ cup toasted almonds

Melt chocolate in cream over hot water. Cook until smooth, stirring occasionally. Combine sugar, flour, and salt; add enough of the chocolate mixture to make a smooth paste. Blend into remaining chocolate mixture. Cook until smooth and slightly thick, about 10 minutes. Remove from heat; stir in the remaining ingredients. Serve hot or cold over ice cream. Makes 2¼ cups. Reheats easily.

Mrs. S. O. Henry, Jr.
Columbia, Louisiana

Brownies

2 sticks butter
2 cups sugar
4 squares, unsweetened
   chocolate, melted
4 eggs, separated
1 cup flour
1 teaspoon baking powder
$\frac{1}{8}$ teaspoon salt
1 teaspoon vanilla
1 cup chopped pecans

Cream butter and sugar; add melted chocolate. Add egg yolks, one at a time beating well after each. Add flour, minus one Tablespoon, baking powder and salt. Fold in stiffly beaten egg whites, vanilla and pecans which have been mixed with reserved flour. Pour in a 9 x 13 inch pan which has been greased on the sides only and lined with brown paper. Bake in a 325 degree oven 40 to 45 minutes. When cool, turn out on waxed paper. Sprinkle with powdered sugar and cut into squares.

Mrs. M. S. Dixon

Chewy Brownies

2 squares bitter sweet
  chocolate
2 sticks butter
2 cups sugar
2 eggs
1 cup flour
1 cup chopped nuts
1 teaspoon vanilla

Melt chocolate with butter in a double boiler or on low heat. Remove from heat. Add sugar and beaten eggs. Stir quickly. Fold in flour, vanilla and nuts. Bake at 300 degrees for about 45 to 55 minutes in a greased 9 x 6 inch pan. Do not over cook. Cool 1 hour and cut into squares.

Mrs. Vic Mitchell

Chocolate Peppermint Cookies
Delicious and frosty in the summer,
beautiful for giving during the holiday season.

'COOKIE:
2 squares unsweetened chocolate
1/2 cup butter
2 eggs
1 cup sugar
1/4 teaspoon peppermint extract
1/2 cup flour
Pinch of salt
1/2 cup chopped nuts

FROSTING:
1 cup confectioners' sugar
2 Tablespoons butter
1 Tablespoon evaporated milk
1/2 teaspoon peppermint extract
A drop or two of green food
  coloring

GLAZE:
2 squares unsweetened chocolate
2 Tablespoons butter

Melt chocolate and butter. Add eggs which have been beaten with sugar. Stir in remaining cookie ingredients and bake in a buttered 8 or 9 inch square cake pan at 350 degrees for 15 minutes. Cool. Mix frosting ingredients, spread on cookies and chill. Melt butter and chocolate for glaze. Spread over frosting. Store in the refrigerator in warm weather. This recipe easily doubles.

Mrs. Wesley Shafto, Sr.

Double Frosted Brownies
Brownies for the most elegant of parties -
simply delicious

2 squares unsweetened
  chocolate
1/2 cup butter
2 eggs
1 cup sugar
1/2 cup flour
1/4 teaspoon salt
1 teaspoon vanilla
1/2 cup chopped nuts

FROSTING:
1 1/2 cups sugar
1/2 cup Half and Half
1/3 cup butter
1 teaspoon vanilla
3 squares unsweetened
  chocolate

Melt chocolate with the butter. Beat eggs, add sugar and mix well. Stir into chocolate mixture. Mix flour and salt; blend into the egg and chocolate mixture. Add vanilla and nuts. Spread in a greased 11 x 7 x 1 1/2 inch pan. Bake for 20 to 25 minutes at 350 degrees. While brownies are cooling prepare frosting. Put sugar, cream and butter in a heavy saucepan. Bring to boil and cook to 236 degrees or soft ball stage. Cool. Add vanilla and beat until creamy. Top brownies with frosting. Melt 3 squares of chocolate and spread on frosting. Refrigerate until firm. Cut into small squares.

Mrs. Dan Sartor

Fudge Frosted Brownies

1/2 cup butter
1 cup sugar
2 eggs, at room temperature
2-1 ounce squares unsweetened
  chocolate, melted
1 teaspoon vanilla
1/2 cup flour
1/2 cup pecans

FROSTING:
1 cup confectioners' sugar,
  sifted
1 Tablespoon cocoa
2 Tablespoons cream
1 Tablespoon butter

Cream butter and sugar well. Add two eggs and beat thoroughly. Blend in melted chocolate and vanilla. Stir in flour and nuts. Pour into a greased 8 x 8 x 2 inch pan. Bake in 325 degree oven for 35 minutes. Let cool. Cook frosting ingredients over low heat until mixture boils around the edge of the pan. Beat until it is of spreading consistency. Easily doubles.

Mrs. Arthur Emerson

Heavenly Hash Brownies

2 sticks butter
4 Tablespoons cocoa
4 eggs
2 cups sugar
1 1/2 cups flour
2 cups nuts
Pinch of salt
2 teaspoons vanilla
Large bag of small marshmallows

ICING:
6 Tablespoons butter
3/4 cup Pet milk
6 cups powdered sugar, 1 1/2
  boxes
3/4 cup cocoa

In a saucepan melt butter and add cocoa. Beat the eggs and add sugar. Mix with the butter and cocoa. Add the flour, nuts, salt and vanilla, mixing well. Bake in two greased 8 x 8 inch square pans at 350 degrees for 20 minutes and test for doneness. While brownies are baking, mix all icing ingredients and heat over boiling water. After brownies have baked, remove and immediately cover top with marshmallows. Pour the hot icing over the marshmallows. Cool and cut into squares.

Mrs. James Brown
Ruston, Louisiana

Chocolate Delights

1/2 cup butter
1 egg yolk
2 teaspoons water
1 1/4 cups flour
1 teaspoon sugar
1 teaspoon baking powder
1-12 ounce package of
  chocolate chips

TOPPING:
2 eggs
3/4 cup sugar
6 Tablespoons melted butter
2 teaspoons vanilla
1 cup chopped pecans

Beat butter, egg yolk and water. Sift and stir in flour, sugar and baking powder. Press in a 9 x 13 inch pan; bake 10 minutes at 350 degrees. Sprinkle at once with chocolate chips and return to oven for 1 minute. *TOPPING*: Beat eggs until thick, add sugar and stir in melted butter, vanilla and pecans. Spread on top and bake 30 to 35 minutes at 350 degrees. When cool, cut into small squares.

Mrs. Tommy Godfrey

Chocolate Cookies

1 large package chocolate
   chips
3 Tablespoons sugar
1 can condensed milk
1 stick butter
1 cup chopped nuts, optional
1 teaspoon vanilla
1 cup flour

Melt chips, sugar, condensed milk and butter in a double boiler. Remove from fire. Add nuts, vanilla and flour. Drop by teaspoonsful onto a greased cookie sheet. Bake at 350 degrees for 10 to 15 minutes. Let set on sheets for 2 to 3 minutes. Remove and place on cake racks to cool.

Mrs. W. J. Hodge, Jr.

Fudge Squares

2 cups sugar
1½ sticks butter
3 squares melted bitter
   chocolate
4 eggs, whole
1 cup sifted flour
Pinch of salt
1 Tablespoon vanilla
1 cup chopped pecans
Confectioners' sugar

Butter a long rectangular cake pan. Cream the butter and sugar. Mix in the melted chocolate and eggs. Add the sifted flour and salt gradually. Add the vanilla and pecans. Bake at 325 degrees. Test with a straw. Cut into squares while hot and sprinkle with sifted confectioners' sugar, rubbing it in.

Mrs. Ralph B. King, Sr.

Mocha Cookies

1 cup butter
½ cup sugar
2 cups chopped pecans
1¾ cups flour
2 teaspoons vanilla
2 teaspoons instant coffee
Dash of salt
Confectioners' sugar

Cream butter and granulated sugar. Dredge nuts in flour. Mix all ingredients together except confectioners' sugar. Mixture will be very dry. Make balls 1 inch in diameter. Bake on an ungreased cookie sheet 15 to 20 minutes at 325 degrees. Let cool and roll in confectioners' sugar. Store in jar. Best after kept a few days. Roll again in sugar before serving. Makes 100 cookies.

Mrs. Joe Wheeler

Hello Dollies
Quick, easy and delicious

Graham cracker crust
1 cup chocolate chips
1 cup coconut
1 cup pecans, chopped
1 can condensed milk

Make a graham cracker crust and press into the bottom of a 9 x 9 inch pan. Layer the chocolate chips, coconut and pecans. Pour condensed milk over top of layered ingredients. Bake at 350 degrees for 25 to 30 minutes. Cook and cut in squares.

Mrs. T. B. Godfrey

Swiss Chews

1-6 ounce package chocolate
  bits
1 egg
½ cup brown sugar, firmly
  packed
½ teaspoon salt
1 teaspoon vanilla
½ cup chopped almonds

Melt chocolate over hot water. Let cool for 5 minutes. Beat egg until thick. Beat in sugar until very thick. Fold in melted chocolate and other ingredients. Drop by a teaspoon onto a greased cookie sheet. Bake at 325 degrees for 10 minutes. Makes 2 dozen.

Mrs. Charles Rountree
Oklahoma City, Oklahoma

A Chocolate Chip Kiss

2 egg whites
⅔ cup sugar
1 teaspoon vanilla
Pinch of salt
1 cup broken pecans
1-6 ounce package chocolate
  chips

Preheat oven 350 to 400 degrees. Beat egg whites until stiff. Blend in sugar, add vanilla and salt. Fold in pecans and chocolate chips. Drop on shiny side of foil on a cookie sheet. Put cookies in oven, *turn heat off*, and leave overnight. If too sticky, leave out in air to dry. Snow white and they melt in your mouth.

Mrs. Carrick Inabnett

Cowboy Cookies
A favorite for children, young or old

1 cup butter
1 cup brown sugar
1 cup white sugar
2 eggs
1 teaspoon vanilla
2 cups flour
1 teaspoon soda
½ teaspoon salt
½ teaspoon baking powder
2 cups rolled oats
1 small package semi-sweet
  chocolate chips
½ cup chopped nuts

Cream sugars, butter, eggs, and vanilla until fluffy. Sift dry ingredients and stir in. Add oatmeal, chocolate chips and nuts. Drop by a teaspoonful on a cookie sheet. Bake at 350 degrees for 12 minutes. Makes 8 to 9 dozen.

Mrs. Tom King, Sr.

Chinese New Year Cookies

1-6 ounce package semi-sweet
  chocolate bits
1-6 ounce package butterscotch
  pieces
1-7 ounce can salted peanuts
1-3½ ounce can Chinese
  noodles

Melt chocolate and butterscotch pieces in top of double boiler over hot, not boiling, water. Stir occasionally until smooth. Remove from heat; stir in nuts and noodles. Drop from a teaspoon on a wax paper covered cookie sheet. Do not bake. Easy and fun for children to do on a rainy afternoon. Yield 3 dozen.

Mrs. Jim Geisler

中國新年食并干

Pecan Crisp Cookies

½ cup shortening
½ cup butter
1 box light brown sugar
2 eggs
2½ cups flour
¼ teaspoon salt
½ teaspoon soda
1 teaspoon vanilla
1 cup pecans, finely chopped

Cream shortening and butter thoroughly; gradually add brown sugar and cream well. Add *well beaten* eggs. Reduce speed of mixer and add the flour that has been sifted with salt and soda. Add vanilla. Stir in finely chopped pecans. Drop from the tip of teaspoon onto a greased cookie sheet, two inches apart. Top with pecan halves. Bake at 350 degrees for about 10 minutes. Makes 5 to 6 dozen.

Mrs. Naomi E. Crawford
Winnfield, Louisiana

Sand Tarts

1 cup soft butter
5 Tablespoons sugar
1 Tablespoon vanilla
2¾ cups flour, sifted
½ cup chopped nuts
Pinch of salt

Cream butter and sugar together. Add vanilla, flour, nuts and salt. This will be rather dry, but you just work it with your fingers until blended. Roll into small balls and bake at 350 degrees for 15 to 20 minutes but not too brown. Roll in powdered sugar and cool. You can also press the balls flat and leave a thumb print, if you wish. Fill with jelly after baking.

Mrs. Dan Vanderhoeven

Helen Corbitt's Sand Tarts

½ pound butter
½ cup confectioners' sugar, sifted
2 cups sifted cake flour
1 cup finely chopped pecans
1½ teaspoons vanilla
Sifted confectioners' sugar

Cream butter and sugar. Stir in flour, nuts and vanilla. Mix well. Shape in crescents and bake at 325 degrees for 15 to 20 minutes or until lightly browned. Roll in powdered sugar while still warm.

Ice Box Cookies

1 cup butter
2 cups sugar
½ cup brown sugar, firmly packed
2 eggs
4 cups sifted flour
3 teaspoons baking powder
¼ teaspoon salt
1 Tablespoon vanilla
2 cups finely chopped nuts

Cream butter and sugars. Mix in beaten eggs. Sift flour with baking powder and salt, add to egg mixture. Stir in vanilla and nuts. Make dough into rolls about the diameter of a fifty cent piece. Wrap in wax paper and refrigerate overnight. Slice thinly; bake on cookie sheet at 350 degrees until light brown. Remove from pan and cool. Keep in tightly closed container.

Mrs. T. M. Sayre
Rayville, Louisiana
Mrs. George M. Snellings III

Tea Time Tassies

PASTRY:
2-3 ounce packages cream cheese
1 cup butter
2 cups flour

FILLING:
1½ cups light brown sugar
2 Tablespoons melted butter
2 teaspoons vanilla
Dash of salt
2 eggs, beaten
1⅓ cups chopped nuts

Mix pastry dough with your hands. Roll into a big ball and chill 1 hour. Make into 1 inch balls and press to fit small ungreased muffin tins. *FILLING*: Mix sugar, butter and vanilla. Add salt and beaten eggs. Fold in nuts and pour into uncooked pastry shells. Bake at 350 degrees until done, about 20 to 25 minutes.

Mrs. W. J. Hodge, Jr.

Pecan Puffs

1 egg white
¼ teaspoon salt
¼ teaspoon soda
1 cup light brown sugar
3 cups pecans

Beat egg white until stiff. Add salt, soda and sugar. Mix well. Coat pecans with mixture. Spoon one puff at a time on a slightly greased cookie sheet. Bake in a 300 degree oven for 30 to 40 minutes until brown. Let stand and cool for awhile before removing from cookie sheet. Makes a large amount. These can be frozen, but make sure they are cold before freezing.

Mrs. Ed Brown
Mrs. John C. Theus

Caramel Cookies

2 sticks butter
1 package dark brown sugar
2 eggs
1½ cups sifted flour
2 teaspoons baking powder
2 cups chopped pecans
Dash of salt
2 teaspoons vanilla
Powdered sugar

Mix butter and brown sugar in a double boiler and melt. Cool the mixture and add eggs one at a time *beating well after each*. Add flour and baking powder. Mix well. Stir in pecans, salt and vanilla. Pour into a greased and floured 13 x 9 x 2 inch baking dish. Bake in a 350 degree oven for 25 to 30 minutes. Let cool, dust with powdered sugar and cut into squares.

Mrs. John G. Snelling
Mrs. G. M. Mott

Golden Maple Roll-Ups

½ cup white corn syrup
½ cup brown sugar, packed
½ cup butter
¼ teaspoon maple flavoring
¾ cup instant type flour,
   Wondra
½ cup nuts, chopped fine

Heat oven to 325 degrees. In a medium saucepan, heat corn syrup, brown sugar and butter. Stir in maple flavoring and flour; add nuts. Drop by level teaspoonsful, 4 inches apart, onto a greased cookie sheet. Bake 6 or 7 minutes. Remove from oven; let stand 1 minute. Remove, one at a time from the cookie sheet; quickly roll the cookie around the handle of a wooden spoon. If the cookies get too hard to roll, reheat in the oven a minute or two. Repeat with remaining dough. Cool. Store in a tightly closed cookie tin. These can be made a week in advance. They may also be frozen for up to two months.

Mrs. Dan Sartor

Toffee Treats

1 cup butter
1 cup brown sugar
1 egg yolk
1 teaspoon vanilla
¼ teaspoon salt
2 cups flour, sifted
1-6 ounce package semi-sweet
   chocolate bits, melted
½ cup nuts, chopped fine

Preheat oven to 375 degrees. Cream butter and sugar until fluffy; beat in egg yolk and vanilla. Blend in salt and flour. Pat dough evenly into a greased 10½ x 15½ inch jelly roll pan. Cover with melted chocolate; sprinkle with nuts. Bake for 15 to 20 minutes. Cut while still warm.

Mrs. E. F. Worthen

Best Peanut Butter Cookies

½ cup dark brown sugar
½ cup white sugar
1 stick butter
1 egg
1 cup peanut butter
½ teaspoon salt
½ teaspoon soda
1½ cups sifted flour
½ teaspoon vanilla

Cream sugars and butter. Beat in egg, peanut butter, salt, and soda. Blend in flour. Add vanilla. Roll dough into small balls and place on a greased cookie sheet. Flatten with a fork. Bake 12 to 15 minutes at 350 degrees or until slightly brown on edges. Makes 60 cookies.

Mrs. George Ellis

Crunchy Peanut Butter Cookies

½ cup butter
½ cup crunchy peanut butter
½ cup sugar
½ cup brown sugar
1 egg
1¼ cups flour
¾ teaspoon soda
½ teaspoon baking powder
¼ teaspoon salt
Oatmeal

Cream butter and peanut butter. Add sugars gradually; cream well. Add beaten egg, flour, soda, baking powder and salt. Blend well. Chill dough, then form into balls the size of a nickel. Flatten balls with a fork dipped in flour, making a criss-cross pattern. Bake at 350 degrees for 10 to 12 minutes. Add a handful of oatmeal to dough for crunchy cookies.

Mrs. W. J. Hodge, Jr.

Oatmeal Cookies

2 sticks butter
1 cup brown sugar
1 cup white sugar
2 whole eggs
1½ cups sifted flour
1 teaspoon salt
1 teaspoon baking soda
1 teaspoon vanilla
3 cups oatmeal
1 cup chopped pecans

Cream butter and sugars together. Add eggs and beat until fluffy. Sift together dry ingredients and slowly add to mixture. Add vanilla. Fold in pecans and oatmeal. Drop by a spoonful onto a greased cookie sheet. Bake at 350 degrees for 10 to 15 minutes or until lightly browned. Dough is easier to work with if chilled. The dough may be rolled into small cookie sized balls and frozen on a cookie sheet until firm. These may then be stored in small container in the freezer to cook a few at one time. Makes about four dozen.

Mrs. Don Phillips
Mrs. Dan Vanderhoeven
Bastrop, Louisiana

Butterscotch Drop-Oatmeal Cookies

1 cup shortening, part
  butter adds flavor
¾ cup white sugar
¾ cup brown sugar
1 egg
1 Tablespoon water
2 cups flour
1 teaspoon soda
1 teaspoon salt
1 teaspoon vanilla
1 package butterscotch
  chips
¾ cup nuts, chopped
2 cups oatmeal

Cream together shortening and sugars. Add egg and water. Sift flour, soda and salt. Add to mixture. Stir in vanilla, chips, nuts and oatmeal. Drop by a teaspoon onto an ungreased cookie sheet. Bake at 350 degrees 10 to 12 minutes. Makes 6 or 7 dozen.

Mrs. Bill Wilson

Spicy Oatmeal Cookies
Chewy good — molasses is the secret.

½ cup Crisco shortening
1½ cups sugar
½ cup molasses
2 eggs
1¾ cups flour
1 teaspoon salt
1 teaspoon soda
1 teaspoon cinnamon
2 cups oatmeal
1½ cups raisins
¾ cup chopped nuts

Cream shortening, sugar and molasses. Add eggs. Sift dry ingredients and stir in. Add oatmeal, nuts and raisins. Drop by small spoonsful on a greased cookie sheet. Bake at 350 to 375 degrees for 8 to 10 minutes. Makes about 8 dozen.

Mrs. Don McBride

Fresh Apple Cookies

½ cup Crisco shortening
1½ cups brown sugar,
  firmly packed
½ teaspoon salt
½ teaspoon nutmeg
1 teaspoon cloves
1 teaspoon cinnamon
1 egg
2 cups sifted flour
1 teaspoon soda
1 cup finely chopped
  unpeeled apples
1 cup raisins
1 cup chopped pecans
¼ cup milk

VANILLA SPREAD:
2½ Tablespoons milk
1½ cups sifted
  confectioners' sugar
1 Tablespoon butter
⅛ teaspoon salt
¼ teaspoon vanilla

Cream first seven ingredients. Sift flour and soda; add to mixture. Stir in apples, raisins, pecans and milk. Blend well. Drop from a teaspoon onto a greased cookie sheet. Bake at 400 degrees 12 to 15 minutes. While cookies are baking, heat milk for vanilla spread until steaming. Remove from heat and add all other ingredients. Beat until creamy. Spread on cookies while hot. Makes 5 to 6 dozen.

Mrs. John Stephens
Metarie, Louisiana

Doris Keller's Banberry Tarts

3 sticks butter
1 cup sugar
2 egg yolks
1 teaspoon vanilla
4 cups flour
Jelly of your choice, preferably
  mayhaw

Cream butter and sugar. Mix in egg yolks, flour and vanilla. Roll balls the size of marbles. Indent with your thumb and fill with a dab of jelly. Bake at 350 degrees for 10 to 15 minutes.

Mrs. Tom Keller
Baton Rouge, Louisiana

Cottage Cheese Pockets

½ cup butter
½ cup Crisco
1 cup cottage cheese, drained
2 cups sifted flour
Favorite preserves or pureed fruit

Cream shortening and butter. Add cottage cheese and blend in flour. Roll in waxed paper and refrigerate overnight. Roll as thin as possible. Cut into 2 inch squares. Fill with ½ teaspoon of preserves; fold over and seal edges pressing with a fork. Bake at 350 degrees until lightly browned.

Mrs. R. M. Kobs
Mt. View, Oklahoma

Date Balls

1 pound chopped dates
1 stick butter
2 egg yolks
⅔ cup sugar
1 teaspoon vanilla
2 cups Rice Krispies
1 cup chopped pecans
1 can coconut

Using the chopped sugar rolled packaged dates really makes this quick and easy! Cook dates, butter, yolks, sugar and vanilla in a heavy iron skillet, stirring constantly until the mixture boils. Let boil, stirring, for 5 minutes. Add Rice Krispies and nuts. Shape into bite size balls, then roll in coconut.

Mrs. Charles Brown, Jr.

Lemon Loves

1 cup flour
½ cup butter
2 Tablespoons sugar
1 cup sugar
5 Tablespoons flour
½ teaspoon baking powder
2 eggs
3 Tablespoons lemon juice

FROSTING:
1½ cups sifted powdered sugar
½ stick butter
2 to 3 teaspoons lemon juice

Mix first three ingredients. Press into a 9 x 9 inch pan and bake at 350 degrees for 15 minutes. Sift sugar, flour and baking powder. Beat eggs with lemon juice. Mix with flour and pour in crust. Bake at 350 degrees for 25 minutes. Remove from oven and frost with powdered sugar creamed with butter and enough lemon juice to make a spreading consistency.

Mrs. Charles Hamaker

Coconut Cookies

2 sticks butter
1/2 cup sugar
2 cups flour
1 teaspoon vanilla
1-3 ounce can Baker's
Angel Flake coconut
Confectioners' sugar

Cream butter and sugar thoroughly. Add flour, vanilla and coconut. Roll by hand into small balls. Put on a cookie sheet about an inch apart. Flatten these balls with a fork which has been dipped in cold water. Bake at 350 degrees for 20 to 25 minutes. Cool the cookies and dust with powdered sugar. This makes about 4 dozen. These are very simple to make but very, very good.

Mrs. Bishop Johnston III

Coconut — Corn Flake Cookies

3 egg whites
1 cup sugar
1 cup Angel Flake coconut
1 teaspoon vanilla
1 cup chopped pecans
4 cups corn flakes

Beat whites stiff, adding sugar a little at a time. Add coconut, vanilla, chopped nuts and crushed corn flakes. Drop on greased cookie sheets in small amounts, using fingers to keep from spreading. Bake about 45 minutes in a 200 or 225 degree oven. Take up with spatula while warm. When cold, put in tight tins. They keep well. Makes several dozen cookies.

Mrs. C. Rupert Evans
Lake Providence, Louisiana

Orange Coconut Balls

1 small can frozen orange
juice, undiluted
1 box powdered sugar
1 stick butter
1 large package vanilla wafers
1 large can Angel Flake
coconut

Leave orange juice in refrigerator overnight to thaw. Cream sugar and butter. Crush vanilla wafers fine; add to sugar mixture. Blend in orange juice mixing well. Form into small balls and roll in coconut. Refrigerate. Makes about 100 balls.

Mrs. Dick Taylor
Ruston, Louisiana

Toasted Coconut Balls
Pretty for teas and coffees

1 cup soft butter
1/2 cup powdered sugar
1/4 teaspoon salt
1 teaspoon almond extract
2 cups sifted flour
1 beaten egg white
Baker's Toasted Coconut
Crunchies, 41/2 ounce size

Mix butter with sugar until creamy. Add salt, almond extract and flour. Mix well. Refrigerate until easy to handle. Form into tiny balls, less than 1 inch in diameter. Dip in beaten egg white and then in toasted coconut. Place on ungreased baking sheet. Bake about 12 minutes or until light brown on the bottom. Makes 4 to 5 dozen.
Variation: Use two teaspoons vanilla extract instead of almond extract. Dip unbaked balls in finely chopped pecans instead of coconut.

Mrs. Leonard Bunch

Lizzies
Great for that "just a bite of fruitcake"

8 ounces golden raisins
8 ounces currants or dark raisins
1 pound diced candied fruit
and peel
8 ounces candied lemon peel
8 ounces candied cherries
4 cups chopped nuts
1 cup brown sugar
1 stick butter
4 beaten eggs
3 cups flour
3 teaspoons soda
1 teaspoon allspice
1 teaspoon cinnamon
1 teaspoon nutmeg
3 Tablespoons milk
1 cup bourbon

Have fruits and nuts chopped. Soak raisins in hot water to plump; drain. Cream sugar and butter. Add well beaten eggs. Sift flour, soda and spices. Add alternately with mixture of bourbon and milk. Add fruit and nuts to batter mixing well to coat all. These are darling baked in tiny muffin tins with paper liners or drop by teaspoonsful onto lightly greased cookie sheets. Bake 15 to 20 minutes in a 275 degree oven. If baked in paper liners decorate tops with a small dollop of hard sauce.

Mrs. Don Irby

Snickerdoodles

1 stick butter
1 stick oleo
1½ cups sugar
2 eggs, beaten well
2¾ cups sifted flour
2 teaspoons cream of tartar
1 teaspoon soda
1 teaspoon salt
2 Tablespoons sugar
2 Tablespoons cinnamon

Cream butter, oleo and sugar. Add eggs and beat well. Sift all dry ingredients except cinnamon and sugar; add to egg mixture. Mix thoroughly and put in the refrigerator overnight. Roll into balls the size of a walnut; roll in cinnamon and sugar mixture. Bake on a greased cookie sheet at 375 degrees for 8 to 10 minutes. Let stand a minute before removing from cookie sheet. Makes 5 to 6 dozen.

Mrs. J. Y. Abraugh
Rayville, Louisiana

Mincemeat Fudge Bars

1 stick butter
1½ squares unsweetened
chocolate
2 eggs
1 cup sugar
½ cup prepared mincemeat
1 teaspoon vanilla
¾ cup flour
¼ teaspoon salt
½ cup pecans, chopped

Melt butter and chocolate in the top of a double boiler. In mixer bowl, beat eggs and add sugar. Add mincemeat and vanilla. Blend in flour, salt and nuts. Add chocolate mixture. Bake in an 8 x 10 inch pan at 350 degrees for 30 minutes. Cool. Cut into bars. Roll in powdered sugar.

Mrs. Charles Hamaker

Almond Macaroons

1-8 ounce can Reese
almond paste
¾ cup sugar
Pinch of salt
3 egg whites, unbeaten
½ teaspoon almond extract

Beat paste to soften; add other ingredients alternately. Line cookie sheets with brown paper and force small amounts of dough through a pastry tube or drop from a teaspoon two inches apart. Smooth tops with pastry brush moistened with water. Bake at 400 degrees for 15 to 20 minutes until golden and puffed. Store in an airtight tin.

Scotch Shortbread

1 pound butter
6 cups flour
1½ cups sugar
½ cup cornstarch

Have butter at room temperature. Place in a large mixing bowl and sift in the dry ingredients. Take hands and mix up the dough. Work it until nothing sticks to the bowl. Pat out in pie tins about ½ inch thick. Prick with fork to make a pattern of small wedges. Bake at 350 degrees until the edges start to brown. Never cut with a knife, just break on pricked lines. Use as a dessert or London tea time. Red cake decorator beads may be sprinkled on top if desired.

Mrs. Oliver Vreeland

Butter Crisp Cookies

⅓ cup butter
¼ cup sugar
1 egg yolk
¼ teaspoon almond extract
Dash of salt
1 cup minus 2 Tablespoons
    sifted enriched flour

Cream butter and sugar. Add egg yolk, almond extract and salt. Beat well. Gradually add flour to creamed mixture, mixing to a smooth dough. *Don't chill.* Force dough through cookie press onto ungreased baking sheet. Bake in a moderate oven, 375 degrees, about 8 to 10 minutes or until golden brown. Makes about 3 dozen tea size cookies.

Mrs. Dan Sartor

Orange Spritz Cookies
The secret: a cold cookie sheet

2½ cups sifted flour
¼ teaspoon salt
¼ teaspoon soda
1 cup Crisco
½ cup sugar
½ cup brown sugar, packed
1 to 2 teaspoons grated
    orange rind
2 Tablespoons orange juice
1 teaspoon vanilla
1 medium egg, unbeaten

FROSTING:
¾ cup confectioners' sugar,
    sifted
½ teaspoon vanilla
3 to 4 teaspoons orange juice
1 teaspoon finely grated orange
    rind

Sift flour, salt and soda. Mix shortening with sugars, rind, juice, vanilla and egg. Beat until very light and fluffy. Gradually add flour mixture, mixing well after each addition. Refrigerate dough for 30 minutes. Fill cookie press and press onto ungreased cold cookie sheet. Bake at 400 degrees for 10 to 12 minutes or until lightly browned. *FROSTING:* Mix all ingredients well until smooth and of frosting consistency, adding a few more drops of juice if needed. Spoon on cookies. Makes about 6 to 7 dozen.

Miss Harriet Swift
Marietta, Georgia

Madelines
A very delicate cookie dropped into special shell-shaped molds. A favorite of all!

4 eggs
1½ cups sugar
1 heaping teaspoon finely
    grated lemon rind or more
1 teaspoon vanilla
2 cups flour, sifted
1½ cups clarified sweet cream
    butter

Melt 4 sticks of butter over low heat and continue until foam disappears from the top and a light brown sediment is on the bottom of the pan. Pour off the clear butter, measure 1½ cups and let cool. Any remaining may be stored indefinitely in the refrigerator. *Have eggs at room temperature.* Mix eggs, sugar, and lemon rind in a large bowl. Place the bowl over a wide mouth pot containing 1 to 2 inches water, but not touching the bowl. Place over low heat. Do not let boil. When egg mixture feels slightly warm to your finger, remove and start beating at high speed until they are light, fluffy, and tripled in bulk; they will look like whipped cream. Add vanilla. Carefully fold in flour followed by melted cooled butter. Fill well buttered Madeline molds about ⅔ full. Bake about 10 minutes at 425 degrees or until golden. Rebutter molds before each use. Dust with powdered sugar. These will melt in your mouth.

Note: To produce the best Madeline, directions must be followed. Don't cheat! It does make a difference.

Mrs. Don Irby

457

Frozen Candied Fruit Cookies
A good holiday cookie

1 cup butter
1 cup sifted confectioners'
 sugar
1 egg
2½ cups flour
¼ teaspoon cream of tartar
1 cup of candied cherries or
 any kind of candied fruit
 desired
½ cup candied fruit or
 citron, chopped
½ cup chopped pecans

Cream butter and sugar well; beat in the egg. Stir in the dry ingredients. Blend in pecans, fruit and cherries. Form in rolls 1½ inches in diameter. Wrap in plastic wrap and *freeze*. Thinly slice cookies and bake in preheated 375 degree oven on a greased cookie sheet 6 to 8 minutes. These cookies will not slice unless they are frozen. Marvelous for using fruit left from your fruit cake baking. Makes about 10 dozen.

Mrs. Clark Boyce

Holiday Sugar Cookies

2½ cups flour
1½ teaspoons baking powder
Pinch of salt
1 cup butter
1¼ cups sugar
2 eggs
1 teaspoon vanilla

Sift flour, baking powder and salt. Cream butter and sugar well. Blend in eggs and vanilla. Add sifted dry ingredients. Chill in the refrigerator at least 4 hours. Work with cool dough. Roll out thin on a floured board. Bake at 400 degrees for 5 or 6 minutes until lightly brown around edges. This dough is very short and must be rolled gently so it will not stick. Makes about 5 dozen.

Mrs. Clarence Roberts

Sugar Cookies

1 cup butter
2 cups sugar
2 eggs
2 teaspoons vanilla
4 cups sifted flour
2 teaspoons baking powder
½ teaspoon salt

Cream butter and sugar. Add eggs, mixing well. Add vanilla. Mix in flour, sifted with salt and baking powder, kneading toward the last if necessary. Refrigerate one hour. Roll out a little over ¼ inch thick. Bake at 375 degrees until lightly browned. Try dusting your board with a combination of flour and sugar. It prevents sticking and you won't work in additional flour which hardens and toughens cookies. Makes about 3 dozen.

Mrs. Dan Sartor

Gingerbread Men, Rabbits and Clowns

½ cup butter
½ cup sugar
½ cup molasses
¼ cup water
2½ cups sifted flour
¾ teaspoon salt
¼ teaspoon nutmeg
½ teaspoon soda
¾ teaspoon ginger
⅛ teaspoon allspice

FROSTING:
1 small package jiffy frosting
1 Tablespoon butter
1½ cups confectioners' sugar
Food coloring

Cream sugar and butter. Blend in the remaining ingredients. Cover and chill 2 to 3 hours before rolling out on a lightly floured board. Roll ¼ inch thick and cut in desired shapes. Cook 10 to 12 minutes at 375 degrees. Remove at once and cool. Keep in a tightly closed tin. FROSTING: Prepare one small package jiffy frosting. Blend in butter and sugar. More hot water may be added to thin. Add food coloring. Makes 15 to 18.

Mrs. Carrick Inabnett

Viennese Marzipan Stars
Just as the name implies, heavenly! Do try these!

COOKIE:
⅓ cup sweet butter
¼ cup canned Reese almond
   paste
⅓ cup sugar
1 egg yolk
1 cup flour, sifted
¼ teaspoon almond extract

MARZIPAN:
1-8 ounce can almond paste
½ stick butter
2 Tablespoons light corn
   syrup
¼ teaspoon almond extract
2¼ cups confectioners'
   sugar

GLAZE:
6 squares semi-sweet chocolate
½ stick butter
½ cup Half and Half
1 cup sifted confectioners'
   sugar

Cream butter and almond paste in mix master beating until smooth. Stir in sugar and egg yolk. Mix in flour and almond extract; chill. Roll ¼ inch thick and cut with star cookie cutter. Bake at 350 degrees for 10 minutes on a buttered cookie sheet. Let cookies cool. While dough is chilling, make the marzipan by beating almond paste and butter until creamy. Add corn syrup and extract. Gradually work in 2¼ cups confectioners' sugar and beat until smooth. Knead lightly on board a few minutes. If very sticky, add a little more sugar. Store in refrigerator until ready to use. After cookies are baked and cooled, roll out 1 cup marzipan between 2 sheets of waxed paper. Using the *same cutter*, cut marzipan stars and press on cookies. In the top of a double boiler over hot water, melt chocolate with butter. Add cream and stir until mixture is well blended. Remove from heat and add sifted sugar. Let the mixture cool until slightly thickened and pour over cookies on a wire rack. Chill cookies and store in refrigerator in sealed container.

*Really worth every bit of the effort; make hearts for Valentines and decorated ovals at Easter. Makes about 30 cookies.

Mrs. Don Irby

Dutch St. Nicholas Cookies

1 cup dark brown sugar
3 Tablespoons milk
3 cups sifted flour
1½ teaspoons cloves
1½ teaspoons cinnamon
¾ teaspoon ginger
¾ teaspoon nutmeg
⅛ teaspoon baking powder
⅛ teaspoon salt
1¼ cups butter
¼ cup slivered almonds

In small bowl, combine sugar and milk. Stir until smooth. Into a large bowl sift flour with spices, baking powder and salt. Cut in butter until mixture is like corn meal. Add sugar mixture and almonds. Mix well. Wrap in foil and refrigerate until needed. If using wooden molds, thoroughly dust with flour and press enough dough in to fill completely. Trim around edge. Invert lightly greased cookie sheet over mold and turn both together until mold is on top. Tap lightly until dough slips onto cookie sheet. Bake 20 to 30 minutes at 350 degrees or until light brown. *Note*: These cookies may also be rolled out on a lightly floured surface and cut with cookie cutters.

Gretchen's Springerle

4 eggs, separated
1 pound, 3¼ cups, confectioners' sugar
1 teaspoon baking powder
¼ teaspoon salt
Flour to make a stiff dough, have 4 cups on hand
1 or 2 teaspoons anise seeds, or to taste
Grated rind of 1 lemon

Beat yolks at high speed until light and fluffy. Gradually sift in one cup sugar, mixing continuously at medium speed. Beat whites until stiff; sift in another cup of sugar, beating gently. Pour yolk mixture into whites; beat at low speed, sifting in the rest of the sugar. Beat until bubbles begin to rise. Sift baking powder and salt with one cup flour. Add with anise seed and lemon rind, beating at low speed. Add enough of remaining flour to make stiff dough. Cover and chill several hours. Roll out ¼ inch thick. Cut out or press with springerle board and cut around pictures. Bake at 300 degrees for 30 to 40 minutes. When cool, remove from baking sheet. These cookies will be almost white, just delicately colored. If you like a softer cookie, make these a couple of weeks in advance. My family prefers them when fresh at which time they are HARD and very crunchy. Keeps for weeks in a tin. We usually cut them in Christmas shapes for a traditional Christmas cookie. Makes 4 dozen cookies.

Mrs. Ed Long

Speculaas

3 cups sifted flour
4 teaspoons baking powder
1 Tablespoon cinnamon
1 teaspoon cloves
1 teaspoon nutmeg
½ teaspoon ground anise seed
½ teaspoon salt
½ teaspoon ginger
2 sticks butter
1½ cups packed brown sugar
3 Tablespoons milk or brandy
2 to 3 packages blanched slivered almonds
2 beaten egg whites

Sift all dry ingredients. Cream butter and sugar; add milk or brandy, the brandy is delicious. Stir and work into the flour mixture. Form the dough in a ball and knead lightly on a slightly floured board. Roll out dough ¼ inch thick. Cut dough in 2½ inch rectangles with a sharp knife. Mix almonds and egg whites together and spread over rectangles. Place on a cookie tin. Bake at 375 degrees, 12 to 15 minutes. A real Dutch treat for the holidays. These may also be cut in shapes and decorated. More anise seed may be added if more flavor is desired.

Mrs. Don Irby

NOTES

Fairis Youngblood's Divinity

4 cups sugar
1 cup white Karo
1 cup water
1/8 teaspoon salt
4 egg whites
1/2 stick butter
1 teaspoon vanilla
2 cups pecans

In a heavy boiler put sugar, Karo, water and salt.
Cook to the hard ball stage using a candy thermometer. Turn fire off and let sit while you beat the egg
whites very stiff and dry. Beat with mixer at medium
speed while pouring the hot syrup into the egg whites.
Mixture must be poured slowly in a very fine stream.
Continue beating and add the soft butter and vanilla.
Beat until the candy will hold its shape and then add
the chopped cold or frozen pecans. Spoon a little out
on wax paper to see if it will hold its shape. If it
does not, continue to beat by hand until it will drop
by spoonsful onto wax paper.

Mrs. Thomas Youngblood

Chocolate Candy

3 packages German's chocolate
1 pound marshmallows
1 Tablespoon cream
3 cups lightly toasted pecans,
    lightly salted

Melt chocolate and marshmallows in a double boiler. Add cream and stir well. Add pecans and drop by teaspoonsful on waxed paper.

Mrs. John Carroll

Fudge

2½ cups sugar
⅔ cup cocoa
1 small can evaporated milk
¼ cup water
¼ cup Karo
1 stick butter
2 teaspoons vanilla
1 cup chopped nuts

Place sugar, cocoa, milk, water and Karo in heavy saucepan. Stir over low heat until sugar and cocoa are dissolved. Remove spoon. Cook slowly until soft ball stage or 234 degrees. Remove from heat; add vanilla, butter and nuts. Have sink partially full of cold water, place pan in water and beat more or less until the fudge begins to lose its glossy sheen. Pour into a well-buttered 9 inch square pan.

Mrs. Lionel V. Swift
Marietta, Georgia

Five Pound Fudge

4½ cups sugar
1 stick butter
1 tall can evaporated milk
Pinch of salt
Bottle Hipolite marshmallow
18 ounce semi-sweet chocolate
    chips
4 cups chopped pecans

Place sugar, butter, milk and salt in heavy aluminum pan. Stir well and bring to a boil. Stir constantly, as it scorches easily, on lowest heat to maintain boil for 8 minutes by the clock. Immediately pour marshmallow, chocolate chips and pecans, which you have already mixed together, into the cooked mixture. Mix well and set out by Tablespoonsful on wax paper. There is so much fudge that it is well to have two people for this part of the operation as it cools quickly. You may pour into large pans and cut when cool. Freezes beautifully. Note: Set Hipolite in warm water for easy removal.

Mrs. Fred Polen

Heavenly Hash

30 large marshmallows, cut up
2 small packages chocolate chips
1 cup nuts
1 can condensed milk

Cut up marshmallows and place in a buttered pan. Melt chocolate chips over hot water. Remove from heat and add condensed milk and nuts. Pour over marshmallows. Let set several hours or over night before cutting.

Mrs. Dan Sartor

Date Loaf

2 cups sugar
1 cup milk
1 pound pitted dates, cut in
    pieces
4 Tablespoons butter
2 cups chopped pecans

Cook sugar and milk to soft ball stage. Add dates and cook to hard ball stage. Remove from fire and add butter and nuts; beat until it cools. Pour onto a wet cloth and shape into a loaf. When cold, slice. If date loaf is sticky after slicing you can roll in powdered sugar.

Mrs. J. E. Brown
Lake Providence, Louisiana

Yam Candy

2 cups sugar
1/2 cup evaporated milk
1 cup pecans
1/2 cup cooked yams, mashed
1/2 stick butter
1/2 teaspoon vanilla

Bring sugar and milk to a boil, takes 2 to 3 minutes. Add pecans and yams. Cook until it starts to sugar. Remove from fire and add butter and vanilla. Cover and let cool. Beat and pour in buttered dish or pan.

Aunt Bill's Brown Candy

3 pints white sugar
1 pint light cream
1/4 teaspoon soda
1/4 pound butter
1 Tablespoon vanilla
3 to 4 cups nuts

Melt 1 pint sugar in heavy skillet stirring constantly with wooden spoon, 1/2 hour or until light brown in color. Pour remaining 2 pints of sugar together with light cream into a deep heavy kettle and set it over a low fire to cook. When sugar in skillet is melted, begin pouring it into the kettle of boiling cream and sugar keeping it at a very low heat and stirring across the bottom of the kettle all the time. Continue cooking and stirring until mixture forms a firm ball when dropped in cool water. Remove from heat and add soda; stir vigorously. Add butter and beat in with vanilla and nuts. Let set 20 minutes. Pour into a buttered pan and cool. Cut in squares.

Mrs. Ray Harkins
San Antonio, Texas

Divinity

2 cups sugar
½ cup hot water
½ cup light corn syrup
¼ teaspoon salt
2 stiffly beaten egg whites
1 teaspoon vanilla
Chopped pecans, optional
Candied cherries, quartered

Combine sugar, water, corn syrup, and salt in saucepan. Cook stirring until sugar is dissolved. Cook uncovered, without stirring until mixture reaches soft ball, 238 degrees. Meanwhile in a large bowl of electric mixer, at high speed, beat egg whites until stiff peaks form. In a thin stream, pour half of hot syrup over egg whites, beating constantly, at high speed, until stiff peaks form when beater is raised. Continue cooking the rest of the syrup to 256 degrees or a hard ball forms in cold water. In a thin stream, pour hot syrup into meringue, beating constantly with a wooden spoon. Beat in vanilla and nuts, if used. Continue beating until mixture is stiff enough to hold shape. Drop by a heaping Tablespoon onto waxed paper, lifting and twirling spoon to form a peak. If divinity becomes too stiff, add a few drops of hot water to bring back to desired consistency. While peaks are still moist, decorate with candied cherries. Makes 1½ dozen.

Mrs. Charles Wilkins

Peanut Butter Balls

4 sticks butter
2 boxes powdered sugar
1 quart crunchy peanut butter
1 cup ground pecans
2½ -6 ounce packages
    semi-sweet chocolate drops
1 block parafin

Mix first four ingredients and roll into balls 1 inch in diameter. Chill until firm. Melt chocolate drops and parafin in double boiler. Leave over hot water while dipping balls. Insert a tooth pick into a ball and dip into chocolate. Drain on waxed paper. Makes 150 balls. A sure hit with the children!

Mrs. Jennings Wilkins

Peanut Butter Candy

2 cups white sugar
1 cup brown sugar
1 cup hot water
½ cup white Karo syrup
2 egg whites
¼ teaspoon salt
½ teaspoon vanilla
Peanut butter

Cook sugars, water and Karo until it spins a thread. Pour over egg whites that have been well beaten with a pinch of salt. Beat until stiff enough to roll out like dough. Roll on a board floured with powdered sugar. Spread with peanut butter and roll up like a jelly roll. Chill and cut crosswise in small pieces.

Mrs. Ralph King, Jr.

Peanut Brittle I

1 cup sugar
⅔ cup white Karo
½ cup water
1 cup shelled raw peanuts
1 teaspoon soda
1 teaspoon vanilla
1 teaspoon butter

Cook sugar, Karo, and water until it reaches hard crack stage. Mixture will crack or pop when dropped in cold water. Add peanuts, stirring constantly; cook until syrup is golden in color and peanuts are done. Remove from stove; add soda, vanilla, and butter. Stir slightly and pour into buttered pan.

Mrs. Dave Aron

Peanut Brittle II

2 cups sugar
1 cup white Karo
½ cup water
2 Tablespoons butter
2 cups raw peanuts
1 teaspoon vanilla
1 teaspoon soda

Cook sugar, Karo and water in big kettle until it reaches crack stage, 275 degrees on a candy thermometer. Add peanuts, stirring until syrup turns light brown in color. Remove from fire and add vanilla, soda and butter. Stir until butter melts. Pour out in small portions on greased foil. Pull from outer edges and stretch brittle while cooling.

Mrs. Jennings Wilkins

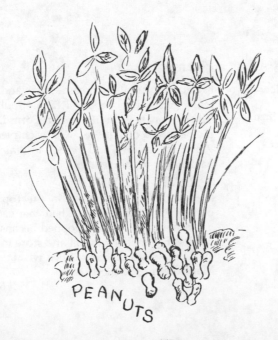

PEANUTS

Penuche

The art of candy making was a well kept secret of days gone by. This is a recipe from one of Monroe's former leading hostesses, Polly Barringer. She compiled her recipes in a book considered to be over 100 years old. This is a recipe for Penuche with a few modern suggestions given in the method.

2 cups sugar
1 cup light cream
2 Tablespoons butter
1 cup sugar
2 Tablespoons butter
2 cups nuts

Boil sugar, cream and butter until thick; soft ball stage. Cook 1 cup of sugar and butter until caramel. Stir caramel into first mixture. Beat, adding chopped nuts, and continue beating until waxy and pour onto buttered slab to harden.

From the files of Polly Barringer

Mexican Pecan Candy

1 cup milk
2 cups sugar
3 Tablespoons white Karo
2 cups pecan halves
2 Tablespoons butter
1/2 teaspoon vanilla

Mix milk, sugar, Karo, pecans, and boil to 240 degrees on a candy thermometer. Remove from fire, cool to lukewarm, and add butter and vanilla. Beat lightly until mixture begins to thicken. Drop by spoonsful onto wax paper. You must work fast taking it up so it will look smooth. These are pralines in appearance, and are often called Mexican pralines.

Mrs. Bill Hardy

Pecan Logs

1-7 1/2 ounce jar marshmallow creme
1 pound powdered sugar, sifted
1 teaspoon vanilla
1/4 teaspoon almond extract
CARAMEL COATING:
1 pound Kraft caramels
2 Tablespoons hot water
6 cups chopped pecans

Knead marshmallow cream, sugar and flavorings. It really gets hard, but it will take up all of the sugar. The harder they get, the better. Form into a ball and divide into 6 or 7 pieces. Roll each piece until about 7 or 8 inches long and 3/4 inch in diameter. Put in a pan and set in the freezer.

CARAMEL COATING:
Melt caramels and water in the top of a double boiler. Stir until smooth. Then coat each of the rolls in caramel and roll in chopped pecans. Let set until hard. Wrap each log in foil and store in tin container. Will keep several weeks. Slice when ready to serve. Makes about 150 slices.

Mrs. Dave Aron

Pralines

3 cups sugar
1 cup water
1 teaspoon vinegar
3 cups pecans
1 Tablespoon butter

Combine sugar, water and vinegar and cook to soft ball stage, 236 degrees, on a candy thermometer. Add nuts and butter and remove from heat. Beat until mixture begins to thicken and drop from a teaspoon onto waxed paper. Cool. Makes 3 dozen pralines.

Mrs. Charles Wilkins

Creamy Pralines

2 cups sugar
1 small can Pet milk
1/2 cup white Karo
1/4 teaspoon baking soda
1/2 stick butter
1 teaspoon vanilla
2 cups pecans

Mix first four ingredients and cook in double boiler. Stir frequently and test in cold water for soft ball. Remove from fire at this point and add butter and vanilla and beat with spoon until shine has gone and it is cool. Add 2 cups pecans and drop on wax paper.

Mrs. W. J. Hodge, Jr.

Creole Pralines

2 cups granulated sugar
1 cup brown sugar
1 stick butter
1 cup milk
2 Tablespoons Karo
4 cups pecan halves

Put all ingredients except pecans in a 3 quart saucepan and cook for about 20 minutes after boiling starts, stirring occasionally. Add the pecans and cook the mixture until the liquid forms a soft ball when a little is dropped into cold water. Stir well and then drop by spoonsful on waxed paper. Place a few sheets of newspaper beneath the waxed paper.

Senator Allen Ellender

Sweet Maupin's Episcopalian Candy

1 pound dark brown sugar
1 cup water
½ stick of butter
2 cups of pecan halves,
   broken .
Pinch of salt

Boil sugar and water until a soft ball forms when tested in ice water. Add butter and remove from heat. Stir in 2 cups of pecans and a pinch of salt. Beat until a bit dropped on a buttered plate or wax paper does not run. Drop from a teaspoon. Note: Never substitute margarine for butter.

Caramel Candy

1 pint whipping cream
1¾ cups light corn syrup
2 cups sugar
¾ cup butter
1 cup nuts
½ teaspoon vanilla

Mix cream, syrup, sugar and butter in a heavy saucepan. Cook until 246 to 248 degrees on a candy thermometer. Remove from heat and beat in vanilla. Pour over chopped nuts that have been put in a 9 x 9 inch square. Cool and cut into squares; wrap individually in small pieces of wax paper. Before wrapping, caramels may be rolled in additional finely chopped nuts.

Mrs. Dan Sartor

Crazy Crunch

2 quarts popped corn
1½ cups pecans
⅔ cup almonds
1⅓ cups sugar
1 cup butter
½ cup Karo light syrup
1 teaspoon vanilla

Pop corn and mix with nuts on cookie sheets. Combine sugar, butter and Karo in a 1½ quart saucepan. Bring to boil over medium heat, stirring until sugar is dissolved. Continue cooking and stir occasionally for 10 to 15 minutes or until mixture turns light caramel color. Remove from heat and stir in vanilla. Pour over corn and nut mixture and mix rapidly.

Mrs. Sol Johnston
San Antonio, Texas

Pop Corn Balls

1 cup sugar
⅓ cup white corn syrup
⅓ cup water
¼ cup butter
½ teaspoon salt
1 teaspoon vinegar
1 teaspoon vanilla
3 quarts popped corn

Combine sugar, syrup, water, butter, vinegar, and salt. Cook, stirring until sugar is dissolved. Continue cooking without stirring until syrup reaches 270 degrees or forms a brittle ball when dropped in cold water. Add vanilla. Pour syrup over popped corn, stirring until all kernels are covered. Grease hands and shape into balls. Makes 12. Do not double recipe. It is best to make several small batches.

Mrs. Dan Sartor

Red Candy Apples

3 cups sugar
½ cup light corn syrup
½ cup water
1 teaspoon cinnamon extract
1 teaspoon red food coloring
8 apples

Cook sugar, corn syrup, and water until it reaches 285 degrees on a candy thermometer. Remove from fire, add cinnamon, food coloring and stir until color is blended. Insert wooden sticks into the top of the apples and dip into mixture. Drain apples on buttered pan, wax paper or foil.

Mrs. Jennings Wilkins

Tea Strawberries

1 small package strawberry jello
½ can Eagle Brand milk
½ pound coconut
Red food coloring

Mix together above ingredients. Reserve a small amount of the jello powder. Let mixture stand in refrigerator for two days. Shape into strawberries and roll in the reserved jello powder. Use a touch of green icing for stems. Suggestions: May use cloves for stem and make red apples, or use orange jello for oranges or pumpkins.

Mrs. Buck Stewart

NOTES

INDEX

489

The watercolor prints which separate the sections of this book are by a local artist, Mrs. Lucy Sartor, and depict the by-gone days of the cotton country.

Sets of these 8 prints are avaiable for $3.00 per set. They are suitable for framing and make lovely gifts.

Send your check to:
COTTON BAYOU PUBLICATIONS:
P. O. Box 7138
Monroe, Louisiana 71211-7138

If you love the
Cotton Country
collection, then . . .

It's time
to Celebrate

Invitations to Dine in Cotton Country Style

The Junior League of Monroe, Inc.
THANKS YOU FOR BUYING
THE COTTON COUNTRY COLLECTION
and
CELEBRATIONS ON THE BAYOU

Cotton/Bayou Publications
P. O. Box 7138
Monroe, Louisiana 71211-7138
1-800-256-4888
FAX # 1-318-325-1814

COTTON COUNTRY _____ copies $16.95 each _____

CELEBRATIONS _____ copies $19.95 each _____

"SECRETS TO SOUTHERN COOKING" Video

_____ copies $ 9.00 each _____

_____ Sets of Section Page Prints $ 3.00 each _____

Louisiana residents add 4% tax

Add shipping and handling $ 3.50 each _____

Add gift wrap $ 1.00 each _____

Total _____

Make check payable to:

_____ Cotton/Bayou Publications or

Please charge to: _____ Master Card _____ Visa

Card Number _____

Expiration Date _____

Name _____

Address _____

City _____

State _____ Zip _____

Telephone (_____) _____

Gift from _____

Mail gift to _____

Address _____

City _____

State _____ Zip _____

Telephone (_____) _____

Gift card reads _____

Proceeds from the sales of these cookbooks are used to support the many community projects of the Junior League of Monroe, Inc.

The Junior League of Monroe, Inc.
THANKS YOU FOR BUYING
THE COTTON COUNTRY COLLECTION
and
CELEBRATIONS ON THE BAYOU

Cotton/Bayou Publications
P. O. Box 7138
Monroe, Louisiana 71211-7138
1-800-256-4888
FAX # 1-318-325-1814

COTTON COUNTRY _____ copies $16.95 each _____

CELEBRATIONS _____ copies $19.95 each _____

"SECRETS TO SOUTHERN COOKING" Video

_____ copies $ 9.00 each _____

_____ Sets of Section Page Prints $ 3.00 each _____

Louisiana residents add 4% tax

Add shipping and handling $ 3.50 each _____

Add gift wrap $ 1.00 each _____

Total _____

Make check payable to:

_____ Cotton/Bayou Publications or

Please charge to: _____ Master Card _____ Visa

Card Number _____

Expiration Date _____

Name _____

Address _____

City _____

State _____ Zip _____

Telephone (_____) _____

Gift from _____

Mail gift to _____

Address _____

City _____

State _____ Zip _____

Telephone (_____) _____

Gift card reads _____

Proceeds from the sales of these cookbooks are used to support the many community projects of the Junior League of Monroe, Inc.

Please list stores and their addresses in your area who might be interested in carrying our book.

_____

_____

_____

_____

_____

_____

_____

_____

_____

_____

_____

_____

Please list stores and their addresses in your area who might be interested in carrying our book.

_____

_____

_____

_____

_____

_____

_____

_____

_____

_____

_____

_____